EIGHTH EDITION

Drugs, Behavior, and Modern Society

CHARLES F. LEVINTHAL

Hofstra University

PEARSON

Boston Columbus Indianapolis New York San Francisco Upper Saddle River
Amsterdam Cape Town Dubai London Madrid Milan Munich Paris Montréal Toronto
Delhi Mexico City São Paulo Sydney Hong Kong Seoul Singapore Taipei Tokyo

Editor in Chief: Ashley Dodge
Acquisitions Editor: Susan Hartman
Director of Marketing: Brandy Dawson
Executive Marketing Manager: Kelly May
Marketing Coordinator: Courtney Stewart
Managing Editor: Denise Forlow
Program Manager: Reena Dalal
Senior Operations Supervisor: Mary Fischer
Operations Specialist: Diane Peirano
Art Director: Jayne Conte
Cover Designer: Bruce Kenselaar

Cover Image: efendy / Shutterstock
Director of Digital Media: Brian Hyland
Digital Media Editor: Rachel Comerford
Digital Media Project Manager:
 Tina Gagliostro
**Full-Service Project Management and
 Composition:** Revathi Viswanathan/
 PreMediaGlobal
Printer/Binder: Courier/Kendallville
Cover Printer: Courier/Kendallville
Text Font: Electra Lt Std-Regular, 10 pts

Credits and acknowledgments borrowed from other sources and reproduced, with permission, in this textbook appear on appropriate page within text (or on page 429).

Library of Congress Cataloging-in-Publication Data

Levinthal, Charles F.
  Drugs, behavior, and modern society / Charles F. Levinthal, Hofstra University. — Eighth edition.
    pages cm
  Includes index.
  ISBN-13: 978-0-205-95933-4
  ISBN-10: 0-205-95933-4
  1. Drugs. 2. Drug abuse. 3. Drugs—Physiological effect. 4. Psychotropic drugs. 5. Psychopharmacology. I. Title.
  HV5801.L49 2014
  362.29—dc23

                                                              2013013402

10 9 8 7 6 5
V011

ISBN-10:   0-205-95933-4
ISBN-13: 978-0-205-95933-4

For my grandsons

Aaron Matthew Levinthal
and
Michael Samuel Levinthal

BRIEF CONTENTS

CONTENTS

CHAPTER 5

Opioids: Opium, Heroin, and Opioid Pain Medications   118

Drugs and Behavior Today

After you have completed this chapter, you should have an understanding of

▶ Basic terminology concerning drugs and drug-taking behavior

▶ The origins and history of drugs and drug-taking behavior

▶ Present-day patterns of drug use in the United States

▶ Risk factors and protective factors for drug-taking behavior

▶ Current problems with club drugs and the nonmedical use of prescription pain relievers and prescription stimulant medications

Mike was seventeen, soon to be a high school senior—an age when life can be both terrific and terrifying. He looked at me with amazement, telling me by his expression that either the question I was asking him was ridiculous, or the answer was obvious. "Why do kids do drugs?" I had asked.

"It's cool," he said. "That's why. Believe me, it's important to be cool. Besides, in my life, drugs just make me feel better. Smoking some weed, chilling out with a little Vicodin, spinning with some Addies—it's a way of getting away from stuff. You know that everybody does it. At least all of my friends do it. And it's easy to get them. A helluva lot easier than beer."

The conversation was over. But as he started to leave, Mike seemed to notice the concern on my face. "Don't worry about me," he said with a smile, "I can handle it. I can handle it just fine."

There is no question that we live in a world where drugs are all around us. Thousands of Internet web sites offering information about drug use are just a click away. We are continually bombarded with news about drug-related arrests of major drug traffickers and ordinary citizens, news about popular celebrities and their latest involvement with drugs, news about drugs intercepted and confiscated at our borders and widespread drug use in the major cities and small towns of America.

It also seems impossible to avoid the reality of drugs in our personal lives. One in four adults in the United States, according to one survey, report that drugs have been a cause of trouble in their family. At a time when the economy and related matters dominate our concerns about the present and the future, about two out of three Americans continue to worry about drug use either a fair amount of time or a great deal. In school, you have been taught the risks involved in drug use, and most of you have contended with the social pressure to engage in drug-taking behavior with your friends. You may or may not have been successful in doing so. You also may have noticed your local pharmacy starting to look increasingly like a bank, with the installation of panic alarms, bulletproof glass, and security cameras, as pharmacists turn to protecting themselves from people robbing them for their supplies of oxycodone and other prescription pain medications.[1]

Making matters more complicated and difficult for us, drug-related problems in our contemporary society extend beyond illegal drugs such as heroin, cocaine, amphetamines, LSD and other hallucinogens, and (except for certain U.S. states) marijuana. In fact, while many of these drugs continue to wreak havoc on lives and communities throughout America, it can be argued that the adverse effects associated with legally sanctioned drugs such as alcohol, nicotine, and certain prescription and nonprescription medications are more far-reaching. The abuse of these drugs affects far greater numbers of people, despite our efforts to regulate their use. Here are some facts about *legally sanctioned* drugs as we proceed through the second decade of the twenty-first century in America:

■ Regular consumption of alcohol often begins in junior high school or earlier, despite the fact that twenty-one is the minimum legal age for purchasing alcoholic beverages. In the United States alone, more than 38 million adults, 1 in 6 in the population, admit to having binged on alcohol at least four times in the last month, with more than 80,000 deaths each year attributed to excessive drinking. One in 10 children and teenagers in the United States (about 7.5 million) live with at least one parent who has an alcohol problem. On college campuses nationwide, binge drinking continues to be a major problem and a significant factor in date-rape assaults and other forms of violent behavior (Chapter 8). We pay a heavy price for problems associated with chronic alcohol abuse and alcoholism on a social and personal level (Chapter 9).

■ About one in eleven high school seniors report smoking cigarettes daily, despite the fact that it is illegal for those younger than 18 years old (19 years old in some U.S. states) to purchase tobacco products. While the current prevalence rate is less than half the prevalence rate in 1990s when the figure was about 1 in 5, underage smoking remains a significant public-health issue (Chapter 10)—for good reason. Nearly 80 percent of all adult smokers smoked their first cigarette and became regular smokers before they were 18 years old.[2]

■ Prescription drug abuse, particularly with respect to pain medications such as oxycodone and hydrocodone (Chapter 5), has reached epidemic proportions. In New York State alone, prescriptions for pain medication have risen 82 percent from 2007 to 2010, along with significant increases in hospital admissions and deaths due to nonmedical use of these drugs. Since 2008, unintentional drug poisoning (principally from prescription medications) has

by the numbers . . .

61,533	On an average day in 2011, the number of U.S. adolescents, aged 12 to 17 years old, who binged on alcohol
3,192	The number in 2011 who smoked a cigarette for the first time. Average age: 17.2 years old.
449,000,000	The number of results that come up from searching the word "drugs" on Google.®

Source: Information from the Google® search engine, 2013. Substance Abuse and Mental Health Services Administration (2012). Results from *The 2011 National Survey on Drug Use and Health: Detailed Tables.* Rockville, MD: Substance Abuse and Mental Health Services Administration, Tables 2.73A and 4.6B.

become the leading cause of injury death among people 25 to 64 years old, *exceeding fatalities due to motor vehicle accidents*. Nationwide, more than 700 pharmacies in 2012 experienced an armed robbery specifically for prescription drugs, about twice as many as in 2006.[3]

It will be important, therefore, to address the issues of drugs that are legally sanctioned in our society as well as drugs that are not.

Whether we like it or not, the decision to use drugs of all types and forms, legally sanctioned or not, has become one of life's choices in America, as well as in societies around the world. Every segment of society is affected. The availability of drugs and the potential for drug abuse present a challenge for people of all ages, from the young to the elderly. The consequences of drug-taking behavior can be observed in the workplace and retirement communities as well as on street corners, in school yards, and on college campuses. Drug use is going on in the homes of every community, large or small. The social and personal problems associated with drug use extend in one way or another to men and women of all ethnic and racial groups, geographic regions, and socioeconomic levels. No groups and no individuals should believe themselves exempt.[4]

The purpose of this book is to answer your questions and address your concerns about the wide range of drugs and the many forms of drug-taking behavior in our society today. You might even find answers to questions you never thought about.

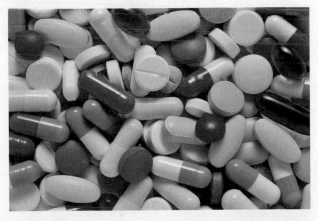

The nonmedical use of prescription medications has become a significant public health concern. In 2011, an estimated 24 million Americans over the age of 26 reported using a pain medication for nonmedical reasons at some point in their lifetime.

Social Messages about Drug Use

Unfortunately, we live in a social environment that sends us mixed messages about drug-taking behavior. The images of Joe Camel, the Marlboro Man, and the Virginia Slims Woman in print advertisements for cigarettes are remnants of an increasingly distant past, but at one time they were iconic (and highly effective) symbols in marketing campaigns designed to convey the attractiveness of smoking to the public, particularly to young people. They are gone now as a result of federal regulations over cigarette advertising that were established in 1998. For decades, warning labels on cigarette packs and public service announcements have cautioned us about the serious health hazards of tobacco use, but the fact remains that about one in four adult Americans today are current cigarette smokers, and the prevalence rate has been slow to decline (see Chapter 10).

Beer commercials during telecasts of football games and other athletic events are designed to be entertaining and to associate beer drinking with a lifestyle filled with fun, friendship, sex, and romance, but we are expected to abide by the tagline at the end of the ad to "drink responsibly" or "know when to say when." The ramifications of the social messages inherent in these commercials are significant. It has been established that the degree of positive expectancies about alcohol (viewing drinking as a way of gaining social acceptance, for example) predicts the onset age of drinking and the tendency to engage in high risk alcohol use over time (see Chapter 8).

Major political figures, including U.S. presidents and vice presidents, as well as candidates for these offices and a host of public officials on local and national levels, have admitted smoking marijuana earlier in their lives. In recent years, regulatory policy in some U.S. states has changed dramatically, making marijuana legally available either for medical purposes or general use by adults. Yet the U.S. federal government position on marijuana remains unchanged, stipulating that the drug is an illegal substance, officially classified since 1970 as a Schedule I controlled substance, defined as a drug with a high potential for abuse and no accepted medical use—in the same category as heroin (see Chapters 2 and 7).

Anti-drug media campaigns are designed to discourage young people from becoming involved with drugs in general. At the same time, we observe a never-ending stream of sports figures, entertainers, and other high-profile individuals engaging in drug-taking behavior. Even though the careers of these people are frequently jeopardized, and in some instances, lives are lost (see Chapter 2), powerful pro–drug-use messages continue to influence us. These messages come from the entertainment industry and traditional media sources, as well as from web sites on the Internet.[5] As confusing and often contradictory as these messages are, they represent the present-day drug scene in America.

Two Ways of Looking at Drugs and Behavior

In the chapters ahead, we will look at the subject of drugs and behavior in two basic ways.

First, we will examine the biological, psychological, and sociological effects of consuming certain types of drugs. The focus will be on the study of specific substances that alter our feelings, our thoughts, our perceptions of the world, and our behavior. These substances are referred to as **psychoactive drugs** because they have the ability to alter the functioning of the brain and hence produce changes in our behavior and experience.

Psychoactive drugs that traditionally receive the greatest amount of attention are referred to as **illicit (illegal) drugs**. Criminal penalties are imposed in the United States on their possession, manufacture, or sale. The best-known examples are heroin, cocaine, and (except in some U.S. states) marijuana, as well as a wide range of so-called "club drugs," such as methamphetamine (meth), Ecstasy, LSD, PCP, ketamine, and GHB. Other equally important psychoactive substances, however, are **licit (legal) drugs**, such as alcohol, nicotine, caffeine, and certain prescription medications. In the cases of alcohol and nicotine, legal access carries a minimum-age requirement.

Second, we will focus on the complex interplay of circumstances in our lives that lead to drug-taking behavior. We will examine the possibility that drug use is, at least in part, a consequence of how we feel about ourselves in relation to our family, friends, and acquaintances, to our life experiences, and to the community in which we live. We will also examine the biological factors that may predispose us to drug-taking behavior. An exploration into the reasons why some individuals engage in drug-taking behavior, whereas others do not, will be a primary topic of discussion.

Understanding the interplay between drug-taking behavior and society is essential when we consider the dangerous potential for drug use to become **drug dependence**. As many of us know all too well, a vicious circle can develop in which drug-taking behavior fosters more drug-taking behavior, in a spiraling pattern that can be extremely difficult to break. Individuals showing signs of drug dependence display intense cravings for the drug and, in many cases, require increasingly greater quantities to get the same, desired effect. They become preoccupied with their drug-taking behavior, and it becomes evident that their lives have gotten out of control (see Chapter 2).

Ultimately, an understanding of drug dependence requires an examination of biological as well as psychological and sociological factors (see Figure 1.1). On a biological level, the use of psychoactive drugs modifies the functioning of the brain, both during the time when

> **psychoactive drugs:** Drugs that affect feelings, thoughts, perceptions, or behavior.
>
> **illicit drugs:** Drugs whose manufacture, sale, or possession is illegal.
>
> **licit drugs:** Drugs whose manufacture, sale, or possession is legal.
>
> **drug dependence:** A condition in which an individual feels a compulsive need to continue taking a drug. In the process, the drug assumes an increasingly central role in the individual's life.

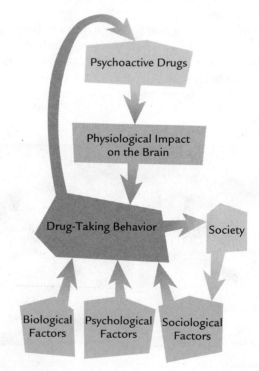

FIGURE 1.1

The Biopsychosocial Model: Understanding the interplay of drugs, behavior, and society.

the drug is present in the body and later, when the drug-taking behavior stops. Drug dependence, therefore, produces long-lasting brain changes. As Alan Leshner, former director of the National Institute on Drug Abuse (NIDA), has put it, a "switch" in the brain seems to be thrown following prolonged drug use. It starts as a voluntary behavior, but once that switch is thrown, a pattern of drug dependence takes over. On a psychological and sociological level, drug dependence can be viewed as the result of a complex interaction of the individual and his or her environment. We cannot fully understand the problem of drug dependence without being aware of the social context in which drug-taking behavior occurs. As we will see in Chapter 17, the recognition that drug dependence can be defined in terms of biological, psychological, and social components has important implications for designing effective treatment programs.[6]

Which drugs have the greatest potential for creating drug dependence? How can someone escape drug dependence once it is established? What factors increase or decrease the likelihood of drug-taking behavior in the first place? These are among the questions we will consider next, as we examine the impact of drugs and drug-taking behavior on our lives.

A Matter of Definition: What Is a Drug?

Considering the ease with which we speak of drugs and drug use, it seems that it should be relatively easy to explain what we mean by the word **drug**. Unfortunately, there are significant problems in arriving at a clear definition.

The standard approach is to characterize a drug as *a chemical substance that, when taken into the body, alters the structure or functioning of the body in some way*. In doing so, we are accounting for examples such as medications used for the treatment of physical disorders and mental illnesses, as well as for alcohol, nicotine, and the typical street drugs. Unfortunately, however, this broad definition could also refer to ordinary food and water. Because it does not make much sense for nutrients to be considered drugs, we need to refine our definition by adding the phrase *excluding those nutrients considered to be related to normal functioning*.

But we may still be on slippery ground. We can now effectively eliminate the cheese in your next pizza from being considered a drug, but what about some exotic ingredient in the sauce? Sugar is safely excluded, even though it has significant energizing (and therefore behavioral) effects on us, but what about the cayenne pepper that burns your tongue? Where do we draw the line between a drug and a nondrug? It is not an easy question to answer.

We can learn two major lessons from this seemingly simple task of defining a drug. First, there is probably no perfect definition that would distinguish drugs from nondrugs without leaving a number of cases that fall within some kind of gray area. The best we can do is to set up a definition, as we have, that handles most of the substances we are likely to encounter. However, significant practical difficulties may still arise. As we will see in Chapter 14, the fact that dietary supplements are currently not regulated in the United States has resulted from a governmental decision that these particular substances are not to be considered drugs in the same category as prescription or nonprescription (over-the-counter) medications. Whether or not this distinction is an arbitrary one continues to be a matter of debate.

The second lesson is more subtle. We often draw the distinction between drugs and nondrugs not in terms of their physical characteristics but, rather, in terms of *whether the substance in question has been intended to be used primarily as a way of inducing a bodily or psychological change*.[7] By this reasoning, if the pizza maker intended to put that spice in the pizza to make it taste better, the spice might not be considered a drug; it would simply be another ingredient in the recipe. If the pizza maker intended the spice to intoxicate you or quicken your heart rate, then it might be considered a drug (See Health Line on page 6).

Ultimately, the problem is that we are trying to reach a consensus on a definition that fits our intuitive sense of what constitutes a drug. We may find it difficult to define pornography, but (as has been said in the halls of the U.S. Supreme Court) we know it when we see it. So it may be with drugs. Whether we realize it or not, when we discuss the topic of drugs, we are operating within a context of social and cultural values, a group of shared feelings about what kind of behavior (that is, what kind of drug-taking behavior) is right and what kind is wrong.

The judgments we make about drug-taking behavior even influence the terminology we use when referring to that behavior. When we say "drug misuse" and "drug abuse," for example, we are implying that something wrong is happening, that a drug is producing some harm to the physical health or psychological well-being of the drug user or to society in general.

drug: A chemical substance that, when taken into the body, alters the structure or functioning of the body in some way, excluding those nutrients considered to be related to normal functioning.

Health Line

Defining Drugs: Olive Oil, Curry Powder, and a Little Grapefruit?

An ever-increasing number of reminders about the blurriness of the distinction between drugs and nondrugs come from research on the chemical properties of specific foods we eat on a daily basis. For example, in 2005 it was found that freshly pressed olive oil contains large amounts of *oleocanthal*, a compound that inhibits the activity of cyclooxygenase enzymes in exactly the same way as ibuprofen, a popular nonsteroidal anti-inflammatory medication (see Chapter 14). Essentially, olive oil reduces inflammation in the body in a drug-like manner. By this definition, olive oil could be classified as a drug.

This discovery provides a biochemical clue to understanding the well-documented but puzzling health benefits of a Mediterranean (olive oil-based) diet, which leads to a lower risk of cancer, heart disease, and other chronic disorders, despite its heavy emphasis on fat and salt. This particular diet may also lower the risk of clinical depression.

Another example is the spice *turmeric*, used commonly in most commercial curry powders, as well as adding the bright yellow color in many mustards. The active ingredient of turmeric, called curcumin, has been credited with several medicinal benefits. Curcumin apparently has antioxidant, anti-inflammatory, antiviral, antibacterial, and antifungal properties with potential benefits in the treatment of cancer, diabetes, arthritis, Alzheimer's disease, and other chronic disorders. In 2005 alone, nearly 300 technical and scientific papers cited the drug-like activity of curcumin—three times the number reported in 2000. If the regulatory hurdles established by the U.S. Food and Drug Administration with respect to long-term safety can be overcome, curcumin could provide an inexpensive alternative to several currently available prescription drugs.

Still another example is grapefruit. A common flavonoid called *naringenin*, found in grapefruit, has a specific inhibitory effect on the secretion of hepatitis C virus from infected liver cells. Nontoxic amounts of naringenin reduced hepatitis C virus secretion by as much as 80 percent. People taking certain prescription medications have to be careful if they are eating grapefruit at the same time. The interaction effects will be covered in Chapter 3.

As we continue to learn more about the therapeutic or drug-interacting effects of common foods and spices, the customary exclusion of nutrients in the definition of drugs becomes increasingly problematic. In the future, we might be hearing people say that they are taking olive oil, curry powder, or a little grapefruit extract for "medicinal reasons."

Sources: Beauchamp, G. K.; Keast, R. S. J.; More, D.; Lin, J.; Pika, J.; Han, Q.; Lee, C. H.; Smith, A. B.; and Breslin, P. A. S. (2005). Phytochemistry: Ibuprofen-like activity in extra-virgin olive oil. *Nature*, 437, 45–46. Hampton, Tracy (2008, April 2). Grapefruit compound battles hepatitis C. *Journal of the American Medical Association*, 1532. Sanchez-Villegas, A.; Delgado-Rodriguez, M.; Alonso, A.; Schlatter, J., et al. Association of the Mediterranean dietary pattern with the incidence of depression. *Archives of General Psychiatry*, 66, 1090–1098. Stix, G. (2007, February). Spice healer. *Scientific American*, pp. 66–69.

But by what criteria do we say that a drug is being misused or abused? We cannot judge on the basis of whether the drug is legal or illegal, since decisions about the legality of a psychoactive drug are more often made as a result of historical and cultural circumstances than on the physical properties of the drug itself. Tobacco, for example, has deeply rooted associations in American history, dating to the earliest colonial days. Although it is objectionable to many individuals and harmful to the health of the smoker and others, tobacco is nonetheless a legal commodity, although its commercial availability is limited to adults. Alcohol is another legal commodity, available within the bounds of the law, even though it can be harmful to individuals who become inebriated and to others who may be affected by the drinker's drunken behavior. The difficulty of using a criterion based on legality is further complicated by differences in religious attitudes toward these substances in some societies in the world.

Instrumental Drug Use/Recreational Drug Use

It is useful to base our discussion about drug abuse and misuse by answering a simple but fundamental question: What is the intent or motivation of the drug user with respect to this kind of behavior? In terms of the intent of the individual, drug-taking behavior can be classified as either instrumental or recreational.[8]

By **instrumental use**, we mean that a person is taking a drug with a specific socially approved goal in mind. The user may want to stay awake longer, fall asleep more quickly, or recover from an illness. If you are a medical professional on call over a long period of time or a

instrumental use: Referring to the motivation of a drug user who takes the drug for a specific purpose other than getting "high."

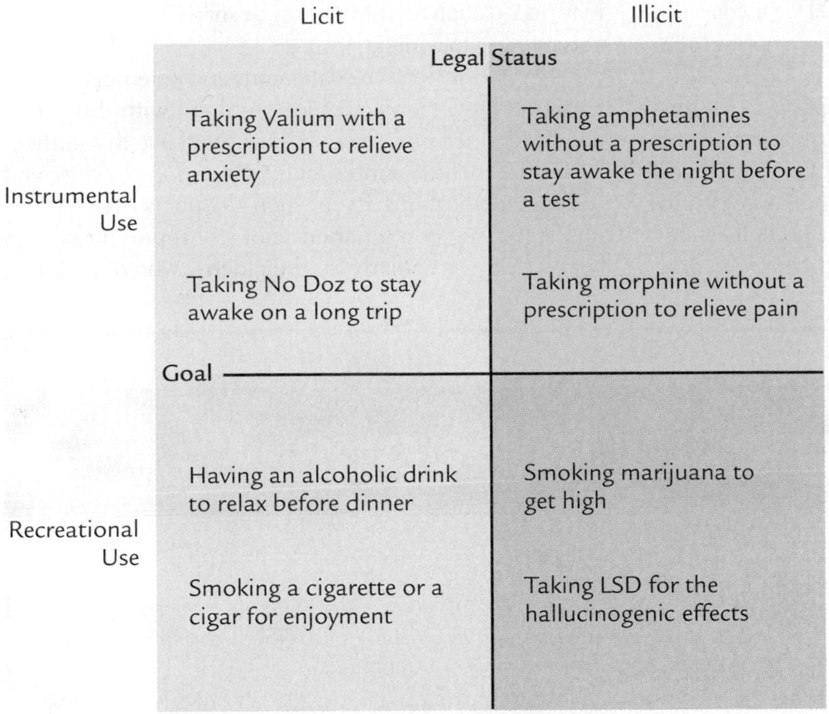

FIGURE 1.2

Four categories of drug-taking behavior, derived from combinations of the user's goal and the drug's legal status.

Source: Adapted from Goode, E. (2008). *Drugs in American Society* (7th ed.). New York: McGraw-Hill, p. 14.

	Licit	Illicit
Legal Status		
Instrumental Use	Taking Valium with a prescription to relieve anxiety	Taking amphetamines without a prescription to stay awake the night before a test
	Taking No Doz to stay awake on a long trip	Taking morphine without a prescription to relieve pain
Recreational Use	Having an alcoholic drink to relax before dinner	Smoking marijuana to get high
	Smoking a cigarette or a cigar for enjoyment	Taking LSD for the hallucinogenic effects

(Goal →)

long-distance truck driver, your taking a drug with the goal of staying alert is considered acceptable by most people. Recovering from an illness and achieving some reduction in pain are goals that are unquestioned. *In these cases, drug-taking behavior occurs as a means toward an end that has been defined by our society as legitimate.*

The legal status of the drug itself or whether we agree with the reason for the drug-taking behavior is not the issue here. The instrumental use of drugs can involve prescription and nonprescription, or over-the-counter, drugs that are licitly obtained and taken for a particular medical purpose. Examples include an antidepressant prescribed for depression, a cold remedy for a cold, an anticonvulsant drug to control epileptic seizures, and insulin to maintain the health of a person with diabetes. But the instrumental use of drugs can also involve drugs that are illicitly obtained, such as an amphetamine or other stimulant drug that has been procured by illegal means to help a person stay awake and alert after hours without sleep.

In contrast, **recreational use** means that a person is taking the drug not as a means to a socially approved goal but for the purposes of experiencing the effect of the drug itself. The motivation is to enjoy a pleasurable feeling or positive state of mind. *Whatever happens as a consequence of recreational drug-taking behavior is viewed not as a means to an end, but as an end onto itself.* Drinking alcohol and smoking tobacco are two examples of licit recreational drug-taking behavior.

Involvement with street drugs, in the sense that the goal is to alter one's mood or state of consciousness, falls into the category of illicit recreational drug-taking behavior.

Although this four-group classification scheme, as shown in Figure 1.2, can help us in understanding the complex relationship between drugs and behavior, there will be instances in which the category is less than clear. Drinking an alcoholic beverage, for example, is considered recreational drug-taking behavior under most circumstances. If it is recommended by a physician for a specified therapeutic or preventive purpose (see Chapter 8), however, the drinking might be considered instrumental in nature. Thus, whether drug use is judged to be recreational or instrumental is determined in no small part by the circumstances under which the behavior takes place.

Drug Misuse or Drug Abuse?

How do the terms **drug misuse** and **drug abuse**, fit into this scheme? Drug misuse typically applies to cases in which

recreational use: Referring to the motivation of a drug user who takes the drug only to get "high" or achieve some pleasurable effect.

drug misuse: Drug-taking behavior in which a prescription or over-the-counter drug is used inappropriately.

drug abuse: Drug-taking behavior resulting in some form of physical, mental, or social impairment.

a legal prescription or over-the-counter (OTC) medication is used inappropriately. Many instances of drug misuse involve instrumental goals. For example, drug doses may be increased beyond the level of the prescription in the mistaken idea that if a little is good, more is even better. Or doses may be decreased from the level of the prescription to make the drug supply last longer. Drugs may be continued longer than they were intended to be used; they may be combined with some other drug; or a prescription drug may (in violation of instructions) be shared by family members or given to a friend.

Drug misuse can be dangerous and potentially lethal, particularly when alcohol is combined with drugs that depress the nervous system. Drugs that have this particular feature include antihistamines, antianxiety drugs, and sleeping medications. Even when alcohol is not involved, however, drug combinations can still represent serious health risks, particularly for the elderly, who often take a

Drugs . . . in Focus

Drug Abuse and the College Student: An Assessment Tool

In a research study conducted at Rutgers University, a cutoff score of five or more "yes" responses to the following twenty-five questions in the Rutgers Collegiate Substance Abuse Screening Test (RCSAST) was found effective in correctly classifying 94 percent of young adults in a clinical sample as problem users and 89 percent of control individuals as nonproblem users. It is important, however, to remember that the RCSAST does not by itself determine the presence of substance abuse or dependence (see Chapter 2). The RCSAST is designed to be used as one part of a larger assessment battery aimed at identifying which young adults experience problems due to substance use and specifically what types of problems a particular individual is experiencing. Here are the questions:

1. Have you gotten into financial trouble as a result of drinking or other drug use?
2. Is alcohol or other drug use making your college life unhappy?
3. Do you use alcohol or other drugs because you are shy with other people?
4. Has drinking alcohol or using other drugs ever caused conflicts with close friends of the opposite sex?
5. Has drinking alcohol or using other drugs ever caused conflicts with close friends of the same sex?
6. Has drinking alcohol or using other drugs ever damaged other friendships?
7. Has drinking alcohol or using other drugs ever been behind your losing a job (or the direct reason for it)?
8. Do you lose time from school due to drinking and/or other drug use?
9. Has drinking alcohol or using other drugs ever interfered with your preparations for exams?
10. Has your efficiency decreased since drinking and/or using other drugs?
11. Do you drink alcohol or use other drugs to escape from worries or troubles?
12. Is your drinking and/or using other drugs jeopardizing your academic performance?
13. Do you drink or use other drugs to build up your self-confidence?
14. Has your ambition decreased since drinking and/or drug using?
15. Does drinking or using other drugs cause you to have difficulty sleeping?
16. Have you ever felt remorse after drinking and/or using other drugs?
17. Do you drink or use drugs alone?
18. Do you crave a drink or other drug at a definite time daily?
19. Do you want a drink or other drug the next morning?
20. Have you ever had a complete or partial loss of memory as a result of drinking or using other drugs?
21. Is drinking or using other drugs affecting your reputation?
22. Does your drinking and/or using other drugs make you careless of your family's welfare?
23. Do you seek out drinking/drugging companions and drinking/drugging environments?
24. Has your physician ever treated you for drinking and/or other drug use?
25. Have you ever been to a hospital or institution on account of drinking or other drug use?

Source: Bennett, M. E.; McCrady, B. S.; Frankenstein, W.; Laitman, L. A.; Van Horn, D. H. A.; and Keller, D. S. (1993). Identifying young adult substance abusers: The Rutgers Collegiate Substance Abuse Screening Test. *Journal of Studies in Alcohol, 54,* 522–527. Reprinted with permission of the authors of the RCSAST.

large number of separate medications. This population is especially vulnerable to the hazards of drug misuse.

In contrast, drug abuse is typically applied to cases in which a licit or illicit drug is used in ways that produce some form of physical, mental, or social impairment (See Drug in Focus on p. 8). The primary motivation for individuals involved in drug abuse is recreational. Drugs with abuse potential include not only the common street drugs but also legally available psychoactive substances, such as caffeine and nicotine (stimulants), alcohol and inhaled solvents (depressants), and a number of prescription or OTC medications designated for medical purposes but used by some individuals exclusively on a recreational basis. In Chapter 5, we will examine concerns about the abuse of opioid pain medications such as Vicodin, OxyContin, and Percocet, among others. In these particular cases, the distinction between drug misuse and drug abuse is particularly blurry. When there is no intent to make a value judgment about the motivation or consequences of a particular type of drug-taking behavior, we will refer to the behavior simply as *drug use*.

Before examining the major role that drugs and drug-taking behavior play in our lives today, however, it is important to examine the historical foundations of drug use. We need to understand why drug-taking behavior has been so pervasive over the many centuries of human history, and why drug-taking behavior remains so compelling for us in our contemporary society. We also need to understand the ways in which our society has responded to problems associated with drug use. How have our attitudes toward drugs changed over time? How did people feel about drugs and drug-taking behavior one hundred years ago, fifty years ago, twenty years ago, or even ten years ago? These are questions that we will now address.

Drugs in Early Times

Try to imagine the accidental circumstances under which a psychoactive drug might have been discovered. Thousands of years ago, perhaps a hundred thousand years ago, the process of discovery would have been as natural as eating, and the motivation as basic as simple curiosity. In cool climates, next to a cave dwelling may have grown a profusion of blue morning glories or brightly colored mushrooms, plants that produce hallucinogens similar to LSD. In desert regions, yellow-orange fruits grew on certain cacti, the source of the hallucinogenic drug peyote. Elsewhere, poppy plants, the source of opium, covered acres of open fields. Coca leaves, from which cocaine is made, grew on shrubs along the mountain valleys throughout Central and

In a wide range of world cultures throughout history, hallucinogens have been regarded as having deeply spiritual powers. Under the influence of drugs, this modern-day shaman communicates with the spirit world.

South America. The hardy cannabis plant, the source of marijuana, grew practically everywhere.

Some of this curiosity may have been sparked by observing the unusual behavior of animals as they fed on these plants. Within their own experience, people made the connection, somewhere along the line, between the chewing of willow bark (the source of modern-day aspirin) and the relief of a headache or between the eating of the senna plant (a natural laxative) and the relief of constipation.[9]

Of course, some of these plants made people sick, and many of them were poisonous and caused death. However, it is likely that the plants that had the strangest impact on humans were the ones that produced hallucinations. Having a sudden vision of something totally alien to everyday life must have been overwhelming, like a visit to another world. Individuals with prior knowledge about such plants, as well as about plants with therapeutic powers, would eventually acquire great power over others in the community.

The accumulation of knowledge about consciousness-altering substances would mark the beginning of **shamanism**, a practice among primitive societies, dating back by some estimates more than forty thousand

shamanism: The philosophy and practice of healing in which diagnosis or treatment is based on trancelike states, on the part of either the healer (shaman) or the patient.

years, in which an individual called a **shaman** acts as a healer through a combination of trances and plant-based medicines, usually in the context of a local religious rite. Shamans still function today in remote areas of the world, often alongside practitioners of modern medicine. As we will see in Chapter 6, hallucination-producing plants of various kinds play a major role in present-day shamanic healing.

With the development of centralized religions in Egyptian and Babylonian societies, the influence of shamanism gradually declined. The power to heal through one's knowledge of drugs passed into the hands of the priesthood, which placed greater emphasis on formal rituals and rules than on hallucinations and trances.

The most dramatic testament to the development of priestly healing during this period is a 65-foot-long Egyptian scroll known as the **Ebers Papyrus**, named after a British Egyptologist who acquired it in 1872. This mammoth document, dating from 1500 B.C., contains more than eight hundred prescriptions for practically every ailment imaginable, including simple wasp stings and crocodile bites, baldness, constipation, headaches, enlarged prostate glands, sweaty feet, arthritis, inflammations of all types, heart disease, and cancer. More than a hundred of the preparations contained castor oil as a natural laxative; some contained "the berry of the poppy," which we now recognize as the Egyptian reference to opium. Other ingredients were quite bizarre: lizard's blood, the teeth of swine, the oil of worms, the hoof of an ass, putrid meat with fly specks, and crocodile dung (excrement of all types being highly favored for its ability to frighten off the evil spirits of disease).[10]

How successful were these strange remedies? It is impossible to know because no records were kept on what happened to the patients. Although some of the ingredients (such as opium and castor oil) had true medicinal value, much of the improvement from these concoctions may have been psychological rather than physiological. In other words, improvements in the patient's condition resulted from the patient's *belief* that he or she would be helped—a phenomenon known as the **placebo effect**. Psychological factors have played a critical role throughout the history of drugs. The importance of the placebo effect as an explanation of some drug effects will be examined in Chapter 3.

Along with substances that had genuine healing properties, some psychoactive drugs were put to less positive use. In the early Middle Ages, Viking warriors ate the mushroom *Amanita muscaria*, known as fly agaric, and experienced a tremendous increase in energy, which resulted in wild behavior in battle. They were called Berserkers because of the bear skins they wore, but this is the origin of the word "berserk" as a reference to reckless and violent behavior. At about the same time, witches operating on the periphery of European society created "witch's brews," mixtures made of various plants such as mandrake, henbane, and belladonna, creating strange hallucinations and a sensation of flying. The toads that they included in their recipes didn't hurt either: We know now that the sweat glands of certain toads contain a chemical related to dimethyltryptamine (DMT), a powerful hallucinogenic drug (see Chapter 6).[11]

Drugs in the Nineteenth Century

By the end of the nineteenth century, the medical profession had made significant strides with respect to medicinal healing. Morphine was identified as the active ingredient in opium, a drug that had been in use for at least three thousand years and had become the physician's most reliable prescription for the control of pain due to disease and injury. The invention of the syringe made it possible to deliver the morphine directly and speedily into the bloodstream. Cocaine, having been extracted from coca leaves, was used as a stimulant and antidepressant. Sedative powers to calm the mind or induce sleep had been discovered in bromides and chloral hydrate.

There were also new drugs for specific purposes or particular diseases. Anesthetic drugs were discovered that made surgery painless for the first time in history. Some diseases could actually be prevented through the administration of vaccines, such as the vaccine against smallpox introduced by Edward Jenner in 1796 and the vaccine against rabies introduced by Louis Pasteur in 1885. The discovery of new pharmaceutical products marked the modern era in the history of healing.[12]

The social picture of drug-taking behavior during this time, however, was more complicated. By the 1890s, prominent leaders in the medical profession and social reformers had begun to call attention to societal problems resulting from the widespread and uncontrolled access to psychoactive drugs. Remedies called

shaman (SHAH-men): A healer whose diagnosis or treatment of patients is based at least in part on trances. These trances are frequently induced by hallucinogenic drugs.

Ebers Papyrus: An Egyptian document, dated approximately 1500 B.C., containing more than eight hundred prescriptions for common ailments and diseases.

placebo (pla-CEE-bo) effect: Any change in a person's condition after taking a drug, based solely on that person's beliefs about the drug rather than on any physical effects of the drug.

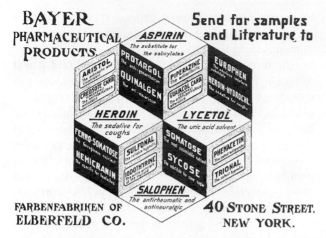

BAYER
PHARMACEUTICAL
PRODUCTS.

Send for samples
and Literature to

ASPIRIN
The substitute for
the salicylates

ARISTOL

CREOSOTE CARB

PROTARGOL

QUINALGEN

PIPERAZINE

GUAIACOL CARB

EUROPHEN

HEROIN-HYDROCHL.

HEROIN
The sedative for
coughs

LYCETOL
The uric acid solvent

FERRO-SOMATOSE

HEMICRANIN

SULFONAL

IODOTHYRINE

SOMATOSE

SYCOSE

PHENACETIN

TRIONAL

SALOPHEN
The antirheumatic and
antineuralgic

FARBENFABRIKEN OF
ELBERFELD CO.

40 STONE STREET,
NEW YORK.

Around 1900, heroin was advertised as a completely safe remedy for common ailments, along with aspirin. No one knows how many people became dependent on heroin as a result.

patent medicines, sold through advertisements, peddlers, or general stores, contained opium, alcohol, and cocaine and were promoted as answers to virtually all common medical and nonmedical complaints.

Opium itself was cheap, easily available, and completely legal. Most people, from newborn infants to the elderly, in the United States and Europe "took opium" during their lives. The way in which they took it, however, was a critical social factor. The respectable way was to drink it, usually in a liquid form called *laudanum*. By contrast, the smoking of opium, as introduced by Chinese immigrants imported for manual labor in the American West, was considered degrading and immoral. Laws prohibiting opium smoking began to be enacted in 1875. In light of the tolerant attitude toward opium drinking, the strong emotional opposition to opium smoking may be viewed as more anti-Chinese than anti-opium.[13]

Like opium, cocaine was in widespread use and was taken quite casually in a variety of forms during this period. The original formula for Coca-Cola, as the name suggests, contained cocaine until 1903 (see Chapter 4), as did Dr. Agnew's Catarrh Powder, a popular remedy for chest colds. In the mid-1880s, Parke, Davis, and Company (since 2002, merged with Pfizer, Inc.) was selling cocaine and its botanical source, coca, in more than a dozen forms, including coca-leaf cigarettes and cigars, cocaine inhalants, a coca cordial, and an injectable cocaine solution.[14]

A Viennese doctor named Sigmund Freud, who was later to gain a greater reputation for his psychoanalytic theories than for his ideas concerning psychoactive drugs, promoted cocaine as a "magical drug." In an influential paper published in 1884, Freud recommended cocaine as a safe and effective treatment for morphine addiction. When a friend and colleague became heavily addicted to cocaine, Freud quickly reversed his position, regretting for the rest of his life that he had been initially so enthusiastic in recommending its use (see Chapter 4).[15]

Drugs and Behavior in the Twentieth Century

By 1900, the promise of medical advances in the area of drugs was beginning to be matched by concern about the dependence that some of these drugs could produce. For a short while after its introduction in 1898, heroin (a derivative of morphine) was completely legal and considered safe. Physicians were impressed with its effectiveness in the treatment of coughs, chest pains, and the respiratory difficulties associated with pneumonia and tuberculosis. This was an era in which antibiotic drugs were unavailable, and pneumonia and tuberculosis were among the leading causes of death.[16]

Some physicians even recommended heroin as a treatment for morphine addiction. Its powerful addictive properties, however, soon became evident. The enactment of laws restricting access to heroin and certain other psychoactive drugs, including marijuana, would eventually follow in later years, a topic discussed further in Chapter 2.

At the beginning of the twentieth century, neither the general public nor the government considered alcohol a drug. Nonetheless, the American temperance movement dedicated to the prohibition of alcohol consumption, led by the Women's Christian Temperance Union and the Anti-Saloon League, was a formidable political force. In 1920, the Eighteenth Amendment to the U.S. Constitution took effect, ushering in the era of national Prohibition, which lasted for thirteen years.

Although successful in substantially reducing the rates of alcohol consumption in the United States, as well as the number of deaths from alcohol-related diseases, Prohibition also succeeded in establishing a nationwide alcohol distribution network dominated by sophisticated criminal organizations.[17] Violent gang wars arose in major American cities as one group battled another for control of the liquor trade.

By the early 1930s, whatever desirable health-related effects Prohibition may have brought were perceived to be overshadowed by the undesirable social changes that had come along with it. Since its end in 1933, the social problems associated with the era

patent medicine: Historically, a drug or combination of drugs sold through peddlers, shops, or mail-order advertisements.

of Prohibition have often been cited as an argument against the continuing restriction of psychoactive drugs in general.

Drugs and Behavior from 1945 to 1960

In the years following World War II, for the first time, physicians were able to control bacteria-borne infectious diseases through the administration of antibiotic drugs. Although *penicillin* had been discovered in a particular species of mold by Alexander Fleming in 1928, techniques for extracting large amounts from the mold were not perfected until the 1940s. Also during that time, Selman Waksman found that a species of fungus had powerful antibacterial effects; it was later to be the source of the drug *streptomycin*.

In the field of psychiatry, advances in therapeutic drugs did not occur until the early 1950s, when quite accidentally a group of psychoactive drugs were discovered that relieved schizophrenic symptoms without producing heavy sedation. The first of these, **chlorpromazine** (brand name: Thorazine), reduced the hallucinations, agitation, and disordered thinking common to schizophrenia. Soon after, there was a torrent of new drugs, forming the basis not only for the treatment of schizophrenia but also the

> **chlorpromazine (chlor-PRO-mah-zeen):** An antipsychotic (antischizophrenia) drug. Brand name is Thorazine (THOR-a-zeen).

treatment of mental illness in general. It was a revolution in psychiatric care, equivalent to the impact of antibiotics in medical care a decade earlier.

In the recreational drug scene of post–World War II America, a number of features stand out. Smoking was considered romantic and sexy, and smoking was commonplace. In 1955, regular cigarette smoking involved more than half of all male adults and more than one-quarter of all female adults in the United States. It was the era of the two-martini lunch; social drinking was at the height of its popularity and acceptance. Cocktail parties dominated the social scene. There was little or no public awareness that alcohol or tobacco use constituted drug-taking behavior. In contrast, the general perception of certain drugs such as heroin, marijuana, and cocaine was simple and negative: They were considered bad, they were illegal, and "no one you knew" had anything to do with them. Illicit drugs were seen as the province of criminals, the urban poor, and nonwhites.[18] The point is that an entire class of drugs were, during this period, outside the mainstream of American life. Furthermore, an atmosphere of fear and suspicion surrounded people who took such drugs. Nonetheless, for the vast majority of Americans, drugs were not considered an issue in their lives.

Drugs and Behavior after 1960

During the 1960s, basic premises of American life—the beliefs that working hard and living a good life would

The famous Woodstock Festival concert drew an estimated 500,000 people to a farm in upstate New York in the summer of 1969. According to historian David Musto, the peacefulness of such a gigantic gathering is considered to have been due, at least in part, to the widespread use of marijuana, as opposed to alcohol.

bring happiness and that society was stable and calm—were being undermined by disturbing events: President John F. Kennedy was assassinated in 1963; Dr. Martin Luther King Jr. and Senator Robert Kennedy were gunned down in 1968. We worried about the continuing Cold War, nuclear annihilation, and Vietnam.

College students, in particular, found it difficult to be as optimistic about the future as their parents had been. To many of them, the reality of the Vietnam War represented all that had gone wrong with the previous generation.[19] At the same time, many young people were searching for new answers to old problems, and their search led to experimentation with drugs that their parents had been taught to fear. The principal symbol of this era of defiance against the established order, and indeed against anyone over thirty years old, was marijuana.

No longer would marijuana be something foreign to middle-class America. Along with other drugs such as LSD, stimulants ("uppers"), and depressants ("downers"), marijuana became part of the lives of sons and daughters in our own families and in our own neighborhoods. Adding to the turbulence of this period was a disturbing increase in heroin abuse across the country. The issues surrounding drug abuse, once a problem associated with minority populations, inner cities, and the poor, were now too close to our personal lives for most of us to ignore.

One of the governmental responses to these events, particularly the increase in heroin dependence, was to finance basic research related to the effects of drugs on the brain. The timing could not have been better because during the 1970s, a new branch of science, called **neuroscience**, was being established. Its intent was to bring together researchers from formerly separate scientific fields in a new collaborative effort to understand the relationship between brain functioning and human behavior. In the area of drug research, pharmacologists (those who specialize in the study of drugs) were joined by biochemists, psychologists, and psychiatrists, among others. One of the important discoveries that emerged from this era was the identification of receptors in the brain that are tailored specifically for drugs taken into the body. The findings of neuroscience research will be discussed in Chapter 3 and in several of the chapters that follow.

With the decade of the 1980s, however, came significant changes in the mood of the country, dominated by a reaction to the social and political attitudes of earlier decades. The focus of media attention was on the image of the "yuppie," a young, upwardly mobile professional. The political climate grew more conservative in all age groups. In the area of drugs, concerns about heroin dependence were being overshadowed by a new fixation on cocaine. At first, cocaine took on an aura of glamor, and (because it was so expensive) cocaine became a symbol of material

success. The media spotlight shone on a steady stream of celebrities in entertainment and sports who used cocaine. Not long after, however, the very same celebrities who had accepted cocaine into their lives were experiencing the dark consequences; many were in rehabilitation programs, and some had died from cocaine overdoses.

To make matters worse, a smokable and cheap form of cocaine called crack succeeded in extending the problems of cocaine dependence to the inner cities of the United States, to segments of American society

Quick Concept Check 1.1

Understanding the History of Drugs and Behavior

Check your understanding of the changes in drug-taking behavior over history by matching the statement (on the left) with the appropriate historical period (on the right).

1. Opium and castor oil are first documented as therapeutic drugs.

2. Marijuana use symbolizes a generation's defiance of establishment values.

3. Waksman discovers the antibacterial effects of streptomycin.

4. Opium use extends to all levels of Western society.

5. Cocaine use is at its peak as a symbol of glamor and material success.

6. Heroin is first introduced as a treatment for morphine addiction.

7. Widespread use of antischizophrenic drugs in mental hospitals begins.

8. Vaccines against smallpox and rabies are introduced.

a. approximately 1500 B.C.

b. late 1700s to late 1880s

c. late 1800s

d. late 1940s

e. mid-1950s

f. late 1960s to early 1970s

g. early 1980s

Answers: 1. a   2. f   3. d   4. b   5. g   6. c   7. e   8. b

neuroscience: The scientific study of the nervous system, undertaken as a collaborative effort among researchers from many scientific disciplines.

that did not have the financial resources to afford cocaine itself. In the glare of intense media attention, crack dependence soon took on all the aspects of a national nightmare. Fortunately, by the end of the 1990s, the extent of crack abuse had greatly diminished, and the urban violence and social upheaval associated with it had declined. Nonetheless, the legacy of this era continues to be felt to the present day.[20]

Present-Day Attitudes Toward Drugs

Attitudes toward drug-taking behavior in the twenty-first century are quite different from those that prevailed at an earlier time. First, there is a far greater awareness today that a wide range of psychoactive drugs, whether they are licit or illicit, qualify as substances with varying levels of potential for misuse and abuse. The "war on drugs," in America, declared officially in 1971 and still ongoing today, is no longer a war on a particular drug, such as heroin in the 1970s or cocaine in the 1980s. We are now fully aware of the widespread personal and social difficulties created by the abuse of alcohol, steroids, inhalants, and nicotine, as well as the misuse of prescription pain medications, prescription stimulants, and over-the-counter medications of all kinds. In short, the battles being waged today are against a wide range of drug misuse and abuse, involving licit as well as illicit substances.

A second difference in attitudes toward drug-taking behavior is related to the history of such behavior in our society since the late 1960s. It is important to recognize that in 1980, about two-thirds of high school seniors had reported illicit drug use (principally marijuana smoking) at some time in their lives. They were born toward the end of the "baby boom" generation (technically defined as those born between 1946 and 1964) and were the first group to have grown up during the explosion of drug experimentation. Now, as the parents of teenagers in the twenty-first century, they face the challenge of dealing with the present-day drug-taking behavior of their children.

What has been the effect, if any, on drug-taking behavior among children of parents who were involved in drug use at an earlier time? With respect to marijuana use, studies have resulted in two major conclusions. First, parents of this particular generation have a more accepting attitude of drug use than an older generation and are more resigned to the idea that their own children would engage in illicit drug-taking behavior. Second, there is no evidence that the prior use of marijuana by parents is related to the extent of present marijuana use by their children. Indeed, the far stronger association lies between adolescent marijuana use and the adolescent's own personal attitude toward the lack of harm involved.[21]

Patterns of Drug Use in the United States

How is it possible to obtain information that would give us a statistical picture of drug-taking behavior today? Assuming that we cannot conduct large-scale random drug testing, the only alternative we have is simply to ask people about their drug-taking behavior through self-reports. We encourage honesty and arrange the data-collection procedure so as to convince the respondents that their answers are confidential, but the fact remains that any questionnaire is inherently imperfect because there is no way to verify the truthfulness of what people say about themselves. Nevertheless, questionnaires are all we have, and the statistics on drug use are based on such survey measures.

One of the best-known surveys, referred to as the Monitoring the Future study, has been conducted by the University of Michigan every year since 1975. Typically, nearly fifty thousand American students in the eighth, tenth, and twelfth grades participate in a nationally representative sampling each year, as well as more than seven thousand American college students and adults between nineteen and fifty years old.

The advantage of repeating the survey with a new sample year after year is that it enables us to examine trends in drug-taking behavior over time and compare the use of one drug relative to another over the years. We can assume that the degree of overreporting and underreporting stays relatively constant over the years and does not affect interpretation of the general trends.

Survey questions concerning drug use have been phrased in four basic ways:

- Whether an individual has ever used a certain drug in his or her lifetime. The percentage of those saying "yes" is referred to as the lifetime prevalence rate.
- Whether an individual has used a certain drug over the past year. The percentage of those saying "yes" is referred to as the annual prevalence rate.
- Whether an individual has used a certain drug within the past thirty days. The percentage of those saying "yes" is referred to as the past-month prevalence rate.
- Whether an individual has used a certain drug on a daily basis during the previous thirty days. The percentage of those saying "yes" is referred to as the daily prevalence rate.

You can see that these questions distinguish three important degrees of involvement with a given drug. The first question focuses on the extent of experimentation, including individuals who may have taken a drug only once or twice in their lives but may have stayed away from it ever since. The second and third questions focus on the extent of current but moderate drug use, and the fourth question focuses on the extent of heavy drug use. What do the numbers tell us?

Illicit Drug Use among High School Seniors

Understanding the present-day drug-taking behavior among U.S. high school seniors is not an easy task. In order to see the total picture, we have to look to the past as well as the present, and make some educated guesses as to the future based on current trends.

As seen in Figure 1.3, it has been something of a roller-coaster ride since the Michigan survey began in 1975. The early statistics were indeed scary. By the end of the 1970s, prevalence rates for illicit drug use had reached historically high levels. About one-half of high school seniors reported smoking marijuana or using an illicit drug of some kind in the past year. At that time and continuing into the mid-1980s, 12 percent (one in eight seniors) reported using cocaine or crack cocaine in the past year. Fortunately, annual prevalence rates for illicit drug use among high school seniors showed a steep decline through the 1980s, ending at a historically low level (27 percent) around 1992. But at that point, a dramatic reversal occurred. Prevalence rates took a sharp upward turn during the decade of the 1990s. From 2000 to most recent figures in 2011, rates have been fairly steady at around 38 to 40 percent. The bottom line is that, in terms of illicit drug use in this demographic group, the present is somewhere between the worst (in 1979) and the best (in 1992).

Looking at the numbers more closely, however, we can see the current pattern of drug use among high school seniors in a somewhat different light. If we examine the annual prevalence rates for the use of illicit drugs *other than marijuana*, the trend is down from about 20 percent in 2000 to about 18 percent in 2011.

This good news, however, is counterbalanced by a more complicated trend with respect to using marijuana

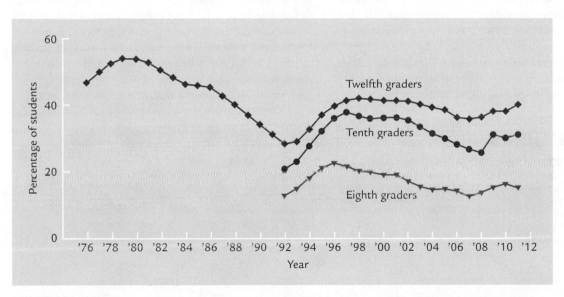

FIGURE 1.3

Trends in annual prevalence of illicit drug use among eighth, tenth, and twelfth graders. Updated statistical information from the University of Michigan survey is available at the end of December of each calendar year through the web site: www.monitoringthefuture.org.

Note: There were no significant changes in 2012 with respect to the annual prevalence rate in eighth, tenth, or twelfth graders. For current information, consult the web site for the Monitoring the Future study.

Source: Johnston, L.D.; O'Malley, P.M.; Bachman, J.G.; and Schulenberg, J.E. (2012). *Monitoring the Future: National Survey Results on Drug use, 1975–2011,* Vol. I: Secondary School Students 2011. Ann Arbor, MI: Institute for Social Research, The University of Michigan, Table 2-2.

alone. In 2000, about 37 percent of seniors reported smoking marijuana in the past year, having risen steadily through the 1990s. In the next few years, the prevalence rate declined. By 2006, however, the trend reversed itself (again). In 2011, annual marijuana use stood at 36 percent (essentially the level observed in 2000). This percentage had risen for the fourth straight year. The rate of *daily* marijuana smoking in 2011 stood at 6.6 percent, the highest it has been since 1981.

In other words, approximately one out of three high school seniors used marijuana over the past year and one out of sixteen seniors used marijuana daily in 2011.[22]

Illicit Drug Use among Eighth Graders and Tenth Graders

Since 1991, the Michigan survey has collected extensive information about illicit drug use among students as early as the eighth grade. As Figure 1.3 shows, the upward trend in the percentages of annual drug use among eighth and tenth graders in the years from 1991 to 1996 parallels a similar trend among high school seniors. At the time, the data from these two groups reflected a level of drug involvement that was quite alarming. Drug-abuse professionals were left to speculate about the negative effect on still younger children, as they observed the drug-taking behavior of their older brothers and sisters. In general, as you would expect, changes in the trend of prevalence rates among high school seniors have been preceded, four years or so earlier, by the shifting prevalence rates among eighth graders.[23]

Illicit Drug Use among College Students

According to the Michigan survey, when compared to high school seniors, college students reported in 2011 a roughly equivalent annual prevalence rate (36 percent) in the use of illicit drugs in general. As it has been the case for younger people, illicit drug use was clearly dominated by marijuana smoking. Table 1.1 shows the lifetime, annual, and 30-day prevalence rates among college students with respect to five major types of drugs: the use of marijuana, hallucinogens, and cocaine, as well as the nonmedical use of prescription stimulant medications and prescription pain medications.[24]

Alcohol Use among High School and College Students

Not surprisingly, the prevalence percentages related to the use of alcohol are much higher than for illicit drugs. Whereas about 25 percent of high school seniors in 2011 reported use of illicit drugs in the past month, 40 percent drank an alcoholic beverage in the past month, and 22 percent reported an instance of binge drinking, defined as having five or more drinks in a row at least once in the past two weeks. These figures are at historic lows, down substantially from those found in surveys conducted in 1980, when 72 percent of high school seniors reported that they had consumed alcohol in the past month, and 41 percent reported binge drinking.[25]

TABLE 1.1

Percentage of five types of drug use among college students, aged 19–22

	EVER IN LIFETIME	IN PAST TWELVE MONTHS	IN PAST THIRTY DAYS
Marijuana	46.6	33.2	19.4
Hallucinogens	6.9	4.1	0.8
Cocaine	5.5	3.3	1.2
Prescription pain medication*	12.4	6.2	2.1
Prescription stimulant medication**	13.4	9.3	4.5

*Nonmedical use of prescription pain medications include Vicodin, OxyContin, and Percocet.

**Nonmedical use of prescription stimulant medications include Adderall and Ritalin.

Note: For current information, consult the web site for the Monitoring the Future study: www.monitoringthefuture.org.

Source: Johnston, L. D.; O'Malley, P. M.; Bachman, J. G.; and Schulenberg, J. E. (2012). *Monitoring the Future: National survey results on drug use, 1975-2011.* Vol. II: College students and adults ages 19–50. Ann Arbor, MI: Institute for Social Research, The University of Michigan, Tables 2-1, 2-2, 2-3, 8-1, 8-2, and 8-3.

The general decline in alcohol use and heavy drinking among adolescents from 1980 to 2011, particularly since the mid-1990s, stems from a number of factors. National campaigns to reduce drunk driving, the encouragement of nondrinking designated drivers, as well as a general personal disapproval of binge drinking, have all played a role. An additional factor is the reduced accessibility to alcohol for this age group; all U.S. states have now adopted a twenty-one-years-or-older requirement. While efforts to reduce underage drinking by enforcing restrictions of alcohol sales to minors have been credited with reducing adolescent alcohol use, however, the statistics show that more work needs to be done. In 2011, 59 percent of eighth graders found it "fairly easy" or "very easy" to obtain alcoholic beverages, down from 71 percent in 2000.[26] About 89 percent of seniors reported the same, down from 95 percent in 2000. The drinking habits of college students, however, have shown relatively little change since the mid-1990s. In 2011, 64 percent of college students surveyed drank at least once in the previous month, and 36 percent reported an instance of binge drinking.[27]

Tobacco Use among High School and College Students

Roughly 10 percent of high school seniors in 2011 had established a regular habit of nicotine intake by smoking at least one cigarette every day. In fact, nicotine remains the drug most frequently used on a daily basis by high school students, although present-day rates are substantially lower than those observed when the Michigan survey began in 1975. More than twice as many high school seniors (27 percent) smoked cigarettes at that time. From the mid-1990s, there has been a steady decline in smoking rates in eighth and tenth graders as well as seniors, owing to the national attention directed toward cigarette smoking among young people. Nonetheless, in 2011, about 4 percent of seniors and 2 percent of tenth graders reported smoking at least half a pack of cigarettes per day—a strikingly high level for these age groups, considering the legal obstacles they face when attempting to obtain cigarettes.[28]

It is true that somewhat fewer college students smoke cigarettes than high school seniors, but the reason is not a matter of a change in smoking behavior from high school to college. It is a reflection of differences between the two populations. Non–college-bound seniors are about three times more likely than college-bound seniors to smoke at least a half pack of cigarettes per day. Therefore, the difference in smoking

rates between seniors and college students is chiefly a result of excluding the heavier smokers in the survey as students progress from secondary to postsecondary education. In 2011, about 7 percent of college students smoked cigarettes on a daily basis, with about 3 percent smoking more than half a pack per day.[29]

Drug Use and Drug Perceptions

The decision to engage in a specific form of drug-taking behavior is intermeshed with individual perceptions about the drug in question. How risky would it be to use a particular drug? How dangerous would it be? These questions have been asked of high school seniors in the Michigan survey since 1975, and the relationship is clear. Figure 1.4 shows an almost exact "mirror-image" in the trends over more than 35 years between the perceived risk of harm in regular marijuana smoking and the 30-day prevalence rate.[30] In the 1990s, there was a steady decline in the percentages of high school students, college students, and young adults who regarded regular drug use (regular marijuana use in particular) as potentially dangerous. These responses contrasted with reports beginning in 1978 that had shown a steady increase in such percentages. At the time, Lloyd Johnston, chief researcher for the Michigan survey, offered one possible reason for this reversal:

> This most recent crop of youngsters [in 1996] grew up in a period in which drug use rates were down substantially from what they had been 10 to 15 years earlier. This gave youngsters less opportunity to learn from others' mistakes and resulted in what I call "generational forgetting" of the hazards of drugs.[31]

Also troubling during much of the 1990s were changes in the way our society dealt with the potential risks of drug use. Drug abuse prevention programs in schools were scaled back or eliminated because of a lack of federal funding, parents were communicating less with their children about drug use, anti-drug public service messages were less prominent in the media than they were in the 1980s, and media coverage in this area declined. At the same time, the cultural influences of the music and entertainment industry were, at best, ambivalent on the question of drug-taking behavior, particularly with respect to marijuana smoking (see Chapter 7). All these elements can be seen as having contributed to the upward trend in drug use during this period.

Another question has been asked in the Michigan survey: Would you experience disapproval if you used a particular drug? Not surprisingly, the likelihood of using

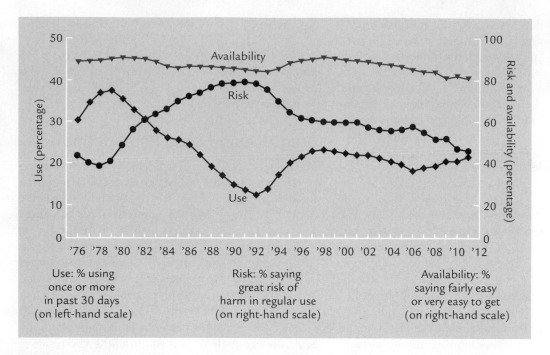

Use: % using
once or more
in past 30 days
(on left-hand scale)

Risk: % saying
great risk of
harm in regular use
(on right-hand scale)

Availability: %
saying fairly easy
or very easy to get
(on right-hand scale)

FIGURE 1.4

Trends in perceived availability of marijuana, perceived risk of marijuana use, and prevalence of marijuana use in the past month for high school seniors.

Note: There were no significant changes in 2012 with respect to any of these measures. For current information, consult the web site for the Monitoring the Future study: www.monitoringthefuture.org.

Source: Johnston, L. D.; O'Malley, P. M.; Bachman, J. G.; and Schulenberg, J. E. (2012). *Monitoring the Future: National survey results on drug use, 1975-2011,* Vol. I: Secondary school students 2011. Ann Arbor, MI: Institute for Social Research, The University of Michigan, Tables 2-3, 8-3, and 9-8.

a drug is inversely related to how much disapproval might be experienced. This is particularly the case in the life of an adolescent, when peer approval is such an important element in guiding his or her behavior.

The two types of drug perception, the perception of possible risk or danger and the perception of disapproval, are useful indices in predicting future trends in drug use, since shifts in perception often precede in time the observed changes in behavior. A lower level of disapproval of marijuana smoking, for example, may reflect a lower perception of riskiness, which might in turn be reflected later in an increased prevalence rate.[32]

Illicit Drug Use among Adults Aged Twenty-Six and Older

A comprehensive report of the prevalence rates of illicit drug use among Americans in several age groups across the life span is made possible by the National Survey on Drug Use and Health (formerly the National Household Survey on Drug Abuse). Table 1.2 shows the estimated number of illicit drug users aged twenty-six or older in the United States in 2011. About 11 percent of this population (more than 21 million people) reported using an illicit drug over the past twelve months, about 8 percent (more than 15 million people) used marijuana or hashish, and about 4 percent (more than 8 million people) engaged in the nonmedical (recreational) use of a prescription-type pain reliever, tranquilizer, stimulant, or sedative. As with the results of the Michigan survey, however, there are some limitations on the interpretation of these estimates. Neither patients institutionalized for medical or psychiatric treatment nor homeless people are included in the collection of sample data.[33]

TABLE 1.2

Illicit drug use during the past year among persons in the United States aged 26 or older in 2011

	ESTIMATED NUMBERS OF USERS
Any illicit drug	21,484,000
Marijuana and hashish	15,632,000
Cocaine	2,064,000
Crack	490,000
Heroin	335,000
Hallucinogens	1,098,000
LSD	135,000
Ecstasy	590,000
Methamphetamine	703,000
Inhalants	540,000
Nonmedical use of any psychotherapeutic medication (not including over-the-counter drugs)	8,542,000
Pain relievers	6,306,000
OxyContin	776,000
Antianxiety medications	3,080,000
Sedatives	314,000
Any illicit drug other than marijuana	10,422,000

Source: Substance Abuse and Mental Health Services Administration (2012). Results from the 2011 National Survey on Drug use and Health: Detailed tables. Rockville, MD: Substance Abuse and Mental Health Services Administration, Tables 1.7A and 1.8A.

Making the Decision to Use Drugs

Why do young people turn to drugs in the first place? What factors influence the drug-taking behavior that we see in all these statistics?

When high school seniors reported their personal reasons for taking drugs, the most frequently occurring responses among the classes of 1983 and 1984 were "to have a good time with my friends" (65 percent), "to experiment or see what it's like" (54 percent), "to feel good or get high" (49 percent), and "to relax or relieve tension" (41 percent). These responses were similar to reasons given by the class of 1976 in earlier surveys, and there is no reason to suspect significant differences today.[34]

Is there any way of predicting which individuals may be inclined to take drugs and which individuals are likely to stay drug-free? One way of thinking about predicting

drug use is to consider any given person as having a certain degree of vulnerability to drug-taking behavior. This vulnerability seems to be shaped by two separate groups of factors in a person's life. The first are **risk factors**, which make it more likely that a person might be involved with drugs; the second are **protective factors**, which make it less likely that a person might be involved with drugs.

Together, risk factors and protective factors combine to give us some idea about the likelihood that drug-taking behavior will occur. The emphasis, however, should be on the phrase "some idea." We still would not know for certain which individuals would use drugs and which would not. An understanding of risk factors and protective factors in general and knowledge about which factors apply to a given individual are useful pieces of information in the development of effective drug abuse prevention programs (see Chapter 16).

Specific Risk Factors

Certain factors that may appear to be strong risk factors for drug-taking behavior in general (socioeconomic

risk factors: Factors in an individual's life that increase the likelihood of involvement with drugs.

protective factors: Factors in an individual's life that decrease the likelihood of involvement with drugs and reduce the impact that any risk factor might have.

Peer influence is a major factor in predicting the extent of drug-taking behavior during adolescence. It can represent either a risk factor or a protective factor for drug abuse.

status, for example) turn out to have an association that is far from simple and may depend on the particular drug under discussion. The most reliable set of risk factors consists of psychosocial characteristics that reflect a tendency toward nonconformity within society. Young people who take drugs are more inclined to attend school irregularly, have poor relationships with their parents, or get into trouble in general. Sociologists refer to such individuals as members of a *deviant subculture*.[35]

The effects of being a participant in a socially deviant subculture are highlighted by the increased probability that an individual will display some level of drug-taking behavior. For example, the odds of youths aged twelve to seventeen using marijuana during the past year are more than six times (6.25 times, to be precise) greater among those who had at least a few close friends who tried or used marijuana than among those who did not have such friends (the second listed risk factor in Table 1.3). Note

TABLE 1.3

Major risk factors and protective factors: Odds ratios for marijuana use over the past year among youths aged 12–17 as related to specific questions about the social context of marijuana smoking

RISK FACTOR	REPRESENTATIVE QUESTION	ODDS RATIO
Antisocial behavior	*"How many times have you gotten a serious into fight at school or at work?"*	7.10
Friends' marijuana use	*"How many friends would you say use marijuana?"*	6.25
Perceived prevalence of marijuana use in school	*"How many of the students in your grade in school would you say use marijuana?"*	4.78
Individual attitudes toward marijuana use	*"How would you feel [positively] about someone your age trying marijuana?"*	4.47
Friends' attitudes toward marijuana use	*"How do you think your close friends would feel [positively] about your trying marijuana?"*	4.37

Note: By definition, risk factors have odds ratios greater than 1. Behavior is more likely to occur if a risk factor is present, through a multiplier designated by the odds ratio. The higher the odds ratio above one, the stronger the risk factor. By definition, protective factors have odds ratios less than 1. Behavior is less likely to occur if a protective factor is present, through a multiplier designated by the odds ratio. The lower the odds ratio below one, the stronger the protective factor.

PROTECTIVE FACTOR	REPRESENTATIVE QUESTION	ODDS RATIO
Sanctions against substance use in school	*"How much trouble do you think a student in your grade would be in if he or she got caught using an illegal drug?"*	0.28
Parents as sources of social support	*"Would you select your mother or father as a source of social support?"*	0.40
Commitment to school	*"Do you like going to school?"*	0.45
Religiosity	*"How many times did you attend religious services?"*	0.47
Extracurricular activities	*"Have you participated in at least two extracurricular activities in or out of school?"*	0.52

Source: Wright, D., and Pemberton, M. (2004). *Risk and protective factors for adolescent drug use: Findings from the 1999 National Household Survey on Drug Use.* Rockville, MD: Substance Abuse and Mental Health Services Administration, Chapter 3 and Appendix A.

however, that in the case of marijuana use, we are speaking of an increased *probability* that it will occur, not necessarily a cause-and-effect relationship.

As shown in Table 1.3, other leading risk factors for marijuana use include the perceived prevalence of marijuana use by friends in and out of school and one's own attitude and the attitude of friends toward marijuana smoking. By contrast, economic deprivation, as measured by a household income under $20,000, fails to be a risk factor for marijuana use.[36]

Specific Protective Factors

Protective factors provide the basis for someone to have stronger resistance against the temptations of drugs, to have a degree of resilience against engaging in a drug-taking life-style, despite the presence of risk factors in that person's life.[37] It is important that we not see these protective factors as simply the inverted image, or the negation, of opposing risk factors. Rather, each group of factors operates independently of the other. One way of thinking about protective factors is to view them as a kind of insurance policy against the occurrence of some future event that you hope to avoid.[38] For example, the third protective factor listed in Table 1.3 shows an odds ratio of 0.45, indicating that youths aged twelve to seventeen who answer "yes" to the question "Do you like going to school?" are about one-half (0.45, to be precise) as likely to have tried or used marijuana during the past year as youths who answer "no."

Protective factors can serve as a buffering element among even high-risk adolescents, giving them a greater degree of resilience against drug-taking behavior and a higher resistance to drug use than they would have had otherwise. Leading protective factors include a commitment to conventionality in one form or another and a degree of social support from one's family.

Obviously the more protective factors in our lives, the better our chances of resilience with respect to drug-related problems. In one study, protective factors were examined in one thousand high-risk male and female adolescents in the seventh and eighth grades, and information was collected on their drug use later in high school. As the number of protective factors increased, the resistance of these students to drug use increased as well. With six or more such factors in their lives, as many as 56 percent of the high-risk adolescents showed a resistance to drug use three years later. In contrast, only

20 percent of the youths with three or fewer protective factors were drug-free.[39]

Present-Day Concerns

What does the future hold with respect to psychoactive drugs and drug-taking behavior? One certainty is that specific drugs will continue to come into and fall out of favor. New drugs will appear on the scene, and others may reappear like ghosts from the past, sometimes in new forms and involving new faces in the drug underground.[40]

Club Drugs

A serious concern in today's drug scene has been the popularity of so-called "club drugs," a term that originally referred to substances ingested at all-night dance parties ("raves"), dance clubs, and bars. Today, the term designates a loosely defined category of recreational psychoactive drugs that are used by young people, primarily in a social setting. Examples of club drugs include MDMA (Ecstasy), GHB, ketamine, Rohypnol, methamphetamine, and LSD. When used in combination with alcohol, as they often are, these drugs carry considerably increased health risks, beyond their own individual toxicities. Because many club drugs are colorless, tasteless, and odorless, they can be slipped unobtrusively into drinks by individuals who want to intoxicate or sedate others. The potential danger of sexual assault, therefore, is a major problem.[41] Drugs in Focus examines the major features of these six club drugs. A more detailed discussion will follow in Chapter 4 (methamphetamine), Chapter 6 (LSD, MDMA, and ketamine), and Chapter 13 (GHB and Rohypnol).

Nonmedical Use of Prescription Pain Relievers

Although present-day prevalence rates among adolescents and young adults for several categories of illicit drugs are much lower than rates observed in earlier years (see Figure 1.2), the incidence of nonmedical (recreational) use of prescription pain relievers has risen to alarmingly high levels and has become a major social problem. In 2011, about 3.4 million young adults, aged eighteen to twenty-five years, in the United States used prescription pain relievers

Drugs . . . in Focus

Facts about Club Drugs

MDMA (methylenedioxymethamphetamine)

- Street names: Ecstacy, XTC, X, E, Adam, Clarity, Lover's Speed, Hug Drug, Euphoria, M&M
- Variations: MDA (methylenedioxyamphetamine), MDEA (methylenedioxyethylamphetamine)
- Forms: Tablet or capsule
- Behavioral effects: Appetite suppression, excitation, perceptual distortions
- Physiological effects: Increased heart rate and blood pressure, dehydration
- Length of effect: 3 to 6 hours
- Toxicity: Marked increase in body temperature; possible heart attack, stroke, or seizure (see Chapter 6)

GHB (gamma-hydroxybutyrate)

- Street names: Grievous Bodily Harm, G, Liquid X, Liquid Ecstasy, Georgia Home Boy, Goop Soup
- Variations: Gamma-butyrolactone (GBL)
- Forms: Clear liquid, tablet, capsule, or white powder
- Behavioral effects: Intoxication, euphoria, sedation, anxiety reduction
- Physiological effects: Central nervous system depressant, stimulation of growth-hormone release
- Length of effect: Up to 4 hours
- Toxicity: Overdoses produce drowsiness, loss of consciousness, impaired breathing, coma, potential death. GHB greatly potentiates the sedative action of alcohol (see Chapter 13).

Ketamine

- Street names: K, Special K, Vitamin K, Ket
- Variations: None
- Forms: Liquid, white powder snorted or smoked with marijuana or tobacco, intramuscular injection
- Behavioral effects: Dreamlike state of consciousness, hallucinations
- Physiological effects: Increased blood pressure, potential seizures, and coma
- Length of effect: 1 hour
- Toxicity: Impaired attention and memory, impaired motor coordination, disorientation (see Chapter 6)

Rohypnol (flunitrazepam)

- Street names: Roofies, Rophies, Roche, Rope, Forget-me pill

- Variations: None
- Forms: Tablet dissolvable in beverages
- Behavioral effects: Sedation
- Physiological effects: Decreased blood pressure, visual disturbances, gastrointestinal disturbances
- Length of effect: 8 to 12 hours
- Toxicity: Anterograde amnesia (loss of memory for events experienced under its influence). Rohypnol effects are greatly potentiated by alcohol (see Chapter 13).

Methamphetamine

- Street names: Speed, Ice, Meth, Crystal, Crystal Meth, Crank, Fire, Glass, Ice, Rock Candy
- Variations: Amphetamines, with varying degrees of similarity
- Forms: Many forms; methamphetamine can be smoked, snorted, injected, or orally ingested.
- Behavioral effects: Increased alertness and energy
- Physiological effects: Increased heart rate and blood pressure, decreased appetite
- Length of effect: Several hours
- Toxicity: Possible heart attack or cardiovascular collapse, seizures, cerebral hemorrhage, and coma (see Chapter 4)

LSD (lysergic acid diethylamide)

- Street names: Acid, Boomers, Yellow Sunshines, Barrels, Blotters, Cubes, Domes, Lids, Wedges
- Variations: Hallucinogens, with varying degrees of similarity
- Forms: Crystalline material soluble in water
- Behavioral effects: Distortions of visual perceptions, distortions of time and space
- Physiological effects: Increased heart rate and blood pressure, sweating, tremors
- Length of effect: 30 to 90 minutes, though effects might last several hours
- Toxicity: Numbness, nausea (see Chapter 6)

Sources: Brands, B.; Sproule, B.; and Marshman, J. (1998). *Drugs and drug abuse: A reference text.* Toronto: Addiction Research Foundation. Ricaurte, G. A., and McConn, U. D. (2005). Recognition and management of complications of new recreational drug use. *Lancet, 365,* 2137–2145.

recreationally in the past year; about 1.2 million used them on a recreational basis during the previous month.[42] Hydrocodone (brand name: Vicodin), oxycodone (brand names: Percodan, Percocet), and controlled-release oxycodone (brand name: OxyContin) have been the principal drugs involved (see Chapter 5).

Nonmedical Use of Prescription Stimulant Medications

For decades, individuals with attention deficit disorder (ADD) have been successfully treated with a number of prescription stimulant medications, principally methylphenidate (brand name: Ritalin) and a combination of dextroamphetamine and levoamphetamine (brand name: Adderall). Concern has grown, however, about two principal forms of drug misuse. The first is the practice of taking these drugs at higher doses than prescribed or combining them with alcohol. The second is the practice of diverting these drugs (that is, transferring the medication of one patient for whom it is prescribed to another individual for whom it is not prescribed), either by selling them or giving them away to friends. Nonmedical use of Adderall is of special interest because of the high prevalence rates among college students (see Chapter 4). In 2011, approximately four million (one in nine) young adults, 18 to 25 years old, reported nonmedical use of Adderall at least once in their lifetime.[43]

In these cases, the drug-taking behavior has been either recreational (to achieve a state of euphoria) or instrumental (to be able to study late into the night).

Nonmedical Use of Over-the-Counter Cough-and-Cold Medications

In 2011, approximately 5 percent of high school seniors reported taking OTC cough-and-cold medications, such as Coricidin HBP Cough and Cold Tablets, Robitussin products, and NyQuil, containing the cough suppressant dextromethorphan (abbreviated DXM or DM) in the past year for the purpose of getting high, a practice commonly referred to as "robo-tripping" or "skittling." The alcohol content (up to 10 percent) in many of these products compounds the health-related problems. The easy availability of dextromethorphan

for people of all ages and the increased risk of brain damage, seizure, and death associated with high doses of dextromethorphan are matters of great concern in today's drug scene.[44]

Why Drugs?

If the history of drug-taking behavior teaches us anything, it is that there will always be an attractiveness about the drug experience, an enticement to enter into a totally different state of consciousness. For a time, they can make us feel euphoric, light-headed, relaxed, or powerful, and there is little doubt that all this feels good. There may be nonpharmacological ways of arriving at these states of mind, but drugs are easy and quick. Some drugs give us the feeling that we are seeing or hearing things in a more intense way. No matter whether we are young or old, rich or poor, drugs enable us to retreat from a state of stress. Some drugs permit us to feel no pain.

Unfortunately, in every generation there will be young people who seek some form of temporary release from an unhappy existence, seeking some form of rebellion against traditional values as a validation of their personal journey in life. And there will be those who will use drugs to have a good time with their friends. There will be young people who are simply willing to try anything new, including drugs. Their curiosity to find out "what it's like" brings us full circle to the earliest times in human history, when we nibbled on the plants in the field just to find out how they tasted. In the modern era, drug experimentation is neither a new nor a singular phenomenon; it can involve an alcoholic drink, an inhaled solvent from some household product, a cigarette, or an illicit drug.

As we will see in Chapter 3, drug experimentation has everything to do with neural circuitry deep in our brains and the release of a neurotransmitter called dopamine, a neurochemical that is at the heart of our feelings of pleasure and reward. Release of dopamine at crucial moments is like a bold-face signal that "this event is worth remembering." Natural rewards affect dopamine activity in the same way, but psychoactive drugs can do it more powerfully. In doing so, these drugs can "hijack" a natural process in our brains.[45]

The personal and social problems associated with drug-taking behavior are examined in Chapter 2.

PORTRAIT

From Oxy to Heroin: The Life and Death of Erik

Erik lived in a suburban Long Island, New York, community, and heroin killed him in 2008 at the age of 19. His mother, Linda D., never imagined what she was up against. "You worry," she has said, "about them smoking pot. You worry about them driving recklessly. You worry about them not using their seat belt. You worry about that phone call in the middle of the night. You don't worry about heroin. Because it didn't exist in my mindset."

In the last few years, the reality of heroin in the suburbs and small towns of America, previously considered to be immune from its deadly reach, has hit home with a sudden and unexpected vengeance. As a director of a local drug counseling center has expressed it, "They're starting younger, they're starting with more substances, they have better access, everything is cheaper, and they have more money." You would call that a perfect storm.

Heroin arrests have doubled; rehabilitation-facility admissions of those 21 and under for prescription pain reliever dependence have tripled or quadrupled in many cases.

In the case of Erik, it began after an emergency appendectomy with a prescription for Vicodin. Erik gradually entered into a shadowy world of drug-taking behavior. Finding new supplies of Vicodin, then shifting to OxyContin, was easy. "It sounded grimy and sleazy," a teenager would say in reference to her own dependence on prescription pain relievers, "but at the time it was just what I did. Everyone knows someone who can get them for you."

At some point in early 2008, according to Linda, "The oxys dried up." Erik turned from pills to heroin. "It started at a party," she has said. "Someone said to him, 'Oh, try this.'" By May, Linda and her husband realized Erik was using heroin.

In the weeks that followed, they tried to convince him to get help. The family's insurance covered Erik's first trip to a rehabilitation facility in upstate New York, but when Erik left after three days, the insurance company told the family that he had used up their "once in a lifetime" rehabilitation coverage. They tried to convince public hospitals to admit Erik, but he was denied. In the meantime, Erik's parents were finding injection needles around the house and discarded rubber tubing. They desperately tried to cobble together funds to pay for rehabilitation, but they didn't succeed in time. Erik died in July.

Sources: Lefrowitz, M. (2009, June 14). Heartbreak of addiction hits home. *Newsday*, pp. A4–A6. Archibold, R. C. (2009, May 31). In heartland death, traces of heroin's spread. *New York Times*, pp. 1, 24.

Summary

Social Messages about Drug Use

- Unfortunately, we live in a social environment that sends us mixed messages with respect to drug use. Cigarette smoking is still often portrayed in a positive light in movies and other forms of entertainment media, despite persistent reminders of health hazards related to tobacco use. Beer commercials on television constitute popular forms of entertainment as well as effective marketing tools, despite the fact that alcohol abuse and alcoholism continue to present serious personal and societal problems. Prominent political figures admit to experiences with marijuana earlier in their lives, while marijuana remains officially classified by the U.S. government as a drug with a high potential for abuse and no accepted medical use.

- Anti-drug campaigns in the media compete with pro–drug-use messages arising from the entertainment industry as well as Internet web sites.

Two Ways of Looking at Drugs and Behavior

- Psychoactive drugs are those drugs that affect our feelings, perceptions, and behavior. Depending on the intent of the individual, drug use can be considered either instrumental or recreational.

- Drug misuse refers to cases in which a prescription or over-the-counter drug is used inappropriately. Drug abuse refers to cases in which a licit or illicit drug is used in ways that produce some form of impairment.

Drugs in Early Times

- Probably the earliest experiences with psychoactive drugs came from tasting naturally growing plants. Individuals with knowledge about such plants were able to attain great power within their cultures.

- Ancient Egyptians and Babylonians in particular had extensive knowledge of both psychoactive and non-psychoactive drugs. Some of these drugs had genuine beneficial effects.

Drugs in the Nineteenth Century

- Medical advances in the 1800s succeeded in the isolation of active ingredients within many psychoactive substances. For example, morphine was identified as the major active ingredient in opium.

- Psychoactive drugs were in widespread use, principally in the form of patent medicines. Only by the end of the century were the risks of drug dependence beginning to be recognized.

Drugs and Behavior in the Twentieth Century

- Increased concern about the social effects of drug dependence led to restrictive legislation regarding the use of morphine, heroin, cocaine, and marijuana.

- Social pressure from the temperance movement resulted in the national prohibition of alcohol consumption in the United States from 1920 to 1933.

- After 1945, important strides were made in the development of antibiotics and psychiatric drugs.

- By the 1940s and 1950s, illicit drugs such as heroin, cocaine, and marijuana were outside the mainstream of American life.

- In the 1960s and 1970s, the use of marijuana and hallucinogenic drugs spread across the nation, along with an increase in problems related to heroin.

- A decline in heroin abuse in the 1980s was matched by an increase in cocaine abuse and the emergence of crack as a cheap, smokable form of cocaine.

Present-Day Attitudes Toward Drugs

- It is now recognized that a wide range of psychoactive drugs, licit or illicit, qualify as potential sources of misuse and abuse.

- Individuals born toward the end of the "baby boom" generation were the first group to have grown up during the explosion of drug experimentation in the 1960s and 1970s. Now, as the parents of teenagers at the beginning of the twenty-first century, they face the difficult challenge of dealing with the present-day drug-taking behavior of their children. Interestingly, there appears to be no relationship between prior marijuana use among parents and marijuana use by their children.

Patterns of Drug Use in the United States

- In 2011, approximately one out of three high school seniors used marijuana over the past year and one out of sixteen seniors used marijuana on a daily basis. Marijuana smoking represents the overwhelming proportion of illicit drug use in this population.

- The prevalence rate in 2011 for alcohol use in the past month among high school seniors was 40 percent and among college students was 64 percent. Roughly 10 percent of high school seniors and 7 percent of college students smoked at least one cigarette every day in 2011.

- In 2011, more than 21 million Americans aged twenty-six or older had used an illicit drug of some kind during the past twelve months. More than 15 million Americans used marijuana or hashish, and more than 8 million Americans engaged in the recreational use of a prescription pain reliever during this time period.

Making the Decision to Use Drugs

- Risk factors for drug-taking behavior in adolescence include a tendency toward nonconformity within society and the influence of drug-using peers.

- Protective factors for drug-taking behavior include an intact home environment, a positive educational experience, and conventional peer relationships.

Present-Day Concerns

- Predictions regarding future drugs and drug-taking behaviors are largely founded on patterns from the past. New drugs will undoubtedly come on the scene; old drugs that are out of favor might regain popularity.

- A serious concern in recent years has been the emergence of a group of drugs referred to as club drugs. They include MDMA (Ecstasy), GHB, ketamine, Rohypnol, methamphetamine, and LSD.

- Relatively high prevalence rates for recreational use of prescription drugs and over-the-counter drugs among young people have raised serious concerns. Examples of abused drugs in these categories include prescription pain medications such as Percocet, Vicodin, and OxyContin; prescription stimulant medications such as Ritalin and Adderall; and dextromethorphan in popular over-the-counter cough-and-cold remedies.

Key Terms

chlorpromazine, p. 12
drug, p. 5
drug abuse, p. 7
drug dependence, p. 4
drug misuse, p. 7

Ebers Papyrus, p. 10
illicit drugs, p. 4
instrumental use, p. 6
licit drugs, p. 4
neuroscience, p. 13

patent medicine, p. 11
placebo effect, p. 10
protective factors, p. 19
psychoactive drugs, p. 4
recreational use, p. 7

risk factors, p. 19
shaman, p. 10
shamanism, p. 9

Endnotes

1. The Gallup Organization (2011, March 21). Americans' worries about economy, budget top other issues. Wax, P. M. (2002). Just a click away: Recreational drug web sites on the Internet. *Pediatrics*, 109, 96.

2. Johnston, L. D.; O'Malley, P. M.; Bachman, J. G.; and Schulenberg, J. E. (2012, December 19). Decline in teen smoking continues in 2012. University of Michigan News Service, Ann Arbor, MI, Table 1. Centers for Disease Control and Prevention (2012, January 13). Vital signs: Binge drinking prevalence, frequency, and intensity among adults—United States, 2010. *Morbidity and Mortality Weekly*, 61, 14–19. Substance Abuse and Mental Health Services (2012, February 16). More than 7 million children live with a parent with alcohol problems. *Data Spotlight*. Rockville, MD: Substance Abuse and Mental Health Services Administration. The path to smoking addiction starts at very young ages. Campaign for Tobacco-Free Kids, Washington DC. Accessed at www. tobaccofreekids.org/research/factsheets/pdf/0127.pdf.

3. Courtesy of the Drug Enforcement Administration, U.S. Department of Justice, Washington, DC, 2013. Kleinfeld, N. R. (2012, January 12). Prescriptions of oxycodone rose sharply in New York. *New York Times*, p. A22. National Institute on Drug Abuse (2011, October). Prescription drug abuse and addiction. *NIDA Research Report Series*. Rockville MD: National Institute on Drug Abuse. Warner, M; Chen L. H.; Makuc, D. M.; Anderson, R. N.; Miniño (2011, December). Drug poisoning deaths in the United States, 1980-2008. *NCHS Data Brief*, No. 81. Atlanta: Centers for Disease Control and Prevention. Updated information from the Centers for Disease Control and Prevention, 2012.

4. Centers for Disease Control and Prevention (2012, January). *Binge drinking: Nationwide problem, local solutions*. Atlanta, GA: Centers for Disease Control and Prevention. Substance Abuse and Mental Health Services Administration (2009, December 29). Illicit drug use among older adults. *The NSDUH Report*, Figures 1 and 2. Substance Abuse and Mental Health Services Administration (2010, February 18). Substance use among black adults. *The NSDUH Report*, Figures 2 and 3.

5. Forman, R. F. (2003). Availability of opioids on the Internet. *Journal of American Medical Association*, 290, 889. Levy, C. J. (2005, October 9). Drink, don't drink. *New York Times*, p. 14. Primack, B. A.; Dalton, M. A.; Carroll, M. V.; Agarwal, A. A.; and Fine, M. J. (2008). Content analysis of tobacco, alcohol, and other drugs in popular music. *Archives of Pediatrics and Adolescent Medicine*, 162, 169–175. Snyder, L. B., and Nadorff, P. G. (2010). Youth substance use and the media. In L. M. Scheier (Ed.), *Handbook of drug use etiology: Theory, methods, and empirical findings*. Washington, DC: American Psychological Association, pp. 475–491.

6. Leshner, A. I. (1998, October). Addiction is a brain disease—and it matters. *National Institute of Justice Journal*, 2–6. Wise, R. A. (2000). Addiction becomes a brain disease. *Neuron*, 26, 27–31.

7. Jacobs, M. R., and Fehr, K. O'B. (1987). *Drugs and drug abuse: A reference text*. Toronto: Addiction Research Foundation, pp. 3–5.

8. Goode, E. (2008). *Drugs in American society* (7th ed.). New York: McGraw-Hill College, pp. 13–19.

9. Caldwell, A. E. (1970). *Origins of psychopharmacology: From CPZ to LSD*. Springfield, IL: C. C. Thomas, p. 3. Muir, H. (2003, December 20; 2004, January 9). Party animals. *New Scientist*, pp. 56–59.

10. Bryan, C. P. (1930). Labate, B. C. (2011). Consumption of ayahuasca by children and pregnant women: Medical controversies and religious perspectives. *Journal of Psychoactive Drugs*, 43 (1), 27–35. Metzner, R. (1998). Hallucinogenic drugs and plants in psychotherapy and shamanism. *Journal of Psychoactive Drugs*, 30, 333–341.

11. Grilly, D. M., and Salamone, J. D. (2012). *Drugs, brain, and behavior* (6th ed.). Boston: Pearson Education, p. 321.

12. Sneader, W. (1985). *Drug discovery: The evolution of modern medicines*. New York: Wiley, pp. 15–47.

13. Levinthal, C. F. (1988). *Messengers of paradise: Opiates and the brain*. New York: Anchor Press/Doubleday, pp. 3–25.

14. Bugliosi, V. (1991). *Drugs in America: The case for victory*. New York: Knightsbridge Publishers, p. 215.

15. Freud, S. (1884). Über Coca (On Coca). *Central-blatt für die gesammte Therapie*. Translated by S. Pollak (1884). St. Louis Medical and Surgical Journal, 47.

16. Inciardi, J. A. (2002). *The war on drugs III*. Boston: Allyn and Bacon, p. 24.

17. Aaron, P., and Musto, D. (1981). Temperance and prohibition in America: A historical overview. In M. H. Moore and D. R. Gerstein (Eds.), *Alcohol and public policy*. Washington, DC: National Academy Press, pp. 127–181.

18. Helmer, J. (1975). *Drugs and minority oppression*. New York: Seabury Press. Schlosser, Eric (2003). *Reefer madness: Sex, drugs, and cheap labor in the American black market*. Boston: Houghton Mifflin, p. 245. Smoking prevalence among U.S. adults, 1955–2007. U.S. Centers for Disease Control and Prevention, Atlanta, GA.

19. Cantor, N. F. (1969). *Western civilization: Its genesis and destiny*. Vol. 2. New York: Scott, Foresman.

20. Courtwright, D. (2001). *Forces of habit: Drugs and the making of the modern world*. Cambridge, MA: Harvard University Press. Egan, Timothy (1999, February 28). War on crack retreats, still taking prisoners. *New York Times*, pp. 1, 22–23.

21. Kandel, D. B.; Griesler, P. C.; Lee, G.; Davies, M.; and Schaffsan, C. (2001). *Parental influences on adolescent marijuana use and the baby boom generation: Findings*

from the *1976–1996 National Household Survey on Drug Abuse*. Rockville, MD: Substance Abuse and Mental Health Services Administration. Merlino, A. C.; O'Malley, P. M.; Schulenberg, J. E.; Bachman, J. G.; and Johnston, L. D. (2004). Substance use among adults 35 years of age: Prevalence, adulthood predictors, and impact of adolescent substance use. *American Journal of Public Health*, 94, 96–102. Wallace-Wells, B. (2012, December 3) The truce on drugs: What happens now that the war has failed? *New York Times Magazine*, pp. 30–35, 104–106.

22. Johnston, L. D.; O'Malley, P. M.; Bachman, J. G.; and Schulenberg, J. E. (2012a). *Monitoring the Future: National survey results on drug use, 1975–2011. Vol. I: Secondary school students 2011*. Ann Arbor, MI: Institute for Social Research, The University of Michigan. Tables 2-2 and 2-4. Johnston, L. D.; O'Malley, P. M.; Bachman, J. G.; and Schulenberg, J. E. (2012b). *Monitoring the Future: National survey results on drug use, 1975–2011. Vol. II: College students and adults ages 19–50, 2011*. Ann Arbor, MI: Institute for Social Research, The University of Michigan.

23. Johnston, O'Malley, Bachman, and Schulenberg, *Monitoring the Future*, Vol. I, Table 2-2.

24. Johnston, O'Malley, Bachman, and Schulenberg, *Monitoring the Future*, Vol. II, Tables 2-1, 2-2, and 2-3.

25. Johnston, O'Malley, Bachman, and Schulenberg, *Monitoring the Future*, Vol. I, Tables 5-2 and 5-4.

26. Ibid, Tables 9-6 and 9-8.

27. Johnston, O'Malley, Bachman, and Schulenberg, *Monitoring the Future*, Vol. II, Tables 2.3, 2.4, 9-3, and 9-4.

28. Johnston, O'Malley, Bachman, and Schulenberg, *Monitoring the Future*, Vol. I, Table 2-4.

29. Johnston, O'Malley, Bachman, and Schulenberg, *Monitoring the Future*, Vol. II, Table 2-4.

30. Johnston, O'Malley, Bachman, and Schulenberg, *Monitoring the Future*, Vol. I, Tables 2-3, 8-1, and 9-8.

31. Johnston, L. D. (1996, December 19). The rise in drug use among American teens continues in 1996. News release from the University of Michigan, Ann Arbor, pp. 6–7.

32. Johnston, L. D.; O'Malley, P.M.; Bachman, J. G.; and Schulenberg, J. E. (2011, December 14). Marijuana use continues to rise among U.S. teens, while alcohol use hits historic lows. University of Michigan News Service, Ann Arbor, MI. Johnston, O'Malley, Bachman, and Schulenberg, *Monitoring the Future*, Vol. I, Table 8-6.

33. Substance Abuse and Mental Health Services Administration. (2012). *Results from the 2011 National Survey on Drug Use and Health: Detailed tables*. Rockville, MD: Substance Abuse and Mental Health Services

Administration, Tables 1.22A, 1.22B, 1.27A, 1.27B, 1.52A, and 1.52B.

34. Johnston, L., and O'Malley, P. M. (1986). Why do the nation's students use drugs and alcohol? Self-reported reasons from nine national surveys. *The Journal of Drug Issues*, 16, 29–66.

35. Goode, *Drugs*, pp. 73–75.

36. Wright, D., and Pemberton, M. (2004). *Risk and protective factors for adolescent drug use: Findings from the 1999 National Household Survey on Drug Abuse*. Rockville, MD: Substance Abuse and Mental Health Services—Administration, Chapter 3 and Appendix A.

37. Scheier, L. M.; Botvin, G. J.; and Baker, E. (1997). Risk and protective factors as predictors of adolescent alcohol involvement and transitions in alcohol use: A prospective analysis. *Journal of Studies in Alcohol*, 58, 652–667.

38. Wright and Pemberton, *Risk and protective factors*, Chapter 3 and Appendix A.

39. Smith, C.; Lizotte, A.J.; Thornberry, T. P.; and Krohn, M. D. (1995). Resilient youth: Identifying factors that prevent high-risk youth from engaging in delinquency and drug use. In J. Hagan (Ed.), *Delinquency and disrepute in the life course*. Greenwich, CT: JAI Press, pp. 217–247.

40. Inciardi, *War on drugs*. Archibald, R.C. (2009, May 31). In heartland death, traces of heroin's spread. *New York Times*, pp. 1, 24.

41. Substance Abuse and Mental Health Services Administration (2004, July). Club drugs, 2002 update. *The DAWN Report*. Rockville, MD.: Substance Abuse and Mental Health Services Administration, pp. 1–4.

42. Substance Abuse and Mental Health Services Administration (2008, June 19). Nonmedical use of pain relievers in substate regions: 2004 to 2006. *The NSDUH Report*, pp. 1–4. Substance Abuse and Mental Health Services Administration, *Results from the 2011 National Survey on Drug Use and Health: Detailed tables*, Table 1.56A.

43. Substance Abuse and Mental Health Services Administration, *Results from the 2011 National Survey on Drug Use and Health: Detailed tables*, Tables 7-23A and 7-23B.

44. Substance Abuse and Mental Health Services Administration (2008). *The abuse of prescription and over-the-counter drugs*. Rockville, MD: Substance Abuse and Mental Health Services Administration. Substance Abuse and Mental Health Services Administration (2007, January 10). Misuse of over-the-counter cough and cold medications among persons aged 12 to 25. *The NSDUH Report*, pp. 1–4.

45. Friedman, R. A. (2010, Augusut 31). Lasting pleasures, robbed by drug abuse. *New York Times*, p. D6.

Drug-Taking Behavior: Personal and Social Issues

I'm a park ranger assigned to a small community park, basically three manicured baseball fields and about four acres of woods, in the middle of a moderate-income-to-affluent suburban town. About a hundred yards into the woods is a hangout where the debris includes a home-made bong used to smoke drugs and lots of needles. Heroin used to be the last thing on the minds of public safety officers and unarmed park rangers like myself just a few years ago. Now we find heroin even in cars outside youth baseball games, less than twenty yards away from kids and parents. Last night, a young man was spotted wandering around the park. We knew that he had been arrested with 77 pills about three weeks ago. But there he was again, looking dazed and disoriented. Fresh needle marks were seen on the inside of both his arms; his car smelled of marijuana. He was clean and his car was clean, so the police had to let him go. "We'll see him again," the police officer said.

Three hours later, he was spotted outside an all-night fast-food place hustling OxyContin.

Ask someone whether drugs present a major problem in the United States today, and you will get a loud, clear, affirmative answer.[1] We all recognize that drug-taking behavior, specifically the abuse of either illicit or licit drugs, seriously undermines America's family life, economy, public health, and public safety. But sometimes it is difficult to appreciate how big of a problem it really is—in economic terms and in our personal lives:

- Each year, we spend in the United States approximately $25 billion on health care for either specialty services, behavioral consequences, or prevention of alcohol and illicit drug abuse. Health care costs associated with tobacco use add another $96 billion annually.

- Each year, we incur more than 106,000 premature deaths from alcohol and illicit drug abuse, representing nearly $90 billion in productivity losses and more than 3 million years of "potential life lost." These numbers are far greater when you consider the number of premature deaths, productivity loss, and years of potential life lost as a result of tobacco use (see Chapter 10).[2]

Agreeing that we have a problem and seeing the enormous impact, however, are only the first steps. If we are to expend our energies, as well as public funds, on ways to reduce "the drug problem," it is important to know or at least reach some degree of consensus about where the problems are and which problems are most deserving of our efforts. Here is where people disagree and controversy exists. This chapter will concern itself with the specific aspects of drugs that are known to present significant problems for individuals and for society in general. It will then explore the response our society has made to these problems, in the form of governmental policy.

At the outset, it should be emphasized that the real culprits are not the drugs per se but rather certain forms of drug-taking behavior. If a drug, for example, were totally without any redeeming value (let us say it was extremely poisonous), most people would simply avoid it. It would be a "non-issue." It would have no street value (other than perhaps to a terrorist), and no one would object to measures that restricted access to it. It would be a totally "bad" drug, but in terms of drug use, few people would care about it at all.

When we characterize heroin and cocaine as "bad drugs" (that is, drugs for which we need some governmental restriction of access), we are essentially saying that society has calculated the perceived risks of heroin or cocaine use against any potential social benefits. Heroin and other drugs such as opium and morphine are excellent painkillers and have been used medically in many countries of the world for a long time. In the case of opium, we are speaking of thousands of years of medical use. Cocaine is an excellent local anesthetic and has been used in a large number of medical procedures in the United States. Nonetheless, society has decided that these positive applications in medicine are outweighed by the negative consequences for the general public, on both a personal and a social level.

The advantage of focusing on drug-taking behavior rather than simply on drugs themselves can be highlighted by a bizarre but true story from the mid-1970s. At that time, a number of male patients were being treated for alcoholism in a Veterans Administration hospital in California. In one ward, a patient was observed moving his bed into the men's room. Shortly afterward, several of his fellow patients, one by one, did the same.

What was behind this curious behavior? Evidently these men, deprived of alcohol after years of alcohol abuse, had discovered that drinking huge amounts of water (more than seven gallons a day) produced a "high" by altering the acid-to-base balance of their blood. They had found a highly dangerous but psychologically effective way of getting drunk. The fact that they were also urinating approximately the same amount of water each day accounted for their decision to move into the men's room.[3] The point of the story is that in this case, water had become a psychoactive substance without technically being a drug (recall the definition from Chapter 1). Once again, it is useful to focus on specific behaviors and their consequences, rather than on the substance itself.

by the numbers . . .

34 Percentage of approximately 2.5 million drug-related emergency department visits in the United States in 2011 that were due to the nonmedical use of prescription or non-prescription drugs alone.

720 Number of armed robberies of pharmacies in the United States in 2012, about twice as many as reported in 2006.

148 Percentage increase in the number of emergency department visits in the United States in 2011 due to the nonmedical use of a prescription or OTC medication, relative to 2004.

Sources: Substance Abuse and Mental Health Services Administration (2013). *Drug Abuse Warning Network, 2011: National estimates of drug-related emergency department visits*. Rockville, MD: Substance Abuse and Mental Health Services Administration. Armed robbery pharmacy incidents courtesy of the U.S. Department of Justice, 2013.

In this chapter, our examination of personal and social concerns associated with drug-taking behavior will focus on three main questions:

- What are the potential risks to one's physical health and to the health of others?
- What are the potential risks for physical and psychological dependence?
- What is the connection between drug-taking behavior and violence and crime?

Drug Toxicity

When we say that a drug is toxic, we are referring to the fact that it may be dangerous or poisonous or may in some way be interfering with a person's normal functioning. Technically, any substance, no matter how benign, has the potential for **toxicity** if the **dose**—the amount in which the substance is taken—is high enough. The question of a drug's safety, or its relative safety when compared to other drugs, centers on the possibility that it may be toxic at relatively low doses. We certainly do not want people to harm themselves accidentally when taking the drug in the course of their daily lives. When there is a possibility that the *short-term* effects of a particular drug will trigger a toxic reaction, then this drug is identified as having some level of **acute toxicity**.

To understand the concept of toxicity in more detail, we need to examine an S-shaped graph called the **dose-response curve** (Figure 2.1a). Let us assume we have the results of data collected from laboratory tests of a hypothetical sleep-inducing drug. Increases in the dose level of the drug will produce the desired sleep-inducing effect in an increasingly large percentage of a test population of mice. At 10 milligrams (mg), 50 percent of the population has fallen asleep; at 50 mg, 100 percent has done so. There is always some variability in individual reactions to any drug; some mice may be internally resistant to the drug's effect, while others may be quite susceptible. We cannot predict *which specific animal* might fall asleep with 10 mg of the drug, only that the probability of a given animal doing so is 50 percent.

We define the **effective dose (ED)** of a drug having a specific effect on a test population in terms of probabilities, from 0 percent to 100 percent. For example, the ED50 of a drug refers to the effective dose for 50 percent of the population; ED99 refers to the effective dose for 99 percent of the population. In this case, the ED numbers refer to the drug's effect of producing sleep on a specific proportion of the population being exposed to the drug. The same drug may be producing other effects (muscular relaxation,

for instance) at lower doses; these drug effects would have their own separate dose-response curves. Remember that we are looking at the properties of a specific drug *effect* here, not at the overall properties of the drug itself.

Now we can look at Figure 2.1b, where the effective dose-response curve is represented next to another S-shaped dose-response curve, also gathered from laboratory testing, only in this case the "response" is death. It makes sense that the second curve should be shifted to the right because the **lethal dose (LD)** would generally require a higher dosage of a drug than the dosage necessary to produce a nonlethal effect.

Emphasis should be placed on the word "generally," because the lethal dose-response curve may overlap with the effective dose-response curve (as it does in this example). In the example shown, although a 100-mg dose needs to be taken to kill 50 percent of the test population, a dose of as little as 50 mg (or less) is lethal for at least a few of them. The LD50 of a drug refers to the lethal dose for 50 percent of the population; LD1 refers to a relatively lower dose that is lethal for only 1 percent of the population.

In order to arrive at an idea of a drug's overall toxicity, we need to combine the effective and lethal doses of a drug in a ratio. The ratio of LD50/ED50 is called the **therapeutic index.** For example, if the LD50 for a drug is 450 mg, and the ED50 is 50 mg, then the therapeutic index is 9. In other words, you would have to take nine times the dose that would be effective for half of the population in order to incur a 50 percent chance of death in that population.

---

toxicity (tox-IS-ih-tee): The physical or psychological harm that a drug might present to the user.

dose: The quantity of drug that is taken into the body, typically measured in terms of milligrams (mg) or micrograms (μg).

acute toxicity: The physical or psychological harm a drug might present to the user immediately or soon after the drug is ingested into the body.

dose-response curve: An S-shaped graph showing the increasing probability of a certain drug effect as the dose level rises.

effective dose (ED): The minimal dose of a particular drug necessary to produce the intended drug effect in a given percentage of the population.

lethal dose (LD): The minimal dose of a particular drug capable of producing death in a given percentage of the population.

therapeutic index: A measure of a drug's relative safety for use, computed as the ratio of the lethal dose for 50 percent of the population to the effective dose for 50 percent of the population.

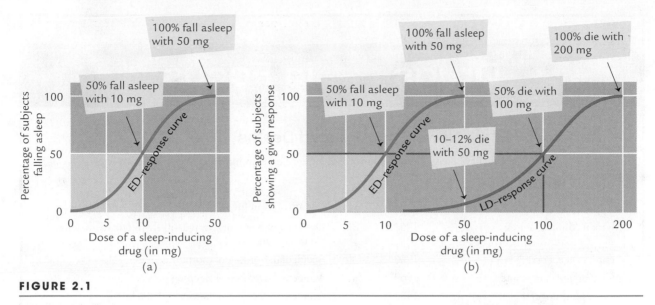

FIGURE 2.1

(a) An effective dose (ED)–response curve, and (b) an ED–response curve (left) alongside a lethal dose (LD)–response curve (right).

It can be argued that a 50 percent probability of dying represents an unacceptably high risk even for a drug that has genuine benefits. To be more conservative in the direction of safety, the ratio of LD1/ED99 is often calculated. Here we are calculating the ratio between the dose that produces death in 1 percent of the population and the dose that would be effective in 99 percent. Naturally, this second ratio, called the **margin of safety**, should be as high as possible. As before, the higher the ratio, the greater the difference between effectiveness and lethality. In other words, the wider the margin of safety, the safer (less toxic) the drug in question. Clearly, the margin of safety for the hypothetical drug examined in Figure 2.1 would present serious toxicity issues.

The therapeutic index and the margin of safety are helpful measures when considering the toxicity of drugs that are manufactured by recognized pharmaceutical companies and regulated by the U.S. Food and Drug Administration (FDA), keeping in mind the possibility that a person might intentionally or unintentionally take a higher-than-recommended dose of the drug. But what about the toxicity estimates in the consumption of illicit drugs? The unfortunate reality of street drugs is that the buyer has no way of knowing what he or she has bought until the drug has been used, and then it is frequently too late. It is an extreme case of *caveat emptor* ("Let the buyer beware").

Few if any illicit drug sellers make a pretense of being ethical businesspeople; their only objective is to make money and avoid prosecution by the law. Frequently, the drugs they sell are diluted with either inert or highly dangerous ingredients. Adulterated heroin, for example, may contain a high proportion of milk sugar as inactive filler and a dash of quinine to simulate the bitter taste of real heroin, when the actual amount of heroin that is being sold is far less than the "standard" street dosage. At the other extreme, the content of heroin may be unexpectedly high and may lead to a lethal overdose, or the adulterated product may contain animal tranquilizers, arsenic, strychnine, insecticides, or other highly toxic substances.[4] Cocaine, LSD, marijuana, and all the other illicit drugs that are available to the drug abuser, as well as look-alike drugs that are unauthorized copies of popular prescription medications, present hidden and unpredictable risks of toxicity. Even if drugs are procured from a friend or from someone you know, these risks remain. Neither of you is likely to know the exact ingredients. The potential for acute toxicity is always present.

Given the uncertainty that exists about the contents of many abused drugs, what measure or index can we use to evaluate the effects of acute toxicity on individuals in our society? The natural tendency is to look first to the news headlines; think of all the well-known public figures who have died as a direct consequence of drug misuse or abuse (see Drugs . . . in Focus on page 32).

margin of safety: The ratio of a lethal dose for 1 percent of the population to the effective dose for 99 percent of the population.

Drugs . . . in Focus

Acute Toxicity in the News: Drug-Related Deaths

The following famous people have died either as a direct consequence or as an indirect consequence of drug misuse or abuse.

Name	Year of Death	Age	Reasons Given for Death
Marilyn Monroe, actress	1962	36	Overdose of Nembutal (a sedative-hypnotic medication); circumstances unknown
Lenny Bruce, comedian	1966	40	Accidental overdose of morphine
Judy Garland, singer and actress	1969	47	Accidental overdose of sleeping pills
Janis Joplin, singer	1970	27	Accidental overdose of heroin and alcohol
Jimi Hendrix, singer and guitarist	1970	27	Accidental overdose of sleeping pills
Elvis Presley, singer and actor	1977	42	Cardiac arrhythmia suspected to be due to an interaction of antihistamine, codeine, and Demerol (a painkiller), as well as Valium and several other tranquilizers
John Belushi, comedian and actor	1982	33	Accidental overdose of heroin combined with cocaine
David A. Kennedy, son of U.S. senator Robert F. Kennedy	1984	28	Accidental interaction of cocaine, Demerol, and Mellaril (an antipsychotic medication)
Len Bias, college basketball player	1986	22	Cardiac-respiratory arrest from accidental overdose of cocaine
River Phoenix, actor	1993	23	Cardiac-respiratory arrest from accidental combination of heroin and cocaine
Jonathan Melvoin, keyboardist for the Smashing Pumpkins rock band	1996	34	Accidental overdose of heroin
Chris Farley, comedian and actor	1998	33	Accidental overdose of heroin and cocaine
Bobby Hatfield, singer, the Righteous Brothers	2003	63	Heart failure following overdose of cocaine
Mitch Hedberg, comedian	2005	37	Heart failure due to "multiple drug toxicity," including heroin and cocaine
Heath Ledger, actor	2008	28	Acute intoxication from combined use of six prescription medicines for pain, anxiety, insomnia, and nasal congestion
Michael Jackson, songwriter and entertainer	2009	50	Cardiac arrest due to an intramuscular administration of propofol (brand name: Diprivan), possibly interacting with a number of antianxiety medications
Greg Giraldo, comedian	2010	44	Accidental overdose of prescription medication and alcohol
Amy Winehouse, singer	2011	27	Accidental alcohol poisoning, resulting from a lethal blood-alcohol concentration of 0.42 percent
Whitney Houston, singer and actress	2012	48	Accidental drowning, with chronic cocaine use and heart disease as contributing factors.

Note: Celebrities whose drug-related deaths have been attributed to the toxicity of nicotine, tars, or carbon monoxide in tobacco products are not included in this listing.

Source: Various media reports.

Quick Concept Check 2.1

Understanding Dose-Response Curves

Check your understanding of dose-response curves and the toxicity of drugs by answering the questions below.

The following three sets of dose-response curves show the effective and lethal responses to three drugs, A, B, and C.

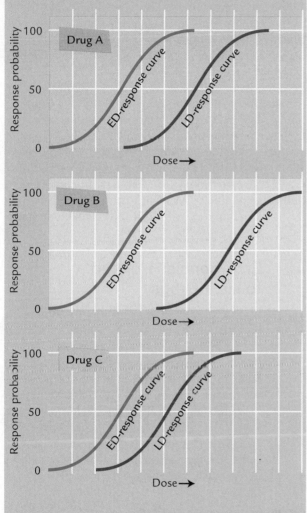

Which of the three drugs would be considered the least toxic? Which would be considered the most toxic?

Answer: Drug B is the least toxic drug. Drug C is the most toxic drug.

Such examples, however, can be misleading. Celebrities are not necessarily representative of the drug-using population in general, and the drugs prevalent among celebrities, because of their expense, may not represent the drugs most frequently encountered by the rest of society. To have some idea of the toxic effects of psychoactive drugs in a broader context, we have to turn to the institutions that contend with drug toxicity on a daily basis: the emergency departments of hospitals around the country. As we will see, the drugs involved in hospital emergencies are not necessarily the ones that are associated with *illicit* drug use.

The DAWN Reports

The U.S. government currently gathers data concerning drug-related medical emergencies in major metropolitan hospitals through a program called the **Drug Abuse Warning Network (DAWN)**. Two basic types of information are reported. The first concerns the number of times an individual visits an emergency department (ED, not to be confused with the ED used to indicate "effective dose") for any reason that is connected to recent drug use. These **drug-related ED visits** involve a wide range of drug-related situations: suicide attempts, malicious poisoning, overmedication, and adverse reactions to medications, as well as the use of illicit drugs, the use of dietary supplements, and the nonmedical use of prescription or over-the-counter (OTC) drugs. The second type of information concerns the number of *drug-related deaths*, as determined by a coroner or medical examiner.[5]

Approximately 2.5 million ED visits in the United States in 2011 (one-half of the total number of drug-related ED visits) were associated with either drug abuse or drug misuse, with an average of two drugs being reported in a given drug-related ED visit. About a third of the time, a drug-related ED visit involved more than one drug, and in some cases, there were five or more drugs mentioned at the time. The circumstances of drug-taking behavior involving multiple drugs is referred to as **polydrug use**.

Drug Abuse Warning Network (DAWN): A federal program in which metropolitan hospitals report the incidence of drug-related lethal and nonlethal emergencies.

drug-related ED visit: An occasion on which a person visits an emergency department (ED) for a purpose that is related to recent drug use.

polydrug use: Drug-taking behavior involving multiple drugs.

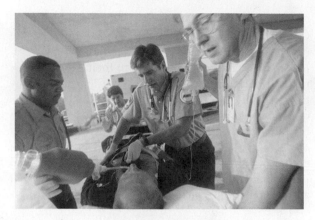
Emergency medical service (EMS) crews frequently have to deal with drug-related cases.

Figure 2.2 shows the distribution of ED visits associated with either drug abuse or drug misuse with respect to seven circumstances. The percentage of these ED visits involving prescription or OTC medications alone (34 percent) was greater than the percentage involving illicit drugs alone (27 percent), and the percentage involving medications in some combination (57 percent) was greater than the percentage involving illicit drugs in some combination (51 percent).[6] The proportion

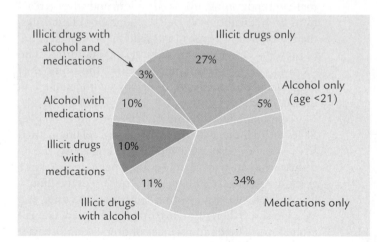

FIGURE 2.2

Distribution of drug-related emergency department visits in 2011 by type of drug involvement. Here, and in the accompanying text discussion, ED stands for "emergency department."

Source: Substance Abuse and Mental Health Services Administration (2013). *Drug Abuse Warning Network, 2011: National estimates of drug-related emergency department visits, 2004–2011.* Rockville, MD: Substance Abuse and Mental Health Services Administration.

of drug-related ED visits involving alcohol use (see Figure 2.2) requires some explanation. Statistics about ED visits *related to the use of alcohol alone* are limited in the DAWN reporting system to such use by individuals younger than twenty-one years of age. In other words, such medical emergencies are resulting, by definition, from underage drinking. DAWN statistics are not collected for ED visits involving alcohol use alone by individuals who are twenty-one years old or older.

There is a very good reason for this exclusion. If all emergencies related to alcohol use alone were reported, the numbers would far exceed those related to any other drug. Considering the number of alcohol-related automobile accidents and alcohol-related personal injuries that end up in emergency departments each year (see Chapter 8), the examination of ED visits related to other circumstances would be totally obscured if all alcohol-related ED visits were included.

An important message in the DAWN statistics is the considerable toxicity that is reflected in the alcohol-in-combination category of ED visits. In these circumstances, the ingestion of alcohol has occurred in conjunction with the ingestion of another drug, regardless of one's age. About one-fourth (24 percent) of drug-related ED visits in 2011 involved some use of alcohol in combination with either an illicit drug, with a prescription or nonprescription medication, or with an illicit drug and a medication.[7]

Emergencies Related to Illicit Drugs

What types of illicit drugs are most likely to result in an ED visit? Among drug-abuse and drug-misuse ED visits reported in 2011, the largest number involved cocaine (40 percent), followed by marijuana (36 percent), heroin (21 percent), and methamphetamine (13 percent). Notice that the percentages for these drugs add up to more than 100 percent, because of the involvement of two or more drugs at a time. In general, patients admitted for an illicit-drug-related ED visit in 2011 were about twice as likely to be male as female.[8]

Drug-Related Deaths

Current DAWN statistics on the number of drug-related deaths in the United States are not reported on a nationwide basis but instead in terms of selected metropolitan areas. This presents certain challenges in drawing conclusions about lethality of drug-taking behavior in a particular region of the country. For example, a similar number of drug-related deaths in 2010 in metropolitan Washington, DC, and metropolitan Denver, Colorado (353 versus 356), with very different populations (5.5 million versus 2.5 million), is indicative of a substantially greater drug problem in Denver as compared to Washington, DC. In mathematical terms, we are using two different denominators in arriving at the prevalence rate.

In addition, a particular metropolitan area in the DAWN survey may have a somewhat different "profile" in terms of five drugs most frequently reported in drug-related death cases. Despite these differences, however, a number of generalizations can still be made, based on the 2010 statistics.

- It is far more common for drug-related deaths to be a result of multiple-drug (polydrug) use than a result of single-drug (monodrug) use.

- In nearly all metropolitan areas surveyed in the DAWN report, an opioid drug (heroin, morphine, methadone, or opioid pain medication) is the most frequently reported drug involved in a drug-related death incident.

- Cocaine is typically reported in 2010 among the top three drugs in these circumstances, while it had been the most frequently reported in earlier years.

- Alcohol (that is, alcohol in combination with some other drug) is commonly in second or third place and is almost always in the "top five."

- Medications used to treat anxiety or depression are almost always among the top five most frequently reported drugs in drug-related death cases. However, the presence of these categories of licit drugs in the "top five" listing should be interpreted carefully. The amounts ingested in these circumstances far exceed the recommended dosage levels and have been, like alcohol, combined with one or more other drugs.

- Marijuana is far less prominent in drug-related deaths, and when there are reports of its involvement, it is almost exclusively in the context of multiple-drug rather than single-drug use.

- Methamphetamine use as a cause of a drug-related death is largely underestimated in the DAWN statistics, because of reliance on reports from large metropolitan areas rather than from smaller, rural areas in the United States, where methamphetamine has been a significant public health concern (see Chapter 4).[9]

Judging Drug Toxicity from Drug-Related Deaths

The finding that the use of heroin or cocaine alone is frequently involved in drug-related deaths is particularly striking when you consider that heroin and cocaine users constitute a relatively small proportion of the total number of illicit drug users, and certainly of the general population. The fact that there are more instances of drug-related deaths resulting from heroin use than instances of cocaine use *underestimates* the potential lethality of heroin, since there are far fewer heroin users than cocaine users in the United States. In contrast, the rare association of marijuana with a drug-related death actually *overestimates* its potential lethality, given its widespread use within a much larger group of people.

In short, a judgment about the relative toxicity of illicit drugs requires an understanding of how frequently a particular drug is used in the general population. All other facts being equal, if one illicit drug produces twice as many deaths as a second drug, but the number of users of the first drug is twice that of the second, then the toxicity levels of the two drugs should be considered equivalent.

Demographics and Trends

By examining DAWN statistics over the last thirty years or so, we can arrive at some idea of the changes that have taken place in the frequency of specific drug-related medical emergencies. For example, a dramatic increase in the number of cocaine-related emergencies occurred in the 1980s as a result of the rise of cocaine abuse and crack cocaine abuse. A decade later, an upturn in heroin-related emergencies took place during the 1990s, as the purity of available heroin increased and the availability of heroin use without a needle injection caused heroin-related emergency rates to rise.

In the mid-1990s, significant concerns emerged about the increase in ED visits arising from the use of illicit club drugs such as Ecstasy, GHB, ketamine, LSD, and methamphetamine. More recently, the class of drugs that have raised the greatest concern among health care professionals include opioid prescription medications, also known as narcotic analgesics (see Chapter 5). In 2009, more than 15,000 people in the United States died from these medications, four times more than in 1999. The principal medications of this type are methadone, oxycodone (brand name: Percocet), controlled-release oxycodone (brand name: OxyContin), and hydrocodone (brand name: Vicodin).[10]

From Acute Toxicity to Chronic Toxicity

Through the DAWN surveys, we can appreciate the extent of acute toxicity involved in the ingestion of a particular drug, but we are unable to get an illuminating picture of the negative consequences of using a particular drug over a long period of time. Examples of **chronic toxicity** can be found in a wide range of psychoactive drugs, either legally or illegally obtained. Ironically, it is the chronic use of alcohol and tobacco, both of

> **chronic toxicity:** The physical or psychological harm a drug might cause over a long period of use.

which are legally available in our society, that causes by far the greatest adverse health effects. As we will see in Chapters 9 and 10, the number of people who die each year as a result of drinking alcohol or smoking tobacco far outstrips the number of fatalities from the abuse of illicit drugs (Figure 2.3).

A number of important issues with respect to drug-taking behavior will be examined in the chapters ahead. What exactly are the problems associated with *chronic* drug use? What is the most productive way of looking at drug dependence in general? How has our society responded to the problems of drug-taking behavior over the years? How successful have we been in dealing with these problems? What new strategies are there to handle drug-related problems in a more effective way?

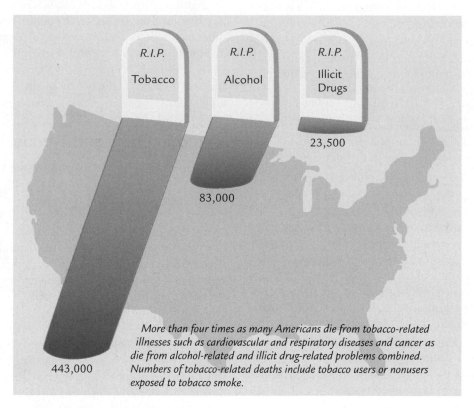

R.I.P. Tobacco

R.I.P. Alcohol

R.I.P. Illicit Drugs

23,500

83,000

443,000

More than four times as many Americans die from tobacco-related illnesses such as cardiovascular and respiratory diseases and cancer as die from alcohol-related and illicit drug-related problems combined. Numbers of tobacco-related deaths include tobacco users or nonusers exposed to tobacco smoke.

FIGURE 2.3

U.S. deaths per year from tobacco, alcohol, and illicit drug use.

Sources: Centers for Disease Control and Prevention (2008, November 14). Cigarette smoking-attributable morbidity, years of potential life lost, and productivity losses—United States, 2000–2004. *Morbidity and Mortality Weekly Report, 57*, 1226–1228. Harwood, H. (2011, October 23). Recent findings on the economic impacts of substance abuse. Presented at the American Psychological Association 2011 Science Leadership Conference, Psychological Science and Substance Abuse, Washington DC, Slide 12. Mokdad, A.H.; Marks, J.S.; Stroup, D. F.; and Gerberding, J.L. (2004). Actual causes of death in the United States, 2000. *Journal of the American Medical Association, 291*, 1238–1245.

Behavioral Tolerance and Drug Overdose

Legend has it that in the first century B.C., King Mithridates VI of Pontus, a region of modern-day Turkey near the Black Sea, grew despondent following a series of defeats by the Romans and decided to commit suicide by poison. The problem was that no amount of poison was sufficient, and the grim task had to be completed by the sword. It turned out that Mithridates, having lived in fear of being poisoned by his rivals, had taken gradually increasing amounts of poison over the course of his life to build up a defense against this possibility. By the time he wanted to end his life by his own hand, he could tolerate such large doses that poisoning no longer presented any threat to his life. This royal case is the first recorded example of drug tolerance. In fact, the phenomenon originally was called *mithridatism*, and several celebrated "poisoners" of history, including the notorious Lucretia Borgia in the early sixteenth century, were later to use the same strategy.[11]

The concept of **tolerance** refers to the capacity of a drug dose to have a gradually diminished effect on the user as the drug is taken repeatedly. Another way of viewing tolerance is to say that over repeated administrations, a drug dose needs to be increased to maintain an equivalent effect.

A common illustration of drug tolerance is the effect of caffeine in coffee. When you are first introduced to caffeine, the stimulant effect is usually quite pronounced; you might feel noticeably "wired" after a 5-ounce cup of coffee containing approximately 100 mg of caffeine (see Chapter 11). But after several days or perhaps a few weeks of coffee drinking the effect is greatly diminished; you may need to be on the second or third cup by that time, consuming 200 to 300 mg of caffeine, to duplicate the earlier reaction. Some individuals who drink coffee regularly have developed such high levels of tolerance to caffeine that they are able to sleep comfortably even after several cups of coffee, while individuals who drink coffee less often may find themselves awake through the night after a single cup.

The danger that the tolerance effect presents is the possibility of death by drug overdose, which is frequently the cause of accidental drug-related deaths listed in the DAWN reports. Individuals involved in drug abuse are often taking drug doses that are precariously close to the LD-response curve amounts, as described earlier. These dosage levels may be sustainable by a drug abuser who has grown tolerant to the drug over repeated administrations but quite lethal to an individual being introduced to the drug for the first time.

In understanding the possibility of drug overdose, it is useful to look at the *interaction* between the actual amount of the drug taken and other factors involved in the drug-taking behavior. Although, as already noted, the number of previous times the drug has been used is crucial, another important factor is the setting within which the drug-taking behavior occurs. There is strong evidence that tolerance effects are maximized when the drug-taking behavior occurs consistently in the same surroundings or under the same circumstances. We speak of this form of tolerance as **behavioral tolerance**.[12]

To have a clear idea of behavioral tolerance, we first have to understand the basic facts of Pavlovian conditioning, upon which behavioral tolerance is based.

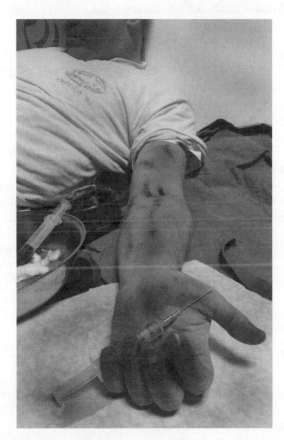

A heroin abuser suffering from a possibly lethal heroin overdose immediately after injection.

---

tolerance: The capacity of a drug to produce a gradually diminished physical or psychological effect upon repeated administrations of the drug at the same dose level.

behavioral tolerance: The process of drug tolerance that is linked to drug-taking behavior occurring consistently in the same surroundings or under the same circumstances. Also known as *conditioned tolerance*.

Suppose you consistently heard a bell ring every time you had a headache. Previously, bells had never had any negative effect on you. The association between the ringing bell and the pain of the headache, however, would become strong enough that the mere ringing of a bell would now give you a headache—perhaps less painful than the ones you had originally, but a headache nonetheless; this effect is Pavlovian conditioning at work.

A pioneering study by the psychologist Shepard Siegel showed a similar phenomenon occurring with drug-taking behavior. In his experiment, one group of rats was injected with doses of morphine in a particular room over a series of days and later tested for tolerance to that dose in the same room. Predictably, they displayed a lessened analgesic effect as a sign of morphine tolerance. A second group was tested in a room other than the one in which the injections had been given. No tolerance developed at all. They reacted as if they had never been given morphine before, even though they had received the same number of repeated injections as the first group.

In a more extreme experiment, Siegel tested two groups of rats that were administered a series of heroin injections with increasingly higher dosages. Eventually both groups were surviving a dosage level that would have been lethal to rats experiencing the drug for the first time. The difference in the groups was related to the environment in which these injections were given. One group received these injections in the colony room where they lived. When the second group were receiving their injections, they were in a room that looked quite different and were hearing 60-decibel "white noise." Siegel then administered a single LD100 dose of heroin, normally a level that should have killed them all. Instead, rats administered this extremely high dosage in the same room in which they had received the earlier heroin injection series showed only a 32 percent mortality rate. When the room was different, however, the mortality rate doubled (64 percent). In both groups, more rats survived than if they had never received heroin in the first place, but the survival rate was influenced by the environment in which the heroin was originally administered.

Siegel explained the results of his studies by assuming that environmental cues in the room where the initial injections were given elicited some form of effect *opposite* to the effect of the drug. In the case of heroin, these compensatory effects would partially counteract the analgesic effect of the drug and protect the animal against dying from potentially high dosage levels.

The phenomenon of behavioral tolerance, also referred to as *conditioned tolerance* because it is based on the principles of Pavlovian conditioning, explains why a heroin abuser may easily suffer the adverse consequences of an overdose when the drug is taken in a different environment from the one more frequently encountered or in a manner different from his or her ordinary routine.[13] An individual's tolerated dose of heroin can vary widely; amounts in the range of 200 to 500 mg may be lethal for a first-time heroin abuser, while amounts as high as 1,800 mg may not even be sufficient to make a long-term heroin abuser sick.[14] You can imagine how dangerous it would be if the conditioned compensatory responses a heroin abuser had built up over time were suddenly absent.

Quick Concept Check 2.2

Understanding Behavioral Tolerance through Conditioning

Check your understanding of behavioral tolerance as proposed by Shepard Siegel by answering the following questions.

1. Suppose you have a rat that has been placed in an environment where it had been repeatedly injected with morphine. You now inject that rat with a saline solution (a substance that has no physiological effect). Assuming that morphine will make a person less sensitive to pain, how will this animal react to the saline injection? Will the rat be less sensitive to pain, will it be more sensitive to pain, or will there be no effect? Explain your answer.

2. If King Mithridates VI had changed palaces from time to time during his reign, what would have been the effect on his eventual level of drug tolerance to poison when he chose to attempt suicide?

Answers: 1. The rat will now be more sensitive to pain. The exposure to an environment associated with morphine injections will have induced a conditioned compensatory effect: a heightened sensitivity to pain. The saline injection produces no physiological effect of its own; however, because it is given in that same environment where the morphine was administered, the conditioned effect will remain, and the rat's reaction will be hyperalgesia. (The experiment has been performed, by the way, and this predicted outcome does occur.)

2. The king would probably have died. He would not have been able to develop a sufficient level of drug tolerance to avoid succeeding in his suicide attempt.

Behavioral tolerance also helps to explain why a formerly drug-dependent individual is strongly advised to avoid the surroundings associated with his or her past drug-taking behavior. If these surroundings provoked a physiological effect opposite to the effect of the drug through their association with prior drug-taking behavior, then a return to this environment might create internal changes and feelings of craving that only drugs could reverse. In effect, environmentally induced withdrawal symptoms would increase the chances of a relapse. The fact that conditioning effects have been demonstrated with respect not only to heroin but to alcohol, cocaine, nicotine, and other dependence-producing drugs as well makes it imperative that the phenomenon of behavioral tolerance be considered during the course of drug abuse treatment and rehabilitation.[15]

Another perspective on drug tolerance, based on physiological changes that occur as result of repeated drug administrations, will be discussed in Chapter 3.

Physical and Psychological Dependence

When we refer to the idea of dependence in drug abuse, we are dealing with a person who has a strong compulsion to continue taking a particular drug. Two possible models or explanations for why drug dependence occurs can be considered. The first is referred to as physical dependence, and the second is referred to as psychological dependence. The two models are not mutually exclusive; the abuse of some drugs can be a result of both physical and psychological dependence, and the abuse of others can be a result of psychological dependence alone.

Physical Dependence

The concept of **physical dependence** originates from observations of heroin abusers, as well as of those who abuse other opioid drugs, who developed strong

physical dependence: A model of drug dependence based on the idea that the drug abuser continues the drug-taking behavior to avoid the consequences of physical withdrawal symptoms.

physical symptoms following withdrawal: a runny nose, chills and fever, inability to sleep, and hypersensitivity to pain. For barbiturate abusers in a comparable situation, symptoms include anxiety, inability to sleep, and sometimes lethal convulsions.[16] For chronic alcoholic abusers, abstention can produce tremors, nausea, weakness, and tachycardia (a rapid heart rate). If severe, symptoms may include delirium, seizures, and hallucinations.[17]

Although the actual symptoms vary with the drug being withdrawn, the fact that we observe physical symptoms at all suggests strongly that some kind of physical need, perhaps as far down as the cellular level, develops over the course of drug abuse. It is as though the drug, previously a foreign substance, has become a normal part of the nervous system, and its removal and absence become abnormal.

From this point of view, it is predictable that the withdrawal symptoms would involve symptoms that are opposite to effects the drug originally had on the body. For example, heroin can be extremely constipating, but eventually the body compensates for heroin's intestinal effects. Abrupt abstinence from heroin leaves the processes that have been counteracting the constipation with nothing to counteract, so the result of withdrawal is diarrhea. You may have noticed a strong resemblance between the action/counteraction phenomena of withdrawal and the processes Siegel has hypothesized as the basis for behavioral tolerance.

Psychological Dependence

The most important implication of the model of physical dependence, as distinct from psychological dependence, is that individuals involved in drug abuse continue their drug-taking behavior at least in part *to avoid the feared consequences of withdrawal.* This idea can form the basis for a general model of drug dependence only if physical withdrawal symptoms appear consistently for every drug considered as a drug of abuse. It turns out, however, that a number of abused drugs (cocaine, hallucinogens, and marijuana, for example) do not produce significant physical withdrawal symptoms, and the effects of heroin withdrawal are more variable than we would expect if physical dependence alone were at work.

It is possible that drug abusers continue to take the drug not because they want to avoid the symptoms of withdrawal but because they crave the pleasurable effects of the drug itself. They may even feel that they need the drug to function at all. This is the way one heroin abuser has expressed it:

> I'm just trying to get high as much as possible. . . . If I could get more money, I would spend it all on drugs. All I want is to get loaded. I just really like shooting dope. I don't have any use for sex; I'd rather shoot dope. I like to shoot dope better than anything else in the world.[18]

A majority of heroin abusers (between 56 percent and 77 percent in one major study) who complete the withdrawal process after abstaining from the drug experience relapse into their former pattern of abuse.[19] If physical dependence were the whole story, these phenomena would not exist. The withdrawal symptoms would have been gone by that time, and any physical need that might have been evident before would no longer be present.

When we speak of **psychological dependence,** we are offering an explanation of drug abuse based not on the attempt of abusers to avoid unpleasant withdrawal symptoms but on their continued desire to obtain pleasurable effects from the drug. Unfortunately, we are faced here with a major conceptual problem: The explanation by itself is circular and tells us basically nothing. If I were to say, for example, that I was taking cocaine because I was psychologically dependent on it, then I could just as easily say that I was psychologically dependent on cocaine because I was abusing it. Without some *independent* justification, the only explanation for the concept of psychological dependence would be the behavior that the concept was supposed to explain!

Fortunately, there is independent evidence for the concept of psychological dependence, founded chiefly upon studies showing that animals are as capable of self-administering drugs of abuse as humans are. Using techniques developed in the late 1950s, researchers have been able to insert a **catheter** into the vein of a freely moving laboratory animal and arrange the

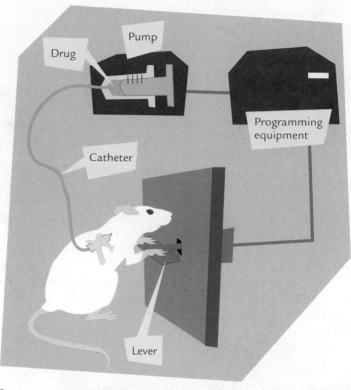

FIGURE 2.4

A simplified depiction of how drugs are self-administered in rats. The rat's pressure on a lever causes the pump to inject a drug through a catheter implanted into its vein.

equipment so that the animal can self-administer a drug intravenously whenever it presses a lever (Figure 2.4). It had been well known that animals would engage in specific behaviors to secure rewards such as food, water, or even electrical stimulation of certain regions of the brain. These objectives were defined as positive reinforcers because animals would learn to work to secure them. The question at the time was whether animals would self-administer drugs in a similar way. Could drugs be positive reinforcers as well?

The experiments showed clearly that animals would self-administer drugs such as cocaine and other stimulants, despite the fact that these drugs would not ordinarily produce physical symptoms during withdrawal. In one study, rats pressed the lever as many as 6,400 times for one administration of cocaine; others were nearly as eager for administrations of amphetamines.[20] Interestingly, a number of other drugs were aversive, judging from the reluctance of animals to work for them. Hallucinogens such as LSD, antipsychotic

psychological dependence: A model of drug dependence based on the idea that the drug abuser is motivated by a craving for the pleasurable effects of the drug.

catheter (CATH-eh-ter): A device to deliver intravenous injections of a drug in a free-moving human or animal.

drugs, and antidepressant drugs were examples of drugs that animals clearly did not like.[21]

By connecting the concept of psychological dependence to general principles of reinforcement, it is possible for us to appreciate the powerful effects of abused drugs. When an animal is presented with a choice of pressing a lever for food or pressing a lever for cocaine, cocaine wins hands down—even to the point of the animal starving to death.[22] When the effects of heroin are compared with those of cocaine, the differences are dramatic:

> *Those rats that self-administer heroin developed a stable pattern of use, maintained their pretest weight, continued good grooming behavior, and tended to be in good health. Their mortality rate was 36 percent after thirty days. Those self-administering cocaine . . . exhibited an extremely erratic pattern of use, with "binges" of heavy use alternating with brief periods of abstinence. They lost 47 percent of their body weight, ceased grooming behavior, and maintained extremely poor physical health. After thirty days, 90 percent were dead.*[23]

In the final analysis, from the standpoint of treating individuals who abuse drugs, it might not matter whether there is physical dependence or psychological dependence going on. According to many experts in the field, the distinction between physical and psychological dependence has outgrown its usefulness in explaining the motivation behind drug abuse. Whether the discontinuation of an abused drug does induce major physical withdrawal symptoms (as in the case of heroin, alcohol, and barbiturates) or does not (as in the case of cocaine, amphetamines, and nicotine), the patterns of compulsive drug-taking behavior are remarkably similar. If the pattern of behavior is the same, then there can be common strategies for treatment. Chapter 3 will examine the current understanding that most, if not all, drugs of abuse are linked together by virtue of common neurochemical processes in the brain.

Diagnosing Drug-Related Problems: The Health Professional's Perspective

Health professionals in the United States use the *Diagnostic and Statistical Manual of Mental Disorders* (referred to as the "DSM"), issued under the auspices of the American Psychiatric Association, as the official standard for defining and diagnosing a wide range of psychological problems. Since the 1980s, the hallmark feature has been that the diagnosis of a psychological disorder is determined on the basis of a number of behavioral criteria. In the case of problems associated with drug-taking behavior, one criterion might be that a person has been observed to have failed "to fulfill major role obligations at work, school, or home within a 12-month period." A specific example would be the "neglect of children or one's household."

In addition, the phrase "substance use" has been used throughout, instead of "drug use." The rationale for this decision is that confusion often exists in the public mind about what is defined as a drug (see Chapter 1) and what is not—particularly in the instance of alcohol or tobacco use. From 2000 to 2013, the fourth edition (text revision) of the DSM (referred to as DSM-IV-TR) defined two psychological disorders associated with drug-taking behavior: **substance abuse** and the more severe condition **substance dependence** (see Table 2.1). For example, one of the possible criteria for substance dependence is the observation that the person would try to stop a recurrent pattern of drug-taking behavior and repeatedly relapse into further drug use. Diagnoses of substance abuse and substance dependence were classified under the general heading of *substance-related disorders*.

A new revision of the DSM (called DSM-5) was issued in 2013, with two major changes involving drug-taking behavior. First, the four possible criteria previously listed for the diagnosis of substance abuse and the seven possible criteria for the diagnosis of substance dependence have been essentially combined into one set of eleven criteria for a newly established diagnosis called **substance use disorder**. A minimum of two criteria

substance abuse: A diagnostic term used in the DSM-IV-TR for clinical psychologists, psychiatrists, and other health professionals to identify an individual who continues to take a psychoactive drug despite the fact that the drug-taking behavior creates specific problems for that individual.

substance dependence: A diagnostic term used in the DSM-IV-TR for clinical psychologists, psychiatrists, and other health professionals to identify an individual with significant signs of a dependent relationship with a psychoactive drug.

substance use disorder: A diagnostic term used in the DSM-5 for clinical psychologists, psychiatrists, and other health professionals to identify an individual with significant problems that are associated with some form of drug-taking behavior.

TABLE 2.1

Summarizing the criteria for substance dependence and substance abuse, according to the DSM-IV-TR (prior to 2013) and substance use disorder, according to DSM-5 (effective 2013)

CRITERIA FOR SUBSTANCE DEPENDENCE

Three or more of the following conditions must have occurred within a 12-month period, lasted for more than a month or occurred repeatedly over a longer period of time:

1. **Tolerance:** Either the substance has been taken in increasingly large doses to produce the desired effect or a diminished effect has been experienced over time from the same amount of the substance.

2. **Withdrawal:** Psychological or physiological symptoms arise when use is stopped or use has continued in order to relieve or avoid these symptoms.

3. **Unintentional use in excessive amounts:** The substance is often taken in larger amounts or over a longer period of time than has been intended by the user.

4. **Persistent intentions or efforts to cut down on substance use:** There are frequent attempts to quit or reduce substance use and repeated failures (relapses) in doing so.

5. **Preoccupation:** A great deal of time is spent in behaviors that are necessary to obtain the substance, use the substance, or recover from its adverse effects.

6. **Reduction in fulfilling important personal responsibilities:** Social, occupational, or recreational obligations are not fully met or abandoned in order to engage in substance use. Examples include quitting a job or neglecting the care of a child.

7. **Continuing substance use even though there are major substance-related social or health problems:** Examples include continuance of cocaine use despite recognition of a cocaine-induced depression or continuance of drinking despite recognition that an ulcer condition would be made worse.

CRITERIA FOR SUBSTANCE ABUSE

Individuals meeting the criteria for substance abuse must never have met the criteria for substance dependence for this class of substance.

One or more of the following conditions must have occurred within a 12-month period:

1. **Recurring failure to meet major role obligations at work, school, or home due to substance use:** Examples include repeated absenteeism at work, school suspensions or expulsions, or neglect of members of one's household.

2. **Recurrence of substance use in physically hazardous situations or circumstances:** Examples include driving while intoxicated or operating a machine while impaired by substance use.

3. **Recurrent legal difficulties related to substance use:** Examples include arrests for disorderly conduct or other disruptive substance-related behaviors.

4. **Continuing substance use even though the individual is aware of persistent social, occupational, psychological or physical problems that would result or be made more difficult by the use of the substance:** Examples include physical fights or spousal arguments related to substance use.

> **DSM-5 criteria for substance use disorder**
> Criteria for substance use disorder in DSM-5 are nearly identical to the criteria for substance dependence and substance abuse in DSM-IV-TR combined into a single list, with two exceptions. The DSM-IV-TR criterion, recurrent legal difficulties, for substance abuse has been deleted and a new criterion, craving or a strong desire or urge to use the substance, has been inserted as a replacement.
>
> Two or more of these criteria must have occurred within a 12-month period of time for a diagnosis of substance use disorder.

Note: Substances include alcohol (see Chapter 9), amphetamines, caffeine, cannabis, cocaine, hallucinogens, inhalants, opioids, phencyclidine, seduative-hypnotics, and anxity-reducing medications in DSM-IV-TR and in addition, tobacco in DSM-5.

Sources: American Psychiatric Association (2013). *Highlights of changes from DSM-IV-TR to DSM-5.* Washington, DC: American Psychiatric Association. American Psychiatric Association (2000). *Diagnostic and statistical manual of mental disorders, text revision* (4th ed.). Washington DC: American Psychiatric Association.

has been established for an individual to be identified as having a substance use disorder. Second, the DSM-5 has set a severity-of-symptoms scale for this condition. The presence of two or three criteria is considered to reflect a mild level of substance use disorder, four or five criteria for a moderate level, and six or more for a severe level.

In the circumstance in which only one particular drug is involved, a substance use disorder is identified in the context of that drug. As examples, the DSM-5 allows for the possibility of a diagnosis of stimulant use disorder (see Chapter 4), opioid use disorder (see Chapter 5), hallucinogen use disorder (see Chapter 6), cannabis use disorder (see Chapter 7), or alcohol use disorder (see Chapter 9). While it may take some time for health professionals to adapt to the new DSM-5 guidelines, the change to a single diagnosis has been considered an improvement over guidelines in the previous editions of the DSM, in that it is simpler to use in the clinical treatment of substance-related problems.[24]

Special Circumstances in Drug Abuse

The discussion so far has dealt with drug-abuse problems, specifically the problems of acute and chronic toxicity, that affect only the drug user. Unfortunately, other people are frequently involved as well. Consider two special circumstances related to drug abuse that require discussions of their own: the problems of drug abuse in pregnancy and drug use in association with HIV infection.

Drug Abuse in Pregnancy

Prior to the 1960s, doctors and scientists regarded the placenta joining the bloodstream of a pregnant woman with that of the developing fetus as a natural barrier protecting the fetus from toxic substances in the mother. We now know that the idea of a "placental barrier" is clearly wrong. During gestation, nearly all drugs cross the placenta and affect the unborn child.

It is clear that women who do engage in the consumption of licit or illicit drugs during pregnancy are at increased risk for obstetrical complications and for premature labor and delivery. They are also more likely to suffer loss of the fetus through spontaneous abortions (miscarriages) and stillbirths than are women who abstain from drugs. The greater the extent of drug-taking behavior, the more likely that there will be adverse consequences.

The timing of drug use during a pregnancy has a great deal to do with the specific risks to the fetus. Drug use during the early weeks of pregnancy, from the fourth to the eighth week following conception, is more likely to increase the risks of spontaneous abortions and physical malformations in the newborn than drug use later in the pregnancy. Drug use after the eighth month of pregnancy is frequently associated with growth retardation, prematurity and low birth weight, and neurological

damage to the infant.[25] These warnings are generalizations, cutting across many categories of psychoactive substances. Health Line examines the specific risks associated with specific categories of drugs.

Approximately 26 percent of women in the United States report having smoked cigarettes in the past month during the first trimester of pregnancy; approximately 18 percent report consuming alcohol, and 7 percent report binge drinking, and approximately 8 percent report smoking marijuana during this time, despite the adverse effects on early prenatal development (see Chapters 7 and 8). These past-month prevalence rates decline significantly over the second and third trimesters but then rise among nonpregnant women with children under three months of age, suggesting that there is a resumption in drug use among mothers in the three months after childbirth.[26]

Drug Abuse and HIV Infection

One of the hazards associated with drug use by injection is the spread of disease when needles are shared. In the past, the contamination has primarily involved infectious hepatitis, a serious liver disease. Since the late 1970s, however, attention has turned to the potential spread of the human immunodeficiency virus (HIV) responsible for acquired immunodeficiency syndrome (AIDS). Since HIV-infected individuals may not show discernible AIDS symptoms for a considerable period of time (the median interval being ten years), there is unfortunately ample opportunity for contaminating others, either through sexual contact or via some direct exchange of bodily fluids.

It is estimated that about one in six injection-drug users (IDUs) in the U.S. have been infected with HIV. HIV-infection prevalence rates among IDUs exceed 40 percent, however, in at least nine other countries of the world.[27] On a domestic and international level, injection-drug use remains a significant public health risk factor for the spread of HIV infection and AIDS.[28]

In an effort to reduce the risk of HIV infection among injecting drug users, needle-exchange programs have been established so that IDUs might have the opportunity to trade in their used needles for sterile ones. These services are now available in thirty-eight U.S. states as well as the District of Columbia and Puerto Rico. The U.S. Department of Health and Human Services officially endorsed needle-exchange programs in 1998 as an effective part of a comprehensive strategy to reduce the incidence of HIV transmission, having estimated that needle-exchange programs can reduce new cases of HIV infection by one-third without increasing the use of illicit drugs. While a twenty-one-year-old

Health Line

Effects of Psychoactive Drugs on Pregnant Women and Newborns

In addition to the adverse effect of psychoactive drugs on fetal development and pregnancy in general, a number of such drugs carry very specific risks. Here is a review of these effects.

Alcohol

- Fetal effects: Impairment in the supply of fetal oxygen and stimulation of excess prostaglandins possibly causing fetal malformations.
- Pregnancy effects: Risk of miscarriage during the second trimester of pregnancy if the mother consumed as few as one or two drinks a day.
- Newborn effects: Signs of alcohol withdrawal upon birth if the mother drank heavily. Fetal alcohol syndrome involving retardation of postnatal growth and nervous system, abnormal craniofacial features, and numerous organ abnormalities.

Tobacco

- Fetal effects: Reduced oxygen supply compounded by carbon monoxide that interferes with the blood's ability to carry oxygen throughout the body.
- Pregnancy effects: Increased frequency of spontaneous abortions and fetal death.
- Newborn effects: Increased risk of physical defects and lower birth weight. Also a higher risk that infants born to mothers who smoke will die before their first birthday.

Marijuana

- Fetal effects: Increased carbon monoxide levels in mother's blood, particularly in the last trimester, resulting in reduced oxygen in fetal blood.
- Pregnancy effects: Inconsistent findings, although there is a tendency for more males to be conceived than females if either parent is a heavy marijuana smoker.
- Newborn effects: Some evidence for abnormal sleep and arousal patterns if mother has used marijuana.

Cocaine or Crack Cocaine

- Fetal effects: Constriction of blood vessels, which reduces normal fetal blood flow and causes urogenital malformations.
- Pregnancy effects: High rates of spontaneous abortion and early separation of the placenta from the uterine wall, resulting in increased numbers of stillbirths. Increased risks of early onset of labor and preterm delivery.
- Newborn effects: Increased risk of intrauterine growth retardation: lower birth weight and smaller length and head circumference. Tendency to be jittery and easily startled. Fewer discernible withdrawal symptoms than in newborns exposed to heroin or other narcotics in utero.

Methamphetamine

- Fetal effects: Unknown but likely to be similar to effects of cocaine.
- Pregnancy effects: Increased risk of premature birth, fetal distress during delivery.
- Newborn effects: Growth retardation, lethargy, increased difficulty to arouse, and, once aroused, increased autonomic reactivity. Long-term effects largely unknown.

Heroin or Morphine

- Fetal effects: Reduced oxygen supply to the fetus, as well as reduced pancreatic, liver, and intestinal functioning.
- Pregnancy effects: In 10 to 15 percent of pregnant women using heroin, development of toxemia, a poisoning of the blood between the mother and the fetus.
- Newborn effects: Retardation of intrauterine growth. Likelihood of lung problems, brain hemorrhages, and respiratory distress. Risk for perinatally transmitted HIV infection and the development of AIDS. Dramatic withdrawal symptoms usually beginning forty-eight to seventy-two hours after delivery.

Prescription Drugs

- Accutane (isoretinoin): Major birth defects associated with this antiacne medication and vitamin A derivative.
- Tetracycline antibiotics: Possibility of permanent discoloration of a child's teeth.
- Salicylates (aspirin products): Possibility of bleeding in the mother or fetus and of delay in delivery if taken close to term or prior to delivery.
- Dilantin (phenytoin): Increased risk of heart malformations, cleft lip, and mental retardation associated with this and other anticonvulsants.
- Antianxiety drugs: Possible depression of respiration in newborn when taken during labor. Fourfold increase in cleft palates and malformations of the heart and limbs when taken during early pregnancy.
- Paxil (paroxetine): Increased risk of birth defects when this antidepressant is taken during the first trimester of pregnancy.
- Barbiturates: Birth defects resembling fetal alcohol syndrome associated with long-acting barbiturates such as phenobarbital. Withdrawal symptoms in the newborn four to seven days after delivery.

Sources: Cook, P. S.; Peterson, R. C.; and Moore, D. T. (1990). *Alcohol, tobacco, and other drugs may harm the unborn.* Rockville, MD: Office of Substance Abuse Prevention. U.S. Food and Drug Administration, 2009. Smith, L. M., et al. (2008). Prenatal methamphetamine use and neonatal neurobehavioral outcome. *Neurotoxicology and Teratology, 30,* 20–28.

Mobile needle-exchange centers are available in those communities that permit needle-exchange programs.

ban on federal funding for needle-exchange programs was lifted in 2009, the ban was reinstated in 2011.[29]

Drugs, Violence, and Crime

Important questions often end up being the most complicated ones to answer. Consider the question of whether illicit drugs cause violence and crime. We can look at the news headlines reporting acts of social violence linked to the world of illicit drugs and the impact of those acts on our society: innocent children killed in the cross fire of rival drug gangs, thousands of crimes against individuals and property to pay for a continuing pattern of drug abuse, terrorization of whole communities by drug dealers. Illicit drugs and crime are bound together in a web of greed and callous disregard for human life.

The association clearly exists. We can draw on information gained from a recently revised version of the Arrestee Drug Abuse Monitoring (ADAM) Program, known as ADAM II, conducted on an annual basis since 2007 by the U.S. Department of Justice. In ADAM II, a sampling of males who have been arrested for a serious offense in ten selected U.S. metropolitan sites (a sampling of regions around the country) are tested through urinalysis within 48 hours of arrest for ten major number of illicit drugs.

Not surprisingly, ADAM II statistics indicate that drug use among an arrestee population is much higher than in the general U.S. population. In 2011, all cities reported a majority of arrestees testing positive for at least one of ten illicit drugs. The percentage varied, however, from 65 percent in Denver, Colorado and Charlotte, North Carolina to 78 percent in Sacramento, California. From 15 percent

(in Charlotte) to 37 percent (in Sacramento) of arrestees tested positive for more than one substance. Generally speaking, the substances most commonly identified at testing were, in descending order of their incidence, marijuana, cocaine, opioids, and methamphetamine.[30]

ADAM II statistics confirm our suspicions about the correlation between drug use and criminal behavior, but do they establish a causative relationship? In other words, do drugs actually *cause* violent behavior and crime? If they do, which drugs have a greater responsibility than others? Are illicit drugs necessarily more problematic with respect to violent behavior and crime than licit drugs such as alcohol? As we will see in the discussion that follows, the relationship between drugs and societal problems such as violence and crime can be broken down into three specific categories: pharmacological violence, economically compulsive violence, and systemic violence.

Pharmacological Violence

Pharmacological violence is an act of violence committed by an offender who is under the direct influence of a psychoactive drug. The implication is that a specific drug caused violent or criminal behavior while the drug was actually present in the individual's system. Although the ADAM II statistics reflect the fact that a large proportion of people have some illicit drug in their system at the time of arrest, we are unable to say whether the offense was committed *as a direct result of the influence of that drug*. The main criticism of evidence related to pharmacological explanations is that the detection period in a standard urinalysis test for an illicit drug can range from two to four days in the case of cocaine and from several days to two months in the case of marijuana (see Chapter 12). Therefore, testing positive for a drug at the time of arrest indicates only that the individual *might* have become violent or have been motivated to commit a crime while under the influence of the drug, assuming that the drug has the potential for creating a violence-producing or crime-producing effect in the first place.

In some instances, the physiological nature of the drug itself makes it quite unlikely that pharmacological violence would occur. For example, marijuana by itself, for example, makes the user more passive than active, indeed the marijuana smoker typically is quite mellow in circumstances in which there may be some interpersonal conflict.

---

pharmacological violence: Violent acts committed while under the influence of a particular psychoactive drug, with the implication that the drug caused the violence to occur.

Heroin produces a passive state of mind that reduces the inclination toward violent behavior. In fact, as rates of heroin abuse rise, the incidence of crimes against individuals (as opposed to crimes against property) declines.[31]

On the other hand, psychoactive stimulants such as amphetamines and cocaine or the hallucinogenic PCP (known as angel dust) produce an "on-edge" manner and a social paranoia that can be the context for violent behavior, although there is no current evidence that these drugs specifically stimulate violent behavior. Yet even in such cases, we need to be careful in the interpretation of studies reporting violent behavior in unselected populations. In a study conducted at an Atlanta medical center, more than half of all patients being treated for acute cocaine intoxication were reported to be aggressive, agitated, and paranoid just prior to and at the time of hospital admission. It is impossible to determine whether these patients were mentally unstable to begin with, prior to their taking cocaine. People who have long-standing psychological problems may be overrepresented in any population of cocaine abusers or of drug abusers in general.[32]

Crack cocaine has the dubious reputation of making the crack smoker irritable, suspicious, and inclined to lash out at another person at the slightest provocation.[33] Whether these effects are due to being under the influence of the drug, however, is unclear. Tendencies toward violence are observed during times of *crack withdrawal* as well as crack intoxication.

Of all the psychoactive drugs we could consider, the one with the most definitive and widely reported linkage to violent behavior is alcohol. In this case, the violence is clearly pharmacological, since the effects of being drunk from the ingestion of alcohol are apparent almost immediately. On a domestic level, males involved in spouse abuse commonly report having been drinking or having been drunk during many of the times that abuse has occurred. Moreover, violent crime outside the home is strongly related to alcohol intoxication. The more violent the crime, the greater the probability that the perpetrator of the crime was drunk while committing it. Studies show that at least a majority of sexually aggressive acts (rapes and attempted rapes) are committed while the offender is drunk (see Chapter 8).[34]

Does the chronic, long-term use of drugs cause individuals to engage in criminal behavior in general? There is little evidence that drugs *cause* an increase in one's general inclination toward antisocial behavior. In other words, it is not true that drugs alone are capable of changing the personality of the user, turning him or her from some kind of upstanding pillar of society into a public menace. As discussed in Chapter 1, social risk factors can be identified that lead toward deviant behavior, as defined by societal norms, and that deviant behavior includes both drug abuse and criminal behavior. One aspect of that deviant behavior cannot be considered the cause of the other. Frequently, individuals with the greatest chance of abusing drugs have a socioeconomic profile that also produces the greatest chance of criminal behavior: a low level of education or scant regard for education, a broken family, little or no social supervision, and low social status.[35] As one researcher has put it,

> Teenagers who begin illegal drug use are also likely to have committed other criminal acts beforehand, whether or not they have been caught. It is likely that this relationship may be sufficient to explain the higher crime rate of marijuana users. It is not so much that marijuana use causes crime (except, of course, the crime of using the drug), but that those who use marijuana are also the type of people more likely to commit criminal acts.[36]

Economically Compulsive Violence

Economic explanations of the relationship between drug use and crime suggest that illicit drug users feel compelled to commit crimes to obtain money to buy drugs and continue a pattern of drug abuse. We can speak of the possibility of **economically compulsive violence,** if the violent act stems from the costliness of the drug-taking behavior.

Several studies show economic considerations to be a major component of the link between drugs and crime. A 1990 study of crack users in the Miami area showed that 59 percent participated in a total of 6,669 robberies over a twelve-month period, averaging thirty-one robberies per individual, or roughly one every twelve days. Yet even though the majority of these robberies were carried out to buy drugs, we cannot assume that they all involved the classic picture of break-ins and holdups. A large percentage involved the theft of drugs from drug dealers or other users, or the users themselves being victims of a drug robbery.[37] Nonetheless, a large proportion of the crimes committed to obtain drug money involved violent acts directed toward individuals within the

economically compulsive violence: Violent acts that are committed by a drug abuser to secure money to buy drugs.

community. Particular targets included store-keepers, children, and the elderly.

When robbery is the means for financing drug abuse, the extent of this crime has been shown to be closely related to market conditions at the time. When heroin prices are high, for example, the level of property crime goes up; when heroin prices are low, the crime level goes down. In other words, heroin abusers steal more to maintain a stable consumption of heroin if the drug becomes more expensive to obtain. Therefore, deliberate elevation of drug prices, when accomplished by reducing the supply, not only fails to reduce the incidence of abuse but also tends to increase the incidence of criminal behavior among drug abusers.[37]

The type of crime a drug user commits under these circumstances is typically related to gender. Males are more likely to commit crimes against persons (muggings) and property (burglary, car theft) or violate drug laws (illicit drug distribution and trafficking), whereas females are more likely to commit crimes against the public order, such as prostitution. One study, for example, found that 64 percent of female crack users exchanged sex for money to buy drugs and that 24 percent reported trading sex for drugs. Among women who bartered sex for crack cocaine, many of them would remain in the "crack houses" for extended periods of time, providing sexual favors to multiple customers to secure a continuous supply of the drug.[38]

Systemic Violence

A third important source of social violence and criminal behavior is inherent within the drug world itself. A substantial number of drug users, as their drug use becomes more intense, involve themselves in drug distribution and a criminal subculture that uses violence as a means of maintaining control over its "business."

Researchers use the term **systemic violence** to refer to the violence that arises from characteristic features of drug dealing (Figure 2.5). Systemic violence can result from such situations as territorial disputes over illicit drug distribution, the consequences of selling inferior grades of the illicit drug, or fraudulent handling of funds from drug sales (referred to as "messing up the money").

systemic violence: Violence that arises from the traditionally aggressive patterns of behavior within a network of illicit drug trafficking and distribution.

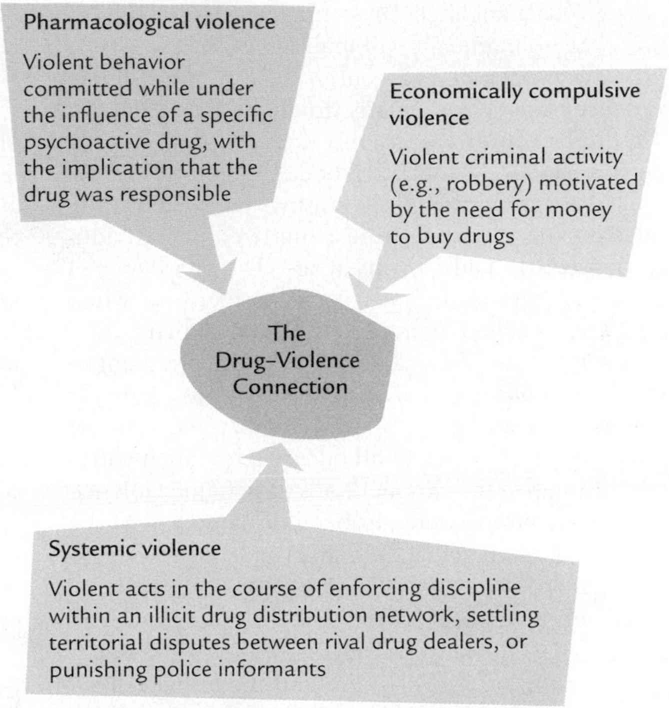

Pharmacological violence

Violent behavior committed while under the influence of a specific psychoactive drug, with the implication that the drug was responsible

Economically compulsive violence

Violent criminal activity (e.g., robbery) motivated by the need for money to buy drugs

The Drug–Violence Connection

Systemic violence

Violent acts in the course of enforcing discipline within an illicit drug distribution network, settling territorial disputes between rival drug dealers, or punishing police informants

FIGURE 2.5

The tripartite framework: Three aspects of drugs and violence.

Source: Goldstein, P. (1985, Fall). The drug-violence nexus: A tripartite framework. Journal of Drug Issues, 493–506.

The best illustrations of systemic violence can be seen in the behavior of two categories of gangs: (1) outlaw motorcycle gangs primarily in Western U.S. states, notably the Hell's Angels, the Outlaws, the Bandidos, and the Pagans, and (2) street gangs in urban communities, such as the Crips and the Bloods in Los Angeles. Since the late 1980s, law enforcement authorities as well as researchers have recognized both organizations as having become the "new faces of organized crime" in America.[39]

In contrast to the popular image of mythic figures rebelling against the norms of society or misunderstood social misfits, members of outlaw motorcycle gangs typically have a history of violent behavior and criminal records that include offenses such as drug trafficking, racketeering, brawling, weapons possession, and homicide. Traditionally, outlaw motorcycle gangs have been principal dealers and traffickers of methamphetamine. In fact, methamphetamine is often referred to as "crank" because motorcyclists would hide the drug in the crank-shafts of their motorcycles. While their association with methamphetamine continues today, their present-day drug involvement has been documented as extending to trafficking in marijuana, cocaine, and PCP.[40]

The association between street gangs and systemic violence became particularly striking in the 1980s during the height of crack cocaine abuse in inner-city neighborhoods. In contrast to outlaw motorcycle gangs, the largest proportion of street gangs involved in drug sales during this time were comprised of individuals between 15 and 16 years of age. The prevalence of gang members aged 18 years or older increased when drug sales reached higher levels. White and Hispanic/Latino gang members tended to be more prevalent in neighborhoods where drug involvement is relatively low, and African American gang members tended to be more prevalent in neighborhoods where drug involvement is high. The extreme levels of systemic violence during this period were attributed in large part to the drug distribution activities of street gang members and their leaders.[41]

The question of which factor causes the other cannot be easily answered. It is quite possible that a combination of self-selection and modeling behavior is occurring here. Inherently violent individuals may be useful in maintaining tight discipline in groups that focus on drug taking and drug selling; they may be useful as combatants in territorial disputes in general.[42]

Given the link between the distribution of crack cocaine and systemic violence, particularly as pertaining to street gangs, it should not be surprising that a decline in the prevalence of crack abuse, first observed in the latter part of the 1990s, would be accompanied by a decline in homicide rates and violent crime in the areas where crack abuse had been dominant. Community-based policing procedures focused on breaking up drug gangs and large street-level drug markets, thereby changing the pattern of drug buying and selling. An expert in the area of criminal justice has put it this way:

In addressing the connections between drug-taking behavior and crime, it is important to include patterns of criminal behavior that are associated with affluent populations as well as impoverished ones. The spread of illicit drug dependence to higher socioeconomic levels of society, since the 1970s, has led to an increase in white-collar crimes of fraud and embezzlement that are motivated by the need for drug money. In such cases, we are speaking of economically compulsive acts. Though generally nonviolent in nature, these criminal acts involve substantially greater amounts of lost revenue than the burglaries and robberies common to poorer neighborhoods.

Governmental Policy, Regulation, and Laws

How should we as a society respond to the social problems of drug-taking behavior? We are faced with an overwhelming flood of illicit drugs entering the United States from around the world, only a small fraction of which are ever identified, much less confiscated, despite the well-publicized drug seizures.[43]

We can express our moral outrage that the situation has become so bad, that drug abuse is costing society such huge amounts of money and wasting so many lives. Social despair is so well entrenched in some portions of society that solutions seem to be nonexistent. The official responses that U.S. society has made through its history, in terms of regulatory controls over drugs, can be understood more clearly in terms of its attitudes toward drug-taking behavior and drug users than in terms of the drugs themselves.

Efforts to Regulate Drugs, 1900–1970

Until about 1900 in the United States, the governmental attitude toward addictive behavior was one of **laissez-faire,** roughly translated as "allow [people] to do as they please," which meant there was little regulation or control. It was a well-ingrained philosophy, going back to our early days as a nation, that government should stay out of the lives of its citizens. Nonmedical use of morphine, for example, was not considered respectable, and in some circles was seen as immoral, but it was no more disreputable than heavy drinking.[44]

Prior to the twentieth century, there were movements to ban alcoholic consumption but none to ban the wholesale use of opium, morphine, heroin, or cocaine. The only exception was the strong opposition to the smoking of opium, an attitude directed principally toward Chinese immigrants in the western states, as noted in Chapter 1. By the turn of the century, however, a wave of reform sentiment began to sweep the country. In 1905, the popular magazine *Collier's* uncovered the fraudulent claims and improper labeling of patent medicines that contained large amounts of alcohol, opium, morphine, and cocaine. Large-scale abuses in the meatpacking industry, publicized

laissez-faire (LAY-say FAIR) (Fr.): The philosophy of exerting as little governmental control and regulation as possible.

in 1906 in Upton Sinclair's novel *The Jungle*, turned the stomach of the American public and quickly pressured President Theodore Roosevelt and Congress to take action.

The result was enactment of the Pure Food and Drug Act. This 1906 law required that food and drug manufacturers list the amounts of alcohol or "habit-forming" drugs, specified as any opium-related drug or cocaine, on the label of the product, but the sale and the use of any of these substances were left unrestricted. The law was the first of a series of legislative controls over food, drinks, drugs, and eventually cosmetics. As Chapter 14 will describe, this legislation eventually evolved into the establishment of the present-day U.S. Food and Drug Administration.

The second major piece of legislation in the early part of the century was the Harrison Act of 1914. This new law concerned itself with opium-related drugs (defined as narcotics) and cocaine. The law was designed to regulate drug abuse essentially through a process of governmental taxation. The act required anyone importing, manufacturing, selling, or dispensing these drugs to register with the Treasury Department, pay a special tax, and keep records of all transactions. From a constitutional perspective, the Harrison Act was a tax law, similar to laws regulating the sale of alcohol. As you can imagine, the difficulties in abiding by the law would soon become virtually insurmountable. Drug-taking behavior that involved these drugs was now driven, from a societal point of view, underground.

Under the Harrison Act, opium, morphine, and heroin were defined as "narcotics," but cocaine was not. Nonetheless, cocaine was often referred to as a narcotic as well, despite the fact that cocaine has totally different psychological and physiological properties (see Chapter 4). Making matters worse, in the years after the enactment of the Harrison Act, several restricted drugs, including marijuana and the hallucinogenic peyote, were also referred to as narcotics without regard to their pharmacological or psychological characteristics. Today, many people still think of *any* illegal drug as a narcotic, and for many years the bureau at the Treasury Department charged with drug-enforcement responsibilities was called the Federal Bureau of Narcotics (FBN), and its agents were known on the street as "narks."

By 1933, as the Prohibition Era ended, the attention of drug-enforcement policymakers, led by Harry Anslinger, the newly installed FBN director, turned from the control of alcohol consumption to the publicizing of marijuana as a major public menace. Congressional committees heard testimony from police claiming that marijuana, now called the "killer weed," aroused people to commit all sorts of violent crime. Movies produced and released in the 1930s, such as *Reefer Madness* (now a cult classic) and *Marihuana: Weed with Roots in Hell*, depicted the moral slide of supposedly innocent young people after they were introduced to marijuana. The result was the Marijuana Tax Act of 1937, after which growers, sellers, and buyers of marijuana were subject to tax. State laws made possession of marijuana illegal (see Chapter 7).

The 1960s saw a number of amendments to the enforcement laws then in effect, as new drugs of abuse came onto the scene. The Federal Bureau of Narcotics became the Federal Bureau of Narcotics and Dangerous Drugs, and Anslinger, whose tenure as director rivaled that of FBI director J. Edgar Hoover in longevity and power, retired in 1962.

Rethinking the Approach toward Drug Regulation, 1970–Present

The Comprehensive Drug Abuse Prevention and Control Act of 1970 organized the control of drugs under five classifications called *schedules of controlled substances*, based on their potential for abuse (see Table 2.2). Since 1970, these categories have defined the extent to which various drugs are authorized to be available to the general public in the United States. Schedules I and II refer to drugs presenting the highest level of abuse potential, and Schedule V refers to drugs presenting the least. All drugs, except those included under Schedule I, are legally available on either a prescription or an over-the-counter basis.

Under the system establishing schedules of controlled substances, drugs that are considered more dangerous and more easily abused are subject to progressively more stringent restrictions on their possession, the number of prescriptions that can be made, or the manner in which they can be dispensed. In the case of Schedule I drugs (heroin, LSD, mescaline, and marijuana, for example), no acceptable medical use has been authorized by the U.S. government, and availability of these drugs is limited to research purposes. The federal penalties for possession and sale of Schedule I drugs, as well as those for violating the restrictions set for other controlled substances, will be examined in Chapter 17.

The 1970 law shifted the responsibility of drug enforcement from the Treasury Department to the Justice Department, ending the long era of attempts

TABLE 2.2

The five schedules of controlled substances in the Comprehensive Drug Abuse Prevention and Control Act

SCHEDULE I

High potential for abuse. No accepted medical use. Research use only; separate records must be maintained, and the drugs must be stored in secure vaults.

Examples: heroin, LSD, mescaline, marijuana, PCP

SCHEDULE II

High potential for abuse. Some accepted medical use, though use may lead to severe physical or psychological dependence. Prescriptions must be written in ink, or typewritten, and signed by a medical practitioner. Verbal prescriptions must be confirmed in writing within 72 hours and may be given only in a genuine emergency. No prescription renewals are permitted. Separate records must be maintained, and the drugs must be stored in secure vaults.

Examples: codeine, morphine, cocaine, methadone, amphetamines, short-acting barbiturates

SCHEDULE III

Some potential for abuse. Accepted medical use, though use may lead to low-to-moderate physical dependence or high psychological dependence. Prescriptions may be oral or written. Up to five prescription renewals are permitted within 6 months.

Examples: long-acting barbiturates, narcotic solutions (for example, paregoric or tincture of opium in alcohol) or mixtures (for example, 1.8% codeine)

SCHEDULE IV

Low potential for abuse. Accepted medical use. Prescriptions may be oral or written. Up to five prescription renewals are permitted within 6 months.

Examples: antianxiety drugs and sedative-hypnotics (for example, Valium and Klonopin)

SCHEDULE V

Minimal abuse potential. Widespread medical use. Minimal controls for selling and dispensing.

Examples: prescription cough medicines not containing codeine, laxatives

Source: Drug Enforcement Administration, U.S. Department of Justice, Washington, DC.

to regulate drug-taking behavior through taxation. As prevention and treatment programs for drug abuse were set up and funds were allocated for educational material, the emphasis started to shift from penalties on the drug user to penalties on drug dealing. In 1988, the Anti-Drug Abuse Act imposed penalties for money laundering when associated with drug smuggling and sales. Under this act, a new cabinet-level position, a "drug czar," was established to coordinate the efforts of the many federal agencies and departments that were by now involved in drug regulation and drug-law enforcement. Overall strategic planning and implementation of drug policy in the United States now originates from the White House Office of National Drug Control Policy.

Drug Law Enforcement and Global Politics

The enforcement picture today is far more complex than it was a few decades ago, when the focus was chiefly on the "supply" side (the availability of drugs) of the problem, without much consideration of the "demand" side (the dependence of individuals on drugs capable of being abused). Treatment and prevention programs in the 1980s represented only 30 percent of the federal budget allocated to controlling drug abuse. More recently, the amount allotted to treatment and prevention has increased somewhat, but about 60 percent of funds in the $25.6 billion drug-control budget are still directed toward efforts to reduce the supply of illicit drugs.[45]

A large proportion of the drug-control budget, approximately $6 billion annually, is expended internationally and at our borders to hold back the continuing influx of illicit drugs into the country. The primary federal agencies involved in this effort are the Drug Enforcement Administration (DEA), the U.S. Customs and Border Patrol Agency, the U.S. Coast Guard and other branches of the U.S. military, and the Immigration and Naturalization Service (INS). In addition, government agents are stationed in more than forty foreign countries, working with the Department of Defense and the Department of State, to limit the exportation of illicit drugs at the source (Portrait).

In recent years, however, our attempts to stem the flood of illicit drugs into the United States have been complicated by a number of economic and

PORTRAIT

Pablo Escobar—Formerly Known as the Colombian King of Cocaine

Pablo Escobar, one of the most powerful, profitable, and violent organized crime bosses in history, began his career as a small-time criminal in the slums of Medellin, Colombia. At age twenty-six, Escobar was arrested for possession of thirty-nine pounds of cocaine, his first and only drug bust. He was never tried for the crime; the arresting officer was mysteriously murdered, and nine judges refused to hear the case because of death threats.

The infamous Medellin Cartel, created by Escobar, would become the first modern-day cocaine trafficking alliance. Organized along the lines of a large corporation, the cartel was vertically integrated and controlled virtually all aspects of the cocaine business from manufacturing and smuggling to wholesale distribution of cocaine in the United States. Escobar's election to the Colombian Congress in 1982 gave him immunity from arrest. But not long after, he came to realize that more power in Colombia could be gained through violence and bribes than through politics.

By 1984, Escobar had controlled over 80 percent of the Colombian drug trade, and it was estimated that Escobar himself was making over $2.75 billion a year. He had "earned" a place on the *Forbes* magazine list of the wealthiest people in the world. Projecting himself as "a man of the people," Escobar built housing for the poor, schools, hospitals, and even a soccer stadium.

Despite the cultivated image of Robin Hood, however, was a man intent on using violence and assassination to maintain his power and the cartel's domination over the life of Colombia. The nation would come to resemble an armed camp. Police officers, judges, public officials, and journalists were in constant fear of being assassinated. Public bombings and drive-by shootings were common occurrences. Escobar himself is alleged to have been behind the murder of three presidential candidates, a Colombian attorney general, more than 200 judges, 100 police officers, and dozens of journalists. He is alleged to have been responsible for the bombing of a Colombian jetliner, resulting in 107 deaths. In 1990, Escobar offered a bounty of $4,000 for each police officer killed in Colombia. During the following month, 42 city police officers were murdered.

In a desperate response to this reign of terror, the Colombian government offered drug traffickers immunity from extradition to the United States if they surrendered themselves to authorities. The traffickers were promised shorter prison terms in Colombia itself.

In 1991, at the age of forty-one, Pablo Escobar turned himself in, having agreed to be placed in a specially built Colombian prison. However, it was a prison that evidently was not secure enough to hold him imprisoned for long. Within months, Escobar escaped, and in one of the most famous manhunts in history, Escobar managed for a while to elude search teams comprised of an elite Colombian police commando squad, members of the U.S. Central Intelligence Agency (CIA), and agents of the Drug Enforcement Administration (DEA). In 1993, authorities finally caught up with him. In a final confrontation, a barrage of gunfire ended his life.

Within months of Escobar's death, the Cali Cartel, a long-standing rival to the Medellin Cartel, had taken over the cocaine business in Colombia. But its newfound dominance was soon to end. Cali Cartel leaders were arrested in Colombia in 1997 and later extradited to the United States. In 2006, a plea agreement included a judgment of forfeiture in the amount of $2.1 billion to be levied against Cali Cartel narcotic-related assets as well as businesses around the world.

Today, cocaine trafficking is controlled by more than 300 "mini-cartels" in the Andean region in association with criminal organizations in Mexico, where approximately 72 percent of cocaine available in U.S. is transported.

Sources: Brooke, J. (1990, June 7). In the capital of cocaine, savagery is the habit. *New York Times*, p. 4. Drug Enforcement Administration (2006, September 26). Cali cartel leaders plead guilty to drug and money laundering conspiracy charges. News release. Washington, DC: U.S. Department of Justice. Fedarko, K. (1993, December 13). Escobar's dead end. *Time*, p. 46. Lyman, M. D., and Potter, G. W. (2000). *Organized crime.* Upper Saddle River, NJ: Prentice Hall. Watson, R., and Katel, P. (1993, December 13). Death on the spot: The end of a drug king. *Newsweek*, pp. 18–21.

political factors on a global scale. Despite its status as a principal U.S. trading partner, the country of Mexico, immediately to our south, remains a major drug-trafficking route not only for cocaine from South America and heroin originating from Mexico itself, but also as a source of marijuana, methamphetamine, and illegal prescription medications (Figure 2.6). An escalation of violence among rival Mexican drug traffickers has engulfed that country and spilled over into U.S. border towns.[46] Efforts to

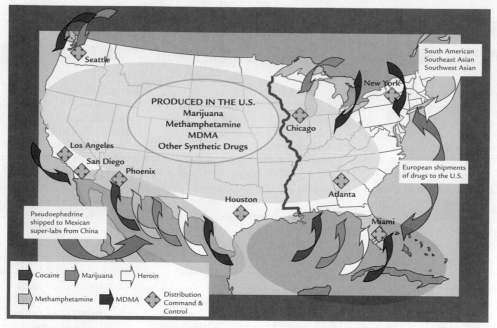

FIGURE 2.6

Drug smuggling entry points into the United States for cocaine, marijuana, heroin, MDMA (Ecstasy), and methamphetamine. Much of the entry from Mexico originates in Colombia and other South American countries.

Source: Drug Enforcement Administration (2011). *FY 2012 Performance budget congressional submission.* Washington, DC: Drug Enforcement Administration, U.S. Department of Justice, p. 12.

reduce the cultivation of opium in the rugged, mountainous areas of Afghanistan, presently the supplier of approximately 94 percent of the world's supply of heroin, have been intertwined with efforts to control the political influence of regional warlords, whether they have terrorist associations or not. The interconnected and sometimes opposing goals of America's drug-control policy and global foreign policy continue to be a major challenge in the effort to regulate drug-taking behavior both in the United States and around the world.[47]

We are more than 40 years into the "war on drugs" declared officially by President Nixon in 1971; the price tag for this war has exceeded $400 billion. Each year more money is requested to carry on the fight, but the struggle continues to be frustrating in the extreme, and the nation grows increasingly battle-weary

(see Point/Counterpoint I, pages 58–59). Although the expenditures are up by more than 1,400 percent since 1981, there is no clear-cut correlation between budget allocations from year to year and the availability of illicit drugs. Many experts in the field of drug abuse view the solution not to be in foreign countries, at U.S. borders, or in U.S. prisons, but to be in the communities of the United States. A recommendation gaining increasing support would shift the emphasis from "use reduction" to "harm reduction," acknowledging that drugs may never be absent from our society (Health Line).[48]

The public policy issues surrounding the "demand" side of the drug-abuse equation, particularly as it pertains to prevention and treatment, will be considered in greater detail in Chapter 16 (see the Portrait on page 384) and Chapter 17.

Members of the U.S. Coast Guard law enforcement team gather in Miami around more than 5,000 pounds of cocaine seized from a Honduran fishing boat off the coast of Colombia. The drugs were discovered hidden in compartments within the fuel tank, and eight Colombians were arrested. The 110-foot boat was later towed to Miami and confiscated.

Health Line

Harm Reduction as a National Drug-Abuse Policy

To say that we are waging a "war on drugs" is, in effect, communicating how serious we are in dealing with the problems of drug abuse in the United States. Using the metaphor of warfare, we recognize that there is an acknowledged enemy (drug misuse and abuse), there are victims or casualties (us), there are resources at our disposal to fight the necessary battles (federal and state governments, communities, parents, etc.), and there is a high price to pay (billions of dollars of federal funds each year).

The implications of this real-life struggle, such as our overall strategy and ultimate goals, are also drawn in metaphorical terms. Do we want total victory and complete annihilation of the enemy? Or do we want some kind of negotiated settlement, some type of compromise that gives us a semblance of peace and tranquility? If it is the former, then we require a total elimination of abusive drug-taking behavior in America, often expressed as "zero tolerance." If it is the latter, then we require a good

deal less. We desire, in that case, only a reduction of the harmful consequences of abusive drug-taking behavior, knowing full well that total elimination is unrealistic and perhaps unattainable. The second alternative is referred to as the harm reduction approach. Whether we should choose a harm reduction or a zero tolerance approach is at the core of our debate on a national drug-abuse policy.

The harm reduction approach in drug policy has its historical roots in the libertarian philosophy of the nineteenth-century philosopher John Stuart Mill, who argued that the state (i.e., the government) did not have the duty to protect individual citizens from harming themselves. As Mill expressed it,

> The only purpose for which power can be rightfully executed over any member of a civilized community, against his will, is to prevent harm to others. His own good, either physical or moral, is not a sufficient warrant. . . . Over himself, over his own body and mind, the individual is sovereign.

(Continued)

It is readily evident, however, that drug-taking behavior does indeed harm other people. The question, according to those advocating a harm reduction strategy, is to look for policies that reduce the harm that drugs do, both directly to the drug user and indirectly to others.

Examples of the harm reduction approach include needle-exchange programs to lower the incidence of HIV infection among intravenous drug abusers, methadone maintenance programs for the treatment of heroin abusers (see Chapter 5), efforts to reduce the incidence of driving while under the influence of alcohol (see Chapter 8), and the use of nicotine patches to avoid the adverse health effects of cigarette smoking on the smoker and those around the smoker (see Chapter 10). A more controversial application of the harm reduction approach is the suggestion that we attempt to reduce an individual's heavy drug use down to a level of occasional use, rather than no use at all.

Sources: Denning, P.; Little, J.; and Glickman, A. (2003). *Over the influence: The harm reduction guide for managing drugs and alcohol.* New York: Guilford Press. How did we get here? History has a habit of repeating itself (2001, July 28–August 3). *Economist*, pp. 4–5. Quotation of John Stuart Mill on page 5. Levinthal, C. F. (2003). Question: Should harm reduction be our overall goal in fighting drug abuse? *Point/Counterpoint: Opposing perspectives on issues of drug policy.* Boston: Allyn and Bacon, pp. 70–73. Marlatt, G. A. (Ed.) (2002). *Harm reduction: Pragmatic strategies for managing high-risk behaviors.* New York: Guilford Press.

Summary

Drug Toxicity

- A drug's harmful effects are referred to as its toxicity. Acute toxicity can be measured in terms of either a drug's therapeutic index or its margin of safety, each of which can be computed from its effective dose-response and lethal dose-response curves.

The DAWN Reports

- Drug Abuse Warning Network (DAWN) statistics, which reflect drug-related lethal and nonlethal emergencies in major metropolitan hospitals in the United States, offer another measure of acute drug toxicity. In general, DAWN statistics show that cocaine and narcotic drugs are both highly toxic and that many emergencies involve drugs being taken in combination with alcohol. There are also recent concerns about the increasing number of emergencies associated with club drugs and opioid pain medications.

Behavioral Tolerance and Drug Overdose

- A tolerance effect is the capacity of a drug to have a gradually diminished effect over repeated administrations; in effect, a greater dose has to be taken to maintain the original effect of the drug. Tolerance effects can be quite dangerous, because experienced drug users often end up taking potentially lethal dose levels.
- The setting within which drug-taking behavior occurs is an important factor in behavioral tolerance. Behavioral tolerance effects are based on the principles of Pavlovian conditioning.

Physical and Psychological Dependence

- Drugs can be viewed in terms of a physical dependence model, in which the compulsive drug-taking behavior is tied to an avoidance of withdrawal symptoms, or a psychological dependence model, in which the drug-taking behavior is tied to a genuine craving for the drug and its highly reinforcing effects on the user's body and mind.

Psychiatric Definitions

- The American Psychiatric Association currently recognizes two major conditions associated with drug-taking behavior: substance dependence and substance abuse. The broader term "substance" is used instead of "drug," because there is often confusion in the public mind about what is defined as a drug and what is not.

Special Circumstances in Drug Abuse

- Increasing attention has been directed toward the harmful effects that drug abuse has on pregnant women, in terms of problems both with the pregnancy itself and with the neural development of the fetus.
- There is also concern about the increased risk of HIV infection (and the spread of AIDS) among intravenous drug users when needles are shared.

Drugs, Violence, and Crime

- There is an overall association between the taking of illicit drugs and crime, but careful analysis indicates that the drug with the closest connection to social violence is alcohol, and that heroin and marijuana cause the user to be less inclined toward violent behavior rather than more so.

- It is clear that drug abuse prompts many drug users to commit criminal acts (generally property theft) to support the drug habit. It is also clear that there is a considerable violence inherent in the trafficking and distribution of illicit drugs, through the criminal behavior of outlaw motorcycle gangs and street gangs in urban communities.

Governmental Policy, Regulation, and Laws

- Since the beginning of the twentieth century, U.S. society's philosophy toward drug-taking behavior has been that we should restrict it by reducing the availability of illicit drugs and making it as difficult as possible for the potential drug user to engage in drug-taking behavior.
- The Harrison Act of 1914 was the first of several legislative efforts to impose criminal penalties for the use of opioids (principally heroin) and cocaine and eventually the use of marijuana, hallucinogens, and several other types of psychoactive drugs.

- The Comprehensive Drug Act of 1970 organized the federal control of drugs under five classifications called schedules. Overall planning and implementation of drug policy in the United States now originate from the White House Office of Drug Control Policy.

Enforcement of Drug Laws on a Global Scale

- Today's drug-law-enforcement program in the United States places considerable emphasis on the interdiction of drugs entering the country and less emphasis on the treatment and prevention of drug abuse.
- Attempts to reduce the influx of illicit drugs into the United States are complicated by a series of economic and political factors on a global scale, particularly with respect to international relations with nations such as Mexico and Afghanistan that have been involved either in drug cultivation or in trafficking. The intertwining and sometimes opposing goals of America's drug-control policy and global foreign policy continue to be a major challenge.

Key Terms

acute toxicity, p. 30
behavioral tolerance, p. 37
catheter, p. 40
chronic toxicity, p. 36
dose, p. 30
dose–response curve, p. 30
Drug Abuse Warning
   Network (DAWN), p. 33

drug-related ED visit,
   p. 33
economically compulsive
   violence, p. 46
effective dose (ED), p. 30
laissez-faire, p. 48
lethal dose (LD), p. 30
margin of safety, p. 31

pharmacological
   violence, p. 45
physical dependence,
   p. 39
polydrug use, p. 33
psychological dependence,
   p. 40
substance abuse, p. 41

substance
   dependence, p. 41
substance use
   disorder, p. 41
systemic violence, p. 47
therapeutic index, p. 30
tolerance, p. 37
toxicity, p. 30

Endnotes

1. The Gallup Organization (2005, April 5). Drug use still among Americans' top worries. Gallup Organization, Princeton, NJ. The Gallup Organization (2007, October 19). Little change in public's view of the U.S. drug problem. Gallup Organization, Princeton, NJ. Kleiman, M. A. R.; Caulkins, J. P; Hawken, A. (2011). *Drugs and drug policy: What everyone needs to know.* New York: Oxford University Press.

2. Harwood, H. (2011, October 23). Recent findings on the economic impacts of substance abuse. Presented at the American Psychological Association 2011 Science Leadership Conference, Psychological Science and Substance Abuse, Washington, DC.

3. Cummings, N. A. (1979). Turning bread into stone: Our modern antimiracle. *American Psychologist, 34,* 1119–1129.

4. Treaster, J. B., and Holloway, L. (1994, September 4). Potent new blend of heroin ends eight very different lives. *New York Times,* pp. 1, 37.

5. Substance Abuse and Mental Health Services Administration (2013). *Drug Abuse Warning Network: National estimates of drug-related emergency department visits 2004–2011.* Rockville, MD: Substance Abuse and Mental Health Services Administration, Excel files. Substance Abuse and Mental Health Services Administration (2012). *Drug Abuse Warning Network, 2010: Area profiles of drug related mortality.* Rockville, MD: Substance Abuse and Mental Health Services Administration.

6. Substance Abuse (2013), *Drug Abuse Warning Network, National estimates.* Excel files.

7. Ibid.

8. Ibid.

9. Substance Abuse, *Area profiles of drug-related mortality*, pp. 59–60 and 67–68.

10. Centers for Disease Control and Prevention (2012, July). *Prescription painkiller overdoses*. Atlanta, GA: Centers for Disease Control and Prevention. Centers for Disease Control and Prevention (2011, November). *Prescription painkiller overdoses in the US*. Atlanta, GA: Centers for Disease Control and Prevention.

11. Lankester, E. R. (1889). Mithridatism. *Nature*, 40, 149.

12. Siegel, S. (1990). Drug anticipation and the treatment of dependence. In B. A. Ray (Ed.), *Learning factors in substance abuse* (NIDA Research Monograph 84). Rockville, MD: National Institute on Drug Abuse, pp. 1–24.

13. Gerevich, J.; Bácskai, E.; Farkas, L.; and Danics, Z. (2005). A case report: Pavlovian conditioning as a risk factor of heroin "overdose" death. *Harm Reduction Journal*, 2. Siegel, S. (1975). Evidence from rats that morphine tolerance is a learned response. *Journal of Comparative and Physiological Psychology*, 89, 489–506.

14. Brecher, E. M., and the editors of Consumer Reports. (1972). *Licit and illicit drugs*. Mount Vernon, NY: Consumers Union.

15. Siegel, S. (1999). Drug anticipation and drug addiction. The 1998 H. David Archibald Lecture. *Addiction*, 94, 1113–1124.

16. Jaffe, J. H. (1985). Drug addiction and drug abuse. In A. G. Gilman, L. S. Goodman, T. W. Rall, and F. Murad (Eds.), *The pharmacological basis of therapeutics*. New York: Macmillan, pp. 532–581.

17. Blum, K. (1991). *Alcohol and the addictive brain*. New York: Free Press, p. 17.

18. Pinel, J. P. J. (2003). *Biopsychology* (5th ed.). Boston: Allyn and Bacon, p. 398.

19. Shalev, U.; Grimm, J.W.; and Shaham, Y. (2002). Neurobiology of relapse to heroin and cocaine seeking: A review. *Pharmacological Reviews*, 54, 1–42.

20. Pickens, R., and Thompson, T. (1968). Cocaine-reinforced behavior in rats: Effects of reinforcement magnitude and fixed-ratio size. *Journal of Pharmacology and Experimental Therapeutics*, 161, 122–129.

21. Hoffmeister, F. H., and Wuttke, W. (1975). Psychotropic drugs as negative reinforcers. *Pharmacological Reviews*, 27, 419–428. Yokel, R. A. (1987). Intravenous self-administration: Response rates, the effect of pharmacological challenges and drug preferences. In Michael A. Bozarth (Ed.), *Methods of assessing the reinforcing properties of abused drugs*. New York: Springer-Verlag, pp. 1–34.

22. Johanson, C. E. (1984). Assessment of the abuse potential of cocaine in animals. In J. Grabowski (Ed.), *Cocaine: Pharmacology, effects, and treatment of abuse*. Rockville, MD: National Institute on Drug Abuse, pp. 54–71.

23. Quotation from Goode, E. (1999). *Drugs in American society* (5th ed.). New York: McGraw-Hill, p. 47. Data from Bozarth, M.A., and Wise, R.A. (1985). Toxicity associated with long-term intravenous heroin and cocaine self-administration in the rat. *Journal of the American Medical Association*, 254, 81–83.

24. American Psychiatric Association (2013). *Diagnostic and statistical manual* (5th ed.). Washington, DC: American Psychiatric Association. American Psychiatric Association (2000). *Diagnostic and statistical manual, Text Revision* (4th ed.). Washington, DC: American Psychiatric Association, pp. 191, 197, and 199.

25. Cook, P. S.; Petersen, R. C.; and Moore, D. T. (1990). *Alcohol, tobacco, and other drugs may harm the unborn*. Washington, DC: Office of Substance Abuse Prevention.

26. Substance Abuse and Mental Health Services Administration (2009, May 21). Substance use among women during pregnancy and following childbirth. *The NSDUH Report*, 1–4. Substance Abuse and Mental Health Services Administration (2012). *Results from the 2011 National Survey on Drug Use and Health: Detailed tables*. Rockville, MD: Substance Abuse and Mental Health Services Administration, Tables 6.73B, 6.75B, 6.76B, and 6.77B.

27. Mathers, B. M.; Degenhardt, L.; Phillips, B.; Wiessing, L., et al. (2008). Global epidemiology of injecting drug use and HIV among people who inject drugs: A systematic review. *Lancet*, 372, 1733–1745.

28. Centers for Disease Control and Prevention (2011, June 24). *HIV surveillance in injection drug users*. Atlanta, GA: Centers for Disease Control and Prevention.

29. An agreement on spending; Editorial (2011, December 17). *New York Times*, p. A24. Righting a wrong, much too late: Editorial (2009, December 26). *New York Times*, p. A22. Centers for Disease Control and Prevention (2010, November 19). Syringe exchange programs—United States 2008. *Morbidity and Mortality Weekly Report*, 59, 1488–1491.

30. Office of National Drug Control Policy (2012, May) ADAM II *2011 annual report. Arrestee Drug Abuse Monitoring Program II*. Washington, DC: Office of National Drug Control Policy, Executive Office of the President, Appendix C.

31. De La Rosa, M.; Lambert, E. Y.; and Gropper, B. (1990). Introduction: Exploring the substance abuse–violence connection. In *Drugs and violence: Causes, correlates, and consequences* (NIDA Research Monograph 103). Rockville, MD: National Institute on Drug Abuse, pp. 1–7.

32. Roth, J. A. (1994, February). Psychoactive substances and violence: Research brief. Washington, DC: National Institute of Justice. Tyner, E. A., and Fremouw, W. J. (2008). The relation of methamphetamine use and violence: A critical review. *Aggression and Violent Behavior*, 13, 285–297.

33. Gold, M. S. (1991). *The good news about drugs and alcohol: Curing, treating and preventing substance abuse in the new age of biopsychiatry*. New York: Villard Books.

34. Bureau of Justice Statistics (2010, September). *Alcohol and crime: Data from 2002 to 2008.* Washington, DC: U.S. Department of Justice, Table 29. Bushman, B. J. (1993, October). Human aggression while under the influence of alcohol and other drugs: An integrative research review. *Current Directions in Psychological Science*, pp. 148–152. Foran, H. M., and O'Leary, K. D. (2008). Alcohol and intimate partner violence: A meta-analytic review. *Clinical Psychology* Review, 28, 1222–1234. Kuhns, J. B., and Clodfelter, T. A. (2009). Illicit drug-related psychopharmacological violence: The current understanding within a causal context. *Aggression and Violent Behavior, 14,* 69–78. Mohler-Kuo, M.; Dowdall, G. W.; Koss, M. P.; and Wechsler, H. (2004). Correlates of rape while intoxicated in a national sample of college women. *Journal of Studies on Alcohol, 65,* 37–45.

35. Galea, S.; Nandi, A.; and Vlahov, D. (2004). The social epidemiology of substance use. *Epidemiologic Reviews,* 26, 36–52.

36. Inciardi, J. A. (1990). The crack–violence connection within a population of hard-core adolescent offenders. In M. De La Rosa, E. Y. Lambert, and B. Gropper (Eds.), *Drugs and violence: Causes, correlates, and consequences* (NIDA Research Monograph 103). Rockville, MD: National Institute on Drug Abuse, pp. 92–111. Quotation on pp. 98–99.

37. Silverman, L. P., and Spruill, N.L. (1977). Urban crime and the price of heroin. *Journal of Urban Economics, 4,* 80–103.

38. Inciardi, J. A. (1995). Crack, crack house sex, and HIV risk. *Archives of Sexual* Behavior, 24, 249–269. McCoy, V. H.; Inciardi, J. A.; Metsch, L. R.; Pottieger, A.; and Saum, C.A. (1995). Women, crack, and crime: Gender comparisons of criminal activity among crack cocaine users. *Contemporary Drug Problems, 22* (3), 435–452. Surrat, H. L.; Inciardi, J. A.; Kurtz, S. P.; and Kiley, M. C. (2004). Sex work and drug use in a subculture of violence. *Crime and Delinquency, 50,* 43–59.

39. Barker, T., and Human, K. M. (2009). Crimes of the Big Four motorcycle gangs. *Journal of Criminal Justice, 37,* 174–179. Bellair, P. E., and McNulty, T. L. (2009). Gang membership, drug selling, and violence in neighborhood context. *Justice Quarterly, 26,* 644–669. Howell, J. C., and Decker, S. H. (1999, January). The youth gangs, drugs, and violence connection. *OJJDP Juvenile Justice Bulletin.* Washington DC: Office of Juvenile Justice and Delinquency Prevention, U.S. Department of Justice. McDermott, E. J. (2006, Winter). Motorcycle gangs: The new face of organized crime. *Journal of Gang Research, 13,* 27–36.

40. McDermott, Motorcycle gangs.

41. Bellair and McNulty, Gang membership. Howell, J. C., and Gleason, D. K. (1999, December). Youth gang drug trafficking. *OJJDP Juvenile Justice Bulletin.* Washington DC: Office of Juvenile Justice and Delinquency Prevention, U.S. Department of Justice. Decker, S.; Katz, C. M.; and Webb, V. J. (2008). Understanding the black box of gang organization: Implications for involvement in violent crime, drug sales, and violent victimization. *Crime and Delinquency, 54,* 153–172.

42. Office of Juvenile Justice and Delinquency Prevention (1999, July). *1996 National Youth Gang Survey. Summary.* Washington, DC: U.S. Department of Justice, pp. 38–39.

43. Bugliosi, V. T. (1991). *Drugs in America: A citizen's call to action.* New York: Knightsbridge Publishing, p. 25.

44. Brecher. *Licit and illicit drugs,* pp. 6–7.

45. Office of National Drug Control Policy (2012, February). *Executive summary. National Drug Control Strategy: FY 2013 Budget Summary.* Washington, DC: White House Office of National Drug Control Policy.

46. Eckholm, E. (2010, January 25). Border tribe feels stuck in middle of drug war. *New York Times,* A1, A10. Luhnow, D., and De Cordoba, J. (2009, December 23). Hit men kill Mexican hero's family. *Wall Street Journal,* p. A1. Malkin, E. (2009, December 23). Vengeful fury in drug war chills Mexico. *New York Times,* pp. A1, A12. Mazzetti, M., and Thompson, G. (2011, August 28). U.S. widens role in Mexican fight. *New York Times,* pp. A1, A3. Rubin, A. J. (2012. January 2). In Afghanistan, poppy growing proves resilient. *New York Times,* pp. A1, A8.

47. Forero, J. (2006, August 19). Colombia's coca survives U.S. plan to uproot it. *New York Times,* pp. A1, A8. Lacey, M. (2008, December 5). Hospitals now a theater in Mexico's drug war. *New York Times,* pp. A1, A18. Moreau, R., and Yousafkai, S. (2006, January 9). A harvest of treachery. *Newsweek,* pp. 32 35. National Drug Intelligence Center (2011, August). *National Drug Threat Assessment 2012.* Washington, DC: U.S. Department of Justice.

48. Gray, J. P. (2001). *Why our drug laws have failed and what we can do about it: A judicial indictment of the war on drugs.* Philadelphia: Temple University Press. Goldstein, A. (2001). *Addiction: From biology to drug policy* (2nd ed.). New York: Oxford University Press, pp. 307–328. Treaster, J. B. (1992, June 14). Twenty years of war on drugs. *New York Times,* p. E7.

Point/Counterpoint I

Should We Legalize Drugs in General?

The following discussion of viewpoints represents the opinions of people on both sides of the controversial issue of the legalization of drugs. Read them with an open mind. You don't have to come up with the final answer, nor should you necessarily agree with the argument you heard last. Many of the ideas in this discussion come from the sources listed.

POINT

Legalization would get the problem under some degree of control. The "war on drugs" does nothing but increase the price of illicit drugs to what the market will bear, and it subsidizes the drug dealers and drug barons around the world. If we legalize drugs, we can take the profit out of the drug business because legalization would bring the price down dramatically. We could regulate drug sales, as we do now with nicotine and alcohol, by setting up centers that would be licensed to sell cocaine and heroin, as well as sterile syringes, while any drug sales to minors would remain a criminal offense. Regulations would also ensure that drugs maintained standards of purity; the health risks of drug contamination would be avoided.

COUNTERPOINT

Legalization is fundamentally immoral. How can we allow people to run to the nearest store and destroy their lives? Don't we as a society have a responsibility for the health and welfare of people in general? If the drugs (pure or impure) were available, the only effect would be to increase the number of drug abusers. When Britain allowed physicians to prescribe heroin to "registered" addicts, the number of heroin addicts rose fivefold (or more according to some informal estimates), and there were then cases of medical abuse as well as drug abuse. A few unscrupulous doctors were prescribing heroin in totally inappropriate amounts, and a new drug culture was created.

POINT

How moral is the situation now? We have whole communities living at the mercy of drug dealers. Any increase in drug users would be more than compensated for by the gains of freedom from such people. Even if the sale of crack were kept illegal, conceding that this drug is highly dangerous to society, we would have an 80 percent reduction in the black market for drugs, a substantial gain for the welfare of society. We can't guarantee that our inner cities would no longer be places of hopelessness and despair, but at least we would not have the systemic violence associated with the drug world. Besides, with all the money saved from programs set up to prevent people from getting hold of illicit drugs, we could increase the funding for drug treatment programs for all the drug abusers who want them and for research into ways of understanding the nature of drug dependence.

COUNTERPOINT

No doubt, many drug abusers seek out treatment and want to break their drug dependence. Perhaps there may be some individuals who seek treatment under legalization because there would no longer be a social stigma associated with drug abuse, but many drug abusers have little or no long-term commitment to drug treatment. In the present situation, the illegality of their behavior enables us to compel them to seek and stay in treatment, and we can monitor their abstinence by periodic drug testing. How could we do this if using the drug were legal? Besides, how would we approach the education of young people if drugs were legal? We could not tell them that cocaine would give them cancer or emphysema, as we warn them of the dangers of nicotine, only that it would prevent them from being a productive member of society and would have long-term effects on their brains. If the adults around them were allowed to take cocaine, what would be the message to the young? Simply wait until you're twenty-one?

POINT

We already have educational programs about alcohol abuse; the message for heroin and cocaine abuse would be similar. The loss of productivity due to any increased availability of drugs would not be as significant as the present loss of productivity we have with alcohol and cigarettes. With the tax revenues obtained from selling drugs legally, we could have money for more extensive anti-drug advertising. We could send a comprehensive message to our youth that, in terms of addressing the problems in their lives, there are alternatives to psychoactive substances. In the meantime, we would be removing the "forbidden fruit" factor in drug-taking behavior. Drugs wouldn't be a big deal.

COUNTERPOINT

Arguing that people take drugs because they are forbidden or hard to get ignores the basic psychological allure of drugs. If you lowered the price of a very expensive sports car, would fewer people want to buy one? Of course not. People would want a fast car because they like fast cars, just as people will still want to get high on drugs. Legalizing currently illicit drugs would only encourage the development of more dangerous drugs in the future. Look at what happened with crack. Cocaine was bad enough, but when crack appeared on the scene, the situation grew far worse.

POINT

It can be argued that crack was marketed because standard cocaine powder was too expensive for people in the inner cities. If cocaine had been legally available, crack might never have been created because the market would not have been there. Even with crack

remaining illegal under a legalization plan, there is at least the possibility that the appeal of crack would decline. The trend lately is that illegal drugs are getting stronger, while legal drugs (alcoholic beverages and cigarettes) are getting weaker as people become more health-conscious. Legalization might make presently illicit drugs weaker in strength, as public opinion turns against them. The main problem we face is that spending 60 percent of a multibillion-dollar drug-law-enforcement program on the "supply" side of the question, and only 40 percent on reducing the demand for drugs, is not working. If one source of drugs is controlled, another source takes its place. The link between drugs and crime is a direct result of the illegality of drugs. It's not the drug addicts who are destroying the country; it's the drug dealers. Right now, the criminals are in charge. We have to change that. Only legalization would take away their profits and refocus our law-enforcement efforts on other crimes that continue to undermine our society.

COUNTERPOINT

The frustration is understandable, but let's not jump into something merely because we're frustrated. We can allocate more funds for treatment without making drugs legal. We can increase funds for

scientific research without making drugs legal. We need a more balanced program, not an entirely new one. Polls do not indicate general support for drug legalization. Between 60 percent and 80 percent of the U.S. public supports continued prohibition of drugs. Most citizens appear to recognize that legalization would make a bad situation worse, not better.

Critical Thinking Questions for Further Debate

1. Suppose you were a legislator considering new regulatory laws with respect to psychoactive drugs. What would be your argument in favor of making a distinction between "hard drugs" such as heroin, cocaine, and methamphetamine, and "soft drugs" such as marijuana and hallucinogens? On what basis would you make such a distinction?

2. Suppose that social regulations based on a Harm Reduction approach were implemented and the consequence was that drug abuse became more prevalent. Would you revert to a Zero Tolerance approach or reexamine the assumptions of the Harm Reduction approach and alter it to produce more positive societal effects?

Point/Counterpoint II can be found on pages 116–117.

Sources: Dennis, R. J. (1990, November). The economics of legalizing drugs. *The Atlantic,* 126–132. Goldstein, A. (2001). *Addiction: From biology to drug policy* (2nd ed.). New York: Oxford University Press. Goode, E. (1997). *Between politics and reason: The drug legalization debate.* New York: St. Martin's Press. Gray, J. P. (2001). *Why our drug laws have failed and what we can do about it.* Philadelphia: Temple University Press. Levinthal, C. F. (2003). *Point/Counterpoint: Opposing perspectives on issues of drug policy.* Boston: Allyn and Bacon, Chapter 1. Wilson, J. Q. (1990, February). Against the legalization of drugs. *Commentary,* 21–28.

How Drugs Work in the Body and on the Mind

You can think of addiction as a form of "learning gone bad."

Drugs can infiltrate into the brain because they can speak the brain's own language.

Neurochemical pathways and synaptic processes have no choice but to respond to drugs as they do to chemicals and signals that occur naturally in the brain, which are far gentler and have served us well for millions of years.

Meanwhile, drugs are hijacking the brain. They ambush, alter, corrupt, infest, curtail. They commandeer brain processes, reshape networks. And their demands escalate over time.

The results are not pretty. The brain is now a mess. Not surprisingly, life is now a mess.

Reflections on substance abuse from the perspective of neuroscience[1]

You might have heard of the classic public-service announcement, which aired frequently on television in the late 1980s:

> *This is your brain (image of an egg held in hand).*
> *This is drugs (image of a sizzling frying pan).*
> *This is your brain on drugs (image of the egg frying in pan).*
> *Any questions?*[2]

Giving the viewer considerable "food for thought," this message had an immediate impact on the American public: Don't do drugs because drugs will fry your brain. The creators of this message were speaking metaphorically, of course. In effect, they were saying that certain classes of drugs have a devastating impact on the human brain. Therefore, stay away from them.

It was (and still is) an important message to convey, though it can be argued that there are better ways to persuade people not to do something than by seeing scary images. Nonetheless, those who felt the impact of watching that egg fry found the experience hard to forget.

At the same time, an equally important message is that there are other classes of drugs that have enormously beneficial effects on the brain. Drugs are used to treat major mental illnesses such as schizophrenia and depression (see Chapter 15) and play a major role in reducing pain and relieving feelings of anxiety (see Chapters 5 and 13). Whether drugs in general have a positive or a negative effect on us depends, at least in part, on how they interact with physiological processes in the body.

As noted in Chapter 1, psychoactive drugs affect our behavior and experience through their effects on brain functioning. Therefore, our understanding of drugs and their effects is closely connected with the progress we have made in our understanding of the ways drugs work in the brain. This chapter will describe the basic functions of the nervous system and the ways in which drugs alter these functions. It will serve as a foundation for understanding specific classes of drugs covered in the chapters that follow.

A reasonable place to start is to ask the question: How do drugs get into the body in the first place?

How Drugs Enter the Body

There are four principal routes through which drugs can be delivered into the body: *oral administration, injection, inhalation,* and *absorption through the skin or membranes.* In all four delivery methods, the goal is for the drug to be absorbed into the bloodstream. In the case of psychoactive drugs, a drug effect depends not only on its reaching the bloodstream but on its reaching the brain as well.

Oral Administration

Ingesting a drug by mouth, digesting it, and absorbing it into the bloodstream through the gastrointestinal tract is the oldest and easiest way of taking a drug. On the one hand, oral administration and reliance on the digestive process for delivering a drug into the bloodstream provides a degree of safety. Many naturally growing poisons taste so vile that we normally spit them out before swallowing; others will cause us to be nauseated, and the drug will be expelled through vomiting. In the case of hazardous substances that are not immediately rejected, we can benefit from the fact that the absorption process for orally administered drugs is relatively slow. Generally speaking, it takes between five and thirty minutes after ingestion for most of the absorption process to be completed. Therefore, there is at least a little time after accidental overdoses or suicide attempts to induce vomiting or pump the stomach.

On the other hand, the gastrointestinal tract contains a number of natural barriers that slow down or, in some cases, prevent the absorption of certain drugs that we might actually want to absorb. One such barrier is related to a drug's alkalinity or acidity (defined as its pH value). The interior of the stomach is highly acidic, and the fate of a particular drug depends on how it reacts with that environment. Weakly acidic drugs such as aspirin are absorbed better in the stomach than highly alkaline drugs such as morphine, heroin, and cocaine. Insulin

---

by the numbers . . .

100 billion	Estimated number of neurons in the human brain
10–100 trillion	Estimated number of synapses in the human brain
20–25	Approximate wattage of a light bulb, equivalent to the total electrical power generated by the brain

Sources: Drachman, D. (2005). Do we have brain to spare? *Neurology, 64,* 2004–2005. Kety, S. (1961). Energy metabolism of the brain during sleep. In G. E. W. Wolstenhome and M. O'Connor (Eds.). *CIBA Foundation Symposium on the nature of sleep.* Boston: Little, Brown, pp. 375–381. Thompson, R. F. (1993). *The brain: A neuroscience primer* (2nd ed.). New York: Freeman, pp. 75, 299.

Alcohol is easily absorbed into the bloodstream and the brain. For other orally consumed drugs, however, absorption is relatively slow, because they must first be processed by the digestive system.

is destroyed by stomach acid, so it cannot be administered orally, whereas a neutral (neither acidic nor alkalinic) substance, such as alcohol, is readily absorbed at all points along the gastrointestinal tract. In the case of alcohol, the brain gets the message very quickly.

If it survives the stomach and gets to the small intestine, the drug still needs to proceed from that point into the bloodstream. The membrane separating the intestinal wall from blood capillaries is made up of two layers of fat molecules, making it necessary for substances to be *lipid-soluble* (soluble in fats) in order to pass through. Even after successful absorption into blood capillaries, however, substances must then pass through the liver for a "screening process" before being released into the general circulation. Enzymes in the liver are capable of breaking down (metabolizing) the molecular structure of certain drugs, thus reducing the amount that eventually enters the bloodstream. This function of the liver, referred to as *first-pass metabolism*, plays an essential role in protecting us from potentially toxic substances that might have been ingested by mouth. A further barrier, which separates the bloodstream (circulatory system) from brain tissue itself, will be discussed in a later section.

As a result of all these natural barriers, orally administered drugs need to be ingested at deliberately elevated dose levels, to allow for the fact that some proportion of the drug will not make it through to the bloodstream. We can try to compensate for the loss of the drug during digestion, but we are often only making an educated guess. The internal state of the gastrointestinal tract changes constantly over time, making it either more or less likely that a drug will reach the circulatory system. The presence or absence of undigested food,

whether the undigested food interacts with the chemical nature of the drug, and the activity level of specific liver enzymes that control the absorption of the drug into the bloodstream are examples of factors that make it difficult to make exact predictions about the strength of the drug when it finally enters the bloodstream (see Chapter 14).

Injection

One solution to the problems of oral administration is to bypass the digestive process entirely and deliver the drug more directly into the bloodstream through a hypodermic syringe and needle.

A very fast means of injection is an **intravenous (i.v.)** injection, as the drug is delivered into a vein without any intermediary tissue. An intravenous injection of heroin in the forearm, for example, arrives at the brain in less than fifteen seconds. The effects of abused drugs delivered in this way, often called *mainlining*, are not only rapid but also extremely intense. In a medical setting, intravenous injections provide a great deal of control over dosage and the opportunity to administer multiple drugs at the same time. The principal disadvantage, however, is that the effects of intravenous drugs are irreversible. In the event of a mistake or unexpected reaction, there is no turning back unless some other drug (called an *antidote*) is available that can counteract the first one. In addition, repeated injections through a particular vein may cause the vein to collapse or develop a blood clot.

With **intramuscular (i.m.)** injections, the drug is delivered into a large muscle (usually in the upper arm, thigh, or buttock) and is absorbed into the bloodstream through the capillaries serving the muscle. Intramuscular injections have slower absorption times than intravenous injections, but they can be administered more rapidly in emergency situations. Our exposure to intramuscular injections comes early in our lives when we receive the standard schedule of inoculations against diseases such as measles, diphtheria, and typhoid fever. Tetanus and flu shots are also administered in this way.

A third injection technique is **subcutaneous (s.c. or sub-Q)** delivery, in which a needle is inserted into the tissue just underneath the skin. Because skin has a less abundant blood supply relative to muscle, a subcutaneous injection has the slowest absorption time of all

intravenous (i.v.): Into a vein.
intramuscular (i.m.): Into a muscle.
subcutaneous (s.c. or sub-Q): Underneath the skin.

the injection techniques. It is best suited for situations in which it is desirable to have a precise control over the dosage and a steady absorption into the bloodstream. The skin, however, may be easily irritated by this procedure. As a result, only relatively small amounts of a drug can be injected under the skin, compared to the quantity that can be injected into a muscle or vein. When involved in drug abuse, subcutaneous injections are often referred to as *skin-popping*.

All injections require a needle to pierce the skin, so there is an inherent risk of bacterial or viral infection if the needle is not sterile. The practice of injecting heroin or cocaine with shared needles, for example, promotes the spread of infectious hepatitis and HIV (see Chapter 2). When administered orally, drugs do not have to be any more sterile than the foods we eat or the water we drink.

Inhalation

Next to ingesting a drug by mouth, the simplest way of receiving its effects is to inhale it in some form of gaseous or vaporous state. The alveoli within the lungs can be imagined as a huge surface area with blood vessels lying immediately behind it. Our bodies are so dependent on the oxygen in the air we breathe that we have evolved an extremely efficient system for getting oxygen to its destinations. As a consequence of this highly developed system, the psychoactive effect of an inhaled drug is even faster than a drug delivered through intravenous injection. Traveling from the lungs to the brain takes only five to eight seconds.

One way of delivering a drug through inhalation is to burn it and breathe in the smoke-borne particles in the air. Drugs administered through smoking include nicotine from cigarettes, opium, tetrahydrocannabinol (THC) from marijuana, free-base cocaine, crack cocaine, and crystallized forms of methamphetamine. Drugs such as paint thinners, gasoline, and glues can also be inhaled because they evaporate easily and the vapors travel freely through the air. In medical settings, surgical anesthetics are administered through inhalation because the concentration of the drug can be precisely controlled.

The principal disadvantage of inhaling smoked drugs, as you probably expect, arises from the long-term hazards of breathing particles in the air that contain not only the active drug but also tars and other substances produced by the burning process. In general, emphysema, asthma, and lung cancer can result from smoking (see Chapter 10). It is also possible, in any form of drug inhalation, that the linings leading from the throat to the lungs will be severely irritated over time.

Drugs administered by smoking and consumed by inhalation are absorbed extremely quickly, aided by a very efficient delivery system from the alveoli in the lungs to the bloodstream and from the bloodstream to the brain. Two men engaged in smoking crack cocaine are depicted here.

Absorption through the Skin or Membranes

Drug users over the ages have been quite creative in finding other routes through which drugs can be administered. One way is to sniff or snort a drug in dust or powder form into the nose. Once inside the nose, it adheres to thin mucous membranes and dissolves through the membranes into the bloodstream. This technique, referred to as an **intranasal** administration, is commonly used in taking snuff tobacco or cocaine. Prescription medications are becoming increasingly available in

intranasal: Applied to the mucous membranes of the nose.

nasal-spray formulations, avoiding the need for needle injections or difficult-to-swallow pills.

Snuff tobacco, chewing tobacco, and cocaine-containing coca leaves can also be chewed without swallowing over a period of time or simply placed in the inner surface of the cheek and slowly absorbed through the membranes of the mouth. Nicotine chewing gums, available for those individuals who wish to quit tobacco smoking, work in a similar way. Nitroglycerin tablets for heart disease patients are typically administered **sublingually**, with the drug placed underneath the tongue and absorbed into the bloodstream.

At the opposite end of the body, medicines can be inserted as a suppository into the rectum, where the suppository gradually melts and the medicine is absorbed through thin rectal membranes into the bloodstream. This method is less reliable than oral administration, but it may be necessary if the individual is vomiting or unconscious at the time.

Another absorption technique involves a **transdermal patch**, which allows a drug to slowly diffuse through the skin. Transdermal patches have been used for long-term administration of nitroglycerin, estrogen, nicotine, and medications for motion sickness, Parkinson's disease, and Alzheimer's disease. Newly developed procedures to enhance the process of skin penetration include the promising technique of administering low-frequency ultrasound, which allows large molecules, such as those of insulin, to pass through the skin. Insulin administration is an especially interesting application because, until now, the only effective way of getting it into the bloodstream has been through needle injection.

Alternative methods under development include small silicon chip patches containing a grid of microscopic needles that painlessly pierce the skin and allow the passage of large molecules into the bloodstream. Other techniques involve a mild electric current that propels the medication through the skin or the application of medication with special compounds that help the medication slip through skin pores. Advantages in nanotechnology have made it possible to provide "smart patches" that can be programmed to schedule specific doses of transdermal medication that match the fluctuating needs of the patient.[3]

Drugs . . . in Focus summarizes the various ways in which drugs can be administered into the body.

How Drugs Exit the Body

Having reviewed how a drug is absorbed into the bloodstream and, in the case of a psychoactive drug, into the brain, we can now consider the ways in which the body eliminates it. The most common means of elimination is through excretion in the urine after a series of actions in the liver and kidneys. Elimination also occurs through excretion in exhaled breath, feces, sweat, saliva, or (in the case of nursing mothers) breast milk.

The sequence of metabolic events leading to urinary excretion begins with a process called **biotransformation**, chiefly through the action of specific enzymes in the liver. The products of biotransformation, referred to as **metabolites**, are structurally modified forms of the original drug. Generally speaking, if these metabolites are water-soluble, they are passed along to the kidneys and eventually excreted in the urine. If they are less water-soluble, then they are reabsorbed into the intestines and excreted through defecation. On rare occasions, a drug may pass through the liver without any biotransformation at all and be excreted intact. The hallucinogenic drug *Amanita muscaria* is an example of this kind of drug (see Chapter 6).

A number of factors influence the process of biotransformation and urinary excretion and, in turn, the rate of elimination from the body. For most drugs, biotransformation rates will increase as a function of the drug's concentration in the bloodstream. In effect, the larger the quantity of a drug, the faster the body "tries" to get rid of it. An exception, however, is alcohol, for which the rate of biotransformation is constant, no matter how much alcohol has been ingested (see Chapter 8).

The activity of enzymes required for biotransformation may be increased or decreased by the presence

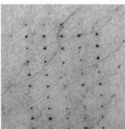

This skin patch contains a rectangular array of 50 microneedles, each 620 microns in length and thinner than a human hair. Tiny, painless epidermal punctures are created by pressing the needles against the skin. Each puncture acts as a conduit for medication to flow evenly from the skin patch into dermal capillaries and the bloodstream.

sublingual: Applied under the tongue.

transdermal patch: A device attached to the skin that slowly delivers the drug through skin absorption.

biotransformation: The process of changing the molecular structure of a drug into forms that make it easier for the body to excrete it.

metabolite (me-TAB-oh-lite): A by-product resulting from the biotransformation process.

Drugs . . . in Focus

Ways to Take Drugs: Routes of Administration

Oral Administration (by Mouth)

- Method: By swallowing or consuming in eating or drinking
- Advantages: Slow absorption time; possibility of rejecting poisons and overdoses
- Disadvantages: Slow absorption time; no immediate effect
- Examples: Medications in pill form, marijuana (baked in food), amphetamine and methamphetamine, barbiturates, LSD (swallowed or licked off paper), PCP, opium, methadone, codeine, caffeine, alcohol

Injection (by Hypodermic Syringe)

Intravenous Injection

- Method: By needle positioned into a vein
- Advantages: Very fast absorption time; immediate effects
- Disadvantages: Cannot be undone; risks of allergic reactions
- Examples: PCP, methamphetamine, heroin, methadone, morphine

Intramuscular Injection

- Method: By needle positioned into a large muscle
- Advantages: Quicker to administer than an intravenous injection
- Disadvantages: Somewhat slower absorption time than an intravenous injection; risk of piercing a vein by accident
- Examples: Vaccine inoculations

Subcutaneous Injection

- Method: By needle positioned underneath the skin
- Advantages: Easiest administration of all injection techniques
- Disadvantages: Slower absorption time than an intramuscular injection; risk of skin irritation and deterioration
- Examples: Heroin and other narcotics

Inhalation (by Breathing)

Smoking

- Method: By burning drug and breathing smoke-borne particles into the lungs
- Advantages: Extremely fast absorption time
- Disadvantages: Effect limited to time during which drug is being inhaled; risk of emphysema, asthma, and lung cancer from inhaling tars and hydrocarbons in the smoke; lung and throat irritation over chronic use
- Examples: Nicotine (from tobacco), marijuana, hashish, methamphetamine, ice or crystal methamphetamine, free-base cocaine, crack cocaine, PCP, heroin, and opium

Vaporous Inhalation

- Method: By breathing in vapors from drug
- Advantages: Extremely fast absorption time
- Disadvantages: Effect limited to time during which drug is being inhaled; lung and throat irritation over chronic use
- Examples: Surgical and dental anesthetics, paint thinners, gasoline, cleaning fluid

Absorption (through Skin or Membranes)

- Method: By positioning drug against skin, inserting it against rectal membrane, snorting it against mucous membranes of the nose, or placing it under the tongue or against the cheek so it diffuses across into bloodstream
- Advantages: Quick absorption time
- Disadvantages: Irritation of skin or membranes
- Examples: Cocaine, amphetamine, methamphetamine, nicotine patches and gums, naltrexone (an opioid antagonist, see Chapter 5), snuff tobacco, coca leaves

of other drugs in the body. As a result, the physiological effect of one drug may interact with the effect of another, creating a potentially dangerous combination. An individual's age can also be a factor. Because enzyme activity levels in the liver decline after the age of forty, older people eliminate drugs more slowly than younger people. We will look at the consequences of drug interactions and individual differences in the next section of this chapter.

Finally, it is important to point out that drugs are gradually eliminated from the body at different rates simply on the basis of their chemical properties. In general, fat-soluble drugs are eliminated more slowly than water-soluble drugs. The index of how rapidly or slowly a particular drug is eliminated is referred to as its **elimination half-life**, defined as the amount of time it takes for the drug in the bloodstream to decline to 50 percent of its original concentration level. As an example, suppose the elimination half-life of Drug X is one hour. After one hour, the drug concentration would be one-half of the original; after two hours, it would be one-fourth of the original. After five hours, the concentration would be about three percent (1/32th) of the original.

Many drugs, such as cocaine and nicotine, have elimination half-lives of only a few hours; marijuana and some prescription medications are examples of drugs with much longer half-lives.[4] Understanding the variation in the elimination rates of drugs and their metabolites is extremely important in the development of drug-testing procedures to detect drug-taking behavior, a topic to be examined in Chapter 12.

Factors Determining the Behavioral Impact of Drugs

If a drug is administered repeatedly, the timing of the administrations plays an important role in determining the final result. When two drugs are administered close together in time, we must also consider how these drugs might interact with each other in terms of their acute effects. The chronic effects of two drugs might interact as well. Finally, it is possible that the same drug at the same dosage taken by two individuals might have different effects by virtue of some inherent characteristic (such as body weight, gender, ethnicity) of the drug user.

---

elimination half-life: The length of time it takes for a drug to be reduced to 50 percent of its equilibrium level in the bloodstream.

latency period: An interval of time during which the blood levels of a drug are not yet sufficient for a drug effect to be observed.

Timing

All drugs, no matter how they are delivered, share some common characteristics when we consider their effects over time. There is initially an interval (the **latency period**) during which the concentration of the drug is increasing in the bloodstream but is not yet high enough for the behavioral effect of the drug to be detected. How long this latency period lasts is related generally to the absorption time of the drug. As the concentration of the drug continues to rise, the effect becomes stronger. A stage is eventually reached when the effect attains a maximum strength, even though the concentration in the blood continues to rise. This point is unfortunately the point at which the drug may produce undesirable side effects. One solution to this problem is to administer the drug in a time-release form (designated as controlled-release, extended-release, or sustained-release formulations). In this approach, a large dose is given initially to enable the drug effect to be felt; then smaller doses are programmed to be released at specific intervals afterward to postpone, up to twelve hours or so, the decline in the drug's concentration in the blood. The intention is to keep the concentration of the drug in the blood within a "therapeutic window"—high enough for the drug to be effective but low enough to avoid any toxic effects. When drugs are administered repeatedly, there is a risk that the second dose will boost the concentration of the drug in the blood too high before the effect of the first dose has had a chance to decline (Figure 3.1).

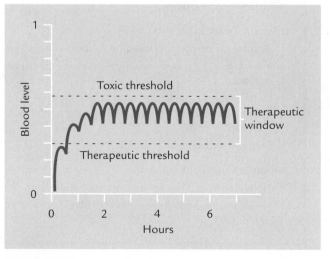

FIGURE 3.1

The therapeutic window. Time-release drugs are formulated to administer the drug in small amounts over time to stay above the threshold for a therapeutic effect but below the threshold for toxicity.

Drug Interactions

Two basic types of interactions may occur when two drugs are mixed together. In the first type, two drugs in combination may produce an acute effect that is greater than the effect of either drug administered separately. In some cases, the combination effect is merely *additive*. For example, if the effect of one drug alone is equivalent to a 4, and the effect of another drug is a 6, then the combined additive effect is equivalent to a value of 10.

In other cases, however, the acute combination effect is *hyperadditive*, with the combined effect exceeding the sum of the individual drugs administered alone, as in the two drugs in the first example combining to a value of 13 or more. Any hyperadditive effect produced by a combination of two or more drugs is referred to as **synergism**. In some synergistic combinations, one drug may even double or triple the effect of another. It is also possible that one drug might have no effect at all unless it is taken simultaneously with another. This special form of synergism is called **potentiation**; it is as though a drug with no effect at all by itself, when combined with a drug having an effect of 6, produces a result equivalent to a 10. The danger of such interactions is that the combined effect of the drugs is so powerful as to become toxic. In extreme cases, this toxicity can be lethal.

In the second type of interaction, two drugs can be *antagonistic* if the acute effect of one drug is diminished to some degree when administered with another—a situation comparable to a drug with the effect of 6 and a drug with the effect of 4 combining to produce an effect of 3. Later chapters discuss drugs that are totally antagonistic to each other, in that the second exactly cancels out, or neutralizes, the effect of the first. Health Alert (page 68) warns that dangerous interactions can result not only from drug–drug combinations but from food–drug combinations as well.

Cross-Tolerance and Cross-Dependence

If you were taking a barbiturate (a sedation-producing drug that acts to depress bodily functioning) for an extended length of time, and you developed a tolerance for its effect, you might also have developed a tolerance for another depressant drug, even though you had never taken the second one. In other words, it is possible for a tolerance effect for one drug to automatically induce a tolerance for another. This phenomenon, referred to as **cross-tolerance**, is commonly observed in the physiological and psychological effects of alcohol, barbiturates, and a class of antianxiety medications called benzodiazepines (Chapter 13). As a result of cross-tolerance, an

alcoholic will have already developed a tolerance for a barbiturate, or a barbiturate abuser will need a greater amount of an anesthetic when undergoing surgery.

We can view the interconnectedness of depressant drugs in another way as well. If withdrawal symptoms of one drug are relieved by administering another drug, then the two drugs show **cross-dependence**. In effect, one drug can substitute for whatever physiological

---

Quick Concept Check 3.1

Understanding Drug Interactions

Check your understanding of drug interactions by assuming the following values represent the effects of Drugs A, B, and C, when taken individually:

- Drug A   0
- Drug B   20
- Drug C   35

Identify the type of drug interaction when the following values represent the effect of two drugs in combination.

1. Drug A combined with Drug B   30
2. Drug B combined with Drug C   55
3. Drug A combined with Drug C   15
4. Drug B combined with Drug C   85
5. Drug B combined with Drug C   0
6. Drug A combined with Drug B   20

Answers: 1. potentiation   2. additive   3. antagonistic
4. synergistic (hyperadditive)   5. antagonistic
6. additive

---

 synergism (SIN-er-jih-zum): The property of a drug interaction in which the combination effect of two drugs exceeds the effect of either drug administered alone.

potentiation: The property of a synergistic drug interaction in which one drug combined with another drug produces an enhanced effect when one of the drugs alone would have had no effect.

cross-tolerance: A phenomenon in which the tolerance that results from the chronic use of one drug induces a tolerance effect with regard to a second drug that has not been used before.

cross-dependence: A phenomenon in which one drug can be used to reduce the withdrawal symptoms following the discontinuance of another drug.

HEALTH ALERT!

Adverse Effects of Drug–Drug and Food–Drug Combinations

It would be impossible to list every known drug–drug interaction or food–drug interaction. Nonetheless, here are some examples. Any adverse reaction to a combination of drugs or a combination of a drug with something eaten should be reported to your physician immediately. An awareness of adverse interactions is particularly important for elderly patients, who tend to be treated with multiple medications. The best advice is to ask your physician whether alcohol, specific foods, or other medications might alter the effect of your medication.

Hyperadditive Effects

- Alcohol with barbiturate-related sleep medications, cardiovascular medications, insulin, anti-inflammatory medications, antihistamines, painkillers, antianxiety medications

Septra, Bactrim, or related types of antibiotics with Coumadin (an anticoagulant)

Tagamet (a heartburn and ulcer treatment medication) with Coumadin

- Aspirin, Aleve, Advil, Tylenol, or related painkillers with Coumadin

Plendil (a blood pressure medication) and Procardia (an angina treatment), as well as Zocor, Lipitor, and Mevacor (all cholesterol-lowering medications), with grapefruit juice

Lanoxin (a medication for heart problems) with licorice

Lanoxin with bran, oatmeal, or other high-fiber foods

Antagonistic Effects

Morphine/heroin with naloxone or naltrexone

Norpramin or related antidepressants with bran, oatmeal, or other high-fiber foods

Soy products and certain vitamin K–rich vegetables (such as broccoli, cabbage, and asparagus) with Coumadin

Possible Toxic Reactions

Internal bleeding by a combination of Parnate and Anafranil (two types of antidepressants)

Elevated body temperature by a combination of Nardil (an antidepressant) and Demerol (a painkiller)

Excessive blood pressure or stroke by a combination of Parnate, Nardil, or other monoamine-oxidase inhibitors (MAOIs) used to treat depression with cheddar cheese, pickled herring, or other foods high in tyramine

Agitation or elevated body temperature by a combination of Paxil, Prozac, Zoloft, or related antidepressants with Parnate, Nardil, or other monoamine-oxidase inhibitors (MAOIs) used to treat depression

Irregular heartbeat, cardiac arrest, and sudden death by a combination of Hismanal or Seldane (two antihistamines) with Nizoral (an antifungal drug)

Note: The hyperadditive effects of grapefruit on certain medications can be dangerous or useful, depending on the circumstances. If grapefruit enhances the effect of the cholesterol-reducing medication Lipitor, for example, it is possible that drinking grapefruit juice might allow the patient to take less Lipitor (reducing costs and possible side effects) and still receive the same level of benefit. Combinations of this kind, however, should be administered only under the close supervision of one's physician.

> **Where to go for assistance:**
> www.drugs.com/drug-interactions.php
> Register free and check out any combination of prescription or OTC drugs for potential adverse interactions.

Sources: Graedon, J., and Graedon, T. (2000, October 16). Say "aaah": The people's pharmacy; drugs and foods can interact adversely. *Los Angeles Times,* p. 2. Graedon, J., and Graedon, T. (1997). *Deadly drug interactions.* New York: St. Martin's Press. *PDR: Guide to drug interactions, side effects, and indications* (2007). Montvale, NJ: PDR Network. Sorensen, J. M. (2002). Herb–drug, food–drug, nutrient–drug, and drug–drug interactions: Mechanisms involved and their medical implications. *Journal of Alternative and Complementary Medicine, 8,* 293–308.

---

effects have been produced by a second drug that has been discontinued. Unfortunately, cross-dependence provides a means for continuing an abused drug in the guise of a new one. If someone wanted to conceal a pattern of drinking from the family, for example, a dose of diazepam (Valium), an antianxiety medication, might suffice as a substitute for that "morning eye opener."[5]

Later in this chapter, we will examine the physiological mechanism that underlies the phenomena of cross-tolerance and cross-dependence.

Individual Differences

Some variations in drug effects may be related to an interaction between the drug itself and specific characteristics of the person taking the drug. One characteristic is an individual's weight. In general, a heavier person will require a greater amount of a drug than a lighter person to obtain an equivalent drug effect, all other things being equal. It is for this reason that drug dosages are expressed as a ratio of drug amount to a person's body weight. This ratio is typically expressed in metric terms, such as milligrams-per-kilogram (mg/kg).

Another characteristic is gender. Even if a man and a woman are exactly the same weight, differences in drug effects can still result on the basis of gender differences in body composition and sex hormones. Women have, on average, a higher proportion of fat, due to a greater fat-to-muscle ratio, and a lower proportion of water than men. When we look at the effects of alcohol consumption in terms of gender, we find that the lower water content (a factor that tends to dilute the alcohol in the body) in women makes them feel more intoxicated than men, even when the same amount of alcohol is consumed.

Relative to men, women also have reduced levels of enzymes that break down alcohol in the liver, resulting in higher alcohol levels in the blood and a higher level of intoxication.[6] We suspect that the lower level of alcohol biotransformation may be related to an increased level of estrogen and progesterone in women. Whether gender differences exist with regard to drugs other than alcohol is presently unknown.

Still another individual characteristic that influences the ways certain drugs affect the body is ethnic background. About 50 percent of all people of Asian descent, for example, show low levels of one of the enzymes that normally breaks down alcohol in the liver shortly before it is excreted. With this particular deficiency, alcohol metabolites tend to build up in the blood, producing a faster heart rate, facial flushing, and nausea.[7] As a result, many Asians find drinking quite unpleasant.

Ethnic variability can be seen in terms of other drug effects as well. It has been found that Caucasians have a faster rate of biotransformation of antipsychotic and antianxiety medications than Asians and, as a result, end up with relatively lower concentrations of drugs in the blood. One consequence of this difference is in the area of psychiatric treatment. Asian schizophrenic patients require significantly lower doses of antipsychotic medication for their symptoms to improve, and they experience medication side effects at much lower doses than do Caucasian patients. Since other possible

factors (such as diet, lifestyle, and environment) do not account for these differences, we can speculate that these differences have a genetic basis.[8]

In some cases, differences in the physiological response to a particular drug can explain differential patterns of drug-taking behavior. For example, researchers have recently found that African Americans have a slower rate of nicotine metabolism following the smoking of cigarettes, relative to whites. This finding might be the reason why African Americans, on average, report smoking fewer cigarettes per day than whites. If we assume that an equivalent level of nicotine needs to be maintained in both populations, fewer cigarettes smoked but a higher level of nicotine absorbed per cigarette will produce the same effect as a greater number of cigarettes smoked but a lower nicotine level absorbed per cigarette. Consequently, African American smokers may be taking in and retaining relatively more nicotine per cigarette, and as a result not having to smoke as many cigarettes per day.[9] Concerns about the specific dangers of nicotine intake among African Americans will be examined further in Chapter 10.

Introducing the Nervous System

Before we can begin to deal with the specific impact of drugs on the brain, we need first to understand some basic facts about the overall organization of the *nervous system*, of which the brain is a part.

In simplest terms, the nervous system is designed to do two basic things: take in information from the environment around us and control our bodily responses so that we can live effectively in that environment. But, of course, we do a lot more than that. We interpret the information coming in, try to make sense of it, remember some of it for a later time, and more than occasionally generate some information on our own in a process called thinking.

We can understand these different functions in terms of divisions within the nervous system. In general, the nervous system is divided into the **central nervous system (CNS)**, consisting of the brain and the spinal cord, and the **peripheral nervous system**,

> **central nervous system (CNS):** The portion of the nervous system that consists of the spinal cord and the brain.
>
> **peripheral nervous system:** The portion of the nervous system that consists of nerves and nerve fibers that carry information to the central nervous system and outward to muscles and glands.

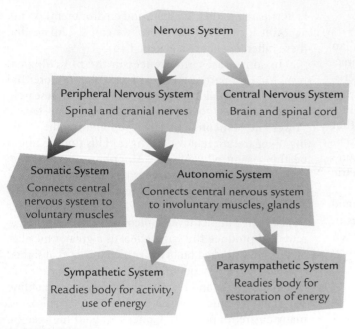

FIGURE 3.2

An "organizational chart" of the nervous system.

surface of your skin, an effect that produces a reddening color and a feeling of warmth. As some of us know from personal experience, blushing often occurs when we do not want it to, and it is difficult to make it go away. And yet it is a reaction to a situation that has been processed through our sensory pathways and interpreted within the brain; in this case, some emotional content has triggered this autonomic response.

If we were to take the time to execute deliberate commands to breathe regularly, to have our hearts beat at an appropriate rate, or to carry out the thousands of changes that our internal organs make, we would not last very long. The autonomic control that has evolved is a product of the interplay of two subsystems, each delivered to smooth and cardiac muscles and to glands through its own set of nerve fibers. These subsystems are referred to as the **sympathetic** and **parasympathetic branches of the autonomic nervous system**.

consisting of all the nerves and nerve fibers that connect the CNS to the environment and to our muscles and glands (Figure 3.2).

The Peripheral Nervous System

The peripheral nervous system is essentially the system that brings information in and, after processing in the CNS, executes our behavioral response to that information. On the input side, it includes the visual pathway, the auditory pathway, and other channels of sensory information about the world around us. On the output side, motor pathways in the peripheral nervous system that control our reactions to that world generate two basic types of responses.

The first type, called a *somatic* response, is a voluntary reaction executed by skeletal muscles that are attached to bone. When you lift your arm, for example, you have executed a series of motor commands that ultimately results in contractions of flexor and extensor muscles. In this case, the movement is deliberate, conscious, and controlled.

A second type of reaction, called an *autonomic response*, is usually involuntary and executed by smooth muscles that form the walls of arteries, veins, capillaries, and internal organs, as well as cardiac muscles that form the walls of the heart. When you blush, for example, the capillaries are dilating, or enlarging, underneath the

Sympathetic and Parasympathetic Responses

Autonomic responses are divided into two general categories (Figure 3.3). The first is oriented toward dealing with some kind of emergency or stress. If we are in a situation that is perceived as a threat to our internal well-being or to our survival, the sympathetic system is in charge. During times of *sympathetic activation*, the heart rate goes up, blood pressure goes up, the bronchi in the lungs dilate to accommodate a greater amount of oxygen, the pupil dilates to allow more light into the eye, and other bodily systems alter their level of functioning, so we are in a better position to fight, to flee, or simply to feel frightened. At the same time, the gastrointestinal tract is inhibited. It makes sense that we should not be digesting our lunch when we are battling for our lives.

The second category of response is totally opposite to the first. We cannot be "on alert" all our lives; we need some time to regroup our forces, to orient ourselves toward a state of calm and rest necessary for

sympathetic branch of the autonomic nervous system: The portion of the autonomic nervous system that controls bodily changes that deal with stressful or emergency situations.

parasympathetic branch of the autonomic nervous system: The portion of the autonomic nervous system that controls the bodily changes that lead to increased nurturance, rest, and maintenance.

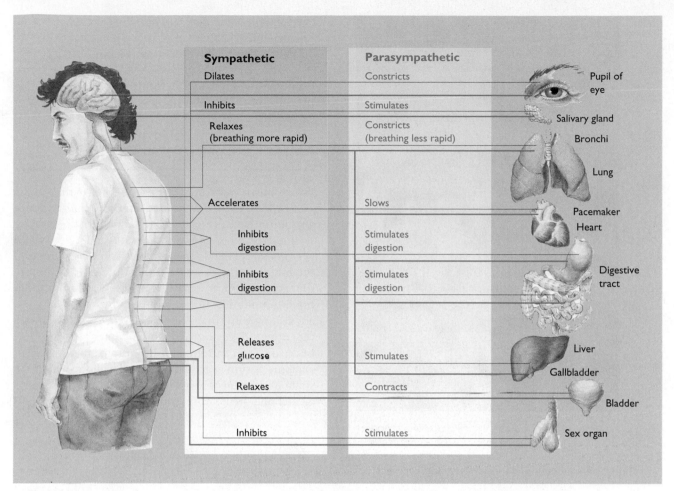

Sympathetic	Parasympathetic	
Dilates	Constricts	Pupil of eye
Inhibits	Stimulates	Salivary gland
Relaxes (breathing more rapid)	Constricts (breathing less rapid)	Bronchi
		Lung
Accelerates	Slows	Pacemaker Heart
Inhibits digestion	Stimulates digestion	Digestive tract
Inhibits digestion	Stimulates digestion	
Releases glucose	Stimulates	Liver Gallbladder
Relaxes	Contracts	Bladder
Inhibits	Stimulates	Sex organ

FIGURE 3.3

Functions of the sympathetic and parasympathetic branches of the autonomic nervous system.

Source: Baron, R. A. (2008). *Psychology: From science to practice.* Englewood Cliffs, NJ: Prentice Hall, p. 73. Reproduced by permission of Pearson Education, Inc.

nurturance and internal maintenance. Heart rate and blood pressure now go down, bronchi and pupils constrict, and the gastrointestinal tract is now excited rather than inhibited. These and other changes constitute *parasympathetic activation* and are an important counterpoint to the activation of the sympathetic system.

Some psychoactive drugs produce autonomic changes, in addition to their direct effects on the brain. They may produce a swing toward sympathetic activation (as with stimulants) or a swing toward parasympathetic activation (as with depressants).

The Central Nervous System

The central nervous system, located along the central axis of the body, consists of the *spinal cord* and

the *brain*. It is here that interpretations of our sensory input occur, and the intricate processing of information is accomplished. Some of our sensory nerves, such as those originating at locations from the neck down, enter the CNS at the level of the spinal cord; others, such as those nerves coming from our eyes and ears, enter at the level of the brain. Complex information entering at the spinal cord is carried by neural pathways upward into the brain for further processing; the processing of simpler information may not involve the brain at all, resulting instead in merely reflexive responses.

The most important part of the CNS, of course, is the brain. It is nearly impossible to overestimate its role in our everyday lives. Every gesture we make, every feeling, every experience we have of our surroundings,

During emergency situations, specific bodily changes are produced through stimulation of the sympathetic branch of the autonomic nervous system. First responders often function under prolonged sympathetic activation.

every insight or memory, is a result of a complex, beautifully modulated pattern of activity among approximately 100 billion specialized cells called **neurons**. We owe our entire cognitive universe—all of what we are or think we are—to the functioning of these cells. It is here that psychoactive drugs do their work, for good or for bad.

Understanding the Brain

Proceeding upward from the spinal cord, starting at the point where the CNS enlarges into the brain, neuroanatomists have classified brain tissue into three major sections: the *hindbrain*, the *midbrain*, and the *forebrain* (Figure 3.4). The older and more primitive systems of the brain tend to be underneath the newer and more sophisticated ones, so as we travel upward from hindbrain to midbrain to forebrain on our quick tour, we are dealing with structures that have evolved ever more recently and have greater involvement in complex behaviors. You can think of this arrangement in brain anatomy as similar to an archaeological dig, where the strata of previous civilizations extend downward into greater and greater antiquity. Understanding the brain

neuron: The specialized cell in the nervous system designed to receive and transmit information.

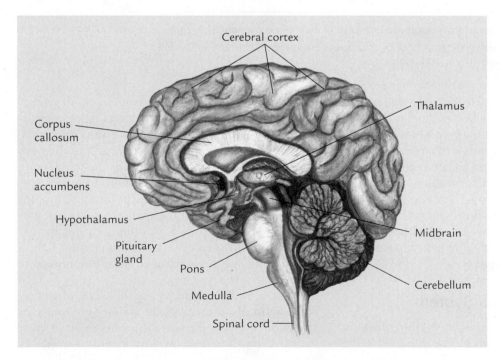

FIGURE 3.4

Basic structures of the human brain, viewed from the side.

Source: Modified from Kalat, J. W. (2007). *Biological psychology* (9th ed.). Belmont, CA: Wadsworth/ Thomson Learning. Reproduced by permission. www. cengage.com/permissions.

in terms of the orderliness of its development over the span of evolutionary history helps to make sense of its complexity.

The Hindbrain

At the top of the spinal cord, neural tissue suddenly widens and enlarges into the hindbrain. The *medulla* lies at the point of the hindbrain where this enlargement has just begun. It is essentially the coordinator of the basic life-support systems in our body. Blood pressure is controlled here, as are the rhythms of breathing, heart rate, digestion, and even vomiting. Death would be seconds away, were it not for the normal functioning of the medulla. Unfortunately, it is highly sensitive to opioids (Chapter 5), alcohol (Chapter 8), barbiturates, and other depressants (Chapter 13). When levels of any of these drugs are excessive in overdose cases, the respiratory controls in the medulla are inhibited, and death can result from asphyxiation (lack of breathing). Even if a person survives, the lack of oxygen in the blood while he or she is not breathing can result in severe brain damage. On a more positive note, the vomiting center in the medulla is sensitive to the presence of poisons in the blood and is able to initiate vomiting to get rid of unwanted and potentially harmful substances.

Another hindbrain structure, situated just above the medulla, is the *pons*. We can view the pons in terms of our ability to maintain the necessary level of alertness to survive. Within the pons are structures that determine when we sleep and when we wake up, as well as the main portion of a structure called the *reticular formation* that energizes the rest of the brain to be alert to incoming information. Drugs affecting the patterns of our sleep influence centers in the pons and reticular formation.

Behind the medulla and the pons in the hindbrain is the *cerebellum*, an important structure for the maintenance of balance and for the execution of smooth movements of the body. The dizziness and lack of coordination we experience after consuming alcohol are attributable in large part to alcohol's depressive effect on the cerebellum.

The Midbrain

The midbrain, located just above the hindbrain, is a center for the control of important sensory and motor reflexes, as well as for the processing of pain information.

Without a specific region of the midbrain called the *substantia nigra*, we would not be able to control the movements of our bodies effectively. The muscular tremors and other motor difficulties characteristic of Parkinson's disease is a result of degeneration of the substantia

nigra. Unfortunately, symptoms that resemble Parkinson's disease have been frequently observed in patients taking antipsychotic medications for the treatment of schizophrenia. Efforts to develop antipsychotic medications without this adverse side effect will be explored in Chapter 15.

The Forebrain

Finally, in the uppermost section of the brain, are the most recently evolved systems in the brain, collectively referred to as the forebrain. One of these forebrain systems, lying immediately above the midbrain, includes the *hypothalamus* and the *limbic system*. It is through these structures that we are able to carry out the motivational and emotional acts that ensure our survival as a species. Feeding behavior, drinking behavior, and sexual behavior are controlled by the hypothalamus.

The limbic system surrounds the hypothalamus and plays a central role in organizing emotional behavior during times of stress. Experimental lesions in points within the limbic system can turn a tame animal into a raging monster or a wild animal into a docile one. Not surprisingly, theories about the basis for psychological dependence have focused on the limbic system. Some of these ideas will be explored later in the chapter. Drugs that deal with symptoms of anxiety, depression, and schizophrenia affect regions within the limbic system.

The second forebrain system, and the most important from the standpoint of understanding human behavior, is a two-sided, wrinkled sheet of neural tissue, with a thickness approximately equivalent to the height of a capital letter on this page. Overhanging nearly all of the brain, the hemispheres of the **cerebral cortex** resemble a giant walnut, an association that prompted early physicians in the Middle Ages to prescribe walnuts as medicine for diseases of the brain (obviously a nutty idea).

When we arrive at the cerebral cortex (or cortex, for short), we have arrived at the pinnacle of the brain both functionally and spatially. Specific regions of the cerebral cortex are concerned with processing visual, auditory, and somatosensory (touch) information, while other regions control the organization of complex and precise movements.

A large percentage of cortical tissue is devoted to the task of associating one piece of information with another. In the human brain, more than 80 percent of the cortex, called the *association cortex*, concerns itself with the integration of information. Of all the areas within the association cortex, the most recently evolved is a region closest

cerebral cortex: The portion of the forebrain devoted to a high level of information processing.

Understanding Drugs and Brain Functioning

Check your understanding of the relationship between certain psychoactive drugs and functions of the brain by matching the part of the brain most likely to be affected by a given drug, given the description of its behavioral effects.

PSYCHOACTIVE DRUG EFFECTS	BRAIN AREAS AFFECTED
1. Drug X changes the pattern of your sleep.	cerebral cortex
2. Drug Y interferes with your intellectual functioning.	medulla
3. Drug Z raises your general arousal level.	cerebellum
4. Drug U interferes with your ability to control food intake.	pons
5. Drug V interferes with your ability to breathe.	hypothalamus
6. Drug W makes you very dizzy.	reticular formation

Answers: 1. pons   2. cerebral cortex   3. reticular formation   4. hypothalamus   5. medulla   6. cerebellum

to the front of the brain called the *prefrontal cortex*. Our higher-order, intellectual abilities (often referred to as *executive functioning*), as well as our personality characteristics, emerge from activity in this region. It has been speculated that a dysfunction in the prefrontal cortex may be associated with a loss of personal control with respect to the abuse of alcohol and other drugs.[10]

Understanding the Neurochemistry of Psychoactive Drugs

Gaining some perspective about brain anatomy lays the foundation for an understanding of *where* certain psychoactive drugs are active, but it does not help us to understand *how* they work. To answer this second question, we need to know something about neurons themselves, the specialized cells designed to communicate information within the nervous system. As we will see, our understanding of neuronal communication has been critical for the insights we have gained into the nature of drug abuse.

Introducing Neurons

It is hard to imagine the enormous complexity of the human brain on a cellular level. There are an estimated 100 billion neurons in the adult brain, and an estimated 10 to 100 trillion structures (called synapses) where these neurons communicate with each other. A cubic millimeter of cerebral cortex alone contains roughly a billion synapses![11]

Not surprisingly, the brain is the most complex organ of the body. So how can we possibly begin to understand the brain amidst such complexity? Or rather, are our own brains sophisticated enough to understand how our brains work?

Fortunately, the task is not as insurmountable as it seems. The neuron itself, as the basic unit of the nervous system, can be understood in relatively simple terms. Imagine the neuron at any moment in time as a tiny device that is either on or off, like a light switch. There is no intermediate state. In this respect, the nervous system is digital like a computer, since a computer consists simply of electrical circuits that are permitted only two states, open or closed. In terms of the neuron, the "on" state is accomplished by the generation of a *nerve impulse*. Just as the neuron is the basic unit that forms the structure of the nervous system, the nerve impulse is the basic event that forms the language of the nervous system.

The unique role of the neuron is to receive information and to transmit information, a task that it carries out through its three principal components: the *cell body,* the *dendrites,* and the *axon* (Figure 3.5). The cell body comprises the bulk of the neuron and contains the nucleus and other elements that various other types of cells in the body (such as muscle cells, skin cells, and blood cells) also exhibit.

The feature that makes the neuron specialized for communication purposes is the appendages that extend from the cell body, some of them rather short and one quite long. The short ones are called dendrites and represent the part of the neuron that receives information from the outside. The long appendage, called the axon, is the part that transmits information outward. The axon is essentially the carrier of the messages of the neuron.

When a nerve impulse is generated, it travels down the length of the axon at speeds up to 120 meters per second (roughly 270 miles per hour) until it reaches the axon's end point. If we followed the nerve impulse down the length of the axon, starting from the cell body (sometimes a distance of up to three feet), we would see

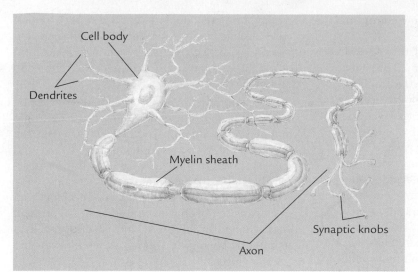

FIGURE 3.5

Basic structure of a neuron. The axon is shown surrounded by the myelin sheath, which increases the transmission speed of nerve impulses.

Cell body

Dendrites

Myelin sheath

Synaptic knobs

Axon

that, toward its end, the axon diverges like the branches of a tree. At the terminal point of each of these branches are small button-like structures called *synaptic knobs*. If nothing else happened here, the nerve impulse would sputter out like a wet fuse. But, of course, there is more to the story. By virtue of junctures between neurons called **synapses**, nerve impulses from one neuron can influence the emission of nerve impulses in other neurons. This process is referred to as *neuronal communication*.

Neuronal Communication

Located inside the synaptic knob are synaptic vesicles (basically container units) that store millions of chemical molecules called **neurotransmitters**. When the nerve impulse reaches the synaptic knob, it causes neurotransmitters to be released out of the vesicles. The neurotransmitters then migrate across the intervening gap between two neurons and quickly arrive at the other ("receiving") side.

On the surface of the receiving neuron are special structures called *receptors*. The receptor can be imagined as having an internal shape that is specifically designed to match the external shape of the neurotransmitter. The successful communication of neurons at the synapse depends on the neurotransmitter and receptor shape "fitting together," like a key successfully fitting into a lock (Figure 3.6). If there is a "match," *receptor*

synapse (SIN-apse): The juncture between neurons. It consists of a synaptic knob, the intervening gap, and receptor sites on a receiving neuron.

neurotransmitter: A chemical substance that a neuron uses to communicate information at the synapse.

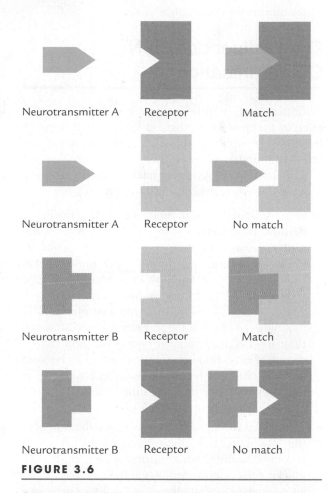

Neurotransmitter A   Receptor   Match

Neurotransmitter A   Receptor   No match

Neurotransmitter B   Receptor   Match

Neurotransmitter B   Receptor   No match

FIGURE 3.6

Communication between neurons depends on a match between neurotransmitter and receptor. The "key and lock" concept is a simplified way of understanding the general process of receptor binding.

binding has occurred. Neuron A has now communicated with Neuron B.

Receptor binding produces one of two possible changes in the receiving neuron: excitation or inhibition. Excitation means that there is an *increase* in the number of nerve impulses per second that are emitted by the receiving neuron; inhibition means that there is a *decrease*. Whether receptor binding produces an excitatory or inhibitory effect depends on the nature of the receptor at the synapse. Some neurotransmitters are referred to as excitatory neurotransmitters because they bind to excitatory receptors; other neurotransmitters are referred to as inhibitory neurotransmitters because they bind to inhibitory receptors.

Having produced either an excitatory or inhibitory effect, neurotransmitters now return back to the vesicles in the synapse knob. Once this is accomplished, conditions at the synapse are ready for the process of neuronal communication to begin once more.

Drug Influences on Neuronal Communication

With these facts in mind, we can understand the influence of psychoactive drugs on brain functioning in terms of the three basic stages of neuronal communication: (1) neurotransmitter release, (2) receptor binding, and finally (3) the "returning back" of the neurotransmitter to the synaptic knob for future use.

- One way that drugs can influence the functioning of neurons is by increasing the quantity of neurotransmitters released into the synapse from the synaptic knob. With more neurotransmitter molecules at work, excitatory or inhibitory changes in the receiving neuron can be enhanced. Some drugs bear such a close structural resemblance to a neurotransmitter that they can arrive at the receptor and act as though they are the "real thing." In other words, a greater degree of excitation or inhibition can occur because both the drug and the neurotransmitter are arriving at the receptor sites at the same time (and the receptors are unable to tell the difference).

- A second way that drugs can influence the functioning of neurons is by diminishing the likelihood of receptor binding. Some drugs accomplish this by blocking the neurotransmitter at the receptor site. In an analogy to football, the drug acts like a defensive back preventing a wide receiver from catching a forward pass from the quarterback.

- Because neurons emit nerve impulses in very rapid succession, neurotransmitters cannot remain in the

receptor for more than a millisecond or two. In most cases, once the neurotransmitter binds to the receptor, it is simply expelled and transported in its intact form back to the synaptic knob. This process is referred to as **reuptake** (Figure 3.7).

- The speed of reuptake can be modified by a specific drug, with important consequences for neuronal communication. If reuptake is slowed down a bit, the neurotransmitter remains in the receptor longer, and receptor binding is enhanced. Conversely, if reuptake is sped up a bit, the neurotransmitter remains in the receptor a shorter period of time, and receptor binding is diminished. Cocaine and some antidepressant drugs accomplish their stimulant effects (see Chapters 4 and 15) by slowing down or even blocking the reuptake process.

- In some cases, receptor binding is followed by the neurotransmitter being broken apart by specific enzymes in the synapse and "reconstructed" back in the synaptic knob for future use. Drugs that inhibit these enzymes cause the breakdown process to be diminished. The neurotransmitter remains longer in the receptor, and receptor binding is enhanced.

Major Neurotransmitters in Brief: The Big Seven

More than fifty neurotransmitters have been identified as functioning in the brain, but fortunately we can understand the essential neurochemical basis for psychoactive drugs and the impact on behavior on the basis of the seven most prominent neurotransmitters.

- **Acetylcholine** was the first molecule to have been firmly established as a neurotransmitter. There are two types of receptors that are sensitive to acetylcholine.

The first type, *muscarinic receptors*, so named because they are responsive to the drug muscarine, are located in the parasympathetic autonomic nervous system. If a drug is antimuscarinic, that means it interferes with the role of acetylcholine in stimulating parasympathetic reactions of the body. Examples are atropine and scopolamine (see Chapter 6). A short-acting atropine-like solution, topically applied to the eyes, is used by ophthalmologists during an eye examination to cause the

---

reuptake: The process by which a neurotransmitter returns from the receptor site to the synaptic knob.

acetylcholine (a-SEE-til-KOH-leen): A neurotransmitter active in the parasympathetic autonomic nervous system, cerebral cortex, and peripheral somatic nerves.

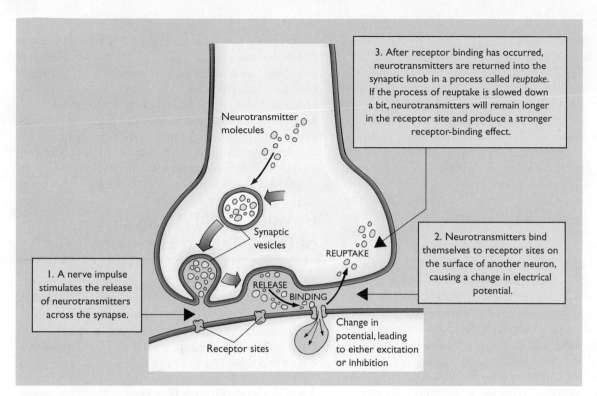

FIGURE 3.7

A close-up view of a single synapse, showing the sequence of major events in neuronal communication: (1) neurotransmitter release, (2) receptor binding, (3) reuptake.

pupils to dilate by inhibiting the parasympathetic tendency for the pupils to constrict, making it possible to examine the retina. The second type, *nicotinic receptors*, so named because they are responsive to nicotine (see Chapter 10), are found near the end points of motor neurons, where skeletal muscles are innervated, as well as throughout the cerebral cortex. Some antinicotinic drugs, such as the poison *curare*, affect these motor neurons so dramatically that the body can become paralyzed within seconds. Deficiencies in acetylcholine or in nicotinic receptors have been tied to Alzheimer's disease, a condition resulting in memory loss and disorientation.

– **Norepinephrine**, the second major neurotransmitter, is concentrated in the hypothalamus and limbic system but is also found throughout the brain. In the peripheral nervous system, it is the principal neurotransmitter for sympathetic autonomic activation, but its role there is independent of its effects in the brain. Norepinephrine helps to regulate our mood states; Chapter 15 will discuss how drugs that boost the levels of norepinephrine also help relieve symptoms of depression.

– **Dopamine**, the third major neurotransmitter, affects three important aspects of our behavior. The first aspect is motor control: the ability to start a movement when we want to; to stop it when we want to; and to execute the movement in a smooth, precisely determined manner. Specifically, Parkinson's disease is a result of a degeneration of dopamine-releasing neurons in the substantia nigra of the midbrain. The second aspect is emotionality. Problems in dopamine releasing neurons in the cortex and limbic system are strongly suspected to be at the root of schizophrenia. The role of dopamine in schizophrenia and efforts to develop drugs that relieve schizophrenic symptoms will be discussed in Chapter 15. Third, as we will see shortly, dopamine in the brain plays a major role in producing the craving that encourages a continuing pattern of compulsive drug-taking behavior.

norepinephrine (NOR-ep-ih-NEH-frin): A neurotransmitter active in the sympathetic autonomic nervous system and in many regions of the brain.

dopamine (DOPE-ah-meen): A neurotransmitter in the brain whose activity is related to emotionality and motor control.

Serotonin, the fourth neurotransmitter, is concentrated in the pons and medulla, in the limbic system, and in the cortex. At the level of the hindbrain, serotonin plays an important role in regulating patterns of sleep. At the level of the limbic system, it shares with norepinephrine responsibility for establishing appropriate mood levels, avoiding wild swings upward that result in mania or wild swings downward that result in depression. As you can predict, many drugs that relieve mania and depression act upon serotonin-releasing neurons. Several hallucinogenic drugs, such as LSD, stimulate serotonin-releasing neurons in the cortex, a topic that will be explored further in Chapter 6.

It should be noted that the technical name for serotonin is 5-hydroxytryptamine (abbreviated 5-HT), and receptors sensitive to serotonin are frequently called 5-HT receptors. Being aware of this terminology is helpful when reviewing the research literature on serotonin in neuronal communication (see earlier section), but it will not be employed here. Any future references to this neurotransmitter will be expressed using the name serotonin, rather than its biochemical equivalent.

Gamma aminobutyric acid (GABA), the fifth neurotransmitter, is an important inhibitory neurotransmitter throughout the brain. Antianxiety medications, often referred to as *tranquilizers*, stimulate GABA-releasing neurons, providing a reduction in feelings of stress and fear, as will be discussed in Chapter 13. Since this neurotransmitter is a major source of inhibitory control, it should not be surprising that GABA deficiencies are associated with an increased tendency to suffer epileptic seizures.

Glutamate, the sixth major neurotransmitter, is also widely distributed throughout the brain and functions as an excitatory neurotransmitter in the brain, causing neurons to be more active. There is increasing evidence of a close connection between glutamate activity and the abuse potential of several psychoactive drugs. The exact relationship, however, appears to depend on the specific subtype of glutamate receptor. On the one hand, the action of two dissociative anesthetics with hallucinogenic properties, phencyclidine (PCP, also known as angel dust) and ketamine, is associated with the blocking of one subgroup of glutamate receptors (see Chapter 6). On the other hand, recent pharmacological research has pointed to the activation of another subgroup of glutamate receptors as a critical element in drug craving and drug-abuse relapse with respect to cocaine, nicotine, alcohol, and heroin. As a result, the current development of new medications that block glutamate receptors of the latter type shows great promise in drug-abuse treatment.[12]

The seventh major neurotransmitter is actually a group of neurotransmitters, collectively known as endorphins. Because they bear a remarkable resemblance to morphine and other opioids, **endorphins** act as natural brain-produced painkillers (see Chapter 5). Another group of brain-produced chemicals called endocannabinoids bear a close resemblance to the active ingredient in marijuana (see Chapter 7). An understanding of neurochemicals such as endorphins and endocannabinoids help to shed light on the mechanisms for the psychoactive effects of opioids and marijuana respectively (Drugs . . . in Focus).

Physiological Aspects of Drug-Taking Behavior

There are three important concepts related to drug-taking behavior that arise from the physiology of the nervous system. The first is the blood–brain barrier, the second is the physiological basis for drug tolerance, and the third is the current hypothesis that psychological dependence is directly related to activity in a specific area of the brain.

The Blood–Brain Barrier

Mentioned earlier in the chapter was a barrier that restricts the passage of drugs and other molecules from the bloodstream to the brain. This exclusionary system is called the **blood–brain barrier**. Because it is important to maintain a level of stability in the brain, we are quite fortunate that this "gatekeeper" keeps the environment of the brain free from the biochemical ups and downs that are a fact of life in the bloodstream. The key factor in determining whether a drug passes

serotonin (SER-ah-TOH-nin): A neurotransmitter in the brain whose activity is related to emotionality and sleep patterns.

gamma aminobutyric acid (GABA) (GAM-ma a-MEEN-o-byoo-TEER-ik ASS-id; GAB-AH): An inhibitory neurotransmitter in the brain. Antianxiety drugs tend to facilitate the activity level of GABA in the brain.

glutamate (GLU-ta-mate): An excitatory neurotransmitter in the brain. Glutamate receptors are associated with actions of PCP and ketamine and with feelings of drug craving.

endorphins (en-DOR-fins): A class of chemical substances, produced in the brain and elsewhere in the body, that mimic the effects of morphine and other opioid drugs.

blood–brain barrier: A system whereby some substances in the bloodstream are excluded from entering the nervous system.

Drugs . . . in Focus

Endorphins, Endocannabinoids, and the "Runner's High"

There has been great progress in our understanding of how specific psychoactive drugs (opioids and marijuana, respectively) work at a biochemical level in the brain. The essential message from neuroscience research is that these drugs produce their physiological and behavioral effects by virtue of triggering chemicals and receptors that have existed in our brains throughout our evolutionary history. They shed light on how the brain works on a day-to-day basis and at crucial times in our lives.

Endorphins, for example, have been related to the underlying process of pain control. Under stressful circumstances, people can become temporarily analgesic (relatively insensitive to pain) without any external drugs. There are well-documented cases of soldiers who have ignored their injuries during the heat of battle, athletes who are unaware of their pain until the game is over, and individuals in primitive societies who endure painful religious rituals without complaint. Increased levels of endorphins are believed to contribute to these phenomena.

In another line of evidence, the effects of the Chinese technique of analgesic acupuncture (the inserting of needles into the skin at precisely defined points in the body to relieve pain) have been found to be completely reversible by naloxone (a specific antagonist to endorphins, see Chapter 5). It is reasonable, therefore, to conclude that the beneficial effects of acupuncture result from increased levels of endorphins.

Endorphin levels measured in the placental bloodstream of pregnant women near to the time of childbirth are greatly elevated from levels normally present in non-pregnant women, and they reach a peak during labor itself.

It is believed that, as a result, women in labor are enduring less pain than they would experience if these endorphin levels were unchanged. In other words, endorphins may protect them against an even greater amount of discomfort.

With respect to the "runner's high," the feeling of calm and euphoria that many individuals report following prolonged exercise, endorphins may play a role. But recently, attention has been drawn to another group of brain produced chemicals called **endocannabinoids**, so called because they mimic the physiological effects of cannabis products such as marijuana. The *endo* prefix in both endorphins and endocannabinoids refers to the fact that these chemicals are produced and operate internally rather than consequences of drugs brought in from outside the nervous system.

It has been found that fifty minutes of hard running on a treadmill or riding on a stationary bicycle significantly increases increased levels of endocannabinoids in the blood. Since endocannabinoids are small molecules, they can pass through the blood-brain barrier (to be described later in the chapter) and produce the calming and free-form sense of well-being that is associated with marijuana. Experiments have yet to be carried out that would establish a causal link between activation of endocannabinoids in the brain and the subjective experience of a "runner's high," but the circumstantial evidence is certainly intriguing.

Sources: Boecker, H.; Sprenger, T.; Spilker, M.B.; Henrikson, G.; et al. (2008). The runner's high: Opioidergic mechanisms in the human brain. *Cerebral Cortex, 18*, 2325–2531. Dietrich, A., and McDaniel, W.F. (2004). Endocannabinoids and exercise. *British Journal of Sports Medicine, 38*, 536-541.

through the blood–brain barrier is the degree to which that drug is *fat-soluble*.

Despite the obstacles, many types of drugs easily pass into the brain: nicotine, alcohol, cocaine, barbiturates, and caffeine, to name a few. Penicillin, by contrast, does not cross the blood-brain barrier because it is not fat-soluble. Consequently, penicillin can be used as an antibiotic treatment only for infections outside the brain.[13]

The presence of a blood–brain barrier is an issue not only for the study of psychoactive drugs but also for certain medical treatments. For example, one of the effective treatments for Parkinson's disease is administration of the drug L-Dopa, a shortened name for levodopa. The reason for using this drug stems from the root cause of Parkinson's disease: a

endocannabinoids (EN-doh-ca-NAB-ih-noids): Brain-produced chemicals that mimic the effects of the active ingredient in marijuana and other cannabis products.

dopamine deficiency in the substantia nigra. Taking dopamine itself is of no help, since its lack of fat-solubility excludes it from getting to the brain. Fortunately, L-Dopa, a metabolic precursor to dopamine, is fat-soluble. Therefore, L-Dopa can enter the brain and then change into dopamine. As a result, there is a rise in dopamine levels in the brain, and the symptoms of Parkinson's disease are relieved. Unfortunately, as dopamine receptors continue to degenerate over a period of years, L-Dopa treatment becomes increasingly ineffective.[14]

It has recently become possible to create fat-soluble molecules in the laboratory rather than finding them in nature. Pharmacologists have succeeded in combining protein-based drugs that are presently excluded by the blood–brain barrier with a fatty acid, enabling the drugs to slip through into the brain. It may be possible in the future to design special proteins ("smart proteins") that not only ferry drugs across the barrier but also regulate the release of the drugs once they are in the brain.[15]

Biochemical Processes Underlying Drug Tolerance

The last chapter considered the phenomenon of drug tolerance as a behavioral effect accomplished through Pavlovian conditioning. Tolerance can also be examined in terms of two types of physiological processes, one occurring in the liver and the other occurring in the neuron itself.

In the first type, called _metabolic (dispositional) tolerance,_ a drug may facilitate, over repeated administrations, the processes that produce the drug's biotransformation in the liver. The rate of alcohol elimination, for example, increases over time if alcohol is ingested repeatedly over an extended period. When the liver breaks down the drug faster than it had initially, a smaller amount is left available for absorption into the blood. In the case of alcohol, the habitual drinker feels less of an alcoholic effect and compensates by increasing the amount consumed.

In the second type of physiological process, called _cellular (pharmacodynamic) tolerance,_ changes occur in the synapses of neurons themselves. Receptors that have been stimulated by the drug over time may become less sensitive to neurotransmitters that ordinarily affect them. As a result, the excitatory or inhibitory effect on the receiving neuron may be diminished. It is important to note that repeated blocking of receptors by a drug over time may cause a compensatory

reaction, such as an increase in the number of receptors or an increase in the amount of neurotransmitter released.[16]

Instances of cross-tolerance and cross-dependence can be explained by the fact that we are dealing with multiple drugs that bind to the same receptors in the brain. Imagine that two or more drugs activated different sites on the same receptor; the receptor itself would then not be able to "tell them apart." As far

Quick Concept Check 3.3

Understanding Cross-Tolerance and Cross-Dependence

Check your understanding of cross-tolerance and cross-dependence by answering the following questions. Suppose you have two receptors in the brain, as shown here.

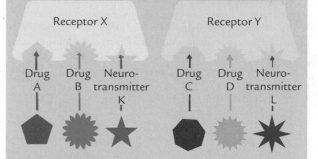

Notice that Receptor X has three binding sites, one for drug A, one for drug B, and one for neurotransmitter K. Receptor Y also has three binding sites, one for drug C, one for drug D, and one for neurotransmitter L.

On the basis of this information, indicate whether the following pairs of drugs show cross-tolerance and cross-dependence with each other.

1. drug A and drug B	yes	no
2. drug A and drug C	yes	no
3. drug B and drug C	yes	no
4. drug C and drug D	yes	no
5. drug B and drug D	yes	no
6. drug A and drug D	yes	no

Answers: 1. yes   2. no   3. no   4. yes   5. no   6. no

as the receptor was concerned, the effect would be the same. The neuronal effects of the drugs over an extended period of time would be equivalent and interchangeable, producing the effects of cross-tolerance and cross-dependence. In general, drugs that have similar psychoactive effects share common receptors.

Physiological Factors in Psychological Dependence

Amphetamines, cocaine, heroin, alcohol, and nicotine may be very different from a pharmacological standpoint, but they are remarkably similar in the way people and animals react to them. There is a tremendous feeling of satisfaction as these drugs enter the bloodstream and the brain, and an intense craving for repeating the experience. The parallels are numerous enough to suggest the existence of a common physiological process in the brain that links them all together. It is not a coincidence that there is a system of neurons near the hypothalamus and limbic system that animals will work hard to stimulate electrically. We cannot say how they are feeling at the time, but their behavior indicates that they want to "turn on" this region of their brains.

Two of the key elements in the rewarding effect of these psychoactive drugs are dopamine and a grouping of neurons lying in a region of the limbic system called the **nucleus accumbens**. When laboratory animals are injected with amphetamines, heroin, cocaine, alcohol, or nicotine, for example, there is a release of dopamine in the nucleus accumbens, and since dopamine acts as an inhibitory neurotransmitter, the activity level of neurons in the nucleus accumbens goes down.

Administration of any substance that interferes with the action of dopamine in this region eliminates the desire of animals to work for the self-administration of these abused drugs. Although we cannot say, of course, that these animals no longer experience feelings of craving as a result, you will recall that self-administration behavior in animals closely parallels the pattern of human behavior that characterizes psychological dependence. Therefore, these studies can be used to understand the neural changes caused by drug abuse. Considering the evidence now in hand, a persuasive argument can be made that dopamine-related processes in the nucleus accumbens underlie the reinforcing effects of many abused drugs. There is also research showing an involvement of the nucleus accumbens with compulsive gambling and compulsive eating disorders.[17]

It is not hard to see the applications to the real-world treatment of drug dependence. Drugs that affect activity in the nucleus accumbens are currently being developed to reduce the feelings of craving that cause drug-dependent individuals to relapse (Health Line).[18]

Research on the influence of dopamine and dopamine receptors in drug dependence has provided an insight into the question of why some individuals may be more susceptible than others to drug-taking behavior. In one study, twenty-three drug-free men with no history of drug abuse were given doses of methylphenidate (brand name: Ritalin), a psychoactive stimulant when ingested by adults. Twelve of the men experienced a pleasant feeling, nine felt annoyed or distrustful, and two felt nothing at all. Measurements of a subclass of dopamine receptors in the brains of these subjects showed a consistent pattern. The men with the least concentration of dopamine receptors were the ones experiencing pleasant effects. It is reasonable to hypothesize that those individuals with the fewest dopamine receptors might be the most vulnerable to drug abuse. A reasonable hypothesis is that their drug-taking behavior as a matter of compensating for an inadequate number of dopamine receptors necessary to experience pleasurable feelings without drugs (see Portrait, page 84).[19]

We now understand that individual differences observed in dopamine receptor concentrations are, in part, genetically based. In the case of nicotine, it is estimated that genetics accounts for about 75 percent of the inclination to begin smoking, for about 60 percent of the tendency to become dependent on nicotine, and for about 54 percent of the ability to quit. Analyses of the human genome have revealed specific gene sites that increase the risk of alcohol abuse and the risk of abuse of a variety of illicit substances, including marijuana.

On the other hand, it is clear that there is an interplay between genetic and environmental influences in this area, and the total picture is bound to be complex.

nucleus accumbens (NEW-clee-us ac-CUM-buns): A region in the limbic system of the brain considered to be responsible for the rewarding effects of several drugs of abuse.

They were thirty-two former cigarette smokers, reporting a minimum of five cigarettes a day for two years or more. They had all suffered some degree of brain injury. They had all reported how difficult it was to stop smoking. Sixteen of the smokers, however, found themselves capable of stopping easily following their injury. Why were these particular sixteen individuals so lucky?

It turns out that it was considerably more likely for these smokers to quit smoking if brain damage had included a prune-shaped area under the frontal lobes of the cerebral cortex called the *insula*. Twelve out of thirteen with insula damage quit easily, whereas only four out of nineteen with damage that did *not* include the insula were able to do so. The insula-damage group had an odds ratio, regarding their likelihood of smoking cessation, of approximately 22 (see Chapter 2). In other words, they were twenty-two times more likely to stop cigarette smoking than the non-insula-damage group.

This relatively small study, reported in 2007, has had a major impact on our understanding of the neurological basis for drug dependence. A neuroimaging study in a group of drug abusers, for example, has shown increased insula activity to be correlated with subjective feelings of drug craving when they viewed a series of drug-related images. In a study of animals made dependent on amphetamine, the inactivation of the insula in their brains has been shown to prevent their urge to seek out amphetamine in their laboratory environment. An accumulating body of research points to the importance of the insula in the neural circuitry that not only maintains substance dependence but also the complex decision-making process that underlies urges for pleasurable outcomes in our lives.

Sources: Carey, B. (2007, January 26). In clue to addiction, a brain injury halts smoking. *New York Times,* pp. A1, A18. Contreras, M.; Ceric, F.; and Torrealba, F. (2007). Inactivation of the interoceptive insula disrupts drug craving and malaise induced by lithium. *Science, 318,* 655–658. Naqvi, N., and Bechara, A. (2010). The insula and drug addiction: An interoceptive view of pleasure, urges, and decision-making. *Brain Structure and Function, 214,* 435–450. Naqvi, N. H.; Rudrauf, D.; Damasio, H.; and Bechara, A. (2007). Damage to the insula disrupts addiction to cigarette smoking. *Science, 315,* 531–534.

For example, genetic influences in substance abuse in general have been found to be more prominent among people in early to middle adulthood and less prominent among adolescents, for whom social environmental factors are dominant.[20]

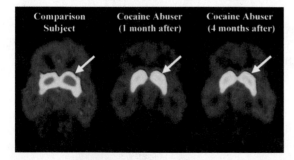

This is literally "your brain on drugs." PET scans from a drug-free subject (left), a detoxified cocaine abuser one month after detoxification (middle), and a detoxified cocaine abuser four months after detoxification (right). The absence of orange-colored areas in the PET scans in the middle and on the right indicates lower levels of dopamine activity.

Psychological Factors in Drug-Taking Behavior

This chapter has considered the physiological effects of psychoactive drugs, down to the level of a single neuron in the brain. It has also pointed out that certain physiological factors (such as weight and gender) must be taken into account to predict particular drug effects. Yet even if we controlled these factors completely, we would still frequently find a drug effect in an individual person to be different from time to time, place to place, and situation to situation. Predictions about how a person might react would be far from perfectly accurate.

Therefore, a good way of thinking about an individual's response to a particular drug is to consider the drug effect as a three-way interaction of the drug's pharmacological properties (the biochemical nature of the substance), the individual taking the drug (set), and the immediate environment within which drug-taking behavior is occurring (setting) (Figure 3.8). Whether

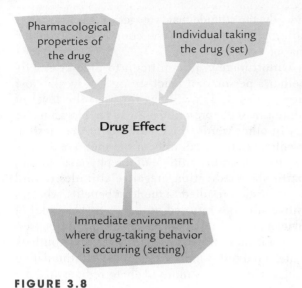

Pharmacological properties of the drug

Individual taking the drug (set)

Drug Effect

Immediate environment where drug-taking behavior is occurring (setting)

FIGURE 3.8

Viewing a psychoactive drug effect as a three-way interaction.

one or more of these factors dominate in the final analysis seems to depend on the dosage level. Generally speaking, the higher the drug dose, the greater the contribution made by the pharmacology of the drug itself; the lower the dose, the greater the contribution of individual characteristics of the drug-taker or environmental conditions.[21]

Expectation Effects

One of the most uncontrollable factors in drug-taking behavior is the set of expectations a person may have about what the drug will do. If you believe that a drug will make you drunk or feel sexy, the chances are increased that it will do so; if you believe that smoking a marijuana joint makes you high, the chances are increased that it will. In the most extreme case, you might experience a drug effect even when the substance you ingested is completely inert—that is, pharmacologically ineffective. Any inert (inactive) substance is referred to as a **placebo** (from the Latin, "I will please"), and the physical reaction to it is referred to as the *placebo effect.*

Of course, the reverse is true as well. You can imagine the impact of negative expectations in drug-taking behavior. When feelings are strong that a drug will have

placebo (pla-SEE-bo): Latin term translated "I will please." Any inert substance that produces a psychological or physiological reaction.

no effect on you, the chances are lessened that you will react to it.

The concept of a placebo goes back to the earliest days of pharmacology. The bizarre ingredients prescribed in the Ebers Papyrus (see Chapter 1) were effective to the extent that people *believed* that they were effective, not as a consequence of any known factor in these ingredients. No doubt, the placebo effect was strong enough for medical symptoms to diminish. During the Middle Ages, in one of the more extreme cases of the placebo effect, Pope Boniface VIII reportedly was cured of kidney pains when his personal physician hung a gold seal bearing the image of a lion around the pope's thigh.[22] However, it would be a mistake to think of the placebo effect as involving totally imaginary symptoms or totally imaginary reactions. Physical symptoms, involving specific bodily changes, can occur on the basis of placebo effects alone. How likely is it that a person will react to a placebo? The probability varies from drug to drug, but in the case of morphine, the data are very clear. A 1959 review of studies in which morphine or a placebo was administered

The likelihood of a placebo effect is maximized when the patient has a substantial level of trust in the expertise of the physician prescribing a drug.

in clinical studies of pain concluded that a placebo-induced reduction in pain occurred 35 percent of the time. Considering that morphine itself had a positive result in only 75 percent of the cases, the placebo effect was a very strong one.

In a more recent placebo study reported in 2008, volunteer subjects were asked to judge the intensity of electric shocks before and after ingesting a pill that contained no active ingredients. Half of the subjects were told the pill was a drug selling for $2.50 each, and the other half were told the pill cost a "discounted" ten cents. The percentage of subjects reporting a reduction in pain was greater with the expensive pill (85 percent) than with the cheaper pill (62 percent). In both cases, a placebo effect was observed. Higher-priced pills were assumed to be more effective than cheaper pills, even though in both cases they were physiologically inert.[23]

Evidently, the attitude that "you get what you paid for" is alive and well, even in the context of drug-taking behavior.

Unfortunately, it is difficult to predict exactly whether a person will react strongly or weakly to a placebo. We do know, however, that the level of enthusiasm of the prescribing physician plays a major role. In other words, the credibility of the messenger enhances the credibility of the message. In one study that varied the attitude of the physician toward a particular medication, negative attitudes toward the medication resulted in the least benefits, whereas positive attitudes resulted in the most. The color of a placebo can also be a factor. A yellow antidepressant pill is more likely to evoke a "sunnier" outlook on life; a red pill is more likely to have a stimulating effect; a green pill is more likely to reduce anxiety;

PORTRAIT

Nora D. Volkow—A Scientist-General in the War on Drugs

It is one thing to speculate about the effects of drug abuse on the brain, to assert that the transition from initially being a voluntary drug user to becoming a compulsive drug user is a matter of subtle but significant brain changes. It is quite another thing to have shown the physical effects themselves.

Using a brain scanning technique called positron emission tomography (PET), neural activity in the human brain can be captured in graphic detail (see images on page 82). Nora D. Volkow, Director of the National Institute on Drug Abuse (NIDA) and her research colleagues have shown that chronic cocaine abuse leads to the loss of about 20 percent of the dopamine receptors in the nucleus accumbens. This effect appears to be long-lasting, enduring for up to four months after the last cocaine exposure, even though the cocaine abuser no longer has cocaine in his or her system. Volkow estimates that a comparable decline in dopamine receptors would take at least 40 years to accomplish in a drug-free brain.

It is not surprising that the nucleus accumbens, with its rich concentration of dopamine receptors, would be the site of this dramatic change. Dopamine and the nucleus accumbens have been associated with feelings of reward and pleasure in a wide range of behavioral activities, from drug use to compulsive exercising to gambling. The irony is that it may be precisely those individuals who have fewer dopamine receptors who may be inclined to engage in drug-taking behavior in the first place; the drug exposure evidently makes the deficit worse.

But then there is a fundamental question: What creates the intense craving for specific drugs once an individual has been first exposed to them? An important clue can be found in the research of Anna R. Childress and her associates at the University of Pennsylvania. When chronic drug abusers were shown video segments of drug-associated paraphernalia (a picture of a syringe or a mound of white powder),

PET scans of their brains revealed increased activity in an area of the limbic system. It is reasonable to hypothesize that the association between activation of the limbic system and stimulation of dopamine-sensitive neurons in the nucleus accumbens may be a significant factor in the triggering of drug craving in cases of chronic drug abuse.

Sources: Childress, A.R.; Mozley, D.; McElgin, W.; Fitzgerald, J.; Reivich, M.; et al. (1999). Limbic activation during cue-induced cocaine craving. *American Journal of Psychiatry, 156,* 11–18. Volkow, N.D.; Wang, G-J.; Fowler, J.S.; Logan, J.; Gatley, S.J.; Hitzemann, R.; et al. (1997). Decrease in striatal dopaminergic responsiveness in detoxified cocaine-dependent subjects. *Nature, 386,* 830–833. Volkow, N., and Li, T.K. (2004, December). Drug addiction: The neurobiology of behaviour gone awry. *Nature Reviews/Neuroscience,* 963–970. Zuger, A.(2011, June 14). Nora D. Volkow: A general in the drug war. *New York Times,* pp. D1, D4.

and, not surprisingly, a pill with a trademark brand imprinted on it is more likely to be effective in general than a generic version.[24]

It is not at all clear how the placebo effect is accomplished. In the case of pain relief, there is evidence that we have the natural ability to increase levels of endorphins in the bloodstream and the brain from one moment to the next, but the nature of our ability to alter other important substances in our bodies is virtually unknown. Placebo studies have shown a 33 percent increase in lung capacity among asthmatic children who inhaled a bronchodilator containing a placebo instead of medication and the development of skin rashes in people who have been exposed to fake poison ivy, to name a few examples of placebo-induced physiological reactions. Placebo research forces us to acknowledge the potential for psychological control over physiological processes in our bodies.[25]

Drug Research Procedures

Given the power of the placebo effect in drug-taking behavior, it is necessary to be very careful when carrying out drug research. For a drug to be deemed truly effective, it must be proved to be better not only in comparison to a no-treatment condition (a difference that could conceivably be attributed to a placebo effect) but also in comparison to an identical-looking drug that lacks the active ingredients of the drug being evaluated. For example, if the drug under study is in the shape of a round red pill, another round red pill without the active ingredients of the drug (called the *active placebo*) must also be administered for comparison.

The procedures of these studies also have to be carefully executed. Neither the individual administering the drug or placebo nor the individual receiving the drug or placebo should know which substance is which. Such precautions, referred to as a **double-blind** procedure, represent the minimal standards for separating the pharmacological effects of a drug from the effects that arise from one's expectations and beliefs.[26] We will return to the issue of interactions between drug effects and expectations in Chapter 8 when we consider behaviors associated with alcohol intoxication.

double-blind: A procedure in drug research in which neither the individual administering a chemical substance nor the individual receiving it knows whether the substance is the drug being evaluated or an active placebo.

Summary

How Drugs Enter the Body

- There are four basic ways to administer drugs into the body: oral administration, injection, inhalation, and absorption through the skin or membranes. Each of these imposes constraints on which kinds of drugs will be effectively delivered into the bloodstream.

How Drugs Exit the Body

- Most drugs are eliminated from the body through urinary excretion. Drugs are broken down for elimination by the action of enzymes in the liver. An index of how long this process takes is called the elimination half-life.

Factors Determining the Behavioral Impact of Drugs

- Factors that influence the physiological effect of a drug include the time elapsed since its administration, drug interactions when it is administered with other drugs at about the same time, and the personal characteristics of the individual consuming the drug.

- An individual's weight, gender, and ethnic background can play a definite role in the behavioral and physiological effects of a drug.

Introducing the Nervous System

- Understanding the organization of the nervous system helps us to understand where psychoactive drugs are working in our bodies.

- The nervous system consists of the peripheral nervous system and the central nervous system, with the latter divided into the brain and the spinal cord. Autonomic nerves control our cardiac and smooth muscles to respond either to stress (sympathetic activation) or to demands for nurturance and renewal (parasympathetic activation).

Understanding the Brain

- Within the brain are three major divisions: the hindbrain, midbrain, and forebrain. The forebrain is the most recently evolved region of the brain; it controls the most complex behaviors and processes the most complex information.
- Many drugs affect all levels of the brain, in one way or another.

Neuronal Communication and Drug Effects

- Understanding the functioning of neurons and their interaction through neuronal communication helps us to understand how psychoactive drugs work in our bodies.
- In general, drugs work at the neuronal level by altering the three basic stages of neuronal communication: (1) neurotransmitter release, (2) receptor binding, and (3) the returning of the neurotransmitter back to the synaptic knob for future use.
- While neuronal communication involves essentially only two kinds of messages, excitation or inhibition, there are dozens of neurotransmitters that accomplish this task. The seven major neurotransmitters

are acetylcholine, norepinephrine, dopamine, serotonin, gamma aminobutyric acid (GABA), glutamate, and a group of neurochemicals called endorphins.

Physiological Aspects of Drug-Taking Behavior

- Three important issues need to be understood in looking at the physiological effect of drugs: the extent to which drugs pass from the bloodstream to the brain, the extent to which tolerance effects occur, and the extent to which a drug influences neuronal activity in the region of the nucleus accumbens in the brain.

Psychological Factors in Drug-Taking Behavior

- Although the physiological actions of psychoactive drugs are becoming increasingly well understood, great variability in the effect of these drugs remains, largely because of psychological factors.
- The most prominent psychological factor is the influence of personal expectations on the part of the individual consuming the drug. The impact of expectations on one's reaction to a drug, a phenomenon called the placebo effect, is an important consideration in drug evaluation and research.

Key Terms

acetylcholine, p. 76
biotransformation, p. 64
blood–brain barrier, p. 78
central nervous system (CNS), p. 69
cerebral cortex, p. 73
cross-dependence, p. 67
cross-tolerance, p. 67
dopamine, p. 77
double-blind, p. 85
elimination half-life, p. 66

endocannabinoids, p. 79
endorphins, p. 78
gamma aminobutyric acid (GABA), p. 78
glutamate, p. 78
intramuscular (i.m.), p. 62
intranasal, p. 63
intravenous (i.v.), p. 62
latency period, p. 66
metabolite, p. 64
neuron, p. 72

neurotransmitter, p. 75
norepinephrine, p. 77
nucleus accumbens, p. 81
parasympathetic branch of the autonomic nervous system, p. 70
peripheral nervous system, p. 69
placebo, p. 83
potentiation, p. 67
reuptake, p. 76

serotonin, p. 78
subcutaneous (s.c. or sub-Q), p. 62
sublingual, p. 64
sympathetic branch of the autonomic nervous system, p. 70
synapse, p. 75
synergism, p. 67
transdermal patch, p. 64

Endnotes

1. Monaghan, P. (2012, March 2). Nota bene: This is your brain on drugs. Review of Lewis, M. (2012). *Memoirs of an addicted brain.* New York: Public Affairs. Phrase quotation from M. Lewis.
2. Public-service message, "Frying Pan." Partners for a Drug-free America, New York, 1987.
3. Benson, H. A. E., and Watkinson, A. C. (2012). *Topical and transdermal drug delivery: Principles and Practice.* Hoboken, NJ: Wiley. Grilly, D. M., and Salamone, J. D. (2012). *Drugs, brain, and behavior* (6th ed.). Boston: Pearson Education, pp. 44–49. National Institute on Drug Abuse (20111, November). Nanotechnology

powers smart skin patch. *NIDA Notes.* Bethesda, MD: National Institute on Drug Abuse.

4. Julien, R. M.; Advokat, C. D.; and Comaty, J. E. (2011). *A primer of drug action* (12th ed.). New York: Worth, pp. 27–32.3. McKim, W. A., and Hancock, S. D. (2013). *Drugs and behavior: An introduction to behavioral pharmacology* (7th ed.). Boston: Pearson, pp. 18–24.

5. Lickey, M. E., and Gordon, B. (1991). *Medicine and mental illness.* New York: Freeman, p. 323.

6. Frezza, M.; DiPadova, C.; Pozzato, G.; Terpin, M.; Baraona, E.; and Lieber, C. S. (1990). High blood alcohol levels in women: The role of decreased gastric alcohol dehydrogenase activity and first-pass metabolism. *New England Journal of Medicine, 322,* 95–99.

7. Nakawatase, T. V.; Yamamoto, J.; and Sasao, T. (1993). The association between fast-flushing response and alcohol use among Japanese Americans. *Journal of Studies on Alcohol, 54,* 48–53.

8. Johnson, R. C., and Nagoshi, C. T. (1990). Asians, Asian-Americans and alcohol. *Journal of Psychoactive Drugs, 22,* 45–52. Levy, R. (2010). Medication use by ethnic and racial groups: Policy implications. *Journal of Pharmaceutical Health Services Research, 1,* 15–22.

9. Haiman, C. A.; Stram, D. O.; Wilkens, L. R.; et al. (2006). Ethnic and racial differences in the smoking-related risk of lung cancer. *New England Journal of Medicine, 354,* 333–342. Perez-Stable, E. J.; Herrera, B.; Jacob III, P.; and Benowita, N.L. (1998). Nicotine metabolism and intake in black and white smokers. *Journal of the American Medical Association, 280,* 152–156.

10. Perry, J. L.; Joseph, J. E.; Yang, J.; Zimmerman, R. S.; et al. (2011). Prefrontal cortex and drug abuse vulnerability: Translation to prevention and treatment interventions. *Brain Research Reviews, 65,* 124–149.

11. Alonso-Nanclares, L.; Gonzalez-Soriano, J.; Rodriguez, J. R., and DeFelipe, J. (2008). Gender differences in human cortical synaptic density. *Proceedings of the National Academy of Sciences U.S.A., 105,* 14615–14619. Drachman, D. (2005). Do we have brain to spare? *Neurology, 64,* 2004–2005. Thompson, R. F. (1993). *The brain: A neuroscience primer* (2nd ed.). New York: Freeman, p. 3.

12. Heidbreder, C. A., and Hagan, J. J. (2005). Novel pharmacotherapeutic approaches to the treatment of drug addiction and craving. *Current Opinion in Pharmacology, 5,* 107–118. Kalivas, P. W. (2009). The glutamate homeostasis hypothesis of addiction. *Nature Reviews Neuroscience, 10,* 561–571.

13. Julien, Advokat, and Comaty, pp. 17–19

14. Grilly and Salamone, pp. 172–177. Whitten, L. (2010, October). Medications that normalize brain glutamate reduce drug-seeking in rats. *NIDA Notes,* pp. 1, 13–15.

15. Kumar, P.; Wu, H.; McBride, J. L.; et al. (2007). Transvascular delivery of small interfering RNA to the central nervous system. *Nature, 448,* 39–43. Jeffrey, P., and Summerfield, S. (2010). Assessment of the blood-brain barrier in CNS drug discovery. *Neurobiology of Disease, 37,* 33–37.

16. Grilly and Salamone, pp. 103–108; Julien, Advokat, and Comaty, pp. 446–447.

17. Potenza, M. N. (2008). The neurobiology of pathological gambling and drug addiction: An overview and next findings. *Philosophical Transactions of the Royal Society, Biological Sciences, 363,* 3181–3189. Russo, S. J.; Dietz, D. M.; Dumitriu, D.; Morrison, J. R., et al (2010). The addicted synapse: Mechanisms of synaptic and structural plasticity in nucleus accumbens. *Trends in Neuroscience, 33,* 267–276.

18. Volkow, N. D.; Fowler, J. S.; Wang, G-J.; and Swanson J. M. (2004). Dopamine in drug abuse and addiction: Results from imaging studies and treatment implications. *Molecular Psychiatry, 9,* 557–569.

19. Volkow, N. D.; Wang, G-J.; Fowler, J. S.; Logan, J.; Gatley, S. J.; et al. (1999). Prediction of reinforcing responses to psychostimulants in humans by brain dopamine D2 receptor levels. *American Journal of Psychiatry, 156,* 1440–1443.

20. Agrawal, A., and Lynskey, M. T. (2008). Are there genetic influences on addiction? Evidence from family, adoption and twin studies. *Addiction, 103,* 1069–1081. Agrawal, A.; Pergadia, M. L.; Saccone, S. F.; Lynskey, M. T.; Wang, J. C.; et al. (2008). An autosomal linkage scan for cannabis use disorders in the Nicotine Addiction Genetics Project. *Archives of General Psychiatry, 65,* 713–722. Kendler, K. S.; Schmitt, E.; Aggen, S. H.; and Prescott, C. A. (2008). Genetic and environmental influences on alcohol, caffeine, cannabis, and nicotine use from early adolescence to middle adulthood. *Archives of General Psychiatry, 65,* 674–682. Price, Uhl, G. R.; Qing-Rong, L.; Drgon, T.; Johnson, C.; et al (2008). Molecular genetics of successful smoking cessation. *Archives of General Psychiatry, 65,* 683–693.

21. Goode, E. (1999). *Drugs in American society* (5th ed.). New York: McGraw-Hill College, p. 9.

22. Kornetsky, C. (1976). *Pharmacology: Drugs affecting behavior.* New York: Wiley, p. 23. Morris, D. B. (1999). Placebo, pain, and belief: A biocultural model. In A. Harrington (Ed.), *The placebo effect: An interdisciplinary exploration.* Cambridge, MA: Harvard University Press, pp. 187–207. Shapiro, A. K., and Shapiro, E. (1997). *The powerful placebo: From ancient priest to modern physician.* Baltimore: Johns Hopkins University Press.

23. Beecher, H. K. (1959). *Measurement of subjective responses: Quantitative effects of drugs.* New York: Oxford University Press. Waber, R. L.; Shiv, B.; Carmon, Z.; and Ariely, D. (2008). Commercial features of placebo and therapeutic efficacy. *Journal of the American Medical Association, 299,* 1016–1017.

24. Benedetti, F. (2002). How the doctor's words affect the patient's brain. *Evaluation and the Health Professions, 25,* 369–386.

25. De la Fuente-Fernández, R., and Stoessl, A. J. (2002). The biochemical bases for reward: Implications for the placebo effect. *Evaluation and the Health Professions, 25,* 387–398. Levinthal, C. F. (1988). *Messengers of paradise: Opiates and the brain.* New York: Anchor Press/ Doubleday. Talbot, M. (2000, January 9). The placebo prescription. *New York Times Magazine,* pp. 34–39, 44, 58–60. Wager, T. D. (2005). The neural bases of placebo effects in pain. *Current Directions in Psychological Science, 14,* 175–179.

26. Quitkin, F. M. (1999). Placebos, drug effects, and study design: A clinician's guide. *American Journal of Psychiatry, 156,* 829–836.

The Major Stimulants: Cocaine and Amphetamines

**After you have completed
this chapter, you should
have an understanding of**

▶ The history of cocaine

▶ How cocaine works in the
brain

▶ Patterns of cocaine abuse

▶ Treatment programs for
cocaine abuse

▶ The history of amphetamines

▶ How amphetamines work in
the brain

▶ Patterns of methamphetamine
abuse

▶ Stimulant treatment for
attention-deficit/hyperactivity
disorder (ADHD)

S.F. is a brilliant young physician attending a case conference at a metropolitan medical center where he is a resident. He has been on call for thirty-six hours and cannot
concentrate on the presentation. S.F. is lonely, depressed,
and overworked. All he can think about is his fiancée,
Martha, who is several hundred miles away. He knows that
her father will not permit her to marry until he is able to
support her, and with his debts and meager salary, that
could take years.

He excuses himself from the conference, takes a
needle syringe from the nurses' station, and locks himself in a bathroom stall. He fills the syringe with cocaine
and plunges the needle into his arm. Within seconds,
the young doctor feels a rush of euphoria. His tears dry
up; he regains his composure and quickly rejoins the
conference.

*—The date is 1884, the place is Vienna,
and the physician is Sigmund Freud.*

The time, place, and identity of S.F. in this fictionalized clinical vignette are based on the life of Sigmund Freud. It may have surprised you to know that the founder of psychoanalysis started out as a physician interested more in the workings of the brain and the stimulant effects of cocaine than the deep recesses of the unconscious mind.[1] It is worth commenting that the year could have been 1984 (or any other year since then) instead of 1884, and the individual involved could have been anyone twenty-eight years old, as Freud was at the time, or some other age. Freud was extremely lucky; he never became dependent on cocaine, although a close friend did—and countless numbers of people have succumbed to cocaine dependence since Freud's time.

The story of cocaine is both ancient and modern. Although its origins stretch back more than four thousand years, cocaine abuse continues to represent a major portion of the present-day drug crisis. For this reason, it is important to understand its history, the properties of the drug itself, and why it has the ability to control and ultimately, in many cases, destroy a person's life. This chapter will focus not only on cocaine but also on another group of stimulant drugs referred to collectively as amphetamines, the most prominent example being methamphetamine (meth). Although cocaine and amphetamines are distinct in terms of their pharmacology (their characteristics as biochemical substances), there are enough similarities in their behavioral and physiological effects to warrant their being discussed together. The emphasis will be on issues surrounding abuse and dependence. With respect to amphetamines and amphetamine-like drugs, we will examine an important medical application, the treatment for attention-deficit/hyperactivity disorder (ADHD).

In general, cocaine and amphetamines represent two major classes of psychoactive stimulants, drugs that energize the body and create intense feelings of euphoria. Other, less powerful stimulants, such as nicotine, caffeine, and clinical antidepressants, will be discussed in later chapters.

The History of Cocaine

Cocaine is derived from small leaves of the coca shrub (*Erythroxylon coca*) grown primarily in the high-altitude rain forests and fields that run along the slopes of the Peruvian and Bolivian Andes in South America, although coca cultivation can be found in other regions of the world with similar climate and soil conditions.

Like many other psychoactive drugs, cocaine use has a long history. We can trace the practice of chewing coca leaves, which contain about 2 percent cocaine, back to the Inca civilization, which flourished from the thirteenth century until its conquest by the Spaniards in 1532, as well as to other Andean cultures dating back five thousand years. According to tradition, coca was a gift from the god Inti to the Incas, allowing them to endure a harsh life in the Andes without suffering.[2]

To this day, coca chewing is part of the culture of this region. It is estimated that about 2 million Peruvian men (called *acullicadores*) who live in the Andean highlands, representing 90 percent of the male population in that area, chew coca leaves.[3] Coca is blended with chalk, lime, and ash to achieve the desired effects, whether the goal is to fight fatigue or simply relax with friends.[4]

This age-old practice produces few instances of toxicity or abuse. The reason lies in the very low doses of cocaine that chewed coca leaves provide; in this form, absorption from the digestive system is slow, and relatively little cocaine enters the bloodstream and is distributed to the brain (Chapter 3). A much more serious problem is the availability of a coca paste containing a much higher percentage of cocaine mixed with tobacco

by the numbers . . .

3.9 million	Americans, aged 12 or older, who reported in 2011 having used cocaine during the past year
625,000	Americans, aged 12 or older, who reported in 2011 having used crack cocaine during the past year
92	Percentage of 50 one-dollar bills randomly sampled from five U.S. cities that have been found to be contaminated with detectable levels of cocaine. Drug contamination begins with contact during drug deals and snorting, then transfers from bill to bill in money-counting machines in banks.

Sources: Substance Abuse and Mental Health Services Administration (2012). *Results from the 2011 National Survey on Drug Use and Health: Detailed tables.* Rockville, MD: Substance Abuse and Mental Health Services Administration, Table 1.1A. Jenkins, A.J. (2001). Drug contamination of U.S. paper currency. *Forensic Science International, 121,* 189–193.

---

cocaine: An extremely potent and dependence-producing stimulant drug derived from the coca leaf.

and smoked as a cigarette (referred to as a *bazuco*). Now delivered directly from the lungs to the brain, this form of coca ingestion is more likely to produce abuse and dependence. Making matters worse, dangerously high levels of kerosene, gasoline, and ether are involved in the coca-refining process and end up as adulterants in the cigarettes themselves.[5]

Cocaine in Nineteenth-Century Life

Coca leaves were brought back to Europe from the Spanish colonies soon after the conquest of the Incas in 1533, but their potency was nearly gone after the long sea voyage. Perhaps, it was said at the time, the legendary effects of coca were merely exaggerations. Coca leaves were ignored for three hundred years.

By the late 1850s, however, the active ingredient of the coca plant had been chemically isolated. In 1859, the German chemist Alfred Niemann observed its anesthetic effect on his tongue and its bitter taste and named it "cocaine." Interest in the drug was renewed, and by the 1860s the patent medicine industry in the United States and Europe (see Chapter 1) had lost no time in taking advantage of cocaine's appeal.

By far the most successful commercial use of cocaine in the nineteenth century was a mixture of coca and wine invented in 1863 by a Corsican chemist and businessman, Angelo Mariani. We know now that the combination of

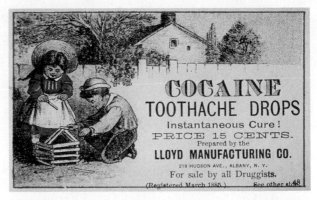

In the late nineteenth century, cocaine products were used by children as well as adults.

alcohol and cocaine produces a metabolite with an elimination half-life up to five times longer than that of cocaine alone, so the intoxicating mixture tends last quite a while (Health Alert). No wonder "Vin Mariani" became an instant sensation and an enormous commercial success.

In a stroke of marketing genius, Mariani also invented the concept of celebrity endorsement. Over the next few decades, advertisements for Vin Mariani carried testimonials from satisfied customers such as U.S. President William McKinley, Thomas Edison, the surgeon general of the U.S. Army, General Ulysses S. Grant, actress Sarah Bernhardt, Jules Verne, the Prince of Wales, the czar of Russia, and Popes Pius X and

HEALTH ALERT!

Cocaine after Alcohol: The Risk of Cocaethylene Toxicity

The risks of dying from cocaine arise from the drug's powerful excitatory effects on the body, such as abnormal heart rhythms, labored breathing, and increased blood pressure. The toxicity potential for any of these toxic reactions is unfortunately increased when alcohol is already in the bloodstream. The biotransformation of cocaine and alcohol (ethanol), when they are ingested in combination, produces a metabolite called *cocaethylene*. One effect of cocaethylene is a three- to fivefold increase in the elimination half-life of cocaine. As a result, cocaine remains in the bloodstream for a much longer time. More important, cocaethylene has a specific excitatory effect on blood pressure and heart rate that is greater than that produced by cocaine alone.

The combination of alcohol and cocaine is associated with a prolonged and enhanced euphoria, but it also brings an eighteen- to twenty-fivefold increased risk of immediate death. The fact that 62 to 90 percent of cocaine abusers are also abusers of alcohol makes the dangers of cocaethylene toxicity a significant health concern.

Where to go for assistance:

http://drugabuse.gov/infofacts/cocaine.html

This web site is sponsored by the National Institute of Drug Abuse and contains a comprehensive examination of cocaine risks, including the combination of cocaine with alcohol.

Sources: Andrews, P. (1997). Cocaethylene toxicity. *Journal of Addictive Diseases, 16,* 75–84. Harris, D. S.; Everhart, E. T.; Mendelson, J.; and Jones, R. T. (2003). The pharmacology of cocaethylene in humans following cocaine and ethanol administration. *Drug and Alcohol Dependence, 72,* 169–182.

Leo XII, to name just a few of Mariani's fans. Frederic Bartholdi, designer of the Statue of Liberty, wrote in a letter to Mariani that if he had been drinking Vin Mariani while designing the statue, it would have been more than three times taller.[6] We can only assume that he meant his remark to be complimentary.

Meanwhile, in the United States, Atlanta pharmacist John Pemberton was successful in selling an imitation form of Vin Mariani that he called French Wine Cola. In 1885, however, as a concession to the American temperance movement (see Chapter 8), he took out the alcohol, added carbonated water, and reformulated the basic mixture to combine the coca with the syrup of the African kola nut containing about 2 percent caffeine. Coca-Cola was born.

On the strength of the beverage containing both coca and caffeine, early advertisements for Coca-Cola emphasized the drink as a stimulating "brain tonic" that made you feel more productive and as a remedy for such assorted nervous ailments as sick headaches

In the late nineteenth century, the Coca-Cola Company advertised its beverage in medicinal terms. A company letterhead of this period spoke of Coca-Cola as containing "the tonic properties of the wonderful coca plant."

and melancholia (in the nineteenth-century, the term was used to mean depression).[7] The medicinal slant to the early promotion of Coca-Cola is probably the reason why soda fountains began to appear in drugstores.[8]

A number of competing brands with similar formulations soon sprang up, with names such as Care-Cola, Dope Cola, Kola Ade, and Wiseola.[9] Eventually, public pressure brought about official restrictions on the patent medicine industry, which, by the beginning of the twentieth century, was marketing more than fifty thousand unregulated products.[10] The Pure Food and Drug Act of 1906 specified that all active ingredients, including cocaine, had to be listed on patent medicine labels. In Canada, the Proprietary and Patent Medicine Act of 1908 banned cocaine from patent medicines entirely, but in the United States no further restrictions on cocaine sales or use were imposed until the Harrison Act of 1914 (see Chapter 2).

Increasingly aware of a rising tide of public sentiment against cocaine, the Coca-Cola Company changed the formula in 1903 from regular coca leaves to de-cocainized coca leaves, which eliminated the cocaine itself but retained the coca flavoring that remains to this day (see Drugs . . . in Focus on page 93). The "pause that refreshed" America would henceforth be due only to the presence of sugar and caffeine.

In the meantime, cocaine was becoming a major factor in the practice of medicine. In the United States, William Halsted, one of the most distinguished surgeons of the time and one of the founders of the Johns Hopkins School of Medicine, studied the effect of cocaine in anesthetizing nerves and whole limbs. In the process, he acquired a cocaine habit of his own (which was replaced several years later by dependence on morphine). It was in Europe, however, that the psychological implications of cocaine were explored most extensively, ironically through the triumphs and tribulations of Sigmund Freud.

Freud and Cocaine

In 1884, Freud was a struggling young physician, given to bouts of depression and self-doubt but nonetheless determined to make his mark in the medical world. He had read a report by a German army physician that supplies of pure cocaine helped soldiers endure fatigue and feel better in general. Freud secured some cocaine for himself and found the experience exhilarating; his depression lifted, and he felt a new sense of boundless energy. His friend and colleague Dr. Ernst von Fleischl-Marxow, taking morphine and enduring a painful illness, borrowed some cocaine from Freud and reported favorable results as well.

What Happened to the Coca in Coca-Cola?

Every day, in a drab factory building in suburban Maywood, New Jersey, a select team of employees of the Stepan Company carries out a chemical procedure that has been one of the primary responsibilities of the company since 1903. They remove cocaine from high-grade coca leaves. The remainder, technically called "decocainized flavor essence" is then shipped to the Coca-Cola Company as part of the secret recipe for the world's favorite soft drink.

Each year, the Stepan Company is legally sanctioned by the U.S. government (and carefully monitored by the Drug Enforcement Administration) to receive shipments of about 175,000 kilograms of coca leaves from Peruvian coca farms, separate the cocaine chemically, and produce about 1,750 kilograms of high-quality cocaine. Its annual output is equivalent to approximately 20 million hits of crack, worth about $200 million if it were to make it to the illicit drug market. Fortunately, the Stepan Company has an impeccable security record.

In case you are wondering what happens to the cocaine after it is removed from the coca leaves, it turns out that Stepan is the official distributor of cocaine to its legitimate market in the world of medicine for use as a local anesthetic.

As a result, the Stepan Company essentially has it both ways. It is the exclusive U.S. supplier of cocaine for use in medical settings, as well as the decocainized coca in your next can of Coke.

Sources: Inciardi, J. A. (2002). *The war on drugs III.* Boston: Allyn and Bacon, p. 21. Miller, M. W. (1994, October 17). Quality stuff: Firm is peddling cocaine, and deals are legit. *Wall Street Journal,* pp. A1, A14.

Before long, Freud was distributing cocaine to his friends and his sisters, and he even sent a supply to his fiancée Martha Bernays. In the words of Freud's biographer Ernest Jones, "From the vantage point of our present knowledge, he was rapidly becoming a public menace."[11] We can gain some perspective on the effect cocaine was having on Freud's behavior at this time through an excerpt from a personal letter to Martha:

> Woe to you, my Princess, when I come. I will kiss you quite red and feed you till you are plump. And if you are forward you shall see who is the stronger, a gentle little girl who doesn't eat enough or a big wild man who has cocaine in his body [underlined in the original]. In my last severe depression I took coca again and a small dose lifted me to the heights in a wonderful fashion. I am just now busy collecting the literature for a song of praise to this magical substance.[12]

Within four months, his "song of praise" essay, "Über Coca" ("Concerning Coca"), was written and published.

Unfortunately, the sweetness of Freud's romance with cocaine soon turned sour. Freud himself escaped becoming dependent on cocaine, although later in his life he clearly became dependent on nicotine (see Chapter 10). His friend Fleischl was not so lucky. Within a year, Fleischl had increased his cocaine dose to twenty times the amount Freud had taken and had developed a severe cocaine-induced psychosis in which he experienced hallucinations that snakes were crawling over his skin (an example of a phenomenon now referred to as **formication**). Fleischl suffered six years of agony and anguish until his death. By 1887, Freud had retracted his earlier stance on the drug.

The story of Freud's infatuation with cocaine and his later disillusionment with it can be seen as a miniature version of the modern history of cocaine itself.[13] From 1880 to 1910, the public reaction to cocaine went from wild enthusiasm to widespread disapproval. A similar cycle of attitudes swept the United States and the world a century later.

formication: Hallucinatory behavior produced by chronic cocaine or amphetamine abuse, in which the individual feels insects or snakes crawling either over or under the skin.

Acute Effects of Cocaine

Although the effects of cocaine on the user vary in degree with the route of administration, the purity of the dose, and the user's expectations about the experience, certain features remain the same. The most prominent reaction is a powerful burst of energy. If the cocaine is injected intravenously or smoked, the extremely intense effect (often referred to as a "rush" or "high") is felt within a matter of seconds and lasts only five to ten minutes. If the drug is snorted through the nose, the effect is less intense than when injected or smoked but lasts somewhat longer, approximately 15 to 30 minutes.

Users also experience a general sense of well-being, although in some instances cocaine may precipitate a panic attack.[14] As levels of cocaine diminish, their mood changes dramatically. The user becomes irritable, despondent, and depressed. These aftereffects are uncomfortable enough to produce a powerful craving for another dose.

Cocaine's effect on sexual arousal is often cited as the basis for its purported allure as an aphrodisiac. On the one hand, interviews of cocaine users frequently include reports of spontaneous and prolonged erections in males and multiple orgasms in females during initial doses of the drug. On the other hand, cocaine's reputation for increasing sexual performance (recall Freud's reference in his letter to Martha) may bias users toward a strong expectation that there will be a sexually stimulating reaction, when in reality the effect is a much weaker one. As one cocaine abuser expressed it, "Everybody says that it's an aphrodisiac. Again, I think some people say it because it's supposed to be. I think that it's just peer group identification. . . . I never felt that way. I was more content to sit there and enjoy it."[15] The fact is that chronic cocaine use results in decreased sexual performance and a loss of sexual desire, as the drug essentially takes the place of sex.

Cocaine produces a sudden elevation in the sympathetic branch of the autonomic nervous system (see Chapter 3). Heart rate and respiration are increased, while appetite is diminished. Blood vessels constrict, pupils in the eyes dilate, and blood pressure rises. The cocaine user may start to sweat and appear suddenly pale. The powerful sympathetic changes can lead to a cerebral hemorrhage or heart failure. Cardiac arrhythmia results from cocaine's tendency to bind to heart tissue itself. While adverse cardiovascular effects are the most significant medical consequences of cocaine use, adverse effects have been observed in practically every organ in the body. As you may recall from Chapter 2, cocaine is the drug most often involved in drug-related hospital emergency department visits and one of the drugs most frequently involved in drug-related deaths.[16]

The extreme effects of cocaine on bodily organs, particularly the heart, stem from its ability not only to excite the sympathetic system but to inhibit the parasympathetic system as well (Health Alert). Given the high level of sympathetic arousal, it is not surprising that motor skills are adversely affected. In a study of drivers showing reckless behavior on the road, those found to have been under the influence of cocaine were wildly overconfident in their abilities, taking turns too fast or

A *Time* magazine cover story (July 6, 1981) depicted cocaine in a manner that was long on "status" and short on "menace." It described the social phenomenon in this way: "In part precisely because it is such an emblem of wealth and status, coke is the drug of choice for perhaps millions of solid, conventional and often upwardly mobile citizens—lawyers, businessmen, students, government bureaucrats, politicians, policemen, secretaries, bankers, mechanics, real estate brokers, and waitresses."

HEALTH ALERT!

The Physical Signs of Possible Cocaine Abuse

- Dilated (enlarged) pupils
- Increased heart rate
- Increased irritability
- Paranoia
- Sneezing and irritability in the nose (if cocaine has been snorted)
- Feelings of depression
- Insomnia
- Decreased appetite and significant weight loss

> **Where to go for assistance:**
> www.cocaine.org/cokalc.htm
> A variety of informative articles can be found on cocaine abuse and combinations with other drugs through this web site.

weaving through traffic. One highway patrol officer called this behavior "diagonal driving. They were just as involved in changing lanes as in going forward." Yet they would pass the standard sobriety tests (such as walking a straight line) that are designed to detect alcohol intoxication.[17]

Chronic Effects of Cocaine

Repeated and continued use of cocaine produces undesirable mood changes that can be alleviated only when the person is under the acute effects of the drug. Chronic cocaine abusers are often irritable, depressed, and paranoid. As was true in Fleischl's experience with cocaine, long-term abuse can produce the disturbing hallucinatory experience of formication. The sensation of "cocaine bugs" crawling on or under the skin can become so severe that abusers may scratch the skin into open sores or even pierce themselves with a knife to cut out the imaginary creatures. These hallucinations, together with feelings of anxiety and paranoia, make up a serious mental disorder referred to as **cocaine psychosis**.

When snorted, cocaine causes bronchial muscles to relax and nasal blood vessels to constrict; the opposite effects occur when the drug wears off. As the bronchial muscles contract and nasal blood vessels relax, chronic abusers endure continuously stuffy or runny noses and bleeding of nasal membranes. In advanced cases of this problem, the septum of the nose can develop lesions or become perforated with small holes, both of which present serious problems for breathing.

cocaine psychosis: A set of symptoms, including hallucinations, paranoia, and disordered thinking, produced by chronic use of cocaine.

Medical Uses of Cocaine

When applied topically on the skin, cocaine has the ability to block the transmission of nerve impulses, deadening all sensations from the area. The use of cocaine as an anesthetic for nasal, lacrimal duct (tear duct), and throat surgery remains its only legitimate medical application.[18]

Even though cocaine is available for use in these situations, other topical anesthetics are typically preferred because they present fewer problems in their use. One disadvantage of cocaine is that it might inadvertently be absorbed into the bloodstream, leading to an acute cocaine response that is unrelated to the anesthetic effect. Another problem is that cocaine produces intense vasoconstriction (constriction of blood vessels). This can be helpful in reducing bleeding during a surgical procedure, but the intensity of the vasoconstriction may have undesirable side effects. Finally, the local anesthetic effects are brief because cocaine breaks down so rapidly and requires reapplications to remain effective. Local anesthetics, such as lidocaine (brand name: Xylocaine), have the advantage of being active over a longer period of time and not causing the problems associated with cocaine.

How Cocaine Works in the Brain

Cocaine greatly enhances the activity of dopamine in the brain. The actual effect is to block the reuptake process at the synapse, so dopamine stimulates the postsynaptic receptors longer and to a greater degree. Unlike the amphetamines (discussed later in this chapter), the structure of cocaine does not resemble the structure of dopamine, so why cocaine should block its reuptake so effectively is not at all clear. Nonetheless, what has been determined is that the acute effect of euphoria experienced through cocaine is directly related to an increase in dopamine activity in the region of the brain that controls pleasure and reinforcement in general: the nucleus accumbens (see Chapter 3). The current scientific thinking is that this alteration in brain chemistry has a profound effect on an individual's decision-making skills and an individual's potential for developing a dependence on cocaine (or some other drug of abuse).

Chronic cocaine abuse, however, leads to the loss of about 20 percent of the dopamine receptors in this region of the brain over time. The depletion of dopamine receptors among long-term cocaine abusers has been observed up to four months after the last cocaine exposure, even though the cocaine abuser no longer has cocaine in his or her system. As a result, there is a tendency toward a decline in the experience of pleasure from natural reinforcers. In fact, cocaine abusers frequently report that their craving for cocaine no longer stems from the pleasure they felt when taking it initially. Their lives may be in a shambles, and the acute effects of euphoria from cocaine may no longer be strong, but they still crave the drug more than ever. In other words, there is now a disconnection between "liking" and "wanting."[19]

One feature of cocaine is quite unlike that of other psychoactive drugs. Although cocaine abusers, over repeated cocaine exposures, develop a pattern of drug tolerance to its euphoric effect, they develop a pattern of sensitization (a heightened responsiveness) with respect to motor behavior and brain excitation. This phenomenon, referred to as the **kindling effect**, makes cocaine particularly dangerous because cocaine has the potential for setting off brain seizures. Repeated exposure to cocaine can lower the threshold for seizures, through a sensitization of neurons in the limbic system over time. As a result of the kindling effect, deaths from cocaine overdose may occur from relatively low dose levels.[20]

Present-Day Cocaine Abuse

The difficult problems of cocaine abuse in the United States and around the world mushroomed during the early 1970s and continue to the present day, although the incidence of abuse is down from peak levels reached around 1986. In ways that resembled the brief period of enthusiasm for cocaine in 1884, attitudes during the early period of this "second epidemic" were incredibly naive. Fueled by media reports of use among the rich and famous, touted as the "champagne of drugs," cocaine became synonymous with a life of wealth, glamour, and sophistication. A *Time* magazine cover story in 1981 depicted cocaine as long on "status" and short on "menace." The article concluded there was such a close identification with wealth and social accomplishment that cocaine was considered the drug of choice ". . . for perhaps millions of solid, conventional and often upwardly mobile citizens—lawyers, businessmen, students, government bureaucrats, politicians, policemen,

kindling effect: A phenomenon in the brain that produces a heightened sensitivity to repeated administrations of some drugs, such as cocaine. This heightened sensitivity is the opposite of the phenomenon of tolerance.

secretaries, bankers, mechanics, real estate brokers, and waitresses."[21] At the same time, the medical profession at this time was surprisingly naive about risks of cocaine use. The widely respected *Comprehensive Textbook of Psychiatry* (1980) stated the following: "If it is used no more than two or three times a week, cocaine creates no serious problem. . . . At present chronic cocaine use does not usually present a medical problem."[22]

These attitudes changed dramatically as events in the 1980s unfolded. The death of actor-comedian John Belushi in 1982, followed by the drug-related deaths of other entertainers and sport figures (see Drugs . . . in Focus, page 32) produced a reversal of opinion about the safety and desirability of cocaine. The greatest influence, however, was the arrival of crack cocaine on the drug scene in 1985, which will be examined in the next sections.

From Coca to Cocaine

To understand the full picture of present-day cocaine abuse, it is necessary to examine the various forms that cocaine can take, beginning with the extraction of cocaine from the coca plant itself (Figure 4.1). During the initial extraction process, coca leaves are soaked in various chemical solvents so that cocaine can be drawn out of the plant material. Leaves are then crushed, and alcohol is percolated through them to remove extraneous matter. After sequential washings and a treatment with kerosene, the yield is cocaine that is approximately 60 percent pure. This coca paste is, as mentioned earlier, combined with tobacco and smoked in many South American countries.

Cocaine in this form, however, is not water-soluble and therefore cannot be injected into the bloodstream. An additional step of treatment with oxidizing agents and acids is required to produce a water-soluble drug. The result is a white crystalline powder called **cocaine hydrochloride**, about 99 percent pure cocaine and classified chemically as a salt. When in the form of cocaine hydrochloride, the drug can be injected intravenously or snorted. The amount injected at one time is about 16 mg. Intravenous cocaine also can be combined with heroin in a highly dangerous mixture called a *speedball*.

If cocaine is snorted, the user generally has the option of two methods. In one method, a tiny spoonful of cocaine is carried to one nostril while the other nostril is shut, and the drug is taken with a rapid inhalation. In the other method, cocaine is spread out on a highly polished surface (often a mirror) and arranged with a razor blade in several lines, each containing from 20 to 30 mg. The cocaine is then inhaled into one nostril by means of a straw or rolled piece of paper. During the early 1980s, a $100 bill was a fashionable choice (see photo on page 95), drawing attention to the level of income necessary to use cocaine in the first place.[23]

From Cocaine to Crack

Options for using cocaine widened with the development of **free-base cocaine** during the 1970s and **crack cocaine** (or simply **crack**) during the mid-1980s. In free-base cocaine, the hydrochloride is removed from the salt form of cocaine, thus liberating it as a free base. The aim is to obtain a smokable form of cocaine, which, by entering the brain more quickly, produces a more intense effect. The technique for producing free-base cocaine, however, is extremely hazardous, as it is necessary to treat cocaine powder with highly flammable

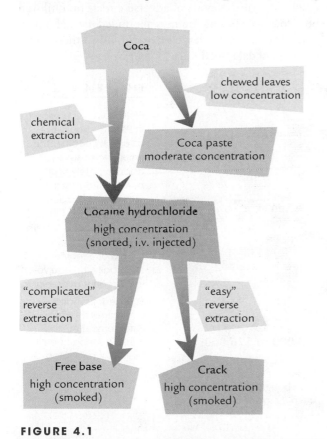

FIGURE 4.1

Steps in producing various forms of cocaine from raw coca.

---

cocaine hydrochloride: The form of cocaine that is inhaled (snorted) or injected into the bloodstream.

free-base cocaine: A smokable form of cocaine.

crack cocaine or crack: A smokable form of cocaine.

Public demonstrations in urban communities in the 1980s and 1990s were one way of responding to the desolation and misery resulting from crack cocaine abuse.

agents, such as ether. If the free base still contains some ether residue, igniting the drug will cause it to explode into flames.

Crack cocaine is the result of a cheaper and safer chemical method, but the result is essentially the same: a smokable form of cocaine. Treatment with baking soda yields small rocks, which can then be smoked in a small pipe. A cracking noise accompanies the burning, hence the name "crack."

How dangerous is crack? There is no question that the effect of cocaine when smoked exceeds the effect of cocaine when snorted; for some users, it even exceeds the effect of cocaine when injected. Inhaling high-potency cocaine (the purity of cocaine in crack averages about 75 percent) into the lungs, and almost immediately into the brain, sets the stage for a pattern of psychological dependence. And at a price of $5 to $10 per dose, cocaine is no longer out of financial reach. The answer is that crack is very dangerous indeed.

At its height of popularity in metropolitan regions of America, crack cocaine had major societal impact on communities where prevalence rates were high. As discussed in Chapter 2, the enormous monetary profits from the selling of crack caused inner-city crime and violence to skyrocket (Figure 4.2). Women who were crack abusers found that their drug cravings overwhelmed their maternal instincts, resulting in their neglecting the basic needs of their children, either in postnatal or prenatal stages of life. In New York, for example, the number of reported cases of child abuse and neglect increased from 36,000 in 1985 to 59,000 in 1989, a change largely attributed to the introduction of crack. Alarming reports of adverse effects on children born to crack-abusing mothers abounded, though initial concerns have been largely discounted in the light of subsequent data (see Drugs . . . in Focus).[24]

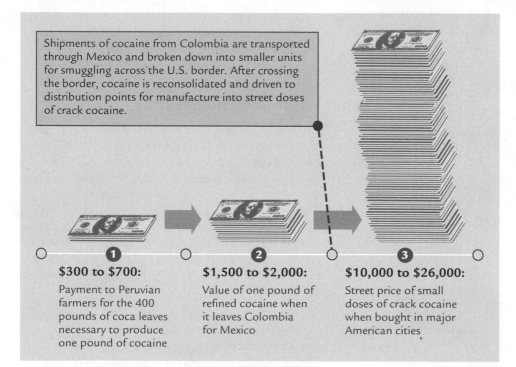

Shipments of cocaine from Colombia are transported through Mexico and broken down into smaller units for smuggling across the U.S. border. After crossing the border, cocaine is reconsolidated and driven to distribution points for manufacture into street doses of crack cocaine.

① $300 to $700: Payment to Peruvian farmers for the 400 pounds of coca leaves necessary to produce one pound of cocaine

② $1,500 to $2,000: Value of one pound of refined cocaine when it leaves Colombia for Mexico

③ $10,000 to $26,000: Street price of small doses of crack cocaine when bought in major American cities

FIGURE 4.2

From coca farm prices in Peru to street prices as crack cocaine. The value increases by approximately 8600 percent, from as little as $300 to as much as $26,000 for the 400 pounds of coca required to produce the one pound of cocaine and eventually the equivalent amount of crack.

Source: Information courtesy of the Drug Enforcement Administration, U.S. Department of Justice, Washington, DC.

Drugs . . . in Focus

Crack Babies Reevaluated: What Really Are the Effects?

In the late 1980s, at the height of the crack abuse explosion, one particularly alarming possibility posed by public health officials focused on the children of women who had been crack abusers during their pregnancies (the newborns subjected to this abuse are frequently referred to as "crack babies"). Might these innocents incur long-term mental and physical deficits later in life as a result of *in utero* exposure to cocaine? The early signs were not promising. These newborns had lower birth weights and smaller head circumferences, and they displayed tremors, excessive crying, disturbed sleep patterns, and diminished responsiveness, all of which are abnormalities typical of cocaine exposure. The question remained whether there would be deficits in social skills and mental ability when these infants grew older.

Unfortunately there is no simple answer. The main difficulty is the fact that most of the mothers who were cocaine abusers during their pregnancies were more accurately polydrug abusers; they typically abused alcohol, marijuana, and tobacco as well as cocaine. Studies comparing cocaine-exposed and non-cocaine-exposed children, therefore, must control for prenatal exposure to other drugs, gestational age and size at birth, ethnicity, and gender, as well as other factors such as the socioeconomic status and intelligence level of the mother. When these factors are taken into account, some differences in cognitive functioning remain and appear to continue being observed as these children progress through their education. The differences that are observed, however, are relatively small, and the contribution of the other possible factors to these differences are typically greater than the contribution of prenatal cocaine exposure alone. In general, boys seem to be more affected by prenatal cocaine exposure than girls.

The consensus among health professionals, therefore, is that developmental difficulties of children as they progress through childhood and adolescence can be the result of many risk factors (see Chapter 1), including inadequate prenatal care, poor nutrition, poor parenting, poverty, and exposure to stressors in everyday living, as well as exposure to licit drugs such as alcohol and nicotine. Cocaine exposure itself prior to their birth has an adverse effect, but apparently not a unique one.

Why the unusually intense interest in the effects of *in utero* exposure to cocaine, when the evidence is so much stronger with respect to the more widely available licit drugs, alcohol (Chapter 9) and nicotine (Chapter 10)? As expressed in an editorial in the *Journal of the American Medical Association* in 2001, a case can be made that the issues in the late 1980s and 1990s extended beyond concerns about public health. To those who viewed drug users in general, and pregnant drug users in particular, with reprehension and distain, the "crack baby" was a symbol. From their perspective, women exposing their unborn children to cocaine were individuals who were selfish enough to cause irreparable damage to an innocent unborn child for the sake of getting high. This image, promoted by the mass media, made it easier to argue for a simplistic, punitive response to the complex causes of drug use.

Sources: Bennett, D. S.; Bendersky, M.; and Lewis, M. I. (2008). Children's cognitive ability from 4 to 9 years old as a function of prenatal cocaine exposure, environmental risk, and maternal verbal intelligences. *Developmental Psychology, 44,* 919–928. Chavkin, W. (2001, March 28). Cocaine and pregnancy—time to look at the evidence. *Journal of the American Medical Association, 285,* 1626 1628. Lumeng, J. C.; Cabral, H. J.; Cannon, K.; Heeren, T.; and Frank, D. A. (2007). Prenatal exposures to cocaine and alcohol and physical growth patterns to age 8 years. *Neurotoxicology and Teratology, 29,* 446–457. Oke, S. (2009, January 29). The epidemic that wasn't. *New York Times,* p. D1.

Although crack abuse remains a problem, the number of new crack abusers has declined substantially, particularly in the inner-city communities of the United States. In 1998, whereas 36 percent of all males over thirty-six years old who were arrested in New York had used crack, little more than 4 percent of those fifteen to twenty years old had done so. A principal reason for this change has been the current stigmatized image of the "crack head," considered a social loser in his or her community.[25]

Patterns of Cocaine Abuse

In 2011, the National Survey on Drug Use and Health estimated that approximately 37 million Americans aged 12 or older had used cocaine at some time in their lives, 3.9 million had used it during the past year, and 1.4 million had used it during the past month. Approximately 8.2 million Americans had used crack at some time in their lives, 625,000 had used it during the past year, and 228,000 had used it during the past month. The past-month prevalence rates for cocaine and crack have declined by more than 40 percent and 45 percent, respectively, compared to 2005.[26]

Although the incidence of cocaine abuse in the United States is substantially lower than it has been in the past, the incidence of medical emergencies associated with cocaine use, as measured through the DAWN statistics, remain substantial. In 2011, approximately 505,000 cocaine-related ED visits were reported by metropolitan hospitals, representing the largest share (40 percent) of all ED visits involving an illicit drug. It is evident, therefore, that the absolute numbers of current cocaine and crack abusers have declined, but the dangers remain the same.[27]

In the meantime, variations of cocaine continue to emerge. A cheap formulation called paco has created significant social problems in Argentina and other regions of South America (see Drugs . . . in Focus).

Treatment Programs for Cocaine Abuse

Treating cocaine abuse presents difficulties that are peculiar to the power of cocaine itself. This is the way one treatment expert has put it:

Coming off cocaine is one of the most anguished, depressing experiences. I've watched people talk

Drugs . . . in Focus

Paco: A Cheap Form of Cocaine Floods Argentine Slums and Beyond

Paco is a shortened name for "pasta de cocaine" (cocaine paste), but it is actually just a chemical by-product that is left over (and usually discarded) when coca is converted to coca paste along the way to being transformed into high-grade cocaine hydrochloride. It is essentially lab trash, but unfortunately it has become the center of a major public health and social problem in the impoverished neighborhoods of Buenos Aires and other metropolitan ghettos in Argentina—a problem comparable, according to public health officials, to the epidemic of crack cocaine in American cities during the 1980s.

Like crack, paco is smoked so that psychoactive effects are felt within seconds (Chapter 3). In addition, even by the standards of the Argentine poor, paco is extraordinarily cheap. One dose costing the equivalent of about thirty cents produces a powerful high that lasts for two minutes or so. Abusers frequently smoke twenty to fifty (some up to 100) paco cigarettes, or as many as they can afford, during an average day. Its toxicity is augmented by paco contaminants such as solvents and chemicals like kerosene and rat poison. Paco dependence is rampant.

Paco abusers are referred to as *muertos vivientes* ("the undead"). They will sell anything they have or can get their hands on to buy paco. Attempts to control the flow of cocaine paste and the availability of paco from neighboring Bolivia, where coca is grown, have largely failed. Recently, Brazil has had to contend with the spillover of paco abuse from Argentina, while becoming a prime customer for cocaine itself. Presently, Brazil is the second largest consumer of cocaine in the world, after the United States.

Sources: Bale, A. (2011, February 21). Paco: Drug epidemic sweeping the streets of Argentina. *The Argentina Independent.* Accessed through http://argentinain dependent.com. Barrionuevo, A. (2008, February 23). Cheap cocaine floods a slum in Argentina, devouring lives. *New York Times*, pp. A1, A6. Hearn, K. (2006, April 5). Abuse of the highly addictive cocaine by-product "paco" is causing officials to revamp drug laws. *Christian Science Monitor*, p. 4. Ryzik, M. (2007, June 10). Cocaine: Hidden in plain sight. *New York Times*, Section 9, pp. 1, 9.

about coming off freebase, and one of the things I noticed was the nonverbal maneuvers they use to describe it. It looks like they're describing a heart attack. They have fists clenched to the chest. You can see that it hurts. They can re-create that hurt for you because it's a devastating event. They'll do almost anything to keep from crashing on cocaine. And on top of that, they'll do just about anything to keep their supply coming. Post-cocaine anguish is a strong inducement to use again—to keep the pain away.[28]

The varieties of treatment for cocaine abuse all have certain features in common. The initial phase is detoxification and total abstinence: The cocaine abuser aims to achieve total withdrawal with the least possibility of physical injury and minimal psychological discomfort. During the first twenty-four to forty-eight hours, the chances are high that there will be profound depression, severe headaches, irritability, and disturbances in sleep.[29]

In severe cases involving a pattern of compulsive use that cannot be easily broken, the cocaine abuser needs to be admitted for inpatient treatment in a hospital facility. The most intensive interventions, medical supervision with psychological counseling, can be made in this kind of environment. The early stages of withdrawal are clearly the most difficult, and the recovering abuser can benefit from around-the-clock attention that only a hospital staff can give.

The alternative approach is an outpatient program, under which the individual remains at home but travels regularly to a facility for treatment. An outpatient program is clearly a less expensive route to take, but it works only for those who recognize the destructive impact of cocaine dependence on their lives and enter treatment with a sincere desire to do whatever is needed to stop.[30]

PORTRAIT

Robert Downey Jr. and Others— Cleaning Up after Cocaine

Since 2008, we have known Robert Downey Jr. through an astounding run of professional success. Through his blockbuster movies—*Iron Man*, in 2008, *Sherlock Holmes* in 2009, *Iron Man 2* in 2010, *Sherlock Holmes: A Game of Shadows* in 2011, Ironman 3 in 2013—Downey essentially "owns" two Hollywood franchises that have no end in sight (see photo on the right).

It is easy to forget the way that Downey's life was going in the 1990s. In 1999, Downey had spent a year in prison after being convicted on charges of cocaine possession. Upon his release, he was featured on the successful *Ally McBeal* TV show, only to be fired in 2000. His drug-abuse problems had first begun making headlines in 1996, when he was found with cocaine, heroin, and a pistol in his car. By January 2003, Downey, at the age of thirty-seven, could remark that he was "a little older" and "mildly wiser" at the premiere of a new film, his first since he had completed a yearlong court-ordered drug

rehabilitation program in 2002. At the time, he was about one year into a three-year probation period, after pleading no-contest to cocaine possession and being under the influence during a November 2000 arrest in a Palm Springs hotel (see photo on the left).

Downey's self-destructive lifestyle appears to be behind him, a tribute to successful substance abuse treatment. Yet, like any recovering substance abuser, he acknowledges the fragility of his current life:

I don't understand that somehow everything was going to turn out O.K. from this lousy, exotic, and dark triple chapter of my life. . . . I don't think I will ever go that fast again.

There are well-known casualties of the struggle over cocaine abuse— River Phoenix in 1993, Chris Farley in 1998, and Mitch Hedberg in 2005,

all of them having died from a lethal combination of cocaine and heroin. Fortunately, however, Downey is not alone in his continuing recovery over substance abuse. Actors and actresses (Drew Barrymore, Samuel L. Jackson, Michael Douglas, Kelsey Grammer) and musicians (Eric Clapton, Steven Tyler, David Bowie) are among many celebrities who have gone from bad times to good, whether their substance of abuse was cocaine or heroin or alcohol or some combination of all three. Chapter 17 will deal with the issues of substance abuse treatment and the important role that treatment programs play in the lives of people at all levels of society.

Sources: Carr, D. (2008, April 20). Been up, been down. Now? Super. *New York Times*, pp. 1, 13. Quotation on page 13. Downey's back, older and "mildly wiser" (2003, January 21). Kidd, C. (2009, February 8). Robert Downey, Jr. *New York Times*, p. MM45. Lemonick, M.D. (2000, December 11). Downey's downfall. *Time*, p. 97.

For cocaine abusers who have failed in previous attempts in outpatient treatment or for those who are in denial of their cocaine dependence, an inpatient approach may be the only answer. For most abusers, long after they have apparently "kicked the habit," it is important to stay away from places where cocaine and other drugs are prevalent, and to stay away from former friends and other stimuli that can act as environmental triggers to resume drug-taking behavior. You may recall that these precautions are crucial, given the power of conditioned environmental cues (Chapter 2) for relapse.[31] A prominent psychiatrist has expressed the phenomenon as a "kind of pathologic learning [that] lies at the heart of compulsive drug use. . . . the individual is vulnerable in these deeply encoded associations that can set off a craving, seemingly out of the blue."[32]

A third alternative is a combined approach in which a shortened inpatient program of seven to fourteen days is followed by an intensive outpatient program that continues for several months.

Whether on an inpatient or an outpatient basis, there are several approaches for treatment. One alternative is the self-help support group Cocaine Anonymous, modeled after the famous twelve-step Alcoholics Anonymous program (see Chapter 9). In this program, recovering cocaine abusers meet in group sessions, learn from the life experiences of other members, and gain a sense of accomplishment from remaining drug-free in an atmosphere of fellowship and mutual support. In another drug-treatment option, cocaine abusers meet with cognitive-behavioral therapists, who teach them new ways of acting and thinking in response to their environment. During the course of cognitive-behavioral therapy, cocaine abusers are urged to avoid situations that lead to drug use, recognize and change irrational thoughts, manage negative moods, and practice drug-refusal skills. While the success rates of both approaches are approximately the same for patients in cocaine-abuse treatment overall, some evidence suggests that a cocaine abuser's personal characteristics may affect the kind of treatment that will work best (Figure 4.3). Whatever the approach taken, however, it is clear that an intensive relearning process has to go on, because many long-term cocaine abusers cannot remember a life without cocaine.[33]

Today, pharmacological approaches in cocaine-abuse treatment, as well as the combination of pharmacological and behavioral approaches, are being vigorously pursued. A promising example of a purely pharmacological strategy is development of the compound gamma vinyl-GABA (vigabatrin), currently FDA-approved for the treatment of epilepsy. Essentially, it has been established that vigabatrin "short-circuits" the reinforcing effect of cocaine by preventing the sudden surge of dopamine in the brain when cocaine is administered. Animals that have become cocaine-dependent no longer self-administer cocaine after taking vigabatrin and are no longer attracted to locations that have been

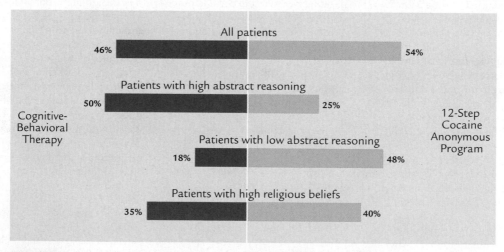

FIGURE 4.3

Percentage of patients achieving four consecutive weeks of cocaine abstinence, comparing two types of treatment.

Source: Adapted from Shine, B. (2000, March). Some cocaine abusers fare better with cognitive-behavioral therapy, others with 12-step programs. *NIDA Notes, 15* (1), 9.

associated with cocaine in the past, implying that animals are not better able to resist the conditioned cues for chronic cocaine use. In 2009, randomized double-blind, placebo-controlled trials involving a sample of long-time cocaine abusers showed that fourteen out of fifty (28%) of abusers treated with vigabatrin showed negative urine tests for cocaine lasting for nine weeks, whereas only 4 out of fifty three (7.5%) treated with a placebo did so. Twelve subjects in the vigabatrin group and two subjects in the placebo group remained abstinent for thirteen weeks, the full-length of the study. Interestingly, among subject reporting prior alcohol use, 44 percent in the vigabatrin group reported abstinence from alcohol, compared to six percent in the placebo group.[34]

The potential for relapse is particularly challenging among recovering cocaine abusers, primarily as a result of powerful conditioned cues that have been associated with the drug. A specialist in cocaine abuse rehabilitation tells this story: "A woman was doing well in treatment. Then one day she was changing her baby's diaper. She used baby powder and the sight of the white powder induced a tremendous craving for cocaine."[35] The continuing investigation of treatment and prevention approaches to cocaine abuse, emphasizing the drug craving factor, reflects a general orientation toward reducing the negative impact of drug-taking behavior on the individual and society (the "demand" side), as opposed to reducing the availability of the drugs themselves (the "supply" side).

Amphetamines

One of humanity's fondest dreams is to have the power of unlimited endurance, to be able to banish fatigue from our lives, to be fueled by endless energy as though we had discovered some internal perpetual-motion machine. We all have wanted, at some time in our lives, to be a super-hero. Cocaine, as we know, gives us that illusion. The remainder of this chapter will examine another powerful drug source for these feelings of invincibility: amphetamines. As we will see, the attractions and problems of abuse associated with cocaine and amphetamines are quite similar.

The Different Forms of Amphetamines

To understand amphetamine abuse, both past and present, it is necessary to know something about the molecular structure of amphetamines themselves.

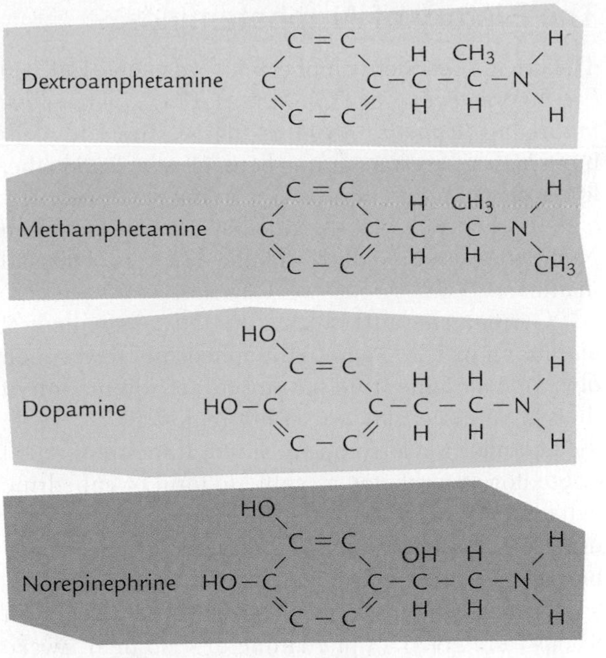

FIGURE 4.4

The molecular structure of dextroamphetamine, methamphetamine, dopamine, and norepinephrine. Notice the chemical similarities.

Amphetamine can be represented chiefly as a specific arrangement of carbon (C), hydrogen (H), and nitrogen (N) atoms (Figure 4.4, shown above), either in a "right-handed" version or a "left-handed" version (mirror image). The more potent version is the right-handed form, called dextroamphetamine or **d-amphetamine** (brand name: Dexedrine). It is stronger than the left-handed form, called levoamphetamine or l-amphetamine, which is not commonly available by itself. It is, however, combined with d-amphetamine in the medication Adderall.

A modified form of d-amphetamine, formulated by substituting CH_3 (called a methyl group) for H at one end, is called **methamphetamine**. This slight change in the formula allows for a quicker passage across the blood–brain barrier. Methamphetamine, often called *meth*, *speed*, or *crank*, has been the primary form of amphetamine abused in recent years.

d-amphetamine: Shortened name for dextroamphetamine, a potent form of amphetamine marketed under the brand name Dexedrine.

methamphetamine: A type of amphetamine once marketed under the brand name Methedrine. Methamphetamine abusers refer to it as meth, speed, or crank.

The History of Amphetamines

The origin of modern amphetamines dates back almost five thousand years to a Chinese medicinal herb called *ma huang* (*Ephedra vulgaris*) that was used to clear bronchial passageways during bouts of asthma and other forms of respiratory distress. According to Chinese legend, this herb was first identified by the Emperor Shen Nung, who also is credited with the discovery of tea and marijuana.

German chemists isolated the active ingredient of *ma huang* in 1887, naming it ephedrine. It was soon obvious that ephedrine mimicked the stimulation of the sympathetic nervous system in general. In 1932, the pharmaceutical company Smith, Kline and French Laboratories marketed a synthetic form of ephedrine called **amphetamine** under the brand name Benzedrine as a nonprescription CNS stimulant appetite suppressant and bronchial dilator.

During World War II, both U.S. and German troops were given amphetamine to keep them awake and alert. Japanese kamikaze pilots were on amphetamine during their suicide missions. The advantages over cocaine, the other stimulant drug available at the time, were twofold: Amphetamine was easily absorbed into the nervous system from the gastrointestinal tract, so it could be taken orally; and its effects were much longer-lasting. After the war, amphetamine use was adapted for peacetime purposes. Amphetamine, often referred to as *bennies*, was a way for college students to stay awake to study for exams and for long-distance truck drivers to fight fatigue on the road. In the meantime, the word got around that amphetamine produced euphoria as well, and soon amphetamine became popular for recreational purposes. People found ways of opening up the nonprescription amphetamine inhalers, withdrawing the contents, and getting high by drinking it or injecting it intravenously. Since each inhaler contained 250 mg of amphetamine, there was enough for several powerful doses. During the early 1960s, injectable amphetamines could be bought with forged prescriptions or even by telephoning a pharmacy and posing as a physician. By 1965, amendments to federal drug laws tightened the supply of prescription amphetamines, requiring manufacturers, wholesalers, and pharmacies to keep careful records of amphetamine transactions, but amphetamines soon became available from illegal laboratories.[36]

Amphetamine abuse in the United States reached a peak around 1967, declining slowly over the 1970s as other drugs of abuse, notably cocaine, grew in popularity. By 1970, 10 percent of the U.S. population over fourteen years of age had used amphetamine, and more than 8 percent of all drug prescriptions were for amphetamine in some form.[37] For about two decades afterward, amphetamine abuse steadily faded from prominence in the drug scene. Cocaine and later crack cocaine became the dominant illicit stimulants of abuse. Only since the mid-1990s has amphetamine abuse, in the form of methamphetamine abuse, resurfaced as a significant social concern.

How Amphetamines Work in the Brain

We can get a good idea of how amphetamines work in the brain by looking carefully at the molecular structures of dopamine and norepinephrine alongside d-amphetamine and methamphetamine in Figure 4.4. Note that there are only slight differences among them. Because of the close resemblance to dopamine and norepinephrine, it is not hard to imagine amphetamines increasing the activity level of these two neurotransmitters. Specifically, amphetamines cause increased amounts of dopamine and norepinephrine to be released from synaptic knobs and also slow down their reuptake from receptor sites. As described in Chapter 3, dopamine figures prominently in regions of the brain (notably the nucleus accumbens) associated with positive reinforcement. The euphoric effects of amphetamines, and the craving for them during abstinence, are considered to result from changes in dopamine activity. In this sense, amphetamines and cocaine share a common neurochemical mechanism.

Acute Effects of Amphetamines

The acute behavioral effects of amphetamine, in either d-amphetamine or methamphetamine form, closely resemble those of cocaine, and the adverse medical consequences are similar as well. However, amphetamine effects extend over a longer period of time. For intervals of eight to twenty-four hours, there are signs of increased sympathetic autonomic activity, such as faster breathing and heart rate as well as hyperthermia (increased body temperature) and elevated blood pressure. Users experience feelings of euphoria and invincibility, decreased appetite, and an extraordinary boost in alertness and energy. Adverse and potentially lethal

amphetamine (am-FEH-ta-meen): A family of ephedrine-based stimulant drugs.

bodily changes include convulsions, chest pains, and stroke. In 2011, approximately 103,000 of drug-related ED visits in the United States were attributable specifically to methamphetamine abuse, accounting for about two-thirds of visits related to stimulant abuse in general.[38]

Chronic Effects of Amphetamines

The chronic effects of amphetamine abuse are both bizarre and unpleasant, particularly in the case of methamphetamine. Heavy methamphetamine abusers may experience formication hallucinations similar to those endured by cocaine abusers. They may become obsessed with the delusion that parasites or insects have lodged in their skin and so attempt to scratch, cut, or burn their skin in an effort to remove them. It is also likely that they will engage in compulsive or repetitive behaviors that are fixated upon ordinarily trivial aspects of life; an entire night might be spent, for example, counting the corn flakes in a cereal box. Compulsive jaw movements and teeth grinding can cause significant dental damage over time.[39]

The most serious societal consequence of methamphetamine abuse is the appearance of paranoia, wildly bizarre delusions, hallucinations, tendencies toward violence, and intense mood swings. In the words of one health professional, "It's about the ugliest drug there is."[40] Because the symptoms have been observed with the chronic abuse of amphetamines of any type, they are referred to collectively as **amphetamine psychosis**. The possibility that methamphetamine abusers may not have slept for three to five days increases their tendency toward extremely irritable, paranoid, and potentially violent behavior. These symptoms, which are called "tweaking" by the drug-abuse community, are displayed by up to 50 percent of methamphetamine abusers and present particular challenges to law-enforcement officers who have to deal with abusers under these circumstances. The close resemblance to paranoid schizophrenia has led to speculation that the two conditions may have a common underlying neurochemical basis: an overstimulation of dopamine-releasing

neurons in those regions in the brain that control emotional reactivity.[41]

A study of heavy methamphetamine abusers has shown changes in chemical metabolites in those regions of the brain that are associated with Parkinson's disease, suggesting that their methamphetamine exposure may predispose this group to acquiring Parkinson symptoms later in life. Fortunately, however, recent evidence indicates that chemical changes in the brain in chronic methamphetamine abusers can be at least partially reversed by abstinence from the drug for a year or more.[42]

Methamphetamine Abuse

In the United States, the emergence of widespread methamphetamine abuse was intermingled with the marijuana and LSD scene during San Francisco's "Summer of Love and Peace" in 1967. Almost from the beginning, however, speed freaks—as methamphetamine abusers were called—whose behaviors were anything but loving or peaceful became the outcasts of that society:

> These wild-eyed, manic burnout cases would blither on endlessly, rip off anything not welded in place, then go into fits of erratic and violent behavior. . . . They were shunned by other sorts of drug users, and ended up congregating with the only segment of the population who could stomach their company— other speed freaks.[43]

In the meantime, prescription amphetamines, widely administered during the 1960s for weight control and as a way to combat drowsiness, resulted in large numbers of abusers from practically every segment of society. Even though d-amphetamine was classified as a Schedule II drug in 1970 and the number of d-amphetamine prescriptions decreased by 90 percent from 1971 and 1986, the pills were still out there, and people found ways to continue an abuse pattern of drug-taking behavior.

Present-Day Patterns of Methamphetamine Abuse

As crack cocaine became increasingly associated with the urban poor and powder cocaine with upscale affluence in the 1980s, amphetamine abuse declined dramatically. In the 1990s, however, as crack cocaine and powder cocaine abuse began to diminish,

amphetamine psychosis: A set of symptoms, including hallucinations, paranoia, and disordered thinking, resulting from high doses of amphetamines.

A public-service campaign against meth abuse aims to reach young adults.

My job.
My friends.
My future.

I lost everything to meth.

800 662 HELP
methresources.gov

methamphetamine abuse reemerged on the drug scene. Once identified with the countercultural 1960s, methamphetamine became a major stimulant of abuse in the United States, and its popularity is now concentrated among working-class people rather than among the poor or the affluent.

Administered by snorting, injecting, or smoking, methamphetamine became one of the few drugs reported to be as prevalent as, or more prevalent than, other illicit drugs in areas outside America's inner cities. In 2011, the National Survey on Drug Use and Health estimated that approximately 12 million Americans aged 12 or older had used methamphetamine at some time in their lives, 1,033,000 had used it during the past year, and 439,000 had used it during the past month.[44]

In the early 1990s, distribution of methamphetamine was dominated by organized criminal groups operating out of southern California and Mexico, with trafficking routes extending through several U.S. states, including Arizona, Colorado, Iowa, Missouri, Nebraska, North Dakota, and Texas. As mentioned in Chapter 2, the slang term "crank" harkens back to the days of motorcycle gangs who distributed methamphetamine, hiding the drug in the crankshaft. By the late 1990s, however, thousands of "homegrown" methamphetamine laboratories proliferated in small towns and rural areas throughout the nation. They were typically situated in mobile homes, campers, vans, and easily hidden farm sheds, making their detection by law enforcement agencies extremely difficult. Toxic residue from methamphetamine manufacture, approximately five pounds of waste for every pound of methamphetamine produced, seeped into the soil and contaminated rivers and streams. Children suffered from inhaling the toxic fumes emitted during the process of methamphetamine manufacture, from the risks of fire and explosions,

and from abuse and neglect by methamphetamine-dependent parents (see Drugs . . . in Focus).

As a response to the methamphetamine abuse problem, a strenuous effort was made to reduce the availability of common products used to manufacture methamphetamine. Because liquid anhydrous ammonia, commonly used as a farm fertilizer, is an ingredient in the "methamphetamine recipe," fertilizer dealers have installed security systems to protect their supplies from theft. Retail outlets are now required by federal law to limit the sales of numerous cold remedies (Sudafed, Tylenol Cold, and others) that contain pseudoephedrine—an essential ingredient in the making of methamphetamine. A number of products that have formerly been "over-the-counter" (see Chapter 14) are now "behind-the-counter." Customers cannot buy more than the equivalent of approximately seventy 60-mg pseudoephedrine tablets per day and must provide photo identification upon purchase and sign a logbook recording the transaction. This simple move in Oregon in 2006 succeeded in reducing the number of domestic lab seizures by 95 percent from 2005 to 2009. In general, federal authorities reported a sharp decline in the number of domestic methamphetamine laboratory seizures between 2004 and 2008, but in 2010 the amount of seizures of methamphetamine itself as well as prevalence rates had turned upward again. Methamphetamine from nondomestic sources, specifically Mexico, has also increased.[45]

It should be noted that in recent years, methamphetamine has become an increasingly problematic club drug in New York, Los Angeles, and other major cities (see Chapter 1). A smokable form of methamphetamine hydrochloride called **ice** (also referred to as *crystal meth*), its

ice: A smokable form of methamphetamine hydrochloride. It is often referred to as crystal meth because of its quartz-like appearance.

Drugs . . . in Focus

Methamphetamine and the Heartland of America

In 2005, the methamphetamine abuse epidemic in Watauga County, North Carolina, had gotten so bad that it has nicknamed itself "the county that never sleeps." Dozens of methamphetamine laboratories in the region were raided. Every fire emergency was treated as if it were a meth-lab fire.

Watauga County was not alone. A survey of more than 500 county sheriffs in the United States, conducted by the National Association of Counties in 2005, documented the alarming proportions of meth abuse across the country since 2000. Fifty-eight percent of sheriffs in the survey regarded methamphetamine abuse as the biggest drug problem they faced, ahead of concerns about heroin, cocaine, or marijuana. In half of the counties surveyed, one in five current prison inmates had been incarcerated in connection with meth-related crimes. In 17 percent of the counties, more than half of the inmate population had been incarcerated for such crimes. A majority of sheriffs reported that meth use was the major contributing factor to increases in robberies or burglaries, domestic violence, and simple assaults. At the same time, only one in six counties reported having the financial resources to support a meth rehabilitation center or program.

Significant increases were reported in cases in which children needed to be placed out of the home as a result of neglect and abuse by parents who were meth abusers or as a result of a child's proximity to the hazards of meth labs. More than 69 percent of counties in Minnesota reported an increase in meth-related child placements between 2004 and 2005.

Two exacerbating factors have made it particularly difficult for children who are affected by the meth epidemic.

First, meth abuse has been concentrated largely in rural areas, where social service networks are ill-prepared to handle the increased numbers of foster children. Second, the chances of reunifying families torn apart by meth abuse have been considerably lower than in cases involving other forms of drug abuse because of the high rate of relapse among meth abusers in treatment.

In recent years, the picture of meth abuse in America has changed. Federal reports indicate a decline in the number of meth lab seizures, particularly in western U.S. states most dramatically affected by meth abuse, from about 10,000 in 200 to about 4,500 in 2009. This decline is due primarily to the restrictions on acquiring basic ingredients for meth production. The influx of illegal methamphetamine from Mexico, however, has increased. This new drug-trafficking pattern indicates that the number of meth abusers in the United States have not diminished overall (in fact, it has increased), but the availability of the drug has simply shifted from a reliance on domestic laboratories in local communities to foreign sources.

Sources: National Association of Counties (2005, July 5). The meth epidemic in America. Two surveys of U.S. counties: The criminal effect of meth on communities and the impact of meth on children. Washington, DC: National Association of Counties. National Drug Intelligence Center (2011). *National Drug Threat Assessment 2011.* Washington, DC: National Drug Intelligence Center, U.S. Department of Justice, Table B3. Substance Abuse and Mental Health Services Administration (2007, January 26). Methamphetamine use. *The NSDUH Report.* Rockville, MD: Substance Abuse and Mental Health Services Administration. Zernike, Kate (2005, July 11). A drug scourge creates its own form of orphan. *New York Times,* pp. A1, A15.

---

name originating from its quartz-like, chunky crystallized appearance, appeared on the drug scene in Hawaii in the late 1980s, but its abuse did not expand to the mainland to a significant degree until the late 1990s. Unfortunately, the combination of a purity of 98 to 100 percent and a highly efficient delivery route through the lungs produces a high level of potential for dependence and a significant social problem. Another is the association between methamphetamine abuse and increased high-risk sexual behavior among HIV-positive gay or bisexual men.[46]

Methamphetamine-Abuse Treatment

Even though methamphetamine and cocaine are similar in their stimulant effects and both trigger a major elevation in dopamine levels in the brain, the pattern of drug-taking behavior for each type of drug has its own distinctive character. Methamphetamine abusers typically use the drug throughout their waking day, at two- to four-hour intervals, in a pattern that resembles taking medication. Cocaine abusers typically use the drug in the evening and nighttime rather than during the day,

Understanding Patterns of Cocaine and Methamphetamine Abuse

Check your understanding of cocaine or crack cocaine abuse and methamphetamine abuse by identifying each statement as being (a) true with respect to cocaine or crack cocaine *but not* methamphetamine, (b) true with respect to methamphetamine *but not* cocaine or crack cocaine, or (c) true with respect to both cocaine or crack cocaine *and* methamphetamine.

1. Sigmund Freud was an early advocate of its use. _____

2. Formication hallucinations can occur. _____

3. Abuse is reported to be as prevalent as or more prevalent than that of other illicit drugs in areas outside America's inner cities. _____

4. A powerful energizing effect can last up to about 20 to 30 minutes. _____

5. Patterns of abuse can involve smokable forms of the drug. _____

6. Accepted use as a local anesthetic for certain types of surgery. _____

7. Sources for illegal manufacture include ingredients in cold remedies and farm fertilizer. _____

8. Neurochemical effects include an increase in dopamine activity in the brain. _____

Answers: 1. a   2. c   3. b   4. a   5. c   6. a   7. b   8. c

taking it in a continuous (binge-like) fashion until all the cocaine on hand has been exhausted. This latter pattern of drug-taking behavior fits the typical picture of the recreational user.

The duration of response to the two drugs may help to explain the differences in usage. Methamphetamine effects generally last longer than cocaine effects. Therefore, cocaine abusers need relatively more frequent administrations to maintain their "high." On tests that evaluate different forms of cognitive functioning, methamphetamine and cocaine abusers show significant differences in the type of cognitive impairment that is produced. Methamphetamine abusers are impaired on tests of perceptual speed or manipulation

of information, effects observed to a lesser extent among cocaine abusers. The greatest difference between the two groups is observed when tests require both speed and the manipulation of information.[47]

On the other hand, the course of methamphetamine withdrawal—and amphetamine withdrawal in general—is very similar to the course of events described earlier for cocaine. First there is the "crash" when the abuser feels intense depression, hunger, agitation, and anxiety within one to four hours after the drug-taking behavior has stopped. Withdrawal from amphetamines, during total abstinence from the drug, takes between six and eighteen weeks, during which the intense craving for amphetamine slowly subsides.

As in cocaine-abuse treatment, there are inpatient and outpatient programs for methamphetamine abuse, depending on the circumstances and motivation of the abuser. Self-help groups such as Cocaine Anonymous can be useful as well, since the symptoms of amphetamine withdrawal and cocaine withdrawal are nearly identical. Methamphetamine abusers represent approximately one in twelve individuals in treatment for substance abuse, but relatively few methamphetamine abusers attempt treatment, much less succeed in recovery. The reason is that they perceive themselves as remaining in control over their drug use, despite evidence to the contrary. As a major government report has expressed it:

> This perception is particularly dangerous because the crossover from initial use to loss of control is rapid for meth users, and generally they have lost control long before they can acknowledge it . . . . This attitude of denial makes it difficult to convince meth abusers to enter and stay in treatment.[48]

Overall, methamphetamine abusers find it extremely difficult to become drug-free, and their relapse rate is one of the highest for any category of illicit or licit drug abuse. In light of acknowledged difficulties in methamphetamine-abuse treatment, attention has been understandably focused on the prevention of methamphetamine abuse (Health Line).

Medical Uses for Amphetamines and Similar Stimulant Drugs

Although amphetamines in general continue to present potential problems of abuse, there are approved medical applications for amphetamines and amphetamine-like stimulant drugs in specific circumstances. Stimulant drugs are prescribed primarily for elementary-school-age children diagnosed as unable to maintain sufficient attention levels and impulse control in school or as behaviorally hyperactive. These symptoms are collectively referred to as **attention-deficit/hyperactivity disorder (ADHD)**. When there is no evidence of hyperactivity, the designation is shortened to *attention deficit disorder* (ADD).

ADHD is the most common psychological disorder among children. It is estimated that 3 to 10 percent of all school-age children meet the criteria for ADHD. The prevalence rate is three times greater, and the symptoms are generally more severe, for boys than for girls. These children have average to above-average intelligence but typically underperform academically. As many as two-thirds of school-age children with ADHD have at least one other psychiatric disorder, including anxiety and depression.[49]

Despite the public image of ADHD as an exclusively childhood phenomenon, longitudinal studies have shown that ADHD symptoms persist from childhood into adolescence in about 75 percent of cases and into adulthood in about 50 percent of cases. As adults, these individuals are ten times more likely to be diagnosed with an antisocial personality disorder, twenty-five times more likely to have been institutionalized for delinquency, and nine times more likely to serve a prison sentence.[50]

Stimulant Medications for ADHD

Commonly prescribed stimulant medications for the treatment of ADHD include oral administrations of the amphetamine-like drug methylphenidate (brand name: Ritalin), a combination of dextroamphetamine and levoamphetamine (brand name: Adderall), and a combination of dextroamphetamine and the amino acid lysine (brand name, Vyvanse).

For decades, Ritalin dominated the market in prescriptions written for ADHD. Although a growing number of alternative medications are now available for this purpose, Ritalin remains the most recognizable "brand" with respect to ADHD treatment. In this drug's original formulation, the rapid onset and short duration of Ritalin requires two administrations during a school day: one at breakfast and another at lunchtime, supervised by a school nurse. In the evening, blood levels of Ritalin

attention-deficit/hyperactivity disorder (ADHD): A behavioral disorder characterized by increased motor activity and reduced attention span.

decline to levels that permit normal sleep. Adderall has a longer duration of action, making it possible to administer a single dose and avoiding school involvement in treatment. In comparative studies, Ritalin and Adderall have been found to be equivalent in effectiveness.[51]

New drug treatments for ADHD have become available that are essentially variations of the traditional methylphenidate medication. They include a sustained-release formulation (brand name: Concerta), a formulation that produces an initial rapid dose of methylphenidate followed by a second, sustained-release phase (brand name: Metadate), and a chemical variation of methylphenidate that allows for a longer duration of action (brand names: Attenade, Focalin). A methylphenidate patch (brand name: Daytrana), designed to release the drug through the skin slowly over a period of nine hours, was approved in 2006.

Stimulant drugs improve behavior and learning ability in 60 to 80 percent of children who are correctly diagnosed with ADD or ADHD. In 1999, a major study examining the effects of medication over a fourteen-month period found that medication was more effective in reducing ADHD symptoms than behavioral treatment and nearly as effective as a combined approach of medication and behavioral treatment.[52]

One side effect of stimulant medications is a suppression of height and weight gains during these formative years, reducing growth to about 80 to 90 percent of normal levels. Fortunately, growth spurts during the summer, when children are typically no longer taking medication (referred to as "drug holidays"), usually compensate for this problem. Discontinuance of medication, however, has to be carefully monitored. Symptoms such as lethargy, lack of motivation, and, in some cases, depression can occur during this time. A more serious concern is the increased risk of cardiovascular disease due to the effects of stimulant drugs. An FDA-mandated "black box" warning now appears on ADHD medications as a guide for patients and physicians.[53] Fortunately, the main concern about the possible risk of future drug dependence as a result of stimulant treatment has been laid to rest. Childhood and adolescent use of stimulant medication for ADHD is *not* associated with later substance abuse. In fact, there is a nearly two-fold reduction in the risk of future abuse.[54]

Until recently, the phenomenon of *reducing* hyperactivity with methylphenidate and related stimulant drugs, rather than increasing it, had been quite puzzling to professionals in this field. It is now known that orally administered methylphenidate and related stimulant drugs produce a relatively slow but steady increase in dopamine activity in the brain. This change

in brain chemistry is hypothesized to have two effects that are beneficial to an individual with ADHD. First, increased dopamine may amplify the effects of environmental stimulation, while reducing the background firing rates of neurons. Thus, there would be a greater "signal-to-noise" ratio in the brain, analogous to having a stronger radio signal received by a radio that no longer emits a large amount of background static. The behavioral effect would be an improvement in attention and decreased distractibility. Symptoms of ADHD may be a result of not having a sufficient "signal-to-noise" ratio in the processing of information for tasks that require concentration and focus. Second, increased dopamine may heighten one's motivation with regard to a particular task, enhancing the salience and interest in that task and improving performance. An individual might perform better on a task simply because he or she likes doing it. The slow rate of absorption achieved through oral administration (Chapter 3) and the relatively slow action of dopamine release in the brain are two factors that make it possible to avoid an emotional high.[55]

It is commonly assumed that increased dopamine activity accounts for the reduction in ADHD symptoms, but this may not necessarily be the case. In 2003, a selective norepinephrine reuptake inhibitor, atomoxetine (brand name: Strattera) was approved by the Food and Drug Administration (FDA) for the treatment of ADHD in both children and adults. Since Strattera produces an increase in norepinephrine activity in the brain, it is possible that lowered norepinephrine levels play a role in ADHD as well. Strattera has been marketed as a once-a-day nonstimulant medication that reduces ADHD symptoms by increasing norepinephrine levels—not dopamine levels—in the brain. The full story may be either that both norepinephrine and dopamine are jointly involved in ADHD or that ADHD itself may be two separable disorders, one related to dopamine activity and the other related to norepinephrine activity. According to this hypothesis, the symptoms may overlap to such a degree that it is difficult to distinguish the two disorders on a strictly behavioral basis.

Other Medical Applications

Narcolepsy (an unpredictable and uncontrollable urge to fall asleep during the day) is another condition for which stimulant drugs have been applied in treatment. In 1999, modafinil (brand name: Provigil) was approved for treating narcolepsy. The advantage of Provigil over traditional stimulant treatments, such as dextroamphetamine, is that it does not present problems of abuse and produces fewer adverse side effects. In 2009, the

University of Michigan survey included, for the first time, a question about the nonmedical use of Provigil among high school seniors. At that time, the reported lifetime prevalence rate was 1.8 percent, and the rate has held steady since then. Evidently, the current misuse of this drug by adolescents is not a serious problem. Whether greater number of college students have taken to Provigil as a "cognitive enhancer" remains to be determined.[56]

There are also several amphetamine-like drugs available to the public, some of them on a nonprescription basis, for use as nasal decongestants. In most cases, their effectiveness stems from their primary action on the peripheral nervous system rather than on the CNS. Even so, the potential for misuse exists: Some users continue to take these drugs over a long period of time because stopping their use results in unpleasant rebound effects such as nasal stuffiness. This reaction, by the way, is similar to the stuffy nose that is experienced in the chronic administration of cocaine.[57]

Stimulant Medication and Cognitive Enhancement

In 1996, the Swiss pharmaceutical company Ciba-Geigy sent letters to hundreds of thousands of pharmacies and physicians in the United States, warning them to exert greater control over Ritalin tablets and prescriptions to obtain them. The alert came in response to reports that Ritalin was becoming a drug of abuse among young people, who were crushing the tablets and snorting the powder as a new way of getting a stimulant high. Diversion of prescription medications used to treat ADHD was beginning to be a concern.

Since then, the problem of stimulant medication abuse, primarily the nonmedical use of Adderall, has become a major issue in terms of its ability to enhance cognitive and academic performance. Approximately 9 percent of students in a New England liberal arts college reported in 2006 taking stimulants for nonmedical purposes, essentially as a cognitive enhancement. In a surprising (and controversial) survey published in 2008 in *Nature*, one of the world's leading scientific journals, 20 percent of respondents said that they were using some kind of cognitive-enhancement drug. In about two-thirds of these cases, the drug was Ritalin. Fourteen hundred presumably healthy people in sixty countries participated in the survey.

The report has sparked a number of interesting questions. Would the quality of cognitive performance really be enhanced, or would the poppers of "smart pills" simply be able to stay awake for a longer period of time? Given what we know about stimulants in general, it is more likely to be the latter rather than the former. Even if such drugs had a positive effect on performance by virtue of increasing the quantity (if not the quality) of the user's output, there would still be important ethical concerns, both inside and outside academia. In neuroscience laboratories around the world, the quest for "smart pills" is well under way.[58] The debate over their use, misuse, or abuse will surely intensify in the years ahead (see Point/Counterpoint II on pages 116–117).

Summary

The History of Cocaine

- Cocaine, one of the two major psychoactive stimulants, is derived from coca leaves grown in the mountainous regions of South America.

- During the last half of the nineteenth century, several patent medicines and beverages were sold that contained cocaine, including the original (pre-1903) formulation for Coca-Cola.

- Sigmund Freud was an early enthusiast of cocaine as an important medicinal drug, promoting cocaine as a cure for morphine dependence and depression. Soon afterward, Freud realized the strong dependence that cocaine can bring about.

Acute Effects of Cocaine

- Cocaine produces a powerful burst of energy and sense of well-being. In general, cocaine causes an elevation in the sympathetic autonomic nervous system.

Chronic Effects of Cocaine

- Long-term cocaine use can produce hallucinations and deep depression, as well as physical deterioration of the nasal membranes if cocaine is administered intranasally.

Medical Uses of Cocaine

- The only accepted medical application for cocaine is its use as a local anesthetic.

How Cocaine Works in the Brain

● Within the CNS, cocaine blocks the reuptake of receptors sensitive to dopamine and norepinephrine. As a result, the activity level of these two neurotransmitters in the brain is enhanced.

Present-Day Cocaine Abuse

● Compared with the permissive attitude toward cocaine use seen during the 1970s and early 1980s, attitudes toward cocaine use since the second half of the 1980s have changed dramatically.

● The emergence in the mid-1908s of relatively inexpensive, smokable crack cocaine expanded the cocaine-abuse problem to new segments of the U.S. population and made cocaine abuse one of the major social issues of our time.

Treatment Programs for Cocaine Abuse

● Cocaine abusers can receive treatment through inpatient programs, outpatient programs, or a combination of the two. Relapse is a continual concern for recovering cocaine abusers.

Amphetamines

● Amphetamines, the second of the two major psychoactive stimulants, have their origin in a Chinese medicinal herb, used for thousands of years as a bronchial dilator; its active ingredient, ephedrine, was isolated in 1887.

● The earliest form of amphetamine (brand name: Benzedrine) was developed in 1927 as a synthetic form of ephedrine. By the 1930s, various forms of amphetamines, specifically d-amphetamine and methamphetamine, became available around the world.

Acute and Chronic Effects of Amphetamines

● Amphetamine is effective as a general arousing agent, as an antidepressant, and as an appetite suppressant, in addition to its ability to keep people awake for long periods of time.

● The acute effects of amphetamines resemble those of cocaine, but amphetamines (when taken in large doses) have the particular feature of producing symptoms of paranoia, delusions, hallucinations, and violent behaviors, referred to as amphetamine psychosis. The bizarre behaviors of the "speed freak" illustrate the dangers of chronic amphetamine abuse.

Present-Day Patterns of Methamphetamine Abuse

● With the emphasis on cocaine abuse during the 1980s, amphetamine abuse was less prominent in the public mind. Recently, however, there has been a resurgence of amphetamine-abuse cases involving methamphetamine, particularly in nonurban regions of the United States.

● Treatment for methamphetamine abuse generally follows along the same lines as treatment for cocaine abuse.

Medical and Nonmedical Uses for Amphetamines and Similar Stimulant Drugs

● Amphetamine-like stimulant drugs have been developed for approved medical purposes.

● Methylphenidate (brand name: Ritalin), atomoxetine (brand name: Strattera), and dextroamphetamine (brand name: Adderall) are three examples of drugs prescribed for children diagnosed with attention-deficit/hyperactivity disorder (ADHD). Recently, there has been growing concern about the nonmedical use of these medications, either for recreational or "cognitive enhancement" purposes.

● Other medical applications for amphetamine-like drugs include their use as a treatment for narcolepsy and as a means for the temporary relief of nasal congestion.

Key Terms

amphetamine, p. 104	cocaine, p. 90	d-amphetamine, p. 103	kindling effect, p. 96
amphetamine psychosis, p. 105	cocaine hydrochloride, p. 97	formication, p. 93	methamphetamine, p. 103
attention-deficit/ hyperactivity disorder (ADHD), p. 109	cocaine psychosis, p. 95	free-base cocaine, p. 97	
	crack cocaine or crack, p. 97	ice, p. 106	

Endnotes

1. Rosencan, J. S., and Spitz, H. I. (1987). Cocaine reconceptualized: Historical overview. In H. I. Spitz and J. S. Rosencan (Eds.), *Cocaine abuse: New directions in treatment and research*. New York: Brunner/Mazel, p. 5.

2. Inglis, B. (1975). *The forbidden game: A social history of drugs*. New York: Scribner, pp. 49–50. Montoya, I. D., and Chilcoat, H. D. (1996). Epidemiology of coca derivatives use in the Andean region: A tale of five countries. *Substance Use and Misuse, 31*, 1227–1240.

3. Jaffe, J. (1985). Drug addiction and drug abuse. In L. S. Goodman and A. Gilman (Eds.), *The pharmacological basis of therapeutics* (7th ed.). New York: Macmillan, p. 552.

4. Nahas, G. G. (1989). *Cocaine: The great white plague.* Middlebury, VT: Paul S. Eriksson, pp. 154–162.

5. Kusinitz, M. (1988). *Drug use around the world.* New York: Chelsea House Publishers, pp. 91–95.

6. Karch, S. B. (2009). *The pathology of drug abuse* (4th ed.). Boca Raton, FL: CRC Press, pp. 9–19. Nuckols, Caldwell C. (1989). *Cocaine: From dependency to recovery* (2nd ed.). Blue Ridge Summit, PA: Tab Books.

7. Brecher, E. M., and the editors of *Consumer Reports* (1972). *Licit and illicit drugs.* Boston: Little, Brown, p. 270. Weiss, R. D., and Mirin, S. M. (1987). *Cocaine.* Washington, DC: American Psychiatric Press, p. 6.

8. McKim, W. A., and Hancock, S. D. (2013). *Drugs and behavior* (7th ed.). Boston: Pearson,, p. 230.

9. Erickson, P. G.; Adlaf, E. M.; Murray, G. F.; and Smart, R. G. (1987). *The steel drug: Cocaine in perspective.* Lexington, MA: D.C. Heath, p. 9.

10. Musto, D. (1973). *The American disease: Origins of narcotic control.* New Haven, CT: Yale University Press.

11. Jones, E. (1953). *The life and work of Sigmund Freud,* Vol. 1. New York: Basic Books, p. 81. White, W. L. (1998). *Slaying the dragon: The history of addiction treatment and recovery in America.* Bloomington, IL: Chestnut Health Systems, pp. 108–119.

12. Ibid., Jones, p. 84.

13. Brecher, *Licit and illicit drugs,* pp. 272–280.

14. National Institute on Drug Abuse (2010, March). *NIDA InfoFacts: Cocaine.* Bethesda, MD: National Institute on Drug Abuse.

15. Philips, J. L., and Wynne, R. D. (1974). *A cocaine bibliography—nonannotated.* Rockville, MD: National Institute on Drug Abuse, 1974. Cited in E. L. Abel. (1985). *Psychoactive drugs and sex.* New York: Plenum Press, p. 100.

16. Schneir A. B. (2008). Medical consequences of the use of cocaine and other stimulants. In J. Brick, (Ed.), *Handbook of the medical consequences of alcohol and drug abuse* (2nd ed.). New York: Routledge, pp. 344–354. Kaufman, M. J.; Levin, J. M.; Ross, M. H.; Lange, N.; Rose, S. L.; et al. (1998). Cocaine-induced cerebral vasoconstriction detected in humans with magnetic resonance angiography. *Journal of the American Medical Association, 279,* 376–380.

17. Experiment in Memphis suggests many drive after using drugs (1994, August 28). *New York Times,* p. 30.

18. Information courtesy of the American Academy of Otolaryngology—Head and Neck Surgery, March 1998.

19. Volkow, N. D.; Wang, G-J; Fowler, J. S.; Logan, J.; Gatley, S. J.; et al. (1997). Decrease in striatal dopaminergic responsiveness in detoxified cocaine-dependent subjects. *Nature, 386,* 830–833. Volkow, N. D., and Ting-Kai, L. (2004). Drug addiction: The neurobiology of behaviour gone awry. *Nature Reviews/Neuroscience, 5,* 963–970.

20. Robinson, T. E. (1993). Persistent sensitizing effects of drugs on brain dopamine systems and behavior: Implications for addiction and relapse. In S. G. Korenman and J. D. Barchas (Eds.), *The biological basis of substance abuse.* New York: Oxford University Press, pp. 373–402. Weiss and Mirin, *Cocaine,* pp. 48–49.

21. Demarest, M. (1981, July 6). Cocaine: Middle class high. *Time,* pp. 56–63. Quotation on p. 56.

22. Kaplan, H. I.; Freedman, A. M.; and Sadock, B. J. (1980). *Comprehensive textbook of psychiatry.* Vol. 3. Baltimore, MD: Williams & Wilkins, p. 1621.

23. Flynn, J. C. (1991). *Cocaine: An in-depth look at the facts, science, history, and future of the world's most addictive drug.* New York: Birch Lane/Carol Publishing, pp. 38–46.

24. Humphries, D. (1998). Crack mothers at 6: Prime-time news, crack/cocaine, and women. *Violence against Women, 4,* 45–61. Massing, M. (1998). *The fix.* New York: Simon and Schuster, p. 41. Singer, L.T.; Minnes, S.; Short, E.; Arendt, R.; Farkas, K.; et al. (2004). Cognitive outcomes of preschool children with prenatal cocaine exposure. *Journal of the American Medical Association, 291,* 2448–2456.

25. Furst, R. T.; Johnson, B. D.; Dunlap, E.; and Curtis, R. (1999). The stigmatized image of the "crack head": A sociocultural exploration of a barrier to cocaine smoking among a cohort of youth in New York City. *Deviant Behavior, 20,* 153–181.

26. Substance Abuse and Mental Health Services Administration (2012). *Results from the 2011 National Survey on Drug Use and Health: Detailed tables.* Rockville, MD: Substance Abuse and Mental Health Services Administration, Table 1.1A.

27. Substance Abuse and Mental Health Services Administration (2013). *Drug Abuse Warning Network: National estimates of drug-related emergency department visits 2004–2011.* Rockville, MD: Substance Abuse and Mental Health Services, Excel files.

28. Nuckols, *Cocaine,* p. 42.

29. Ibid., pp. 71–72.

30. Weiss and Mirin, *Cocaine,* p. 125.

31. Siegel, S. (1999). Drug anticipation and drug addiction. The 1998 H. David Archibald Lecture. *Addiction, 94,* 1113–1124.

32. Friedman, R. A. (2010, August 31). Lasting pleasures, robbed by drug abuse. *New York Times,* p. D6.

33. Shine, B. (2000, March). Some cocaine abusers fare better with cognitive-behavioral therapy, others with 12-step programs. *NIDA Notes, 15* (1), 9–11.

34. Brodie, J. D.; Case, B. G.; Figuerosa, E.; Dewey, S. L.; Robinson, J. A.; and Laska, E.M. (2009). Randomized, double-blind, placebo-controlled trial of vigabatrin for the treatment of cocaine dependence in Mexican parolees. *American Journal of Psychiatry, 166,* 1269–1277. Sergo, P. (2008, April/May). New weapons against cocaine addiction. *Scientific American Mind,* pp. 54–57.

35. Barnes, D. M. (1988). Breaking the cycle of addiction. *Science, 241*, p. 1029. Whitten, L. (2005, August). Cocaine-related environmental cues elicit physiological stress responses. *NIDA Notes, 20*(1), pp. 1, 6–7.

36. Brecher, *Licit and illicit drugs*, pp. 282–283.

37. Greaves, G. B. (1980). Psychosocial aspects of amphetamine and related substance abuse. In J. Caldwell (Ed.), *Amphetamines and related stimulants: Chemical, biological, clinical, and sociological aspects.* Boca Raton, FL: CRC Press, pp. 175–192.

38. Schneir, *Handbook* , 354-356. Substance Abuse and Mental Health Services Administration (2013). *Drug Abuse Warning Network, National estimates of drug-related emergency department visits 2004–2011.* Rockville, MD: Substance Abuse and Mental Health Services Administration, Excel files.

39. Goode, E. (2005). *Drugs in American society* (6th ed.). New York: McGraw-Hill College, p. 276.

40. Bai, M. (1997, March 31). White storm warning: In Fargo and the prairie states, speed kills. *Newsweek,* pp. 66–67. Quotation by M. A. R. Kleiman, p. 67.

41. Goode, *Drugs in American society*, p. 276. Sheff, D. (2008). *Beautiful boy: A father's journey through his son's addiction.* New York: Houghton Mifflin. Sheff, N. (2008). *Tweak: Growing up with methamphetamine.* New York: Ginee See Books/Atheneum Books for Young Readers, pp. 113–115.

42. Ernst, T. Chang, L.; Leonido-Yee, M.; and Speck, O. (2000). Evidence for long-term neurotoxicity associated with methamphetamine abuse: A 1H MRS study. *Neurology, 54*, 1344–1349. London, E. D.; Simon, S. L.; Berman, S. M.; Mandelhern, M. A.; et al. (2004). Mood disturbances and regional cerebral metabolic abnormalities in recently abstinent methamphetamine abusers. *Archives of General Psychiatry, 61*, 73–84.

43. Young, S. (1989, July). Zing! Speed: The choice of a new generation. *Spin magazine*, pp. 83, 124–125. Reprinted in E. Goode (Ed.) (1992). *Drugs, society, and behavior 92/93.* Guilford, CT: Dushkin Publishing, p. 116.

44. Substance Abuse and Mental Health Services Administration, *Results from the 2011 National Survey on Drug Use and Health: Detailed tables*, Table 1.1A.

45. Butterfield, F. (2004, January 4). Across rural America, drug casts a grim shadow. *New York Times*, p. 10. *Carnevale Associates (2011, March) . Policy Brief: Update: The changing landscape of the methamphetamine* epidemic. Gathersburg, MD: Carnevale Associates. Harris, G. (2005, December 15). Fighting methamphetamine, lawmakers reach accord to curb sales of cold medicines. *New York Times*, p. A33. Johnson, D. (2004, March 8). Policing a rural plague: Meth is ravaging the Midwest. *Newsweek,* p. 41. National Association of Counties (2006, January). *The meth epidemic in America.* Washington, DC: National Association of Counties. National Drug Intelligence Center (2011, August). Drug Enforcement Administration (2013). Methamphetamine lab incidents. Drug Enforcement Administration, U.S. Department of Justice, Washington, DC.

46. Jacobs, A. J. (2004, January 12). The beast in the bathhouse: Crystal meth use by gay men threatens to reignite an epidemic. *New York Times*, pp. B1, B5. Shernoff, M. (2005, July–August). Crystal's sexual persuasion. *The Gay & Lesbian Review*, pp. 24–26.

47. Zickler, P. (2001). Methamphetamine, cocaine abusers have different patterns of drug use, suffer different cognitive impairments. *NIDA Notes*, 16 (5), 11–12.

48. Gawin, F. H., and Ellinwood, E. H. (1988). Cocaine and other stimulants: Action, abuse, and treatment. *New England Journal of Medicine, 318*, 1173–1182. National Institute of Justice (1999, May). *Meth matters: Report on methamphetamine users in five western cities.* Washington, DC: National Institute of Justice, U.S. Department of Justice. Quotation on p. xii.

49. Julien, R. M. (2005). *A primer of drug action* (10th ed.). New York: Worth, pp. 390–405.

50. Findling, R. L. (2008). Evolution of the treatment of attention-deficit/hyperactivity disorder in children. *Clinical Therapeutics, 30*, 942–957. Julien, *A primer of drug action*, pp. 390–391. Wilens, T. E. (2003). Drug therapy for adults with attention-deficit hyperactivity disorder. *Drugs, 63*, 2385–2411. Wilens, T. E., and Fusillo, S. (2007). When ADHD and substance use disorders intersect: Relationship and treatment implications. *Current Psychiatry Reports, 9*, 408–414.

51. Julien, *A primer of drug action*, pp. 395–396.

52. The MTA Cooperative Group (1999). A 14-month randomized clinical trial of treatment strategies for attention-deficit/hyperactivity disorder. *Archives of General Psychiatry, 56*, 1073–1086.

53. Nissen, S. E. (2006, April 6). ADHD drugs and cardiovascular risks. *New England Journal of Medicine,* pp. 1445–1448.

54. Wilens, T. E.; Faraone, S. V.; Biederman, J.; and Gunawardene, S. (2003). Does stimulant therapy of attention deficit/hyperactivity disorder beget later substance abuse? A meta-analytic review of the literature. *Pediatrics, 111*, 179–185.

55. Julien, *A primer of drug action*, p. 395. Volkow, N. D.; Wang, G-J; Kollins, S. H.; Wigal, T. L.; Newcorn, J. H.; et al. (2009). Evaluating dopamine reward pathway in ADHD: Clinical implications. *Journal of the American Medical Association, 302*, 1084–1091.

56. Green, P. M., and Stillman, M. J. (1998). Narcolepsy: Signs, symptoms, differential diagnosis, and management. *Archives of Family Medicine, 7*, 472–478. Johnston, L. D.; O'Malley, P. M.; Bachman, J. G.; and Schulenberg, J. E. (2012a). Monitoring the Future: National survey results on drug use, 1975–2011. Vol. I: Secondary school students 2011. Ann Arbor, MI: Institute for Social Research, The University of Michigan, Table 2-1.Tuller, D. (2002, January 8). A quiet revolution for those prone to nodding off. *New York Times*, p. F7.

57. Julien, R. M. (1998). *A primer of drug action* (8th ed.). New York: Freeman, pp. 141–143.

58. Arria, A. M.; Caldeira, K. M.; O'Grady, K. E.; Vincent, K. B.; et al. (2008). Nonmedical use of prescription stimulants among college students: Associations with attention-deficit-hyperactivity disorder and polydrug use. *Pharmacotherapy, 28,* 156–169. Carroll, B.C.; McLaughlin, T. J.; and Blake, D. R. (2006). Patterns and knowledge of nonmedical use of stimulants among college students. *Archives of Pediatric and Adolescent Medicine, 160,* 481–485. Greely, H.; Sahakian, B.; Harris, J. Kessler, R. C.; Gazzaniga, M.; et al. (2008). Toward responsible use of cognitive-enhancing drugs by the healthy. *Nature, 456,* 702–705. Harris, J., and Quigley, M. (2008). Commentary on "Professor's little helper": Humans have always tried to improve their condition. *Nature, 451,* 521 Schermer, M. (2008). On the argument that enhancement is "cheating." *Journal of Medical Ethics, 34,* 85-88. Stix, G. (2009, October). Turbocharging the brain. *Scientific American,* 46–55 Substance Abuse and Mental Health Services Administration (2009, April 7). Nonmedical use of Adderall among full-time college students. *The NSDUH Report,* pp.1–4. Talbot, M.. (2009, April 27). Brain gain: The underground world of "neuroenhancing" drugs. *New Yorker,* pp. 32–43. Wilens, T. E.; Adler, L. A.; Adams, J.; Sgambati, S. E; Rotrosen, J.; et al. (2008). Misuse and diversion of stimulants prescribed for ADHD: A systematic review of the literature. *Journal of the American Academy of Child and Adolescent Psychiatry, 47,* 21–31.

Point/Counterpoint II

Should Cognitive Performance-Enhancing Drugs Be Used by Healthy People?

The following discussion of viewpoints presents the opinions of people on both sides of the controversial issue of whether cognitive performance-enhancing drugs, originally intended for the treatment of ADHD and other behavioral disorders, should be used by healthy people to enhance their behavior on the job or in an academic or research environment. Read them with an open mind. You don't have to come up with the final answer, nor should you necessarily agree with the argument presented last. Many of the ideas in this feature come from the sources listed.

POINT

In a surprising survey report published in 2008 in *Nature*, one of the world's leading scientific journals, 20 percent of respondents said that they took some kind of cognitive-enhancement drug; about two-thirds of these cases involved Ritalin, an FDA-approved medication for the treatment of attention-deficit/hyperactivity disorder (ADHD), simply to enhance their mental performance. Fourteen hundred presumably healthy people in sixty different countries participated in the survey. This is a ghastly example of scientists and scholars engaging in uncontrolled pharmacological experimentation. Here was evidence of psychostimulant drugs, intended for therapeutic use for a specific disorder, being used by healthy adults to improve their productivity. Isn't anything sacred anymore?

COUNTERPOINT

How is this different from dosing yourself with caffeine with a couple of strong cups of coffee to get through that boring afternoon meeting or that all-nighter to finish a term paper? You are taking a psychoactive drug (caffeine) to enhance your cognitive performance, just as others have been doing for centuries. How is it different from taking a prescribed beta-blocker medication to help reduce situational anxiety?

POINT

Granted that we already engage in a form of cognitive performance enhancement with the consumption of caffeine. But let's talk about a level playing field. Caffeine can be obtained anywhere; it's ubiquitous. In contrast, Ritalin is a prescription drug. Were the pills obtained through prescriptions written for them, and if so, were the prescriptions obtained under false pretenses? This is dishonest at best, illegal at worst. The *Nature* survey reported that a third of the respondents had obtained their drugs through the Internet, where the industry is largely unregulated. They ran the risk of great harm to themselves. They may have ingested all sorts of contaminants. They may have risked dying.

COUNTERPOINT

Health risks from contaminated drugs ordered through the Internet don't seem to be higher in these cases than health risks among people who are ordering their prescriptions online to save money. I don't buy the argument that obtaining cognitive performance-enhancing drugs through the Internet suddenly plunges you into the dark world of illicit drug abuse. Besides, the side effects of Ritalin are relatively mild—moderate increases in heart rate and blood pressure. When these drugs went through the FDA approval process, clinical trials (see Chapter 14) revealed no serious cardiac problems in healthy adults. There was a problem in older adults and in those with preexisting cardiovascular problems, but generally these drugs were deemed safe and effective if you're healthy.

POINT

You're missing a bigger point here. Where is your basic sense of fair play? Not everyone has equivalent access. It's morally wrong to put one person at an advantage over other people who might be without access to these enhancements.

COUNTERPOINT

There isn't equivalent access to SAT-preparation courses either. Yet people don't discount a high SAT score just because someone else couldn't afford the expense of such preparation.

POINT

That may be true, but there is an effort to provide SAT preparation courses and instruction to as wide a population as possible, through a number of community programs. To make the same argument here, you would have to ensure that as many people as possible have access to Ritalin. Isn't this getting absurd?

Until that day comes (and let us hope it will not), how do we make an ultimate judgment about a person's achievements in life? Do we need an asterisk next to someone's Nobel or Pulitzer Prize if it was determined that cognitive performance-enhancing drugs were used? Such a move is being considered for sports records achieved by athletes who were taking anabolic steroids and other performance-enhancing drugs when they set these records. Why not in the case of cognitive performance-enhancing drugs? Conversely, would a disclaimer (perhaps a negative urinalysis) be required on a professor's tenure candidacy file to indicate that her or his productivity was achieved without the aid of cognitive performance-enhancing drugs?

COUNTERPOINT

The current phenomenon of cognitive performance-enhancing drugs such as Ritalin is only the most recent instance in a long history of human enhancement. People have always taken steps to improve the human condition or the circumstances under which they work and serve society. Isn't it an obligation to use one's full potential and resources to the greatest benefit of humanity? If cognitive performance-enhancing drugs advance that process, the drugs are serving humankind.

Consider it a mental form of cosmetic surgery. Besides, it hasn't been scientifically determined that cognitive performance-enhancing drugs actually make you smarter. Probably, at most, they allow you to stay alert longer than you would have under ordinary circumstances. But if their effects turn out to be more profound than that, we need to consider carefully the issues of *responsible use*.

Critical Thinking Questions for Further Debate

1 Suppose you are a new employee in a high-pressure corporation where your co-workers are ingesting a cognitive performance-enhancing drug such as Ritalin to increase their work productivity, but you have a preexisting cardiovascular disorder that would make taking this drug unwise. There is no overt coercion to join in with your co-workers, but you know that you will be at a disadvantage in terms of promotion and salary incentives if you don't. Is this a form of discrimination in the workplace?

2 Suppose you are taking a chemistry exam, and you know that a person next to you took Ritalin in order to study 50 percent longer than you were able to without taking a cognitive performance-enhancing drug. That other person outscores you by a full letter grade. Do you have any recourse in appealing your grade?

Point/Counterpoint III can be found on pages 246–247.

Sources: Carey, B. (2008, March 9). Brain enhancement is wrong, right? *New York Times, Week in Review,* pp. 1–2. Greely, H.; Sahakian, B.; Harris, J.; Kessler, R. C.; Gazzaniga, M.; et al. (2008). Toward responsible use of cognitive-enhancing drugs by the healthy. *Nature, 456,* 702–705. Harris, J., and Quigley, M. (2008). Commentary on "Professor's little helper": Humans have always tried to improve their condition. *Nature, 451,* 521. Monatersky, R.D. (2008, April 25). Some professors pop pills for an intellectual edge. *The Chronicle of Higher Education,* pp. A1, A10. Sahakian, B., and Morein-Zamir, S. (2007). Professor's little helper. *Nature, 450,* 1157–1159. Schermer, M. (2008). On the argument that enhancement is cheating. *Journal of Medical Ethics, 34,* 85–88.

Opioids: Opium, Heroin, and Opioid Pain Medications

I'm 72 years old, a grandmother of five and a great-grandmother too, living alone since my husband passed away five years ago. Since my spinal stenosis surgery a year and a half ago, life is a nightmare. I have to say that OxyContin saved my life, even though I call it a "fake" life. I can do the little things sure, like doing the dishes, straightening up the house for a while, without letting people know that I'm crying inside. But the fact is that I'm 90 percent disabled and miserable all the time. I know it could be worse; if it was, I think I would end it all tomorrow.

So please don't take away my medicine. It's keeping me around. Maybe I'm addicted, I don't know. Maybe if the doctor took away my OxyContin, I would try to get it any way I could. I'd probably be out there with those people who hold up those drugstores.[1]

There is no escaping the love–hate relationship we have with opium and a category of similarly acting drugs that are collectively known as **opioids**. Here is a group of psychoactive drugs with the astonishing ability to banish pain from our lives and, at the same time, the potential for enslaving our minds. This chapter will concern itself with the medical uses and recreational abuses of opioids.

Historically, opioid drugs have been referred to as **narcotics** (from the Greek word for "stupor"), in that they produce a dream-like effect on the user and at higher doses induce a state of sleep. As noted in Chapter 2, the term "narcotic" was used at one time inappropriately to mean *any* illicit psychoactive drug or at least any drug that caused some degree of dependence, including such unlikely examples as cocaine and amphetamine, which are anything but sleep-inducing. Ironically, specific drugs are currently available that have no relationship to opium or opioids but are far more effective in inducing sleep (see Chapter 13).

Opioids can be divided into four broad categories of drugs.

- The first category comprises three natural compounds that are directly extracted from opium itself: morphine, codeine, and thebaine. All opioid derivatives have their origin in these compounds.
- The second category comprises derivative compounds that are created by making specific changes in the chemical composition of morphine. Examples are heroin, hydromorphone (brand name: Dilaudid), oxymorphone (brand names: Numorphan, Opana), and the extended-release form of oxymorphone (brand name: Opana ER).
- The third category comprises derivative compounds that are created by making specific changes in the chemical composition of codeine or thebaine. Examples are oxycodone (brand names: Percodan,

Percocet), the controlled-release form of oxycodone (brand name: OxyContin), and hydrocodone (brand names: Hycodan, Vicodin).

- The fourth category comprises drugs that are not chemically related to any of the natural extracts of opium but rather are synthesized entirely in the laboratory. As a result, they are often referred to as *synthetic opioids*. Examples include methadone, meperidine (brand name: Demerol), propoxyphene (brand names: Darvon, Darvocet), LAAM (brand name: Orlaam), tramadol (brand names: Ultram, Ultracet), and buprenorphine (brand names: Subutex, Suboxone).

Figure 5.1 shows some of the major opioid drugs that are currently available for medical and nonmedical uses.

Opium in History

Like cocaine, the history of heroin and the other opioid drugs can be traced back to faraway times and places. This particular story begins with a method of harvesting of raw **opium** that has not changed much in more than three thousand years. It takes place today in remote villages of Myanmar (formerly Burma), Laos, Thailand, Afghanistan, Kazakhstan, Mexico, Colombia, Peru, and other countries where the weather is hot and labor is cheap. The source is the opium poppy, known by its botanical name as *Papaver somniferum* (literally "the poppy that brings sleep"), an annual plant growing three to four feet high. Its large flowers are typically about four or five inches in diameter and can be white, pink, red, or purple. This variety is the only type of poppy that produces opium; common garden plants such as the red Oriental poppy and the yellow California poppy look similar but do not produce psychoactive effects.

The process is simple. When the petals of the opium poppy have fallen but the seed capsule of the plant underneath the petals is not yet completely ripe, laborers make small, shallow incisions in the capsules, allowing a milky white juice to ooze out during the night. The next day, this substance will have oxidized and hardened by contact with the air. Now they go from plant to plant, collecting the juice onto large poppy

by the numbers . . .

281,000   Number of persons in the United States over 12 years who reported in 2011 having used heroin in the past month

434,000   Number of persons in the United States over 12 years who reported in 2011 having used OxyContin for nonmedical purposes in the past month

Source: Substance Abuse and Mental Health Services Administration (2012). *Results from the 2011 National Survey on Drug Use and Health: Detailed tables.* Rockville, MD: Substance Abuse and Mental Health Services Administration, Table 1.1A.

opioids (OH-pee-oids): Drugs with analgesic (pain reducing) properties that act in the brain like opium.

narcotics: A general term technically referring to opiate-related or opiate-derived drugs. It is often mistakenly used to include several other illicit drug categories as well.

opium: An analgesic and euphoriant drug acquired from the dried juice of the opium poppy.

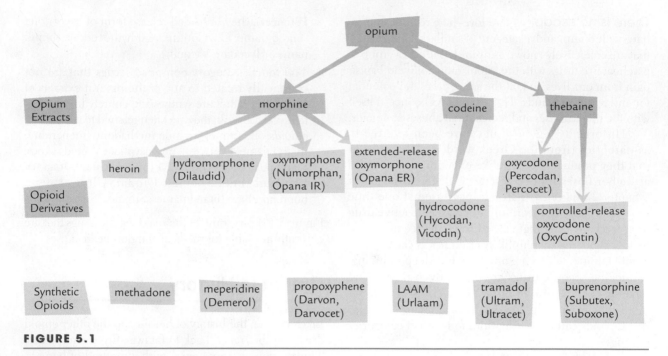

FIGURE 5.1

Classifying major opioid drugs: Opium extracts, opioid derivatives, and synthetic opioids (Brand names are shown in parentheses.)

Note: Hydrocodone can also be derived from thebaine. A more complete listing of opioid pain medications appears in Table 5.2 on page 136.

Sources: Physicians' desk reference (67th ed.) (2013). Montvale, NJ: PDR Network. Raj, P. Prithvi (1996). *Pain medicine: A comprehensive review.* St. Louis: Mosby, pp. 126–153.

leaves. At this point, opium is reddish brown in color and has the consistency of heavy syrup. Later it will darken further and form small gum-like balls.[2]

The first written references to opium date back to the early third century B.C., but we can be fairly sure that it was used for at least a thousand years before that. A ceramic opium pipe has been excavated in Cyprus,

Local villagers harvest opium in a poppy field in the Golestan district of Farah province in Afghanistan.

dating from the Late Bronze Age, about 1200 B.C. Cypriot vases from that era depict incised poppy capsules. Evidence contained in the Ebers Papyrus writings (see Chapter 1) shows that Egyptians were knowledgeable about the medicinal value of opium.[3]

In the second century A.D., Claudius Galen, a famous Greek physician and surgeon to Roman gladiators, recommended opium for practically everything. He wrote that it

> . . . *resists poison and venomous bites, cures chronic headache, vertigo, deafness, apoplexy, dimness of sight, loss of voice, asthma, coughs of all kinds, spitting of blood, tightness of breath, colic, . . . jaundice, hardness of the spleen, . . . urinary complaints, fever, . . . leprosies, the troubles to which women are subject, melancholy, and all pestilences.*[4]

Galen's enthusiasm for the instrumental use of opium is an early example of "over-prescribing." Interestingly, however, there are no records in ancient times that refer to the recreational use of opium or to any problems of opium dependence.[5]

Western Europe was introduced to opium in the eleventh and twelfth centuries by returning crusaders who had learned of it from the Arabs. During the first stirrings of modern medicine in Europe, opium began to be regarded as a therapeutic drug. In 1520, a physician named Paracelsus, promoting himself as the foremost medical authority of his day, introduced a medicinal drink combining opium, wine, and an assortment of spices. He called the mixture *laudanum* (derived from the Latin phrase meaning "something to be praised"), and before long the formula of Paracelsus was being called the "stone of immortality." Even though Paracelsus himself denounced many of the doctrines of Galen and earlier physicians in history, he continued the time-honored tradition of recommending opium for practically every known disease.

In 1680, the English physician Thomas Sydenham, considered the father of clinical medicine, introduced a highly popular version of opium drink similar to that of Paracelsus, called Sydenham's Laudanum. For the next two hundred years or so, the acceptable means of taking opium among Europeans and then Americans would be in the form of a drink, either Sydenham's recipe or a host of variations. Sydenham's enthusiasm for the drug was no less than that of his predecessors. "Among the remedies," he wrote, "which it has pleased Almighty God to give man to relieve his sufferings, none is so universal and so efficacious as opium."[6] The popularity of opium drinking eventually led to the emergence of opium as a major recreational drug in Europe and the United States.

This late-nineteenth-century illustration of young working girls in a New York City opium den was part of a widespread media campaign at the time to outlaw the smoking of opium.

The Opium War

Sometime in the eighteenth century, China invented a novel form of opium use, opium smoking, which eventually became synonymous in the Western mind with China itself. However, for at least eight hundred years before that, the Chinese had used opium only in a very limited way. They took it almost exclusively on a medicinal basis, consuming it orally in its raw state as a highly effective painkiller and treatment for diarrhea (see Table 5.1).

The picture changed dramatically in the eighteenth century, strangely enough, when the British people discovered and fell in love with Chinese tea. Sensing a business opportunity, British merchants in China sought a way to buy Chinese tea and transport it home for a handsome profit. But what could they sell to the Chinese in exchange? The problem was that there were few, if any, commodities that China really wanted from the outside. In their eyes, the rest of the world was populated by "barbarians" with an inferior culture, offering little or nothing the Chinese people needed.

TABLE 5.1	
Symptoms of administering heroin and of withdrawing heroin	
ADMINISTERING	**WITHDRAWING**
Lowered body temperature	Elevated body temperature
Decreased blood pressure	Increased blood pressure
Skin flushed and warm	Piloerection (gooseflesh)
Pupil constriction	Pupil dilation
Constipation	Diarrhea
Respiratory depression	Yawning, panting, sneezing
Drying of secretions	Tearing, runny nose
Decreased sex drive	Spontaneous ejaculations and orgasms
Muscular relaxation	Restlessness, involuntary twitching and kicking movements*
Nodding, stupor	Insomnia
Analgesia	Pain and irritability
Euphoria and calm	Depression and anxiety

*The source of the expression "kicking the habit."

Source: Adapted from Grilly, D. M., and Salamone, J. D. (2012). *Drugs, brain, and behavior* (6th ed.). Boston: Pearson Education, p. 298.

The answer turned out to be opium. In 1773, British forces had conquered Bengal Province in India and suddenly had a monopoly on raw opium. Here was an opportunity to introduce Indian-grown opium to China as a major item of trade. Despite the understandable opposition by the Chinese government, opium soon flooded into the country, smuggled in by local British and Portuguese merchants, which enabled the British government and its official trade representative, the East India Company, to maintain a public image of not being directly involved in the opium trade. Huge quantities of opium found a ready market in southern port cities such as Canton. Not surprisingly, opium smoking and opium dependence soon became a major social problem. Repeated edicts by the Chinese emperor to reduce the use of opium within China or cut the supply line from India failed. The situation was out of control.[7]

In 1839, tensions had reached a peak. In a historic act of defiance against the European powers, including Britain, an imperial commissioner appointed by the Chinese emperor to deal with the opium problem once and for all, confiscated a shipment of opium and burned it publicly in Canton. His courageous act, however, was not appreciated by the British. Events escalated shortly thereafter, until open fighting broke out between Chinese and British soldiers. The Opium War had begun.

By 1842, British artillery and warships had overwhelmed a nation unprepared to deal with European firepower. In a humiliating treaty, China was forced to sign over to Britain the island of Hong Kong and its harbor (until the distant year of 1997), grant to British merchants exclusive trading rights in major Chinese ports, and pay a large amount of money to reimburse Britain for losses during the war. Despite these agreements, fighting broke out again between 1858 and 1860; with French and American forces joining the British. In a treaty signed in 1860, China was required to legalize opium within its borders. The Opium War succeeded in opening up the gates of China, much against its will, to the rest of the world.[8]

Opium in Britain and the United States

To the average British citizen in the mid-1800s, the Opium War in China was purely a trade issue, a faraway conflict with little or no direct impact on one's daily life. Nonetheless, opium itself was everywhere. The important difference between China and Britain with respect to opium was not in the *extent* of its consumption but in the *way* it was consumed. The acceptable form of opium use in Victorian England was opium drinking in the form of laudanum, whereas the Asian practice of opium smoking was linked to a perceived lifestyle of vice and degradation and associated with the very lowest fringes of society. The contrast was strikingly ironic. Opium dens, with all the evil connotations that the phrase has carried into modern times, were the places where opium was *smoked*; the respectable parlors of middle-class British families were the places where opium was *drunk*.

Supplies of British opium were unlimited, cheaper than gin or beer. Medical opinion was at most divided on the question of any potential harm; there was no negative public opinion and seldom any trouble with the police. As long as there were no signs of opium smoking, a chronic opium abuser was considered no worse than a drunkard. Nearly all infants and young children in Britain during this period were given opium, often from the day they were born. Dozens of laudanum-based patent medicines (with appealing names such as Godfrey's Cordial, A Pennysworth of Peace, and Mrs. Winslow's Soothing Syrup) were used to dull teething pain or colic, or merely to keep the children quiet. The administration of opium to babies was particularly attractive in the new, industrial-age lifestyle of female workers, who had to leave their infants in the care of elderly women or young children when they went off to work in the factories.[9]

Out of this climate of acceptance sprang a new cultural phenomenon: the opium-addict writer. Just as LSD and other hallucinogens were to be promoted in the 1960s as an avenue toward a greatly expanded level of creativity and imagination (see Chapter 6), a similar belief was spreading among intellectuals during this period with respect to opium. The leader of the movement was Thomas DeQuincey, and his book *Confessions of an English Opium Eater*, published in 1821, became the movement's bible. It is impossible to say how many people started to use opium recreationally as a direct result of reading DeQuincey's ecstatic revelations about "opium eating" (by which he meant opium drinking in the form of laudanum), but there is no doubt that the book made the practice fashionable. English authors enamored with laudanum included Elizabeth Barrett Browning and Samuel Taylor Coleridge (whose exotic poem *Kubla Khan* was undoubtedly inspired by an "opium high").

In many ways, opium consumption in the United States paralleled its widespread use in Britain. In one survey of thirty-five Boston drugstores in 1888, 78 percent

A nineteenth-century advertising card for Mrs. Winslow's Soothing Syrup, a popular opium remedy, was directed toward young mothers and their children.

of the prescriptions that had been refilled three or more times contained opium. Until 1942, opium poppies were cultivated in Vermont and New Hampshire, in Florida and Louisiana, and later in California and Arizona. Women outnumbered men in opium use during the nineteenth century by as much as 3 to 1. As one historian has succinctly put it, "husbands drank alcohol in the saloon; wives took opium at home."[10]

Throughout the 1800s, opium coexisted alongside alcohol, nicotine (in tobacco products), and cocaine as the dominant recreational drugs of the day. As late as 1897, the Sears, Roebuck mail-order catalog was advertising laudanum for sale for about six cents an ounce. In a clever marketing move directed to alcoholic men, Sears's "White Star Secret Liquor Cure" was advertised as designed to be added to the gentleman's after-dinner coffee so that he would be less inclined to join his friends at the local saloon. In effect, he would probably fall asleep at the table, since the "cure" was opium. If customers became dependent on opium, perhaps as a result of taking the "liquor cure," then fortunately they could order "A Cure for the Opium Habit," promoted on another page of the same catalog. If you guessed that the ingredients in this one included a heavy dose of alcohol, you would be right.[11] Opium dependence was frequently replaced by cocaine abuse (see Chapter 4), and vice versa.

Given the openness of opium drinking in the nineteenth-century United States, we can only surmise that the fanatical reaction against the practice of opium smoking was based on anti-Chinese prejudice. It is clear that intense hostility existed toward the thousands of Chinese men and boys brought to the West in the 1850s and 1860s to build the railroads. Since most of the Chinese workers were recruited from the Canton area, where opium trafficking was particularly intense, the practice of opium smoking was well known to them, and it served as a safety valve for an obviously oppressed society of men. In 1875, San Francisco outlawed opium smoking for fear, to quote a newspaper of the time, that "many women and young girls, as well as young men of respectable family, were being induced to visit the dens, where they were ruined morally and otherwise."[12] No mention was ever made of any moral ruin resulting from drinking opium at home.

A federal law forbidding opium smoking soon followed, whereas the regulation of opium use by any other means failed to receive legislative attention at that time. By the beginning of the twentieth century, however, the desire for social control of opium dens became overshadowed by the emergence of opium-derived drugs that presented a substantially greater threat to society than smoked opium.[13]

Morphine and the Advent of Heroin

In 1803, a German drug clerk named Friedrich Wilhelm Adam Sertürner first isolated a yellowish-white substance in raw opium that turned out to be its primary active ingredient. He called it **morphine**, in honor of Morpheus, the Greek god of dreams. For the first time, more than three-fourths of the total weight of opium (containing inactive resins, oils, and sugars) could be separated out and discarded. Morphine represented roughly 10 percent of the total weight of opium, but it was found to be roughly ten times stronger than raw opium. All the twenty-five or so opiate products that were eventually isolated from opium were found to be weaker than morphine and formed a far smaller proportion of opium. Besides morphine, other major opiate products were **codeine** (0.5 percent of raw opium) and **thebaine** (0.2 percent of raw opium), both of which were found to have a considerably weaker opiate effect.

With the invention of the hypodermic syringe in 1856, morphine could now be injected into the bloodstream rather than administered orally, thus bypassing the gastrointestinal tract and speeding the delivery of effects

morphine: The major active ingredient in opium.

codeine (COH-deen): One of the three active ingredients in opium, used primarily to treat coughing.

thebaine (THEE-bayn): One of three active ingredients in opium.

(see Chapter 3). The new potential of morphine injection coincided with the traumas of the Civil War in the United States (1861–1865) and later of the Franco-Prussian War in Europe (1870–1871). It is not surprising that large numbers of soldiers became dependent on opiates and maintained the condition in the years that followed. After the Civil War, opiate dependence in general was so widespread among Union and Confederate veterans that the condition was often called the "soldier's disease."[14]

Against the backdrop of increasing worry about opiate dependence, a new painkilling morphine derivative called **heroin** was introduced into the market in 1898 by the Bayer Company in Germany, the same company that had been highly successful in developing acetylsalicylic acid as an analgesic drug and marketing it as "Bayer's Aspirin" (see Chapter 14). About three times stronger than morphine, and strangely enough believed initially to be free of morphine's dependence-producing properties, heroin (from the German *heroisch*, meaning "powerful") was hailed as an entirely safe cough suppressant (preferable to codeine) and as a medication to relieve the chest discomfort associated with pneumonia and tuberculosis. In retrospect, it is incredible that from 1895 to 1905, no fewer than forty medical studies concerning injections of heroin failed to recognize its potential for dependence! The abuse potential of heroin, which we now know exceeds that of morphine, was not fully recognized until as late as 1910.[15]

Why is heroin more potent than morphine? The answer lies in its chemical composition. Heroin consists of two acetyl groups joined to a basic morphine molecule. These attachments make heroin more fat-soluble and hence more rapidly absorbed into the brain. Once inside the brain, the two acetyl groups break off, making the effects of heroin chemically identical to that of morphine. One way of understanding the relationship between the two drugs is to imagine morphine as the contents inside a plain cardboard box and the heroin as the box covered with gift wrapping. The contents remain the same, but the wrapping increases the chances that the box will be opened.

Opioids in American Society

The end of the nineteenth century marked a turning point in the history of opium and its derivatives. Opioid dependence would never again be treated

> **heroin:** A chemical derivative of morphine. It is approximately three times as potent as morphine and a major drug of abuse.

casually. By 1900, there were, by one conservative estimate, 250,000 opioid-dependent people in the United States, and the actual number could have been closer to 750,000 or more. If we rely on the upper estimate, then we are speaking of roughly one out of every hundred Americans, *young or old*, living at that time. Compare this figure with the 2011 estimate of 281,000 Americans (aged twelve or older) who have used heroin alone within the past month out of a current population that is roughly four times the population in 1900, and you can appreciate the impact that opioid abuse had on American society in the early twentieth century.[16]

The size of the opioid-abusing population alone at that time probably would have been sufficient grounds for social reformers to seek some way of controlling these drugs, but there was also the growing fear that the problems of opioid abuse were becoming closely associated with criminal elements. There was a gnawing anxiety that opioid drugs were creating a significant disruption in American society. A movement began to build toward instituting some system of governmental regulation.

Opioid Use and Heroin Abuse after 1914

The Harrison Act of 1914 (see Chapter 2) radically changed the face of opioid use and abuse in the United States. It ushered in an era in which the abuser was no longer a victim of drugs worthy of society's sympathy. Instead, he was now viewed as weak, degenerate, and self-indulgent, a "contaminant" infecting his community's social order and, as a result, deserving society's moral outrage and whatever legal sanction it could devise.[17]

The situation, however, did not change overnight. Most important, the 1914 legislation did not actually ban opioids. It simply required that doctors register with the Internal Revenue Service the opioid drugs (as well as cocaine and other coca products) that they were prescribing to their patients and pay a small fee for the right to prescribe such drugs. The real impact of the new law came later, in the early 1920s, as a result of several landmark decisions sent down from the U.S. Supreme Court. In effect, the decisions interpreted the Harrison Act more broadly. Under the Court's interpretation of the Harrison Act, no physician was permitted to prescribe opioids for "nonmedical" use. In other words, it was now illegal for addicted individuals to obtain drugs merely to maintain their habit, even from a physician. Without a legal source for their drugs, opioid abusers were forced to abandon them altogether or turn to illegal means, and the drug dealer suddenly provided the only place where opioids, particularly heroin, could be obtained.

Heroin became the perfect black market drug. It was easier and more profitable to refine it from raw opium overseas and ship it into the country in small bags of odorless heroin powder than it was to transport raw opium with its characteristic odor. In addition, because it had to be obtained illegally, heroin's price tag skyrocketed to thirty to fifty times what it had cost when it was available from legitimate sources.[18]

With the emergence of restrictive legislation, the demographic picture changed dramatically. No longer were the typical consumers of opioid drugs characterized as female, predominantly white, middle-aged, and middle-class, as likely to be living on a Nebraskan farm as in a Chicago townhouse. In their place were young, predominantly white, urban adult males, whose opioid drug of choice was intravenous heroin and whose drug supply was controlled by increasingly sophisticated crime organizations. In the minds of most Americans, heroin and heroin abusers could be comfortably relegated to the social and moral fringes of America.[19]

Heroin Abuse in the 1960s and 1970s

Three major social developments in the 1960s brought the heroin story back into the mainstream of the United States. The first began in late 1961, when a crackdown on heroin smuggling resulted in a significant shortage of heroin on the street. The price of heroin suddenly increased, and heroin dosages became more adulterated than ever before. Predictably, the high costs of maintaining heroin dependence encouraged new levels of criminal behavior, particularly in urban ghettos. Heroin abuse soon imposed a cultural stranglehold on many African American and Latino communities in major U.S. cities.

A second development, beginning in the 1960s, affected the white majority more directly. Fanned by extensive media attention, a youthful counterculture of hippies, flower children, and the sexually liberated swept the country.

It was a time of unconventional fashions and anti-establishment attitudes. In unprecedented numbers, middle- and upper-class people experimented with illegal drugs to get high. They smoked marijuana; tried the new synthetic properties of amphetamines and barbiturates; rediscovered the almost forgotten

product of the coca plant, cocaine; and, for the first time, people from the mainstream of American life began to experiment with derivatives of the opium poppy. Thus, heroin addiction made its insidious way back to the forefront of national concern.[20]

Finally, disturbing reports about heroin abuse began to appear that focused not only on Americans at home but also on American armed forces personnel stationed in Vietnam. Reports beginning in the late 1960s indicated an increasingly widespread recreational abuse of heroin, along with alcohol, marijuana, and other drugs, among U.S. soldiers.

With respect to heroin, the problem was exacerbated given that Vietnamese heroin was 90 to 98 percent pure, compared to 2 to 10 percent pure in the United States at the time, and incredibly cheap to buy. A 250-mg dose of heroin, for example, could be purchased for $10, whereas the standard intravenous dose on the streets of a major U.S. city would amount to only 10 mg. A comparable 250 mg of highly diluted U.S. heroin would have cost about $500. With the purity of heroin supplies so high, most U.S. soldiers smoked or sniffed it to get an effect; some drank it mixed with alcohol, even though most of the drug was lost as it was filtered through the liver en route to the bloodstream.[21]

Military involvement in Vietnam brought U.S. soldiers in contact with unusually potent doses of heroin and other psycho-active drugs.

In 1971, it was estimated from survey data that about 11 percent of American troops were regular users of heroin and about 22 percent had tried it at least once. Beyond the concern for the soldiers overseas, there was the considerable worry that at least one in ten Vietnam veterans would be returning home heroin-dependent and continuing a pattern of heroin abuse. As a response, the military instituted a mandatory program of urinalysis testing (appropriately named Operation Golden Flow), conducted near the end of a soldier's tour of duty. In October 1971, three months of testing showed that about 5 percent of soldiers tested positive for heroin. The percentage of heroin abusers at that time could very well have been higher since there were strong indications that soldiers had voluntarily given up heroin prior to their being shipped home.[22] Fortunately, a comprehensive investigation in 1974 showed that only 1 to 2 percent of Vietnam veterans were regular heroin abusers one year following their return from overseas—approximately the same percentage as those entering the military from the general population.

Even if the original numbers of heroin abusers in Vietnam had been exaggerated in the first place (and evidence now suggests that the story was hyped out of proportion by the media at the time), the low number among returnees presents an interesting question. What happened to those who had been previously heroin abusers after they returned to the United States? It has been proposed that heroin use was specific to involvement in Vietnam. Once returning soldiers were home in the states, the stressful environmental cues and motivational factors for drug abuse were no longer present.[23] Does that mean it is possible to abuse heroin without becoming dependent on it? This question will be addressed later in the chapter.

Heroin and Other Opioids Since the 1980s

At one time, the major source of white powder heroin smuggled into the United States was Turkey, where the opium was grown, and the center of heroin manufacture and distribution was Marseilles in southern France (the infamous French connection, as popularized in the 1970 movie of the same name). International control over the growing of Turkish opium in 1973 closed this route of heroin distribution, but it succeeded only in encouraging other parts of the world to fill the vacuum. The "Golden Triangle" region of Laos, Myanmar (formerly Burma), and Thailand became the principal players in providing the United States with heroin. Joining southeast Asian heroin suppliers were southwest Asian nations such as Afghanistan, Pakistan, and Iran (in the "Golden Crescent"), as well as the central Asian nations of Kazakhstan, Kyrgyzstan, Tajikistan, Turkmenistan, and Uzbekistan that had been, until 1991, regions of the Soviet Union. As a consequence of these new sources, the purity of imported heroin at this time increased from around 5 percent to over 18 percent.[24]

Although the growth of crack cocaine abuse in the 1980s pushed the issue of heroin abuse temporarily off the front page, heroin abuse itself continued in new forms and variations. One significant development was the appearance around 1985 of a relatively pure and inexpensive form of Mexican heroin called **black tar**. In addition, new synthetic forms of heroin were appearing on the street, created in illegal drug laboratories within the United States. One such synthetic drug was derived from **fentanyl**, a prescription narcotic drug. Chemical modifications of fentanyl, anywhere from ten to a thousand times stronger than heroin, were sold under the common name "China White." The risks of overdose death increased dramatically.

At that time, fentanyl derivatives and similar "designer drugs" were legal, owing to a loophole in the drug laws; because they were not chemically identical to heroin, no specific law applied to them. In 1986, the Controlled Substance Analogue Act closed this unfortunate loophole. The laws now state that any drug with a chemical structure or pharmacological effect similar to that of a controlled substance is as illegal as the genuine article. The mid-1990s witnessed still another shift in the pattern of heroin trafficking. The dominant source of white-powder heroin in the United States, judged from the analysis of drug seizures, was no longer Asia but South America, principally Colombia.

Street heroin from South American sources was now both cheaper and purer. Heroin purities exceeded 60 percent, at least ten times more powerful than the typical street heroin in the 1970s. In 1994, a 90-percent-pure brand of heroin circulating in New York City took heroin abusers by surprise; several overdose deaths occurred within a period of five days. Street prices for a milligram of heroin in New York fell from $1.81 in 1988 to as little as 37 cents in 1994. By government estimates,

black tar: A potent form of heroin, generally brownish in color, originating in Mexico.

fentanyl (FEN-teh-nil): A chemical derivative of thebaine, used as a prescription painkiller. The street name for fentanyl and related compounds is China White.

heroin consumption nationwide in 1996 had doubled from a decade earlier. As one writer put it, "If the U.S. auto industry cut the price of its sedans by half and redesigned them to go 180 mph, no one would wonder why sales hit the roof."[25]

In the mid-1990s, there was also a shift in the perception of heroin abuse itself. As the popularity of cocaine abuse declined and the incidence of crack abuse began to ebb, the spotlight once more turned toward the allure of heroin. For a brief time, popular movies (*Pulp Fiction* in 1994, *Trainspotting* in 1995) and fashion photography (Calvin Klein fragrance advertisements in 1996) presented provocative images that glamorized heroin abuse, a phenomenon the media dubbed "heroin chic."

As the potency of heroin increased during the 1990s, a significant change occurred in the way heroin was abused. Due to the availability of increasingly pure heroin, the drug no longer needed to be injected. Instead, it could be snorted (inhaled through the nose) or smoked. New heroin abusers were frequently smoking mixtures of heroin and crack cocaine or heating heroin and inhaling its vapors. These methods of heroin abuse avoided potential HIV infections or hepatitis through contaminated needles, but they did not prevent the dependence that heroin could produce or the risk of heroin overdose.

Unfortunately, heroin snorting or smoking opened the door to new populations of potential heroin abusers who had previously stayed away from the drug because of their aversion to hypodermic needles. University of Michigan surveys from 1991 to 2011 indicate that 1 to 2 percent of all high school seniors reported heroin use at some time in their lives, with a majority of them smoking heroin rather than injecting it. However, the prevalence rate was not uniform across the United States in demographic or geographic terms. The incidence of heroin smoking among young people was and continued to be generally higher than the national average and predominant in suburban communities, particularly in the Northeast.[26]

Although approximately 94 percent of the world's supply of heroin today originates from the opium crop in Afghanistan, relatively little is destined for the United States. The major supplies of U.S. heroin come from opium grown in Colombia and Mexico. Mexico serves as the principal transport route for Colombian heroin (see Chapter 2). At present, Mexico is a major player in opium cultivation, second only to Afghanistan, as Colombian cultivation is on the decline. Whether this pattern of heroin trafficking continues remains to be seen. Illicit drug trafficking, in general, is in constant flux, subject to shifting market demands and the continuing challenges posed by U.S. and international law enforcement agencies.[27]

Quick Concept Check 5.1

Understanding the History of Opium and Opioids

Check your understanding of the historical background for opium and opioids by answering the following question. Imagine yourself to be living as a male adult in the year 1900. Check yes or no to indicate whether the following psychoactive drugs would be available to you.

1. heroin   ☐ yes   ☐ no
2. opium   ☐ yes   ☐ no
3. fentanyl   ☐ yes   ☐ no
4. oxycodone   ☐ yes   ☐ no
5. morphine   ☐ yes   ☐ no

Answers: 1. yes   2. yes   3. no   4. no   5. yes

Effects on the Mind and the Body

Recreational opioid use in the United States involves a range of drugs other than heroin itself, but we will concentrate on acute effects from the perspective of the heroin abuser. We have to be careful, however, to recognize that the specific effects are quite variable. The intensity of a response to heroin changes as a function of (1) the quantity and purity of the heroin taken, (2) the route through which heroin is administered, (3) the interval since the previous dose of heroin, and (4) the degree of tolerance of the user to heroin itself. In addition, there are psychological factors related to the setting, circumstances, and expectations of the user that make an important difference in what an individual feels after taking heroin.[28] Nonetheless, there are several major effects that occur often enough to qualify as typical of the experience.

If heroin is injected intravenously, there is an almost immediate tingling sensation and sudden feeling of warmth in the lower abdomen, resembling a sexual orgasm, for the first minute or two. There is a feeling of intense euphoria, variously described as a "rush" or a "flash," followed later by a state of tranquil drowsiness that heroin abusers often call being "on the nod."

During this period, which lasts from three to four hours, any interest in sex is greatly diminished. In the case of male heroin abusers, the decline in sexual desire is due, at least in part, to the fact that opiates reduce the levels of testosterone, the male sex hormone. Withdrawal symptoms can begin in about four hours. Therefore, maintaining a relatively constant "heroin high" often requires three or four administrations in a given day.[29]

Ironically, an individual's first-time experience with heroin may be considerably unpleasant. Opiates in general cause nausea and vomiting, as the reflex centers in the medulla are suddenly stimulated. Some first-time abusers find the vomiting so aversive that they never try the drug again; others consider the discomfort largely irrelevant because the euphoria is so powerful.

There are a number of additional physiological changes in the body. A sudden release of histamine in the bloodstream produces an often intense itching over the entire body and a reddening of the eyes. Heroin also causes pupillary constriction, resulting in the characteristic "pinpoint pupils" that are used as an important diagnostic sign for narcotic abuse in general. Like sedative-hypnotic drugs (see Chapter 13), heroin reduces the sensitivity of respiratory centers in the medulla to levels of carbon dioxide, resulting in a depression in breathing. At high doses, respiratory depression is a major risk factor that can result in death. Blood pressure is also depressed from heroin intake. A suppression of the immune system over time increases the risk of infectious disease. Finally, a distressing, though nonlethal, effect of heroin is the slowing down of the gastrointestinal tract, causing labored defecation and intense constipation.[30]

How Opioids Work in the Brain

It is useful to view the neurochemical basis for a number of psychoactive drugs in terms of their influence on specific neurotransmitters in the brain. For example, the stimulant effects of cocaine and amphetamine are related to changes in norepinephrine and dopamine (see Chapter 4). In the case of opioid drugs, however, as a result of major discoveries in the 1970s, it is clear that we are dealing with a more direct effect: the activation of receptors in the brain that are specifically sensitive to morphine.

naloxone (nah-LOX-ohn): A pure antagonist for morphine and other opioid drugs. Brand name is Narcan.

During the 1960s, suspicions grew that a morphine-sensitive receptor, or a family of them, exists in the brain. One major clue came from the discovery that small chemical alterations in the morphine molecule would result in a group of new drugs with strange and intriguing properties. Not only would these drugs produce little or no *agonistic* effects—that is, they would not act like morphine—but they would instead act as *opiate antagonists*—that is, they would reverse or block the effects of morphine (Figure 5.2).

The most complete opioid antagonist to be identified, **naloxone** (brand name: Narcan), has turned out to have enormous therapeutic benefits in the emergency treatment of opioid-overdose patients. In such cases, intramuscular or intravenous injections of naloxone reverse the depressed breathing and blood pressure in a matter of a minute or so, an effect so fast that emergency-department specialists view the reaction as "miraculous." The effect lasts for one to four hours. Higher doses of naloxone bring on symptoms that are similar to those observed following an abrupt withdrawal of opioids.

Interestingly, in nondrugged people, naloxone produces only negligible changes, either on a physiological or a psychological level. Only if morphine or other opioid drugs are already in the body does naloxone have an effect.[31]

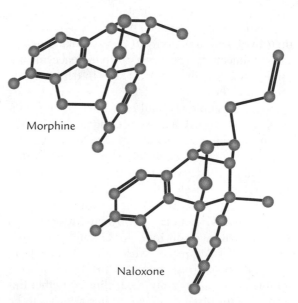

FIGURE 5.2

Only minor differences exist between a morphine molecule and a naloxone molecule. Yet naloxone is a complete antagonist to morphine.

Beyond its practical application, the discovery of naloxone had theoretical implications as well. The argument went as follows: If such small molecular changes could so dramatically transform an agonist into an antagonist, then the drug must be acting on some receptor in the brain that can be easily excited or inhibited. The concept of a special morphine-sensitive receptor fulfilled these requirements.

The actual receptors themselves were discovered in 1973, precisely where you would have expected them to be: in the spinal cord and brain, where pain signals are known to be processed, and in the limbic system of the brain, where emotional behaviors are coordinated. In other words, it was clear that the analgesic and euphoric properties of morphine were due to the stimulation of these receptors.

Why would these receptors exist in the first place? No one seriously considers the possibility that receptors in the brain have been patiently waiting, during millions of years of evolutionary history, for the day that the juice of the opium poppy could finally slip inside them! The only logical answer is that we must be producing our own morphine-like chemicals that activate these receptors.

As a result of a series of important discoveries from 1975 to the early 1980s, three groups of natural morphine-like molecules have been identified: enkephalins, beta-endorphins, and dynorphins. Together, they are known as **endogenous opioid peptides**, inasmuch as they are all (1) peptide molecules (amino acids strung together like a necklace), (2) opium-like in function (hence the word *opioid*), and (3) produced within the central nervous system. Unfortunately, this is such an unwieldy name that more frequently they are simply referred to as *endorphins*.

What can we then conclude about the effect of opiates on the brain? The answer, as we now understand it, is that the brain has the ability to produce its own "opioid" substances, called endorphins, and contains a special set of receptor sites to receive them. By an amazing quirk of fate, the opium poppy yields a similarly shaped chemical that fits into these receptor sites, thus producing equivalent psychological and physiological effects. Naloxone acts as an opioid antagonist because its structural features enable it to fit into these receptor sites, replacing the opioid molecules that have gotten in. The receptors themselves, however, are *inactivated* by naloxone. This is why naloxone can "undo" the acute effects of an opioid drug like heroin.

A long-acting form of naloxone, **naltrexone** (brand name: ReVia, previously marketed as Trexan), administered orally three times per week, has since been found to be a useful medication in the treatment of heroin abuse, mainly for patients who are highly motivated to stop their drug-taking behavior. Such patients include doctors, nurses, and other health professionals who must end a pattern of heroin abuse to retain their licenses and former heroin abusers on parole who are at risk of returning to prison if they suffer a relapse. Injectable slow-release formulations that extend the effects of naltrexone over thirty days or more are presently being investigated, in an effort to free patients from having to rely on a more frequent oral administration schedule. A once-per-month slow-release form of naltrexone (brand name: Vivitrol) has been available for alcohol dependence since 2006 (see Chapter 9). In 2009, a combined naltrexone and extended-release morphine capsule (brand name: Embeda) was introduced to provide a morphine-induced analgesia while reducing the possibility of abuse. The combination makes it impossible to crush and snort the capsules, because crushing releases the naltrexone and counteracts the morphine effect (see pages 137–139 on the problems of OxyContin abuse).[32]

Patterns of Heroin Abuse

The dominant route of administration in heroin abuse is intravenous injection, usually referred to as either *mainlining* or *shooting*. Heroin also can be administered by a variety of other routes. Heroin smoking is popular in Middle Eastern countries and in Asia, but until very recently it has seldom been observed in the United States. Newcomers to heroin may begin their abuse either by snorting the drug through the nose or injecting it subcutaneously (skin-popping). Experienced heroin abusers may snort heroin to avoid using a needle or choose the subcutaneous route when they can no longer find veins in good enough condition to handle an intravenous injection. As mentioned earlier, an oral administration of heroin is usually worthless because absorption is extremely poor. American soldiers in Vietnam who were abusing heroin often took the drug orally, but because of the extremely high purity of the

endogenous opioid peptides (en-DODGE-eh-nus OH-pee-oid PEP-tides): Also known as *endorphins*. A class of chemicals produced inside the body that mimic the effects of opioid drugs.

naltrexone (nal-TREX-ohn): A long-lasting form of naloxone. Brand name prior to 1994 was Trexan; brand name has since been changed to ReVia.

heroin being consumed, their effective dose levels equaled or slightly exceeded levels found on American streets at the time.

Tolerance and Withdrawal Symptoms

A prime feature of chronic heroin abuse is the tolerance that develops, but the tolerance effects themselves do not occur in every bodily system. Gastrointestinal effects of constipation and spasms do not show much tolerance at all, whereas distinctive pupillary responses (the pinpoint feature of the eyes) eventually subside with chronic use. The greatest signs of tolerance are seen in the degree of analgesia, euphoria, and respiratory depression. The intense thrill of the intravenous injection will be noticeably lessened. The overall decline in heroin reactions, however, is dose-dependent. If the continuing dose level is high, then tolerance effects will be more dramatic than if the dose level is low.

The first sign of heroin withdrawal, a marked craving for another fix, generally begins about four to six hours after the previous dose and intensifies gradually to a peak over the next thirty-six to seventy-two hours, with other symptoms beginning a few hours later (Table 5.1). The abuser is essentially over the withdrawal period in five to ten days, though mild physiological disturbances, chiefly elevations in blood pressure and heart rate, are observed as long as six months later. Generally, these long-term effects are associated with a gradual withdrawal from heroin rather than an abrupt one.

The overall severity of heroin-withdrawal symptoms is a function of the dosage levels of heroin that have been sustained. When dosage levels are less than 10 percent, the withdrawal symptoms are comparable to a moderate to intense case of the flu. In more severe cases, the withdrawal process can result in a significant loss of weight and body fluids. With recent increases in the purities of street heroin in the 1990s, the symptoms of withdrawal are greater. Only rarely, however, is the process of heroin withdrawal life-threatening, unlike the withdrawal from barbiturate drugs (see Chapter 13).

It should not be surprising that withdrawal symptoms are essentially the mirror image of symptoms observed when a person is under the influence of heroin. If we are dealing with a group of endorphin-sensitive receptors that are, in the case of the heroin abuser, being stimulated by the opioids coming in from the outside, then it is reasonable to assume that over time, the production of endorphins would decline. Why produce

something on your own when you are getting it from an external source? By that argument, withdrawal from heroin would then be a matter of cutting off those receptors from that external source, resulting in a reaction opposite to the one that would have occurred had the receptors been satisfied in the first place. Over a period of time, coinciding with the withdrawal period for a heroin abuser, we would expect that the normal production of endorphins would reestablish itself and there would be little or no need for the external supply of heroin.

The receptor explanation for heroin dependence sounds reasonable and does account for the presence of withdrawal symptoms, but unfortunately it is an oversimplification for heroin abuse in general. We would expect that once the endorphin-sensitive receptors regain their natural supply of endorphins, heroin abuse should end, but we know that it does not.

In the case of heroin abusers, their tendency to continue taking heroin is propelled by a number of factors. There is, first of all, the combination of fear and distress associated with the prospect of experiencing withdrawal symptoms, along with a genuine craving for the effects themselves, reflecting the physical and psychological dependence that heroin inflicts. In addition, long-term heroin abuse frequently produces such a powerful conditioned-learning effect that the social setting in which the drug-taking behavior has occurred takes on reinforcing properties of its own (see Chapter 2). Even the act of inserting a needle can become pleasurable. Some heroin abusers (called *needle freaks*) continue to insert needles into their skin and experience heroin-like effects even when there is no heroin in the syringe. In effect, the heroin abuser is responding to a placebo. Any long-term treatment for heroin abuse, as will be discussed in a later section, must address a range of physical, psychological, and social factors to be successful.

The Lethality of Heroin Abuse

Considering the numbers of hospital emergencies and deaths associated with heroin abuse (see Chapter 2), you might be surprised that one would question the toxicity of heroin itself. To understand the toxicity of heroin, we first need to separate the effects of chronic heroin abuse from the drug's acute effects. From a long-term perspective with regard to one's physical health, heroin is considered relatively nontoxic, particularly when compared to several other drugs of abuse. Organ systems are not damaged or impaired by even a lifetime of heroin abuse, by virtue of ingesting the drug itself. There are no malformations, tissue damage, or physical deterioration directly tied to the use of any opioid drug, including heroin.[33] A notable exception, however, is found in the case of heroin administered by inhaling the heated heroin vapors (sometimes referred to as "chasing the dragon"). This form of heroin abuse has been linked to leukoencephalopathy, a neurological disease in which a progressive loss of muscle coordination can lead to paralysis and death.[34]

On the other hand, it is abundantly clear that the *practice* of heroin abuse is highly dangerous and potentially lethal. The reasons have to do with a number of situations resulting from heroin administration itself.[35]

- Heroin has a relatively small ratio of LD (lethal dose) to ED (effective dose). Increase a dose that produces a high in a heroin abuser by ten or fifteen times, and you will be in the dosage range that is potentially fatal. As a result, death by overdose is an ever-present risk. If we take into account the virtually unknown potency of street heroin in any given fix, we can appreciate the hazards of a drug overdose. The "bag" sold to a heroin abuser may look like the same amount each time, but the actual heroin content may be anywhere from none at all to 90 percent. Therefore, it is easy to underestimate the amount of heroin being taken in.

- Heroin abusers risk possible adverse effects from any toxic substance that has been "cut" with the heroin. Adding to the complexity, deaths from heroin overdose are frequently consequences of synergistic combinations of heroin with other abused drugs such as stimulants like cocaine or depressants like alcohol, Valium, or barbiturates. In some cases, individuals have smoked crack as their primary drug of abuse and snorted heroin to ease the agitation associated with crack. In other cases, lines of cocaine and heroin are alternately inhaled in a single session, a practice referred to as "criss-crossing."

- It is also possible that some heroin abusers develop unstable levels of tolerance that are tied to the environmental setting in which the heroin is administered. As a result of conditioned tolerance (see Chapter 2), a heroin dose experienced in an environment that has not been previously associated with drug taking may have a significantly greater effect on the abuser than the same dose taken in more familiar surroundings. Consequently, the specific effect on the abuser is highly unpredictable.

- Although the overriding danger of excessive amounts of heroin is the potentially lethal effect of respiratory depression, abusers can die from other physiological reactions. In some instances, death can come so quickly that the victims are found with a needle still in their veins; such deaths are usually due to a massive release of histamine or to an allergic reaction to some filler in the heroin to which the abuser was hypersensitive. Intravenous injections of heroin increase the risks of hepatitis or HIV infections, and unsterile water used in the mixing of heroin for these injections can be contaminated with bacteria.

- An additional risk began to appear during the mid-1980s. In some forms of synthetic heroin illicitly produced in clandestine laboratories in the United States, "manufacturers" failed to remove an impurity called MPTP that destroys dopamine-sensitive neurons in the substantia nigra of the midbrain. As a result, young people exposed to this type of heroin could acquire full-blown symptoms of Parkinson's disease (see Chapter 3) that were virtually identical to the symptoms observed in elderly patients suffering from a progressive loss of dopamine-sensitive neurons in their brains.

Quick Concept Check 5.2

Understanding the Effects of Administering and Withdrawing Heroin

Without looking at Table 5.1, check your understanding of the effects of heroin, relative to withdrawal symptoms, by noting whether the following symptoms are associated with administering heroin or withdrawing it.

SYMPTOM	ADMINISTERING	WITHDRAWING
1. twitching and sneezing		
2. skin flushed and warm		
3. decreased sex drive		
4. yawning and panting		
5. pain and irritability		
6. pupillary constriction		
7. increased blood pressure		
8. diarrhea		
9. analgesia		

Answers: 1. withdrawing   2. administering   3. administering   4. withdrawing   5. withdrawing   6. administering   7. withdrawing   8. withdrawing   9. administering

Heroin Abuse and Society

Over the years, society has had to deal with the reality of drug abuse in many forms, but many people still look upon heroin abuse as the ultimate drug addiction and view the heroin abuser as the ultimate "dope addict." It is true that many heroin abusers fit this image: people driven to stay high on a four- to eight-hour schedule, committing a continuing series of predatory crimes. Yet the actual picture of the present-day heroin abuser is more complex. A major study has shown that although robbery, burglary, and shoplifting accounted for 44 percent of an abuser's income and for nearly two-thirds of that abuser's criminal income, a substantial amount of income came from either victimless crimes (such as pimping or prostitution) or noncriminal activity. Often a heroin abuser would work in some capacity in the underground drug industry and be paid in heroin instead of dollars.[36]

A related question with regard to our image of the heroin abuser is whether controlled heroin abuse is possible. Is heroin abuse a situation that is, by definition, out of control? For most heroin abusers, the answer is yes. Yet for some individuals, heroin may not be a compulsion. The practice of controlled or paced heroin intake is referred to as **chipping**, and the occasional heroin abuser is known as a *chipper*. An important study conducted by Norman E. Zinberg in 1984 analyzed a group of people who had been using heroin on a controlled basis for more than four years.[37] Over the course of one year, 23 percent reported taking heroin less than once a month, 36 percent reported taking it one to three times a month, and 41 percent reported taking it twice a week. Four years of exposure to heroin would seem to have been sufficient time to develop a compulsive dependence, but that did not happen. The observation that most compulsive heroin-dependent individuals never had any period of controlled use implies that controlled heroin abuse actually might not be an early transitional stage that eventually turns into uncontrolled heroin dependence.

Although the Zinberg findings have provided support for the possibility of long-term heroin abuse on a controlled basis, newer evidence from studies of heroin abusers over more than three decades—a period of time

chipping: The taking of heroin on an occasional basis.

detoxification: The process of drug withdrawal in which the body is allowed to rid itself of the chemical effects of the drug in the bloodstream.

much longer than that studied by Zinberg—indicates a somewhat darker scenario. During the 1970s, 1980s, and 1990s, a series of follow-up investigations were carried out on nearly six hundred male heroin abusers who had been admitted to a compulsory drug-treatment program for heroin-dependent criminal offenders from 1962 to 1964. By 1996–1997, only 42 percent of individuals in the original sample, on average about fifty-eight years old at the time, were available for interview. About 9 percent were of unknown status, and 49 percent had died. The most common cause of death (22 percent) was accidental poisoning from heroin adulterants or heroin overdose. Homicide, suicide, or accident accounted for 20 percent of the deaths, with the remainder being related to liver disease, cardiovascular disease, or cancer. Regarding the drug-taking behavior of the survivors, the researchers concluded that heroin dependence had been very difficult for them to avoid. As the principal investigator of the study has expressed it,

> Although many of the survivors reported that they had been able to stop using heroin for extensive periods, fewer than half reported abstinence for periods of more than five years. Abstinence for five years significantly reduced the likelihood of relapse, but even among those who achieved fifteen years of abstinence, a quarter [of them] still relapsed.[38]

Moreover, large proportions of these men were engaged in alcohol, cocaine, or amphetamine abuse as well. The bottom line is this: Dabbling in a drug as potentially dependence-inducing as heroin is an extremely risky business. To paraphrase the words of a nationally prominent drug-abuse counselor, it is equivalent to playing a pharmacological form of Russian roulette.

Treatment for Heroin Abuse

For the heroin abuser seeking treatment for heroin dependence, the two primary difficulties are the short-term effects of heroin withdrawal and the long-term effects of heroin craving. Any successful treatment, therefore, must combine a short-term and a long-term solution.

Heroin Detoxification

Traditionally, it has been possible to make the process of withdrawal from heroin, called **detoxification** ("detox"), less distressing to the abuser by reducing the level of heroin in a gradual fashion under medical supervision, rather than withdrawing from heroin "cold turkey" (a term inspired by the gooseflesh appearance of the abuser's skin during abrupt withdrawal). In medical settings, opioid drugs such as **propoxyphene** (brand name: Darvon), meperidine (brand name: Demerol), or **methadone** are administered orally to replace the heroin initially; then doses of these so-called transitional drugs are decreased over a period of two weeks or so.[39]

Methadone Maintenance

For the heroin abuser seeking out medical treatment for heroin dependence, the most immediate problem is getting the drug out of the abuser's system during detoxification with a minimum of discomfort and distress. In some procedures, the administration of naloxone has been used to speed up withdrawal and reduce the severity of physiological symptoms.

After detoxification, however, the long-term problem of drug dependence remains. The craving for heroin persists, and the abuser most often has little choice but to return to a drug-oriented environment where the temptations to satisfy the craving still exist. Since the mid-1960s, one strategy has been to have a detoxified heroin abuser participate in a program in which oral administrations of the methadone are essentially substituted for the injected heroin. This treatment approach, called **methadone maintenance**, was initiated in New York City through the joint efforts of Vincent Dole, a specialist in metabolic disorders, and Marie Nyswander, a psychiatrist whose interest had focused on narcotic dependence. Their idea was that if a legally and carefully controlled opioid drug was available to heroin abusers on a regular basis, the craving for heroin would be eliminated, their drug-taking lifestyle would no longer be needed, and they could turn to more appropriate social behaviors such as steady employment and a more stable family life. The general philosophy behind this approach to heroin-abuse treatment was that heroin abuse was essentially a chronic metabolic disorder requiring a long-term maintenance drug for the body to "normalize" the drug abuser, in the same way as a diabetic patient would need a maintenance supply of insulin.

There are several advantages of the methadone maintenance approach in heroin-abuse treatment. Since it is a legal, inexpensive narcotic drug (when dispensed through authorized drug-treatment centers), criminal activity involved in the purchase of heroin on the street can be avoided. Methadone is slower acting and more slowly metabolized, so that, unlike heroin, its effects last approximately twenty-four hours and it can be easily absorbed through an oral administration. Because it is an opioid drug, methadone binds to the endorphin-sensitive receptors in the brain (Chapter 3) and prevents feelings of heroin craving, yet the rush of a heroin high is avoided, thanks to its relatively slow rate of absorption by brain tissue.

Typically, clients in the program come to the treatment center daily for an oral dose of methadone, dispensed in orange juice, and the dose is gradually increased to a maintenance level over a period of four to six weeks. The chances of an abuser turning away from illicit drug use are increased if the higher doses of methadone are made conditional on a "clean" (drug-free) urinalysis.[40]

As a social experiment, methadone-maintenance programs have met with a mixture of success and failure. On the one hand, evaluations of this program have found that 71 percent of former heroin abusers who have stayed in methadone maintenance for a year or more have stopped intravenous drug taking, thus reducing the risk of AIDS. In a major study, drug-associated problems declined from about 80 percent to between 17 and 28 percent, criminal behavior dropped from more than 20 percent to less than 10 percent, and there was a slight increase in permanent employment.[41] Although it attracts only a fraction of the heroin-dependent community, methadone maintenance does attract those who perceive themselves as having a negligible chance of becoming abstinent on their own.[42]

Although opioid maintenance programs do help many heroin abusers, particularly those who stay in the program over an extended period of time, there are strong indications that the programs do not reduce the overall vulnerability to drug abuse in general. In other words, methadone blocks the yearning for heroin, but it is less effective in blocking the simple craving to get high. Alcohol abuse among methadone-maintenance clients, for example, ranges

propoxyphene (pro-POX-ee-feen): A synthetic (laboratory-based) opioid useful in reducing pain. Brand names are Darvon, Darvocet.

methadone: A synthetic (laboratory-based) opioid useful in treating heroin abuse.

methadone maintenance: A treatment program for heroin abusers in which heroin is replaced by the long-term intake of methadone.

from 10 percent to 40 percent, suggesting that alcohol may be substituting for opioids during the course of treatment, and one study found that as many as 43 percent of those who had successfully given up heroin had become dependent on alcohol.[43] Furthermore, methadone is sometimes diverted away from the clinics and onto the streets for illicit use. The availability of street methadone remains a matter of great concern.[44]

Alternative Maintenance Programs

Two alternative orally administered maintenance drugs for heroin abusers have been developed that avoid the problems associated with the daily dosage approach of methadone programs. The first is the opioid **LAAM** (levo-alpha-acetylmethadol), marketed under the brand name Orlaam. The advantage of LAAM is its substantially longer duration, relative to methadone, so that treatment clients need to receive the drug only three times a week instead of every day.[45]

The second drug is the opioid **buprenorphine** (brand name: Subutex), also available as a three-times-a-week medication. Both medications have been shown to be useful in treating heroin abuse. To reduce the potential for buprenorphine tablets to be made into an injectable form and abused, buprenorphine is also available in combination with naloxone (brand name: Suboxone). If the tablets are crushed and dissolved into an injectable solution, the combined formulation triggers undesirable withdrawal symptoms.

The advantage of buprenorphine as a heroin-abuse treatment is that it can be prescribed by office-based physicians rather than having to be dispensed through maintenance centers, as is the case with methadone and LAAM. When it is combined with naloxone, the abuse potential of buprenorphine is minimized, and while

long-term blockage of opioid receptors occurs, there is less of an opioid "high." Buprenorphine treatment substantially reduces the cost to public health clinics because it can be administered more widely in less heavily secured medical locations, such as primary-care clinics and physicians' offices. It also reduces the inconvenience and stigmatization faced by treatment clients, particularly for teenage heroin abusers who would be disinclined to seek treatment at facilities that are associated with older people. Continuing advances in the forms of buprenorphine administration have made this option increasingly attractive as a heroin-abuse treatment. (Health Alert).[46]

Behavioral and Social-Community Programs

To help deal with the tremendous social stresses that reinforce a continuation of heroin abuse as well as substance abuse in general, programs called **therapeutic communities** (TCs) have been developed (examples include Daytop Village, Samaritan Village, and Phoenix House). These "mini-communities" are drug-free residential settings based on the idea that stages of treatment and recovery should reflect increased levels of personal and social responsibility on the part of the abuser. Peer influence, mediated through a variety of group processes, is used to help individuals learn and assimilate social norms and develop more effective social skills. Typically, counselors are former heroin abusers or former abusers of other drugs.[47]

Other approaches have been developed that combine detoxification, treatment with naltrexone, psychotherapy, and vocational rehabilitation under a single comprehensive plan of action. These programs, called **multimodality programs**, are designed to focus simultaneously on the multitude of needs facing the heroin abuser, the goal being a successful reintegration into society. As a continuing effort to help the recovering heroin abuser over time, there are also twelve-step group support programs such as Narcotics Anonymous, modeled after similar programs for those recovering from alcohol or cocaine dependence.

Medical Uses of Opioid Drugs

The focus in this chapter has been on the acute effects of opioid drugs in the context of heroin abuse, but it is also important to look at the beneficial

LAAM: The synthetic narcotic drug levo-alpha-acetylmethadol, used in the treatment of heroin abuse. Brand name is Orlaam.

buprenorphine (BYOO-preh-NOR-feen): A synthetic (laboratory-based) opioid used in the treatment of heroin abuse. Brand names are Subutex and (in combination with naloxone) Suboxone.

therapeutic communities: Living environments for individuals in treatment for heroin and other drug abuse, where they learn social and psychological skills needed to lead a drug-free life.

multimodality programs: Treatment programs in which a combination of detoxification, psychotherapy, and group support is implemented.

Sustained-Release Buprenorphine: A New Era in Heroin-Abuse Treatment

When buprenorphine (brand name: Subutex) and its combination with naloxone (brand name: Suboxone) received FDA approval in 2002, a new era of heroin-abuse treatment began. Because buprenorphine is only a partial activator of opioid-sensitive receptors in the brain, as opposed to full activators such as heroin and methadone, clients in treatment are more likely to discontinue their heroin intake without experiencing withdrawal symptoms, and the symptoms that do occur are considerably milder. At the same time, buprenorphine administration avoids the typical heroin effects of euphoria and respiratory depression. There is also no evidence of significant impairment of cognitive or motor performance in the course of long-term buprenorphine maintenance.

In recent years, significant developments have increased the convenience of buprenorphine administration as a heroin-abuse treatment. A sustained-release version of buprenorphine, administered by injection by a certified primary-care physician has made it possible for heroin abusers to obtain treatment only once per month and has lessened the potential for diversion. Federal legislation enacted in 2007 allows a certified physician to treat a caseload of up to one hundred patients. Previous regulations had limited caseloads to no more than thirty

patients. Additionally, a buprenorphine transdermal patch (brand name: Butrans), delivering 5-20 micrograms of buprenorphine hourly over a seven-day period, has been available since 2011 for heroin abuse treatment on an "off-label basis" (see Chapter 14).

Where to go for assistance:

www.buprenorphine.samhsa.gov/about.html

This web site, sponsored by the Substance Abuse and Mental Health Services Administration of the U.S. Department of Health and Human Services, provides extensive information on treatment options and a list of available buprenorphine treatment locations. There are more than eight hundred physicians certified for buprenorphine treatment in New York State alone.

Sources: Martin, K. R. (2004, September). Once-a-month medication for heroin addiction? *NIDA Notes*, p. 9. Mitka, M. (2003). Office-based primary care physicians called on to treat the "new" addict. *Journal of the American Medical Association, 290,* 735–738. Opioid detox study shows buprenorphine improves retention rate for teens (2005, October 10). *Alcoholism and Drug Abuse Weekly*, pp. 1–2. Purdue Pharma (2011, January 21). Butrans transdermal system CIII now available. News and media release. Substance Abuse and Mental Health Services Administration (2007, January/ February). Buprenorphine: Patient limits increase. *SAMHSA Report*, p. 7.

effects that these drugs can have in a medical setting (Table 5.2).

Beneficial Effects

Excluding heroin, which is a Schedule I controlled substance in the United States and therefore unavailable even for medical use, opioid drugs are available as prescription medications (Schedule II controlled substances) for three primary therapeutic purposes: the relief of pain, the treatment of acute diarrhea, and the suppression of coughing.

■ The first and foremost medical use of opioids today is for the treatment of pain. For a patient suffering severe pain following surgical procedures or from burns or cancer, the traditional drug of choice has been morphine. Recently, pain treatment with fentanyl through

a transdermal patch administration (see Chapter 3) has been found to be more effective as an analgesic than morphine in an oral time-release administration and is preferred by patients with chronic pain because the pain relief is achieved with less constipation and an enhanced quality of life. A transdermal buprenorphine patch (brand name: Butrans) has recently become available as well.[48]

■ The second application capitalizes on the effect of opioids in slowing down peristaltic contractions in the intestines that occur as part of the digestive process. As noted earlier, one problem associated with the chronic abuse of heroin, as well as of other opioids, is constipation. However, for individuals with dysentery, a bacterial infection of the lower intestinal tract causing pain and severe diarrhea, this negative side effect becomes desirable. Therefore, the control of diarrhea by an opioid is literally life-saving, since

TABLE 5.2

Major opioid pain medications

GENERIC NAME	BRAND NAME*	RECOMMENDED DOSE FOR ADULTS	GENERIC NAME	BRAND NAME*	RECOMMENDED DOSE FOR ADULTS
morphine	Avinza	30–120 mg (oral, combined immediate release, and extended-release)	hydrocodone	Hycodan	5 mg (oral)
				Vicodin	5 mg (oral) with acetaminophen
	Duramorph	5–10 mg (i.v.)	methadone	Dolophine	5–10 mg (oral, i.v., or s.c.)
	Kadian	10–200 mg (oral, extended-release)	meperidine	Demerol	50–100 mg (oral, i.m., i.v.)
	MS Contin	15–200 mg (oral, controlled-release)	propoxyphene	Darvocet-N	50 mg (oral) with acetaminophen
	Oramorph SR	15–100 mg (oral, sustained-release)		Darvon	65 mg (oral)
	Embeda	20–100 mg morphine/ 0.8–4 mg naltrexone (oral, sustained-release)	fentanyl	Duragesic	12.5–100 mcg/hour (extended-release transdermal patch)
codeine		30–60 mg (oral, i.m., or s.c.)		Actiq	200–1,600 mcg ("lollipop" form),
hydromorphone	Dilaudid	1–8 mg (oral, i.m., i.v., or s.c.)	tramadol	Ultram ER	100–300 mg (oral, extended-release)
oxymorphone	Numorphone	Suppository, injectable			
	Opana IR	5–10 mg (oral, immediate release)			
	Opana ER	5–40 mg (oral, extended release)			
oxycodone	OxyContin	10–80 mg (oral, controlled-release)			
	Percocet	2.5–10 mg (oral) with acetaminophen			
	Percodan	4.5 mg (oral) with aspirin			

*Two forms of buprenorphine are described in Health Alert on page 135). Some opioid drugs are available only under their generic names, and some are available under either their generic or their brand names.

Note: i.v. = intravenous; i.m. = intramuscular; s.c. = subcutaneous.

Source: Physicians' desk reference (67th ed.) (2013). Montvale, NJ: PDR Network.

acute dehydration (loss of water from the body) can be fatal. Fortunately, the opioid medication loperamide (brand name: Imodium), which is available on an over-the-counter basis, effectively controls diarrhea symptoms by its action on the gastrointestinal system.

antitussive: Having an effect that controls coughing.

dextromethorphan (DEX-troh-meh-THOR-fan): A popular non-narcotic ingredient used in over-the-counter cough remedies. The "DM" designation on these preparations refers to dextromethorphan.

Because it cannot cross the blood–brain barrier, loperamide does not produce any psychoactive effects.

■ The third application focuses on the capacity of these drugs to suppress the cough reflex center in the medulla. In cases in which an **antitussive** (cough-suppressing) drug is necessary, codeine is frequently prescribed, either by itself or combined with other medications such as aspirin or acetaminophen (brand name: Tylenol, among others). As an alternative treatment for coughing, a nonopiate drug, **dextromethorphan**, is available in over-the-counter syrups and lozenges, as well as in combination with antihistamines. Unfortunately, the abuse of dextro-methorphan among young people, who are consuming it on a recreational basis, has become a relatively new cause for concern (see Chapter 1).

Prescription Pain Medication Misuse and Abuse

Even though the overall effects of prescription pain medications are beneficial, a number of serious problems should be noted in the context of their legitimate medical use. For example, respiration will be depressed for four to five hours following even a therapeutic dose of morphine, so caution is advised when the patient suffers from asthma, emphysema, or pulmonary heart disease. In addition, opioid medications decrease the secretion of hydrochloric acid in the stomach and reduce the pushing of food through the intestines, a condition that can lead to intestinal spasms. Finally, although opioids have a sleep-inducing effect in high doses, it is not recommended that they be used as a general sedative-hypnotic treatment, unless sleep is being prevented by pain or coughing.[49]

Most importantly, however, is the widespread abuse of opioid medications in which the drugs are used for clearly nonmedical purposes. Medications that have been particularly problematic are the controlled-release form of oxycodone (brand name: **OxyContin**), hydrocodone with acetaminophen (brand name: Vicodin), oxycodone with acetaminophen (brand name: Percocet), and oxymorphone (brand name: Opana). All of these medications are classified in the United States as Schedule II controlled substances, according to the Controlled Substances Act of 1970.

OxyContin Abuse

Introduced in 1995, OxyContin was promoted initially as being relatively safe from potential abuse and more acceptable to the general public because it lacked the social stigma associated with morphine. Its FDA-approved formulation allows OxyContin to be taken orally and absorbed slowly over a period of twelve hours, killing pain without inducing a sudden feeling of euphoria. However, when OxyContin tablets are crushed and then either swallowed or inhaled as a powder, or injected after diluting the powder into a solution, the effect is similar to that of heroin. Even without altering the tablets in any way, some patients have suffered severe withdrawal symptoms, similar to those experienced during heroin withdrawal, when they abruptly stopped taking high-dosage levels of the OxyContin.

Unlike heroin abusers, the demographic features of OxyContin abusers cut across age, socioeconomic status, geographic location, and gender. However, as is the case with methamphetamine (see Chapter 4), communities particularly hard-hit by this form of substance abuse have been located in small towns and rural areas. Driven by widespread opioid prescription drug abuse, twenty U.S. states reported in 2007 that the number of unintentional overdose deaths exceeded deaths to either motor vehicle crashes or suicides, Nationwide, treatment facility admissions in 2008 increased more than threefold, relative to 1998, among abusers aged 18 to 34 years. With many regions lacking the necessary funds for adequate systems to monitor pharmacy sales, abusers have been able to obtain multiple prescriptions for OxyContin and similar medications through the practice of "doctor shopping." Pharmacy robberies, when prescription access fails, are on the rise (see Portrait on page 138).[50]

Responses to OxyContin Abuse

Efforts have been made to reduce OxyContin abuse in a number of ways. An FDA-mandated warning label now states that the drug is as potentially addictive as morphine and that chewing, snorting, or injecting it could be lethal. In 2010, Purdue Pharma, manufacturer of OxyContin, introduced a new formulation (brand name: OxyNeo) containing an added chemical called Remoxy that changed the tablet into a gummy, less easily abusable substance when crushed or dissolved.

Unfortunately, alternative means have been found in an attempt to circumvent these changes. Some abusers have turned to microwaving the new formulation and sniffing the burned remains, a far less convenient but nonetheless viable option.[51] Others have turned to the extended-release form of another opioid medication, oxymorphone (brand name: Opana ER), which can be crushed and dissolved like the original form of OxyContin. In 2012, a new formulation of Opana ER was launched with a modification similar to that implemented with OxyContin, but whether these developments will significantly reduce the abuse of these medications remains to be seen. Clearly, it is extremely difficult to meet the public-health challenge in making effective pain medications available for legitimate reasons and, at the same time, restricting the opportunities for abuse.[52]

OxyContin: A controlled-release form of oxycodone, used in the treatment of chronic pain.

David Laffer—Pharmacy Robber and Killer of Four

Arguably the most famous bank robber in American history, Willie Sutton, was once asked by a reporter in an interview why, over a 40-year criminal career, he robbed banks. "Because that's where the money is," he explained. It's become a famous quote, and probably the most well-known quote by a lifelong criminal.

Today, it's not the banks that are being robbed but the local pharmacies. Why pharmacies? To update Willie Sutton's explanation: "Because that's where the drugs are." To be more specific: "That's where the OxyContin is." From a law enforcement standpoint, pharmacy robberies have gotten totally out of control, in practically every region in America, in states as disparate as Oklahoma, Ohio, California, and Oregon. The Drug Enforcement Administration (DEA) reported more than 700 drug-related pharmacy robberies in 2012. And it has gotten deadly. In 2011, four people were killed during a suburban pharmacy robbery on Long Island, New York. The killer, David Laffer, had acquired nearly 12,000 opioid pain medication pills in the four years leading to the robbery.

From a street sale alone, the 80 mg dosage of OxyContin has become a prime target for theft. A single pill at this dosage goes for $80 on the street, so a heist of even a few bottles can add up to real money. Meanwhile, pharmacists have had to contend with some difficult choices. Do they suspend all sales of Oxy-Contin, depriving the many patients with genuine pain-control issues? Do they institute security measures such as banks do? Do they hire guards around the clock to protect themselves?

Some pharmacies (particularly those that are independently owned) have upgraded their surveillance cameras, installed bulletproof glass-enclosed counters, and buzzers at the door for customers. Time-release locks on the safes used to store narcotics are now in place to reduce the number of burglaries. In one counter-move, a pharmacist in Maine took to attaching a tracking device on specific bottles of OxyContin, reserved for a potential pharmacy robber, that has led successfully to the location of the perpetrator. Some pharmacists have greatly restricted their stock supplies of oxycodone or OxyContin products and have no regrets in telling this to their customers.

Several U.S. states are increasing the minimum jail time for second-degree robbery, when a pharmacist may be threatened but no weapon is shown (a typical scenario in pharmacy robberies), from three months to three years. As a county prosecutor in Washington State has put it, "Word travels fast on the street about what an easy target the pharmacies are and how much profit can be made and what small punishment is attached."

Whatever the course that pharmacies and law-enforcement agencies take, the crisis in prescription drug abuse is bound to continue. It is difficult to battle an increasing trend in the quantity of opioid pain prescriptions that is being reported throughout the nation.

Sources: Goodnough, A. (2011, February 7). Pharmacies under siege from robbers seeking drugs. *New York Times*, p. A14. Peddie, S.; Van Sant, W.; and Lewis, R. (2012, January 8). The fear in the pharmacies. *Newsday*, pp. A3, A4. Brown, J. (2011, June 23). The oxycodone curse. *Newsday*, p. A8.

Abuse of Other Opioid Pain Medications

Vicodin and Percocet are based on opioids (hydrocodone and oxycodone, respectively) that have been available for a longer period of time, and they unfortunately have a longer record of abuse and dependence. An additional problem has been the addition of acetaminophen (up to 1000 mg in the case of one form of Percocet) to the hydrocodone and oxycodone in these medications. This combination is particularly dangerous because excessive dosages of acetaminophen increase the risk of liver toxicity and death (see Chapter 14). In order to reduce the incidence of adverse effects, the FDA ordered in 2011 a limit of 325 mg of acetaminophen when combined with a prescription pain medication.[53]

Prevalence of Nonmedical Use of Opioid Pain Medications

The nonmedical use of opioid pain medications has increased dramatically in recent years. It has been estimated that in 2011, approximately 7.6 million young adults aged eighteen to twenty-five (about 22 percent of individuals in this age group) reported to have used an opioid pain medication for nonmedical reasons in their lifetime. Approximately 2.1 million (6 percent) had used OxyContin, 5.5 million (16 percent) had used Vicodin, and 3.1 million (9 percent) had used Percocet for nonmedical reasons in their lifetime. In 2009, prescription pain medications were responsible for approximately 15,000 deaths in the United States, exceeding the number of deaths due to the overdose of cocaine or heroin.

Nonmedical use of prescription pain medications is also extensive in high schools, though prevalence rates in 2011 were lower than peak level years in 2009. According to the University of Michigan survey, 8 percent of high school seniors in 2011 reported nonmedical use of Vicodin (the most widely used opioid pain medication among this population) during the previous year. The decline in rates of Vicodin abuse may be a reflection of the current media coverage regarding the hazards of opioid pain-medication abuse in general.[54]

Summary

Opium in History

- A drug with a very long history, opium has been used for medicinal and recreational purposes for approximately 5,000 years.
- During the nineteenth century, opium figured in global politics as the instigating factor for the Opium War fought between China and Britain. At the time, opium use was widespread in Britain and the United States at all levels of society.

Morphine and the Advent of Heroin

- The discovery of morphine in 1803 as the principal active ingredient in opium revolutionized medical treatment of pain and chronic diseases.
- At the end of the nineteenth century, heroin was introduced by the Bayer Company in Germany. Initially, it was believed that heroin lacked the dependence-producing properties of morphine.

Opioids in American Society

- The abuse potential of morphine and especially of heroin was not fully realized until the beginning of the twentieth century. Social and political developments in the United States after the passage of the Harrison Act in 1914 drove heroin underground, where it acquired a growing association with criminal life.
- Heroin abuse became associated with African American and other minority communities in urban ghettos after World War II; later, the drug revolution and the military involvement in Vietnam during the 1960s and 1970s brought the issue of heroin abuse to a wider population.

Effects on the Mind and the Body

- The effects of opioids such as heroin include euphoria, analgesia, gastrointestinal slowing, and respiratory depression.
- Respiratory depression is the major risk factor for heroin intake.

How Opioids Work in the Brain

- Since the 1970s, we have known that the effects of morphine and related opioid drugs are the result of the activation of opioid-sensitive receptors in the brain.
- Three families of chemical substances produced by the brain bind to these receptors. These chemicals are collectively known as endorphins.

Patterns of Heroin Abuse

- Chronic heroin abuse is subject to tolerance effects over time. Withdrawal effects include intense craving for heroin and physical symptoms such as diarrhea and dehydration.
- One of the major problems surrounding heroin abuse is the unpredictable content of a heroin dose.

Treatment for Heroin Abuse

- Treatment for heroin abuse includes short-term detoxification and long-term interventions that address the continuing craving for the drug and physical dependence factors in the body.
- Methadone-maintenance programs focus primarily on the physiological needs of the heroin abuser, whereas therapeutic communities and support groups focus on his or her long-term reintegration into society.

Opioid Use, Misuse, and Abuse

- In medical settings, narcotic drugs have been extremely helpful in the treatment of pain, in the treatment of dysentery, and in the suppression of coughing.
- Side effects of opioid medications include respiratory depression, intestinal spasms, and sedation.
- There has been great concern since the late 1990s that opioid pain medications have been diverted to nonmedical purposes and are subject to abuse. Three medications of this type are OxyContin, Vicodin, and Percocet. There are increasing reports of pharmacy robberies, with the intent of securing supplies of opioid pain medication, particularly OxyContin.

Key Terms

antitussive, p. 136
black tar, p. 126
buprenorphine, p. 134
chipping, p. 132
codeine, p. 123
detoxification, p. 132
dextromethorphan,
   p. 136

endogenous opioid peptides,
   p. 129
fentanyl, p. 126
heroin, p. 124
LAAM, p. 134
methadone, p. 133
methadone maintenance,
   p. 133

morphine, p. 123
multimodality programs,
   p. 134
naloxone, p. 128
naltrexone, p. 129
narcotics, p. 119
opioids, p. 119
opium, p. 119

OxyContin, p. 137
propoxyphene, p. 133
thebaine, p. 123
therapeutic communities,
   p. 134

Endnotes

1. Adapted from a composite of anonymous contributors to the Sober Living by the Sea blog, www.soberliving.com/blog.
2. Levinthal, C. F. (1988). *Messengers of paradise: Opiates and the brain.* New York: Anchor Press/ Doubleday, p. 4.
3. Courtwright, D. T. (2001). *Forces of habit: Drugs and the making of the modern world.* Cambridge, MA: Harvard University Press, pp. 31–39. Merlin, M. D. (1984). *On the trail of the ancient opium poppy.* Cranbury, NJ: Associated University Press.
4. Scott, J. M. (1969). *The white poppy: A history of opium.* New York: Funk and Wagnalls, p. 111.
5. Nencini, P. (1997). The rules of drug-taking: Wine and poppy derivatives in the ancient world. VIII. Lack of evidence of opium addiction. *Substance Use and Misuse,* 32, 1581–1586.
6. Levinthal, *Messengers of paradise,* pp. 3–25. Snyder, S. H. (1977). Opiate receptors and internal opiates. *Scientific American,* 236 (3), 44.
7. Beeching, J. (1975). *The Chinese opium wars.* New York: Harcourt Brace Jovanovich, p. 23. Hanes, W. Travis III, and Sanello, F. (2002). *The opium wars.* Napierville, IL: Sourcebooks.
8. Owen, D. E. (1934). *British opium policy in China and India.* New Haven, CT: Yale University Press. Waley, A. (1958). *The opium war through Chinese eyes.* London: Allen and Unwin.
9. DeQuincey, T. (1822/2002). *Confessions of an English opium-eater.* In D. F. Musto (Ed.), *Drugs in America: A documentary history.* New York: New York University, pp. 197–199. Fay, P. W. (1975). *The opium war 1840–1842.* Chapel Hill: University of North Carolina Press, p. 11.
10. Brecher, E. M., and the editors of *Consumer Reports* (1972). *Licit and illicit drugs.* Boston: Little, Brown, p. 17.
11. Kaplan, E. H., and Wieder, H. (1974). *Drugs don't take people; people take drugs.* Secaucus, NJ: Lyle Stuart.
12. Brecher, *Licit and illicit drugs,* pp. 42–43.
13. Levinthal, *Messengers of paradise,* pp. 16–17.
14. Courtwright, D. T. (1982). *Dark paradise: Opiate addiction in America before 1940.* Cambridge, MA: Harvard University Press, p. 47.
15. Inciardi, J. A. (2002). *The war on drugs III.* Boston: Allyn and Bacon, p. 24. Terry, C. E., and Pellens, M. (1928/1970). *The opium problem.* Montclair, NJ: Patterson Smith.
16. Substance Abuse and Mental Health Services Administration (2012). *Results from the 2011 National Survey on Drug Use and Health: Detailed tables.* Rockville, MD: Substance Abuse and Mental Health Services Administration, Table 1.1A.
17. Smith, R. (1966). Status politics and the image of the addict. *Issues in Criminology,* 2 (2), 157–175.
18. Zackon, F. (1986). *Heroin: The street narcotic.* New York: Chelsea House Publishers, p. 44.
19. McCoy, A. W.; with Read, C. B., and Adams, L. P. (1972). *The politics of heroin in southeast Asia.* New York: Harper & Row, pp. 5–6.
20. Zackon, *Heroin,* p. 45.
21. Bentel, D. J.; Crim, D.; and Smith, D. E. (1972). Drug abuse in combat: The crisis of drugs and addiction among American troops in Vietnam. In D. E. Smith and G. R. Gay (Eds.), *It's so good, don't even try it once: Heroin in perspective.* Englewood Cliffs, NJ: Prentice-Hall, p. 58.
22. McCoy, *The politics of heroin,* pp. 220–221.
23. Kuzmarov, J. (2010). *The myth of the addicted army: Vietnam and the modern war on drugs.* Amherst, MA: University of Massachusetts Press. Robins, L. N.; David, D. H.; and Goodwin, D. W. (1974). Drug use by U.S. Army enlisted men in Vietnam: A follow-up on their return home. *American Journal of Epidemiology,* 99 (4), 235–249.
24. Greenhouse, S. (1995, February 12). Heroin from Burmese surges as U.S. debates strategy. *New York Times,* p. 3.
25. Holloway, L. (1994, August 31). 13 heroin deaths spark wide police investigation. *New York Times,* pp. A1, B2.

Leland, J. (1996, August 26). The fear of heroin is shooting up. *Newsweek*, pp. 55–56. Quotation on p. 56.

26. Herbert, K. (2010, January 3). Deadly drug's toll in black and white. *Newsday*, pp. A5–A6. Hernandez, D. (2003, May 23). Heroin's new generation: Young, white, and middle class. *New York Times*, p. 34. Johnston, L. D.; O'Malley, P.M.; Bachman, J. G.; and Schulenberg, J. E. (2012). *Monitoring the Future: National survey results on drug use, 1975–2011*. Vol. I: Secondary school students, 2011. Ann Arbor, MI: Institute for Social Research, The University of Michigan. Table 2-1.Jones, R.G. (2008, January 13). Heroin's hold on the young. *New York Times*, Long Island section, pp. 1, 8. Richey, Warren (1996, October 25). Boycott groups: Klein ads carry scent of "heroin chic." *Christian Science Monitor*, p. 3.

27. National Drug Intelligence Center (2011). *National Drug Threat Assessment 2011*. Washington, DC: U.S. Department of Justice, pp. 26–28.

28. Winger, G.; Hofmann, F. G.; and Woods, J. H. (1992). *A handbook on drug and alcohol abuse: The biomedical aspects*. New York: Oxford University Press, 1992, pp. 44–46.

29. Abel, E. L. (1985). *Psychoactive drugs and sex*. New York: Plenum Press, pp. 175–204.

30. McHugh, P. F., and Kreek, M. J. (2008). The medical consequences of opiate abuse and addiction and methadone pharmacotherapy. In J. Brick (Ed.), *Handbook of the medical consequences of alcohol and drug abuse*, 2nd ed. New York: Routledge, pp. 303–339. Winger, Hofmann, and Woods, *Handbook on drug and alcohol abuse*, pp. 46–50.

31. Julien, R. M. (2005), *A primer of drug action* (10th ed.). New York: Worth, pp. 490–492. Yaksh, T. L., and Wallace, M. S. (2012). In L. L. Brunton, B. A. Chabner, and B. C. Knollman (Eds.), *Goodman and Gilman's The pharmacological basis of therapeutics* (12th ed.). New York: Macmillan, pp. 481–525.

32. Levinthal, *Messengers of paradise*. Mathias, R. (2003, March). New approaches seek to expand naltrexone use in heroin treatment. *NIDA Notes*, 17 (6), p. 8. Self, D. W. (1998). Neural substrates of drug craving and relapse in drug addiction. *Annals of Medicine*, 30, 379–389. Teagle, S. (2007, April). Depot naltrexone appears safe and effective for heroin addiction. *NIDA Notes*, p. 7.

33. Goode, E. (1999). *Drugs in American society* (5th ed.). New York: McGraw-Hill, p. 328. McHugh and Kreek, Medical consequences, pp. 326–327. Strang, J.; Griffiths, P.; and Gossop, M. (1997). Heroin smoking by "chasing the dragon": Origins and history. *Addiction*, 92, 673–684.

34. Buxton, J. A.; Sebastian, R.; Clearsky, L.; Angus, N.; Shah, L.; et al. (2011). Chasing the dragon – characterizing cases of leukoencephalopathy associated with heroin inhalation in British Columbia. *Harm Reduction Journal*, 8, 3.

35. McHugh and Kreek, Medical consequences.

36. Johnson, B. D.; Goldstein, P. J.; Preble, E.; Schmeidler, J.; Lipton, D. S.; et al. (1985). *Taking care of business: The economics of crime by heroin abusers*. Lexington, MA: Lexington Books.

37. Zinberg, N. E. (1984). *Drug, set, and setting: The basis for controlled intoxicant use*. New Haven, CT: Yale University Press, pp. 46–81.

38. Hser, Y. I.; Hoffman, V.; Grella, C.; and Douglas A. M. (2001). A 33-year follow-up of narcotics addicts. *Archives of General Psychiatry*, 58, 503–508. Goode, E. *Drugs in American Society* (8th ed.). New York: McGraw-Hill, pp. 278–281. National Institute on Drug Abuse (2001). 33-year study finds lifelong, lethal consequences of heroin addiction. *NIDA Notes*, 16 (4), 1, 5, 7. Quotation on p. 5. Treaster, J. B. (1992, July 22). Executive's secret struggle with heroin's powerful grip. *New York Times*, pp. A1, B4.

39. Schuckit, M. A. (2006). *Drug and alcohol abuse: A clinical guide to diagnosis and treatment* (6th ed.). New York: Springer, pp. 178-182.

40. Stitzer, M. L.; Bickel, W. K.; Bigelow, G. E.; and Liebson, I.A. (1986). Effect of methadone dose contingencies on urinalysis test results of polydrug-abusing methadone-maintenance patients. *Drug and Alcohol Dependence*, 18, 341–348.

41. Maddux, J. F., and Desmond, D. P. (1997). Outcomes of methadone maintenance 1 year after admission. *Journal of Drug Issues*, 27, 225–238. Sees, K. L.; Delucchi, K. L.; Masson, C.; Rosen, A.; Clark, H. W.; et al. (2000). Methadone maintenance vs. 180-day psychosocially enriched detoxification for treatment of opioid dependence. *Journal of the American Medical Association*, 283, 1303–1310.

42. Office of National Drug Control Policy (2000, April). Methadone. *ONDCP Drug Policy Information Clearinghouse Fact Sheet*. Washington, DC: Office of National Drug Control Policy.

43. Wasserman, D. A.; Korcha, R.; Havassy, B. E.; and Hall, S. M. (1999). Detection of illicit opioid and cocaine use in methadone maintenance treatment. *American Journal of Drug and Alcohol Abuse*, 25, 561–571.

44. Faupel, C. E. (1991). *Shooting dope: Career patterns of hard-core heroin users*. Gainesville: University of Florida Press, pp. 170–173. Gollnisch, Gernot (1997). Multiple predictors of illicit drug use in methadone maintenance clients. *Addictive Behaviors*, 22, 353–366. Substance Abuse and Mental Health Services Administration (2003, January). Narcotic analgesics. *The DAWN report*. Rockville, MD: Substance Abuse and Mental Health Services Administration, Figure 2.

45. Eissenberg, T.; Bigelow, G. F.; Strain, E. C.; Walsh, S. L.; Brooner, R. K.; et al. (1997). Dose-related efficacy of levomethadyl acetate for treatment of opioid dependence: A randomized clinical trial. *Journal of the American Medical Association*, 277, 1945–1951.

46. Martin, K. R. (2004, September). Once-a-month medication for heroin addiction? *NIDA Notes*, 19 (3), p. 9.

Mitka, M. (2003). Office-based primary care physicians called on to treat the "new" addict. *Journal of the American Medical Association, 290*, 735–736. Butrans (buprenorphine) Transdermal System CIII now available. News and media release, Purdue Pharma, January 20, 2011.

47. Martin, S. S.; O'Connell, D. J.; Paternoster, R.; and Bachman, R. D. (2011). The long and winding road to desistance from crime for drug-involved offenders: The long-term influence of TC treatment on re-arrest. *Journal of Drug Issues, 11*, 179-196. National Institute on Drug Abuse (2002). Therapeutic community. *National Institute on Drug Abuse Research Report*. Rockville, MD: National Institute on Drug Abuse.

48. Allan, L.; Hays, H.; Jensen, N.H.; Le Polain de Waroux, B.; Bolt, M.; et al. (2001). Randomised crossover trial of transdermal fentanyl and sustained-release oral morphine for treating chronic non-cancer pain. *British Medical Journal, 322*, 1154–1158.

49. Julien, R. M. (2005). *A primer of drug action* (10th ed.). New York: Worth, pp. 461-500.

50. Meier, B. (2012, April 9). Tightening the lid on pain prescriptions. *New York Times*, pp. A1, A12. Rosenberg, D. (2001, April 9). How one town got hooked. *Newsweek*, pp. 49–50. Tavernise, S. (2011, April 20). Ohio county losing its young to painkillers' grip. *New York Times*, pp. A1, A16. Van Sant, W.; Peddie, S.; and Lewis, R. (2011, December 26). Millions for doctor-shoppers. *Newsday*, pp. A4-A5. Substance Abuse and Mental Health Services Administration (2010, November/December). Rise in treatment admissions for prescription pain relievers. *SAMHSA News*, p. 19.

51. Basbaum, A. I., and Julius, D. (2006, June). Toward better pain control. *Scientific American*, pp. 60–67. Meier, B. (2003, November 23). The delicate balance between pain and addiction. *New York Times*, pp. F1, F6. FDA approves new formulation of OxyContin (2010, April 5). News release from the U.S. Food and Drug Administration, Washington, DC.

52. Goodnough, A., and Zezima, K. (2011, June 16). Drug is harder to abuse, but users persevere. *New York Times*, p. A21. RPT-painkiller Opana, new scourge of rural America (2012, March 12). Reuters News Service.

53. Associated Press (2011, January 23). FDA orders lower doses in prescription painkillers.

54. Centers for Disease Control and Prevention (2012, July). *Vital Signs: Prescription painkiller overdoses.* Atlanta, GA: Centers for Disease Control and Prevention. Centers for Disease Control and Prevention (2011, November 4). Vital signs: Overdoses of prescription opioid pain relievers—United States, 1999-2008. *Morbidity and Mortality Weekly Report , 60*, 1487-1492. Johnston, O'Malley, Bachman, and Schulenberg, *Monitoring the Future*, Table 2-2. Substance Abuse and Mental Health Services Administration, *Results from the 2011 National Survey of Drug Use and Health: Detailed tables*, Tables 1.85A and 1.85B. 1.89A, and 1.89B.

LSD and Other Hallucinogens

I was forced to interrupt my work in the laboratory in the middle of the afternoon and proceed home, being affected by a remarkable restlessness combined with a slight dizziness. At home I lay down and sank into a not unpleasant intoxicated-like condition, characterized by an extremely stimulated imagination. In a dreamlike state with eyes closed . . . I perceived an uninterrupted stream of fantastic pictures, extraordinary shapes with intense, kaleidoscopic play of colors.

—Albert Hofmann, the discoverer of LSD,
reflecting on the day he took a sample of the drug
LSD: My Problem Child *(1980)*

After you have completed this chapter, you should have an understanding of

▶ The classification of hallucinogenic drugs

▶ The history of LSD

▶ Facts and fiction about LSD effects

▶ Prominent hallucinogens other than LSD

▶ The special dangers of MDMA (Ecstasy), phencyclidine (PCP), and ketamine

▶ Current issues concerning *Salvia divinorum* (Salvia) abuse

On an April afternoon in 1943, Albert Hofmann, a research chemist at Sandoz Pharmaceuticals in Basel, Switzerland, went home early from work, unaware that his fingertips had made contact with an extremely minute trace of a new synthetic chemical he had been testing that day. The chemical was **lysergic acid diethylamide (LSD)**, and, as the opening passage indicates, Hofmann unknowingly experienced history's first "acid trip."

Three days later, having pieced together the origin of his strange experience, he decided to try a more deliberate experiment. He chose a dose of 0.25 mg, a concentration that could not, so he thought, possibly be effective. His plan was to start with this dose and gradually increase it to see what would happen.

The dose Hofmann had considered inadequate was actually about five times greater than an average dose for LSD. As he later recalled his experience,

> *My condition began to assume threatening forms. Everything in my field of vision wavered and was distorted as if seen in a curved mirror. I also had the sensation of being unable to move from the spot.*[1]

A little while later, his experience worsened:

> *The dizziness and sensation of fainting became so strong at times that I could no longer hold myself erect, and had to lie down on a sofa. My surroundings had now transformed themselves in more terrifying ways. Everything in the room spun around, and the familiar objects and pieces of furniture assumed grotesque, threatening forms. . . . I was seized by the dreadful fear of going insane. I was taken to another place, another time.*[2]

His experience then became pleasant:

> *Kaleidoscopic, fantastic images surged in on me, alternating, variegated, opening and then closing themselves in circles and spirals. . . . It was particularly remarkable how every acoustic perception, such as the sound of a door handle or a passing automobile, became transformed into optical perceptions. Every sound generated a vividly changing image, with its own consistent form and color.*[3]

Hofmann's vivid remembrances are presented here at length because they succinctly convey some of

lysergic acid diethylamide (LSD) (lye-SER-jik ASS-id di-ETH-il-la-mide): A synthetic, serotonin-related hallucinogenic drug.

hallucinogens (ha-LOO-sin-oh-jens): A class of drugs producing distortions in perception and body image at moderate doses.

by the numbers . . .

566,990	Approximate number of LSD doses in one ounce of pure LSD, based on 50 micrograms as a typical LSD dosage level
1	The number of documented cases of deaths due to LSD ingestion alone, since 1960

Source: Fysh, R. R.; Oon, M. C. H.; Robinson, K. N.; Smith, R. N.; White, P. C.; and Whitehouse, M. J. (1985). A fatal poisoning with LSD. *Forensic Science International, 28,* 109–113.

the major facets of a hallucinogenic drug experience: the distortions of visual images and body sense, the frightening reaction that often occurs when everyday reality is so dramatically changed, and the strange intermingling of visual and auditory sensations. These effects will be considered later in more detail as this chapter explores the bizarre world of hallucinogenic drugs.

Like many of the drugs that have been examined in the preceding chapters, hallucinogenic drugs such as LSD and several others have a story that belongs both in our contemporary culture and in the distant past. Hofmann worked in the modern facilities of an international pharmaceutical company, but the basic material on his laboratory bench was a fungus that has been around for millions of years. It has been estimated that as many as 6,000 plant species around the world have some psychoactive properties.[4] This chapter will focus on a collection of special chemicals called *hallucinogenic drugs* or simply **hallucinogens**, often pharmacologically dissimilar to one another but with the common ability to distort perceptions and alter the user's sense of reality.

A Matter of Definition

Definitions are frequently reflections of one's attitude toward the thing one is defining, and the terminology used to describe hallucinogens is no exception. For those who view these drugs with a "positive spin," particularly for those who took LSD in the 1960s, hallucinogens have been described as *psychedelic*, meaning "mind-expanding" or "making the mind manifest." In cases where a spiritual experience has been reported, such as with the ingestion of *ayahuasca*, hallucinogens have been called *entheogenic*, meaning "generating the divine within." On the other hand, for people who view these drugs with more alarm than acceptance, the popular descriptive adjectives have been *psychotomimetic*, meaning "having the appearance of a psychosis," *psychodysleptic*, meaning "mind-disrupting," or even worse, *psycholytic*, meaning "mind-dissolving."

As a result of all this emotional baggage, describing these drugs as hallucinogenic, meaning "hallucination-producing," is probably the most even-handed way of defining their effects; that is the way they will be referred to in this chapter. Some problems, however, still need to be considered. Technically, a hallucination is the reported perception of something that does not physically exist. For example, a schizophrenic patient might hear voices that no one else hears, and therefore we must conclude (at least the nonschizophrenic world must conclude) that such voices are not real. In the case of hallucinogens, the effect is more complicated because we are dealing with a perceived alteration in the existing physical environment. Some researchers have suggested using the term *illusionogenic* as a more accurate way of describing drugs that produce these kinds of experiences.

We also should be aware of another qualification when we use the term "hallucinogen." Many drugs that produce distinctive effects when taken at low to moderate dose levels turn out to produce hallucinations when either the dose levels are extremely high or drug use is extended over a period of time. Examples of this possibility appeared in Chapter 4 with cocaine and amphetamines and will appear in Chapter 13 with inhalants. Here the category of hallucinogens will be limited to those drugs that produce marked changes in perceived reality at relatively low dosages and over a relatively short time interval.

Classifying Hallucinogens

It is relatively easy to define what hallucinogens are by virtue of their effects on the users, but classifying them can be complicated. In general, most hallucinogens can be classified in terms of the particular neurotransmitter in the brain (see Chapter 3) that bears a close resemblance to the molecular features of the drug. Basically, we are speaking of three possible neurotransmitters: serotonin, norepinephrine, and acetylcholine. A relatively small number of hallucinogens, however, bear no resemblance to any neurotransmitter at all.

Table 6.1 shows the overall four-group classification scheme. The first three categories are (1) hallucinogens

---

TABLE 6.1

Major categories of hallucinogens

CATEGORY	SOURCE
Hallucinogens related to serotonin	
lysergic acid diethylamide (LSD)	a synthetic derivative of lysergic acid, which is, in turn, a component of ergot
psilocybin	various species of North American mushrooms
lysergic acid amide or morning glory seeds	morning glory seeds
dimethyltryptamine (DMT)	the bark resin of several varieties of trees and some nuts native to Central and South America
harmine	the bark of a South American vine
Hallucinogens related to norepinephrine	
mescaline	the peyote cactus in Mexico and the U.S. Southwest
2,5,-dimethoxy-4-methylamphetamine (DOM or, more commonly, STP)	a synthetic, mescaline-like hallucinogen
MDMA (Ecstasy) and MDA	two synthetic hallucinogens
Hallucinogens related to acetylcholine	
atropine	*Atropa belladonna* plant, known as deadly nightshade, and the datura plant
scopolamine (hyoscine)	roots of the mandrake plant, henbane herb, and the datura plant
hyoscyamine	roots of the mandrake plant, henbane herb, and the datura plant
ibotenic acid	*Amanita muscaria* mushrooms
Miscellaneous hallucinogens	
phencyclidine (PCP)	a synthetic preparation, developed in 1963, referred to as angel dust
ketamine (K)	a PCP-like hallucinogen
Salvia divinorum or Salvia	a hallucinogenic Mexican herb, in the mint family

Source: Schultes, R. E., and Hofmann, A. (1979). *Plants of the gods: Origins of hallucinogenic use.* New York: McGraw-Hill.

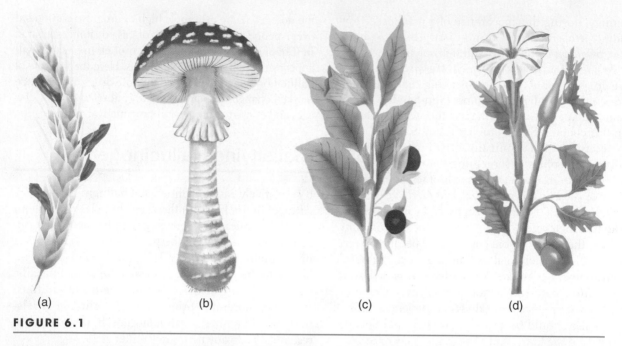

FIGURE 6.1

Botanical sources for four hallucinogenic drugs: (a) *Claviceps tulasne* (ergot), (b) *Amanita muscaria* (ibotenic acid), (c) *Atropa belladonna* (atropine), and (d) *Datura stramonium*, called jimsonweed (atropine, scopolamine, and hyoscyamine). These sources are not shown to the same scale; actually, they differ in size.

that are chemically similar to serotonin (LSD, psilocybin, morning glory seeds, DMT, and harmine), (2) hallucinogens that are chemically similar to norepinephrine (mescaline, DOM, MDMA, and MDA), and (3) hallucinogens that are chemically similar to acetylcholine (atropine, scopolamine, hyoscyamine, and ibotenic acid). The fourth category comprises three hallucinogens (PCP, ketamine, and *Salvia divinorum*) that are chemically unlike any known neurotransmitter; these drugs will be called miscellaneous hallucinogens. Most of these drugs have natural botanical origins (see four examples in Figure 6.1).

Lysergic Acid Diethylamide (LSD)

The most widely known hallucinogen is LSD, which does not exist in nature but is synthetically derived from **ergot**, a fungus present in moldy rye and other grains. One of the compounds in ergot, lysergic acid, is highly toxic, inducing a condition called **ergotism**.

ergot (ER-got): A fungus infecting rye and other grains.

ergotism: A physical and/or psychological disorder acquired by ingesting ergot-infected grains. One form of ergotism involves gangrene and eventual loss of limbs; the other form is associated with convulsions, disordered thinking, and hallucinations.

Historians have surmised that widespread epidemics of ergotism (called St. Anthony's fire) occurred periodically in Europe during the Middle Ages, when extreme famine forced people to bake bread from infected grain (see Drugs . . . in Focus on page 147).

In one particularly deadly episode in 944, an outbreak of ergotism claimed as many as 40,000 lives. The features of this calamity were twofold. One form of ergotism produced a reduction in blood flow toward the extremities, leading to gangrene, burning pain, and the eventual loss of limbs. The other form produced a tingling sensation on the skin, convulsions, disordered thinking, and hallucinations.[5]

Even though the link between this strange affliction and ergot in moldy grain has been known since the 1700s, outbreaks of ergotism have continued to occur in recent times. A major outbreak occurred in Pont-Saint-Esprit, a small French village, in 1951. Hundreds of townspeople went totally mad on a single night:

> *Many of the most highly regarded citizens leaped from windows or jumped into the Rhône, screaming that their heads were made of copper, their bodies wrapped in snakes, their limbs swollen to gigantic size or shrunken to tiny appendages. . . . Animals went berserk. Dogs ripped bark from trees until their teeth fell out.*[6]

Drugs . . . in Focus

Strange Days in Salem: Witchcraft or Hallucinogens?

In the early months of 1692, in Salem, Massachusetts, eight young girls suddenly developed a combination of bizarre symptoms: disordered speech, odd body postures, and convulsive fits. They also began to accuse various townspeople of witchcraft. During the summer, in a series of trials, more than 150 people were convicted of being witches and 20 were executed. Accusations were also made in neighboring villages in the county and in Connecticut. Nothing approaching the magnitude of the Salem witch trials has since occurred in American history.

Over the years, a number of theories have attempted to account for these strange events: a case of adolescent pranks, general hysteria, or some kind of political scapegoating. An interesting and controversial speculation has been advanced that these girls were showing the hallucinogenic and convulsive symptoms of ergotism, acquired from fungus-infected rye grain. Arguments that support this theory include the following:

- Rye grain, once harvested, was stored in barns for months, and the unusually moist weather in the area that year could have promoted the growth of ergot fungus during storage. Of twenty-two Salem households with some afflicted member, sixteen were located close to riverbanks or swamps.

- Children and teenagers would have been particularly vulnerable to ergotism because they ingest more food, and hence more poison, per pound of body weight than do adults.

- The Salem girls as well as the accused "witches" frequently displayed hallucinatory behavior and physical symptoms common to convulsive ergotism.

The role of ergotism in the Salem witch trials of 1692 has been vigorously debated by both historians and pharmacologists. The readings listed below provide more information on this intriguing possibility.

Sources: **In favor:** Caporael, L. R. (1976). Ergotism: The Satan loosed in Salem? *Science, 192,* 21–26. Matossian, M. K. (1982). Ergot and the Salem witchcraft affair. *American Scientist, 70,* 355–357. Matossian, M.K. (1989). *Poisons of the past: Molds, epidemics, and history.* New Haven, CT: Yale University Press, pp. 113–122. **Against:** Spanos, N. P., and Gottlieb, J. (1976). Ergotism and the Salem village witch trials. *Science, 194,* 1390–1394.

Albert Hofmann's professional interest in lysergic acid centered on its ability to reduce bleeding and increase contractions in smooth muscle, particularly the uterus. He was trying to find a nontoxic chemical version that would be useful in treating problems associated with childbirth. The LSD molecule was the twenty-fifth in a series of variations that Hofmann studied in 1938, and his creation was officially named LSD-25 for that reason. He thought at the time that the compound had possibilities for medical use but then went on to other pursuits. He returned to these investigations five years later, in 1943, the year of his famous LSD experience.

The Beginning of the Psychedelic Era

Sandoz Pharmaceuticals applied for Food and Drug Administration (FDA) approval of LSD in 1953. As was common practice at the time, the company sent out samples of LSD to laboratories around the world for scientific study. The idea was that LSD might be helpful in the treatment of schizophrenia by allowing psychiatrists to gain insight into subconscious processes, which this drug supposedly unlocked. One of the researchers intrigued by the potential psychotherapeutic applications of LSD was the psychiatrist Humphrey Osmond of the University of Saskatchewan in Canada, who coined the word "psychedelic" to describe its effects and whose interest also extended to other hallucinogens, such as mescaline.

In 1953, Osmond introduced the British writer Aldous Huxley to mescaline, and Huxley later reported his experiences, under Osmond's supervision, in his essay *The Doors of Experience*. Prior to 1960, LSD was being administered to humans under fairly limited circumstances, chiefly as part of research studies in psychiatric hospitals and psychotherapy sessions on the West Coast. As would be revealed later in court testimony in the 1970s, there were also top-secret experiments conducted by the Central Intelligence Agency (CIA), which was interested in LSD for possible application in espionage work. Word of its extraordinary effects, however, gradually spread to regions outside laboratories or hospitals. One of those who picked up on these events was a young clinical psychologist and lecturer at Harvard University named Timothy Leary.

Leary's first hallucinatory experience (in fact, his first psychoactive drug experience of any kind, other than alcoholic intoxication) was in Mexico in 1960, when he ate some mushrooms containing the hallucinogen psilocybin. This is his recollection of his response:

> *During the next five hours, I was whirled through an experience which could be described in many extravagant metaphors but which was above all and without question the deepest religious experience of my life.*[7]

Back at Harvard, his revelations sparked the interest of a colleague, Richard Alpert (later to be known as Baba Ram Dass). The two men were soon holding psilocybin sessions with university students and whoever else was interested, on and off campus. At first these studies retained some semblance of scientific control. For example, a physician was on hand, and objective observers of behavior reported the reactions of the subjects. Later, these procedures were altered. Physicians were no longer invited to the sessions, and Leary himself began taking the drug at the same time. His argument was that he could communicate better with the subject during the drug experience, but his participation seriously undermined the scientific nature of the studies.

In 1961 Leary, Alpert, and other associates turned to LSD as the focus of their investigations, in their homes and other locations off the Harvard campus. Although these experiments were technically separate from the university itself, public relations concerns on the part of the Harvard administration were mounting. Leary further aggravated the situation through his increasingly incendiary writings. In a 1962 article published in the *Bulletin of the Atomic Scientists*, he suggested that the Soviets could conceivably dump LSD into the water supply and that, to prepare for such an attack, Americans should dump LSD into their own water supply so that citizens would know what to expect. Needless to say, the U.S. government was not amused.

In 1963, after a Harvard investigation, Leary and Alpert were dismissed from their academic positions, making it the first time in the twentieth century that a Harvard faculty member had been fired. As you can imagine, such events brought enormous media exposure. Leary was now "Mr. LSD" (see Portrait), and suddenly the public became acquainted with a class of drugs that had been previously unknown to them.[8]

For the rest of the 1960s, LSD became not only a drug but also one of the symbols for the cultural revolt of a generation of youth against the perceived inadequacies of the established, older generation. Leary himself told his followers that they were "the wisest and holiest generation" and advised them to "turn on, tune in, and drop out."[9] The era has been described in this way:

> *There were psychedelic churches, ashrams, rock festivals, light shows, posters, comic books and newspapers, psychedelic jargon and slang. Every middle-sized city had its enclaves, and there was a drug culture touring circuit. . . . Everyone had his own idea of what was meant by turning on, tuning in, and dropping out—his own set and setting—and the drug culture provided almost as many variations in doctrine, attitude, and way of life, from rational and sedate to lewd and violent, as the rest of society.*[10]

In congressional hearings on LSD use by the nation's youth, scientists, health officials, and law-enforcement experts testified to a growing panic over the drug. Newspaper stories emphasized the dangers with alarmist headlines: "A monster in our midst—a drug called LSD" and "Thrill drug warps mind, kills," among them. Sandoz quietly allowed its LSD patent to lapse in 1966 and did everything it could to distance itself from the controversy. Hofmann himself called LSD his "problem child."

Multicolored images such as these, inspired by the LSD experience, epitomized the psychedelic era of the 1960s.

Timothy Leary—Nutty Professor or Psychedelic Visionary?

For the average college student, the question regarding Timothy Leary might be not "Whatever happened to that guy?" but rather "Who was this guy, anyway?" For those of you who ask the latter question, here is a capsule rendition of the life and times of Timothy Leary. Historians are only starting to come to grips with the complexity of his legacy.

Until 1960, Leary's career was a world apart from what would follow. It had none of the unconventionality that would later characterize his life. As a clinical psychologist, he had written a widely acclaimed textbook and devised a respected personality test (called the Leary). An experience with psilocybin in Mexico in 1960, however, turned his life around. The more extensive his exposure to hallucinogenic drugs became, the more he took on the self-appointed role of Pied Piper for what was referred to then as the "acid generation."

By the middle of the 1970s, Leary had been sentenced to twenty years for marijuana possession (the longest sentence ever imposed for such an offense), had gone to federal prison, had escaped, had evaded the authorities in Algeria, Afghanistan, and Switzerland for a few years, had been recaptured, and finally had been released after a successful appeal of his original conviction. LSD advocacy was no longer on his agenda by this time, and in fact LSD had lost its mystique years earlier. Leary hit the college lecture circuit, talking about space migration and life extension and calling himself a "stand-up philosopher."

In the late 1980s, Leary discovered computers. He formed a software company, marketed a number of successful video games, and viewed interactive computer programming and virtual reality in particular as the consciousness expansion of the 1990s, the newest route to "cerebral stimulation."

Leary never stopped being a social activist, with his own unique brand of opportunism. In 1994, he was detained by the police in an Austin, Texas,

airport for smoking—a cigarette, this time. Leary said that he wanted to draw attention to people being "demonized" by no-smoking restrictions.

A year after his death in 1996, Leary's friends arranged to have his cremated remains delivered by rocket into space. It was estimated that he would orbit Earth every ninety minutes for approximately two years or so, until his "space-hearse" would eventually burn up during reentry. As his followers put it at the time, it was fitting that this would be his "ultimate trip."

Sources: Brozan, N. (1994, May 12). Chronicle: Timothy Leary lights up. *New York Times*, p. D26. Greenfield, R. (2006). *Timothy Leary: A biography.* New York: Harcourt. L., Martin A., and Shlain, B. (1985). *Acid dreams: The complete social history of LSD.* New York: Grove Weidenfeld. Simons, M. (1997, April 22). A final turn-on lifts Timothy Leary off. *New York Times*, pp. A1, A4. Stone, J. (1991, June). Turn on, tune in, boot up. *Discover*, pp. 32–35.

In 1966, LSD was made illegal, later becoming a Schedule I drug, with possession originally set as a misdemeanor and later upgraded to a felony. By the 1970s, LSD had become entrenched as a street drug, and taking LSD had become a component of the already dangerous world of illicit drugs. The story of LSD will be updated in a later section, but first it is important to understand the range of effects that LSD typically produces.

Acute Effects of LSD

LSD is considered one of the most powerful psychoactive drugs known. Its potency is so great that effective dose levels have to be expressed in terms of micrograms (millionths of a gram), often called *mikes*. The typical street dose ranges from 50 to 150 micrograms, though sellers often claim that their product contains more. The effective dose can be as small as 10 micrograms, with only one-hundredth of a percent being absorbed into

the brain. You can appreciate the enormous potency of LSD by comparing these figures to the fact that a single regular-strength aspirin tablet contains 325,000 micrograms of aspirin.[11]

Taken orally, LSD is rapidly absorbed into the bloodstream and the brain, and its effects begin to be felt within thirty to sixty minutes, reaching a peak in about two to four hours. Within four to twelve hours, LSD effects are over.[12]

Surprisingly, given its extreme potency, the toxicity of LSD is relatively low. Generalizing from studies of animals given varying doses of LSD, we can estimate that a lethal dose of LSD for humans would have to be roughly 300 to 600 times the effective dose, a fairly comfortable margin of safety. In 2011, the DAWN statistics showed that less than 0.1 percent of all drug-related emergency department visits were associated with the ingestion of LSD. To this day, there has been only one definitive case in which a death has been attributed solely to an LSD overdose.[13]

A microdot tablet of LSD positioned against a British postage stamp (to the left of the queen) underscores the minute amount necessary for a single dose.

Street forms of LSD may contain color additives or adulterants with specific flavors, but the drug itself is odorless, tasteless, and colorless. LSD is sold on the street in single-dose "hits." It is typically swallowed in the form of powder pellets (microdots) or gelatin chips (windowpanes) or else licked off small squares of absorbent paper that have been soaked in liquid LSD (blotters). In the past, blotters soaked with LSD have been decorated with pictures of mystical symbols and signs, rocket ships, or representations of Mickey Mouse, Snoopy, Bart Simpson, or other popular cartoon characters.

LSD initially produces an excitation of the sympathetic autonomic activity: increased heart rate, elevated blood pressure, dilated pupils, and a slightly raised body temperature. There is an accompanying feeling of restlessness, euphoria, and a sensation that inner tension has been released. There may be laughing or crying, depending on one's expectations and the setting.[14]

Between thirty minutes and two hours later, a "psychedelic trip" begins, characterized by four distinctive features. The best way to describe these effects is in the words of individuals who have experienced them:[15]

- Images seen with the eyes closed.

  Closing my eyes, I saw millions of color droplets, like rain, like a shower of stars, all different colors.

synesthesia: A subjective sensation in a modality other than the one being stimulated. An example is a visual experience when a sound is heard.

- An intermingling of senses called **synesthesia**, which usually involves sounds being perceived as hallucinatory visions.

  I clapped my hands and saw sound waves passing before my eyes.

- Perception of a multilevel reality.

  I was sitting on a chair and I could see the molecules. I could see right through things to the molecules.

- Strange and exaggerated configurations of common objects or experiences.

  A towel falling off the edge of my tub looked like a giant lizard crawling down.

  When my girlfriend was peeling an orange for me, it was like she was ripping a small animal apart.

During the third and final phase, approximately three to five hours after first taking LSD, the following features begin to appear:

- Great swings in emotions or feelings of panic.

  It started off beautifully. I looked into a garden . . . and suddenly, it got terrible . . . and I started to cry. . . . And then, my attention wandered, and something else was happening, beautiful music was turned on. . . . Then suddenly I felt happy.

- A feeling of timelessness.

  Has an hour gone by since I last looked at the clock? Maybe it was a lifetime. Maybe it was no time at all.

- A feeling of ego disintegration, or a separation of one's mind from one's body.

  Boundaries between self and nonself evaporate, giving rise to a serene sense of being at one with the universe. I recall muttering to myself again and again, "All is one, all is one."

Whether these strong reactions result in a "good trip" or a "bad trip" depends heavily on the set of expectations for the drug, the setting or environment in which the LSD is experienced, and the overall psychological health of the individual.

Effects of LSD on the Brain

LSD closely resembles the molecular structure of serotonin. Therefore, it is not surprising that LSD should have effects on receptors in the brain that are sensitive to serotonin (see Chapter 3). As a result of research in the 1980s, it turns out that the critical factor behind LSD's hallucinogenic effects lies in its ability to stimulate a special subtype of serotonin-sensitive receptors called serotonin-2A receptors. In fact, all hallucinogens, even those drugs whose structures do not resemble serotonin, have the ability to excite these receptors. Drugs that specifically block serotonin-2A receptors, leaving all other subtypes unchanged, will block the behavioral effects of hallucinogens. In addition, the ability of a particular drug to produce hallucinogenic effects is directly proportional to its ability to bind to serotonin-2A receptors.[16]

Patterns of LSD Use

The enormous publicity surrounding Timothy Leary and his followers in the 1960s made LSD a household word. As many as fifty popular articles about LSD were published in major U.S. newspapers and magazines between March 1966 and February 1967 alone. By 1970, however, the media had lost interest, and hardly anything was appearing about LSD. Even so, while media attention was diminishing, the incidence of LSD abuse was steadily rising. In four Gallup Poll surveys conducted between 1967 and 1971, the percentage of college students reported to have taken LSD at least once in their lives rose dramatically, from 1 to 18 percent.[17]

From the middle 1970s to the early 1990s, the numbers showed a steady decline. By 1986, the University of Michigan survey indicated that the lifetime incidence of LSD taking among high school seniors was 7 percent, down from 11 percent in 1975. By the end of the 1990s, however, prevalence rates were once again on the rise, reaching and later exceeding the levels of a quarter-century earlier. Since 1997 when the prevalence rate was about 14 percent, LSD use has declined substantially. Four percent of high school seniors in 2011 reported taking LSD at some time in their lives. A parallel trend has been observed in college students.[18]

It should be noted that today's LSD users are different from those of a previous generation in a number of ways. Typical LSD users now take the drug less frequently. And because the dosage of street LSD is presently about one-fourth the level common to the 1960s and 1970s, they remain high for a briefer period of time. Their motivation behind using LSD is also not the same. They report using LSD as a club drug, simply to get high, rather than to explore alternate states of consciousness or gain a greater insight into life. For current users, LSD no longer has the symbolic significance that it had in an earlier time.[19]

Facts and Fiction about LSD

Given the history of LSD use and the publicity about it, it is all the more important to look carefully at the facts about LSD and to unmask the myths. It is useful to examine six basic questions that are frequently asked about the acute and chronic effects of this drug.

Will LSD Produce Substance Dependence?

There are three major reasons why LSD is not likely to result in drug dependence, despite the fact that the experience at times is quite pleasant. First, LSD and other hallucinogens cause the body to build up a tolerance to their effects faster than any other drug category. As a result, one cannot remain on an LSD-induced high day after day, for an extended period of time. Second, LSD is not the drug for someone seeking an easy way to get high. As one drug expert has put it,

> *The LSD experience requires a monumental effort. To go through eight hours of an LSD high—sensory bombardment, psychic turmoil, emotional insecurity, alternations of despair and bliss, one exploding insight upon the heels of another, images hurtling through the mind as fast as the spinning fruit of a slot machine—is draining and exhausting in the extreme.*[20]

Third, the LSD experience seems to control the user rather than the other way around. It is virtually impossible to "come down" from LSD at will. Besides, the unpredictability of the LSD experience is an unpopular feature for those who would want a specific and reliable drug effect every time the drug is taken.

Will LSD Produce a Panic Attack or Psychotic Behavior?

One of the most notorious features of LSD is the possibility of a bad trip. Personal accounts abound of sweet, dreamlike states rapidly turning into nightmares. Perhaps the greatest risks are taken when a person is slipped a dose of LSD and begins to experience its effect without knowing that he or she has taken a drug. But panic reactions may also occur when a person is fully aware of having taken LSD. Although the probability of having a bad trip is difficult to estimate, there are very few regular LSD abusers who have not experienced a bad trip or had a disturbing experience as part of an LSD trip. The best treatment for adverse effects is the companionship and reassurance of others throughout the period when

we should recognize that psychological reactions to LSD are inherently unpredictable, and caution is advised.

Psilocybin and Other Hallucinogens Related to Serotonin

The source of the drug **psilocybin** is a family of mushrooms native to southern Mexico and Central America. Spanish chroniclers in the sixteenth century wrote of "sacred mushrooms" revered by the Aztecs as *teonanacatl* (roughly translated as "God's flesh") and as capable of providing extraordinary visions when eaten. Their psychoactive properties had been known for a long time, judging from stone-carved representations of these mushrooms discovered in El Salvador and dating back to as early as 500 B.C. Today, shamans in remote villages in Mexico and Central America (see Chapter 1) continue the use of psilocybin mushrooms, among other hallucinogenic plants, achieve healing on both physical and spiritual levels.[29]

In 1955, a group of Western observers documented the hallucinogenic effects of the *Psilocybe mexicana* in a native community living in a remote mountainous region of southern Mexico. Three years later, samples worked their way to Switzerland, where Albert Hofmann, already known for his work on LSD, identified the active ingredient and named it psilocybin. As was his habit, Hofmann sampled some of the mushrooms himself and wrote later of his reactions:

> Thirty minutes after my taking the mushrooms, the exterior world began to undergo a Mexican character. . . . I saw only Mexican motifs and colors. When the doctor supervising the experiment bent over me to check my blood pressure, he was transformed into an Aztec priest.[30]

An interesting question is whether the Aztec character of these hallucinogenic effects was simply a result of suggestion, given the social context in which the drug-taking behavior was occurring, or, alternatively, Aztec designs may have been inspired over the centuries by the effects of psilocybin.

Once ingested, psilocybin loses a portion of its molecule, making it more fat-soluble and more easily

Psilocybe mexicana mushrooms, the source of psilocybin.

absorbed into the brain. This new version, called **psilocin**, is the actual agent that works on the brain. Because LSD and psilocin are chemically similar, the biochemical effects are also similar. Cross-tolerance will occur (see Chapter 3). If you develop a tolerance to LSD, you have become tolerant to psilocybin effects, and vice versa.[31]

Far less potent than LSD, psilocybin is effective at dose levels measured in the more traditional units of milligrams, rather than in micrograms. At doses of 4 to 5 mg, psilocybin causes a pleasant, relaxing feeling; at doses of 15 mg and more, hallucinations, time distortions, and changes in body perception appear. A psilocybin trip generally lasts from two to five hours, considerably shorter than an LSD trip.

Individuals who have experienced both kinds of hallucinogens report that, compared to LSD, psilocybin produces effects that are more strongly visual, less emotionally intense, and more euphoric, with fewer panic reactions and less chance of paranoia. On the other hand, experimental studies of volunteers taking high doses of psilocybin have established that the drug produces drastic enough changes in mood, sensory perception, and thought processes to qualify as a psychotic experience.

Like LSD, psilocybin (often called simply "shrooms") has become increasingly available as a drug of abuse. In 2011, about 38 percent of high school seniors reported that non-LSD hallucinogens (including "shrooms") were "fairly easy" or "very easy" to get, whereas about 25 percent felt the same way about LSD itself.[32]

Lysergic Acid Amide (LAA)

In addition to their reverence for psilocybin mushrooms, the Aztecs ingested locally grown morning glory seeds, calling them *ololuiqui*, and used their hallucinogenic effects in religious rites and healing. Like many Native

---

psilocybin (SIL-oh-SIGH-bin): A serotonin-related hallucinogenic drug originating from a species of mushroom.

psilocin (SIL-oh-sin): A brain chemical related to serotonin, resulting from the ingestion of psilocybin.

Health Line
Bufotenine and the *Bufo* Toad

Bufotenine is a drug with a strange past. Found in a family of beans native to Central and South America, bufotenine is better known as a chemical that can be isolated from the skin and glands of the *Bufo* toad, from which it gets its name. As noted in Chapter 1, *Bufo* toads figured prominently in the magical potions of European witches. Evidence also exists that *Bufo* toads were incorporated into the ceremonial rituals of ancient Aztec and Mayan cultures. Largely as a result of these historical references, it has been widely assumed that bufotenine was the primary contributor to the psychoactive effects of these concoctions and that bufotenine itself is a powerful hallucinogen.

It turns out that these conclusions are wrong. The few studies in which human volunteers were administered bufotenine indicate that the substance induces strong excitatory effects on blood pressure and heart rate but no hallucinatory experiences. Some subjects report distorted images with high dosages of the drug, but this might well occur as oxygen is cut off from parts of the body, particularly the optic nerve carrying visual information to the brain. It is likely that whatever hallucinogenic effects *Bufo* toads may produce are brought on by another chemical also found in these toads that functions similarly to the hallucinogen DMT.

Despite the confusion about which substance is responsible for its psychoactive properties, *Bufo* toads continue to fascinate the public. Wildly exaggerated and frequently unsubstantiated accounts of "toad licking" and "toad smoking" periodically circulate in the media. Reportedly, a small group calling themselves Amphibians Anonymous was formed in the late 1980s; the group's motto was "Never has it been so easy to just say no."

The bottom line, however, is that the dangers of consuming toad tissue are substantial. Besides the extreme cardiovascular reactions, toxic effects include a skin condition called **cyanosis** (literally, "turning blue"). Actually, that description may be an understatement. Skin color has been observed to be closer to an eggplant purple.

Sources: Horgan, J. (1990, August). *Bufo* abuse. *Scientific American*, pp. 26–27. Inciardi, J. A. (2002). *The war on drugs III*. Boston: Allyn and Bacon, pp. 4–5. Lyttle, T.; Goldstein, D.; and Gartz, J. (1996). *Bufo* toads and bufotenine: Fact and fiction surrounding an alleged psychedelic. *Journal of Psychoactive Drugs, 28*, 267–290.

American practices, the recreational use of morning glory seeds has survived in remote areas of southern Mexico. In 1961, Albert Hofmann (once again) identified the active ingredient in these seeds as **lysergic acid amide (LAA)** after having sampled its hallucinogenic properties. As the chemical name suggests, this drug is closely related to LSD.

The LAA experience, judging from Hofmann's report, is similar to that of LSD, although LAA is only one-tenth to one-thirtieth as potent, and the hallucinations tend to be dominated by auditory rather than visual images. Commercial varieties of morning glory seeds are available to the public, but to minimize their abuse, suppliers have taken the precaution of coating them with an additive that causes nausea and vomiting if they are eaten.[33]

Dimethyltryptamine (DMT)

The drug **dimethyltryptamine (DMT)** is obtained chiefly from the resin of the bark of trees and nuts native to the West Indies as well as to Central and South America, where it is generally inhaled as a snuff. An oral administration does not produce psychoactive effects. The similarity of this drug's effects to those of LSD and its very short duration gave DMT the reputation, during the psychedelic years of the 1960s, of being "the businessman's LSD." Presumably, someone could take a DMT trip during lunch and be back at the office in time for work in the afternoon.

An inhaled 30-mg dose of DMT produces physiological changes within ten seconds, with hallucinogenic effects peaking around ten to fifteen minutes later. Paranoia, anxiety, and panic also can result at this time, but most symptoms are over in about an hour.[34] A chemical found in *Bufo* toads is similar to DMT (see Health Line).

bufotenine (byoo-FOT-eh-neen): A serotonin-related drug obtained either from a bean plant in Central and South America or from the skin of a particular type of toad.

cyanosis (SIGH-ah-NOH-sis): A tendency for the skin to turn bluish purple. It can be a side effect of the drug bufotenine.

lysergic acid amide (LAA) (lye-SER-jik ASS-id A-mide): A hallucinogenic drug found in morning glory seeds, producing effects similar to those of LSD.

dimethyltryptamine (DMT) (dye-METH-il-TRIP-ta-meen): A short-acting hallucinogenic drug.

Harmine

Among native tribes in the western Amazon region of South America, the bark of the *Banisteriopsis* vine yields the powerful drug **harmine**. A drink containing harmine, called *ayahuasca*, is frequently used by local shamans for healing rites. It is chemically similar to serotonin, like LSD and the other hallucinogens examined so far. Its psychological effects, however, are somewhat different. Unlike LSD, harmine makes the individual withdraw into a trance, and the hallucinatory images (often visions of animals and supernatural beings) are experienced within the context of a dreamlike state. Reports among shamans refer to a sense of suspension in space or of flying, falling into one's body, or experiencing one's own death.[35]

Hallucinogens Related to Norepinephrine

Several types of hallucinogens have a chemical composition similar to that of norepinephrine. As you may recall from Chapter 4, amphetamines are also chemically similar to norepinephrine. Consequently, some of the norepinephrine-related hallucinogens are capable of producing amphetamine-like stimulant effects. This is the case with MDMA (Ecstasy) but not with mescaline or DOM (short for 2,5-dimethoxy-4-methylamphetamine).

Mescaline

The hallucinogen **mescaline** is derived from the **peyote** plant, a spineless cactus with a small, greenish crown that grows above ground and a long carrot-like root. This cactus is found over a wide area, from the southwestern United States to northern regions of South America, and many communities in these regions have discovered its psychoactive properties. Given the large distances between these groups, it is remarkable that

The peyote cactus, source of mescaline.

they prepare and ingest mescaline in a highly similar manner. The crowns of the cactus are cut off, sliced into small disks called buttons, dried in the sun, and then consumed. An effective dose of mescaline from peyote is 200 mg, equivalent to about five buttons. Peak response to the drug takes place thirty minutes to two hours after consumption. Mescaline is still used today as part of religious worship among many Native Americans in the United States and Canada (see Drugs . . . in Focus on page 157).

The psychological and physiological effects of mescaline are highly similar to those of LSD, though some have reported that mescaline hallucinations are more sensual, with fewer changes in mood and the sense of self. Nonetheless, double-blind studies comparing the reactions to LSD and mescaline show that subjects cannot distinguish between the two when dose levels are equivalent. Although the reactions may be the same, the mescaline trip comes at a greater price, as far as physiological reactions are concerned. Peyote buttons taste extremely bitter and can cause vomiting, headaches, and, unless the stomach is empty, distressing levels of nausea.[36]

Today mescaline can be synthesized as well as obtained from the peyote cactus. The mescaline molecule resembles the chemical structure of norepinephrine but stimulates the same serotonin-2A receptors as LSD and other hallucinogens that resemble serotonin. As a result, mescaline and LSD share a common brain mechanism.[37]

DOM

A group of synthetic hallucinogens have been developed that share mescaline's resemblance to amphetamine but do not produce the strong stimulant effects of amphetamine. One example of these synthetic drugs, **DOM**, appeared in the 1960s and 1970s, when it was

harmine (HAR-meen): A serotonin-related hallucinogenic drug frequently used by South American shamans in healing rituals.

mescaline (MES-kul-leen): A norepinephrine-related hallucinogenic drug. Its source is the peyote cactus.

peyote (pay-YO-tay): A species of cactus that is the source for the hallucinogenic drug mescaline.

DOM: A synthetic norepinephrine-related hallucinogenic drug, derived from amphetamine. DOM or a combination of DOM and LSD is often referred to by the street name STP.

Drugs . . . in Focus

Present-Day Peyotism and the Native American Church

Among Native Americans within the United States, the ritual use of peyote buttons, called *peyotism*, can be traced to the eighteenth century, when the Mescalero Apaches (from whom the word *mescaline* was derived) adopted the custom from Mexican Indians who had been using peyote for more than three thousand years. By the late 1800s, peyotism had become widely popular among tribes from Wisconsin and Minnesota to the West Coast. It was not until the early twentieth century, however, that peyote use became incorporated into an official religious organization, the Native American Church of North America, chartered in 1918.

The beliefs of the Native American Church membership, estimated to include anywhere from 50,000 to 250,000 Native Americans in the United States and Canada, combine traditional tribal customs and practices with Christian morality. To them, life is a choice between two roads that meet at a junction. The Profane Road is paved and wide, surrounded by worldly passions and temptations. The Peyote Road is a narrow and winding path, surrounded by natural, unspoiled beauty; it is also a path of sobriety (since alcohol poisons the goodness of the body), hard work, caring for one's family, and brotherly love. Only the Peyote Road leads to salvation. In their weekly ceremonies, lasting from Saturday night until Sunday afternoon, church members swallow small peyote buttons

as a sacrament, similar to the ritual of taking Holy Communion, or drink peyote tea. It is considered sacrilegious to take peyote outside the ceremonies in the church.

The Religious Freedom Restoration Act of 1993 established an exemption from federal and state controlled substance laws when peyote is used for religious purposes in traditional Native American ceremonies. In 2005, a study found that peyote use among church members does not result in impairments on tests of memory, attention, and other aspects of cognitive functioning.

Today, a handful of people are licensed by state and federal authorities to harvest peyote for religious purposes, in south Texas near Laredo. This locale is the only place in the United States where peyote grows in the wild. As one of the harvesters has put it, "This is sacred ground to a lot of Native American tribes. To some, the land here is very holy because it is the home to the sacred peyote."

Sources: Calabrese, J. D. (1997). Spiritual healing and human development in the Native American Church: Toward a cultural psychiatry of peyote. *Psychoanalytic Review, 84*, 237–255. Halpern, J. H.; Sherwood, A. R.; Hudson, J. I.; Yurgelum-Tod, D.; and Pope, H. G. Jr. (2005). Psychological and cognitive effects of long-term peyote use among Native Americans. *Biological Psychiatry, 58*, 624–631. Milloy, Ross E. (2002, May 7). A forbidding landscape that's Eden for peyote. *New York Times*, p. A20. Quotation on p. A20. Morgan, G. (1983). Recollections of the peyote road. In L. Grinspoon and J. B. Bakalar (Eds.), *Psychedelic reflections*. New York: Human Sciences Press, pp. 91–99.

---

frequently combined with LSD and carried the street name of STP. To some, the nickname was a reference to the well-known engine oil additive; to others the letters stood for "serenity, tranquility, and peace" or, alternatively, "super terrific psychedelic." It is roughly eighty times more potent than mescaline, though still far weaker than LSD. At low doses of about 3 to 5 mg, DOM produces euphoria; with higher doses of 10 mg or more, severe hallucinations result, often lasting from sixteen to twenty-five hours. Though similar to LSD in many respects, DOM has the reputation of producing a far greater incidence of panic attacks, psychotic episodes, and other symptoms of a very bad trip. Cases have been reported of STP being added as an adulterant to marijuana.[38]

MDMA (Ecstasy)

Another synthetic norepinephrine-related hallucinogen, abbreviated **MDMA**, first appeared on the scene in the 1980s. Although subject to abuse as a new designer drug, it also became known to a number of psychiatrists who used the drug as part of their therapy, believing that MDMA had a special ability to enhance empathy among their patients. In fact, some therapists at the time

MDMA (Ecstasy): There is a growing consensus of opinion that hallucinogenic drug. There is a growing consensus of opinion of his psychotherapeutic benefits, although there are significant adverse physical and psychological side effects.

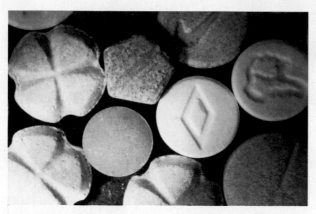

Assorted Ecstasy tablets.

suggested the name *empathogens* (meaning "generating a state of empathy") to describe MDMA and related drugs. Eventually, after several years of hesitations and reversals, the Drug Enforcement Administration (DEA) put MDMA permanently on the Schedule I list of controlled substances, indicating that there is no accepted medical application for the drug. Nonetheless, in recent years, a small number of research laboratories have received permission to produce MDMA and study its effects under closely supervised circumstances. The treatment of post-traumatic stress disorder among veterans of the wars in Iraq and Afghanistan has been identified as a potentially useful therapeutic application. There is an increased interest in MDMA in psychotherapy in general, a possibility that remains for now officially prohibited by virtue of its status as Schedule I controlled substance.[39]

Since the early 1990s, MDMA has become prominent among the new club drugs (see Chapter 1) especially popular at dance clubs and all-night "rave" parties. Widely available under names such as Ecstasy (not to be confused with the stimulant Herbal Ecstasy), E, XTC, X, Essence, Clarity, and Adam, MDMA has the reputation of having the stimulant qualities of amphetamines and the hallucinogenic qualities of mescaline.

HEALTH ALERT!

MDMA Toxicity: The Other Side of Ecstasy

- **Possible Physical Effects**
  Hyperthermia and heatstroke
  Dehydration and electrolyte depletion
  Irregular heartbeat or increased heart rate
  Kidney and liver failure
  Jaw-clenching and other forms of muscle spasms
  Long-term neurochemical changes

- **Possible Psychological Effects**
  Agitation and confusion
  Depression and anxiety
  Long-term impairments in memory recall

Note: As with other illicit drugs, adulterated versions raise significant concerns. In the case of MDMA, adulterants include dextromethorphan (a common cough suppressant) at approximately thirteen times the dose found in over-the-counter cough medications. At this dosage, dextromethorphan itself functions as a hallucinogen and inhibits sweating, increasing the risk of hyperthermia and heatstroke. More powerful hallucinogens and hyperthermic drugs have also been identified as adulterants in MDMA batches.

In 2003, the federal RAVE (Reducing Americans' Vulnerability to Ecstasy) Act was signed into law, making it unlawful to "knowingly open, lease, rent, use, or maintain any place, whether permanently or temporarily for the purpose of manufacturing, distributing, or using any controlled substance." Supporters of the law view it as helping to reduce illicit drug use in dance clubs; opponents view it more as a reflection of prejudice against youth culture.

Where to go for assistance:
www.nida.nih.gov/infofacts/ecstasy.html
This web site is sponsored by the National Institute on Drug Abuse and includes an extensive treatment on the hazards of Ecstasy (MDMA).

Sources: Boils, K. I. (1999). Memory impairment in abstinent MDMA ("Ecstasy") users. *Journal of the American Medical Association, 281,* 494. Chonin, N. (2003, April 27). Congress acts out against club culture. *San Francisco Chronicle,* p. 35. Leshner, A. I. (2002). Ecstasy abuse and control: Hearing before the Senate Subcommittee on Governmental Affairs—July 30, 2001. Statement for the record. *Journal of Psychoactive Drugs, 34,* 133–135. Schwartz, R. H., and Miller, N. S. (1997). MDMA (Ecstasy) and the rave: A review. *Pediatrics, 100,* 705–708. Stryker, J. (2001, September 25). For partygoers who can't say no, experts try to reduce the risks. *New York Times,* p. F5.

The physical health concerns with respect to Ecstasy center on its short-term and long-term toxicity. The principal acute effect is severe hyperthermia (and heatstroke), which can be lethal when one ingests Ecstasy while engaged in the physical exertion in an already overheated environment. The dehydration associated with hyperthermia causes an elevation in blood pressure and heart rate and places a strain on kidney functioning. These problems are compounded by the highly risky practice of "Ecstasy stacking," in which multiple Ecstasy tablets are taken at once or Ecstasy is combined with LSD, alcohol, marijuana, or other drugs. Ecstasy use also has been linked to long-term cognitive impairments and emotional difficulties. Heavy and prolonged Ecstasy use can produce confusion, anxiety, sleep problems, reductions in impulse control, and declines in memory and attention. In general, women show greater behavioral effects from chronic Ecstasy use than do men.[40] The Health Alert feature on page 158 summarizes the major elements of potential toxicity.

In 2011, according to the University of Michigan survey, about 8 percent of high school seniors and about 3 percent of eighth graders reported having taken Ecstasy at some point in their lives. After a sharp rise in prevalence rates observed between 1998 and 2001 in these groups (peaking in 2001 at 12 percent and 5 percent, respectively), Ecstasy use has been on the decline, largely due to publicity about its adverse health effects. However, a worrisome trend began in 2005, with a *decreasing* number of high school seniors and eighth graders judging Ecstasy use to represent a great risk of harm. This trend will be watched carefully in coming years to predict whether a resurgence in the use of Ecstasy as a recreational drug may be on the horizon.[41]

Hallucinogens Related to Acetylcholine

Of the acetylcholine-related hallucinogens, some enhance the neurotransmitter and some inhibit it. Examples include *Amanita muscaria* mushrooms, atropine, scopolamine, and hyoscyamine.

Amanita muscaria

The **Amanita muscaria** mushroom, also called the fly agaric mushroom because of its ability to lure and sedate flies and other insects, grows in the upper latitudes of the Northern Hemisphere, usually among the roots of birch trees. The mushroom has a bright red cap speckled with white dots; the dancing mushrooms in Walt Disney's film *Fantasia* were inspired by the appearance (if not the hallucinogenic effects) of this fungus (see Figure 6.1b).

Amanita mushrooms are one of the world's oldest intoxicants. Many historians hypothesize that this mushroom was the basis for the mysterious and divine substance called soma that is celebrated in the *Rig-Veda*, one of Hinduism's oldest holy books, dating from 1000 B.C. It is strongly suspected that amanita mushrooms were used in Greek mystery cults and were the basis for the legendary "nectar of the gods" on Mount Olympus.[42]

The effects of amanita mushrooms can be lethal if dose levels are not watched very carefully. They produce muscular twitching and spasms, vivid hallucinations, dizziness, and heightened aggressive behavior. It was briefly mentioned in Chapter 1 that Viking warriors were reputed to have ingested amanita mushrooms before sailing off to battle. The drug-induced strength and savagery of these "berserk" invaders were so widely feared that a medieval prayer was written especially for protection from their attacks: "From the intolerable fury of the Norseman, O Lord, deliver us."[43]

The Hexing Drugs and Witchcraft

A number of natural plants contain chemicals that share a common feature: the ability to block the parasympathetic effects of acetylcholine in the body. The drugs with this ability, called *anticholinergic drugs*, produce specific physiological effects. The production of mucus in the nose and throat, and of saliva in the mouth, is reduced. Body temperature is elevated, sometimes to very high fever levels. Heart rate and blood pressure go up, and the pupils dilate considerably. Psychological effects include a feeling of delirium, confusion, and a loss of memory for events occurring during the drugged state.[44] The amnesic property is one of the primary reasons for the minimal street appeal of these drugs.

The principal anticholinergic drugs are **atropine**, **scopolamine** (also called hyoscine), and **hyoscyamine**.

Amanita muscaria (a-ma-NEE-ta mus-CAR-ee-ah): A species of mushroom containing the hallucinogenic drug ibotenic acid.

atropine (AT-tro-peen): An anticholinergic hallucinogenic drug derived from the *Atropa belladonna* plant.

scopolamine (scoh-POL-ah-meen): An anticholinergic hallucinogenic drug. Also called hyoscine.

hyoscyamine (HEYE-oh-SEYE-eh-meen): An anticholinergic hallucinogenic drug found in mandrake, henbane, and various species of the datura plant.

They are found in various combinations and relative amounts in a large number of psychoactive plants. Four of the better known ones are examined here.

- Atropine is principally derived from the **Atropa belladonna** plant, also called deadly nightshade. Its lethal reputation is quite justified, since it is estimated that ingesting only a dozen or so berries is sufficient for death to occur. Through history, atropine has been associated with poisoning, either accidental or not. In the eleventh century, Scottish forces succeeded in destroying an opposing army (English or Scandinavian, records are unclear) by atropine-adulterated shipments of meal. At lower, more benign dose levels, plant extracts can be applied to the eyes, causing the pupils to dilate. Egyptian and Roman women used this technique to enhance their beauty or at least improve their appearance. The term "belladonna" ("beautiful lady") originates from this specific application. The psychological effects of atropine are generally associated with the anticholinergic effects of heart-rate acceleration, light-headedness, and general arousal.

- The **mandrake** plant is an oddly shaped, potato-like plant with a long forked root that has traditionally been imagined to resemble a human body. In ancient times, mandrake was considered to have aphrodisiac properties. According to medieval folklore, mandrake plants supposedly shrieked when they were uprooted, understandably driving people mad.

  Mandrake contains a combination of atropine, scopolamine, and hyoscyamine. Because low doses act as a depressant, mandrake has been used as a sedative-hypnotic drug to relieve anxiety and induce sleep. At higher doses, it produces bizarre hallucinations and muscular paralysis.

- **Henbane** is a strong-smelling herb, native to widespread areas of the Northern Hemisphere, with purple-veined, yellowish flowers and hairy leaves. Its English name, meaning "harmful to hens," originates from the observation that henbane seeds were toxic to chickens and other birds. The lethal possibilities for henbane potions have been described by writers since the days of the Roman Empire. Hamlet's father in Shakespeare's play was supposedly murdered with henbane poison. Lower doses of henbane, however, have been used in a more benign way, as an anesthetic and painkiller. We now know that the predominant drugs in henbane are scopolamine and hyoscyamine.

- Various species of the datura plant, containing a combination of atropine, scopolamine, and hyoscyamine, grow wild in locations throughout the world. In the United States, one particular species, **Datura stramonium**, is called jimsonweed, a contraction of "Jamestown weed" (the name given to it by early American colonists). Consumption of the seeds or berries of jimsonweed produces hypnotic and hallucinogenic effects, together with disorientation, confusion, and amnesia. At high doses, jimsonweed is quite toxic. In recent years, there have been occasional reports of hospitalizations and even deaths among teenagers who have eaten jimsonweed seeds as an inexpensive way to get high.[45]

During medieval times, mixtures of deadly nightshade, mandrake, and henbane were responsible for the psychoactive effects of witches' potions, producing a disastrous combination of physiological and psychological effects. Satanic celebrations of the Black Mass centered on the ingestion of such brews. Atropine, in particular, produced a substantial elevation in arousal, probably leading to the feeling that the person was flying (or at least capable of it), while the hallucinogenic effects enabled the person to imagine communing with the Devil. According to fourteenth-century reports, witches were described as preparing these mixtures as ointments and rubbing them on their bodies and on broomsticks, which they straddled while naked. The chemicals would have been easily absorbed through the skin and the membranes of the vagina. The considerably sanitized Halloween image of a witch flying on a broomstick has been with us ever since.[46]

Miscellaneous Hallucinogens

Three hallucinogens are referred to as miscellaneous hallucinogens because they do not have any chemical resemblance to serotonin, norepinephrine, or acetylcholine. They are phencyclidine, ketamine, and *Salvia divinorum*.

Atropa belladonna (a-TROH-pah BEL-ah-DON-ah): A plant species, also called deadly nightshade, whose berries can be highly toxic. It is the principal source of atropine.

mandrake: A potato-like plant containing anticholinergic hallucinogenic drugs.

henbane: An herb containing anticholinergic hallucinogenic drugs.

Datura stramonium (duh-TOOR-ah strah-MOH-nee-um): A species of the datura family of plants with hallucinogenic properties. In the United States, the plant is called jimsonweed.

Phencyclidine (PCP)

Perhaps the most notorious of all the hallucinogens is **phencyclidine (PCP)**, commonly known as *angel dust*. Technically, PCP is a synthetic depressant, and it was originally introduced in 1963 as a depressant drug by the Parke-Davis pharmaceutical company, under the brand name of Sernyl. It was marketed as a promising new surgical anesthetic that had the advantage of not depressing respiration or blood pressure or causing heartbeat irregularities, as some other anesthetics do. In addition, PCP had a higher therapeutic ratio than many other anesthetics available at that time. By 1965, however, it was withdrawn from human applications after reports that nearly half of all patients receiving PCP showed signs of delirium, disorientation, hallucinations, intense anxiety, or agitation. In 1979, PCP was classified as a Schedule II controlled substance and is still used as an anesthetic for animal surgery.

The weird combination of stimulant, depressant, and hallucinogenic effects makes PCP difficult to classify. Some textbooks treat the discussion of PCP in a chapter on hallucinogens, as is done here, whereas others include it in a chapter on stimulants because some features of PCP intoxication resemble the effect of cocaine. A growing consensus of opinion has it that PCP should be described as a *dissociative anesthetic hallucinogen*, because it produces a feeling of being dissociated or cut off from one's environment.

Acute Effects of PCP

PCP can be taken orally, intravenously, or by inhalation, but commonly it is smoked either alone or in combination with other drugs. Whatever its mode of administration, the results are extremely dangerous, with an unpredictability that far exceeds that of LSD or other hallucinogens. The symptoms may include manic excitement, depression, severe anxiety, sudden mood changes, disordered and confused thought, paranoid thoughts, and unpredictable aggression. Because PCP has analgesic properties as well, individuals taking the drug often feel invulnerable to threats against them and may be willing and able to withstand considerable pain. The mechanism behind PCP effects appears to be the blocking of a specific subtype of glutamate receptor in the brain (see Chapter 3).

Hallucinations also occur, but they are quite different from the hallucinations experienced under the influence of LSD. There are no colorful images, no intermingling of sight and sound, no mystical sense of being "one with the world." Instead, a

prominent feature of PCP-induced hallucinations is the change in one's body image. As one PCP abuser has expressed it:

> *The most frequent hallucination is that parts of your body are extremely large or extremely small. You can imagine yourself small enough to walk through a key hole, or you can be lying there and all of a sudden you just hallucinate that your arm is twice the length of your body.*[47]

Individuals under the influence of PCP also may stagger, speak in a slurred way, and feel depersonalized or

phencyclidine (PCP) (fen-SIGH-klih-deen): A dissociative anesthetic hallucinogen that produces disorientation, agitation, aggressive behavior, analgesia, and amnesia. It has various street names, including angel dust.

detached from people around them. A prominent feature is a prolonged visual stare, often called "doll's eyes."

The effects of PCP last from as little as a few hours to as long as two weeks, and they are followed by partial or total amnesia and dissociation from the entire experience. Considering these bizarre reactions, it is not surprising that PCP deaths occur more frequently from the behavioral consequences of the PCP experience than from its physiological effects. Suicides, accidental or intentional mutilations, drownings (sometimes in very small amounts of water), falls, and threatening behavior leading to the individual being shot are only some of the possible consequences.[48]

Patterns of PCP Abuse

It is strange that a drug with so many adverse effects would be subject to deliberate abuse, but such is the case with PCP. Reports of PCP abuse began surfacing in 1967 among the hippie community in San Francisco, where it became known as the PeaCe Pill. Word quickly spread that PCP did not live up to its name. Inexperienced PCP abusers were suffering the same bizarre effects as had the clinical patients earlier in the decade. By 1969, PCP had been written off as a garbage drug, and it dropped out of sight as a drug of abuse.

In the early 1970s, PCP returned under new street names and in new forms (Table 6.2). No longer a pill to be taken orally, PCP was now in powdered or liquid form. Powdered PCP could be added to parsley, mint, oregano, tobacco, or marijuana, rolled as a cigarette, and smoked. Liquid PCP could be used to soak leaf mixtures of all types, including manufactured cigarettes, which could then be dried and smoked. Many new users have turned to PCP as a way to boost the effects of marijuana. Making matters worse, as many as 120 different designer-drug variations of PCP have been developed in illicit laboratories around the country and the world. The dangers of PCP abuse, therefore, are complicated by the difficulty in knowing whether a street drug has been adulterated with PCP and what version of PCP may be present. Unfortunately, the common practice of mixing PCP with alcohol or marijuana adds to the unpredictability of the final result.[49]

Ketamine

Ketamine, a drug chemically similar to PCP, is also classified as a dissociative anesthetic hallucinogen. Like PCP, ketamine has a mixture of stimulant and

ketamine (KET-ah-meen): A dissociative anesthetic hallucinogen related to phencyclidine (PCP).

TABLE 6.2

Street names for phencyclidine (PCP) and PCP-like drugs

PCP	JET FUEL
angel dust	sherms (derived from the reaction that it hits you like a Sherman tank)
monkey dust	superkools
peep	cyclones
supergrass	zombie dust
killer weed	ketamine
ozone	special K
embalming fluid	
rocket fuel	

Note: In the illicit drug market, PCP and ketamine are frequently misrepresented and sold as mescaline, LSD, marijuana, amphetamine, or cocaine.

Source: Updated from Milburn, H. T. (1991). Diagnosis and management of phencyclidine intoxication. *American Family Physician, 43,* 1293.

---

depressive properties, though its depressive effect is more extreme and does not last as long as that of PCP. Ketamine (brand name: Ketalar) was used as an emergency surgical anesthetic on the battlefield in Vietnam as well as in standard hospital-based operations in which gaseous anesthetics could not be employed. It has also been used occasionally in short surgical procedures involving the head and neck or in the treatment of facial burns where it is not possible to use an anesthetic mask. Adverse side effects, however, have limited its therapeutic use. These problems include unpredictable and sometimes violent jerking and twitching of the body, as well as vivid and unpleasant dreams during and after surgery. During recovery, patients may experience hallucinations and feelings of disorientation. Delayed effects of ketamine, such as nightmares, have been reported to occur for weeks or longer after surgery.[50]

Ketamine abuse began to be reported in the 1980s. More recently, under the names "Special K" and "Vitamin K," it has been included among current club drugs on the scene (see Chapter 1). Its popularity has increased among college students and patrons of dance clubs and all-night "rave" parties. Like PCP, ketamine produces a dreamlike intoxication, accompanied by an inability to move or feel pain. There are also experiences of dizziness, confusion, and slurred speech. As is the case with dissociative hallucinogens, ketamine produces amnesia, in that abusers frequently cannot later

Quick Concept Check 6.2

Understanding PCP

Check your understanding of the effects of PCP by listing three major features of PCP intoxication that are significantly different from the effects of other hallucinogens.

Answer: Correct responses can include any of the following: analgesia, amnesia, prolonged stare, absence of synesthesia, absence of mysticism, unpredictable aggression, extreme disorientation, feelings of being cut off from oneself or the environment.

remember what has happened while under its influence. The primary hazard of acute ketamine ingestion is the depression of breathing. Little is known, however, of the chronic effects of extended ketamine abuse over time, except that experiences of "flashbacks" have been reported. As with PCP, the effects of ketamine are associated with the blocking of specific glutamate receptors.

As with other club drugs that produce depressive effects on the central nervous system, there is the dangerous potential for ketamine to be abused as a "date-rape" drug. Women who may unwittingly take the drug can be rendered incapacitated, without the ability to recall the experience. In 1999, ketamine became classified as a Schedule III controlled substance.[51]

Salvia divinorum

The Mexican herb **Salvia divinorum** (commonly referred to as salvia) has a long tradition as a shamanic treatment for diarrhea, headache, rheumatism, and abdominal discomfort. When smoked, chewed, or brewed as a tea, salvia produces intense visual hallucinations (resembling the effect of psilocybin-containing mushrooms), laughter, and an "out of body," dissociative experience. Its potency approaches that of LSD, but the effects are very short-lived. In one recent study of salvia users, 85 percent reported salvia effects lasting less than fifteen minutes.

Considerable media attention has been directed toward recreational use of salvia. At present, it has not been classified as a controlled substance under the federal Controlled Substances Act. The DEA is currently pursuing the possibility of classification as a Schedule I drug, but until that occurs, salvia remains legally available through numerous Internet web sites. In a growing number of U.S. states and of countries around the world, salvia has been officially classified as an illicit drug, along with other hallucinogens.

According to the 2011 University of Michigan survey, 6 percent of high school seniors reported using salvia in the past year. In a smaller sample of college students reporting in 2006, 23 percent of students had heard of salvia. About 7 percent had used it at some time in their lives, but the prevalence rate plummeted to less than 1 percent when respondents were asked whether they had used it in the last month. The "snapshots" that surveys of this kind reveal are twofold. First, it is virtually certain that extensive media attention has dramatically increased the level of awareness about salvia and its legal availability through Internet sources, so that most adolescents and young adults have heard about it. Second, it is likely that salvia may be attractive to those experimenting with a hallucinogen but not particularly attractive to chronic drug users. The particularly intense and unpredictable character of the salvia experience, as well as its very short duration, will be unpleasant to many. A majority of the first-time salvia users in the college sample said that they would not want to use it again.[52]

Salvia divinorum (SAL-via di-vi-NOR-um) or Salvia: A Mexican leafy herb with short-duration hallucinogenic effects.

Summary

A Matter of Definition

- Hallucinogens are, by definition, drugs that produce distortions of perception and of one's sense of reality. These drugs have also been called psychedelic ("mind-expanding") drugs. In some cases, users of hallucinogens feel that they have been transported to a new reality.

- Other classes of drugs may produce hallucinations at high dose levels, but hallucinogens produce these effects at low or moderate dose levels.

Classifying Hallucinogens

- Hallucinogens can be classified into four basic groups. The first three relate to the chemical similarity between the particular drug and one of three major neurotransmitters: serotonin, norepinephrine, or acetylcholine.

- The fourth, miscellaneous group includes synthetic hallucinogens, such as PCP and ketamine, which bear little resemblance to any known neurotransmitter.

Lysergic Acid Diethylamide (LSD)

- LSD the best-known hallucinogenic drug, belongs to the serotonin group. It is synthetically derived from ergot, a toxic rye fungus that has been documented as being responsible for thousands of deaths over the centuries.
- Albert Hofmann synthesized LSD in 1943, and Timothy Leary led the psychedelic movement that popularized LSD use in the 1960s.
- Although the LSD experience is often unpredictable, certain features are commonly observed: colorful hallucinations, synesthesia in which sounds often appear as visions, a distortion of perceptual reality, emotional swings, a feeling of timelessness, and an illusory separation of mind from body.
- It is now known that LSD effects are due to the stimulation of a subtype of brain receptors sensitive to serotonin, referred to as serotonin-2A receptors.
- In the early 1990s, there was a resurgence in LSD abuse, particularly among young individuals, a trend that began to reverse in 1997.

Facts and Fiction about LSD

- LSD does not produce psychological or physical dependence and has only a slight chance of inducing a panic or psychotic state (provided that there is a supportive setting for the taking of LSD).
- LSD does not elevate one's level of creativity. It does not damage chromosomes (though there remains a chance of birth defects if a woman ingests LSD when she is pregnant), and a relationship between LSD abuse and violent behavior has not been established. Flashback experiences, however, are potential hazards.

Psilocybin and Other Hallucinogens Related to Serotonin

- Other hallucinogens related to serotonin are psilocybin, LAA, DMT, and harmine.

Hallucinogens Related to Norepinephrine

- Mescaline is chemically related to norepinephrine, even though serotonin-2A receptors are responsible for its hallucinogenic effects.
- Two synthetic hallucinogens, DOM and MDMA, are variations of the amphetamine molecule. MDMA (Ecstasy) is currently a popular club drug, but research studies indicate that it poses serious health risks to the user.

Hallucinogens Related to Acetylcholine

- A number of anticholinergic hallucinogens, so named because they diminish the effects of acetylcholine in the parasympathetic nervous system, have been involved in sorcery and witchcraft since the Middle Ages.
- These so-called hexing drugs contain a combination of atropine, scopolamine, and/or hyoscyamine. Sources for such drugs include the deadly nightshade plant, mandrake roots, henbane seeds, and the datura plant family.

Miscellaneous Hallucinogens: Phencyclidine (PCP), Ketamine, and *Salvia divinorum*

- A dangerous form of hallucinogen abuse involves PCP. Originally a psychedelic street drug in the 1960s, PCP quickly developed a reputation for producing a number of adverse reactions.
- PCP reappeared in the early 1970s in smokable forms, either alone or in combination with marijuana. Extremely aggressive tendencies, as well as behaviors resembling acute schizophrenia, have been associated with PCP intoxication.
- Ketamine is popular as a club drug that produces a dream-like intoxication, accompanied by an inability to move or feel pain. Like PCP, ketamine produces amnesia and a potentially hazardous depression in breathing.
- *Salvia divinorum* (or simply Salvia) is a Mexican leafy herb with short-duration hallucinogenic effects when smoked, chewed, or brewed as a tea. It is regarded by the DEA as a "drug of concern," considering its growing popularity as a recreational drug, although it is not presently classified as a Schedule I drug under the Controlled Substances Act.

Key Terms

Endnotes

1. Hofmann, A. (1980). *LSD: My problem child.* New York: McGraw-Hill, p. 17.
2. Ibid., pp. 17–18.
3. Ibid., p. 19.
4. Brophy, J. J. (1985). Psychiatric disorders. In M. A. Krupp, M. J. Chatton, and D. Werdegar (Eds.), *Current medical diagnosis and treatment.* Los Altos, CA: Lange Medical Publications, p. 674.
5. Mann, J. (1992). *Murder, magic, and medicine.* New York: Oxford University Press, pp. 41–51.
6. Fuller, J. G. (1968). *The day of St. Anthony's fire.* New York: Macmillan, preface.
7. Leary, T. (1973). The religious experience: Its production and interpretation. In G. Weil, R. Metzner, and T. Leary (Eds.), *The psychedelic reader.* Secaucus, NJ: Citadel Press, p. 191.
8. Lattin, D. (2010). *The Harvard psychedelic club.* New York: HarperCollins. Lee, M. A., and Shlain, B. (1985). *Acid dreams: The complete social history of LSD.* New York: Grove Weidenfeld, pp. 71–118.
9. Greenfield, R. (2006). *Timothy Leary: A biography.* New York: J. H. Silberman Books/Harcourt. Leary, T. (1968). *High priest.* New York: New American Library, p. 46. Manchester, W. R. (1974). *The glory and the dream: A narrative history of America, 1932–1972.* Boston: Little, Brown, p. 1362.
10. Grinspoon, L., and Bakalar, J. B. (1979). *Psychedelic drugs reconsidered.* New York: Basic Books, p. 68.
11. Brown, F. C. (1972). *Hallucinogenic drugs.* Springfield, IL: C.C. Thomas, pp. 46–49. Goode, E. (2008). *Drugs and American society* (7th ed.). New York: McGraw-Hill, p. 260.
12. Schuckit, M. A. (2006). *Drug and alcohol abuse: A clinical guide to diagnosis and treatment* (6th ed.). New York: Springer, pp. 211–214.
13. Jacobs, M. R., and Fehr, K. O' B. (1987). *Drugs and drug abuse: A reference text* (2nd ed.). Toronto: Addiction Research Foundation, p. 345. Substance Abuse and Mental Health Services Administration (2013). Drug Abuse Warning Network, National estimates of drug-related emergency department visits 2004–2011. Rockville, MD: Substance Abuse and Mental Health Services Administration, Excel files.
14. Brophy, Psychiatric disorders. Jacobs and Fehr, *Drugs and drug abuse,* pp. 337–347.
15. First, third, fourth, and fifth quotations from Goode, *Drugs and American society,* pp. 261–263. Second, sixth, seventh, and eighth quotations from Snyder, S. H. (1986). *Drugs and the brain.* New York: Freeman, pp. 180–181.
16. Aghajanian, G. K., and Marek, G. J. (1999). Serotonin and hallucinogens. *Neuropsychopharmacology, 21 (Suppl. 2),* 16S–23S. Gresch, P. J.; Smith, R. L.; Barrett, R. J.; and Sanders-Bush, E. (2005). Behavioral tolerance to lysergic acid diethylamide is associated with reduced serotonin-2A receptor signaling in rat cortex. *Neuropsychopharmacology, 30,* 1693–1702. Julien, R. M. (2005). *A primer of drug action* (10th ed.). New York: Worth, p. 602.
17. Goode, *Drugs and American society,* p. 259.
18. Brands, B.; Sproule, B.; and Marshman, J. (1998). *Drugs and drug abuse: A reference text.* Toronto, Canada: Addiction Research Foundation, p. 328. Henderson, L. A., and Glass, W. J. (Eds.) (1994). *LSD: Still with us after all these years.* New York: Lexington Books. Johnston, L. D.; O'Malley, P. M.; Bachman, J. G.; and Schulenberg, J. E. (2012). Monitoring the Future: National survey results on drug use, 1975–2011. Vol. I: Secondary school students 2011. Ann Arbor, MI: Institute for Social Research, The University of Michigan, Table 2-1.
19. Goode, *Drugs and American society,* pp. 265–266.
20. Ibid., p. 266.
21. Cohen, S. (1960). Lysergic acid diethylamide: Side effects and complications. *Journal of Nervous and Mental Diseases, 130,* 30–40. Levine, J., and Ludwig, A. M. (1964). The LSD controversy. *Comprehensive Psychiatry, 5 (5),* 314–321.
22. Wells, B. (1974). *Psychedelic drugs: Psychological, medical, and social issues.* New York: Jason Aronson, pp. 170–188.
23. Cohen, M. M., and Marmillo, M. J. (1967). Chromosomal damage in human leukocytes induced by lysergic acid diethylamide. *Science, 155,* 1417–1419.
24. Dishotsky, N. I.; Loughman, W. D.; Mogar, R. E.; and Lipscomb, W. R. (1971). LSD and genetic damage. *Science, 172,* 431–440. Grinspoon and Bakalar, *Psychedelic drugs reconsidered,* pp. 188–191.
25. Brown, *Hallucinogenic drugs,* pp. 61–64. Wells, *Psychedelic drugs,* pp. 104–109.
26. Abraham, H. D. (1983). Visual phenomenology of the LSD flashback. *Archives of General Psychiatry, 40,*

884–889. Schlaadt, R. G., and Shannon, P. T. (1994). *Drugs: Use, misuse, and abuse*. Englewood Cliffs, NJ: Prentice-Hall, p. 273.

27. Halpern, J. H., and Pope, H. G. (1999). Do hallucinogens cause residual neuropsychological toxicity? *Drugs and Alcohol Dependence*, 53, 247–256.

28. Knudsen, K. (1964). Homicide after treatment with lysergic acid diethylamide. *Acta Psychiatrica Scandinavica*, 40 (*Suppl. 180*), 389–395.

29. Metzner, R. (1998). Hallucinogenic drugs and plants in psychotherapy and shamanism. *Journal of Psychoactive Drugs*, 30, 333–341.

30. Hofmann, *LSD*, p. 112.

31. Brown, *Hallucinogenic drugs*, pp. 81–88.

32. Johnston, O'Malley, Bachman, and Schulenberg, *Monitoring the Future*, Table 9-8., Vollenweider, Franz X.; Vollenweider-Scherpenhuyzen, M. F. I.; Babler, A.; Vogel, H.; and Hell, D. (1998). Psilocybin induces schizophrenia-like psychosis in humans via a serotonin-2 agonist action. *Neuroreport*, 9, 3897–3902.

33. Hofmann, *LSD*, pp. 119–127. Schultes, Richard E., and Hofmann, A. (1979). *Plants of the gods: Origins of hallucinogenic use*. New York: McGraw-Hill, pp. 158–163.

34. Brands, Sproule, and Marshman, *Drugs and drug abuse*, pp. 512–513.

35. Frecska, E.; White, K. D.; and Luna, L. E. (2003). Effects of Amazonian psychoactive beverage *ayuhuasca* on binocular rivalry: Interhemispheric switching or interhemispheric fusion? *Journal of Psychoactive Drugs*, 35, 367–374. Grinspoon and Bakalar, *Psychedelic drugs reconsidered*, pp. 14–15. Trichter, S.; Klimo, J.; and Krippner, S. (2009). Changes in spirituality among ayahuasca ceremony novice participants. *Journal of Psychoactive Drugs*, 41, 121–134.

36. Ibid., pp. 20–21. Hollister, L. E., and Sjoberg, B. M. (1964). Clinical syndromes and biochemical alterations following mescaline, lysergic acid diethylamide, psilocybin, and a combination of the three psychotomimetic drugs. *Comprehensive Psychiatry*, 5, 170–178.

37. Jacobs, B. L. (1987). How hallucinogenic drugs work. *American Scientist*, 75, 386–392.

38. Brecher, Edward, and the editors of *Consumer Reports* (1972). *Licit and illicit drugs*. Boston: Little, Brown, pp. 376–377.

39. Carey, B. (2012, November 20). A "party drug" may help the brain cope with trauma. *New York Times*, pp. D1, D6. Metzner, Hallucinogenic drugs and plants. Schmidt, C. J. (1987). Psychedelic amphetamine, methylendioxymethamphetamine. *Journal of Pharmacology and Experimental Therapeutics*, 240, 1–7.

40. Boils, K. I. (1999). Memory impairment in abstinent MDMA ("Ecstasy") users. *Journal of the American Medical Association*, 281, 494. Leshner, A. I. (2002). Ecstasy abuse and control: Hearing before the Senate Subcommittee on Governmental Affairs—July 30, 2001. Statement for the record. *Journal of Psychoactive Drugs*, 34, 133–135. Vollenweider, F. X.; Liechti, M. E.; Gamma, A.; Greer, G.; and Geyer, M. (2002). Acute psychological and neurophysiological effects of MDMA in humans.

Journal of Psychoactive Drugs, 34, 171–184. Wiegand, T.; Thai, D.; and Benowitz, N. (2008). Medical consequences of the use of hallucinogens: LSD, mescaline, PCP, and MDMA ("Ecstasy"). In J. Brick (Ed.), *Handbook of medical consequences of alcohol and drug use* (2nd ed.). New York: Routledge, pp. 473-490.

41. Cloud, J. (2000, June 5). The lure of Ecstasy. *Time*, pp. 62–68. Feuer, A. (2000, August 6). Distilling the truth in the Ecstasy buzz. *New York Times*, pp. 25, 28. Johnston, O'Malley, Bachman, and Schulenberg, *Monitoring the Future*, Table 2-1. Martins, Silvia, S.; Mazzotti, G.; and Chilcoat, H. D. (2005). Trends in Ecstasy use in the United States from 1995 to 2001: Comparison with marijuana users and association with other drug use. *Experimental and Clinical Psychopharmacology*, 13, 244–252.

42. Wasson, R. G. (1968). *Soma: Divine mushroom of immortality*. New York: Harcourt, Brace and World.

43. Cohen, S. (1964). *The beyond within: The LSD story*. New York: Atheneum, p. 17.

44. Ramachandran, V. S., and Hubbard, E. M. (2003, May). Hearing colors, tasting shapes. *Scientific American*, pp. 52–59.

45. Clark, Jason D. (2005). The roadside high: Jimson weed toxicity. *Air Medical Journal*, 24, 234–237. Schultes and Hofmann, *Plants of the gods*, pp. 35, 106–111.

46. Mann, J. (1992). *Murder, magic, and medicine*. New York: Oxford University Press, pp. 79–82. Schultes and Hofmann, *Plants of the gods*, pp. 86–91.

47. James, J., and Andresen, E. (1979). Sea-Tac and PCP. In H. V. Feldman, M. H. Agar, and G. M. Beschner (Eds.), *Angel dust: An ethnographic study of PCP users*. Lexington, MA: Lexington Books, p. 133.

48. Grinspoon and Bakalar, *Psychedelic drugs reconsidered*, pp. 32–33. Petersen, R. C., and Stillman, R. C. (1978). Phencyclidine: An overview. In R. C. Petersen and R. C. Stillman (Eds.), *Phencyclidine (PCP) abuse: An appraisal* (NIDA Research Monograph 21). Rockville, MD: National Institute on Drug Abuse, pp. 1–17. Robbins, *Hallucinogens*, pp. 12–14. Seeman, P.; Ko, F.; and Tallerico, T. (2005). Dopamine receptor contribution to the action of PCP, LSD and ketamine psychotomimetics. *Molecular Psychiatry*, 10, 877–883.

49. Trends in PCP-related emergency department visits (2004, January). *The DAWN Report*, pp. 1–4.

50. Brands, Sproule, and Marshman, *Drugs and drug abuse*, pp. 523–525.

51. Ibid. Feds classify ketamine as controlled substance (1999, August 2). *Alcoholism and Drug Abuse Weekly*, p. 7.

52. Braiker, B. (2008, May 19). Old herb, new controversy. *Newsweek*, pp. 40–41. González, D.; Riba, J.; Bouso, J. C.; Gómez-Jarabo, G.; et al. (2006). Pattern of use and subjective effects of *Salvia divinorum* among recreational users. *Drug and Alcohol Dependence*, 85, 157–162. Johnston, O'Malley, Bachman, and Schulenberg, *Monitoring the Future*, Table 2-2. Julien, *A primer of drug action*, p. 619. Khey, D.N.; Miller, B.L.; and Griffin, O.H. (2008). *Salvia divinorum* use among a college student sample. *Journal of Drug Education*, 38, 297–306.

Marijuana

The sprawled body of a young girl lay crushed on the sidewalk the other day after a plunge from the fifth story of a Chicago apartment house. Everyone called it suicide, but actually it was murder. The killer was a narcotic known to America as marijuana, and to history as hashish. It is a narcotic used in the form of cigarettes, comparatively new to the United States and as dangerous as a coiled rattlesnake. . . .

How many murders, suicides, robberies, criminal assaults, holdups, burglaries, and deeds of maniacal insanity it causes each year, especially among the young, can be only conjectured. . . .

That youth has been selected by the peddlers of this poison as an especially fertile filed makes it a problem of serious concern to every man and woman in America.

—Harry J. Anslinger, Commissioner, Federal Bureau of Narcotics, in the opening of an article in the widely-read periodical, The American Magazine, *published in July 1937.*[1]

It is fair to say that few other drugs have been so politicized in the history of the twentieth century. Marijuana has been frequently praised by one side, or (judging from the Anslinger quotation) demonized by the other, on the basis of emotionally charged issues rather than an objective view of research data, and sometimes with little regard for the facts. The pro-marijuana faction has tended to dismiss or downplay reports of potential dangers and to emphasize the benefits; the anti-marijuana faction has tended to do the opposite, arguing that marijuana should continue to be classified by the U.S. federal government as a Schedule I controlled substance, along with heroin and LSD. It is the drug that everyone brings up when debating the successes or failures of the decades-long war on drugs. Marijuana has often been regarded, in cultural terms, as a reflection of an individual's attitude toward the establishment. This makes it even more critical that we look at the effects of marijuana as dispassionately as possible.

Think of *Cannabis sativa*, known to the general public as the marijuana plant, as a scrawny weed with an attitude. Whether it is hot or cold, wet or dry, cannabis will grow abundantly from seeds that are unbelievably hardy and prolific. Under ordinary circumstances, it needs little or no cultivation. A handful of cannabis seeds, tossed on the ground and pressed in with one's foot, will usually anchor and become plants. Its roots devour whatever nutrients there are in the soil, as historian Ernest Abel has expressed it, "like a vampire sucking the life blood from the earth."[2]

by the numbers . . .

107,842,000	Estimated number of Americans who reported in 2011 that they had smoked marijuana sometime in their lifetime.
18,071,000	Estimated number of Americans who reported in 2011 that they had smoked marijuana in the previous month.
18	Number of U.S. states in 2012 that have authorized marijuana smoking for the relief of pain and discomfort or for the control of nausea and weight loss, when prescribed by a physician.

Source: Substance Abuse and Mental Health Services Administration (2012). *Results from the 2011 National Survey on Drug Use and Health. Detailed tables.* Rockville, MD: Substance Abuse and Mental Health Services Administration, Table 1.1A.

Indeed, marijuana has managed to grow in some unorthodox places. It can be found growing wild in median strips of interstate highways and in ditches alongside country roads, much to the chagrin of local authorities. Its legendary hardiness has spawned urban myths over the years. One of them is the existence of the so-called Manhattan Silver strain, supposedly growing to this day in underground New York sewers, after having been hastily flushed down a toilet during a police raid in the 1960s.[3]

The pharmacological effects of marijuana show something of an independent nature as well. When we consider a category for marijuana, we are faced with an odd assortment of unconnected properties, making it difficult to place marijuana within a traditional classification of psychoactive drugs. Marijuana produces some excitatory effects, but it is not generally regarded as a stimulant. It produces some sedative effects, but a user faces no risk of slipping into a coma or dying. It produces mild analgesic effects, but it is not related chemically to opioid drugs. It produces hallucinations at high doses, but its structure does not resemble that of LSD or any other drug formally categorized as a hallucinogen (see Chapter 6). Marijuana is clearly a drug in a league of its own.

A Matter of Terminology

Although *marijuana* (sometimes spelled *marihuana*) is commonly referred to as a synonym for "cannabis," the two terms need to be differentiated. Cannabis is the shortened botanical term for the hemp plant **Cannabis sativa**. With a potential height of about eighteen feet, cannabis has sturdy stalks, four-cornered in cross-section, that have been commercially valuable for thousands of years in the manufacture of rope, twine, shoes, sailcloth, and containers of all kinds. Pots made of hemp fiber discovered at archaeological sites in China date the origins of cannabis cultivation as far back as the Stone Age. It is arguably the oldest cultivated plant not used for food.[4]

Spaniards brought cannabis to the New World in 1545, and English settlers brought it to Jamestown, Virginia, in 1611, where it became a major commercial crop, along with tobacco. Like other eighteenth-century farmers in the region, George Washington grew cannabis in the fields of his estate at Mount

Cannabis sativa (CAN-uh-bus sah-TEE-vah): A plant species, commonly called hemp, from which marijuana and hashish are obtained.

Vernon. Entries in his diary indicate that he maintained a keen interest in the improvement of strains of cannabis, but there is no reason to believe he was interested in anything more than producing a better-quality rope.

Marijuana, however, is obtained not from the stalks of the cannabis plant but from its serrated leaves. The key psychoactive factor is contained in a sticky substance, or resin, that accumulates on these leaves. Depending on the growing conditions, cannabis will produce either a greater amount of fiber or a greater amount of resin. In a cool, humid climate, such as North America, less resin is produced, but the fiber is stronger and more durable. In a warmer, less humid climate—such as North Africa—the fiber content is weak, but so much resin is produced that the plant looks as if it is covered with dew. Therefore, depending on environmental factors, you are getting a stronger rope or a stronger high.[5]

As many as eighty separate chemical compounds, called **cannabinoids**, have been identified from cannabis resin. Among these, the chief psychoactive compound and the active ingredient that produces the intoxicating effects is **delta-9-tetrahydrocannabinol (THC)**. The isolation and identification of THC in 1964 was a major step toward understanding the effects on the brain of marijuana and similar preparations obtained from *Cannabis sativa*.

Knowing these facts, we can categorize various forms of cannabis products in terms of their origin within the cannabis plant and resulting THC concentration. The first and best known of these products, **marijuana**, consists of leaves and occasionally flowers of the cannabis plant that are first dried and then shredded. During the 1960s and 1970s, the typical THC concentration of street marijuana imported from Mexico was about 1 to 2 percent. Since the early 1990s, however, THC concentrations have steadily risen to about 10 percent, primarily because of advanced outdoor and indoor cultivation methods. Marijuana, smoked as a cigarette, is the form of cannabis most familiar to North Americans.

A more potent form of marijuana is obtained by cultivating only the unpollinated, or seedless, portion of the cannabis plant. Without pollination, the cannabis plant grows bushier, the resin content is increased, and a greater THC concentration, up to 15 percent, is achieved. This form is called **sinsemilla**, from the Spanish meaning "without seed."

Another cannabis product, **hashish**, is achieved when the resin itself is scraped from cannabis leaves and then dried. Either smoked by itself or in combination

A Mexican harvester gathers his crop of *Cannabis sativa*, later to be processed into marijuana or hashish.

with tobacco, hashish can have a THC concentration as high as 24 percent. The most potent forms of cannabis are **hashish oil** and **hashish oil crystals**, produced by boiling hashish in alcohol or some other solvent and filtering out the alcohol, which leaves a residue with a THC concentration ranging from 15 to 60 percent.[6]

cannabinoids (can-NAB-ih-noids): Any of several dozen active substances in marijuana and other cannabis products.

delta-9-tetrahydrocannabinol (THC) (DEL-tah-9-TEH-trah-HIGH-dro-CAN-a-bih-nol): The active psychoactive ingredient in marijuana and hashish.

marijuana: The most commonly available psychoactive drug originating from the cannabis plant. The THC concentration ranges from approximately 1 to 6 percent. Also spelled marihuana.

sinsemilla (SIN-sih-MEE-yah): A form of marijuana obtained from the unpollinated or seedless portion of the cannabis plant. It has a higher THC concentration than regular marijuana, as high as 15 percent.

hashish (hah-SHEESH): A drug containing the resin of cannabis flowers. The THC concentration ranges from approximately 8 to 14 percent.

hashish oil: A drug produced by boiling hashish, leaving a potent psychoactive residue. The THC concentration ranges from approximately 15 to 60 percent.

hashish oil crystals: A solid form of hashish oil.

The History of Marijuana and Hashish

The first direct reference to a cannabis product as a psychoactive agent dates from 2737 B.C. in the writings of the mythical Chinese emperor Shen Nung. The focus was on its powers as a medication for rheumatism, gout, malaria, and (strangely enough) absent-mindedness. Mention was made of its intoxicating properties, but the medicinal possibilities evidently were considered more important. In India, however, its use was clearly recreational. The most popular form, in ancient times as well as in the present day, can be found in a syrupy liquid made from cannabis leaves called **bhang**, with a THC potency usually equal to that of a marijuana joint in the United States.[7]

The Muslim world also grew to appreciate the psychoactive potential of cannabis, encouraged by the fact that, in contrast to its stern prohibition of alcohol consumption, the Koran did not specifically ban its use. It was here, in a hot, dry climate conducive to maximizing the resin content of cannabis, that hashish was born, and its popularity spread quickly during the twelfth century from Persia (Iran) in the east to North Africa in the west.

Hashish in the Nineteenth Century

In Western Europe, knowledge about hashish or any other cannabis product was limited until the beginning of the nineteenth century. Judging from the decree issued by Pope Innocent VIII in 1484 condemning witchcraft and the use of hemp in the Black Mass, we can assume that the psychoactive properties of cannabis were known by at least some portions of the population. Nonetheless, there is no evidence of widespread use.

By about 1800, however, cannabis had become more widely known and was the subject of a popular craze. One reason was that French soldiers who had served in Napoleon's military campaigns in Egypt brought hashish back with them to their homes in France. Another reason was a wave of romanticism that swept Europe, including an increased interest in exotic stories of the East, notably the *Arabian Nights* and the tales of Marco Polo, which contained references to hashish.

In Paris during the 1840s, a small group of prominent French artists, writers, and intellectuals formed the Club des Hachichins ("Club of the Hashish-Eaters"),

bhang: A liquid form of marijuana popular in India.

A merchant sits outside his bhang shop in North India. *Bhang ki thandai* is a popular cold drink prepared with bhang combined with almonds, spices, milk, and sugar. *Bhang lassi,* a mixture of bhang and iced yogurt, is another popular drink. It is traditional for many Hindus to drink bhang during religious festivals, particularly in Bengal during the Kali Puja (Festival of Kali, the Mother Goddess).

where they would gather, in the words of their leader, "to talk of literature, art, and love" while consuming hashish. The recipe consisted of a concentrated cannabis paste mixed with butter, sweeteners, and flavorings such as vanilla and cinnamon. Members included Victor Hugo, Alexandre Dumas, Charles Baudelaire, Eugéne Delacroix, and Honoré de Balzac.

Marijuana and Hashish in the Twentieth Century

Chances are that anyone living in the United States at the beginning of the twentieth century would not have heard of marijuana, much less hashish. By 1890, cotton had replaced hemp as a major cash crop in southern states, although cannabis plants continued to grow wild along roadsides and in the fields. Some patent medicines during this era contained marijuana, but it was a small percentage compared with the number containing opium or cocaine (see Chapter 1).[8]

It was not until the 1920s that marijuana smoking began to be a social phenomenon. Some historians have related the appearance of marijuana as a recreational drug to societal changes brought on by Prohibition (see Chapter 8), when it was suddenly difficult to obtain good-quality liquor at affordable prices. Recreational use was taken up primarily by jazz musicians and people in show business. "Reefer songs" became the rage of the jazz world; even the mainstream clarinetist and bandleader Benny Goodman had his popular hit "Sweet Marihuana Brown." Marijuana clubs, called *tea pads*, sprang up in the major cities; more than five hundred were estimated to have opened in Harlem alone, outnumbering the speakeasies where illegal alcohol was dispensed. These marijuana establishments were largely tolerated by the authorities because at that time marijuana was not illegal and patrons showed no evidence of making a nuisance of themselves or disturbing the community. In the culture of the time, marijuana was not considered a threat at all.[9]

The Anti-Marijuana Crusade

The picture started to change by the end of the 1920s and early 1930s. Even though millions of people had never heard of the marijuana, much less smoked it, the drug suddenly became widely known as a "killer weed." An intense anti-marijuana media campaign in print and in the movies (see Chapter 2), orchestrated by the Federal Bureau of Narcotics (FBN), had succeeded in convincing the American public that marijuana was a pestilence singlehandedly destroying a generation of American youth. These efforts, however, could not have been as successful as they were without a significant demographic change occurring in American society at the time. The practice of smoking marijuana and the cultivation of cannabis plants for that purpose had been filtering slowly into the United States since 1900 as a result of the migration of Mexican immigrants. They entered the country through towns along the Mexican border and along the Gulf Coast. In Mexican communities, marijuana was a casual part of Mexican life, a mild euphoriant, and often a folk remedy for headaches.

Once in the United States, however, these immigrant communities were met with considerable hostility, and the smoking of an alien and foreign-sounding substance did not smooth their reception, particularly as their numbers increased. In effect, it would be a social rerun of the Chinese-opium panic of the 1870s (see Chapter 5)

This advertising poster for the 1942 film *Devil's Harvest* depicted the supposed evils of smoking marijuana.

but with the Mexicans on the receiving end. Unsubstantiated rumors about the violent behavioral consequences of marijuana smoking among Mexicans began to spread. In addition, social and economic upheavals during the Depression made it particularly convenient to vent frustrations on an immigrant group perceived as competing for a dwindling number of American jobs and straining an already weak economy. Anti-marijuana-themed movies with provocative titles such as *Reefer Madness* and *Marihuana: Weed with Roots in Hell* were produced and distributed during the late 1930s and early 1940s with the encouragement of the FBN.

Considering the mounting hysteria against marijuana smoking and cannabis use in general during this period, it is not surprising that the Marijuana Tax Act of 1937 had little difficulty gaining support in Congress. As with the Harrison Act of 1914, the regulation of marijuana was accomplished indirectly. The act did not ban marijuana; it merely required everyone connected with marijuana, from growers to buyers, to pay a tax. It was a deceptively simple procedure that, in effect, made it virtually impossible to comply with the law. In the absence of compliance, a person was in violation of the act and therefore subject to arrest. It was the state's responsibility to make possession of marijuana or any other product of *Cannabis sativa* illegal. Shortly after the tax act of 1937 was imposed, all of the states adopted a uniform law that did just that.

The official stance of the federal government continued to be that marijuana smoking was tied to antisocial behavior. Harry Anslinger, FBN director, wrote in 1953:

> Those who are accustomed to habitual use of the drug are said eventually to develop a delirious rage after its administration during which they are temporarily, at least, irresponsible and prone to commit violent crimes. . . . Much of the most irrational juvenile violence and killing that has written a new chapter of shame and tragedy is traceable directly to this hemp intoxication.[10]

Over time, the "pharmacological violence" theory (see Chapter 2) would fade into oblivion, in the absence of any evidence to support it. In its place, a new conceptualization of marijuana smoking would be introduced by the FBN: the gateway theory. According to this idea, marijuana was dangerous because its abuse would lead to the abuse of heroin, cocaine, or other illicit drugs. This gateway hypothesis will be closely examined later in the chapter.

The severity of criminal penalties for involvement with marijuana steadily increased. State judges frequently had the option of sentencing a marijuana seller or user to life imprisonment. In Georgia, a second offense of selling marijuana to a minor could be punishable by death.

Ironically, in 1969, more than three decades after its passage, the U.S. Supreme Court ruled the 1937 Marijuana Tax Act unconstitutional *precisely because marijuana possession was illegal*. The argument was made that requiring a person to pay a tax (and that was all that the 1937 act concerned) in order to possess an illegal substance amounted to a form of self-incrimination, which would violate that person's rights under the Fifth Amendment to the Constitution. The case in question here was brought to the high court by none other than Timothy Leary (see the Portrait in Chapter 6), and the court's decision succeeded in overturning a marijuana conviction judged against him.[11]

---

reefer: A marijuana cigarette.

joint: A marijuana cigarette.

Challenging Old Ideas about Marijuana

Prior to 1960, arrests and seizures for possession of marijuana were relatively rare and attracted little or no public attention. The social consensus was that marijuana was a drug that could be comfortably associated with, and isolated to, ethnic and racial minorities. It was relatively easy for most Americans to avoid the drug entirely. In any event, involvement with marijuana during the 1950s was a deviant act, in an era when there was little tolerance for personal deviance.

By the mid-1960s, this consensus began to dissolve. Marijuana smoking suddenly was an attraction on the campuses of U.S. colleges and universities, affecting a wide cross section of the nation. Strangely enough, the bizarre effects depicted in the anti-marijuana movies failed to occur! At the same time, the experimental use of drugs, particularly marijuana, by young people set the stage for a wholesale questioning of what it meant to respect authority, on an individual as well as a governmental level. We will turn to the more recent issues of medical marijuana and marijuana decriminalization later in the chapter.

Acute Effects of Marijuana

In the United States, THC is usually ingested by smoking a hand-rolled marijuana cigarette referred to as a **reefer**, or, more commonly, a **joint**. Exactly how much THC is administered depends on the specific THC concentration level in the marijuana (often referred to as its quality), how deeply the smoke is inhaled into the lungs, and how long it is held in the lungs before being exhaled. In general, an experienced smoker will consume more THC than a novice smoker by virtue of being able to inhale more deeply and hold the marijuana smoke in his or her lungs longer, for twenty-five seconds or more, thus maximizing THC absorption into the bloodstream.

The inhalation of any drug into the lungs produces extremely rapid absorption, as noted in earlier chapters, and marijuana is no exception. In the case of THC, effects are felt within seconds. Peak levels are reached in the blood within ten minutes and start to decline shortly afterward. Behavioral and psychological effects generally last from two to three hours. At this point, low levels of THC linger for several days because they are absorbed into fatty tissue, and excretion from fatty tissue is notoriously slow.[12]

One implication arising from a slow elimination rate is that the residual THC, left over from a previous administration, can intensify the effect of marijuana on a subsequent occasion. In this way, regular marijuana smokers often report a quicker and more easily obtained high, achieved with a smaller quantity of drug, than more intermittent smokers.[13]

It is also important to see the implication of slow marijuana elimination with regard to drug testing. Urine tests for possible marijuana abuse typically measure levels of THC metabolites (broken-down remnants of THC); because of the slow biotransformation of marijuana, these metabolites are detectable in the urine even when the smoker no longer feels high or shows any behavioral effects. Metabolites can remain in the body for several days after the smoking of a single joint and for several weeks later if there has been chronic marijuana smoking. Some tests are so sensitive that a positive level for marijuana can result from passive inhalation of marijuana smoke–filled air in a closed environment, even though the THC levels in these cases are substantially below levels that result from active smoking. The bottom line is that marijuana testing procedures generally are unable to indicate *when* marijuana has been smoked (if it has been smoked at all), only that exposure to marijuana has occurred (see Chapter 12).[14]

Acute Physiological Effects

Immediate physiological effects after smoking marijuana are relatively minor. It has been estimated that a human would need to ingest a dose of marijuana that was from twenty thousand to forty thousand times the effective dose before death would occur.[15] Nonetheless, there is a dose-related increase in heart rate during early stages of marijuana ingestion, up to 160 beats per minute when dose levels are high. Blood pressure either increases, remains the same, or decreases, depending primarily on whether the individual is standing, sitting, or lying down.[16] A dilation of blood vessels on the cornea resulting in bloodshot eyes peaks about an hour after smoking a joint. Frequently there is a drying of the mouth and an urge to drink.

Other physiological reactions are inconsistent, and at least part of the inconsistency can be attributed to cultural and interpersonal influences. For example, the observation that marijuana smoking makes you feel extremely hungry and crave especially sweet things to eat (often referred to as "having the munchies") generally holds true in studies of North Americans but not

for Jamaicans, who consider marijuana an appetite suppressant.

Likewise, North Americans often report enhanced sexual responses following marijuana use, whereas in India marijuana is considered a sexual depressant. These reactions, being subjective in nature, can very well be influenced in one direction or the other by the mind-set (expectations) of the marijuana smoker going into the experience. A good example is the effect on sexual responses. If you believe that marijuana turns you on sexually, the chances are that it will.

Although expectations undoubtedly play a prominent role here, we should be aware of the possibility that varying effects also may be due to differences in the THC concentration of the marijuana being smoked. In the case of sexual reactivity, studies of male marijuana smokers have shown that low-dose marijuana tends to enhance sexual desire, whereas high-dose marijuana tends to depress it, even to the point of impotence. It is quite possible that the enhancement results from a brief rise in the male sex hormone testosterone and that the depression results from a rebound effect that lowers testosterone below normal levels. Typically, the THC concentration in India is higher than that in North America. As a result, we would expect different effects on sexual reactivity. The same argument could be made with respect to the differences in marijuana's effect on appetite.[17]

In 2011, approximately 456,000 drug-related emergency department (ED) visits in the DAWN statistics (see Chapter 2) involved marijuana, making it the second highest category, behind cocaine. In one fourth of these cases, marijuana was the only drug present in the patient's system at the time. Marijuana-related emergency department incidents had increased by about 21 percent from 2009 and about 62 percent from 2004, most likely due to the higher THC concentrations in marijuana and greater numbers of marijuana smokers.[18]

Acute Psychological and Behavioral Effects

In Chapter 5, it was noted that a first-time heroin abuser frequently finds the experience more aversive than pleasurable. With marijuana, it is common for a first-time smoker to feel no discernible effects at all. It takes some practice to be able to inhale deeply and keep the smoke in the lungs long enough (up to forty seconds) for a minimal level of THC to take effect, particularly when smoking low-quality marijuana. Novices often have to be "instructed" to focus on some aspect of the intoxicated state to start to feel intoxicated, but the psychological reactions, once they do occur, are fairly predictable.

The marijuana high, as the name implies, is a feeling of euphoria and well-being. Marijuana smokers typically report an increased awareness of their surroundings, as well as a sharpened sense of sight and sound. They often feel that everything is suddenly very funny, and even the most innocent comments or events can set off uproarious laughter. Usually mundane ideas can seem filled with profound implications, and the individual may believe that her or his creativity has been increased. As with LSD, however, no objective evidence shows that creativity is enhanced by marijuana. Commonly, time seems to pass more slowly while a person is under the influence of marijuana, and events appear to be elongated in duration. Finally, marijuana smokers frequently report that they feel sleepy and sometimes dreamy. Relatively low THC concentrations in a marijuana joint are not sufficient to be particularly sleep-inducing, though stronger cannabis preparations with higher THC can have strong sleep-inducing effects, particularly when combined with alcohol.[19]

At the same time, marijuana produces significant deficits in behavior. The major deficit is a decline in the ability to carry out tasks that involve attention and memory. Speech becomes increasingly fragmented and disjointed; individuals often forget what they, or others, have just said. The problem is that marijuana typically causes such a rush of distracting ideas to come to mind that it is difficult to concentrate on new information coming in. By virtue of a diminished focus of concentration, the performance of both short-term and long-term memory tasks is impaired. In general, these difficulties increase in magnitude as a direct function of the level of THC in the marijuana.[20]

Not surprisingly, complex motor tasks such as driving a car are more poorly performed while a person is under the influence of marijuana. It is not necessarily a matter of reaction time; studies of marijuana smokers in automobile simulators indicate that they are as quick to respond as control subjects. The problem arises from a difficulty in attending to peripheral information and making an appropriate response while driving.[21] One researcher has put it this way:

> Marijuana-intoxicated drivers might be able to stop a car as fast as they normally could, but they may not be as quick to notice things that they should stop for. This is probably because they are attending to internal events rather than what is happening on the road.[22]

Given these observations in the laboratory and on the road, marijuana use is a significant risk factor for an automobile accident. Surveys that have examined accident rates among drivers testing positive for THC in their bloodstreams have shown them to be about three to seven times more likely to be involved in an accident than drivers testing negative for THC or alcohol.[23]

An additional problem is that the decline in sensorimotor performance can persist well past the point at which the marijuana smoker no longer feels high, particularly in cases of chronic heavy marijuana use. Significant impairments in attention and memory tasks have been demonstrated among heavy marijuana users (daily smokers) twenty-four hours after they last used the drug. Therefore, the possibility exists that some important aspects of behavior can be impaired following marijuana smoking, even when an individual is not aware of it. This effect is likely to be result of the very slow rate at which marijuana is eliminated from the body.[24]

Acute psychological reactions such as paranoia and increased anxiety can occur with marijuana use. However, more severe schizophrenia-like symptoms such as delusions, hallucinations, depersonalization, confusion, and disorientation are far less frequently observed (see Drugs . . . in Focus). If these symptoms

---

Quick Concept Check 7.1

Understanding the Effects of Marijuana

Check your understanding of the effects of marijuana by checking off the response (on the right) that you think is appropriate to each circumstance related to marijuana or other cannabis products (on the left).

CIRCUMSTANCE	INCREASES THE EFFECT	DECREASES THE EFFECT
1. The resin content in the cannabis is low.	_____	_____
2. You have decided to inhale more deeply.	_____	_____
3. You are smoking hashish instead of marijuana.	_____	_____
4. This is the first time you have ever smoked marijuana.	_____	_____
5. The THC concentration level is relatively high.	_____	_____

Answers: 1. decreases the effect   2. increases the effect
3. increases the effect   4. decreases the effect
5. increases the effect

Drugs . . . in Focus

The Neurochemical "Yin and Yang" of Cannabis

Considering the large number of cannabinoids in the cannabis plant, it should not be surprising that individually they might have different neurochemical and behavioral effects. Recent studies indicate that two of the cannabinoids have diametrically opposite effects. The first and best known cannabinoid, THC, is the principal psychoactive component, resulting in the marijuana high. It is also considered to be associated with acute symptoms of paranoia and increased anxiety, as well as occasional schizophrenia-like reactions, although these reactions tend to occur only when THC-concentrations are high. On the other hand, cannabidiol (CBD) is associated with opposite effects, producing a reduction in anxiety and fewer instances of severe emotional problems. In effect, CBD can be understood as having a "neuroprotective" effect, making it less likely that adverse emotional reactions will occur. Because of the opposing properties of these cannabinoids, different strains of marijuana may have various psychological effects, depending upon the ratio of THC and CBD.

A 2008 study analyzed hair samples of individuals in three groups: nonusers of cannabis, users testing positive for both CBD and THC, and users testing positive for THC alone. There was a greater incidence of hallucinations and delusions in the THC-only group, relative to the other groups, with the THC+CBD group showing no greater incidence than nonusers.

It was not possible in this study to examine the behaviors of individuals who tested positive for CBD alone, since there are no strains of natural cannabis that have this property. Nonetheless, it is possible that future research will result in the creation of synthetic forms of cannabis containing CBD alone, with the potential for treating individuals suffering from schizophrenia and related disorders (see Chapter 15).

Source: Morgan, C. J., and Curran, H. V. (2008). Effects of cannabidiol on schizophrenia-like symptoms in people who use cannabis. *British Journal of Psychiatry, 192,* 306–307.

---

do occur, they are generally short-lasting and more likely to occur among individuals with preexisting personality disorders. Reports of a substantially higher incidence of psychiatric problems arising from THC exposure in India and North Africa indicate that there is a significant "dose-dependent" effect in the association between emotional problems and cannabis use in its various forms.[25]

Effects of Marijuana on the Brain

When THC was isolated in 1964 as the primary agent for the intoxicating properties of marijuana, the next step was to find out specifically how THC affected the brain to produce these effects. In 1990, the mechanism was discovered. Just as with morphine, special receptors in the brain are stimulated specifically by THC. They are concentrated in areas of the brain that are important for short-term memory and motor control. Unlike morphine-sensitive receptors, however, THC-sensitive receptors are not found in the lower portions of the brain that control breathing. As a result, no matter how high the THC concentration in the brain, there is no danger of accidental death by asphyxiation.

Once we have identified a specific receptor for a drug, the question inevitably becomes, "Why is it there?" As noted in Chapter 5, when the morphine-sensitive receptor was discovered, it made sense to speculate about a natural morphine-like (opioid) substance that would fit into that receptor. The same speculation surrounded the discovery of the THC-sensitive receptor until 1992, when researchers isolated a natural substance, dubbed **anandamide**, that activates this receptor and appears to produce the same effects as THC in the brain.

anandamide (a-NAN-duh-mide): A naturally occurring chemical in the brain that fits into THC-sensitive receptor sites, producing many of the same effects as marijuana.

The functions of anandamide and THC-sensitive receptors remain largely a mystery. One study has found that THC stimulates neurons in the nucleus accumbens in rats, the same area that is affected by a host of other psychoactive drugs, including heroin, cocaine, and nicotine (Chapter 3). The effect, however, is much weaker than with drugs that produce strong signs of dependence. Animals will self-administer marijuana in laboratory studies and, in fact, are able to discriminate high-potency from low-potency marijuana, but their behavior is not as compulsive as that observed with heroin, cocaine, or nicotine.[26]

Chronic Effects of Marijuana

Is chronic marijuana smoking harmful over a period of time? What is the extent of tolerance and dependence? Are there long-term consequences for organ systems in the body? Does marijuana lessen one's potential as a productive human being in society? Does marijuana abuse lead to the abuse of other drugs? These are questions to be considered next.

Tolerance

It is frequently reported that experienced marijuana smokers become intoxicated more quickly and to a greater extent than inexperienced smokers when exposed to marijuana joints with equivalent THC concentrations. For many years, this observation suggested that repeated administrations of marijuana produced sensitization, or reverse tolerance (a greater sensitivity), rather than tolerance (a lesser sensitivity). If this were true, then we would have been faced with the troubling conclusion that marijuana operates in a way totally opposite to that of any other psychoactive drug considered so far. As it turns out, when animals or humans are studied in the laboratory, marijuana smoking shows tolerance effects that are consistent and clear-cut.

Why, then, is the experience of humans outside the laboratory different from that of animals? One important factor is the way we measure the quantity of THC consumed. Reaching an effective high from marijuana requires some degree of practice. For example, novice marijuana smokers may not have mastered the breathing technique necessary to allow the minimal level of THC to enter the lungs. They may have to smoke a relatively large number of marijuana joints initially before they achieve a high. Later, when they have acquired the technique, they may need fewer joints to accomplish

the same effect. In these circumstances, a calculation of the number of joints consumed does not reflect the amount of THC ingested. If you were to control the THC content entering the body, as is done in laboratory studies, you would find the predictable results of tolerance over repeated administrations.

Another factor that complicates tolerance studies is the slow elimination rate of marijuana. Regular marijuana smokers are likely to have a residual amount of THC still in the system. This buildup of THC would elevate the total quantity of THC consumed with every joint and induce a quicker high. Once again, the impression of sensitization is false; the enhanced effects result from an accumulation of THC in the body. When dosage levels are controlled, the results indicate a consistent pattern of tolerance rather than sensitization. In general, tolerance effects following repeated administrations of THC are greater as the dosage level of THC increases.[27]

Withdrawal and Dependence

Withdrawal symptoms after discontinuance of marijuana smoking (that is, evidence of physical dependence) are observed in both short-term and long-term marijuana users, even when relatively low levels of THC are ingested. In one study, abstinence from smoking marijuana cigarettes with approximately 2 to 3 percent THC levels or equivalent oral doses of THC, administered four times a day over a four-day period, resulted in feelings of irritability, stomach pain, anxiety, and loss of appetite. These symptoms began within forty-eight hours and lasted at least two days.[28] Chronic marijuana users who have ingested higher levels of THC show negative physical symptoms that are more severe and long lasting, resembling the withdrawal symptoms associated with the chronic use of tobacco. These symptoms, however, are substantially milder than those associated with the chronic use of heroin (Chapter 5) or alcohol (Chapter 9).[29]

There is also evidence of marijuana craving, indicating a degree of psychological dependence in some marijuana smokers, but it is difficult to measure the extent of these feelings or to determine whether these effects are due to circumstances in which marijuana is used in conjunction with other drugs. As was pointed out earlier, any definitive judgment about the possibility of psychological dependence, or about the extent to which psychological dependence may occur in the average marijuana smoker, must be made on the basis of research studies involving THC concentrations that are typical of currently available marijuana.[30]

Cardiovascular Effects

THC produces significant increases in heart rate, but there is no conclusive evidence of adverse effects in the cardiovascular functioning in young, healthy people. The reason why the emphasis is on a specific age group is that most of the studies looking at possible long-term cardiovascular effects have involved marijuana smokers under the age of thirty-five; little or no information has been compiled about older populations. For those people with preexisting disorders such as heart disease, high blood pressure, or arteriosclerosis (hardening of the arteries), it is known that the acute effects of marijuana on heart rate and blood pressure can worsen their condition.

Respiratory Effects and the Risk of Cancer

The technique of marijuana smoking involves the deep and maintained inhalation into the lungs of unfiltered smoke on a repetitive basis—probably the worst possible scenario for incurring chronic pulmonary problems. In addition, a marijuana joint (when compared with a tobacco cigarette) typically contains about the same levels of tars, 50 percent more hydrocarbons, and an unknown amount of possible contaminants (Table 7.1). Joints are often smoked more completely because the smoker tries to waste as little marijuana as possible.

Given all these factors, marijuana smoking presents several risks. One of the immediate consequences affects the process of breathing. When marijuana is inhaled initially, the passageways for air entering and leaving the lungs widen, but after chronic exposure, an opposite reaction occurs. As a result, symptoms of asthma and other breathing difficulties are increased. Overall, even though the effects of a single inhalation of marijuana smoke present greater problems than a single inhalation of tobacco smoke, we need to remember that the patterns of consumption are far from comparable. All things considered, one joint is roughly equivalent to five cigarettes in terms of the amount of carbon monoxide intake and to four cigarettes in terms of tar intake. The use of a water pipe reduces the harm somewhat, but the risks are still present.

In the respiratory tracts of heavy marijuana smokers, molecular abnormalities have been identified that resemble the changes in the respiratory tracts of cigarette smokers. The effect of a single marijuana joint is equivalent to that of up to five tobacco cigarettes in this regard. However, marijuana smoking does not increase the risk of developing emphysema, a chronic lung disease associated with tobacco smoking (see Chapter 10). A recent study has indicated occasional and low cumulative marijuana use, even over a period of more than twenty years (1985–2006), does not produce adverse effects on lung capacity as indicated by standard pulmonary breathing tests.

Does smoking marijuana produce a higher incidence of cancer? Given the number of known carcinogens in marijuana smoke, the potential for an increased risk of cancer exists. However, there is no definitive evidence of increases in lung cancer rates among marijuana smokers, after controlling for tobacco use. But it may still be too soon to answer the question of increased risk of cancer in general. Marijuana smokers who were twenty years old in the late 1960s have only recently reached the peak ages when cancers appear, and they smoked marijuana containing relatively low THC concentrations at the time. Those individuals more recently exposed to higher-potency marijuana, such as those whose marijuana experience began in the late 1990s, are substantially younger, and it will be decades before they reach an age at which the incidence of cancer becomes a significant concern. Fortunately, there is the possibility, as is the case with cigarette smoking (see Chapter 10), that the risk of cancer declines after a person stops smoking marijuana.[31]

TABLE 7.1

A comparison of the components of marijuana and tobacco smoke

COMPONENT	MARIJUANA	TOBACCO
Carbon monoxide (mg)	17.6	20.2
Carbon dioxide (mg)	57.3	65.0
Ammonia (micrograms)	228.0	178.0
Acetaldehyde (micrograms)	1,200.0	980.0
Acetone (micrograms)*	443.0	578.0
Benzene (micrograms)*	76.0	67.0
Toluene (micrograms)*	112.0	108.0
THC (tetrahydrocannabinol) (micrograms)	820.0	—
Nicotine (micrograms)	—	2,850.0
Naphthalene (nanograms)	3,000.0	1,200.0

*See Chapter 13 for information about the health risks of inhaling some of these chemicals.

Source: Julien, R. M. (2001). *A primer of drug action* (9th ed.). New York: Worth, p. 317.

Nonetheless, it is important to point out that an overwhelming proportion of young marijuana smokers do not go on to use other illicit drugs. As expressed in a 1999 newspaper editorial on this point, "millions of baby boomers . . . once did, indeed, inhale. They later went into business, not cocaine or heroin."[42]

The Association Question

From a statistical perspective, the association between marijuana use and subsequent use of other illicit drugs is not controversial. Generally speaking, marijuana smokers are several times more likely to consume illicit drugs such as cocaine and heroin during their lifetimes than are people who never smoked marijuana. The greater the frequency of marijuana smoking and the earlier an individual first engages in marijuana smoking, the greater the likelihood of his or her becoming involved with other illicit drugs in the future.

A precise determination of the magnitude of risk involved in marijuana use requires studies that take into account a range of genetic and environmental variables that might act as risk factors or protective factors for drug-taking behavior (see Chapter 1). A 2003 study set out to control for these variables by investigating a specific subpopulation of twins; one member of each twin pair reported marijuana use by the age of seventeen, and the other reported no marijuana use at all. Examining twins enabled the researchers to calculate the increased risk of future drug-taking behavior when environmental factors (in the case of fraternal twins) and both environmental and genetic factors (in the case of identical twins) were controlled. Results showed that early marijuana users were about two and one-half times more likely to use heroin later in life, four times more likely to use cocaine or other stimulants, and five times more likely to use hallucinogens. In general, they were twice as likely to become alcoholic and twice as likely to develop any form of illicit drug abuse or dependence.

The question of whether future twin studies using this approach will find the increased risk from marijuana use to be *higher than the increased risk from alcohol or tobacco use* remains unanswered. In any case, the fact that marijuana use is one of the risk factors for illicit drug use in other forms reinforces the need to develop intervention programs for marijuana users that might discourage subsequent drug use, as well as prevention programs for youths to reduce the incidence of marijuana use in the first place.[43]

In the final analysis, however, the statistical relationship between marijuana smoking and other forms of drug-taking behavior may simply reflect the sequential pattern of drug use among multiple-drug (polydrug) users. Essentially, they begin using high-prevalence drugs (such as alcohol, tobacco, and/or marijuana) earlier than they begin using low-prevalence drugs (such as cocaine and/or heroin). This effect can be viewed as due not to the drugs themselves but, rather, to the relative differences in prevalence rates. Numerous statistical relationships exist between other types of common and uncommon behaviors in our lives:

> *For example, most people who ride a motorcycle (a fairly rare activity) have ridden a bicycle (a fairly common activity). Indeed, the prevalence of motorcycle riding among people who have never ridden a bicycle is probably extremely low. However, bicycle riding does not cause motorcycle riding, and increases in the former will not lead automatically to increases in the latter.*[44]

The Causation Question

The strongest form of the gateway hypothesis relates to the possibility of a causal link between marijuana smoking and the use of other illicit drugs. With respect to the causation issue, Erich Goode, a sociologist and drug-abuse researcher, has distinguished between two schools of thought, which he calls the intrinsic argument and the sociocultural argument.

The *intrinsic argument* asserts that some inherent property of marijuana exposure itself leads to physical or psychological dependence on other illicit drugs. According to this viewpoint, the pleasurable sensations induced by marijuana create a biological urge to consume more potent substances, through a combination of drug tolerance and drug dependence.

In contrast, the *sociocultural argument* holds that the relationship exists not because of the pharmacological effects of marijuana but because of the activities, friends, and acquaintances that are associated with marijuana smoking. In other words, the sociocultural explanation asserts that those who smoke marijuana tend to have friends who not only smoke marijuana themselves but also abuse other drugs. These friends are likely to have positive attitudes toward substance abuse in general and to provide opportunities for drug experimentation.

Professionals in the drug-abuse field have concluded that if any such causal link exists, the result is socioculturally based rather than related to the pharmacological properties of marijuana itself. The consensus is that any early exposure to psychoactive substances in general, and to illicit drugs such as marijuana in particular, represents a "deviance-prone pattern of behavior" that will be reflected in a higher incidence of exposure to psychoactive drugs of many types later in life. It is interesting to note that early adolescent marijuana use among males also increases the risk in late adolescence of delinquency, having multiple sexual partners, not always using condoms during sex, perceiving drugs as not harmful, and having problems with cigarettes and alcohol. Generally speaking, marijuana smokers show a greater inclination toward risk-taking behavior and are more unconventional with regard to social norms.[45]

Patterns of Marijuana Smoking

From as early as their days in elementary school, most young Americans have had to come to terms with marijuana as a pervasive element in their lives. Just as nearly all adolescents have had to decide whether to drink and whether to smoke cigarettes, they also have had to decide whether to smoke or not smoke marijuana.

Marijuana is undoubtedly the dominant illicit drug in U.S. society today, used by 80 percent of current illicit drug users (Figure 7.2). For more than six out of ten illicit drug users, marijuana is the *only* illicit drug being used. From the National Survey on Drug Use and Health conducted in 2011, it is estimated that an astounding 108 million Americans, about 42 percent of the U.S. population over the age of twelve, have smoked marijuana at least once during their lives. More than 18 million Americans are estimated to have smoked marijuana within the past thirty days. About 48 percent of individuals between 18 and 20 years old in 2011 had smoked marijuana at least once in their lives; about 22 percent had done so in the past month.[46]

Among high school seniors surveyed in 2011, 36 percent reported having smoked marijuana in the past year, 23 percent reported having done so in the past month, and 7 percent smoked on a daily basis. Among eighth graders, 13 percent reported smoking marijuana in the past year and 7 percent in the past month.[47]

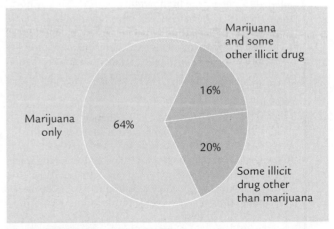

FIGURE 7.2

Types of drugs used by illicit drug users aged twelve or older in the past month in 2011.

Source: Substance Abuse and Mental Health Services Administration (2012). *Results from the 2011 National Survey on Drug Use and Health: National findings.* Rockville, MD: Substance Abuse and Mental Health Services Administration, p. 13.

Causes for Concern

Current prevalence rates among young people are substantially lower than those in the 1970s. Nonetheless, there is some concern that marijuana smoking rates are increasing. In other words, the "roller-coaster ride" of marijuana use monitored over the decades (see Figure 1.3) appears to be entering a new upward phase. In 2009, Lloyd Johnston of the University of Michigan survey cautioned that "a key belief about the degree of risk associated with marijuana use has been in decline among young people . . . and the degree to which teens disapprove of use of the drug has recently begun to decline."[48] In 2011, less than half of high school seniors judged "regular marijuana smoking" as representing "great risk," whereas seniors in 1992 had judged it as representing "great risk" by a three-to-one margin.[49]

A second concern with regard to present-day marijuana use has to do with an increased potency in the cannabis products that are available. As noted earlier, a typical marijuana joint in the psychedelic era several decades ago contained approximately 1 to 2 percent THC; the average concentration has now risen above 6 percent to as high as 10 percent and, in the case of recent strains of sinsemilla, as high as 15 percent. It is reasonable to assume that the adverse effects of chronic marijuana smoking will be more intense than the relatively mild symptoms associated with marijuana use in the past. In addition, there are new synthetic forms of marijuana that can produce serious adverse side-effects (Health Alert). A third concern applies to any illicit street drug: the possibility for adulteration. As emphasized in earlier chapters, what you think you are buying is not always what you get. Each year brings with it a new group of ingredients, some of them newly introduced drugs and others merely inventive creations from already available materials, ready to be combined with marijuana either to weaken its effects or to change the overall psychoactive result by some synergistic or other interactive effect.

HEALTH ALERT!

A Synthetic Marijuana called Spice

In 2010, the Drug Enforcement Administration was alerted to a new leafy-herb product, marketed under the name "spice" (alternately, "K2") that began to be available through smoke shops and other small retail outlets. Since spice has been sold officially as a "herbal incense" and therefore as a legal commodity, retailers were able to curt the law prohibiting sale of marijuana itself. In actuality, spice contains a powerful cannabinoid called JWH-018, which can bind with THC receptors at a rate four times greater than THC itself. As a consequence, administration of spice results in a powerful marijuana-like high. Standard drug testing screening for THC metabolites (see Chapter 12) cannot be used for individuals smoking spice, though specialized tests to include detection of JWH-018 are presently being developed. An estimated 11,000 of the 4.9 million drug-related emergency department visits in 2010 were linked to spice.

In 2011, the DEA executed its emergency scheduling authority (under the Controlled Substance Act) to include JWH-018 and other similar cannabinoids as Schedule I controlled substances, as they have for THC in natural marijuana. Emergency physicians had reported individuals ingesting spice with serious side effects that included convulsions, anxiety attacks, elevated heart rate and blood pressure, vomiting, and disorientation.

Recently, most U.S. states and many countries have recently made spice and similar products illegal within their jurisdiction. However, it is likely that spice has moved underground and will become still another option within the illicit drug community.

Where to go for assistance:

http://www.drugabuse.gov/publications/drugfacts/spice-synthetic-marijuana

This web site, issued by the National Institute on Drug Abuse, provides up-to-date information on the health effects and patterns of abuse of spice. Prevention and treatment strategies are also provided.

Sources: Substance Abuse and Mental Health Services Administration (2012, December 4). First-of-its-kind report find that street forms of "synthetic marijuana" products linked to thousands of hospital emergency department visits each year. *SAMHSA News Release.* Rockville, MD: Substance Abuse and Mental Health Services Administration. U.S. Drug Enforcement Administration (2011, March 1). Chemicals used in "spice" and "K2" type products now under federal control and regulation. DEA Office of Public Affairs, Washington, DC.

Medical Marijuana

Even though the medicinal benefits of marijuana have been noted for thousands of years, strong anti-marijuana sentiment in the United States made it difficult until the 1970s to conduct an objective appraisal of its clinical applications. Early research in the effectiveness of marijuana to reduce intraocular (within the eye) pressure and dilate bronchioles in the lungs suggested uses as a possible therapy for glaucoma and asthma, respectively. However, new prescription medications have been shown to be as effective as marijuana in the treatment of these disorders. Today, the focus has turned toward the treatment of chronic pain, muscle spasticity, nausea, and weight loss.

Muscle Spasticity and Chronic Pain

Evidence that marijuana is useful in the treatment of muscle spasticity and lack of mobility associated with neurological diseases such as multiple sclerosis (MS) comes largely from subjective reports. In a randomized placebo-controlled study of MS patients taking oral capsules of THC or whole cannabis extract, no significant improvements were observed through objective measures of mobility but about two-thirds of the patients reported that they felt significant relief from muscle spasticity and associated chronic pain. In addition, patients frequently report relief from cancer-related pain as well as phantom limb pain (a phenomenon in which pain is experienced as coming from a limb that had been amputated). In many cases, they cite the superiority of smoked marijuana to any other form of treatment (Portrait).[50]

PORTRAIT

Marcy Dolin—Marijuana Self-Medicator

In a *New York Times Magazine* article, photographer Steve LaBadessa vividly recalls meeting 71-year-old Marcy Dolin in her Rohnert Park, California, home in 2011. Unlike many people using medical marijuana who were reluctant to talk to him—much less allow a photographer to take a picture at such short range—Marcy wasn't shy at all. But being in such close proximity took its toll on the photographer. There was so much smoke in the room that LaBadessa had to sit in his car for a while afterward to recuperate before driving home.

Dolin had been a marijuana smoker for about 35 years to treat her multiple sclerosis symptoms. Today, she typically smokes eight joints a day and eats a marijuana cookie before bedtime. "It takes the pain and muscle spasms away," she said. "Without it, I would be living on morphine and other horrible drugs. I couldn't do that to my family. That's no life, and I would have ended it. That's the truth."

She used to take Neurontin but she couldn't stop crying, and it put her in a depressed fog. She had been warned that she might be arrested but she couldn't care less about that.

The medical marijuana issue assumed national importance in the 1990s after California voters in 1996 passed the Compassionate Use Act, legalizing marijuana for medical use within the state, the first U.S. state to have done so. After the Drug Enforcement Administration (DEA) seized doctor-prescribed marijuana from the home of a patient, advocates of medical marijuana sued the DEA and then–U.S. Attorney General John Ashcroft in federal district court and won. However, in the 2005 U.S. Supreme Court case *Raich v. Ashcroft*, the legal status of medical marijuana within the state of California was overturned in favor of arguments that federal regulations prohibiting marijuana use under any circumstances were paramount.

The litigant was Angel McClary Raich who had become permanently disabled in 1995, with multiple diagnoses that included an inoperable brain tumor, life-threatening wasting syndrome, chronic pain disorders, seizure disorder, nausea, and scoliosis (a painful back condition). After her physician recommended cannabis use as a medication for her symptoms, Raich became one of the fourteen "medical necessity" patients at the Oakland Cannabis Buyers' Cooperative who were represented in the court cases that led up to the Supreme Court decision.

As of 2012, eighteen U.S. states and the District of Columbia have legalized medical marijuana, and two states have legalized its recreational use. In 2009, the federal government issued a "non-interference" policy with respect to medical marijuana use within states that allow it. Nonetheless, the legal challenges and drug enforcement conflicts between state's rights and federal prerogatives regarding marijuana use continue.

Sources: LaBadessa, S. (2011, March 20). Self-medicator, Rohnert Park, Calif. *New York Times Magazine*, p. 23. Who Is Angel McClary Raich? Angel Wings Patient Outreach, Inc. Web Site, angeljustice.org. Declaration of Frank Henry Lucido, M.D., In Support of the Plaintiff Angel McClary Raich, October 20, 2002, U.S. District Court for the Northern District of California.

Nausea and Weight Loss

Chemotherapy in the course of cancer treatment produces an extreme and debilitating nausea, lack of appetite, and loss of body weight, symptoms that are clearly counterproductive in helping an individual contend with an ongoing fight against cancer. AIDS patients suffer from similar symptoms, as do those diagnosed with the gastrointestinal ailment Crohn's disease. Under these circumstances, standard antiemetic (antivomiting) drugs are frequently ineffective. The beneficial effect of marijuana, specifically THC, as an antiemetic drug when treatment by traditional antiemetic medications have failed, is an important therapeutic application.[51]

At the same time, the use of marijuana per se as a therapeutic agent has distinct disadvantages. First, the typical administration through smoking presents a significant health risk to the lungs. Second, because marijuana is insoluble in water, suspensions in an injectable form cannot be prepared. Since 1985, however, two legal prescription drugs containing THC or a variation of it have been made available in capsule form and classified as Schedule II controlled substances. **Dronabinol** (brand name: Marinol) is essentially THC in a sesame oil suspension; **nabilone** (brand name: Cesamet) is a synthetic variation of THC. Both drugs have been shown to be clinically effective against nausea, although the personal reactions of patients taking these drugs vary considerably.[52]

The Medical Marijuana Controversy

Even though Marinol and Cesamet are presently in use, U.S. federal authorities have resisted the reclassification of marijuana itself or of any other cannabis product from the Schedule I category of controlled substances (drugs that have no medical application) to the Schedule II category (which includes morphine and cocaine). Only a handful of "compassionate use" applications have been approved, and the entire program for reviewing new applications was curtailed in 1992.

Despite opposition from federal authorities, advocacy for the medical application of marijuana has grown

> **dronabinol (droh-NAB-ih-nol):** A prescription drug containing delta-9-tetrahydrocannabinol (THC). Brand name is Marinol.
>
> **nabilone (NAB-ih-lone):** A prescription drug containing a synthetic variation of delta-9-tetrahydrocannabinol (THC). Brand name is Cesamet.

considerably. Unfortunately, the facts about medical marijuana sometimes have been lost in a thicket of politics and opposing ideologies. A case in point is the interpretation of a major report on the possibility of using marijuana as a medical treatment, issued by the Institute of Medicine, a branch of the National Academy of Sciences, in 1999. In its preface, the report began by acknowledging the problems involved:

> *Although marijuana smoke delivers THC and other cannabinoids to the body, it also delivers harmful substances, including most of those found in tobacco smoke. In addition, plants contain a variable mixture of biologically-active compounds and cannot be expected to provide a precisely defined drug effect. For these reasons, this report concludes that the future of cannabinoid drugs lies not in smoked marijuana, but in chemically-defined drugs that act on the cannabinoid systems that are a natural component of human physiology.*[53]

In focusing on the report's preface, the federal Office of National Drug Control Strategy has emphasized the potential health risks of marijuana *smoking* and the imprecision of its administration as a justification for the continued prohibition of marijuana for medical purposes. Largely ignored has been one of the report's main conclusions within the report itself.

> *Until a nonsmoked, rapid-onset cannabinoid drug delivery system becomes available, we acknowledge that there is no clear alternative for people suffering from chronic conditions that might be relieved by smoking marijuana, such as pain or AIDS wasting.*[54]

In effect, the report concluded that, although smoked marijuana could not be recommended for long-term use, short-term use appeared to be suitable for treating specific conditions when patients failed to respond well to traditional medications.

As of 2012, eighteen U.S. states (Alaska, Arizona, California, Colorado, Connecticut, Delaware, Hawaii, Maine, Massachusetts, Michigan, Montana, Nevada, New Jersey, New Mexico, Oregon, Rhode Island, Vermont, and Washington) and the District of Columbia have authorized marijuana smoking for the relief of pain and discomfort or the control of nausea and weight loss, when prescribed by a physician. In New Jersey, tight restrictions on medical marijuana have been established: Patients must suffer from specific diseases such as cancer and glaucoma and must demonstrate severe or chronic pain, nausea, seizures, muscle spasms, or wasting syndrome (loss of weight or body mass).

In addition, two U.S. states approved in 2012 the legalization of recreational marijuana use, with specific regulatory safeguards. In Colorado, adults over 21 can grow up to six marijuana plants in a private secure area and possess up to an ounce of marijuana, although public use is banned. In Washington, adults over 21 can buy and possess up to an ounce of marijuana from a state-licensed system of marijuana growers, processors, and stores. Standardized testing procedures for driving under the influence will be implemented.[55]

How would the contradictory positions in the statutes of states and the federal government regarding medical marijuana be reconciled? In a significant reversal of federal enforcement policy, the U.S. Department of Justice announced in 2009 that

> It will not be a priority to use federal resources to prosecute patients with serious illnesses or their caregivers who are complying with state laws on medical marijuana, but we will not tolerate drug traffickers who hide behind claims of compliance with state law to mask activities that are clearly illegal.[55]

In effect, the Department of Justice has returned the question of medical marijuana to the jurisdiction of the states without altering its official stance on a federal level that marijuana is a controlled substance without medical use. At the same time, it has signaled the requirement that the states set up regulations that limit marijuana use to legitimate medical circumstances. Recently, U.S. states with medical marijuana laws have had to contend with federal drug enforcement campaigns, when the lines have blurred between legal and illegal marijuana use. How the federal government will handle the newly established legalization of marijuana in Colorado and Washington remains to be seen.[56] Meanwhile, public opinion in favor of medical marijuana in general has increased steadily over the years, judging from the more than one-third of U.S. states authorizing the practice. In a national CBS News poll conducted in 2011, 77 percent of American adults favored legalizing the possession of small amounts of marijuana for medicinal purposes.[57]

Canada has officially approved the medicinal use of marijuana since 2001. It is legal for Canadian patients to grow and smoke marijuana if their symptoms have been certified by a physician as warranting this treatment. It is also permitted, under these circumstances, to request marijuana, free of charge, from government-operated cannabis farms in Manitoba. In 2005, the FDA-equivalent agency in Canada approved the prescription use of Sativex, a liquid spray derived from the cannabis plant. In 2006, the FDA approved clinical testing of Sativex

A DEA officer supervises the confiscation of a small-scale marijuana crop.

for potential sale in the United States. By providing a nonsmoking means of administration, this formulation circumvents arguments that medical marijuana smoking presents increased risks of smoking-related diseases (see Chapter 10).[58]

The Issues of Decriminalization and Legalization

What, then, should public policy be toward marijuana smoking in the United States today? To deal with this question, we need first to review how public policy with respect to marijuana regulation has evolved since the 1970s. As described earlier, the dramatic emergence during the 1960s of marijuana as a major psychoactive drug initiated a slow but steady reassessment of myths that had been attached to it for decades. By 1972, the American Medical Association and the American Bar Association had proposed a liberalization of laws regarding the possession of marijuana. In 1972, the National Commission on

Marijuana and Drug Abuse, authorized by the Comprehensive Drug Abuse Prevention and Control Act of 1970, encouraged state legislators around the country to consider changes in their particular regulatory statutes related to marijuana.[59] Since that time, several states, including California, Oregon, Colorado, Minnesota, and North Carolina, have adopted some form of decriminalization laws with respect to the possession of marijuana in small amounts (usually less than an ounce or so). Essentially, **decriminalization** has meant that possession under these circumstances is considered a civil (noncriminal) offense, punishable by a fine rather than imprisonment.

You may find it surprising or not surprising (depending on your personal views) that official decriminalization has not been demonstrated to result in an upturn in the incidence of marijuana smoking. Statistics drawn from states that either have or have not decriminalized show little or no difference.[60] In addition, attitude surveys conducted in California before and after the enactment of

---

decriminalization: The policy of making the possession of small amounts of a drug subject to a small fine but not criminal prosecution.

---

such statutes indicate that the acceptance of marijuana among college students actually declined following decriminalization.[61]

Marijuana legalization is different from decriminalization in that it allows anyone over the age of 21 to purchase marijuana for his or her own use, typically with regulations similar to the use of alcohol. As with recent voter referendum results regarding medical marijuana, public support for marijuana legalization tends to be mixed. In 2010, a California state referendum to legalize marijuana was defeated by a 54 to 46 percent vote. In 2012 elections, Colorado and Washington voters approved legalized marijuana use by adults, but Oregon voters rejected it. Nonetheless, support for such a policy is steadily growing. From the late 1970s to the mid-1990s, acceptance of marijuana legalization had never exceeded 25 percent. According to a 2013 Pew Research Center national poll, 52 percent of Americans now favor legalizing marijuana, while 45 percent are opposed, marking the first time that those in favor have gained the majority. Legalization is favored by 70 percent of those who have ever tried marijuana and 89 percent of those who have tried it in the past year.[62]

Summary

A Matter of Terminology

- Marijuana is one of several products of *Cannabis sativa*, or the common hemp plant, grown abundantly throughout the world.

- Various cannabis products are distinguished in terms of the content of cannabis resin and, in turn, the concentration of THC, the active psychoactive agent.

The History of Marijuana and Hashish

- The earliest records of marijuana come from Chinese writings nearly five thousand years ago; the use of hashish originated in North Africa and Persia in the ninth or tenth century A.D.

- In the United States, marijuana was available in patent medicines during the late 1800s, but its popularity did not become extensive until the 1920s.

- Federal and state regulation of marijuana began in the 1930s; penalties for possessing and selling marijuana escalated during the 1940s and 1950s.

- The emergence of marijuana on American college campuses and among American youth in general during the late 1960s, however, forced a reexamination of public policy regarding this drug, leading to a more lenient approach in the 1970s.

Acute Effects of Marijuana

- Because marijuana is almost always consumed through smoking, the acute effects are rapid, but because it is absorbed into fatty tissue, its elimination is slow. It may require days or weeks (in the case of extensive exposure to marijuana) for THC to leave the body completely.

- Acute physiological effects include cardiac acceleration and a reddening of the eyes. Acute psychological effects, with typical dosages, include euphoria, giddiness, a perception of time elongation, and increased hunger. There are impairments in attention and memory, which interfere with complex visual–motor skills such as driving an automobile.

- The acute effects of marijuana are now known to be due to the binding of THC at special receptors in the brain.

Chronic Effects of Marijuana

- Chronic marijuana use produces tolerance effects; there is no physical dependence when doses are moderate, and only a mild psychological dependence.

- Carcinogenic effects are suspected because marijuana smoke contains many of the same harmful components that tobacco smoke does, and in the case of marijuana smoking, inhalation is deeper and more prolonged.

The Amotivational Syndrome and the Gateway Hypothesis

- The idea that there exists an "amotivational syndrome," characterized by general apathy and an indifference to long-range planning, as a result of the pharmacological effects of chronic marijuana use has been largely discredited. An alternative explanation for the behavioral changes is that chronic marijuana users are involved in a deviant subculture that tends to undermine traditional values of school achievement and long-term aspirations.

- Another idea that has been related to chronic marijuana use is the gateway hypothesis, which asserts that marijuana inherently sets the stage for future patterns of drug abuse. Research studies have indicated that the use of alcohol and cigarettes precedes marijuana use and that marijuana use precedes the use of other illicit drugs. In addition, marijuana use and the subsequent use of other illicit drugs are statistically correlated. However, there is little evidence that some inherent property of marijuana exposure itself leads to physical or psychological dependence on other drugs.

Patterns of Marijuana Smoking

- The current prevalence rate of marijuana smoking among adolescents and young adults is lower than in the late 1970s. However, in 2011, 36 percent of high school seniors reported smoking marijuana in the past year.

- Other areas of concern are the considerably greater potency of marijuana that is now available and the continuing potential risk of marijuana adulteration.

Medical Marijuana, Decriminalization, and Legalization

- Marijuana has been useful in the treatment of glaucoma and asthma, but its most effective application to date has been in the treatment of symptoms of nausea and weight loss. As of 2012, eighteen U.S. states had approved medical marijuana. In 2009, a significant reversal of federal policy on medical marijuana occurred when the U.S. Department of Justice announced that it would not be a national priority to use federal resources to prosecute patients with serious illnesses or their caregivers who are complying with state laws on medical marijuana. However, the federal government is still officially on record as classifying marijuana as a Schedule I controlled substance, indicating that it is considered to have no medical use.

- Present public policy in the United States toward marijuana smoking has evolved to the point of essentially decriminalizing the possession of marijuana in small amounts. A majority of Americans now support marijuana legalization, and two U.S. states (Colorado and Washington) have enacted statutes to that effect.

Key Terms

amotivational syndrome, p. 178
anandamide, p. 175
bhang, p. 170
cannabinoids, p. 169

Cannabis sativa, p. 168
decriminalization, p. 186
delta-9-tetrahydrocannabinol (THC), p. 169
dronabinol, p. 184

gateway hypothesis, p. 179
hashish, p. 169
hashish oil, p. 169
hashish oil crystals, p. 169

joint, p. 172
marijuana, p. 169
nabilone, p. 184
reefer, p. 172
sinsemilla, p. 169

Endnotes

1. Anslinger, H. J.; with Cooper, C. R. (1937, July). Marihuana: Assassin of youth. *American Magazine*, pp. 18–19, 150-153. Reprinted in Musto, D. F. (2002). *Drugs in America: A documentary history*. New York: New York University Press, pp. 433-440.

2. Abel, E. L. (1980). *Marihuana, the first twelve thousand years*. New York: Plenum Press, p. ix.

3. Bloomquist, E. R. (1968). *Marijuana*. Beverly Hills, CA: Glencoe Press, pp. 4–5.

4. Abel, *Marihuana*, p. 4. Palfai, T., and Jankiewicz, H. (1991). *Drugs and human behavior*. Dubuque, IA: W. C. Brown, p. 452.

5. Abel, *Marihuana*, pp. x–xi.

6. Goode, E. (2012). *Drugs in American society* (8th ed.). New York: McGraw-Hill, p. 208. National Drug Intelligence Center (2009). *Domestic cannabis cultivation assessment 2009*. Washington, DC: U.S. Department of Justice, p. 4. National Drug

Intelligence Center (2008). *National drug threat assessment: 2009.* Washington, DC: U.S. Department of Justice, p. 18. *Pulse check: Marijuana report.* Washington, DC: White House Office of Drug Control Policy.

7. Abel, *Marihuana*, p. 12.

8. Bonnie, R. J., and Whitebread, C. H. (1974). *The marihuana conviction: A history of marihuana prohibition in the United States.* Charlottesville, VA: University Press of Virginia, p. 3.

9. Abel, *Marihuana*, pp. 218–222.

10. Anslinger, H. J., and Tompkins, W. F. (1953). *The traffic in narcotics.* New York: Funk & Wagnalls, pp. 37–38. Cited in Inciardi, J. A. (2002). *The war on drugs III.* Boston: Allyn and Bacon, p. 46.

11. Lee, M. A., and Shlain, B. (1985). *Acid dreams: The complete social history of LSD.* New York: Grove Weidenfeld.

12. Julien, R. M. (2005). *A primer of drug action* (10th ed.). New York: Worth, pp. 565–567.

13. Ibid., p. 566.

14. *Allen and Hanbury's athletic drug reference* (1992). Research Triangle Park, NC: Clean Data, p. 33. Wadler, G. I., and Hainline, B. (1989). *Drugs and the athlete.* Philadelphia: F. A. Davis, pp. 208–209.

15. Grinspoon, L., and Bakalar, J. B. (1997). Marihuana. In J. H. Lowinson, P. Ruiz, R. B. Millman, and J. G. Langrod (Eds.), *Substance abuse: A comprehensive textbook* (3rd ed.). Baltimore, MD: Williams and Wilkins, pp. 199–206.

16. Jones, R. T. (1980). Human effects: An overview. In R. C. Petersen (Ed.), *Marijuana research findings: 1980* (NIDA Research Monograph 31). Rockville, MD: National Institute on Drug Abuse, p. 65.

17. Grilly, D. M. (2006). *Drugs and human behavior* (5th ed.). Boston: Allyn and Bacon, p. 268.

18. Substance Abuse and Mental Health Services Administration (2013). *Drug Abuse Warning Network, National estimates of drug-related emergency department visits 2004–2011.* Rockville, MD: Substance Abuse and Mental Health Services Administration, Excel files.

19. Winger, G.; Hofmann, F. G.; and Woods, J. H. (1992). *A handbook on drug and alcohol abuse* (3rd ed.). New York: Oxford University Press, pp. 123–125.

20. Budney, A. J.; Moore, B. A., and Vandrey, R. (2008). Health consequences of marijuana use. In J. Brick (Ed.), *Handbook of the medical consequences of alcohol and drug abuse* (2nd ed.). New York: Routledge, pp. 265–272. Hooker, W. D., and Jones, R. T. (1987). Increased susceptibility to memory intrusions and the Stroop interference effect during acute marijuana intoxication. *Psychopharmacology, 91,* 20–24. Ilan, A. B.; Gevins, A.; Coleman, M.; ElSohly, M. A.; and de Wit, H. (2005). Neurophysiological and subjective profile of marijuana with varying concentrations of cannabinoids. *Behavioural Pharmacology, 16,* 487–496.

21. Delong, F. L., and Levy, B. I. (1974). A model of attention describing the cognitive effects of marijuana. In

L. L. Miller (Ed.), *Marijuana: Effects on human behavior.* New York: Academic Press, pp. 103–117. Gieringer, D. H. (1988). Marijuana, driving, and accident safety. *Journal of Psychoactive Drugs, 20,* 93–101.

22. McKim, W. A., and Hancock, S. D. (2013). *Drugs and behavior* (7th ed.). Boston: Pearson, p. 323.

23. Ramaekers, J. G.; Berghaus, G.; van Laar, M.; and Drummer, O. H. (2004). Dose related risk of motor vehicle crashes after cannabis use. *Drugs and Alcohol Dependence, 73,* 109–119.

24. Block, R. I. (1997). Editorial: Does heavy marijuana use impair human cognition and brain function? *Journal of the American Medical Association, 275,* 560–561. Pope, H. G., Jr., and Yurgelun-Todd, D. (1996). The residual cognitive effects of heavy marijuana use in college students. *Journal of the American Medical Association, 275,* 521–527.

25. Budney, Moore, and Vandrey, *Handbook,* pp. 261–265. Hall, W.; Degenhardt, L.; and Teesson, M. (2004). Cannabis use and psychotic disorders: An update. *Drug and Alcohol Review, 23,* 433–443. Julien, *A primer of drug action,* pp. 568–572. McKim and Hancock, *Drugs and behavior,* p. 328.

26. Ameri, A. (1999). The effects of cannabinoids on the brain. *Progress in Neurobiology, 58,* 315–348. Chait, L. D., and Burke, K. A. (1994). Preference for high- versus low-potency marijuana. *Pharmacology, Biochemistry, and Behavior, 49,* 643–647. Tanda, G.; Pontieri, F. E.; and Di Chiara, G. (1997). Cannabinoid and heroin activation of mesolimbic dopamine transmission by a common μ_1 opioid receptor mechanism. *Science, 276,* 2048–2049. Wickelgren, I. (1997). Research news: Marijuana: Harder than thought? *Science, 276,* 1967–1968.

27. Abood, M., and Martin, B. (1992). Neurobiology of marijuana abuse. *Trends in Pharmacological Sciences, 13,* 201–206.

28. Haney, M.; Ward, A. S.; Comer, S. D.; Foltin, R. W. and Fischman, M. W. (1999a). Abstinence symptoms following oral THC administration in humans. *Psychopharmacology, 141,* 385–394. Haney, M.; Ward, A. S.; Comer, S.D.; Foltin, R. W. and Fischman, M. W. (1999b). Abstinence symptoms following smoked marijuana in humans. *Psychopharmacology, 141,* 395–404.

29. Budney, A. J.; Hughes, J. R.; Moore, B. A.; and Vandrey, R. (2004). Review of the validity and significance of cannabis withdrawal syndrome. *American Journal of Psychiatry, 161,* 1967–1977.

30. Duffy, A., and Milin, R. (1996). Case study: Withdrawal syndrome in adolescent chronic cannabis users. *Journal of the American Academy of Child and Adolescent Psychiatry, 35,* 1618–1621. Julien, R. M. (2001). *A primer of drug action* (9th ed.). New York: Worth, pp. 320–322.

31. Mehra, R.; Moore, B. A.; Crothers, K.; Tetrault, J.; and Fiellin, D. A. (2006). The association between marijuana smoking and lung cancer: A systematic review. *Archives of Internal Medicine, 166,* 1359–1367. Pletcher, M. J.;

Vittinghoff, E.; Kalhan, R.; Richman, J.; Safford, M., et al. (2012). Association between marijuana exposure and pulmonary function over 20 years. *Journal of the American Medical Association, 307,* 173–181. Schuckit, M. (2006). *Drug and alcohol abuse: A clinical guide to diagnosis and treatment* (6th ed.) New York: Springer, pp. 197–205.

32. Committee on Substance Abuse, American Academy of Pediatrics (1999). Marijuana: A continuing concern for pediatricians. *Pediatrics, 104,* 982–985. Friedman, H.; Newton C.; and Klein, T. W. (2003). Microbial infections, immunomodulation, and drugs of abuse. *Clinical Biochemistry Reviews, 16,* 209–219.

33. Brands, B.; Sproule, B.; and Marshman, J. (Eds.) (1998). *Drugs and drug abuse: A reference text* (3rd ed.). Toronto: Addiction Research Foundation. Budney, Moore, and Vandrey, *Handbook,* p. 258. Committee on Substance Abuse, Marijuana. Grinspoon and Bakalar, Marihuana, pp. 203–204. Male infertility: Sperm from marijuana smokers move too fast, too early (2003, November 3). *Health and Medicine Week,* pp. 459–460.

34. Grinspoon and Bakalar, Marihuana, p. 203.

35. McGothlin, W. H., and West, L. J. (1968). The marijuana problem: An overview. *American Journal of Psychiatry, 125,* 372.

36. Goode, E. (1999). *Drugs in American society* (5th ed.). New York: McGraw-Hill College, pp. 232–233.

37. Brook, J. S.; Adams, R. E.; Balka, E. B.; and Johnson, E. (2002). Early adolescent marijuana use: Risks for the transition to young adulthood. *Psychological Medicine, 32,* 79–91. Goode, E. (2012). *Drugs in American society* (8th ed.). New York: McGraw-Hill, pp. 219–220. Roebuck, M. C.; French, M. T.; and Dennis, M. L. (2004). Adolescent marijuana use and school attendance. *Economics of Education Review, 23,* 133–141.

38. Goode, E. (2012), *Drugs in American society,* pp. 219–220.

39. Fried, P. A.; Wilkinson, B.; and Gray, R. (2005). Neurocognitive consequences of marihuana—A comparison with pre-drug performance. *Neurotoxicology and Teratology, 27,* 231–239. Pope, H. (2002). Cannabis, cognition, and residual confounding. *Journal of the American Medical Association, 287,* 1172–1174. Solowij, N.; Stephens, R. S.; Roffman, R. A.; Babor, T.; Kadden, R.; et al. (2002). Cognitive functioning of long-term heavy cannabis users seeking treatment. *Journal of the American Medical Association, 287,* 1123–1131.

40. Brook, J. S.; Zhang, C.; and Brook, D. W. (2011). Developmental trajectories of marijuana use from adolescence to adulthood: Personal predictors. *Archives of Pediatric and Adolescent Medicine, 165,* 55–60i. Gruber, S. A.; Dahlgren, M. K.; Sagar, K. A.; Gonenc, A.; and Killogre, W. D. (2012). Age of onset of marijuana use impacts inhibitory processing. *Neuroscience Letters, 511,* 89–94. Yücel, M.; Solowij, N.; Respondek, C.; Whittle, S.; Fornito, A.; et al. (2008). Regional brain abnormalities associated with long-term heavy cannabis use. *Archives of General Psychiatry, 65,* 694–701.

41. Kandel, D. B. (2003). Does marijuana use cause the use of other drugs? *Journal of the American Medical Association, 289,* 482–483. Quotation on p. 482. Kandel, D. B. (Ed.) (2002). *Stages and pathways of drug involvement: Examining the gateway hypothesis.* Cambridge: Cambridge University Press.

42. Cited in Medical marijuana: Editorials debate "gateway" effect (1999, April 12). *American Health Line,* http://www.ahl.com.

43. Kandel, Does marijuana use cause the use of other drugs? Lynskey, M. T.; Hath, A. C.; Bucholz, K. K.; Slutske, W. S.; Madden, P. A. F.; et al. (2003). The escalation of drug use in early-onset cannabis users vs. co-twin controls. *Journal of the American Medical Association, 289,* 427–433. Martin, K. R. (2001). Adolescent treatment programs reduce drug abuse, produce other improvements. *NIDA Notes, 16* (1), 11–12. Martin, K. R. (2001). Television public service announcements decrease marijuana use in targeted teens. *NIDA Notes, 16* (1), 14.

44. Zimmer, L., and Morgan, J. P. (1997). *Marijuana myths, marijuana facts: A review of the scientific evidence.* New York: Lindesmith Center, p. 37.

45. Goode (2012), *Drugs in American society,* pp. 220–225.

46. Substance Abuse and Mental Health Services Administration (2012). *Results from the 2011 National Survey on Drug Use and Health: Detailed tables.* Rockville, MD: Substance Abuse and Mental Health Services Administration, Tables 1.1A, 1.1B, and 1.5B.

47. Johnston, L. D.; O'Malley, P. M.; Bachman, J. G.; and Schulenberg, J. E. (2012). *Monitoring the Future: National survey results on drug use, 1975–2011.* Vol. I: Secondary school students 2011. Ann Arbor, MI: Institute for Social Research, The University of Michigan, Tables 2-2, 2-3, and 2-4.

48. Johnston, L. D.; O'Malley, P. M.; Bachman, J. G.; and Schulenberg, J. E. (2009, December 14). Teen marijuana use tilts up, while some drugs decline in use. University of Michigan News Service, Ann Arbor, p. 1.

49. Johnston, O'Malley, Bachman, and Schulenberg (2012). *Monitoring the Future,* Table 8-3.

50. Budney, Moore, and Vandrey, *Handbook,* pp. 278–282. Consroe, P.; Musty, R.; Rein, J.; Tillery, W.; and Pertwee, R. (1997). The perceived effects of smoked cannabis on patients with multiple sclerosis. *European Neurology, 38,* 44–48. Pertwee, R. (2001). Cannabinoid receptors and pain., *Progress in Neurobiology, 63,* 165–174. Pertwee, R. (2002). Cannabinoids and multiple sclerosis. *Pharmacology and Therapeutics, 95,* 165–174. Zajicek, J.; Fox, P.; Sanders, H.; Wright, D.; Vickery, J.; et al. (2003). Cannabinoids for treatment of spasticity and other symptoms related to multiple sclerosis (CAMS study): multicentre randomized placebo-controlled trial. *Lancet, 362,* 1517–1526.

51. Julien, *A primer of drug action,* pp. 577–579. Vestag, B. (2003). Medical marijuana center opens its doors. *Journal of the American Medical Association, 290,* 877–879.

52. Plasse, T. F.; Gorter, R. W.; Krasnow, S. H.; Lane, M.; Shepard, K. V.; et al. (1991). Recent clinical experience with dronabinol. International conference on cannabis and cannabinoids, Chania, Greece. *Pharmacology, Biochemistry, and Behavior, 40,* 695–700.

53. Institute of Medicine (1999). *Marijuana as medicine: Assessing the science base.* Washington, DC: National Academy Press, p. vii.

54. Updated from Inciardi, *The war on drugs III*, pp. 300–301. Institute of Medicine, *Marijuana as medicine*, p. 8.

55. Johnson, K. (2012, January 27). Marijuana push in Colorado likens it to alcohol. *New York Times*, p. A13. Kocieniewski, D. (2010, January 12). New Jersey vote backs marijuana for severely ill. *New York Times*, pp. A1, A18.

56. Attorney General E. H. Holder Jr. (2009, October 19). Attorney General announces formal medical marijuana guidelines. Washington DC: Office of Public Affairs, U.S. Department of Justice. Eckholm, E. (2011, November 5). California dispensaries moving to block U.S. marijuana crackdown. *New York Times*, p. A17. Johnson, K. (2009, October 26). States pressed into new role on marijuana. *New York Times*, pp. A1, A16. Quenqua, D. (2011, May 31). Putting a crimp in the hookah. *New York Times*, pp. A1, A16. Stout, D.; and Moore, S. (2009, October 20). U.S. won't prosecute in states that allow medical marijuana. *New York Times,* pp. A1, A21.

57. AP-CNBC marijuana poll—Complete results and analysis. CNBC.com, accessed April 20, 2010. Responses to Question 3.

58. Rock announces medical marijuana regulation and progress report on research and domestic supply (2001, July 4). Health Canada news release.

59. National Commission on Marihuana and Drug Abuse (1972). *Marihuana: A signal of misunderstanding.* Washington, DC: Government Printing Office, pp. 151–167.

60. Johnston, L. D. (1980, January 16). Marijuana use and the effects of marijuana decriminalization. Unpublished testimony delivered at the hearings on the effects of marijuana held by the Subcommittee on Criminal Justice, Judiciary Committee, U.S. Senate, Washington, DC, p. 5.

61. Melamede, R. J. (2005). Harm reduction—The cannabis paradox. *Harm Reduction Journal, 2,* 17. Sommer, R. (1988). Two decades of marijuana attitudes: The more it changes, the more it is the same. *Journal of Psychoactive Drugs, 20,* 67–70.

62. Majority now supports legalizing marijuana (2013, April 4). News release, Pew Research Center for the People and the Press, Washington, DC.

Alcohol: Social Beverage/Social Drug

After you have completed this chapter, you should have an understanding of

- How alcoholic beverages are produced
- Alcohol use through history
- The history of alcohol regulation from Prohibition to taxation
- Patterns of alcohol consumption
- The pharmacology of alcohol
- Acute physiological and behavioral effects of alcohol
- Alcohol and health benefits
- Strategies for responsible alcohol consumption

I was invited to address a convention of high school teachers on the topic of drug abuse. When I arrived at the convention center to give my talk, I was escorted to a special suite, where I was encouraged to join the executive committee in a round of drug taking—the drug was a special high-proof single-malt whiskey. Later, the irony of the situation had its full impact. As I stepped to the podium under the influence of a psychoactive drug (the whiskey), I looked out through the haze of cigarette smoke at an audience of educators who had invited me to speak to them because they were concerned about the unhealthy impact of drugs on their students. The welcoming applause gradually gave way to the melodic tinkling of ice cubes in liquor glasses, and I began. They did not like what I had to say.

—*John P. J. Pinel*, Biopsychology *(2011)*

Pinel's experience in this opening vignette sums up the central problem facing American society in its dealings with alcohol use and abuse: the frequent failure to acknowledge that alcohol is indeed a psychoactive drug.[1] You may have heard someone remark, "He drinks a little too much, but at least he's not doing drugs." In the eyes of many people, an alcoholic drink is simply a social beverage. In actuality, it is a social drug.

We can see this problem reflected in a number of ways. College courses that cover drug abuse and its effect on society, perhaps the one you are taking right now, are often entitled "Drugs and Alcohol." Would you personally have expected to cover the effects of alcohol in a course simply entitled "Drugs" in your college catalog? If you answered no, then alcohol had better stay in the course title.

Historically, the U.S. government has had two separate federal agencies under the National Institutes of Health (NIH), one concerned with alcohol abuse (the National Institute on Alcohol Abuse and Alcoholism, NIAAA) and the other concerned with the abuse of other drugs (the National Institute on Drug Abuse, NIDA), a distinction that unfortunately has reinforced the notion that alcohol is somehow a substance that stands apart from (or worse, is less serious than) other drugs of potential abuse. A recommendation to consolidate the two agencies had been made in 2010, with an estimated effective date of 2013. However, in 2012, it was decided that NIAAA and NIDA would remain structurally separate but pursue a "functional integration" in future research and educational programs that deal with multiple forms of substance abuse.[2]

Recognizing the immense impact of alcohol use and alcohol abuse on us individually and on our society, two chapters are devoted to alcohol-related issues. This chapter considers alcohol specifically as a drug, with a unique history and tradition. The next chapter examines the long-term effects, specifically the problems of chronic alcohol abuse and alcoholism. We begin by considering the nature of alcohol itself.

What Makes an Alcoholic Beverage?

Creating **ethyl alcohol**, through a process known as **fermentation**, is a remarkably easy thing to do. Almost every culture in the world, at one time or another, has stumbled on the basic recipe. All you need is organic material with a sugar content (honey, grapes, berries, molasses, rye, apples, corn, sugar cane, rice, pumpkins, to name some examples) left undisturbed in a warm container for a time, and nature does the work. Microscopic yeast cells, floating through the air, land on this material and literally consume the sugar in it, and for every sugar molecule consumed, two molecules of alcohol and two molecules of carbon dioxide are left behind as waste. The carbon dioxide bubbles out, and what remains is an alcoholic beverage, less sweet than the substance that began it all but with a new, noticeable "kick." Basic fermentation results in a beverage with an alcohol content of between 12 and 16 percent, best exemplified by standard grape wine.

The process of fermenting starchy grains such as barley to produce beer, called **brewing**, is somewhat more complicated. The barley is first soaked in water until it sprouts, producing an enzyme that is capable of breaking down the starch into sugar. It is then slowly dried, the sprouts are removed, and the remainder (now called **barley malt**) is crushed into a powder. The barley malt is combined with water, corn, and rice to form a mixture called a **mash**. The water activates the enzyme so that the

---

by the numbers . . .

14 Percentage in 2011 of U.S. college students (one in seven) reporting having 10 or more drinks in a row at least once in the past two weeks.

5 Percentage in 2011 of U.S. college students (one in twenty) reporting 15 or more drinks in a row at least once in the past two weeks.

85 Percentage of instances of alcohol-impaired driving reported in 2010 by persons who also reported binge drinking.

Sources: Centers for Disease Control and Prevention (2011). Alcohol-impaired driving among adults—United States, 2010. *Morbidity and Mortality Weekly Report, 60,* 1351–1356. Johnston, L. D.; O'Malley, P. M.; Bachman, J. G.; and Schulenberg, J. E. (2012). Monitoring the Future: National survey results on drug use, 1975–2011. Vol. II: College students and adults ages 19–50, 2011. Ann Arbor, MI: Institute for Social Research, The University of Michigan, p. 260.

---

ethyl alcohol: The product of fermentation of natural sugars. It is generally referred to simply as *alcohol,* though several types of nonethyl alcohol exist.

fermentation: The process of converting natural sugars into ethyl alcohol by the action of yeasts.

brewing: The process of producing beer from barley grain.

barley malt: Barley after it has been soaked in water, sprouts have grown, sprouts have been removed, and the mixture has been dried and crushed to a powder.

mash: Fermented barley malt, following liquefaction and combination with yeasts.

starches convert into sugars. The addition of yeast to the mash starts the fermentation process and produces an alcohol content of approximately 4.5 percent. The dried blossoms of the hop plant, called *hops*, are then added to the brew for the characteristic pungent flavoring and aroma.

Relying on fermentation alone gives an alcohol concentration of about 15 to 16 percent at best. (An alcohol content above this level starts to kill the yeast and, in doing so, stops the fermentation process.) To obtain a higher alcoholic content, another process, called **distillation**, must occur.

Distillation involves heating a container of some fermented mixture until it boils. Because alcohol has a lower boiling temperature than water, the vapor produced has a higher alcohol-to-water ratio than the original mixture. This alcohol-laden vapor is then drawn off into a special coiled apparatus (often referred to as a *still*), cooled until it condenses back to a liquid, and poured drop by drop into a second container. This new liquid, referred to as **distilled spirits** or simply *liquor*, has an alcohol content considerably higher than 16 percent, generally in the neighborhood of 40 to 50 percent.

It is possible, through further distillations, to achieve an alcohol content of up to 95 percent. At this point, however, the alcohol content of distilled spirits is commonly described not by percentage but rather by the designation "proof." Any proof is twice the percentage of alcohol: An 80-proof whiskey contains 40 percent alcohol; a 190-proof vodka contains 95 percent alcohol.

The three basic forms of alcoholic beverages are wine, beer, and distilled spirits. Table 8.1 shows the sources of some well-known examples.

distillation: A process by which fermented liquid is boiled and then cooled, so that the condensed product contains a higher concentration of alcohol than before.

distilled spirits: The liquid product of distillation, also known as *liquor*.

TABLE 8.1

Prominent alcoholic beverages and their sources

BEVERAGE	SOURCE	BEVERAGE	SOURCE
Distilled spirits		**Wines**	
Brandy	Distilled from grape wine, cherries, or peaches	Red table wine	Fermented red grapes with skins
		White table wine	Fermented skinless grapes
Liqueur or cordial	Brandy or gin, flavored with blackberry, cherry, chocolate, peppermint, licorice, etc. Alcohol content ranges from 20% to 55%	Champagne	White wine bottled before all of the yeast is gone so that remaining carbon dioxide produces a carbonated effect
Rum	Distilled from the syrup of sugar cane or from molasses	Sparkling wine	Red wine prepared like champagne or with carbonation added
Scotch whiskey	Distilled from fermented corn and barley malt	**Fortified wines**	Wines whose alcohol content is raised, or fortified, to 20% by the addition of brandy—for example, sherry, port, Marsala, and Madeira
Rye whiskey	Distilled from rye and barley malt		
Blended whiskey	A mixture of two or more types of whiskey		
Bourbon whiskey	Distilled primarily from fermented corn		
Gin	Distilled from barley, potato, corn, wheat, or rye, and flavored with juniper berries	**Wine-like variations**	
		Hard cider	Fermented apples
Vodka	Approximately 95% pure alcohol, distilled from grains or potatoes and diluted by mixing with water	Sake	Fermented rice
Tequila	Distilled from the fermented juice of the maguey plant	**Beers**	Types of beer vary, depending on brewing procedures.
		Draft beer	Contains 3–6% alcohol
Grain neutral spirits	Approximately 95% pure alcohol, used either for medicinal purposes or diluted and mixed in less-concentrated distilled spirits	Lager beer	Contains 3–6% alcohol
		Ale	Contains 3–6% alcohol
		Malt liquor	Contains up to 8% alcohol

Source: Table compiled by the author.

Alcohol Use through History

Historians point out that fermented honey, called *mead*, was probably the original alcoholic beverage, dating from approximately 8000 B.C. Beer, requiring more effort than simple fermentation, came on the scene much later; the Egyptians established the first official brewery about 3700 B.C. At that time, beer was quite different from the watery forms we know today. It more closely resembled a bread than a beverage, and the process of producing beer was closer to baking than to brewing.

Evidence of the development of wine comes from references to its sale in the Code of Hammurabi, King of Babylonia, recorded about 1700 B.C. Wine making itself, however, appears to have begun more than three thousand years before that. Excavations of an ancient village in modern-day Iran have revealed the remains of wine-stained pottery dating back to as early as 5400 B.C.[3]

The first documented distillation of alcohol was the conversion of wine into brandy during the Middle Ages, at a medical school in Salerno, Italy. With an emphasis on its medicinal applications, the new beverage became known in Latin as **aqua vitae** ("the water of life"), but people quickly caught on to its inebriating possibilities. Brandy became the primary distilled liquor in Europe until the middle of the seventeenth century. At that time the Dutch perfected the process of distilling liquor and flavoring it with juniper berries. A new alcoholic beverage was born: gin.

The enormous popularity of gin throughout Europe marked a crucial point in the history of the impact of alcohol on European society. Because it was easily produced, cheaper than brandy, and faster-acting than wine, gin became an immediate hit for all levels of society, particularly the poorer classes of people. By the mid-1700s, alcohol abuse was being condemned as a major societal problem, and concerns about drunkenness had become a public issue.

The consequences of gin consumption was felt in many parts of Europe, but it was in English cities that the gin epidemic became a genuine crisis. By 1750, consumption in England had grown to twenty-two times the level in 1685, and the social devastation was obvious. In London, infant mortality rose during this period, with only one of four baptized babies between 1730 and 1749 surviving to the age of five, despite the fact that mortality rates were falling in the countryside. In one

The social chaos of "Gin Lane" in London, as interpreted in this engraving by William Hogarth (1697–1764). Notice the falling baby in the foreground as a symbol of rampant child neglect during this time.

section of the city, as many as one in every five houses was a gin shop.

Consumption of other distilled spirits introduced during this period, such as rum and whiskey, added to the overall problem, but gin was undoubtedly the prime culprit. The social impact of gin drinking in England during the first half of the eighteenth century illustrates how destructive the introduction of a potent and easily available psychoactive drug into an urban society already suffering from social dislocation and instability can be. The consequences in many ways mirrored the introduction of crack cocaine into the ghettos of the United States during the 1980s (Chapter 4).[4]

Alcohol in Nineteenth-Century America

From its earliest days as a nation to the nineteenth century, alcohol use was a fact of life in America.[5] Not surprisingly, therefore, the social focus of American communities was the tavern. Not only did taverns serve as public dispensers of alcoholic beverages, but they also served as centers for local business dealings and town politics. Mail was delivered there; travelers could

aqua vitae (AH-kwa VEYE-tee): A brandy, the first distilled liquor in recorded history.

stay the night; elections were held there. As an institution, the tavern was as highly regarded, and as regularly attended as the local church.[6]

By today's standards, it is difficult to imagine the extent of alcohol consumption that was going on during the early decades of American history. In 1830, the average per capita intake was an immoderate five drinks a day, more than three times the level of consumption today. It was common to take "whiskey breaks" at 11 A.M. and 4 P.M. each day (except Sunday), much as we take coffee breaks today. As far as types of liquor were concerned, rum was the favorite in New England and along the North Atlantic coast, but elsewhere whiskey was king. George Washington himself went into the whiskey business at Mount Vernon in 1797, eventually establishing the largest whiskey distillery of his time.[7]

The Rise of the Temperance Movement

In the late 1700s, prominent physicians, writers, and scientists began to consider the adverse effects of alcohol consumption and tried to formulate some kind of social reform to mitigate them. The goal at that time was to reduce the consumption of distilled spirits (liquor) only. It was a temperate attitude toward drinking (hence the phrase **temperance movement**) rather than an insistence on the total prohibition of alcohol in all forms.

In the United States, where the temperance movement was to be stronger than anywhere else, its most influential spokesman was Benjamin Rush, a physician, Revolutionary War hero, and signer of the Declaration of Independence. In his 1785 pamphlet "An Inquiry into the Effects of Ardent Spirits on the Human Mind and Body," Rush vividly described the range of mental and physical dangers associated with excessive alcohol consumption, focusing on the specific dangers of liquor to the citizens of a new democracy:

> *Strong liquor is more destructive than the sword. The destruction of war is periodic, whereas alcohol exerts its influence upon human life at all times and in all seasons. . . . A nation corrupted by alcohol can never be free.*[8]

Rush's efforts did not have a major influence on the drinking habits of American society during his lifetime, but they would serve as an inspiration to political and religious groups around the country who saw alcohol consumption in social and moral terms. In their view, drunkenness led to poverty, a disorderly society, and civil disobedience. In short, it was unpatriotic at best and subversive at worst. When we hear the phrase "demon rum,"

Even though this 1874 Currier and Ives engraving shows a temperance crusader in full battle regalia, relatively few temperance activists resorted to physical violence.

we have to recognize that many Americans during the nineteenth century took the phrase quite literally. Liquor was demonized as a direct source of evil in the world.

The temperance point of view toward liquor, like any other form of scapegoating, spread like wildfire. In 1831, the American Temperance Society reported that nearly 2 million Americans had renounced strong liquor and that more than eight hundred local societies had been established. With a characteristic succinctness, Abraham Lincoln observed, in an 1842 address before a national temperance organization, that prior to the temperance era, the harm done by alcohol was considered to be a result of the "abuse of a very good thing," whereas his contemporaries now viewed the harm as coming "from the use of a bad thing."[9] By the 1850s, twelve U.S. states (about one-third of the nation at the time) and two Canadian provinces had introduced legislation forbidding the sale of "alcoholic" (distilled) drink.

temperance movement: The social movement in the United States, beginning in the nineteenth century, that advocated the renunciation of alcohol consumption.

Whether or not justified in doing so, temperance groups took credit for a dramatic change that was occurring in the levels of alcohol consumption in the United States. From 1830 to 1850, consumption of all types of alcohol plummeted from an annual per capita level of roughly 7 gallons to roughly 2 gallons, approximately today's consumption level. It is quite possible that this decline encouraged the temperance movement to formulate its ultimate goal: a prohibition of alcohol consumption in any form.

The Road to National Prohibition

A major development in the temperance movement was the formation in 1880 of a women's organization called the Woman's Christian Temperance Union (WCTU). Almost from the beginning, its primary target was a highly visible fixture of late-nineteenth-century masculine American life: the saloon. These establishments were now vilified as the source of all the troubles alcohol could bring. It is not difficult to imagine how the saloon would have been seen as a significant threat to American women in general.

> Bars appeared to invite family catastrophe. They introduced children to drunkenness and vice and drove husbands to alcoholism; they also caused squandering of wages, wife beating, and child abuse; and, with the patron's inhibitions lowered through drink, the saloon led many men into the arms of prostitutes (and, not incidentally, contributed to the alarming spread of syphilis).[10]

No wonder the WCTU hated the saloon, and no saloon in the country was safe from their "pray-in" demonstrations, vocal opposition, and in some cases violent interventions. Their influence eventually extended into every aspect of American culture. The WCTU and other anti-alcohol forces, such as the newly formed Anti-Saloon League and National Prohibition Party, were soon electing congressional candidates who pledged to enact national legislation banning alcohol consumption throughout the land.

The Beginning and Ending of a "Noble Experiment"

In December 1917, Congress passed a resolution "prohibiting the manufacture, sale, transportation, or importation of intoxicating liquors," the simple wording that would form the basis for the Eighteenth Amendment to the U.S. Constitution. (Note that it did not specifically forbid purchase or use of alcohol.)

The Volstead Act of 1919 set up the enforcement procedures. By the end of the year, the necessary thirty-six states had ratified the amendment, and Prohibition took effect in January 1920.

Despite its lofty aims, Prohibition was doomed to failure. In the countryside, operators of illegal stills (called "moonshiners" because they worked largely at night) continued their production despite the efforts of an occasional half-hearted raid by Treasury agents (known as "revenooers"). The major cities became centers of open defiance. Liquor, having been smuggled into the country, flowed abundantly as saloons turned into speakeasies and operated in violation of the law.

The early years of Prohibition did, however, show positive effects in the area of public health. Alcohol-related deaths, cirrhosis of the liver, mental disorders, and alcohol-related crime declined in 1920 and 1921, but in a few years, the figures began to creep up again, and the level of criminal activity associated with illegal drinking was clearly intolerable.[11] By the end of the decade, it was obvious to the vast majority of Americans that the "noble experiment" (as it was called at the time) was not working.

In 1933 President Franklin D. Roosevelt, having campaigned on a platform to repeal the Volstead Act, signed the necessary legislation that became the Twenty-first Amendment; ratification was swift. Alcohol was restored as a legal commodity, and its regulation was returned once more to local authorities. Over the years, the states gradually repealed their prohibition laws. Mississippi, in 1966, was the last state to do so.

Present-Day Alcohol Regulation by Taxation

One immediate benefit of repealing Prohibition was the return of federal revenue from taxes on alcohol. Indeed, the impact on a struggling national economy hard hit by the Depression had been one of the arguments advanced by the repeal movement. In 1933 alone, excise taxes on alcohol sales brought in $500 million, which was used to finance social welfare programs during the Depression.

The concept of collecting taxes on the basis of alcohol consumption dates back to the very beginning of the United States as a nation. In 1794, the newly formed U.S. Congress passed a law imposing an excise tax on the sale of whiskey. After a short-lived Whiskey Rebellion in which President Washington had to order federal militia to subdue Appalachian farmers who had refused to pay the new tax, the practice of taxing alcohol was accepted and has continued to the present day as an appropriate way of raising tax money.

Taxes on alcohol sales have been an indirect mechanism for regulating the consumption of alcohol by increasing its price, not unlike taxes on tobacco products (see Chapter 10). More than $8 billion each year is collected from federal excise taxes on alcohol. Total annual revenues exceed $18 billion, when additional excise taxes imposed by all U.S. states and some local communities are included. Today, alcoholic beverages are one of the most heavily taxed consumer products. Approximately 45 percent of the retail price of an average bottle of distilled spirits, for example, is earmarked for federal and state taxes.[12]

It has been proposed that alcohol taxes be set high enough to begin to offset the total societal costs resulting from alcohol abuse. This approach would place a type of "user fee" on the consumption of alcohol and reduce the prevalence of alcohol abuse. In general, studies investigating the effects of price on drinking behavior have shown that increases in retail prices for alcoholic beverages have had a significant effect in reducing consumption both in the general population and high-risk groups such as heavy drinkers, adolescents, and young adults.[13]

The stainless steel tanks of the world's largest wine maker, the Ernest and Julio Gallo Winery, are located in Modesto, California. Nearly 900 million gallons of wine are produced by E. & J. Gallo each year, accounting for approximately one of every three bottles of wine sold annually in the United States.

Patterns of Alcohol Consumption Today

It has been theorized that the earliest systems of agriculture in human history were born of the desire to secure a dependable supply of beer.[14] If this is so, then alcohol, commercialization, and economics have been linked from the very beginning. Today, of course, alcohol is not merely a big business but an enormous business. Americans spend more than $140 billion on the purchase of alcoholic beverages each year, and the alcohol industry spends about $1.7 billion advertising its products. In 2007, more than 40 percent of this advertising budget was devoted to television commercials for beer.[15]

Overall Patterns of Alcohol Consumption

How much do Americans actually drink? The most recent estimate of the annual per capita consumption of pure alcohol for adults in the United States is approximately 2.3 gallons (8.7 liters). This level of consumption amounts to about three-fourths of an ounce per day.[16]

How many alcoholic drinks does this estimated daily amount add up to? To answer this question, it is important first to consider the amount of pure alcohol that is contained in each of four basic types of alcoholic beverages. A person consumes a half-ounce of alcohol when drinking any of the following alcoholic beverages:

- One 5-ounce glass of wine
- One 12-ounce bottle or can of beer
- One 12-ounce bottle of wine cooler
- One shot (1.5-ounce size) of 80 proof liquor

All these quantities are approximately equal to about one-half ounce in terms of pure alcohol, and they are often referred to as "standard drinks."

Based on these equivalencies, the average alcohol consumption in the United States can be approximated as about 1.5 "standard drinks" per day. Bear in mind, however, that a "standard drink" may not be the drink you consume, so it is not necessarily the appropriate unit to use when computing your own personal level of alcohol consumption. Draft beer, for example, is typically dispensed in large glasses that exceed 12 ounces in capacity. A mixed drink in a bar might contain a quantity of liquor that exceeds a standard amount, if the bartender is particularly generous. In either of these circumstances, an individual can be misled into believing that he or she is consuming an "average" amount (in terms of number of drinks) when, in fact, the quantity of alcohol being consumed is considerably larger (Health Line).

Health Line

Multiple Ways of Getting a Standard Drink

A standard alcoholic drink is any drink that contains about 14 grams of pure alcohol (about 0.5 fluid ounce). All of the following seven alcoholic drinks should be considered equivalently as a standard drink.

12 oz of beer or wine cooler	8–9 oz of malt liquor	5 oz of table wine*	3–4 oz of fortified wine (such as sherry or port)	2–3 oz of cordial, liqueur, or aperitif	1.5 oz of brandy (a single jigger)	1.5 oz of spirits (a single jigger of 80-proof gin, vodka, whiskey, etc.)
	8.5 oz shown in a 12 oz glass that, if full, would hold about 1.5 standard drinks of malt liquor		3.5 oz shown	2.5 oz shown		Shown straight and in a highball glass with ice to show level before adding mixer †
12 oz	8.5 oz	5 oz	3.5 oz	2.5 oz	1.5 oz	1.5 oz

There are so many variations in the quantity of an alcoholic beverage being served that it can be confusing to determine how many standard drinks are actually being consumed. Here are some examples of how the number of standard drinks can multiply when quantities increase:

- For beer or wine cooler, the approximate number of standard drinks in
  - 12 oz = 1
  - 16 oz = 1.3
  - 22 oz = 2
  - 40 oz = 3.3
- For malt liquor, the approximate number of standard drinks in
  - 12 oz = 1.5
  - 16 oz = 2
  - 22 oz = 2.5
  - 40 oz = 4.5
- For table wine, the approximate number of standard drinks in
  - a standard 750 mL (25 oz) bottle = 5
- For 80-proof spirits, or "hard liquor," the approximate number of standard drinks in
  - a mixed drink = 1 or more †
  - a pint (16 oz) = 11
  - a fifth (25 oz) = 17
  - 1.75 L (59 oz) = 39

*In recent years it has been common for wines to contain an alcohol concentration of 16 percent. In these instances, 5 ounces of wine would be equivalent to 0.80 ounce of alcohol, which is 33 percent higher than when a 12 percent wine is considered. Another way of thinking about this is that for a drink of wine with 16 percent alcohol concentration to be equivalent to a 12-ounce can of beer or a typical shot of liquor, the quantity of wine consumed should be reduced to approximately 4 ounces. In this chapter, however, we will retain the concept of 5 ounces of wine as representing a standard drink, since it is traditional that alcohol equivalencies are calculated on this basis.

†It can be difficult to estimate the number of standard drinks served in a single mixed drink made with hard liquor. Depending on factors such as the type of spirits and the recipe, one mixed drink can contain from one to three or more standard drinks.

Source: National Institute on Alcohol Abuse and Alcoholism (2005). *Helping patients who drink too much: A clinician's guide.* Bethesda, MD: National Institute on Alcohol Abuse and Alcoholism, p. 12.

Another consideration when looking at statistics based on population averages is the obvious fact that not everyone is "average." There is an enormous disparity in terms of how much alcohol each person actually consumes during a given year. Some people drink no alcohol at all, whereas others drink heavily. *In fact, 80 percent of the total amount of alcohol consumed in the United States each year is consumed by only the 30 percent of Americans who drink—and by only 20 percent of the population (includes non-drinkers) in general.* Drugs . . . in Focus, shown below, provides a concrete illustration of the extremely uneven pattern of alcohol consumption in the United States today.

Looking at the types of alcohol consumed in the United States, beer consumption represents about 67 percent of overall alcoholic consumption and a disproportionate share of heavy alcohol drinking. When five or more 12-ounce beers are consumed in a day,

Drugs . . . in Focus

Visualizing the Pattern of Alcohol Consumption in the United States

To appreciate the uneven pattern of alcohol consumption in the population, try the following demonstration:

Assemble ten people and ten bottles of beer (preferably empty).

Separate three people who hold nothing. They represent the 30 percent of the population that does not drink alcohol at all.

Separate five people; together they hold two bottles. They represent the 50 percent of the population that drinks 20 percent of the total alcohol supply.

Separate the ninth person; this person holds two bottles. This individual represents the 10 percent of the population that drinks another 20 percent of the total alcohol supply.

Separate the tenth person; this person holds a six-pack of bottles. This individual represents the 10 percent of the population that drinks 60 percent of the total alcohol supply.

The Moral of the Story

Twenty percent of the entire population (the ninth and tenth persons in this demonstration) drink 80 percent of the total alcohol consumed in the United States each year. Of those who drink some alcohol, two-sevenths (roughly 30 percent) of them drink 80 percent of the total alcohol consumed each year, while five-sevenths (roughly 70 percent) of them drink the remaining 20 percent. These figures correspond to those expressed in the text.

Figure, p. 30, "A Tale of 10 Beers and 10 People" from *Loosening the Grip: A Handbook of Alcohol Information* (8th ed.) by J. Kinney. Copyright © 2006. Reprinted by permission of The McGraw-Hill Companies.

A Tale of 10 Beers and 10 People

3 drink none

5 share 2 beers

1 drinks 2

1 drinks 6

there is a stronger association with alcohol-related problems than when there are comparable consumption levels of wine or liquor. We can conclude that beer is the most problematic form of alcohol consumption in the United States today.[17]

Problematic Alcohol Consumption among College Students

Not surprisingly, the prevalence of moderate alcohol consumption in college (assessed in terms of those having a drink in the last thirty days) is substantially higher than levels encountered in high school (see Chapter 1), although the establishment of twenty-one as the mandated legal drinking age in all U.S. states has delayed the occurrence of *peak* consumption levels to the junior or senior year. Among young adults, *binge drinking*—defined for men as having five or more alcoholic drinks and for women as having four or more alcoholic drinks over a period of two hours—rises sharply from age eighteen to a prevalence rate of about 28 percent (one in four) among those 18 to 35 years of age. For adults of all ages, the prevalence rate is about 17 percent (one in six).

An extensive series of surveys conducted from 1993 to 2005 on American college campuses have shown a fairly consistent picture of the problematic alcohol consumption of college students in the United States over this period of time. Here are the general findings:

- Overall, approximately 44 percent of college students report having engaged in binge drinking during the two weeks prior to the administration of the survey—41 percent of the women and 49 percent of the men. About one in five students abstains from alcohol, whereas one in four is a frequent binge drinker. About half of college students (48 percent) report that drinking to get drunk is an important reason for drinking. Three students in ten (29 percent) report being intoxicated three or more times in a month.

- College students who drank alcohol at some time over the past year frequently report alcohol-related problems while at college. One in four students report that their drinking had a negative impact on their academic performance. Problems included missing a class, falling behind on course assignments, doing poorly on exams or papers, and receiving lower grades overall.

- One in five students report that, while intoxicated, they engaged in unplanned sexual activity or engaged in unprotected sex. One in three students report that they had done something they regretted while intoxicated.

Binge drinking among college students and other young adults is a common social ritual as well as a continuing social concern.

The surveys have also shed light on the adverse impact of alcohol consumption among college students on *nondrinkers* (defined as either abstainers or nonbinge drinkers). These situations, called secondhand effects (because the individuals themselves were not intoxicated but were affected by those who were), are analogous to the problems of secondhand smoking, which will be examined in Chapter 10. Three in 10 college students (29 percent) report that they were insulted or humiliated by another student who had been drinking. One in five students (19 percent) report having experienced an unwanted sexual advance.

It is estimated that approximately 700 college students between the ages of 18 and 24 die each year from alcohol-related unintentional injuries, principally as a consequence of motor vehicle accidents. The trend toward lower levels of high-risk drinking on college campuses will be reviewed in Chapter 16 in the context of overall substance-abuse prevention.[18]

Alcohol Consumption among Adolescents

Among young people who report some alcohol consumption between the ages of twelve and twenty, *the average age when drinking began is fourteen years*. In the 2011 University of Michigan survey, 33 percent of eighth graders reported that they had consumed alcohol, and 15 percent reported that they had been drunk sometime in their lives. Fortunately, these figures are down significantly when compared to earlier surveys. Approximately 6 percent of students at this age reported consuming more than five drinks on a single occasion in the previous two weeks, a pattern of behavior that is about one-half the percentage reported in the late 1990s.

The major challenge in reducing underage alcohol use has been the continuing access that underage drinkers have to alcoholic beverages, despite the present legal restrictions on alcohol sales. Studies show that more than 40 percent of the estimated 11 million underage drinkers, defined as persons aged twelve to twenty who drank in the past 30 days, were provided free alcohol by adults twenty-one or older. About 6 percent of underage drinkers were given alcohol by their parents in the past month. A majority (54 percent) reported drinking alcohol in someone else's home, and 30 percent drank in their own home.[19]

The Pharmacology of Alcohol

Alcohol is a very small molecule that is moderately soluble in fat and highly soluble in water—all characteristics that make it easily absorbed through the gastrointestinal tract once it is ingested, without needing any digestion. About 20 percent of it is absorbed into the bloodstream directly from the stomach, whereas the remaining 80 percent is absorbed from the upper portion of the small intestine.

On entering the stomach, alcohol acts initially as an irritant, increasing the flow of hydrochloric acid and pepsin, chemicals that aid digestion. Therefore, in small amounts, alcohol can help digest a meal. In large amounts, however, alcohol irritates the stomach lining. This is a concern for those already having stomach problems; preexisting ulcers are worsened by drinking alcohol, and heavy alcohol drinking can produce ulcers.

The irritating effect on the stomach explains why the alcohol proceeds on to the small intestine more quickly when alcohol concentrations are high. The stomach is simply trying to get rid of its irritant. Over time, the chronic consumption of alcohol can produce an inflammation of the stomach (gastritis) or the pancreas (pancreatitis).

Because the small intestine assumes the major share of the responsibilities and acts extremely rapidly (more rapidly than the stomach), the rate of total alcohol absorption is based largely on the condition of the stomach when the alcohol arrives and the time required for the stomach to empty its contents into the small intestine. If the stomach is empty, an intoxicating effect (the "buzz") will be felt very quickly. If the stomach is full, absorption will be delayed as the alcohol is retained by the stomach along with the food being digested, and the passage of alcohol into the small intestine will slow down.

Besides the condition of the stomach, there are other factors related to the alcohol itself and the behavior of the drinker that influence the rate of alcohol absorption. The principal factor is the concentration of alcohol in the beverage being ingested. An ounce of 80-proof (40 percent) alcohol will be felt more quickly than an ounce of wine containing 12 percent alcohol, and of course the level of alcohol in the blood will be higher as well. Also, if the alcoholic beverage is carbonated, as are champagne and other sparkling wines, the stomach will empty its contents faster and effects will be felt sooner. Finally, if the alcohol enters the body at a rapid pace, such as when drinks are consumed in quick succession, the level of alcohol in the blood will be higher because the liver cannot eliminate it fast enough. All other factors being equal, a bigger person requires a larger quantity of alcohol to have equivalent levels accumulating in the blood, simply because there are more body fluids to absorb the alcohol, thus diluting the overall effect.[20]

The Breakdown and Elimination of Alcohol

Its solubility in water helps alcohol to be distributed to all bodily tissues, with those tissues having greater water content receiving a relatively greater proportion of alcohol. The excretion of alcohol is accomplished in two basic ways. About 5 percent will be eliminated by the lungs through exhalation, causing the characteristic "alcohol breath" of heavy drinkers. Breathalyzers, designed to test for alcohol concentrations in the body and used frequently by law-enforcement officers to test for drunkenness, work on this principle. The remaining 95 percent is eliminated in the urine after the alcohol has been biotransformed into carbon dioxide and water.[21]

The solubility of alcohol in fat facilitates its passage across the blood–brain barrier (see Chapter 3). As a result, approximately 90 percent of the alcohol in the blood reaches the brain almost immediately. Unfortunately, alcohol passes the blood–placenta barrier with equal ease, so alcohol intake by women during pregnancy affects the developing fetus. As a result, fetal alcohol levels are essentially identical to those of the mother who is drinking.[22] This important matter will be discussed in the next chapter, when we consider a type of mental and physical retardation called *fetal alcohol syndrome.*

The body recognizes alcohol as a visitor with no real biological purpose. It contains calories but no vitamins, minerals, or other components that have any nutritional value. Therefore, the primary bodily reaction is to break it down for eventual removal, through a process called **oxidation**. This biotransformation process consists of two basic steps. First, an enzyme, **alcohol dehydrogenase** breaks down alcohol into **acetaldehyde**. This enzyme is present in the stomach, where about 20 percent of alcohol is broken down prior to absorption into the bloodstream, and in the liver, where the remaining 80 percent is broken down from accumulations in the blood. Second, another enzyme, **acetaldehyde dehydrogenase**, breaks down acetaldehyde in the liver into **acetic acid**. From there, further

oxidation results in oxygen, carbon dioxide, and calories of energy.

The entire process is determined by the speed with which alcohol dehydrogenase does its work, and for a given individual, it works at a constant rate, no matter how much alcohol needs to be broken down. Imagine a bank at which only one teller window stays open, no matter how long the line of customers grows, and you will understand the limitations under which the body is operating.

The specific rate of oxidation is approximately 100 milligrams of alcohol per hour per kilogram of body weight. To put this in perspective, 8 grams of alcohol will be broken down in an hour if you weigh 176 pounds (80 kilograms), and 5 grams of alcohol will be broken down in an hour if you weigh 110 pounds (50 kilograms). Certain conditions and circumstances, however, can alter this basic biotransformation rate (Health Line).

In terms of alcoholic beverages, the oxidation rate for adults in general is approximately one-third to one-half ounce of pure alcohol an hour. If you sipped (not gulped) slightly less than the contents of one 12-ounce bottle of beer, one 5-ounce glass of wine, or any equivalent portion of alcohol very slowly over an hour's time, the enzymes in the stomach and liver would keep up, and you would not feel intoxicated. Naturally, if you consume larger amounts of alcohol at faster rates of consumption, all bets are off.[23]

It is no secret that alcohol consumption is conducive to the accumulation of body fat, most noticeably in the form of the notorious beer belly. It turns out that alcohol does not have significant effects on the biotransformation of dietary carbohydrates and proteins, so a drinking individual who consumes a healthy diet does not have to worry about getting enough nutrients. Alcohol does, however, reduce the breakdown of fat, so dietary fat has a greater chance of being stored rather than expended. Over time, the accumulation of fat in the liver is particularly serious because it eventually interferes with normal liver function. The potentially life-threatening medical conditions involving the liver will be examined in the next chapter as a prime example of the adverse effects of chronic alcohol consumption.[24]

Measuring Alcohol in the Blood

Alcohol levels in the blood, like levels of any drug, vary considerably not only by virtue of how much is ingested and how long ago, but also as a result of differences in an individual's body size and relative

oxidation: A chemical process in alcohol metabolism.

alcohol dehydrogenase (AL-co-haul DEE-high-DRAW-juh-nays): An enzyme in the stomach and liver that converts alcohol into acetaldehyde.

acetaldehyde (ASS-ee-TAL-duh-hide): A by-product of alcohol metabolism, produced through the action of alcohol dehydrogenase.

acetaldehyde dehydrogenase (ASS-ee-TAL-duh-hide DEE-high-DRAW-juh-nays): An enzyme in the liver that converts acetaldehyde to acetic acid in alcohol metabolism.

acetic acid (a-SEE-tik ASS-id): A by-product of alcohol metabolism, produced through the action of acetaldehyde dehydrogenase.

Health Line

Gender, Race, and Medication: Factors in Alcohol Metabolism

Since enzymes play such a critical role in alcohol breakdown, it is important to consider factors that alter the levels of these enzymes. As mentioned in Chapter 3, two of these factors are gender and ethnicity. In general, women have about 60 percent less alcohol dehydrogenase in the stomach than men; thus their oxidation of alcohol is relatively slower, even when different body weights have been taken into account.

In addition, about 50 percent of all people of Asian descent have a genetically imposed lower level of acetaldehyde dehydrogenase in the liver. As a consequence, acetaldehyde builds up, causing nausea, itching, facial flushing, and cardiac acceleration. The combination of these symptoms, often referred to as *fast-flushing*, makes alcohol consumption very unpleasant for many Asians.

It would be reasonable to expect, then, that those who experienced fast-flushing would drink less alcohol than those who do not. This is true when you look at the population at large. For Japanese American college students who have to contend with peer pressure to drink, however, the relationship between the physiological response and the quantity of alcohol consumed is not nearly as strong. For them, environmental factors encourage alcohol consumption, despite their genetically determined predisposition to get sick. In a similar way, the social life of Japanese businessmen has promoted alcohol consumption, even though many get sick as a result. Unfortunately, accepting an offer from one's boss to go out drinking is part of the social networking required for corporate advancement.

Medications also can influence alcohol breakdown by altering levels of alcohol dehydrogenase in the stomach. Aspirin, for example, when taken on a full stomach, reduces enzyme levels by one-half, causing more alcohol to accumulate in the blood. Among women, aspirin has a greater inhibiting effect than among men, so it is possible that enzyme levels may be reduced to nearly zero if a woman is taking aspirin prior to drinking alcoholic beverages. Gastric ulcer medications also inhibit alcohol dehydrogenase and thus increase the physiological impact of alcohol. Any combination of these factors appears to produce additive effects. (See Table 8.3 on page 207 for other examples of alcohol-medication interactions.)

Sources: Edenberg, H. J. (2007, Winter). The genetics of alcohol metabolism: Role of alcohol dehydrogenase and aldehyde dehydrogenase variants. *Alcohol Research and Health*, 5–37. Frezza, M.; DiPadova, C.; Pozzato, G.; Terpin, M.; Baraona, E.; and Lieber, C. S. (1990). High blood alcohol levels in women: The role of decreased gastric alcohol dehydrogenase activity and first-pass metabolism. *New England Journal of Medicine, 322*, 95–99. Nakawatase, T. V., and Sasao, T. (1993). The association between fast-flushing response and alcohol use among Japanese Americans. *Journal of Studies on Alcohol, 54*, 48–53. Roine, R.; Gentry, T.; Hernandez-Muñoz, R.; Baraona, E.; and Lieber, C. S. (1990). Aspirin increases blood alcohol concentrations in humans after ingestion of ethanol. *Journal of the American Medical Association, 264*, 2406–2408. Scott, D. M., and Taylor, R. E. (2007, Winter). Health-related effects of genetic variations of alcohol-metabolizing enzymes in African Americans. *Alcohol Research and Health*, 18–21.

proportions of body fat. Consequently, we have to consider a specific ratio referred to as the **blood-alcohol concentration (BAC)** when assessing physiological and psychological effects (an alternative term is blood-alcohol level).

The BAC refers to the number of grams of alcohol in the blood relative to 100 milliliters of blood, expressed as a percentage. For example, 0.1 gram (100 milligrams) of alcohol in 100 milliliters of blood is represented by a BAC of 0.10 percent. Table 8.2 (page 204) shows the BAC levels that can be estimated from one's body weight, number of standard drinks consumed, and hours elapsed since starting the first drink.

From these figures, BAC levels typically are considered in terms of three broad categories of behavior: caution (0.01 to 0.05 percent), driving impaired (0.05 to 0.08 percent), and legally drunk (in all U.S. states, 0.08 percent and higher). In effect, you need to compute the accumulated BAC levels for your specific body weight after having a specific number of drinks, and then subtract 0.015 percent BAC for each hour since the drinking occurred.[25]

blood-alcohol concentration (BAC): The number of grams of alcohol in the blood relative to 100 milliliters of blood, expressed as a percentage.

TABLE 8.2

When are you drunk? Calculating your blood-alcohol concentration (BAC) level

					Standard Drinks						
		1	2	3	4	5	6	7	8	9	10
WEIGHT (LB)	100	.029	.058	.088	.117	.146	.175	.204	.233	.262	.290
	120	.024	.048	.073	.097	.121	.145	.170	.194	.219	.243
	140	.021	.042	.063	.083	.104	.125	.146	.166	.187	.208
	160	.019	.037	.055	.073	.091	.109	.128	.146	.164	.182
	180	.017	.033	.049	.065	.081	.097	.113	.130	.146	.162
	200	.015	.029	.044	.058	.073	.087	.102	.117	.131	.146
	220	.014	.027	.040	.053	.067	.080	.093	.106	.119	.133
	240	.012	.024	.037	.048	.061	.073	.085	.097	.109	.122

CAUTION   DRIVING IMPAIRED   LEGALLY DRUNK

Alcohol is "burned up" by your body at .015% per hour, as follows:

Hours since starting first drink	1	2	3	4	5	6
Percent alcohol burned up	.015	.030	.045	.060	.075	.090

To calculate your BAC level correctly, you must consider the number of standard drinks you have consumed, your body weight, and how much time has passed since the first drink. Note that a BAC level of .10% or higher has been, until recently, the standard for drunk driving in most U.S. states. All U.S. states have now adopted the .08% standard.

Source: Updated from *A primer of drug action,* 8th ed., by R. M. Julien, M.D. © 2001 Worth Publishers. Used with permission.

Effects of Alcohol on the Brain

Alcohol is clearly a CNS depressant drug, though it is often misidentified as a stimulant. The reason for this confusion is that alcohol, at low doses, first releases the cerebral cortex from its inhibitory control over subcortical systems in the brain, a kind of double-negative effect. In other words, alcohol is depressing an area of the brain that normally would be an inhibitor, and the result of this "disinhibition" is the illusion of stimulation. The impairment in judgment and thinking (the classic features of being drunk) stems from a loosening of social inhibitions that enable us, under nonalcoholic circumstances, to be relatively thoughtful about the consequences of our actions, as well as relatively civil and well behaved.[26]

As the BAC level increases, the depressive action of alcohol extends downward to lower regions of the brain. Eventually, an inhibition of the respiratory centers in the medulla becomes a distinct possibility, leading to asphyxiation (a loss of breathing). In general, neuronal inhibition is linked to the effect of alcohol on the GABA receptor in the brain. Imagine this receptor as having three components: one sensitive specifically to the neurotransmitter GABA, one sensitive to barbiturates, and one sensitive to a type of antianxiety medication (see Chapter 13). The last component is also sensitive to alcohol, and the research suggests that alcohol acts at this site, making it more difficult for the neuron to be stimulated.[27]

More worrisome than alcohol's depressive effects on the brain, however, is its ability to set up a pattern of psychological dependence. Since the late 1980s, evidence has accumulated that the reinforcing action of alcohol is a result of its influence on dopamine-releasing neurons in the nucleus accumbens of the brain (see Chapter 3). The fact that alcohol shares this effect with other abused drugs, including heroin, cocaine, and nicotine, suggests that treatments for one form of drug abuse can be effective for others. Chapter 9 describes the recent research concerning the use of naltrexone, an opioid antagonist, in the treatment of chronic alcohol abuse.[28]

Acute Physiological Effects

Alcohol can produce a number of *acute* physiological effects; they will be examined here. The physiological effects resulting from *chronic* alcohol consumption will be covered in the next chapter.

Toxic Reactions

First and foremost, we need to be aware of the risk of death by asphyxiation if BAC levels are elevated, generally when they reach 0.50 percent. The therapeutic index for alcohol, as measured by the LD50/ED50 ratio (see Chapter 2), is approximately 6, which is not a very high number. Therefore, caution is strongly advised; the risks of being the "big winner" in a drinking contest should be weighed very carefully. On the one hand, to achieve a lethal BAC level of 0.50 percent, a 165-pound man needs to have consumed approximately twenty-three drinks over a four-hour period.[29] On the other hand, consuming "merely" ten drinks in one hour, a drinking schedule that achieves a BAC level of 0.35 percent, puts a person in extremely dangerous territory. It is important to remember that LD50 is the *average* level for a lethal effect; there is no way to predict where a particular person might be located on the normal curve.

Fortunately, two physiological mechanisms are designed to protect us to a certain degree. First, alcohol acts as a gastric irritant, so the drinker often feels nauseated and vomits. Second, the drinker may simply pass out, and the risk potential from further drinking becomes irrelevant. Nonetheless, there are residual dangers in becoming unconscious; vomiting while in this state can prevent breathing, and death can occur from asphyxiation (Health Alert).

Heat Loss and the Saint Bernard Myth

Alcohol is a peripheral vasodilator, which means that blood vessels near the skin surface enlarge, leading to a greater amount of blood shunted to the skin. The effect gives you the feeling that your skin is warm, which is probably the basis for the myth that alcohol can keep you warm in freezing weather. In truth, however, peripheral dilation causes core body temperature to decrease. In other words, alcohol produces a greater loss in body heat than would occur without it. So if you are marooned in the snow and you see an approaching Saint Bernard with a cask of brandy strapped to its neck, refuse the offer. It will not help and could very well do you harm. (But feel free to hug the dog—that will certainly help.)

HEALTH ALERT!

Emergency Signs and Procedures in Acute Alcohol Intoxication

Emergency Signs

- Stupor or unconsciousness
- Cool or damp skin
- Weak, rapid pulse (more than 100 beats per minute)
- Shallow and irregular breathing rate, averaging around one breath every three or four seconds
- Pale or bluish skin

Note: Among African Americans, color changes will be apparent in the fingernail beds, mucous membranes inside the mouth, or underneath the eyelids.

Emergency Procedures

- Seek medical help immediately.
- Drinker should lie on his or her side, with the head slightly lower than the rest of the body. This will prevent blockage of the airway and possible asphyxiation if the drinker starts to vomit.
- If drinker is put to bed, maintain some system of monitoring until he or she regains consciousness.

Note: There is no evidence that home remedies for "sobering up," such as cold showers, strong coffee, forced activity, or induction of vomiting, have any effect in reducing the level of intoxication. The only factors that help are the passage of time, rest, and perhaps an analgesic if there is a headache.

> **Where to go for assistance:**
> www.emedicinehealth.com/alcohol_intoxication/article_em.htm.
>
> This web site provides consumer health information on a variety of issues related to acute alcohol intoxication. It is owned and operated by WebMD and is part of the WebMD network.

Source: Victor, M. (1976). Treatment of alcohol intoxication and the withdrawal syndrome: A critical analysis of the use of drugs and other forms of therapy. In P. G. Bourne (Ed.), *Acute drug abuse emergencies: A treatment manual.* New York: Academic Press, pp. 197–228.

Diuretic Effects

As concentration levels rise in the blood, alcohol begins to inhibit **antidiuretic hormone (ADH)**, a hormone that normally acts to reabsorb water in the kidneys prior to elimination in the urine. As a result, urine is more diluted and, because large amounts of liquid are typically being consumed at the time, more copious. Once blood-alcohol concentrations have peaked, however, the reverse occurs. Water is now retained in a condition called **antidiuresis**, resulting in swollen fingers, hands, and feet. This effect is more pronounced if salty foods (peanuts or pretzels, for example) were eaten along with the alcohol.

The inhibition of ADH during the drinking of alcoholic beverages can be a serious concern, particularly following vigorous exercise when the body is already suffering from a loss of water and fluid levels are low. Therefore, the advice to the marathoner, whose body may lose more than a gallon of water over the course of a warm three-hour run, is to celebrate the end of the race not with a beer but with nonintoxicating liquids such as Gatorade or similar mineral-rich drinks.[30]

Effects on Sleep

It might seem tempting to induce sleep with a relaxing "nightcap," but in fact the resulting sleep patterns are adversely affected. Alcohol reduces the duration of a phase of sleep called rapid eye movement (REM) sleep (see Chapter 13). Depending on the dose, REM sleep can be either partially or completely suppressed during the night. When alcohol is withdrawn, REM sleep rebounds and represents a higher percentage of total sleep time than before alcohol consumption began. As a result, individuals sleep poorly and experience nightmares.[31]

Effects on Pregnancy

The consumption of alcohol during pregnancy, even in moderation, greatly increases the risk of retardation in the development of the fetus (a serious condition called *fetal alcohol syndrome*, see Chapter 9), and reducing the incidence of this behavior has been a major public health objective since the mid-1990s. From data

antidiuretic hormone (ADH): A hormone that acts to reabsorb water in the kidneys prior to excretion from the body.

antidiuresis: A condition resulting from excessive reabsorption of water in the kidneys.

averaged over 2010 and 2011, it has been estimated that about 9 percent of pregnant women consume alcohol during the past month at some time during their pregnancy, exposing approximately one in eleven fetuses to alcohol *in utero*. National public health goals for the United States (see Chapter 17) have included a reduction of this percentage to 6 percent, an objective that may be achieved in the next decade, given the steady progress being made in this regard. It is fortunate that even relatively brief interventions are effective in helping pregnant women achieve abstinence from alcohol. In one program of this kind, women were five times more likely to have abstained by the third trimester of pregnancy, relative to controls, after a brief (10 to 15 minute) counseling session in a walk-in center.[32]

Interactions with Other Drugs

A major concern in alcohol drinking is the complex interaction of alcohol with a wide range of drugs. As noted in Chapter 2, the DAWN reports of emergency department admissions and deaths show a significant incidence of medical crises arising from the combination of alcohol not only with prescribed medications but also with virtually all the illicit drugs on the street. Opioid drugs, marijuana, and many prescription medicines interact with alcohol such that the resulting combination produces effects that are either the sum of the parts or greater than the sum of the parts. In other cases, the ingestion of medication with alcohol significantly lessens the medication's benefits. Anticoagulants, anticonvulsants, and monoamine oxidase inhibitors (used as antidepressants) fit into this second category. Table 8.3 shows a partial listing of major therapeutic drugs that interact with alcohol and have undesirable, if not dangerous, outcomes. *Given the length of a complete listing, it is fair to say that, whenever any medication is taken, the individual should inquire about possible interactions with alcohol.*

Hangovers

About four to twelve hours after heavy consumption of alcohol, usually the next day, unpleasant symptoms of headache, nausea, fatigue, and thirst may occur; these are collectively known as a *hangover*. At least one such experience has been undergone by 40 percent of all men and 27 percent of all women over the age of eighteen.[33] Why these symptoms occur is not at all clear. The probable explanations at present focus on individual aspects of a hangover, though it is likely that several factors contribute to the total phenomenon.

TABLE 8.3

A partial listing of possible drug-alcohol interactions

GENERIC DRUG (BRAND NAME OR TYPE)	CONDITION BEING TREATED	EFFECT OF INTERACTION
chloral hydrate (Noctec)	Insomnia	Excessive sedation that can be fatal; irregular heartbeat; flushing
glutethimide (Doriden)	Insomnia	Excessive sedation; reduced driving and machine-operating skills
antihypertensives (Apresoline, Diuril)	High blood pressure	Exaggeration of blood pressure-lowering effect; dizziness on rising
diuretics (Aldactone)	High blood pressure	Exaggeration of blood pressure-lowering effect; dizziness on rising
antibiotics (penicillin)	Bacterial infections	Reduced therapeutic effectiveness
nitroglycerin (Nitro-bid)	Angina pain	Severe decrease in blood pressure; intense flushing; headache; dizziness on rising
warfarin (Coumadin)	Blood clot	Changes in the anti-blood clotting effect*
insulin	Diabetes	Excessive low blood sugar; nausea; flushing
disulfiram (Antabuse)	Alcoholic drinking	Intense flushing; severe headache; vomiting; heart palpitations; could be fatal
methotrexate	Various cancers	Increased risk of liver damage
phenytoin (Dilantin)	Epileptic seizures	Changes in drug effectiveness in preventing seizures*
prednisone (Deltasone)	Inflammatory conditions (arthritis, bursitis)	Stomach Irritation
various antihistamines	Nasal congestion	Excessive sedation that could be fatal
acetaminophen (Tylenol)	Pain	Increased risk of liver damage

Note: Warfarin effects and phenytoin effectiveness will be decreased among individuals who are regular alcohol drinkers, while warfarin effects and phenytoin effectiveness will be enhanced (with greater incidence of side effects) among individuals who ingest a few drinks or more immediately prior to taking the drug.

Sources: Brick, J.; Wallen, M. C.; and Lorman, W. J. (2008). Interaction of alcohol with medications and other drugs. In J. Brick (Ed.), Handbook of the medical consequences of drug and alcohol abuse (2nd ed.). New York, Routledge, pp. 527–563. National Institute on Alcohol Abuse and Alcoholism (1995, January). Alcohol alert: Alcohol–medication interactions. No. 27, PH355. Bethesda, MD: National Institute on Alcohol Abuse and Alcoholism.

One factor, beyond the simple fact of drinking too much, is the type of alcohol that has been consumed. Among distilled spirits, for example, vodka has a lower probability of inducing hangovers than whiskey. A possible reason is the relatively lower amount of **congeners**. These substances in alcoholic beverages, including trace amounts of nonethyl alcohol, oils, and other organic matter, are by-products of the fermentation and distillation processes and give the drinks their distinctive smell, taste, and color. A common congener is the tannin found in red wines. Although no harm is caused by congeners in minute concentrations, they are still toxic substances, and they probably contribute to hangover symptoms.[34]

Other possible factors include traces of nonoxidized acetaldehyde in the blood, residual irritation in the stomach, and a low blood sugar level rebounding from the high levels induced by the previous ingestion of alcohol. The feeling of swollenness from the anti-diuresis, discussed earlier, may contribute to the headache pain. The thirst may be due to the dehydration that occurred the night before.

Acute Behavioral Effects

The consumption of alcoholic beverages is so pervasive in the world that it seems almost unnecessary to comment on how it feels to be intoxicated by alcohol. The behavioral effects of consuming alcohol in more than very moderate quantities range from the relatively

congeners (KON-jen-ers): Nonethyl alcohols, oils, and other organic substances found in trace amounts in some distilled spirits.

harmless effects of exhilaration and excitement, talk-ativeness, slurred speech, and irritability to behaviors that have the potential for causing great harm: uncoordinated movement, drowsiness, sensorimotor difficulties, and stupor.[35] Some of the prominent behavioral problems associated with acute alcohol intoxication will be examined in this section.

Blackouts

A **blackout** is an inability to remember events that occurred during the period of intoxication, even though the individual was conscious at the time. For example, a drinker having too much to drink at a party drives home, parks the car on a nearby street, and goes to bed. The next morning, he or she has no memory of having driven home and cannot locate the car. This phenomenon is different from "passing out," which is a loss of consciousness from alcoholic intoxication. In the case of blackouts, consciousness is never lost. Essentially, the alcohol is suppressing specific areas of the brain that are normally responsible for the formation of long-term memory.

Owing to the possibility of blackouts, drinkers can be easily misled into thinking that because they can understand some information given to them during drinking, they will remember it later. The risk of blackouts is greatest when alcohol is consumed very quickly, forcing the BAC to rise rapidly. In a recent e-mail survey of college students to learn more about their experiences with blackouts, approximately half of those who had ever consumed alcohol reported having experienced a blackout at some point in their lives, and 40 percent reported having had at least one experience in the twelve months prior to the survey.[36]

Driving Skills

There is no question that alcohol consumption significantly impairs the ability to drive or deal with automobile traffic, particularly among young people. In 2011, of the 32,367 traffic fatalities that occurred in the United States, 9,878 of them (about 31 percent) were alcohol-related. To put this statistic in perspective, there were approximately 27 alcohol-impaired driving fatalities every day during that year (one instance every 53 minutes).[37]

blackout: Amnesia concerning events occurring during the period of alcoholic intoxication, even though consciousness had been maintained at that time.

Every community has its tragic stories of preventable deaths due to drunk driving. Alcohol is also recognized as a major factor in more than 800 boating fatalities in the United States each year.

Officially, statistics about alcohol-related fatalities are based on conditions in which drivers had a BAC of 0.08 percent or higher, the minimum standard for legal intoxication in all U.S. states, but there were also a number of fatalities resulting from a BAC below that level. It is important to recognize that driving can be impaired and an accident can occur with BAC levels as low as 0.02 to 0.04 percent—well below the "driving while intoxicated" (DWI) threshold.

All these statistics could be viewed as correlational, and not necessarily as proof of a causal relationship between alcohol and automobile accidents, were it not for the data from laboratory-based experiments showing a clear deterioration of sensorimotor skills following the ingestion of alcohol. Reaction times are slower, the coordination necessary to steer a car steadily is hampered, and the ability to stay awake when fatigued is impaired, but the major way that alcohol impairs driving ability is by reducing the drinker's awareness of peripheral events and stimuli.[38] One researcher in this area has expressed the deficit in this way:

> *The overwhelming majority of accidents involving alcohol are not accidents in which tracking is the prime error. Contrary to what most people think, it isn't that people are weaving down the road, which is a sign of very high blood alcohol levels; it's that they have failed to see something. They go through a red light, they fail to see a pedestrian or a motorcyclist, they fail to see that the road is curving. Their perceptual and attentive mechanisms are affected very early, after just one drink. These are the things that are the prime causes of accidents.*[39]

Unfortunately, it is the weaving behavior, or other extreme examples of driving impairments, that most often signals the police to stop a car for a possible DWI violation; other alcohol-based impairments frequently go unnoticed until it is too late.

Preventing Alcohol-Related Traffic Fatalities among Young People

Increasing the minimum age for alcohol sales and standardizing the minimal BAC level for intoxicated driving have had a major impact on the likelihood of traffic fatalities among young people.[40] Now that the minimum legal drinking age is set at twenty-one years and the minimum BAC level for intoxication lowered to 0.08 percent nationwide, there is reason to be cautiously optimistic. According to estimates made by the National Highway Traffic Safety Administration, the reduction of the minimum BAC level to 0.08 percent has saved five hundred lives each year on the nation's highways. More than 700 lives of persons aged eighteen, nineteen, or twenty have been saved each year as a result of laws setting twenty-one as the minimum drinking age. Since 1998, a nationwide minimum level of intoxication for drivers younger than twenty-one years of age has been set at a BAC level of 0.02 percent.[41]

Educational programs in schools and communities emphasizing the advantages of using "designated drivers," as well as public education and lobbying groups such as Mothers Against Drunk Driving (MADD) and Students Against Drunk Driving (SADD), have had positive effects. This chapter's Portrait feature highlights the origins and current aspirations of MADD.

A major goal in reducing alcohol-related fatalities on the road is to prevent an intoxicated individual from getting behind the wheel in the first place. We cannot prevent any intoxicated individual from driving a car,

PORTRAIT

Candace Lightner—Founder of MADD

In 1980, Candace Lightner's thirteen-year-old daughter, Cari, was killed by a hit-and-run intoxicated driver in California. The driver had been out of jail on bail for only two days, a consequence of another hit-and-run drunk-driving crash, and he had three previous drunk-driving arrests and two previous convictions. He was allowed to plea bargain to vehicular manslaughter. Although the sentence was to serve two years in prison, the judge allowed him to serve time in a work camp and later a half-way house.

It was appalling to Lightner that drunk drivers, similar to the one who had killed her daughter, were receiving such lenient treatment, with many of them never going to jail for a single day. Lightner quit her job and started an organization that has become a household name: Mothers Against Drunk Driving (MADD).

Since then, MADD has campaigned for stricter laws against drunk driving, and most of the present DWI legislation around the country is a result of its intense efforts. In addition, MADD acts as a voice for victims of drunk-driving injuries and the families of those who have been killed. From a single act of courage, despite enormous grief, Lightner created an organization that currently boasts more than 3 million members in the United States, with groups in virtually every state and more than four hundred local chapters.

Over the years, MADD has sought to reduce the number of alcohol-related traffic fatalities in a number of directions:

1. More effective enforcement of the minimum-drinking-age law.
2. A "0.00 percent BAC" criterion for drivers under twenty-one, making it illegal to drive with *any* measurable level of blood alcohol in any state.
3. Driver's license suspensions for underage persons convicted of purchasing or possessing alcoholic beverages.
4. Alcohol-free zones for youth gatherings.
5. Criminal sanctions against adults who provide or allow alcoholic beverages at events for underage participants.
6. Mandatory alcohol and drug testing for all drivers in all traffic crashes resulting in fatalities or serious bodily injury.
7. Sobriety checkpoints to detect and apprehend alcohol-impaired drivers and to serve as a visible deterrent to drinking and driving.

Its most recent success has been in the establishment of laws mandating the installation of ignition interlock systems in vehicles driven by individuals convicted of drunk driving in all 50 U.S. states (see page 210).

Sources: Information courtesy of Mothers Against Drunk Driving, Dallas, Texas, 2012. Interview with Candace Lightner.

but we can at least try to prevent an individual who has had a previous DUI arrest from driving while intoxicated. The most widely used technology for preventing such a situation is known as an ignition interlock device. When activated by the detection of a minimum BAC level in the breath of the driver, the ignition interlock will prevent the car from starting. When New Mexico became the first state to require ignition interlocks to be installed after a first DWI offense; alcohol-related fatalities decreased 11 percent in the first year. When Maryland mandated that the system be installed after several DWI arrests, fatalities were reduced by 18 percent. All 50 U.S. states have now enacted some form of ignition interlock law, typically during the period of license suspension and/or a specified time before fully relicensing DWI offenders. Several states mandate the installation of ignition interlock devices even after a first-time DWI offense.[42]

In general, even though we have reason to be somewhat hopeful about reducing alcohol-related traffic fatalities, it is clear that much work remains to be done. The United States presently has one of the most lenient standards for driving while intoxicated among nations in the world (Table 8.4). The number of alcohol-related accidents, particularly among male drivers, whose involvement exceeds that of female drivers by about 2:1, is far too high. Meanwhile, the drinking-and-driving phenomenon is widespread throughout the population. In 2011, approximately 29 million drivers (one in nine drivers in the United States) admitted to driving a motor vehicle over the past year when they thought they were over the legal limit for alcohol and driving. The peak age among males reporting that they were drinking and driving was between 21 and 25, during which approximately at least one in five reported being intoxicated on the road in the past year. Not surprisingly, automobile insurance premiums are considerably elevated for this demographic group.[43]

Alcohol, Violence, and Aggression

It is difficult to avoid sweeping generalizations when confronted with statistics about alcohol and violent behavior both in the United States and around the world (see Chapter 2). In a major study conducted in a community in northwestern Ontario, Canada, and reported in 1991, more than 50 percent of the most recent occasions of physical violence were found to be preceded by alcohol use on the part of the assailant and/or the victims themselves.[44] Other studies show from 50 to 60 percent of all murders being committed when the killer had been drinking. About 40 percent of all acts of male sexual aggression against adult women and from 60 to 70 percent of male-instigated domestic violence occur when the offender has been drunk; more than 60 percent of all acts of child molestation involve drunkenness.[45]

Researchers have advanced three principal ways of accounting for the link between alcohol intoxication and violent behavior. The *disinhibition theory* holds that ingesting alcohol on a pharmacological level impairs normal cortical mechanisms responsible for inhibiting the expression of innate or suppressed aggressive inclinations. The *cognitive-expectation theory* holds that learned beliefs or expectations about alcohol's effects can facilitate aggressive behaviors. The implication is that violence is induced by the act of drinking in combination with one's personal view of how a person is "supposed to respond," rather than by the pharmacological effects of alcohol itself (Drugs . . . in Focus). The *alcohol myopia theory* holds that intoxicated individuals are limited in their capacity to process information, so that they focus only on the most salient cues in their environment. According to this viewpoint, alcohol reduces the ability to attend to all of the subtle social cues that would have normally led to more appropriate behavior.[46]

TABLE 8.4

Blood-alcohol concentration at which drivers in different nations are legally drunk

0.00+	0.02	0.03	0.05	0.08
Czech Republic, Slovakia, Hungary	Norway, Poland, Sweden	Japan, China Germany, Greece, Netherlands,	Argentina, Australia, Costa Rica, Denmark, Finland, France, Italy, Jamaica, New Zealand, Peru, Russia, South Africa, Spain, Thailand	Brazil, Britain, Canada, Chile, Ecuador, Ireland, Hungary Singapore, United States

Source: National Highway Traffic Safety Administration (2000, March). *On DWI laws in other countries.* Washington DC: National Highway Traffic Safety Administration, U.S. Department of Transportation.

Drugs . . . in Focus

Alcohol, Security, and Spectator Sports

In 2005, the National Basketball Association (NBA) issued a new set of security guidelines for all thirty teams, including a "Fan Code of Conduct" specifying that "guests will enjoy the basketball experience free from disruptive behavior, including foul or abusive language or obscene gestures." Acknowledging the connection between disruptive behavior and alcohol, the NBA now bans alcohol sales during the fourth quarter of every game and imposes a 24-ounce limit on the size of alcoholic drinks sold in an arena, with a maximum of two alcoholic drinks per customer. Increased security measures and restrictions on alcohol sales came about after basketball players and fans brawled in the stands and on the court at the end of a game in November 2004 between the Indiana Pacers and the Detroit Pistons. Indiana's Ron Artest went into the seats after being hit by a full cup of beer that had been tossed by a spectator. Alcohol consumption has also come under scrutiny during college and professional football games, where binge drinking at tailgating parties and after-game celebrations frequently results in property damage and sometimes leads to injuries or deaths. At the University of Virginia, a tradition that began in the 1980s has seniors individually drinking a fifth of liquor by kick-off time at the final game of the football season (the so-called "Fourth-Year Fifth"). This practice

was been associated with the deaths of eighteen students between 1990 and 2002. Since 1999, a university organization, Fourth-years Acting Responsibly (FAR), has coordinated an annual campaign to reduce abusive drinking at the final home game, emphasizing that alcohol intoxication is not needed for intense school spirit. A recent YouTube video features the slogan "Be at your best. Responsible. Respectful. Rowdy."

At the same time, more than 20 major colleges have initiated beer sales to legal-age drinkers at football games, acknowledging increased revenue that can be realized to athletic programs in their respective institutions. Presently, the National Collegiate Athletic Association (NCAA) does not have any rules preventing alcohol sales at regular-season events, barring sales only during championship games.

Sources: Eskenazi, G. (2005, December 21). For Patriots and Jets, a sobering experience. *New York Times*, p. D3. Football, tailgating parties, and alcohol safety (2005, October 1). *The NCADI Reporter.* Bethesda, MD: National Clearinghouse for Drug Information. Join Together (2011, August 8). Beer sales becoming more popular at college football games. New York: The Partnership at DrugFree.org. NBA issuing sterner security, beer guidelines. *USA Today.* com, accessed May 8, 2005. University of Virginia video (2008, January 31). Be at your best. Responsible. Respectful. Rowdy. University of Virginia, Charlottesville, VA.

Expectations about the consequences of drug-taking behavior or of any behavior at all, as noted in Chapter 3, are studied experimentally through the placebo research design. Given the prominence of cognitive expectations in alcohol research (based on what people know about alcoholic intoxication), it is necessary to use a variation of this design, called the **balanced placebo design.** Subjects are randomly divided into four groups. Two groups are given an alcoholic drink, with one group being told that they are ingesting alcohol and the other that they are ingesting a nonalcohol substitute that tastes and smells like alcohol. Two other groups are given the nonalcohol substitute, with one group being told that they are ingesting this substitute and the other that they are ingesting alcohol.

Studies using the balanced placebo design have shown clearly that beliefs (mind-sets) concerning the

effects of drinking are more influential in determining a subject's behavior than the more direct physiological effects of the alcohol. In other words, *what they are told they are consuming is more important than what they consume* (Health Line). Unfortunately, for a true test of the cognitive-expectation theory, a balanced placebo design cannot be used with BAC levels above 0.035 percent, because subjects who drink larger quantities are no longer fooled by the deception, and most alcohol-associated acts of violence occur with BAC levels at least six times higher.[47]

> **balanced placebo design:** An experimental design that can distinguish psychological effects (due to subjective expectations) from physiological effects (due to the pharmacology of the drug).

Caffeine, Alcohol, and the Dangers of Caffeinated Alcoholic Drinks

Despite the popular notion that caffeine has a "sobering" effect on an alcohol-intoxicated state of mind, the truth is often quite the opposite. It appears to be a factor of one's expectations. In one study, subjects were told either that caffeine would have a significant "sobering" effect when they were intoxicated with alcohol or that caffeine would have no effect. The participants who were led to expect counteracting effects of alcohol-induced impairments in behavior actually displayed a *greater* level of impairment than those who were led to expect no such counteraction.

Misconceptions about the effect of caffeine on alcohol-impaired behavior have serious ramifications, particularly in light of the short-lived popularity of caffeinated alcoholic drinks. The malt-liquor-based beverage Four Loko combining caffeine with an alcohol content of between 6 and 12 percent appeared on the scene around 2007. The premise of the public outcry against Four Loko was that the caffeine would mask (but not counteract) the effects of alcohol, fooling the drinker into thinking that more alcohol could be consumed. In subsequent years, a number of ED-visits among drinkers of caffeinated alcoholic products occurred, and in some cases elevated BAC levels approached the lethal dose range with respect to alcohol toxicity. As noted above, the expectation that the caffeine in a caffeinated alcohol drink would make you less impaired will tend to exacerbate an already dangerous situation. Under intense pressure from the FDA in late 2010, the manufacturers agreed to remove caffeine and other stimulants from the drink. The beverages were reintroduced in 2011 as a purely alcoholic drink.

Sources: Fillmore, M. T.; Roach, E. L.; and Rice, J. T. (2002). Does caffeine counteract alcohol-induced impairment? The ironic effects of expectancy. *Journal of Studies on Alcohol, 63,* 745–754. Goodnough, A. (2010, October 27). Doctors point to caffeinated alcoholic drinks' dangers. *New York Times,* pp. A12, A14. Tumolillo, M. A. (2010, November 17). Company to drop caffeine from alcoholic drinks. *New York Times,* p. A22.

Sex and Sexual Desire

If they were asked, most people would say that alcohol has an enhancing, or aphrodisiac, effect on sexual desire and performance. The actual effect of alcohol, however, is more complex than what we commonly believe. In fact, it is because of these beliefs that people are frequently more susceptible to the expectations of what alcohol *should* do for them than they are to the actual physiological effects of alcohol.

To examine the complex relationship between alcohol and sex, we need to turn again to studies using the balanced placebo design. The general results from such studies are quite different for men and women. Among men, those who expected to be receiving low levels of alcohol had greater penile responses, reported greater subjective arousal, and spent more time watching erotic pictures, *regardless of whether they did indeed receive alcohol.* When alcohol concentrations rise to levels that reflect genuine intoxication, however, the pharmacological actions outweigh the expectations, and the overall effect is definitely inhibitory. Men who are drunk have less sexual desire and a decreased capacity to perform sexually.

In contrast, expectations among women play a lesser role. They are more inclined to react to the pharmacological properties of alcohol itself, but the direction of their response depends on whether we are talking about subjective or physiological measures. For women receiving increasing alcohol concentrations, measures of subjective arousal increase but measures of vaginal arousal decrease. The pattern of their responses mirrors Shakespeare's observation in *Macbeth* that alcohol "provokes the desire, but it takes away the performance," a comment originally intended to reflect only the male point of view.[48]

Alcohol and Health Benefits

The documented health benefits of moderate levels of alcohol consumption over the last thirty years of research have presented a major dilemma among medical and public health professionals. The crux of the dilemma is that moderate amounts of alcohol can possibly save your life, while immoderate amounts can possibly destroy it. As one writer has expressed it, "Alcohol has become the sharpest double-edged sword in medicine."

It started as an observation that did not seem to make sense. Epidemiological studies of French and other European populations who consumed large amounts of butter, cheese, liver, and other animal fats—a diet associated with elevated cholesterol and an elevated risk for coronary failure—found that these populations had a remarkably low incidence of coronary heart disease. The answer seemed to be that relatively more alcohol was consumed along with their dietary food. The "French paradox" was resolved when later research showed that alcohol increases high-density lipoprotein (HDL) cholesterol (the so-called good cholesterol) levels in the blood, with HDL acting as a protective mechanism against a possible restriction of blood flow through arteries. The greatest benefit was seen in those individuals who had high concentrations of low-density lipoprotein (LDL)

cholesterol (the so-called bad cholesterol) and therefore had the greatest risk for coronary heart disease. It was estimated that consumption of approximately 8 ounces of wine (a bit less than two standard drinks) per day resulted in a 25 percent reduction in the risk of coronary heart disease.

A natural substance in red wine known as *resveratrol* has been identified as a possible factor in explaining the health benefits of drinking red wine. Mice administered resveratrol in very large quantities were higher in endurance levels, relative to controls, and were less susceptible to the elevations in glucose and insulin that normally result from eating a high-fat diet. However, these animals received a daily dosage of resveratrol far larger than a human would ingest from drinking wine, so the question of whether this substance is a key factor remains unsettled. Human intake of resveratrol at comparable dosages would have a significant potential for acute toxicity (Chapter 2).[49]

Whether these health benefits can be attributed specifically to moderate wine (or red wine) consumption or to moderate alcohol consumption in general, remains a controversial issue. The difficulty lies in the fact that wine drinkers tend to have higher socioeconomic status than average alcohol drinkers and typically these people follow healthier lifestyles that reduce the incidence of disease. Yet the evidence for moderate alcohol consumption and health benefits is considerable, extending beyond the risk of coronary heart disease. Moderate alcohol intake reduces the risk of diabetes mellitus, reduces the risk of stroke, and reduces the risk of dementia (possibly by reducing the incidence of mini-strokes or by boosting concentrations of vitamin B_6, which is essential for the formation of essential brain chemicals). Moderate alcohol consumption can also lower the risk of rheumatoid arthritis by up to 50 percent. Of course, the key to the health benefits of alcohol consumption lies in moderation. Moderate drinking has been defined as taking no more than one drink per day for women and no more than two drinks per day for men.[50]

Despite the weight of evidence tilting toward the potential health benefits of alcohol, the medical field remains divided on the question of whether to encourage patients who do not drink alcohol to start at a moderate level of consumption. In some cases, moderate intake is not advisable. Even one drink per day slightly increases the risk for breast cancer in women, and in no circumstances should alcohol be consumed during pregnancy. Some public health researchers are concerned that an endorsement of moderate alcohol drinking may open up a range of possible risks, in effect giving alcohol a kind of "halo effect" that might be confusing to the public. Besides, an argument can be made that moderate alcohol drinking is simply a behavior that coincides with a healthful lifestyle in the first place, rather than a behavior that actually makes you healthy. The official word is found in the newest Dietary Guidelines for Americans, released in 2011 by the U.S. Department of Agriculture and the U.S. Department of Health and Human Services, acknowledging the effect of alcohol in reducing the risk of cardiovascular disease and helping to keep cognitive function intact with age but not recommending that "anyone begin drinking or drink more frequently on the basis of potential health benefits because moderate

HEALTH ALERT!

Guidelines for Responsible Drinking

- **Know how much you are drinking.** Measure your drinks. Beer is often premeasured (unless you are drinking draft beer from a keg), but wine and liquor drinks frequently are not. Learn what a 5-ounce quantity of wine or a 1½-ounce shot of liquor looks like, and use these measures to guide your drinking.

- **Choose beer or wine over liquor.** Beer especially will make you feel fuller more quickly, with a smaller intake of alcohol. But be careful. A 12-ounce beer is equivalent in alcohol content to a 5-ounce glass of wine or a 1-shot drink of liquor.

- **Drink slowly.** One drink an hour stays relatively even with your body's metabolism of the alcohol you consume. Sipping your drinks is a good strategy for slowing down your consumption. If you are a man, you'll look cool; if you are a woman, you'll look refined.

- **Don't cluster your drinking.** If you are going to have seven drinks during a week, don't drink them all on the weekend.

- **Eat something substantial while you are drinking.** Protein is an excellent accompaniment to alcohol. Avoid salty foods because they will make you thirstier and more inclined to have another drink.

- **Drink only when you are already relaxed.** Chronic alcohol abuse occurs more easily when alcohol is viewed as a way to relax. If you have a problem, seek some nondrug alternative.

- **When you drink, savor the experience.** If you focus on the quality of what you drink rather than the quantity you are drinking, you will avoid drinking too much.

- **Never drink alone.** Drinking is never an appropriate answer to social isolation. Besides, when there are people around, there is someone to look out for you.

- **Beware of unfamiliar drinks.** Some drinks, such as zombies and other fruit and rum drinks, are deceptively high in the kinds of alcohol that are not easily detected by taste.

- **Never drive a car after having had a drink.** Driving impairment begins after consumption of very low quantities of alcohol.

- **Be a good host or hostess.** If you are serving alcohol at a party, do not make drinking the focus of activity. Do not refill your guests' glasses. Discourage intoxication and do not condone drunkenness. Provide transportation options for those who drink at your party. Present nonalcoholic beverages as prominently as alcoholic ones. Prior to the end of the party, stop serving alcohol and offer coffee or other warm nonalcoholic beverages and a substantial snack, providing an interval of nondrinking time before people leave.

- **Support organizations that encourage responsible drinking.** If you are on a college campus, get involved with the local chapter of BACCHUS (Boost Alcohol Consciousness Concerning the Health of University Students). If there is no chapter, start one.

Where to go for assistance:

www.indiana.edu/~engs/hints/holiday.html

This web site on sensible, moderate, and responsible alcohol consumption and party hosting is adapted from Engs, R. C. (1987). *Alcohol and other drugs: Self responsibility.* Bloomington, IN: Tichenor.

Sources: Gross, L. (1983). *How much is too much? The effects of social drinking.* New York: Random House, pp. 149–152. Hanson, D. J., and Engs, R. C. (1994). Drinking behavior: Taking personal responsibility. In P. J. Venturelli (Ed.), *Drug use in America: Social, cultural, and political perspectives.* Boston: Jones and Bartlett, pp. 175–181. *Managing alcohol in your life.* Mansfield, MA: Steele Publishing and Consulting.

alcohol intake also is associated with increased risk of breast cancer, violence, drowning, and injuries from falls and motor vehicle crashes."[51]

Strategies for Responsible Drinking

This chapter has focused on the various negative consequences of alcohol consumption on physiological responses and behavior. Yet we need to remember that there are very large numbers of people who drink alcoholic beverages and avoid the adverse effects that have been detailed here. An overwhelming proportion of the population, for example, drink on occasion, enjoy the experience, and have never engaged in any violent or aggressive acts. They drink in moderate amounts, according to the federal guidelines for diet and nutrition. In addition, they avoid situations (such as driving) in which alcohol consumption would impair their performance and endanger their lives. The issue of responsible drinking is an important one; it may not be easy for us to accomplish, but fortunately, guidelines exist that make it easier (Health Alert).[52]

At the same time, it is important to remember that, regardless of how it is consumed, alcohol remains a drug with a significant potential for dependence. It is easy to get hooked. As it has been said, people may plan to get drunk, but no one plans to be an alcoholic. The problems surrounding chronic alcohol abuse and alcoholism are examined in the next chapter.

Summary

What Makes an Alcoholic Beverage?

- Drinkable alcohol is obtained from the fermentation of sugar in some natural products such as grapes, apples, honey, or molasses. The result is some form of wine.
- Beer is obtained from barley, after the starch has first been converted into sugar, fermented along with other grains and hops, and aged.
- To obtain very strong alcoholic beverages, it is necessary to boil the fermented liquid and condense it later by cooling. This process, called distillation, results in alcohol concentrations of up to 95 percent, and the products are known as distilled spirits or liquors.

Alcohol Use through History

- The history of alcohol use dates back many thousands of years; the process of fermentation is very simple, and its discovery was probably accidental.
- Distillation techniques were perfected during the Middle Ages, with brandy being the first distilled spirit. In later centuries, gin gained popularity in Europe, as did whiskey in the United States.
- Serious concern about the adverse consequences of alcohol consumption arose in the late 1700s and took root in the United States as a temperance movement. This movement addressed primarily the drinking of distilled spirits.
- The differentiation among forms of alcohol drinking became blurred during the nineteenth century, as temperance advocates began to promote a total ban on alcohol consumption. National Prohibition was the law in the United States from 1920 to 1933.
- Since the end of Prohibition, government regulation has been carried out chiefly through education and the taxation of alcohol.

Patterns of Alcohol Consumption Today

- The demographics of alcohol consumption reveal a large disparity in the drinking habits of the population. About a third do not drink at all, and only about 30 percent of those who drink account for 80 percent of all the alcoholic beverages consumed in the United States.
- Peak alcohol consumption occurs at ages twenty-one to twenty-two.

The Pharmacology of Alcohol

- Alcohol is a very small molecule, easily soluble in both water and fat. Its absorption into the bloodstream is extremely rapid. The breakdown of alcohol is handled by two special enzymes in the stomach and liver.
- The rate of alcohol biodegradation is constant, so alcohol can leave the body only at a specific pace, no matter what the quantity taken in.
- The effective level of alcohol in the body is measured by the blood-alcohol concentration (BAC) level, which adjusts for differences in body weight and the time since ingestion of the last alcoholic beverage.

Effects of Alcohol on the Brain

- Although alcohol affects several neurotransmitters in the brain, it is presently agreed that the principal effect is stimulation of the GABA receptor.
- Generally, the neural effect of alcohol proceeds downward, beginning with inhibition of the cerebral cortex, then that of lower brain regions. Inhibition of respiratory systems in the medulla, usually accomplished at BAC levels in the neighborhood of 0.50 percent, results in asphyxiation and death.

Acute Physiological Effects

- Alcohol at very high levels produces life-threatening consequences and at moderate levels produces a loss of body heat, increased excretion of water, an increase in heart rate and constriction of coronary arteries, disturbed patterns of sleep, and serious interactions with other drugs.

Acute Behavioral Effects

- On a behavioral level, serious adverse effects include blackouts, significant impairment in sensorimotor skills such as driving an automobile, and an increased potential for aggressive or violent acts. Particular attention has been directed toward these problems within a college student population.
- The relationship between alcohol consumption and sexual desire and performance is a complex one, with differences being observed for men and women.

Alcohol and Health Benefits

- The accumulated evidence of medical research has indicated that there is a reduced risk for coronary heart disease and stroke with moderate consumption of alcohol. Possible health benefits include a reduction of risk for diabetes, dementia, and rheumatoid arthritis.
- Moderate alcohol consumption has been defined as no more than one drink per day for women and no more than two drinks per day for men. There should be zero tolerance for alcohol consumption among pregnant women.

Strategies for Responsible Drinking

- Despite the potential for alcohol consumption to produce adverse effects, most people can drink alcohol in a responsible way that avoids these harmful consequences. However, the risk of alcohol dependence is always present.

Key Terms

acetaldehyde, p. 202
acetaldehyde
  dehydrogenase, p. 202
acetic acid, p. 202
alcohol dehydrogenase,
  p. 202
antidiuresis, p. 206

antidiuretic hormone
  (ADH), p. 206
aqua vitae, p. 194
balanced placebo design,
  p. 211
barley malt, p. 192
blackout, p. 208

blood-alcohol concentration
  (BAC), p. 203
brewing, p. 192
congeners, p. 207
distillation, p. 193
distilled spirits, p. 193
ethyl alcohol, p. 192

fermentation, p. 192
mash, p. 192
oxidation, p. 202
temperance
  movement, p. 195

Endnotes

1. Pinel, J. P. J. (2011). *Biopsychology* (8th ed.). Boston: Allyn and Bacon, p. 384.
2. Statement of NIH Director Dr. Francis Collins on the future of substance use, abuse, and addiction-related research at NIH. News release, National Institutes of Health. Bethesda, MD, November 16, 2012.
3. Gibbons, B. (1992, February). Alcohol: The legal drug. *National Geographic Magazine*, pp. 2–35. McGovern, P. E.; Glusker, D. L.; Exner, L. J.; and Voigt, M. M. (1996). Neolithic resinated wine. *Nature, 381*, 480–481. Roueché, B. (1963). Alcohol in human culture. In S. P. Lucia (Ed.), *Alcohol and civilization.* New York: McGraw-Hill, pp. 167–182. Vallee, B. L. (1998, June). Alcohol in the western world. *Scientific American,* pp. 80–85.
4. Sournia, J. C. (1990). *A history of alcoholism.* Cambridge, MA: Basil Blackwell, pp. 14–50. U.S. Department of Health, Education, and Welfare (1978). *Perspectives on the history of psychoactive substance use,* pp. 67–75.
5. Grimes, W. (1993). *Straight up or on the rocks: A cultural history of American drink.* New York: Simon and Schuster, p. 36. Musto, D. F. (1996, April). Alcohol in American history. *Scientific American,* pp. 78–83.
6. Lender, M. E., and Martin, J. K. (1982). *Drinking in America: A history.* New York: Free Press, pp. 13–14.

7. First in war, peace—and hooch, by George! (2000, December 7). *Newsday*, p. A86. Grimes, *Straight up*, p. 51.

8. Quoted in Sournia, J. C. (1990). *A history of alcoholism*. Cambridge, MA: Basil Blackwell, p. 29.

9. Lincoln, A. (1842/1989). Address to the Washingtonian Temperance Society of Springfield, Illinois. *Speeches and writings, 1832–1858*. New York: Library of America, p. 84.

10. Lender, M. E., and Martin, J. R. (1982). *Drinking in America: A history*. New York: Free Press, p. 107. Okrent, D. (2010). *Last call: The rise and fall of Prohibition*. New York: Scribner.

11. Blocker, J. S. (2006, February). Did Prohibition really work? Alcohol prohibition as a public health innovation. *American Journal of Public Health*, pp. 233–243. Lerner, M. A. (2007). *Dry Manhattan*. Cambridge, MA: Harvard University Press. Musto, D. F. (1996, April). Alcohol in American history. *Scientific American*, pp. 78–83. Sournia, *History of alcoholism*, p. 122.

12. Americans for Tax Reform Center for Fiscal Accountability, Washington, DC, 2012. U.S. Department of Health and Human Services (2000). *Alcohol and health* (Tenth Special Report to the U.S. Congress). Bethesda, MD: National Institute on Alcohol Abuse and Alcoholism, p. 370. *Industry Surveys* (1997, September 11). Alcoholic beverages and tobacco, p. 16.

13. Gruenewald, P. J. (2011). Regulating availability: How access to alcohol affects drinking and problems of youth and adults. *Alcohol Research and Health, 34*, 248–256. Xu, X., and Chaloupka, F. J. (2011). The effects of prices on alcohol use and its consequences. *Alcohol Research and Health, 34*, 236–245.

14. Gibbons, Alcohol, p. 7.

15. Alcohol Policies Project, Center for Science in the Public Interest Fact Sheet, Washington, DC, 2012. Hanson, G. R., and Li, T. K. (2003). Public health implications of excessive alcohol consumption. *Journal of the American Medical Association, 289*, 1031–1032. National Association of Convenience Stores (2008). That's the spirit—U.S. alcohol sales growing. www.nacsonline.com.

16. Statistics on 2009 consumption levels from the National Institute on Alcohol Abuse and Alcoholism, Bethesda, MD.

17. Center for Science in the Public Interest (2008, August 8). Press release: CSPI blasts NCAA decision to keep beer ad. Center for Science in the Public Interest, Washington, DC. Rogers, J. D., and Greenfield, T. K. (1999). Beer drinking accounts for most of the hazardous alcohol consumption reported in the United States. *Journal of Studies on Alcohol, 60*, 732–739.

18. Centers for Disease Control and Prevention (2012, January 13). Vital signs: Binge drinking prevalence, frequency, and intensity among adults—United States, 2010. *Morbidity and Mortality Weekly, 61*, 14–19. Hingson, R. W.; Zha, W.; and Weitzman, E. R. (2009). Magnitude of and trends in alcohol-related mortality and morbidity among U.S. college students ages 18–24, 1998–2005. *Journal of Studies on Alcohol and Drugs, Supplement No. 16*, 12–20. National Institute on Alcohol and Alcohol Abuse (2007). *What colleges need to know now: An update on college drinking research*. Bethesda, MD: National Institute on Alcohol and Alcohol Abuse. National Institute on Alcohol and Alcohol Abuse (2010). Statistical snapshot of college drinking. Bethesda, MD: National Institute on Alcohol and Alcohol Abuse. Wechsler, H., and Nelson, T. F. (2008). What we have learned from the Harvard School of Public Health College Alcohol Study: Focusing attention on college student alcohol consumption and the environmental conditions that promote it. *Journal of Studies on Alcohol and Drugs, 69*, 1–10. ; Wechsler, H.; Lee, J. E.; Kuo, M.; Seibring, M.; Nelson, T. F.; et al. (2002). Trends in college binge drinking during a period of increased prevention efforts: Findings from four Harvard School of Public Health College Alcohol Study Surveys: 1993–2001. *Journal of American College Health, 50*, 203–217.

19. Johnston, L. D.; O'Malley, P. M.; Bachman, J. G.; and Schulenberg, J. E. (2012). Monitoring the Future: National survey results on drug use, 1975–2011. Vol. I: Secondary school students 2011. Ann Arbor, MI: Institute for Social Research, The University of Michigan, Table 2-1. Substance Abuse and Mental Health Services Administration (2008, August 28). Underage alcohol use: Where do young people drink? *The NSDUH Report*. Rockville, MD: Substance Abuse and Mental Health Services Administration. Windle, M., and Zucker, R. A. (2010). Reducing underage and young adult drinking: How to address critical drinking problems during this developmental period. *Alcohol Research and Health, 33*, 29–44.

20. U.S. Department of Health and Human Services (1990). *Alcohol and health*. (The Seventh Special Report to the U.S. Congress). Bethesda, MD: National Institute on Alcohol Abuse and Alcoholism.

21. Julien, R. M. (2005), *A primer of drug action* (10th ed.). New York: Worth, pp. 91–126.

22. Julien, R. M. (2000). *A primer of drug action* (9th ed.). New York: Worth, p. 95.

23. National Institute on Alcohol Abuse and Alcoholism (2007, April). Alcohol alert: Alcohol metabolism: An update. No. 72. Bethesda, MD: National Institute on Alcohol Abuse and Alcoholism. Julien, *A primer of drug action*, pp. 91–97.

24. Suter, P. M.; Schutz, Y.; and Jequier, E. (1992). The effect of ethanol on fat storage in healthy subjects. *New England Journal of Medicine, 326*, 983–987.

25. Hawks, R. L., and Chiang, C. N. (1986). Examples of specific drug assays. In R. L. Hawks and C. N. Chiang (Eds.), *Urine testing for drugs of abuse* (NIDA Research Monograph 73). Rockville, MD: National Institute on Drug Abuse, p. 103. Julien (2000), *A primer of drug action*, pp. 91–97.

26. Levinthal, C. F. (1990). *Introduction to physiological psychology* (3rd ed.). Englewood Cliffs, NJ, Prentice-Hall, pp. 181–184.

27. U.S. Department of Health and Human Services (1994). *Alcohol and health*. (The Eighth Special Report to the U.S. Congress). Bethesda, MD: National Institute on Alcohol Abuse and Alcoholism, pp. 4–6, 4–7.

28. Koob, G. F.; Rassnick, S.; Heinrichs, S.; and Weiss, F. (1994). Alcohol, the reward system and dependence. In B. Jansson, H. Jörnvall, U. Rydberg, L. Terenius, and B. L. Vallee (Eds.), *Toward a molecular basis of alcohol use and abuse*. Basel: Birkhäuser-Verlag, pp. 103–114. Rosenbloom, M. J., and Pfefferbaum, A. (2008). Magnetic resonance imaging of the living brain. Evidence for brain degeneration among alcoholics and recovery with abstinence. *Alcohol Research and Health, 31*, 362–376.

29. Grilly, D. M., and Salamone, J. D. (2012). *Drugs and human behavior* (6th ed.). Boston: Pearson, p. 238.

30. Luks, A., and Barbato, J. (1989). *You are what you drink*. New York: Villiard, pp. 42–43.

31. National Institute on Alcohol Abuse and Alcoholism (1998, July). Alcohol alert: Alcohol and sleep. No. 41. Bethesda, MD: National Institute on Alcohol Abuse and Alcoholism.

32. O'Connor, M. J., and Wahley, S. E. (2007). Brief intervention for alcohol use by pregnant women. *American Journal of Public Health, 97*, 252–258. Substance Abuse and Mental Health Services Administration (2012). Drug Abuse Warning Network, National estimates of drug-related emergency department visits 2004–2010. Rockville, MD: Substance Abuse and Mental Health Services Administration, Excel files. Substance Abuse and Mental Health Services Administration (2012). *Results from the 2011 National Survey on Drug Use and Health: National findings. Detailed tables*. Rockville, MD: Substance Abuse and Mental Health Services Administration, Table 6-76B.

33. Schuckit, M. A. (2006). *Drug and alcohol abuse: A clinical guide to diagnosis and treatment* (6th ed.). New York: Springer, p. 88.

34. Wiese, J. G.; Shlipak, M. G.; and Browner, W. S. (2000). The alcohol hangover. *Annals of Internal Medicine, 232*, 897–902.

35. Brick, J. (2008). Characteristics of alcohol: Definitions, chemistry, measurement, use, and abuse. In J. Brick (Ed.), *Handbook of the medical consequences of alcohol and drug abuse* (2nd ed.). New York: Routledge, pp. 9–19.

36. White, A. M.; Jamieson-Drake, D. W.; and Swartzwelder, H. S. (2002). Prevalence and correlates of alcohol-induced blackouts among college students: Results of an e-mail survey. *Journal of American College Health, 51*, 117–131. White, A. M. (2003). What happened? Alcohol, memory blackouts, and the brain. *Alcohol Research and Health, 23*, 186–196.

37. National Highway Traffic Safety Administration (2012, December). 2011 motor vehicle crashes: Overview. *Traffic Safety Facts: Research Note*, p. 2.

38. Hoyer, W. J.; Semenec, S. C.; and Buchler, N. E. G. (2007). Acute alcohol intoxication impairs controlled search across the visual field. *Journal of Studies on Alcohol and Drugs, 68*, 748–758. National Institute on Alcohol Abuse and Alcoholism (1996, January). Alcohol Alert: Drinking and driving. No. 31, PH362. Bethesda, MD: National Institute on Alcohol Abuse and Alcoholism.

39. Gross, L. (1983). *How much is too much? The effects of social drinking*. New York: Random House, p. 29. Quotation of Dr. H. Moskowitz.

40. National Institute on Alcohol Abuse and Alcoholism (2001, April). Alcohol alert: Alcohol and transportation safety. No. 52. Bethesda, MD: National Institute on Alcohol Abuse and Alcoholism. Wagenaar, A. C.; O'Malley, P. M.; and LaFond, C. (2001). Lowered legal blood alcohol limits for young drivers: Effects on drinking, driving, and driving-after-drinking behaviors in 30 states. *American Journal of Public Health, 91*, 801–803.

41. Substance Abuse and Mental Health Services Administration (2012, November). *Report to Congress on the prevention and reduction of underage drinking*. Rockville, MD: Substance Abuse and Mental Health Services Administration. National Highway Traffic Safety Administration (2009, June). Lives saved in 2008 by restraint use and minimum drinking age laws. *Traffic Safety Facts*. Washington, DC: National Center for Statistics and Analysis, National Highway Traffic Safety Administration. Wald, M. L. (2006, November 20). A new strategy to discourage driving drunk. *New York Times*, pp. A1, A20.

42. National Conference of State Legislatures (2012). State ignition interlock laws. National Conference of State Legislatures, Washington, DC.

43. Hingson, R.; Heeren, T.; Zakocs, R.; Winter, M.; and Wechsler, H. (2003). Age of first intoxication, heavy drinking, driving after drinking and risk of unintentional injury among U.S. college students. *Journal of Studies on Alcohol, 64*, 23–31. National Highway Traffic Safety Administration (2010, August). National survey of drinking and driving attitudes and behaviors. Washington, DC: U.S. Department of Transportation. National Highway Traffic Administration (1999, March). The relationship of alcohol safety laws to drinking drivers in fatal crashes. Washington, DC: U.S. Department of Transportation. Substance Abuse and Mental Health Services Administration, *Results from the 2011 National Survey on Drug Use and Health: Detailed tables*.

44. Abbey, A.; Zawacki, T.; Buck, P. O.; Clinton, A. M.; and McAuslan, P. (2004). Sexual assault and alcohol consumption: What do we know about their relationship and what types of research are still needed? *Aggression and Violent Behavior, 9*, 271–303. Haggård-Grann, U.; Hallqvist, J.; Långström, N.; and Möller, J. (2006). The role of alcohol and drugs in triggering criminal violence: A case-crossover study. *Addiction, 101*, 100–108. Pernanen, K. (1991). *Alcohol in human violence*. New York: Guilford Press, pp. 192–193.

45. Collins, J. J., and Messerschmidt, P. M. (1993). Epidemiology of alcohol-related violence. *Alcohol Health and Research World, 17,* 93–100. Goode, E. (2008). *Drugs in American society* (7th ed.). New York: McGraw-Hill, pp. 343–346. National Institute on Alcohol Abuse and Alcoholism (1997, October). Alcohol alert: Alcohol, violence, and aggression. No. 38. Bethesda, MD: National Institute on Alcohol Abuse and Alcoholism.

46. Giancola, P. R. (2000). Executive functioning: A conceptual framework for alcohol-related aggression. *Experimental and Clinical Psychopharmacology, 8,* 576–597. Giancola, P. R. (2002). Alcohol-related aggression in men and women: The influence of dispositional aggressivity. *Journal of Studies on Alcohol, 63,* 696–708. Grant, N. K., and MacDonald, T. K. (2005). Can alcohol lead to inhibition or disinhibition? Applying alcohol myopia to animal experimentation. *Alcohol and Alcoholism, 40,* 2005. Norris, J.; David, K. C.; George, W. H.; Martell, J.; and Heiman, J. R. (2002). Alcohol's direct and indirect effects on men's self-reported sexual aggression likelihood. *Journal of Studies on Alcohol, 63,* 688–695.

47. Foran, H. M., and O'Leary, K. D. (2008). Alcohol and intimate partner violence: A meta-analytic review. *Clinical Psychology Review, 28,* 1222–1234. Pernanen, K. (1993). Research approaches in the study of alcohol related violence. *Alcohol Health and Research World, 17,* 101–107.

48. Cooper, M. L. (2006). Does drinking promote risky sexual behavior? A complex answer to a simple question. *Current Directions in Psychological Science, 15,* 19–23. Enyeart Smith, T. M., and Wessel, M. T. (2011). Alcohol, drugs, and links to sexual risk behaviors among a sample of Virginia college students. *Journal of Drug Education, 41,* 1–16. Testa, M.; Vanzile-Tamsen, C.; and Livingston, J. A. (2004). The role of victim and perpetrator intoxication on sexual assault outcomes. *Journal of Studies on Alcohol, 65,* 320–329.

49. Mochly-Rosen, D., and Zakhari, S. (2010). The cardiovascular system: What did we learn from the French (paradox)? *Alcohol Research and Health, 33,* 76–86. Rimm, E. B. (2000). Moderate alcohol intake and lower risk of coronary heart disease: Meta-analysis of effects on lipids and haemostatic factors. *Journal of the American Medical Association, 283,* 1269. Wade, N. (2006, November 2). Yes, red wine holds answer. Check dosage. Zuger, A. (2002, December 31). The case for drinking (all together now: in moderation). *New York Times,* pp. F1, F6. Quotation on p. F1.

50. Holahan, C. J.; Schutte, K. K.; Brennan, P. L.; North, R. J., Holahan, C. K., et al. (2012). Wine consumption and 20-year mortality among late-life moderate drinkers. *Journal of Studies of Alcohol and Drugs, 73,* 80–88. Howard, A. A.; Arnsten, J. H.; and Gourevitch, M. N. (2004). Effect of alcohol consumption on diabetes mellitus: A systematic review. *Annals of Internal Medicine, 140,* 211–219. Källberg, H.; Jacobsen, S.; Bengtsson, C.; Pdersen, M.; Padyukov, L.; et al. (2009). Alcohol consumption is associated with decreased risk of rheumatoid arthritis: Results from two Scandinavian case-control studies. *Annals of the Rheumatic Diseases. 68,* 222–227. Mukamal, K. J.; Conigrave, K. M.; Mittleman, M. A.; Carmargo, C. A., Jr.; Stampfer, M. J.; et al. (2003). Roles of drinking pattern and type of alcohol consumed in coronary heart disease in men. *New England Journal of Medicine, 348,* 109–118. Mukamal, K. J.; Kuller, L. H.; Longstreth, W. T.; Mittleman, M. A.; and Siscovick, D. S. (2003). Prospective study of alcohol consumption and risk of dementia in older adults. *Journal of the American Medical Association, 289,* 1405–1413. Reynold, K.; Lewis, L. B.; Nolen, J. D. L.; Kinney, G. L.; Sathya, B.; et al. (2003). Alcohol consumption and risk of stroke: A meta-analysis. *Journal of the American Medical Association, 289,* 579–588.

51. Goldberg, I. (2003). To drink or not to drink? *New England Journal of Medicine, 348,* 163–164. Klatsky, A. (2003, February). Drink to your health? *Scientific American,* pp. 75–81. Rabin, R. C. (2009, June 19). Alcohol's good for you? Some scientists doubt it. *New York Times,* pp. D1, D6. U.S. Department of Agriculture and U.S. Department of Health and Human Services (2010). *Dietary guidelines for Americans, 2010* (7th ed.). Washington DC: U.S. Government Printing Office, p. 31.

52. Darby, W., and Heinz, A. (1991). *The responsible use of alcohol: Defining the parameters of moderation.* New York: American Council on Science and Health, pp. 1–26.

Chronic Alcohol Abuse and Alcoholism

When you live in an alcoholic family, you lie in bed sometimes and imagine how things could be different. You dream that you could actually invite your friends over to hang out at your house. You dream that the family car wouldn't get its fenders bashed in on a regular basis. You dream that the money you made mowing lawns didn't end up missing from your room. You dream that someone had been there at the athletic awards banquet. You dream that you didn't have to plead with them to quit drinking—time after time. You dream that enlisting in the military isn't just a way of getting out of the house. You dream that your life is normal, except that you have no idea what normal is.

—Thoughts of a teenager in an alcoholic family

For chronic abusers of alcohol, there is no need to get out on the street and find a drug dealer. Alcohol consumption is so tightly woven into the social fabric of our lives that it is easy to drink too much too often. Currently, an estimated 18.2 million Americans have a serious long-term problem with alcohol. Considering that for each one of these individuals, it is estimated that four family members are directly affected, the consequences extend to approximately 80 million people in the United States. This chapter will continue the examination of the impact of alcohol in America and specifically deal with the very serious problems associated with chronic alcohol abuse.[1]

Alcoholism: Stereotypes, Definitions, and Life Problems

If you were asked to imagine what an alcoholic looks like, it is likely that you would not form an image of a person employed in a highly responsible position or a teenager. You might be thinking of someone, probably male, homeless and alone, living from day to day in a continual state of inebriation and deteriorating health. Chances are that the characteristics of the person who came to mind would match up with fewer than 5 percent of all alcoholics. It turns out that the demographics of alcoholism include every possible category. Alcoholics can be fourteen or eighty-four years of age, male or female, professional or blue-collar, employed or unemployed. They can be urbanites, suburbanites, or rural residents in any community. Typically, they have jobs, a home, and a family.

What aspects of their behavior tie them all together, allowing us to describe their condition with a single

label? In order to arrive at a general sense of what we mean by an individual being an alcoholic, we need to examine the signs, symptoms, and behaviors that constitute problematic drinking. However, health professionals have abandoned the specific term, alcoholism, as a diagnosis in favor of criterion-based diagnoses, such as alcohol abuse and alcohol dependence or alcohol use disorder (see pages 225–226).

Four basic life problems are tied to the consumption of alcohol: (1) problems associated with a preoccupation with drinking, (2) emotional problems, (3) vocational, social, and family problems, and (4) problems associated with physical health. In short, we are recognizing that **alcoholism** is a complex phenomenon with psychological-behavioral components (problems 1 and 2), social components (problem 3), and physical components (problem 4).

Problems Associated with a Preoccupation with Drinking

The dominant characteristic of alcoholics is their preoccupation with the act of drinking and their incorporation of drinking into their everyday lives. An alcoholic may need a drink prior to a social occasion to feel "fortified." With increasing frequency, such a person sees alcohol as a way of dealing with stress and anxiety. Drinking itself becomes routine, no longer a social affair. The habit of taking a few drinks upon arriving home from work each day is an example of **symptomatic drinking,** in which alcohol is viewed specifically as a way of relieving tension, depression, or some other negative mood state. Also increasing is the incidence of unintentional occasions of severe intoxication and blackouts of events surrounding the time of drinking, a condition quite different from "passing out" from a high BAC level (see Chapter 8).[2]

Traditionally, alcoholism is associated with consumption of a large quantity of alcohol. This sounds pretty obvious and is true of most alcoholics, but not all alcoholics consume alcohol in the same way. Not all of them begin every day with a drink. Many of them drink on a daily basis, but others are spree or binge alcoholics who might become grossly intoxicated at intervals during a given week and totally abstain from drinking the rest of the time. Given these differences in the pattern of

---

by the numbers . . .

6.3	Estimated percentage of U.S. college students (one in sixteen) who meet the criteria for alcohol dependence.
2.1 million	Estimated number of Americans who report that they have worked under the influence of alcohol in the past twelve months, from a national sample of employed adults

Sources: Frone, M. R. (2006). Prevalence and distribution of alcohol use and impairment in the workplace: A U.S. survey. Journal of Studies on Alcohol and Drugs, 67, 147–156. Knight, J. R.; Wechsler, H.; Kuo, M.; Seibring, M.; Weitzman, E. R.; and Schuckit, M. A. (2002). Alcohol abuse and dependence among U.S. college students. Journal of Studies on Alcohol, 63, 263-270.

---

alcoholism: A condition in which the consumption of alcohol has produced major psychological, physical, social, or occupational problems.

symptomatic drinking: A pattern of alcohol consumption aimed at reducing stress and anxiety.

The typical alcoholic American

Doctor, age 54

Farmer, age 35

Unemployed, age 40

College student, age 19

Counselor, age 38

Retired editor, age 86

Dancer, age 22

Police officer, age 46

Military officer, age 31

Student, age 14

Executive, age 50

Taxi driver, age 61

Homemaker, age 43

Bricklayer, age 29

Computer programmer, age 25

Lawyer, age 52

There's no such thing as typical. We have all kinds.
10 million Americans are alcoholic.
It's our number one drug problem.

This poster conveys a powerful message: Alcoholism affects such a diverse group of people that it is virtually impossible to make generalizations about the typical profile of an alcoholic. Here are sixteen examples of individuals with whom many people might not have immediately associated the term "alcoholic."

alcohol consumption, the National Institute on Alcohol Abuse and Alcoholism (NIAAA) has recently established guidelines for "at-risk" or "heavy" drinking *based on both a single-day level and a weekly level of consumption.* Just as binge drinking was defined separately for men and women (Chapter 8), there are two different thresholds for being in the "at-risk" or "heavy" drinking category, depending on gender. These thresholds are:

- More than four drinks on any day and more than 14 drinks per week (for men).
- More than three drinks on any day and more than seven drinks per week (for women).

Individuals drinking more than both the single-day and weekly limits (about nine percent of the adult U.S. population) carry the highest risk for alcoholism-related problems; individuals drinking more than either the single-day or weekly limits (about 19 percent) carry an increased risk.[3]

Another feature often attributed to alcoholics is a loss of control over their drinking. The alcoholic typically craves a drink and frequently engages in compulsive behavior related to alcohol, much in the same way as we have seen in stimulant dependence (Chapter 4) or opioid dependence (Chapter 5), except that in the case of alcoholism, the behavior is often embedded in a social context. There may be a stockpiling of liquor, taking a drink or two before going to a party, or feeling uncomfortable unless alcohol is present. The alcoholic may be sneaking drinks or having drinks that others do not know about, such as surreptitiously having an extra drink or two in the kitchen out of the sight of the party guests.[4] Particularly when the alcoholic is trying to abstain from alcohol or to reduce the quantity of alcohol consumed, his or her thoughts become focused on the possibility of drinking or on ways to rationalize it.[5]

Nonetheless, health professionals disagree about whether all alcoholics are *necessarily* out of control with respect to alcohol consumption. As discussed later in the chapter, this controversy has major implications for choosing the treatment approach in cases of alcohol abuse. If it is true that even a small amount of alcohol will propel a recovering alcoholic back to alcohol abuse, then a primary focus of treatment should be on "no drinking at all"—better known as absolute **abstinence.** If it is not true, then there is the possibility of controlled drinking without the fear of "falling off the wagon." The well-known alcohol treatment program Alcoholics Anonymous, for example, functions under the assumption that an alcoholic must never drink again, even in minute quantities, if recovery is to be sustained over a long period of time.

Emotional Problems

Given that alcohol is a depressant drug on the central nervous system, it should not be surprising that chronic alcohol intake produces depressive symptoms. Serious depressions and thoughts of suicide frequently occur in the midst of heavy drinking. It is estimated that about 40 percent of individuals who meet the criteria for alcohol dependence (see page 225) will have one or more alcohol-induced depressive episodes. Nonetheless, the frequency of severe depressions lasting every day for weeks on end and observed outside of the context of heavy drinking may be no more prevalent in alcoholics than in the general population.[6]

Vocational, Social, and Family Problems

No one questions the potential problems that chronic alcohol abuse can bring to the maintenance of a job or career, social relationships, and a stable family life. These three problem areas frequently intertwine, with trouble in one usually exacerbating trouble in another. A job loss puts stress on marital and family relationships, just as marital and family difficulties put stress on occupational performance.

Numerous clinical studies support the idea of increased domestic instability in the lives of alcoholics, but the true extent of these problems is difficult to assess. Family violence, for example, is frequently examined through cases seen in treatment or social service programs. As a result, these agencies may interpret the domestic behavior of a father not known to have a drinking problem differently from that of a father with a history of alcoholism. A man who drinks heavily and abuses his children may be more likely to be "counted" as an alcoholic than a nonabusive father who consumes just as much alcohol. It is much easier to assess the likelihood of domestic violence or decline in job performance due to acute intoxication than it is to evaluate the influence of chronic abuse of alcohol. Even so, there is no doubt that the cumulative effects of alcoholism on family dynamics are devastating.[7]

Physical Problems

There is also no question that chronic alcohol consumption has a destructive effect on the body. Not surprisingly, a principal site of damage is the brain. Neuroimaging

abstinence: The avoidance of some consumable item or behavior.

procedures, such as CT and MRI brain scans, reveal a consistent link between heavy drinking and physical shrinkage of brain matter, particularly in the cerebral cortex, cerebellum, and regions associated with memory and other cognitive functions. These neurological changes are observed even in the absence of other alcohol-related medical conditions such as chronic liver disease.[8]

Hiding the Problems: Denial and Enabling

The major life problems that serve as rough criteria for determining the condition of alcoholism are often not recognized by alcoholics themselves because of their tendency to deny that their drinking has any influence on their lives or the lives of people around them. When in denial, the alcoholic can be extremely sensitive to any mention of problems associated with drinking. A hangover the next day, for example, is seldom discussed because it would draw attention to the fact that drinking has occurred.[9]

Denial also can be manifest among the people around the alcoholic. Members of an alcoholic's family, for example, may try to function as if life were normal. Through their excuse making and efforts to undo or cover up the frequent physical and psychological damage the alcoholic causes, they inadvertently prevent the alcoholic from seeking treatment or delay that treatment until the alcoholism is more severe. These people are referred to as **enablers** because they enable the alcoholic to function as an alcoholic rather than as a sober person. Both processes of denial and enabling present major difficulties not only in establishing problem-oriented criteria for diagnosing alcoholism but also in introducing necessary interventions. Denial and enabling are clearly relevant processes in the area of alcoholism, but it is not difficult to see that they present problems with regard to treatment for *any* form of substance abuse (see Chapter 17).

Health Line provides a useful self-survey for identifying signs of potential alcoholism.

enablers: Individuals whose behavior consciously or unconsciously encourages another person's continuation in a pattern of alcohol or other drug abuse.

Understanding the Psychology of Alcoholism

Check your understanding of the psychological aspects of alcoholism by matching each quotation or behavioral description (on the left) with the appropriate term (on the right).

1. Brad tries to call his estranged wife on the telephone. She hangs up on him. Now angry and frustrated, Brad takes a drink.

2. Mary stays sober during the workweek, but on the weekend she downs at least two quarts of vodka.

3. "Despite what my family says, I am convinced I am not an alcoholic."

4. "If I'm with her when she's drinking, I can make sure she doesn't overdo her drinking."

5. "I'm going to the theater later. I don't think there will be any liquor there, so I had better have a couple of drinks before I go."

a. denial
b. enabling
c. out-of-control drinking
d. spree or binge drinking
e. symptomatic drinking

Answers: 1. e 2. d 3. a 4. b 5. c

Alcohol Abuse and Alcohol Dependence: The Health Professional's Perspective

As you can see, the problem areas commonly employed in determining the presence of alcoholism are at times quite murky, and often there are nearly as many counterexamples as there are examples. The American Psychiatric Association, through its *Diagnostic and Statistical Manual, Text Revision*, fourth edition (DSM-IV-TR), has attempted to put together as many common features as possible and has established two basic syndromes. It is important to understand these technical definitions, because professionals in the field of alcoholism commonly use the DSM-IV-TR either in their research or in clinical practice.[10]

The first syndrome, referred to as **alcohol abuse,** is characterized as either (1) the continued use of alcohol for at least one month despite the knowledge of having a persistent or recurring physical problem or some difficulty in social or occupational functioning, or (2) the recurring use of alcohol in situations (such as driving) when alcohol consumption is physically hazardous.

The second syndrome, referred to as **alcohol dependence,** is characterized as alcohol abuse that involves any three of the following seven circumstances:

- Consuming alcohol in greater amounts or over a longer period than the person intends
- A persistent desire, or one or more unsuccessful attempts, to cut down or control drinking
- A great deal of time spent drinking or recovering from the effects of drinking
- Alcohol consumption continuing despite knowledge that drinking either causes or exacerbates recurrent physical or psychological problems
- Major social, occupational, or recreational activities given up or reduced because of alcohol
- Marked tolerance or the need to drink more than before to achieve previous levels of intoxication
- Symptoms of alcohol withdrawal or the consumption of alcohol to relieve or avoid withdrawal symptoms

Obviously, individuals who fit the second definition are considered more greatly impaired than those who fit the first. That distinction also was true with regard to the more general criteria for substance abuse and substance dependence (see Chapter 2). At least 15 percent of men and about 10 percent of women in the U.S. have met the criteria for alcohol dependence at some time in their lives. An estimated 10 percent of adults overall and 6 percent of college students have met the criteria for alcohol dependence during the past year.[11]

As noted in Chapter 2, the new DSM-5 revision in 2013 combines the diagnoses of alcohol abuse and alcohol dependence into one diagnosis: *alcohol use disorder.* Like the more general diagnosis of substance use disorder, the new diagnosis of alcohol use disorder is made on the basis of the same behavioral criteria previously identified

alcohol abuse: A syndrome characterized primarily by the continued use of alcohol despite the drinker's knowledge of having a persistent physical problem or some social or occupational difficulty.

alcohol dependence: A syndrome in which alcohol abuse involves a variety of significant physical, psychological, social, and behavioral problems.

with alcohol abuse and alcohol dependence, with the exception that the criterion of "legal problems" has been dropped and the criterion of "craving" has been added.[12]

Physiological Effects of Chronic Alcohol Use

We can now examine what we know about the consequences of long-term (chronic) consumption of alcohol, over and above the acute effects that were discussed in the last chapter.

Tolerance and Withdrawal

As with other CNS depressants, alcohol consumption over a period of time will result in a tolerance effect. On a metabolic level, alcohol dehydrogenase activity during tolerance becomes higher in the stomach and liver, allowing the alcohol to leave the body somewhat faster; on a neural level, the brain is less responsive to alcohol's depressive effects. Therefore, if the level of alcohol consumption remains steady, individuals feel less of an effect.

As a result of tolerance and the tendency to compensate for it in terms of drinking a greater quantity, the chronic alcohol abuser is subject to increased physical risks. There are serious behavioral risks as well; for example, an alcohol-tolerant drinker may consider driving with a BAC level that exceeds the standard for drunk driving, thinking that he or she is not intoxicated and hence not impaired. A person's driving ability, under these circumstances, will be substantially overestimated.

An alcohol-dependent person's abrupt withdrawal from alcohol can result in a range of serious physical symptoms beginning from six to forty-eight hours after the last drink, but estimates of how many people are typically affected vary. Among hospitalized patients, only 5 percent appear to show withdrawal symptoms, whereas studies of alcoholics using outpatient facilities have estimated the percentage to be as high as 18. Although the exact incidence may be somewhat unclear, there is less disagreement about what takes place. Physical withdrawal effects are classified in two clusters of symptoms.

The first cluster, called the **alcohol withdrawal syndrome,** is the more common of the two. It begins with insomnia, vivid dreaming, and a severe hangover; these discomforts are followed by tremors (the "shakes"), sweating, mild agitation, anxiety (the "jitters"), nausea, and vomiting, as well as increased heart rate and blood pressure. In some patients, there are also brief tonic-clonic (grand mal) seizures, as the nervous system rebounds from the chronic depression induced by alcohol. The alcohol withdrawal syndrome usually reaches a peak from twenty-four to thirty-six hours after the last drink and is over after forty-eight hours.

The second cluster, called **delirium tremens (DTs),** is much more dangerous and is fortunately less common. The symptoms include extreme disorientation and confusion, profuse sweating, fever, and disturbing nightmares. Typically, there are also periods of frightening hallucinations, when the individual might see snakes or insects on the walls, ceiling, or his or her skin. These effects generally reach a peak three to four days after the last drink. During this time, there is the possibility of life-threatening events such as heart failure, dehydration, or suicide, so it is critical for the individual to be hospitalized and under medical supervision at all times. The current medical practice for treating individuals undergoing withdrawal is to administer antianxiety medication (see Chapter 13) to relieve the symptoms. After the withdrawal period has ended, the dose levels of the medication are gradually reduced and discontinued.[13]

Liver Disease

Chronic consumption of alcohol produces three forms of liver disease. The first of these is a **fatty liver,** resulting from an abnormal concentration of fatty deposits inside liver cells. Normally, the liver breaks down fats adequately, but when alcohol is in the body, the liver breaks down the alcohol at the expense of fats. As a result, fats accumulate and ultimately interfere with the functioning of the liver. The condition is fortunately reversible, if the drinker abstains. The accumulated fats are gradually metabolized, and the liver returns to normal.

The second condition is **alcoholic hepatitis,** an inflammation of liver tissue causing fever, jaundice

alcohol withdrawal syndrome: The more common of two general reactions to the cessation of alcohol consumption in an alcoholic. It is characterized by physiological discomfort, seizures, and sleep disturbances.

delirium tremens (DTs): The less common of two general reactions to the cessation of drinking in an alcoholic. It is characterized by extreme disorientation and confusion, fever, hallucinations, and other symptoms.

fatty liver: A condition in which fat deposits accumulate in the liver as a result of chronic alcohol abuse.

alcoholic hepatitis (AL-co-HAUL-ik hep-ah-TIE-tus): A disease involving inflammation of the liver as a result of chronic alcohol abuse.

(a yellowing of the skin), and abdominal pain, resulting at least in part from a lower functioning level of the immune system. It is also reversible with abstinence, though some residual scarring may remain.

The third and most serious liver condition is **alcoholic cirrhosis,** characterized by the progressive development of scar tissue that chokes off blood vessels in the liver and destroys liver cells by interfering with the cell's utilization of oxygen. At an early stage, the liver is enlarged from the accumulation of fats, but at later stages it is shrunken as liver cells begin to degenerate (Figure 9.1). Although abstinence helps to prevent further liver degeneration when cirrhosis is diagnosed, the condition is not reversible except by liver transplantation surgery.

Prior to the 1970s, alcoholic cirrhosis was attributed to nutritional deficiencies that are often associated with an alcoholic's diet. We know now that, although nutritional problems play a role, alcohol itself is toxic to the liver. After a pattern of heavy alcohol consumption of many years, it is possible to develop cirrhosis, even when nutrition is adequate. A major cause of liver cell damage is the toxic accumulation of free radicals, molecule fragments that are by-products of acetaldehyde (Chapter 8).

Cirrhosis and other forms of chronic liver disease are collectively ranked as the twelfth leading cause of death in the United States, claiming more than 27,000 lives each year. Most deaths occur in people forty to sixty-five years old. Daily drinkers are at a higher risk of developing cirrhosis than binge drinkers, though this risk may be the result of the relatively larger quantity of alcohol consumed over a long period of time. Generally, patients showing liver damage have been drinking for ten to twenty years. Only 10 to 20 percent of all heavy drinkers develop cirrhosis, however, in contrast to 90 to 100 percent who show evidence of either fatty liver or hepatitis. There may be a genetic predisposition to cirrhosis that puts a subgroup of alcoholics at increased risk.[14]

Cardiovascular Problems

About one in every four alcoholics develops cardiovascular problems owing to the chronic consumption of alcohol. The effects include inflammation and enlargement of the heart muscle, poor blood circulation to the heart, irregular heart contractions, fatty accumulations in the heart and arteries, high blood pressure, and stroke. In these cases, the quantity and frequency of drinking far exceeds the standard of "moderate alcohol consumption" which can be a protective factor with regard to cardiovascular disease (see Chapter 8).[15]

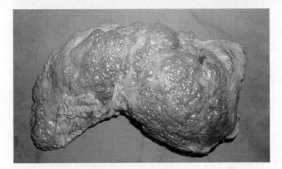

FIGURE 9.1

The dramatic difference between a healthy liver (top) and a cirrhotic liver (bottom).

Cancer

Chronic alcohol abuse is associated with the increased risk of several types of cancers—in particular, cancers of the pharynx and larynx. Nearly 50 percent of all such cancers are associated with heavy drinking. If alcohol abusers also smoke cigarettes, the increased risk is even more dramatic. An increased risk of liver cancer is also linked to chronic alcoholic abuse, whether or not cirrhosis is present as well. In addition, alcohol consumption is associated with breast cancer in women. There is either a weaker association or no association at all with cancers of the stomach, colon, pancreas, or rectum.

Alcohol is not technically considered a carcinogen (a direct producer of cancer), so why the risks are increased in certain cancer types is at present unknown. It is possible that the increased risk is a combined result of alcohol enhancing the carcinogenic effects of other chemicals and, as is true with the development of hepatitis, alcohol depressing the immune system. With a reduced immune

alcoholic cirrhosis (AL-co-HAUL-ik seer-OH-sis): A disease involving scarring and deterioration of liver cells as a result of chronic alcohol abuse.

response, the alcoholic may have a lowered resistance to the development of cancerous tumors.[16]

Dementia and Wernicke-Korsakoff Syndrome

Chronic alcohol consumption can produce longer-lasting deficits in the way an individual solves problems, remembers information, and organizes facts about his or her identity and surroundings. These cognitive deficits are commonly referred to collectively as **alcoholic dementia** and are associated with structural changes in brain tissue. Specifically, there is an enlargement of brain ventricles (the interior fluid-filled spaces within the brain), a widening of fissures separating sections of the cerebral cortex, and a loss of acetylcholine-sensitive receptors. The combination of these effects results in a net decrease in brain mass, as indicated in CT and MRI brain scans, and a decline in overall intelligence, verbal learning and retention, and short-term memory, particularly for middle-aged and elderly alcoholics.

Some 50 to 75 percent of all detoxified alcoholics and nearly 20 percent of all individuals admitted to state mental hospitals show signs of alcohol-related dementia. Through abstinence, it is possible to reverse some of the cognitive deficits and even some of the abnormalities in the brain, depending on the age of the alcoholic when treatment begins. As you might suspect, younger alcoholics respond better than older ones.[17]

A more severe form of cognitive impairment related to chronic alcohol consumption is a two-part disease referred to as **Wernicke-Korsakoff syndrome.** In *Wernicke's encephalopathy*, or simply *Wernicke's disease*, the patient shows confusion and disorientation, abnormal eye movements, and difficulties in movement and body coordination. These neurological problems arise from a deficiency in vitamin B1 (**thiamine**), a nutrient required for neurons in the brain to consume

glucose. Extreme alcoholics may go days or weeks at a time eating practically nothing and receiving calories exclusively from drinking alcoholic beverages.

As a result of thiamine deficiency, large numbers of neurons die in areas of the brain specifically concerned with thinking and movement. About 15 percent of patients with Wernicke's disease, however, respond favorably to large amounts of thiamine supplements in combination with abstinence from alcohol, restoring their previous level of orientation, eye movements, and coordination.

In some cases, Wernicke's disease patients, whether or not they recover from confusion and motor impairments, also display a severe form of chronic amnesia and general apathy called *Korsakoff's psychosis*. Such patients cannot remember information that has just been presented to them and have only a patchy memory for distant events that occurred prior to their alcoholic state. They frequently attempt, through a behavior called **confabulation,** to compensate for their gaps in memory by telling elaborate stories of imagined past events, as if trying to fool others into thinking that they remember more than they actually do.

Thiamine deficiency is linked to Korsakoff's psychosis as well. After being treated with thiamine supplements, about 20 percent of patients completely recover their memory and 60 percent partially recover it. Yet the remaining 20 percent, generally the most severely impaired patients and those with the longest history of alcohol consumption, show little or no improvement and require chronic institutionalization.[18]

Fetal Alcohol Syndrome (FAS)

The disorders just reviewed generally have been associated with consumption of large quantities of alcohol over a long period of time. In the case of the adverse effects of alcohol during pregnancy on unborn children, we are dealing with a unique situation. First of all, we need to recognize the extreme susceptibility of a developing fetus to conditions in the mother's bloodstream. In short, if the mother takes a drink, the fetus takes one, too. And to make matters worse, the fetus does not have sufficient levels of alcohol dehydrogenase to break down the alcohol properly; thus the alcohol stays in the fetus's system longer than in the mother's. In addition, the presence of alcohol coincides with a period of time in prenatal development when critical processes are occurring that are essential for the development of a healthy, alert child.

Although it has long been suspected that alcohol abuse among pregnant women might present serious

---

alcoholic dementia (AL-co-HAUL-ik dih-MEN-chee-ah): A condition in which chronic alcohol abuse produces cognitive deficits such as difficulties in problem solving and memory.

Wernicke-Korsakoff syndrome (VERN-ih-kee KOR-sa-kof SIN-drohm): A condition resulting from chronic alcohol consumption, characterized by disorientation, cognitive deficits, amnesia, and motor difficulty.

thiamine (THY-ah-meen or THY-ah-min): Vitamin B1.

confabulation: The tendency to make up elaborate past histories to cover the fact that long-term memory has been impaired.

The face of a child with fetal alcohol syndrome, showing the wide-set eyes and other features that are characteristic of this condition. The diagnoses of FAS and that of FAE have been subsumed under the more comprehensive term, fetal alcohol spectrum disorders (FASD).

risks to the fetus, a specific syndrome was not established until 1973, when Kenneth L. Jones and David W. Smith described a cluster of characteristic features in children of alcoholic mothers that is now referred to as **fetal alcohol syndrome (FAS).** Their studies, and research conducted since then, have shown clearly that alcohol is **teratogenic**; that is, it produces specific birth defects in offspring by disrupting fetal development during pregnancy, even when differences in prenatal nutrition have been accounted for. Later in life, FAS children show deficits in short-term memory, problem solving, and attentiveness.

Present-day diagnoses of FAS are made on the basis of three groups of observations: (1) prenatal or postnatal growth retardation in which the child's weight or length is below the 10th percentile, (2) evidence of CNS abnormalities or mental retardation, and (3) a characteristic skull and facial appearance that includes a smaller-than-normal head, small wide-set eyes, drooping eyelids, a flattening of the vertical groove between the mouth and nose, a thin upper lip, and a short upturned nose. If only some of these characteristics are observed, the condition is referred to as *partial fetal alcohol syndrome (PFAS).* Currently, FAS and PFAS cases are included in a range of diagnoses in which birth defects have been related to maternal alcohol consumption, collectively referred to as *fetal alcohol spectrum disorders (FASD).*[19]

The incidence of FAS has been estimated to be approximately 0.2 to 1.5 cases per thousand live births in the general U.S. population, but the rates vary greatly within that population. Incidence is generally higher among Native Americans within the United States. In general, the incidence of FASD is estimated to be three times higher than FAS alone.[20]

We do not know at present how alcohol causes FASD, except that the greatest risk is in the first trimester of pregnancy, especially the third week of gestation when craniofacial formation and brain growth are prominent developmental milestones. Concentrated periods of drinking during this time appear to be very damaging to the fetus. For example, if two mothers consumed a similar overall quantity of alcohol during their pregnancies, but Mother A consumed one drink on each of seven days in a week and Mother B consumed all seven drinks on two weekend evenings, then Mother B would have incurred a far greater risk to her child than Mother A (Health Line, page 230).[21]

Although not all alcoholic mothers give birth to babies with FASD, the research findings are clear: Risks are greatly increased when excessive drinking is taking place. Although an occasional drink may have minimal effects, no one has determined a "safe" level of drinking during pregnancy that would make this behavior risk-free. The objective of prevention, therefore, is to educate women to the dangers of drinking at any level and to encourage complete abstinence from alcohol (as well as other psychoactive drugs) during pregnancy. Since 1989, all containers of alcoholic beverages must contain two warning messages, one of which is that "according to the Surgeon General, women should not drink alcoholic beverages during pregnancy because of the risk of birth defects."

Fortunately, it has been possible to reduce prenatal exposure to alcohol through specific public health initiatives. An extensive prevention program, for example, begun in 1982 in a Pueblo tribe in New Mexico, where the incidence of FAS was 4.1 per 1,000 live births, resulted in the incidence decreased to between 1.3 and 1.6 per 1,000 live births for the years 1984 through 1995.[22]

---

fetal alcohol syndrome (FAS): A serious condition involving mental retardation and facial-cranial malformations in the offspring of an alcoholic mother.

teratogenic (TER-ah-tuh-JEN-ik): Capable of producing specific birth defects.

The bad news, however, is that the rates of alcohol consumption among several other high-risk populations in the United States, such as pregnant smokers, unmarried women, women under the age of twenty-five, and women with the fewest years of education, remain substantial despite the fact that about 90 percent of women are aware of the potential harm. Nine percent of pregnant women nationwide continue to consume alcohol (Chapter 8). Unfortunately, FASD continues to be the third leading cause of mental retardation not only in the United States but in the entire Western world, exceeded only by Down syndrome and spina bifida. The fact that the development of alcohol-related fetal defects is entirely preventable makes the incidence of these conditions all the more tragic.[23]

Patterns of Chronic Alcohol Abuse

When we consider the range of direct and indirect costs to society that result from chronic abuse of alcohol, the price we pay is enormous. These costs include the expense of treatment for alcoholism and of medical intervention for alcohol-related diseases, lost productivity from absenteeism and decreases in worker performance, treatment for alcohol-related injuries, and the lost value of future earnings of individuals who die prematurely because of alcoholism. The total costs in the United States are estimated to be about $224 billion annually, even without taking into consideration the incalculable costs of human suffering that are associated with more than estimated

80,000 alcohol-related deaths each year. More than three fourths of these costs and more than one half of these deaths are specific results of binge drinking.[24]

Gender Differences in Chronic Alcohol Abuse

As mentioned earlier, chronic alcohol abuse can be found among both men and women. Nonetheless, there are significant gender differences. For example, among persons aged 18 or older, men outnumber women in the incidence of binge drinking by about two to one and heavy alcohol use by about three to one. Overall, women are more vulnerable to alcohol-related organ damage. Whether this higher risk results from differences in the pattern of drinking or from differences in the way alcohol is processed in a woman's body is at present unknown.[25]

Figure 9.2 shows a state-by-state analysis of alcohol-related problems as measured by the prevalence rate for binge drinking.[26]

Alcohol Abuse among the Elderly

There is a widely held misconception that alcohol abuse is not much of a problem with the elderly. On the basis of careful studies addressing the problem of chronic alcohol abuse among the elderly, it has been estimated that approximately 9 percent of the elderly population have alcohol problems, as indicated by consuming four or more drinks in a single day or more than thirty per month. An analysis of Medicare records has indicated that more people over the age of sixty-five are hospitalized each year for alcohol-related problems than for heart attacks.[27]

One of the reasons for the underreporting of this problem is that we typically use the quantity of alcohol consumed as a primary index of alcoholism, and alcohol consumption does indeed decline with age. Yet, because of the changes in alcohol biotransformation over a lifetime, three drinks consumed at age sixty can be equivalent in their effects to four times as many drinks for someone at age twenty. In addition, the indications of social and occupational problems, traditionally part of the criteria for alcoholism, are often irrelevant for an elderly drinker. There would be no incidence of drunk driving if the person is no longer driving, no job supervisor to notice a decline in work performance, and frequently no spouse to complain of social difficulties. Finally, the occurrence of blackouts or symptoms of Wernicke-Korsakoff syndrome may be misdiagnosed simply as an indication of senility or the onset of Alzheimer's disease.

A number of problems particularly affect the elderly who chronically abuse alcohol. One problem is the risk of the alcohol interacting with the many medications that the elderly typically take. Another is the risk of complications for already existing medical conditions, such as gastrointestinal bleeding, hypertension and cardiac

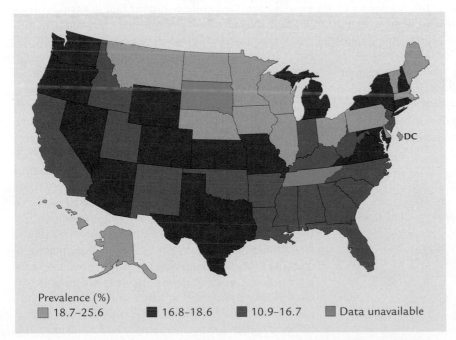

FIGURE 9.2

State-by-state prevalence rates for binge drinking among adults in 2010.

Source: Centers for Disease Control and Prevention (2012). Vital signs: Binge drinking prevalence, frequency, and intensity among adults—United States, 2010. *Morbidity and Mortality Weekly Report, 61,* 14–19.

Prevalence (%)
■ 18.7–25.6   ■ 16.8–18.6   ■ 10.9–16.7   ■ Data unavailable

arrhythmias, osteoporosis, depression, and cognitive impairment-related disorders.

There is growing recognition that treatment programs for alcoholism ought to be tailored to the special needs of the elderly; frequently the traditional treatment programs that benefit much younger individuals do not work well with older people. Many seniors were brought up in an era when highly negative attitudes toward drinking prevailed, so if they are drinking themselves, they feel stigmatized and resist treatment. On a brighter note, however, it has been found that when treatment programs are designed specifically with the elderly in mind, older alcoholics often respond well to treatment.[28]

The Family Dynamics of Alcoholism: A Systems Approach

Alcoholism, like any form of drug abuse, is an especially traumatizing experience for the families involved. For every one person who has a problem with alcohol, there are, on average, at least four others who are directly affected on a day-to-day basis. It is therefore important to examine some of these effects on particular family members. Since the 1950s, a **systems approach** has advocated looking at how the alcoholic and other members of the family interact.[29] We discussed one of these aspects earlier in the chapter in connection with the adverse effects of enabling behavior on the alcoholic. Another important aspect related to an alcoholic's family is the possibility of codependency.

Since the early 1980s, the concept of **codependency** has gained widespread attention as a way of understanding people who live on a day-to-day basis with an alcoholic or any individual with a drug dependence. Definitions vary but most identify four essential features. In members of the family of an alcoholic, therapists have observed (1) an over-involvement with the alcoholic, (2) obsessive attempts to control the alcoholic's behavior, (3) a strong reliance on external sources of self-worth, through the approval of others, and (4) an attempt to make personal sacrifices in an effort to improve the alcoholic's condition.[30]

If people in a relationship with a codependent act badly, the codependent believes that he or she is responsible for their behavior. Because codependency is considered to be a learned pattern of thinking rather than an innate trait, the goal of therapy is to teach the codependent person to detach himself or herself from the alcoholic and begin to meet his or her own needs rather than being controlled by the value judgments of others.[31]

Some professionals, however, have questioned the validity of the codependency concept. They have argued that by labeling a person a codependent, the therapist is promoting feelings of helplessness or victimization in these individuals that might not have existed before. Indeed, the idea of codependency might diminish the person's incentive to begin efforts to take control over his or her life by reinforcing the feeling that he or she is "doomed to suffer." Critics also have pointed out that actual patterns of codependency may not be specific to particular individuals but, rather, occur in practically everyone and that codependency may simply reflect the problems of living in modern society, only now we have found language to describe our tendency to explain our own failures by blaming other people. Nonetheless, despite the criticisms, codependency has become a central concept in therapies that consider family issues in the treatment of alcoholism.[32]

Children of an Alcoholic Parent or Parents

Considering the immense impact that our parents have in our lives, it is understandable that an alcoholic family has distinct negative consequences on the psychological development of the children in that family. As a result, **children of alcoholics (COAs)** have a higher statistical risk of becoming alcoholics than do children of nonalcoholics. Whether this increased risk is genetically or environmentally based is a complex issue that will be reviewed in the next section.

An equally important and independent risk factor may be the specific behavioral and physiological reactions a person has to alcohol itself. Men who at age twenty have a relatively low response to alcohol, in that they need to drink more than other people to feel intoxicated, carry a higher risk of becoming alcoholic by the time they are thirty, regardless of their pattern of drinking at an earlier age and regardless of their parents' drinking. Sons of alcoholics having a low response to alcohol have a 60 percent chance of becoming alcoholics, compared with a 42 percent chance for sons of alcoholics in general. Sons of nonalcoholics having a low

---

systems approach: A way of understanding a phenomenon in terms of complex interacting relationships among individuals, family, friends, and community.

codependency: The concept that individuals who live with a person who has an alcohol (or other drug) dependence suffer themselves from difficulties of self-image and impaired social independence.

children of alcoholics (COAs): Individuals who grew up in a family with either one or two alcoholic parents.

response to alcohol have a 22 percent chance of becoming alcoholics, compared with an 8 to 9 percent chance for sons of nonalcoholics in general.

The combination of these two risk factors—family history and a low response to alcohol—is obviously the worst scenario for a development of alcoholism, at least in males. Nonetheless, we should remember that a large proportion of people still *do not* become alcoholics, even with both risk factors present. The question of what protective factors may account for the resilience of some high-risk individuals with regard to alcoholism continues to be a major subject of alcoholism research.[33]

The Genetics of Alcoholism

For centuries, a common observation has been that alcoholism tends to run in families. Today, a more specific question can be addressed: To what extent is alcoholism genetically determined (through the genes of the parents) and to what extent is it environmentally determined (through the living conditions in which the offspring have been brought up)?

One approach is to examine the inheritance pattern in a family tree. It is impossible, however, to tease out the separate genetic (nature) and environmental (nurture) factors from information of this kind. For more precise answers, we can turn to cases of adopted children and compare the behavior of their lives with the behavior in the lives of either their biological or adoptive parents. In 1981, an extensive research study in Sweden examined the adoption records of approximately three thousand children who had alcoholic biological parents but lived with nonalcoholic adoptive parents. The results showed that a larger percentage of these children become alcoholics than would be seen in the general population. The greater incidence was present even when the children had been raised by their adoptive parents immediately after being born, indicating that a strong genetic component was operating.

There were, however, two subgroups among those children who eventually became alcoholics. One subgroup, called *Type 1 alcoholics*, developed problem drinking later in life and generally functioned well in society. In addition to a genetic predisposition toward alcoholism, there was for this subgroup a strong environmental factor as well. Whether the child was placed in a middle-class or a poor adoptive family influenced the final outcome. A second subgroup, called *Type 2 alcoholics*, developed alcoholism earlier in life and had significant antisocial patterns of behavior. A strong genetic component was operating in this subgroup, and because the socioeconomic status of the adoptive family

TABLE 9.1

Two types of alcoholics

CHARACTERISTICS	TYPE 1	TYPE 2
Usual age at onset	(late onset) after 25	(early onset) before 25
Inability to abstain	infrequent	frequent
Fights and arrests when drinking	infrequent	frequent
Psychological dependence (loss of control)	infrequent	frequent
Guilt and fear about alcoholism	frequent	infrequent
Novelty-seeking personality	low	high
Tendency to use alcohol to escape negative feelings	high	low
Tendency to use alcohol to achieve positive feelings	low	high
Gender	male and female	male only
Extent of genetic influences	moderate	high
Extent of environmental influences	high	low
Serotonin abnormalities in the brain	absent	present

Source: Updated from Cloninger, C. R. (1987). Neurogenetic adaptive mechanisms in alcoholism. *Science, 236,* 410–416.

made no difference in the outcome, we can conclude that environmental factors played a negligible role. Table 9.1 gives a more complete picture of the characteristics associated with Type 1 and Type 2 alcoholics.[34]

The study of twins is another source of information about the genetic and environmental influences in alcoholism. Probably the most important piece of data is the **concordance rate** for alcoholism in pairs of identical twins—that is, how likely one member of a pair is to be alcoholic if the other member is. The concordance rate has been found to be between 50 and 60 percent. If genetics were the whole story in determining the incidence of alcoholism, the concordance rate would have been 100 percent.

If we look closely at the type of alcoholic involved and whether the alcoholic is male or female, the data from twin studies are similar to those found in the

concordance rate: The likelihood that one member of a twin or family relation will have a condition if the other member has it.

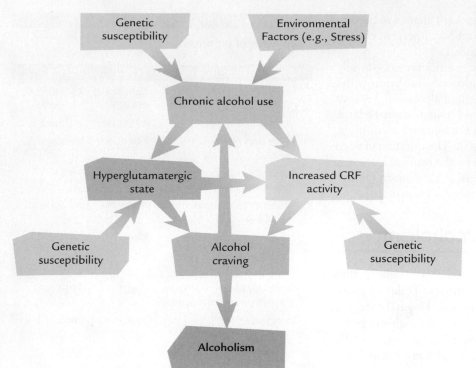

FIGURE 9.3

The contributions of genetic and environmental factors to the development of alcohol abuse and neurochemical adaptations that lead to alcohol craving and the development of alcoholism.

Source: Stacy, D.; Clarke, T-K.; and Schumann, G. (2009). The genetics of alcoholism. *Current Psychiatry Reports, 11*, p. 366.

adoption research. For example, the concordance rate for identical twins has been found to be significantly higher than the concordance rate for fraternal twins when one member of the pair is a male alcoholic whose drinking problems started in adolescence (in other words, a Type 2 alcoholic). For female and male alcoholics whose drinking problems started after adolescence (the Type 1 subgroup), a comparison of concordance rates shows that genetic factors played a lesser role.[35]

Recent studies of alcoholism have brought together genetic and environmental factors by identifying two neurochemical systems in the brain (see Chapter 3). The first system involves the release of corticotropin-releasing factor (CRF) in the hypothalamus. Increased CRF levels have been observed during stress-induced alcohol-drinking behavior and during alcohol withdrawal. The second system involves an increased glutamate activity during alcohol withdrawal, presumably causing behavior related to alcohol craving. In short, studies in both animals and humans have led to the idea that an increased risk of alcoholism may be a result of an interaction between these two systems (see Figure 9.3). It is possible that that abnormal glutamate-related activity may be responsible for increased levels of CRF (Figure 9.3).[36]

The Concept of Alcoholism as a Disease

In contrast to the days when alcoholism was considered a moral failure or worse, the opinion today is that alcoholism is best characterized as a disease, with the consequence being that the alcoholic individual should be treated rather than punished. This viewpoint, by the way, was advanced as early as the 1780s by Benjamin Rush (see Chapter 8). The modern-day concept of alcoholism as a disease can be credited principally to the writings of E. M. Jellinek in the late 1940s. Jellinek proposed that alcohol dependence progressed through a natural sequence of stages, much as a physical illness develops.[37] In more recent interpretations, the disease concept has moved away from the idea that all alcoholics follow a common path (many of Jellinek's ideas have not been confirmed) to a more general focus on the biological factors that might differentiate alcoholics from nonalcoholics. In addition, the disease concept has led to the idea that alcoholics are fundamentally out of control and that abstinence is the only answer to their recovery.[38]

Since 1957, the American Medical Association has defined alcoholism as a disease, and other health organizations have adopted a similar position. Nonetheless, as reasonable as this position might sound, the disease concept has created something of a dilemma among professionals concerned with the treatment of alcohol abuse. It places the burden on physicians to deal with the alcoholic through medical interventions, and unfortunately the medical profession is frequently ill equipped to help. A study in 2000, for example, found that 94 percent of a group of primary care physicians failed to make a correct diagnosis of early-stage alcohol abuse when presented with symptoms typical of this condition. Only a small percentage, approximately one out of five, considered themselves "very prepared" to diagnose alcoholism in the first place.[39]

Important legal considerations also cloud this issue. Can we say, for example, that an alcoholic is legally absolved from a crime or a legal obligation because he or she is afflicted with this disease? These and related issues will be explored later in the chapter in Health Line (page 238) and in Point/Counterpoint III (pages 246–247).

Approaches to Treatment for Alcoholism

Alcoholism, as should be clear at this point, is a study in diversity, and it makes sense that there might be some advantage in matching alcoholics with certain characteristics to specific forms of treatment. One treatment program might be best suited for one subgroup, another for another subgroup. A major eight-year study sponsored by NIAAA, known as Project MATCH, was completed in 1997 to address the relative effectiveness of three psychosocial approaches to alcoholism treatment:

- Cognitive Behavioral Coping Skills Therapy, oriented toward correcting poor self-esteem and distorted, self-defeating thinking.

- Motivational Enhancement Therapy, helping to improve one's readiness to quit drinking.

- Twelve-step Facilitation Therapy, designed to educate clients with the philosophy of Alcoholics Anonymous and encourage their participation.

While improvements were noted for all three treatment approaches, none of the approaches were considered superior to the others in most measures of effectiveness. However, in terms of the percentage maintaining complete abstinence, the Twelve-step facilitation group showed greater improvement than the two other groups, a difference that continued across three years.[40]

Since then, approaches in treatment have gone beyond an exclusive focus on psychosocial issues in alcoholism, taking advantage of an increased understanding of neurochemical changes that occur in the development of alcoholism. Today, both biologically-based and psychosocial-oriented treatments are available, often in conjunction with each other. In this section, we will examine alcoholism treatment in terms of these two broad areas: biological interventions, which involve medications, and psychosocial interventions, such as Alcoholics Anonymous and other self-help programs.

Biologically Based Treatments

The earliest biologically based treatment was the introduction of **disulfiram** (brand name: Antabuse), based on the idea that if a drug induced an aversive reaction when alcohol is consumed, then consumption would be avoided. When applied to alcoholism treatment, the prediction was that the problems of alcoholism would be reduced as a result. Disulfiram, taken orally as a pill once each day, inhibits aldehyde dehydrogenase, allowing acetaldehyde to build up in the bloodstream. Individuals who consume alcohol in combination with disulfiram experience a flushing of the face, rapid heart rate and palpitations, nausea, and vomiting. These effects are brought on not only by consuming alcoholic beverages but also by ingesting alcohol in other forms, such as mouthwashes and cough mixtures, and even by the absorption of aftershave lotions and shampoos through the skin.

Clearly the symptoms caused by a combination of disulfiram and alcohol can be a powerful short-term deterrent to alcoholic drinking, but the question is whether this kind of aversion therapy is an effective treatment over the long run. Careful studies in which disulfiram has been administered to large numbers of alcoholics indicate that it is not effective when it is the sole treatment. One major problem is that alcoholics must take the drug regularly every day, and because disulfiram does nothing to reduce the alcoholic's craving for alcohol, compliance rates are low. The consensus among professionals in this field is that disulfiram can be useful in a subgroup of higher-functioning alcoholics with exceptionally high motivation to quit drinking; for others, disulfiram can be useful as a transitional treatment until other support programs are in place.[41]

> **disulfiram (dye-SULL-fih-ram):** A medication that causes severe physical reactions and discomfort when combined with alcohol. Brand name is Antabuse.

A more direct approach to treatment than aversion therapy has been to reduce the actual craving for alcohol on a neurochemical level. As noted in Chapter 8, evidence suggests that alcohol dependence is related to neural activity in the same dopamine-releasing receptors in the nucleus accumbens that have been implicated in heroin craving, as well as in craving for cocaine and nicotine. This parallel to heroin dependence suggests that opioid receptor antagonists in this region of the brain, such as **naltrexone** (brand name: ReVia) and **nalmefene** (brand name: Revex), should be useful in alcohol-dependence treatment.

An extended-release injectable form of naltrexone (brand name: Vivitrol), administered on a monthly basis, was FDA-approved for alcoholism treatment in 2006. The obvious advantage is that individuals do not have to remember to take their medication on a daily basis. Problems associated with individuals skipping their medication are eliminated, and there can be a more intensive concentration on the counseling component of recovery. The advantage of an extended-release naltrexone for treating alcohol dependence parallels that of extended-release formulations of buprenorphine (Subutex, Suboxone) for treating heroin abuse (Chapter 5). Another approach in treatment has been to focus on the regulation of GABA, in a manner similar to the way gamma vinyl-GABA (Vigabatrin) is used for cocaine-abuse treatment (Chapter 4). **Acamprosate** (brand name: Campral) was FDA-approved in 2004 for this purpose. Recent studies indicate the usefulness of anticonvulsant medications such as topiramate (brand name: Topamax), levetiracetam (brand name: Keppra), and gabapentin (brand name: Neurontin). The combination treatment of gabapentin and naltrexone has shown particular promise.

Still another approach has focused on the role of serotonin levels in the brains of alcoholics. Since

TABLE 9.2

The famous Twelve Steps of Alcoholics Anonymous

1. We admitted we were powerless over alcohol—that our lives had become unmanageable.
2. Came to believe that a Power greater than ourselves could restore us to sanity.
3. Made a decision to turn our will and our lives over to the care of God *as we understood Him*.
4. Made a searching and fearless moral inventory of ourselves.
5. Admitted to God, to ourselves, and to another human being the exact nature of our wrongs.
6. Were entirely ready to have God remove all these defects of character.
7. Humbly asked Him to remove our shortcomings.
8. Made a list of all persons we had harmed and became willing to make amends to them all.
9. Made direct amends to such people wherever possible, except when to do so would injure them or others.
10. Continued to take moral inventory and when we were wrong, promptly admitted it.
11. Sought through prayer and meditation to improve our conscious contact with God, *as we understood Him*, praying only for knowledge of His will for us and the power to carry that out.
12. Having had a spiritual awakening as a result of these steps, we tried to carry this message to alcoholics, and to practice these principles in all our affairs.

Source: The Twelve Steps are reprinted with permission of Alcoholics Anonymous World Services, Inc. (AAWS). Permission to reprint the Twelve Steps does not mean that AAWS has reviewed or approved the contents of this publication, or that AAWS necessarily agrees with the views expressed herein. A.A. is a program of recovery from alcoholism only—use of the Twelve Steps in connection with programs and activities which are patterned after A.A., but which address other problems, or in any other non-A.A. context, does not imply otherwise.

naltrexone (nal-TREX-ohn): A long-lasting opioid antagonist for the treatment of alcoholism. Brand name is ReVia. Brand name for an extended-release injectable form is Vivitrol

nalmefene (nal-MEH-feen): A long-lasting opioid antagonist for the treatment of alcoholism. Brand name is Revex.

acamprosate (A-cam-PRO-sate): A GABA-related drug for the treatment of alcoholism. Brand name is Campral.

ondansetron (on-DANS-eh-tron): A serotonin-related drug for the treatment of alcoholism. Brand name is Zofran.

early-onset (Type 2) alcoholism differs from late-onset (Type 1) alcoholism owing to its association with serotonin abnormalities in the brain (see Table 9.1), a drug that reduces serotonin levels, such as **ondansetron** (brand name: Zofran), typically used as an antinausea medication, should be beneficial in treating this subgroup. This prediction has been confirmed. Among Type 2 alcoholics, Zofran has significantly reduced their drinking behavior and provided a longer period of abstinence.[42]

Bill W. and Dr. Bob—Founders of Alcoholics Anonymous

When they met in the spring of 1935, the backgrounds of William Griffith Wilson (left) and Dr. Robert Smith (right) could not have been more different, but they shared an important problem. They were both alcoholics, and their lives had come apart because of it. Wilson had gone from being a successful businessman, whose investments on Wall Street during the 1920s had made him rich, to a penniless failure after losing his entire fortune in the 1929 crash. Whether rich or poor, he had been a drunk, but his poverty made the condition worse. In 1934 Wilson was admitted to Towns Hospital in New York City and agreed to subject himself to the "belladonna cure," a treatment based on his receiving morphine and the powerful hallucinogen belladonna. Under the influence of this combination of drugs, Wilson experienced "his spiritual awakening." He later wrote,

> In the wake of my spiritual experience there came a vision of a society of alcoholics. If each sufferer were to carry the news of the scientific hopelessness of alcoholism to each new prospect, he might be able to lay every newcomer wide open to a transforming spiritual experience.

For several months, following his newfound mission in life, Wilson sought out drunks to "work on." On a trip to Akron, Ohio, where he was seeking a new job, he was introduced by mutual friends to a proctologist and surgeon named Dr. Robert Smith.

Smith's alcoholism had wrecked a distinguished medical career, and in 1935, he was in severe financial straits. Wilson's determination combined with Smith's desperation led to their taking on the task of keeping each other sober and helping others do the same. On June 10, 1935 (the official date of the founding of Alcoholics Anonymous), Smith took his last drink. By 1939, Wilson had finished writing the Twelve Steps and an extended explanation of the AA philosophy, known today as the "Big Book." Wilson and Smith had discovered that they were most successful in keeping alcoholics abstinent when the latter attended meetings on a regular basis and were assured of complete privacy and anonymity.

Wilson became Bill W., and Smith became Dr. Bob.

It was not until the 1940s that AA began to be nationally known. The *Saturday Evening Post*, one of the leading magazines of the day, gave AA its first real publicity break, publishing an article about the organization that generated an avalanche of responses and a dramatic increase in membership. During this time, AA adopted the an untitled prayer, originally composed by the American theologian Reinhold Niebuhr. It has since been commonly referred to as The Serenity Prayer, recited millions of times in AA and other twelve-step program meetings throughout the world: "God grant me the serenity to accept the things I cannot change, the courage to change the things I can, and the wisdom to know the difference."

Sources: Alcoholics Anonymous comes of age: A brief history of AA (1959). New York: Alcoholics Anonymous World Services. Alibrandi, L.A. (1982). The fellowship of Alcoholics Anonymous. In E. M. Pattison and E. Kaufman (Eds.), *The encyclopedic handbook of alcoholism.* New York: Gardner Press, p. 979. Cheever, S. (2004). *My name is Bill.* New York: Simon and Schuster.

Alcoholics Anonymous

The best-known treatment program for alcoholism is **Alcoholics Anonymous (AA).** Founded in 1935, this organization was conceived basically as a fellowship of alcoholics who wish to rid themselves of their problem drinking by helping one another maintain sobriety. The philosophy of AA is expressed in the famous Twelve Steps (Table 9.2). Members must have acknowledged that they were "powerless over alcohol" and that their lives had become unmanageable, and must have turned their will and their lives over "to the care of God *as we understood Him.*" As the steps indicate, there is a strong spiritual component to the AA program, although the organization vigorously denies that any religious doctrine prevails (Portrait).

AA functions as a type of group therapy with each member oriented toward a common goal: the maintenance of abstinence from alcohol despite a powerful and continuing craving for it. All meetings are completely anonymous (only first names are used in all communications), and the proceedings are dominated by members recounting their personal struggles with alcohol, their efforts to stop drinking, and their support for fellow alcoholics in their own struggles. New members are encouraged to pair up with a sponsor,

> **Alcoholics Anonymous (AA):** A worldwide organization devoted to the treatment of alcoholism through self-help groups and adherence to its principles, which include absolute abstinence from alcohol.

typically a more experienced AA member who has successfully completed the Twelve Steps and can serve as a personal source of support on a day-to-day basis. According to AA, no alcoholic is ever cured but is only recovering, and the process of recovery continues throughout that person's life. In this view alcoholism is a disease, and relapse from sobriety can occur at any moment. The question of whether an alcoholic is totally unable to control his or her drinking is examined in Health Line.

AA has grown to more than 114,000 groups and more than 2 million members worldwide, although it is difficult to get a precise count because the organization is deliberately structured very loosely. Perhaps more important than its size is the powerful impact AA has had not only on the way we deal with alcoholism but also on the way we consider treatment for any compulsive behavior in general. Over the years, the twelve-step program has become a generic concept, as the precepts and philosophy of AA have been widely imitated. There are chapters of Gamblers Anonymous, Nicotine Anonymous, Narcotics or Cocaine Anonymous, and Overeaters Anonymous, all based on the AA model. In addition, there are two specialized fellowship organizations, Al-Anon for relatives and friends of alcoholics and Alateen for teenagers living with an alcoholic family member. These programs adopt a twelve-step approach to identifying and dealing with the dysfunctionality of an alcoholic family.

Health Line
Is Controlled Drinking Possible for Alcoholics?

One of the most intensely debated questions in the field of alcoholism treatment has been whether it is possible for alcoholics to achieve a level of "controlled drinking" without falling back into a state of alcohol dependence.

On one side are well-entrenched organizations such as Alcoholics Anonymous (AA) and the National Institute on Alcohol Abuse and Alcoholism, as well as many other organizations that assert that alcoholism is an irreversible disease, that abstinence is the only answer, and that even the slightest level of alcohol consumption will trigger a cascade of problems that the alcoholic is constitutionally incapable of handling.

On the other side are groups, represented in greater numbers in Canada and Europe than in the United States, asserting that uncontrolled drinking is a reversible behavioral disorder and that for many alcoholics the promotion of total abstinence as a treatment goal is a serious obstacle to their success in rehabilitation. The organization Moderation Management (MM) is an example of this type of therapeutic approach.

Some of the early controlled-drinking studies had so many methodological flaws that the abstinence-only groups were justified in denouncing them. But later research, using carefully randomized assignment of alcoholic subjects to either an abstinence-oriented treatment or a controlled-drinking treatment, has shown that long-term results are comparable for the two groups. This is not to say that the prospects are wonderful for either of them; sadly, the odds against long-term recovery from alcoholism are still higher than the odds in favor of it, no matter what the treatment. But it does appear that controlled drinking can occur.

How many alcoholics can manage to achieve a continued level of nonproblem drinking? Percentages vary from 2 to 10 to 15 percent, although the lower figure is probably more accurate for those individuals with severe alcoholic difficulties. Perhaps a more important point is that no one knows how to predict whether an alcohol abuser will be one of that small number of successful controlled drinkers. Obviously, most alcoholics are convinced that they will be among the lucky ones. How does an alcoholism-treatment counselor handle this? A prominent expert offers one strategy:

> My own perspective is that there is little sense in losing a client by a standoff on this issue. . . . It has been my clinical experience that an unsuccessful trial at "controlled drinking" may be a more persuasive confrontation of the need for abstinence than any amount of argumentation between therapist and client.

Sources: Hester, R. K., and Miller, W. R. (1989). Self-control training. In R. K. Hester and W. R. Miller (Eds.), Handbook of alcoholism treatment approaches. New York: Pergamon Press, pp. 141–149. Miller, W. R. (1989). Increasing motivation for change. In R. K. Hester and W. R. Miller (Eds.), Handbook of alcoholism treatment approaches. New York: Pergamon Press, pp. 67–80. Quotation on p. 77. Sobell, M. B., and Sobell, L. C. (1978). Behavioral treatment of alcohol problems: Individualized therapy and controlled drinking. New York: Plenum.

An anonymous group of men and women at a typical Alcoholics Anonymous meeting.

Despite its stature as the preeminent approach to treatment, there are relatively few scientific appraisals of the overall effectiveness of AA. One of the principal obstacles to evaluation is the anonymity guaranteed to all members, which makes it difficult to conduct well-controlled follow-up studies on how well AA members are doing. Nonetheless, AA is widely regarded in the field of alcohol rehabilitation as a beneficial self-help approach, particularly when it is combined with other treatments, such as individual counseling and medical interventions.[43] It has been pointed out that AA employs four factors that are widely shown to be effective in preventing relapse in alcohol dependence: (1) the imposition of external supervision, (2) the substitution of dependence on a group activity for

Drugs . . . in Focus

The Non-Disease Model of Alcoholism and Other Patterns of Substance Abuse

Despite the "official" description of alcoholism as a disease by the American Medical Association and many international health organizations, the concept of alcoholism as a disease remains controversial and continues to attract vigorous criticism. As Erich Goode has put it, the non-disease theorists assert that alcoholics (as well as other drug abusers) are ". . . not 'sick,' but are rational, problem-solving human beings attempting to carve out a meaningful existence in a harsh and seemingly unyielding environment." Others have warned that the disease model encourages alcoholics to assume a passive stance, depending solely on the advances of modern medicine to save the day, and that acceptance of the disease model often leads to making excuses for one's behavior rather than changing it. As a one-liner expresses it, "There's nothing wrong with being an alcoholic, if you're doing something about it."

The "disease versus non-disease" debate has inevitable consequences for the ways in which we choose to respond to the problem. Non-disease theorists view the prevailing majority opinion as unfortunately leading to a marginalization of alcoholics, reducing them to a small group of afflicted, biologically predestined individuals, rather than seeing these people in the context of the way all of us behave to one degree or another. In the words of

non-disease advocate Stanton Peele, this attitude fosters a "coercive, one-size-fits-all . . . disease treatment system of hospitals, Alcoholics Anonymous, and the twelve steps, which are increasingly administered within the framework of the law enforcement system." He views the disease model as leading to the assumption that all drinking must cease (a position held by AA), instead of to the encouragement of controlled levels of drinking, as advocated by Moderation Management (MM). He also argues that without the disease model of alcoholism and other drug abuse, it is possible to focus on "the larger question of why some people seek to close off their experience through a comforting, but artificial and self-consuming relationship with something external to themselves. In itself, the choice of object is irrelevant to this universal process of becoming dependent."

Further discussion of the disease model of alcoholism can be found in the form of a simulated debate in Point/Counterpoint III on pages 246–247.

Sources: Goode, E. (1999). *Drugs in American society* (5th ed.). New York: McGraw-Hill College, quotation on p. 350. Kinney, J. (2012). *Loosening the grip: A handbook of alcohol information* (12th ed.). New York: McGraw-Hill, pp. 89-92. Peele, S. (1995). Assumptions about drugs and the marketing of drug policies. In W. K. Bickel and R. J. DeGrandpre (Eds.), *Drug policy and human nature*. New York: Plenum, pp. 199–220, first quotation on p. 214. Peele, S., and Brodsky, A. (1975). *Love and addiction*. New York: Taplinger Publishing, second quotation on p. 55.

dependence on drug-taking behavior, (3) the development of caring relationships, and (4) a heightened sense of spirituality.[44]

SMART Recovery

In contrast to AA, the self-help program **SMART Recovery** assumes that people do not need to believe they are "powerless over alcohol" or submit to "a Power greater than ourselves" (phrases taken from the Twelve Steps) to recover from alcoholism. Instead, the dominant philosophy is that individuals have the power themselves to overcome anything, including drinking. Unlike AA, SMART Recovery discourages labeling in general; a person is not required to call himself or herself an alcoholic to achieve success in recovery. The strategy is based on

SMART Recovery: A treatment program for abuse of alcohol and other drugs that emphasizes a nonspiritual philosophy and a greater sense of personal control in the abuser. SMART stands for "Self-Management And Recovery Training."

rational emotive behavior therapy (REBT), an approach developed by the psychologist Albert Ellis that emphasizes rooting out irrational thoughts, emotions, and beliefs that prevent the achievement of personal goals.

Another major difference is that SMART Recovery insists on professional involvement in its program, with a professional adviser (often a clinical psychologist) helping members learn the fundamentals of REBT. No reference is made to God or a higher power; the objective is "NHP (no higher power) sobriety." The goal is that within a year and a half, members will be able to maintain sobriety without going to meetings. In contrast, AA members are encouraged to continue going to meetings for the rest of their lives.

Since 1990, there has been increased interest in secular (nonreligious) approaches to self-help alcoholism treatment such as that practiced by SMART Recovery. Other examples include Men for Sobriety (MFS), Women for Sobriety (WFS), Moderation Management (MM), and Secular Organization for Sobriety (SOS). Nonetheless, recent research has indicated that alcoholics benefit from participation in AA programs, regardless of their religious beliefs (Drugs . . . in Focus).[45]

Chronic Alcohol Abuse and Alcoholism in the Workplace

It has been estimated that about 15 percent of the people in the American work force (19.2 million workers) have used alcohol within two hours of reporting to work or during the workday, worked under the influence of alcohol or worked with a hangover at least once in the previous 12 months. The prevalence rates of alcohol impairment at the workplace are higher among men than women, higher for white employees than minority employees, higher for younger than older employees, and higher for unmarried than married employees. Alcohol impairment is also most frequently reported by individuals in the arts/entertainment/sports/media industries, food preparation and service jobs, and building and grounds maintenance occupations. Individuals with jobs that would be seriously affected if alcohol impairment were present, such as workers in construction/extraction industries and transportation/material-moving industries, do not show a significantly higher prevalence rate of alcohol impairment at work than the work force at large.[46]

Given the adverse impact of chronic alcohol abuse on a range of workplace behaviors, it makes sense that corporations, hospitals, the armed services, and other large organizations should benefit by establishing workplace programs specifically designed for employees who need help. Two major efforts address this problem. The first is employer-sponsored **employee assistance programs (EAPs)**, and the second is union-supported **member assistance programs (MAPs)**. EAPs have been established as a way of increasing the productivity of the organization, whereas MAPs are oriented toward enhancing the welfare of the individual worker.

In either case, a major thrust of workplace interventions has been to change the culture of drinking within the organization. For example, problems arise because employees tend to drink heavily in order to conform to workplace drinking norms. Within a heavy drinking culture, employees are more likely to use alcohol to cope with stress and feelings of alienation. Gender harassment, characterized by behaviors directed at female employees that convey hostile and degrading attitudes toward women, is associated with the proportion of male employees identified as heavy or "at-risk" drinkers,

and the association is stronger when alcohol consumption is considered a common pattern of behavior during lunch or other meal breaks. In other words, a permissive, alcohol-oriented culture at work exacerbates an already serious workplace problem.

Workplace EAPs and MAPs will be examined in Chapter 17 in the larger context of treatment for the substance abuse in general.[47]

---

employee assistance programs (EAPs): Corporate or institutional programs for workers or employees to help them with alcohol or other drug-abuse problems.

member assistance programs (MAPs): Institutional programs for workers or employees to help them with alcohol or other drug-abuse problems, set up by established unions within the organization and tailored to meet the needs of union members.

Summary

Alcoholism: Stereotypes, Definitions, and Life Problems

- Alcoholism is a multidimensional condition that is typically defined in terms of four major life problems: (1) problems associated with a preoccupation with drinking, (2) emotional problems, (3) vocational, social, and family problems, and (4) physical problems.

Alcohol Abuse and Alcohol Dependence

- According to health professionals, alcohol abuse is defined in terms of (1) persistent physical, social, or occupational problems that have become associated with alcohol use and (2) recurring use of alcohol in physically hazardous situations. Alcohol dependence is defined in terms of uncontrolled alcohol intake, unsuccessful efforts to reduce alcohol use, life problems, and alcohol tolerance and withdrawal.

- According to DSM-IV-TR criteria set by the American Psychiatric Association, at least 15 percent of men and about 10 percent of women in the U.S. have met the criteria for alcohol dependence at some time in their lives. An estimated 10 percent of adults overall and 6 percent of college students have met the criteria for alcohol dependence during the past year.

Physiological Effects of Chronic Alcohol Abuse

- Physical effects of alcoholism include tolerance and withdrawal, liver disease, cardiovascular disease,

cancer, and neurological disorders such as Wernicke-Korsakoff syndrome.

- A particular concern is the development of fetal alcohol syndrome (FAS), subsumed under the broader category, fetal alcohol spectrum disorder (FASD) in the offspring of alcoholic mothers. Despite extensive prevention efforts, FASD continues to be the third leading cause of mental retardation not only in the United States but in the entire Western world, exceeded only by Down syndrome and spina bifida.

Patterns of Chronic Alcohol Abuse

- Alcoholics can be found in every age, gender, racial, ethnic, and religious group and in all socioeconomic and geographic categories. Nonetheless, men outnumber women in the incidence of alcoholism by about six to one, although women are more vulnerable to alcohol-related organ damage. The elderly tend to be an underreported group with respect to alcoholism.

- A systems approach to alcoholism examines the complex interacting relationships among individuals, family, friends, and community. The concept of codependency has helped shed light on the specific effects of alcoholism on spouses and other family members. The children of alcoholics (COAs) carry an increased risk of becoming alcoholic as a result of a vulnerability toward alcoholism that is genetically or environmentally based, or both.

The Genetics of Alcoholism

- Studies of adoptions and twins have provided information about the relative influence of genetics and environment on the development of alcoholism.

- A distinction has been made between a male or female alcoholic with drinking problems occurring late in life (Type 1) and a male alcoholic with drinking problems occurring in adolescence (Type 2). The latter subgroup appears to have a greater genetic component in the inheritance pattern.

- Recent studies of alcoholism have brought together genetic and environmental factors by identifying two neurochemical systems: the release of corticotrophin-releasing factor (CRF) in the hypothalamus and abnormal glutamate-related activity in brain areas related to substance craving.

The Concept of Alcoholism as a Disease

- The majority position with respect to alcoholism is that it should be considered a disease and that alcoholics should be treated rather than punished. Since 1957, the American Medical Association has supported this idea.

- Unfortunately, recent surveys of primary care physicians indicate that the medical profession is frequently ill prepared to diagnose alcoholism or supervise effective treatment.

Approaches to Treatment for Alcoholism

- Approaches include biologically based treatments and psychosocial treatments such as the self-help programs of Alcoholics Anonymous (AA).

- Recent biologically based treatments have focused on the reward and craving mechanisms in the brain. Effective treatments include administration of naltrexone, several types of antiseizure medications, and drugs that affect serotonin activity in the brain.

- Objections to certain aspects of the AA philosophy have promoted the growth of other self-help organizations, such as Moderation Management (MM) and SMART Recovery.

Chronic Alcohol Abuse and Alcoholism in the Workplace

- It has been estimated that about 15 percent of the people in the American work force (19.2 million workers) have used alcohol within two hours of reporting to work or during the workday, worked under the influence of alcohol or worked with a hangover at least once in the previous 12 months.

- Corporations and other large organizations have instituted employee assistance programs (EAPs), and unions have instituted member assistance programs (MAPs), to help workers with problems of alcohol abuse or other forms of drug abuse.

Key Terms

abstinence, p. 223
acamprosate, p. 236
alcohol abuse, p. 225
alcohol dependence, p. 225
alcoholic cirrhosis, p. 227
alcoholic dementia, p. 228
alcoholic hepatitis, p. 226
Alcoholics Anonymous (AA), p. 237
alcoholism, p. 221

alcohol withdrawal syndrome, p. 226
children of alcoholics (COAs), p. 232
codependency, p. 232
concordance rate, p. 233
confabulation, p. 228
delirium tremens (DTs), p. 226
disulfiram, p. 235

employee assistance programs (EAPs), p. 241
enablers, p. 224
fatty liver, p. 226
fetal alcohol syndrome (FAS), p. 229
member assistance programs (MAPs), p. 241
nalmefene, p. 236
naltrexone, p. 236

ondansetron, p. 236
SMART Recovery, p. 240
symptomatic drinking, p. 221
systems approach, p. 232
teratogenic, p. 229
thiamine, p. 228
Wernicke-Korsakoff syndrome, p. 228

Endnotes

1. Kinney, J. (2012). *Loosening the grip: A handbook of alcohol information* (10th ed.). New York: McGraw-Hill, pp. 40–41 Chapter opening modified from Kinney, p. 216.
2. Kinney, *Loosening the grip*, pp. 182–185.
3. National Institute on Alcohol Abuse and Alcoholism (2010, April). *Rethinking drinking: Alcohol and your health*. National Institute on Health Publication 10-3770. Bethesda MD: National Institute on Alcohol Abuse and Alcoholism.
4. Kinney, *Loosening the grip*, pp. 193–207.
5. Drobes, D. J., and Thomas, S. E. (1999). Assessing craving for alcohol. *Alcohol Research and Health, 23,* 179–186.
6. Conner, K. R.; Yue, L.; Meldrum, S.; Duberstein, P. R.; and Conwell, Y. (2003). The role of drinking in suicidal ideation: Analysis of Project MATCH data. *Journal of Studies on Alcohol, 64,* 402–408. Schuckit, M. A. (2006). *Drug and alcohol abuse: A clinical guide to diagnosis and treatment* (6th ed.). New York: Springer, p. 72.

7. Hussong, A. M.; Bauer, D.; and Chassin, I. (2008). Telescoped trajectories from alcohol initiation to disorder in children of alcoholic parents. *Journal of Abnormal Psychology, 117,* 63–78. Maiden, R.P. (1997). Alcohol dependence and domestic violence: Incidence and treatment implications. *Alcohol Treatment Quarterly, 15,* 31–50.

8. National Institute on Alcohol Abuse and Alcoholism (2000, April). Alcohol Alert: Imaging and alcoholism: A window on the brain. No. 47. Rockville, MD: National Institute on Alcohol Abuse and Alcoholism. Schacht, J.P.; Anton, R.F.; Myrick, H. (2013). Functional neuroimaging studies of alcohol cue reactivity: A quantitative meta-analysis and systematic review. *Addiction Biology,18,* 121–133.

9. Fishbein, D.H., and Pease, S.E. (1996). *The dynamics of drug abuse.* Needham Heights, MA: Allyn and Bacon, pp. 122–124.

10. American Psychiatric Association (2000). *Diagnostic and statistical manual of mental disorders* (4th ed.). *Text Revision.* Washington, DC: American Psychiatric Association, pp. 213–214.

11. Grant, B.F.; Stinson, F.S.; Dawson, D.A.; Chou, S.P.; Dufour, M.C.; et al. (2004). Prevalence and co-occurrence of substance use disorders and independent mood and anxiety disorders. *Archives of General Psychiatry, 61,* 807–816. Schuckit, *Drug and alcohol abuse,* pp. 90–91.

12. Edwards, A. C.; Gillespie, N. A.; Aggen, S. H.; and Kendler, K. S. (2013). Assessment of a modified DSM-5 diagnosis of alcohol use disorder in a genetically informative population. *Alcoholism: Clinical and Experimental Research, 37,* 443–451.

13. Becker, H. (2008). Alcohol dependence, withdrawal, and relapse. *Alcohol Research and Health, 31,* 348–361. Bayard, M.; Mcintyre, J.; Hill, K.R.; and Woodside, J. (2004). Alcohol withdrawal syndrome. *American Family Physician, 69,* 1443–1450. Schuckit, *Drug and alcohol abuse,* pp. 78–80, 88–90.

14. Centers for Disease Control and Prevention (2012, June 6). Deaths: Leading causes for 2008. *National Vital Statistics Reports, 60,* 1–95, Table D.; Szabo, G., and Mandrekar, P. (2010). Alcohol and the liver. *Alcohol Research and Health, 33,* 87–96. Brick, J. (2008). Characteristics of alcohol: Definitions, chemistry, measurement, use, and abuse. In J. Brick (Ed.), *Handbook of medical consequences of alcohol and drug abuse* (2nd ed.). New York: Routledge, pp. 27–31.

15. Mukamal, K.J.; Tolstrup, J.S.; Friberg, J.; Jensen, G.; and Gronbaek, M. (2005). Alcohol consumption and risk of atrial fibrillation in men and women. *Circulation, 112,* 1736–1742.

16. Bagnardi, V.; Blangliardo, M.; and LaVecchia, C. (2001). Alcohol consumption and the risk of cancer: A meta-analysis. *Alcohol Research and Health, 25,* 263–270. Molina, P.E.; Happel, K.I.; Zhang, P.; Kolls, J.K.; and Nelson, S. (2010). Alcohol and the immune system. *Alcohol Research and Health, 33,* 97–108. Singletary, K.W., and Gapstur, S.M. (2001). Alcohol and breast cancer: Review of epidemiologic and experimental evidence and potential mechanisms. *Journal of the American Medical Association, 286,* 2143–2151.

17. National Institute on Alcohol Abuse and Alcoholism (2001, July). Alcohol Alert: Cognitive impairment and recovery from alcoholism. No. 53. Rockville, MD: National Institute on Alcohol Abuse and Alcoholism. Oscar-Berman, M., and Marinkovic, K. (2003). Alcoholism and the brain: An overview. *Alcohol Research and Health, 27,* 125–133.

18. Ambrose, M. L.; Bowden, S.C.; and Whelan, G. (2001). Thiamin treatment and working memory function of alcohol-dependent people: Preliminary findings. *Alcoholism: Clinical and Experimental Research, 25,* 112–116. Cook, C.C. (2000, May–June Supplement). Prevention and treatment of Wernicke-Korsakoff syndrome. *Alcohol and Alcoholism, 3,* 19–20. Witt, E.D. (1985). Neuroanatomical consequences of thiamine deficiency: A comparative analysis. *Alcohol and Alcoholism, 20,* 201–221.

19. Sokol, R.J.; Delaney-Black, V.; and Nordstrom, B. (2003). Fetal alcohol spectrum disorder. *Journal of the American Medical Association, 290,* 2996–2999. Thomas, J.; Warren, K.; and Hewitt, B.G. (2010). Fetal alcohol spectrum disorders: From research to policy. *Alcohol Research and Health, 33,* 118–126. Wetherill, L., and Foroud, T. (2011). Understanding the effects of prenatal alcohol exposure using three-dimensional facial imaging. *Alcohol Research and Health, 34,* 38–41.

20. Centers for Disease Control and Prevention (2011, December). *Fetal alcohol spectrum disorder: Data and statistics.* Atlanta, GA: Centers for Disease Control and Prevention.

21. National Institute on Alcohol Abuse and Alcoholism (2000, December). Alcohol Alert: Fetal alcohol exposure and the brain. No. 13. Bethesda, MD: National Institute on Alcohol Abuse and Alcoholism, U.S. Department of Health and Human Services (2000). *Alcohol and health,* pp. 300–322.

22. May, P.A. (1998, April). Lessons learned from early studies of alcohol abuse in pregnancy. Presentation at the Early Studies on Prevention of Alcohol Use in Pregnancy Conference, National Institute on Alcohol Abuse and Alcoholism, Bethesda, MD. May, P.A., and Gossage, J.P. (2011). Maternal risk factors for fetal alcohol spectrum disorders. *Alcohol Research and Health, 34,* 16–23. National Institute on Alcohol Abuse and Alcoholism (2004, July). Alcohol Alert: Alcohol—An important women's health issue. Bethesda, MD: National Institute on Alcohol Abuse and Alcoholism.

23. Carroll, L. (2003, November 4). Alcohol's toll on fetuses: Even worse than thought. *New York Times,* pp. F1, F6. Floyd, R.L.; O'Connor, M.J.; Sokol, R.J.; Bertrand, J.; and Cordero, J.F. (2005). Recognition and prevention of fetal alcohol syndrome. *Obstetrics and Gynecology, 106,* 1059–1064. Substance Abuse and Mental Health Services Administration (2012). *Results from the 2011 National Survey on Drug Use and Health: Detailed*

tables. Rockville, MD: Substance Abuse and Mental Health Services Administration, Table 6.76B.

24. Centers for Disease Control and Prevention (2012, January 13). Vital signs: Binge drinking prevalence, frequency, and intensity among adults—United States, 2010. *Morbidity and Mortality Weekly Report, 61*, 14–19.

25. National Institute on Alcohol Abuse and Alcoholism (1999, December). Alcohol Alert: Are women more vulnerable to alcohol's effects? No. 46. Bethesda, MD: National Institute on Alcohol Abuse and Alcoholism. Substance Abuse and Mental Health Services (2011). *Results from the 2010 Survey on Drug Use and Health: Detailed tables*, Table 2.46B.

26. Centers for Disease Control and Prevention (2012). Vital signs: Binge drinking prevalence, frequency, and intensity among adults—United States, 2010. *Morbidity and Mortality Weekly Report, 61*, 14–19, Figure 2.

27. Merrick, E.L.; Horgan, C.M.; Hodgkin, D.; Garrick, D.W.; et al. (2008). Unhealthy drinking patterns in older adults: Prevalence and associated characteristics. *Journal of the American Geriatrics Society, 56*, 214–223.

28. Brody, J.E. (2002, April 2). Hidden plague of alcohol abuse by the elderly. *New York Times*, p. F7. Substance Abuse and Mental Health Services Administration (2007, January/February). Treatment for older adults: What works best? *SAMHSA News*, pp. 1–5.

29. Fisher, G.L., and Harrison, T.C. (2008). *Substance abuse: Information for school counselors, social workers, therapists, and counselors* (4th ed.). Boston: Pearson Education, pp. 199-227. Fields, R. (2010). *Drugs in perspective: Causes, assessment, family, prevention, intervention, and treatment* (7th ed.). New York: McGraw-Hill, pp. 154–173.

30. Doweiko, H.E. (2012). *Concepts of chemical dependency* (8th ed.). Belmont, CA: Brooks/Cole, pp. 297–306. Beattie, M. (2009). *The new codependency: Help and guidance for today's generation*. New York: Simon and Schuster.

31. Fields, pp. 204–233.

32. Hands, M., and Dear, G. (1994). Co-dependency: A critical review. *Drug and alcohol review, 13*, 437–445. Hurcom, C.; Copello, A.; and Orford, J. (2000). The family and alcohol: Effects of excessive drinking and conceptualization of spouses over recent decades. *Substance Use and Misuse, 35*, 473–502.

33. Hall, C.W., and Webster, R.E. (2007). Multiple stressors and adjustment among adult children of alcoholics. *Addiction Research and Theory, 15*, 425–434. Pearson, M. R.; D'Lima, G. M.; and Kelley, M. L. (2011). Self-regulation as a buffer of the relationship between parental alcohol misuse and alcohol-related outcomes in first-year college students. *Addictive Behaviors, 36*, 1309–1312.

34. Cloninger, C.R.; Gohman, M.; and Sigvardsson, S. (1981). Inheritance of alcohol abuse: Cross fostering analysis of adopted men. *Archives of General Psychiatry, 38*, 861–868. Devor, E.J., and Cloninger, C.R. (1989). Genetics of alcoholism. *Annual Review of Genetics, 23*, 19–36.

35. McGue, M.; Pickens, R.W.; and Svikis, D.S. (1992). Sex and age effects on the inheritance of alcohol problems: A twin study. *Journal of Abnormal Psychology, 101*, 3–17. Substance Abuse and Mental Health Services Administration (2009, June 18). Fathers' alcohol use and substance use among adolescents. *The NSDUH Report*. Rockville, MD: Office of Applied Studies, Substance Abuse and Mental Health Services Administration.

36. Nurnberger, J.I., and Bierut, L.J. (2007, April). Seeking the connections: Alcoholism and our genes. *Scientific American*, pp. 46–53. Stacy, D.; Clarke, T-K.; and Schumann, G. (2009). The genetics of alcoholism. *Current Psychiatry Reports, 11*, 364–369.

37. Jellinek, E.M. (1960). *The disease concept of alcoholism*. New Haven, CT: Hillhouse Press. Vaillant, G.E. (1995). *The natural history of alcoholism revisited*. Cambridge, MA: Harvard University Press.

38. George, W.H., and Marlatt, G.A. (1983). Alcoholism: The evolution of a behavioral perspective. In M. Galanter (Ed.), *Recent developments in alcoholism*. Vol. 1. New York: Plenum, pp. 105–138.

39. Maltzman, I. (1994). Why alcoholism is a disease. *Journal of Psychoactive Drugs, 26*, 13–31. National Center on Addiction and Substance Abuse at Columbia University (2000, May). *Missed opportunity: National survey of primary care physicians and patients on substance abuse*. New York: National Center on Addiction and Substance Abuse at Columbia University.

40. Babor, T.F., and Del Boca, F.K. (Eds.) (2003). *Treatment matching in alcoholism*. Cambridge, UK: Cambridge University Press. Cutler, R.B., and Fishbain, D.A. (2005). Are alcoholism treatments effective? The Project MATCH data. *BMC Public Health, 5*, 75. Miller, W.R. (2005). Are alcoholism treatments effective? The Project MATCH data: Response. *BMC Public Health, 5*, 76.:

41. Banys, P. (1988). The clinical use of disulfiram (Antabuse): A review. *Journal of Psychoactive Drugs, 20*, 243–261.

42. Anton, R.F.; Myrick, H.; Wright, T.M.; Latham, P.K.; Baros, A.M.; et al. (2011). Gabapentin combined with naltrexone for the treatment of alcohol dependence. *American Journal of Psychiatry, 168*, 709–717. Fertig, J.B.; Ryan, M.L.; Falk, D.E.; Litten, R.Z.; et al. (2012). A double-blind, placebo-controlled trial assessing the efficacy of levetiracetam extended-release in very heavy drinking alcohol-dependent patients. *Alcoholism: Clinical and Experimental Research*, doi:10.111/j.1530-0277.2-11.01716.x. Johnson, B.A.; Rosenthal, N.; Capece, J. A.; Wiegand, F.; Mao, L.; et al. (2007). Topiramate for treating alcohol dependence: A randomized controlled trial. *Journal of the American Medical Association, 298*, 1641–1651. Scott, L. J.; Figgitt, D. P.; Keam, S. J.; and Waugh, J. (2005). Acamprosate: A review of its use in the maintenance of abstinence in patients with alcohol dependence. *CNS Drugs, 19*, 445–464. Substance Abuse and Mental Health Services Administration (2007, May/June). Treating alcohol dependence: Naltrexone advisory. *SAMHSA News*, p. 14.

43. Hopson, R.E., and Beaird-Spiller, B. (1995). Why AA works: A psychological analysis of the addictive experience and the efficacy of Alcoholics Anonymous. *Alcoholism Treatment Quarterly, 12*, 1–17. Morgenstern, J.; Bux, D.; LaBouvie, E.; Blanchard, K.A.; and Morgan, T.J. (2002). Examining mechanisms of action in a 12-step treatment: The role of 12-step cognitions. *Journal of Studies on Alcohol, 63*, 665–672. White, W.H. (1998). *Slaying the dragon: The history of addiction treatment and recovery in America.* Bloomington, IL: Chestnut Health Systems, pp. 127–177.

44. Forcehimes, A.A. (2004). *De Profundis:* Spiritual transformations in Alcoholics Anonymous. *Journal of Clinical Psychology/In Session, 60*, 503–517. How effective is Alcoholics Anonymous? (2003, December). *Harvard Medical Letter*, p. 7.

45. Ellis, A., and Velten, E. (1992). *When AA doesn't work for you: Rational steps to quitting alcohol.* Fort Lee, NJ: Barricade Press. Kaskutas, L.A. (1996). A road less traveled: Choosing the "Women for Sobriety" program. *Journal of Drug Issues, 26*, 77–94. Schmidt, E. (1996). Rational recovery: Finding an alternative for addiction treatment. *Alcoholism Treatment Quarterly, 14*, 47–57. SMART Recovery (2004). *SMART Recovery handbook.* Mentor, OH: SMART Recovery®. Winzelberg, A., and Humphreys, K. (1999). Should patients' religiosity influence clinicians' referral to 12-step self-help groups? Evidence from a study of 3,018 male substance abuse patients. *Journal of Consulting and Clinical Psychology, 67*, 790–794.

46. Frone, M.R. (2006). Prevalence and distribution of alcohol use and impairment in the workplace: A U.S. national survey. *Journal of Studies on Alcohol and Drugs, 67*, 147–156. Frone, M.R., and Brown, A.L. (2009). Workplace substance-use norms as predictors of employee substance use and impairment: A survey of U.S. workers. *Journal of Studies on Alcohol and Drugs, 71*, 526–534.

47. Bachrach, S.B.; Bamberger, P.A.; and McKinney, V.M. (2007). Harassing under the influence: The prevalence of male heavy drinking, the embeddedness of permissive workplace drinking norms, and the gender harassment of female coworkers. *Journal of Occupational Health Psychology, 13*, 232–250. Substance Abuse and Mental Health Services Administration (2009, April 9). Alcohol treatment: Need, utilization, and barriers. *The NSDUH Report.* Rockville, MD: Office of Applied Studies, Substance Abuse and Mental Health Services Administration. Osilla, K.C.; Zellmer, S.P.; Larimer, M.E.: Neighbors, C.; and Marlatt, G.A. (2008). A brief intervention for at-risk drinking in an employee assistance program. *Journal of Studies on Alcohol and Drugs, 69*, 14–20.

Point/Counterpoint III

Should Alcoholism Be Viewed as a Disease?

The following viewpoints on whether alcoholism is a disease represent both sides of this controversial issue. Read them with an open mind. You don't have to come up with the final answer, nor should you necessarily agree with the last argument you read. Many of the ideas in this feature come from the sources listed.

POINT

Alcohol abuse has recently been defined by the National Institute on Alcohol Abuse and Alcoholism (NIAAA) as existing when three criteria are met: a preoccupation with drinking alcohol, a pattern of compulsive use despite the adverse consequences, and a pattern of relapse to alcohol use. Alcoholics cannot control their drinking; that is their disease. Give a drink to a person who is genetically vulnerable to alcohol, and the consumption of alcohol will make that person an alcoholic, just as a person infected with a type of bacteria might acquire an infectious disease.

COUNTERPOINT

First of all, you're taking considerable liberty with the bacterial infection argument. The research on alcoholism does not show that everyone who acquires the behaviors of alcohol abuse was genetically disposed to it. Controlled drinking is attainable for at least some alcoholics. How do you separate the alcoholics who respond less to genetic factors than to environmental ones, and seem to retain some degree of control over their drinking, from those individuals who do not? Besides, we are not talking about alcohol as some invisible bacteria floating around, waiting to "infect" people without their knowledge. Alcoholics become alcoholic because they consume a substance that later on they no longer can handle. At one time in their lives, they chose to have that first drink; no one person or thing made them do it.

POINT

We accept the fact that the alcoholic is responsible for "that first drink," but we assert that the consequences are not voluntary. The alcoholic is powerless over alcohol, not over his or her alcoholism. The situation is similar to a diabetic being in control over whether a treatment of insulin injections should be taken. The alcoholic can seek treatment.

COUNTERPOINT

You can't have it both ways. Being responsible for the treatment of the disease is not the same as being powerless in the face of alcoholism (one of the main assumptions of Alcoholics Anonymous). Even the Supreme Court has trouble wrestling with the issue. In 1988, it ruled that two alcoholics could not be excluded from claiming educational benefits normally accorded to veterans just because their alcoholism prevented them from applying in the time allowed. The Veterans Administration had refused them, claiming that alcoholism, without physical or mental disorders, is an example of "willful misconduct."

POINT

Not exactly. The Court ruled that the source of the "willful misconduct" was the disease of alcoholism. In doing so, it actually reconfirmed the concept of alcoholism as a disease. The courts typically do not excuse the alcoholic from the consequences of the condition. Instead, they give the person a choice of being punished for his or her offenses or accepting a program of rehabilitation. We cannot go back to the days when drinking too much was considered a moral deficiency.

COUNTERPOINT

If alcoholism is a disease, then it's a very strange one. It may be in a category all its own.

Critical Thinking Questions for Further Debate

1. Suppose that the evidence were overwhelming that moderate alcohol intake was a health-promoting activity and that there were social programs promoting moderate alcohol use through society. How would this work and would you envision any unanticipated consequences? What would be the

effect on efforts to prevent and treat alcohol abuse?

2. Suppose you are an alcohol abuser and have attended several meetings of Alcoholics Anonymous (AA), to no avail. Programs that permit a moderate but nonzero level of alcohol consumption have not worked for you either. What options do you have, assuming you want to stop drinking? Do you go back to AA?

Point/Counterpoint IV can be found on pages 360–361.

Sources: Holden, C. (1987). Is alcoholism a disease? *Science, 238,* 1647. Levinthal, C.F. (2003). *Point/Counterpoint: Opposing perspectives on issues of drug policy.* Boston: Allyn and Bacon, Chapters 5 and 6. Maltzman, I. (1994). Why alcoholism is a disease. *Journal of Psychoactive Drugs, 26,* 13–31. Miller, N., and Toft, D. (1990). *The disease concept of alcoholism and other drug addiction.* Center City, MN: Hazelden Foundation.

CHAPTER 10

After you have completed this chapter, you should have an understanding of

Nicotine and Tobacco Use

I know the old joke. Mark Twain said that quitting smoking was easy and that he should know because he had done it hundreds of times. Well, I should know too. It seems that I've tried to quit hundreds of times too. I realize it's not good for me; I'm no fool. But somehow I keep on smoking. My fellow smokers and I cluster on the sidewalk outside our offices in the mornings and the afternoons, standing out there in the rain and the cold. I feel like an outcast of society, day in and day out. Someday I'll stop, but in the meantime I will just have to contend with the disapproving glances, the inconveniences, the feelings of shame.

—*Anonymous*

In some ways, our attitudes toward tobacco have not changed very much over the years. In the late sixteenth century, when tobacco was first introduced to the Western world, tobacco smoking for some people was a personally objectionable behavior, yet strangely captivating to those who tried it and enjoyed the experience. The same is true today. And in the twenty-first century, we have as much difficulty quitting as they had in Mark Twain's time.

In other ways, however, the times have definitely changed. From the 1920s until the mid-1960s, lighting up and smoking a cigarette was an unquestioned sign of sophistication, encouraged by the intense marketing efforts of tobacco manufacturers. Ashtrays and cigarette lighters were standard on automobile dashboards. There was little or no public recognition that harm would come of smoking—a possibility that was concealed for decades by the tobacco industry. It was an era before surgeon general's reports, Tobacco-Free Kids advertisements, National Smoke-Out Days, and smoke-free restaurants, hotels, and public buildings.

Today, it is no longer a matter of debate that tobacco smoking is a major health hazard, not only to the individual doing the smoking but also to society at large. It is also no longer a matter of debate that the main psychoactive ingredient in tobacco, nicotine, is a major dependence-producing drug. Even the tobacco companies now concede that their product is dangerous.

Yet at the same time, tobacco products are legally sanctioned commodities with an economic significance, both to the United States and to the world. Banning tobacco products would lead us into a Prohibition era comparable to or perhaps exceeding in social upheaval the one experienced with respect to alcohol in the last century (see Chapter 8). How did we arrive at this point, and what lies ahead? This chapter will explore what we now know about the effects of tobacco smoking and other forms of tobacco use, the impact these behaviors have had on American society and the world, and the ways in which we have dealt with the issue of tobacco use over the years. It also will consider current approaches to helping people who choose to stop smoking, and prevention strategies to encourage young people not to start smoking in the first place.

Tobacco Use through History

Shortly after setting foot on the small island of San Salvador on October 12, 1492, Christopher Columbus received from the inhabitants a welcoming gift of large, green, sweet-smelling tobacco leaves. Never having seen tobacco before, Columbus did not know what to make of this curious offering, except to observe in his journal that the leaves were greatly prized by the "Indians." In the first week of November, two members of the expedition ventured to the shores of Cuba, searching at Columbus's insistence for the great khan of Cathay (China). They found no evidence of the khan but did return with reports of natives who apparently were "drinking smoke."

Before long, Columbus's men were "tobacco drinking" as well. One sailor in particular, Rodrigo de Jerez, became quite fond of the practice. He was, in fact, history's first documented European smoker, though he lived to regret it. When Rodrigo returned to Spain, he volunteered to demonstrate the newfound custom to his neighbors, who, instead of being impressed, thought that anyone who could emit smoke from the nose and mouth without burning had to be possessed by the Devil. A parish priest turned Rodrigo over to the Inquisition, which sentenced him to imprisonment for witchcraft. He spent several years in jail, presumably without a supply of tobacco. Rodrigo therefore also may be remembered as the first European smoker to quit cold turkey.[1]

In 1559, the year historians mark as the year tobacco was officially introduced to Europe, the French ambassador to Portugal, Jean Nicot, presented some tobacco plants acquired in the New World to Catherine de Medici, Queen of France as a possible treatment for her migraine headaches (supposedly it helped); the plant was

by the numbers . . .

>300 million	The estimated number of men in China who are regular tobacco smokers, a number exceeding the population of the United States.
5.4 million	The estimated number of people worldwide who die each year from tobacco-related lung cancer, heart disease, and other illnesses.
>8 million	The estimated number of people worldwide who will die each year by 2030, if present trends continue; 80 percent of these deaths will be in developing nations.
100 million	The estimated number of people worldwide in the twentieth century who died prematurely of tobacco-related disease.

Sources: World Health Organization (2010). Tobacco: Key facts. Geneva, Switzerland: World Health Organization. World Health Organization (2009). WHO report on the global tobacco epidemic 2009. Geneva, Switzerland: World Health Organization. World Health Organization (2008). The WHO report on the global tobacco epidemic 2008. Geneva, Switzerland: World Health Organization.

named a century later, *Nicotiana tabacum*, after him. The medical applications, however, quickly became secondary to its recreational use. The practice of smoking tobacco soon became fashionable among European aristocracy.

Not everyone was enthusiastic about this new fad. In 1604, predating a modern-day surgeon general's report by more than 350 years, King James I of England wrote "A Counter-blaste to Tobacco," a lengthy treatise condemning tobacco use. Referring to tobacco as a "stinking weede," he characterized smoking as "a custom loathsome to the eye, hateful to the nose, harmful to the brain, [and] dangerous to the lung." In the first recorded comment on its potential for causing dependence, the king observed that "he that taketh tobacco saith he cannot leave it, it doth bewitch him."

Politics, Economics, and Tobacco

Elsewhere in the world, during the early seventeenth century, the condemnation of tobacco became extreme. In Russia, officials established penalties for smoking that included whipping, mutilation, exile to Siberia, and death. Turkey, Japan, and China tried similar tactics, but not surprisingly, tobacco use continued to spread.[2]

By the end of the seventeenth century even the fiercest opponents of tobacco had to concede that it was here to stay. A sultan of Turkey in 1648 became a smoker himself, and naturally, Turkish penalties for tobacco use vanished overnight; Czar Peter the Great in 1689 pledged to open up Russia to the West, and tobacco suddenly became a welcome symbol of modernism; Japan and China gave up trying to enforce a prohibition that citizens obviously did not want. Even England's James I put aside his personal distain for tobacco when he realized that a new source of revenue could come from taxes imposed on this popular new commodity.[3]

Snuffing and Chewing

One form of tobacco use observed by the early Spanish explorers was the practice of grinding a mixture of tobacco into a fine powder (**snuff**), placing or sniffing a pinch of it into the nose, and exhaling it with a sneeze. By the 1700s, this custom, called **snuffing**, overtook smoking as the dominant European form of tobacco use. Among French

---

snuff: A quantity of finely shredded or powdered tobacco. Modern forms of snuff are available in either dry or moist forms.

snuffing: The ingestion of snuff either by inhalation or by absorption through tissue in the nose.

cigars: Tightly rolled quantities of dried tobacco leaves.

---

aristocrats, both men and women, expensive snuffs, perfumed with exotic scents and carried in jeweled and enameled boxes, became part of the daily routine at the court in France and then in the rest of Europe. Sneezing was considered to clear the head of "superfluous humours," invigorate the brain, and brighten the eyes. In an era when bad smells were constant features of daily living, snuffing brought some degree of relief, not to mention a very effective way of sending nicotine to the brain (see Chapter 3).

Because of their dominance in the rapidly expanding tobacco market, the British colony of Virginia in America prospered greatly. England enjoyed a profitable tobacco trade as a result, but you might say that its development of colonial tobacco growing would eventually backfire. In 1777, when Benjamin Franklin was sent as an envoy to France to gain support against the British in the American War for Independence, a key factor in his success was an offer to deliver prime Virginia tobacco in return for French money. The French liked the idea, and the rest is history. Had it not been for American tobacco, there might not have been a United States of America at all.[4]

In the United States, snuffing was soon replaced by a more rough-and-ready method for using tobacco: chewing. The practice was not totally new; early Spanish explorers had found the natives chewing tobacco as well as smoking it from the earliest days of their conquest, although North American tribes preferred smoking exclusively. Chewing tobacco had the advantage of freeing the hands for work, and its low cost made it a democratic custom befitting a vigorous new nation in the nineteenth century. However, the need to spit out tobacco juices on a regular basis raised the tobacco habit to unimaginable heights of gross behavior. It was enough to make the objections to smoke and the hazards of fire fade into insignificance; now the problem was a matter of public health. Tobacco spitting became a major factor behind the spread of infectious diseases such as tuberculosis. Adding to this unsavory picture was the fact that a man's accuracy in targeting the nearest spittoon was inevitably compromised by his level of alcohol consumption, which was setting all-time records during this period (see Chapter 8).

Cigars and Cigarettes

By the time of the American Civil War, the fashion in tobacco use began to shift once more, as its overall popularity continued to soar. Although the plug of tobacco suitable for chewing was still a major seller and would remain so until the early twentieth century, two new trends emerged, particularly in the growing industrial cities.

The first trend was the popularity of smoking **cigars** (commonly known as "seegars"), tight rolls of dried tobacco leaves. New innovations in curing (drying) tobacco leaves had produced a milder and lighter-quality leaf that was more suitable for smoking than the older forms that had been around since the colonial period. North Carolina, with its ideal soil for cultivating this type of tobacco emerged as the tobacco-growing center of the United States; it continues to do so today. With the advent of cigars, tobacco consumers could combine the feeling of chewing (since the cigar remained in the mouth for a relatively long period of time) and the effects of ingesting tobacco smoke. Pioneers heading west could indulge in foot-long cigars called "stogies," named after the Conestoga wagons that they rode during the long and tedious journey.

The second trend was the introduction of **cigarettes**, rolls of shredded tobacco wrapped in paper. They had become popular among British soldiers returning from the Crimean War in 1856, who had adopted the practice from the Turks. Europe took to cigarettes immediately, but the United States proved a harder sell. Part of the problem was the opposition of a well-entrenched U.S. cigar industry, which did not look kindly on an upstart competitor. Cigar makers did not discourage the circulation of rumors that the cigarette paper wrapping was actually soaked in arsenic or white lead, that cigarette factory workers were urinating on the tobacco to give it an extra "bite," or that Egyptian brands were mixed with crushed camel dung.[5]

An even greater marketing challenge than unsubstantiated rumors was the effeminate image of cigarette smoking itself. A cigarette was looked upon as a dainty, sissy version of the he-man cigar; cigars were fat, long, and dark, whereas cigarettes were slender, short, and light. Well into the beginning of the twentieth century, this attitude persisted. This is what John L. Sullivan, champion boxer and self-appointed defender of American masculinity, thought of cigarettes in 1904:

> Who smokes 'em? Dudes and college stiffs—fellows who'd be wiped out by a single jab or a quick under cut. It isn't natural to smoke cigarettes. An American ought to smoke cigars. . . . It's the Dutchmen, Italians, Russians, Turks, and Egyptians who smoke cigarettes and they're no good anyhow.[6]

The public image of the cigarette eventually would change dramatically; until then, cigarette manufacturers had to rely instead on a powerful marketing advantage: low cost. In 1881, James Bonsack patented a cigarette-making machine that transformed the tobacco industry. Instead of producing at most 300 cigarettes an hour by hand, three machine operators could now turn out 200 a minute, or roughly 120,000 cigarettes a day. This is a snail's pace compared to today's state-of-the-art machines, which can produce more than 10,000 cigarettes a minute,

but in those days, the Bonsack machine was viewed as an industrial miracle. Cigarettes by the end of the 1800s were as cheap as twenty for a nickel.[7]

Tobacco in the Twentieth Century

At the beginning of the twentieth century, Americans could choose from a variety of ways to satisfy their hunger for tobacco and the psychoactive effects it could bring. Cigars and pipes were still the dominant form of tobacco use, but the future favored the cigarette for two basic reasons. First, a growing number of women began to challenge the idea of masculine dominance, and smoking tobacco was one of the privileges of men that women now wanted to share. Not that women smoking was met with immediate acceptance; in one famous case in 1904, a New York City woman was arrested for smoking in

To encourage male cigarette smokers, advertisements drew heavily on an association with baseball players. What is arguably the most famous and most valuable baseball card, depicting 1909 baseball player Honus Wagner, was actually included in a packet of cigarettes, long before baseball cards became associated with bubble gum.

cigarettes: Rolls of shredded tobacco wrapped in paper, today usually fitted at the mouth end with a filter.

public. Nonetheless, as smoking became more common among women, the mild-tasting, easy-to-hold cigarette was the perfect option for them. By the 1920s, advertising slogans such as "Reach for a Lucky instead of a sweet" (a clever effort to promote cigarette smoking as a weight-control aid) as well as endorsements by glamorous celebrities were being designed specifically for the women's market. The second factor was World War I, during which time cigarettes became logical form of tobacco easily taken along to war. Times of tension have always been times of increased tobacco use. When the war was over, the cigarette was, in the words of one historian, "enshrined forever as the weary soldier's relief, the worried man's support, and the relaxing man's companion."[8]

Cigarettes really came into their own in the 1920s, with the introduction of heavily advertised brand names and intense competition among American tobacco companies. Cigarette sales in the United States increased from $45 billion in 1920 to $80 billion in 1925 and $180 billion by 1940.[9]

Health Concerns and Smoking Behavior

A combination of mass-media advertising and the endorsement of smoking by sports celebrities and glamorous people in the entertainment industry enabled the tobacco industry, now dominated by cigarettes, to increase its volume of sales from the 1940s to the 1980s by a steady 9 billion cigarettes each year. The peak in domestic sales was reached in 1981, when approximately 640 billion were sold. Owing to the increase in population, however, per capita consumption in the United States had peaked in 1963 at approximately 4,300 cigarettes per year (roughly twelve cigarettes per day).

Beginning in 1964, per capita consumption began a steady decline to approximately 1,600 per year (roughly four cigarettes per day). The year of the turnaround coincided with the U.S. surgeon general's first report on smoking and health. For the first time, the federal

Health Line

African Americans, Smoking, and Mentholated Cigarettes

It has long been puzzling that African Americans tend to smoke fewer cigarettes than white smokers but carry a higher risk of tobacco-related disorders such as lung cancer and heart disease. One factor that has been used as an explanation is the relatively slower rate of nicotine metabolism among African Americans following cigarette smoking (Chapter 3). African Americans may be taking in and retaining relatively more nicotine per cigarette and, as a result, may not need to smoke as many cigarettes per day to take in an equivalent dose of nicotine.

Recent studies have indicated that a major factor might be the menthol in certain brands of cigarettes. More than 60 percent of African American smokers prefer mentholated brands such as Newport and Kool over non-mentholated brands such as Marlboro and Camel, almost the complete opposite to the pattern of brand preferences among white smokers. Menthol allows smokers to take in more smoke and possibly hold it in longer, essentially canceling any benefit of choosing a "light" or "ultralight" brand to smoke. Relative to other smokers, African Americans who smoked menthol cigarettes had higher levels in their saliva of a specific nicotine by-product. The finding that smokers of mentholated cigarettes are almost twice as likely to relapse after attempts to quit smoking, compared to smokers of nonmentholated cigarettes, is consistent with the relatively higher levels of nicotine intake likely to occur when one is smoking mentholated brands.

The growing evidence of the effect of menthol content in cigarettes on smoking behavior and the implications with regard to smoking cessation have led some to demand that tobacco companies be required to report how much menthol is contained in various cigarette brands, as they now do for levels of nicotine and tar. Others have even called for mentholated cigarettes to be banned altogether. These actions might come about as part of future FDA regulations over tobacco products, as authorized by the Tobacco Control Act of 2009.

Sources: Celebucki, C. C.; Wayne, G. F.; Connolly, G. N.; Pankow, J. F.; and Chang, E. I. (2005). Characterization of measured menthol in 48 U.S. cigarette sub-brands. Nicotine and Tobacco Research, 7, 523–531. Mustonen, T. K.; Spencer, S. M.; Hoskinson, R. A.; Sachs, D. P. L.; and Garvey, A. J. (2005). The influence of gender, race, and menthol content on tobacco exposure measures. Nicotine and Tobacco Research, 7, 581–590. Pletcher, J.; Hulley, B. J.; Houston, T.; Kiefe, C.; Benowitz, N.; et al. (2006). Menthol cigarettes, smoking cessation, atherosclerosis, and pulmonary function. Archives of Internal Medicine, 166, 1915–1922. Samet, J., and Wipfli, H. (2009). Unfinished business in tobacco control. Journal of the American Medical Association, 302, 681–682. Substance Abuse and Mental Health Services Administration (2009, November 19). Use of menthol cigarettes. The NSDUH Report. Rockville, MD: Substance Abuse and Mental Health Services Administration.

government asserted publicly what had been suspected for decades: the link between tobacco smoking and cancer and other serious diseases. A succession of surgeon general's reports since 1964 has produced a number of important developments in tobacco use in America.

- As evidence of health risks accumulated, restrictions on public consumption were instituted. In 1971, all television advertising for tobacco was banned, and in 1984, a rotating series of warning labels (which had been required on all packages of tobacco products since 1966) were required on all print advertisements and outdoor billboards.

- There was a significant change in the type of cigarette smoked by the average smoker. In the 1950s, more and more cigarette smokers chose to smoke *filtered* rather than *unfiltered* cigarettes, in an effort to ingest less of the toxins in tobacco. By the 1990s, about 95 percent of all smokers were using filtered brands. However, after the introduction of filtered cigarettes, the industry *changed* the formulation of the tobacco to a stronger blend with an increased tar content. As a result of a stronger "filter blend" formula in the cigarette, **sidestream smoke**, the smoke directly inhaled by a nonsmoker from a burning cigarette, ended up more toxic when originating from a filtered cigarette than it was from an unfiltered one. In principle, a cigarette filter should have allowed a flow of air through small holes in the filter itself. Because a smoker typically held the cigarette with the fingers covering these holes, however, little or no filtering was accomplished. In the meantime, filtered cigarettes increased tobacco company profits. Filters were only paper and therefore cost considerably less than filling the same space with tobacco.

- As a consequence of the surgeon general's assertion that tar and nicotine were specifically responsible for increased health risks from smoking, new "light" and "mild" cigarette brands were introduced that were low in tar and nicotine (T/N), and the Federal Trade Commission began to issue a listing of tar and nicotine levels in major commercial brands. As later surgeon general's reports indicated, however, smokers canceled out the benefits of switching to low T/N brands by varying the manner in which they smoked low-T/N cigarettes. Smokers took more puffs, inhaled more deeply, and smoked more of such cigarettes so as to get the same amount of nicotine (the same number of nicotine "hits"). Moreover, a greater number of low-T/N cigarettes had to be smoked in order to satisfy the smoker's needs. In 2010, tobacco companies were mandated to change the branding labels to acknowledge that "light" and "mild" brands were no less harmful than regular brands. Marlboro Lights, for example, became Marlboro Gold; Marlboro Ultra Lights became Marlboro Silver.

- In 2007, it was confirmed that cigarette manufacturers had increased the nicotine concentrations in tobacco from 1997 to 2005 by 11 percent and also had modified certain design features of the cigarettes themselves to increase the number of puffs per cigarette during smoking. In the "medium/mild" market category, nicotine levels more than doubled from 1998 to 2005 in nonmentholated cigarettes and rose by 22 percent in mentholated cigarettes (Health Line).[10]

The Tobacco Industry Today

The tobacco industry in the United States, since the early 1990s, has faced continuing challenges from federal governmental agencies, as well as individuals and groups who have sued tobacco companies for damages resulting from the ingestion of their tobacco products. As a result the legal and economic status of the tobacco industry has been altered significantly.

Two major events occurred in the 1990s that would forever change the image of tobacco use in American society. In 1993, the U.S. Environmental Protection Agency (EPA) announced its conclusion from available research that **environmental tobacco smoke (ETS)**, the sidestream smoke in the air that is inhaled by nonsmokers as a result of tobacco smoking, causes lung cancer. Since then, most U.S. states, cities, and communities have enacted laws mandating smoke-free environments in all public and private workplaces, unless ventilated smoking rooms have been provided. It is now commonplace for restaurants, hotels, and other commercial spaces to be completely smoke-free. In 1994, congressional hearings were held on allegations that during the 1970s tobacco companies had suppressed data obtained in their own research laboratories regarding the hazards of cigarette smoking. In 1999, the Philip Morris company issued a statement, formally admitting that there is "overwhelming medical and scientific consensus that cigarette smoking causes cancer, heart disease, emphysema, and other serious diseases in smokers" and that "cigarette smoking is addictive, as that term is most commonly used today." This stance represented a complete reversal of the industry's 1994 congressional

sidestream smoke: Tobacco smoke that is inhaled by nonsmokers from the burning cigarettes of nearby smokers. Also referred to as environmental tobacco smoke.

environmental tobacco smoke (ETS): Tobacco smoke in the atmosphere as a result of burning cigarettes; also called sidestream or secondary smoke.

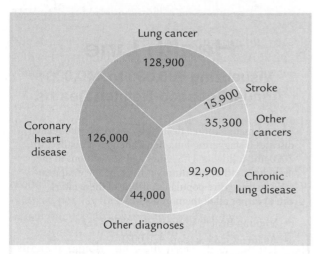

FIGURE 10.1

The distribution of approximately 443,000 U.S. deaths attributed each year to tobacco use or secondhand smoke from tobacco use.

Source: Centers for Disease Control and Prevention (2008, November 14). Cigarette smoking–attributable morbidity, years of potential life lost, and productivity losses—United States, 2000–2004. *Morbidity and Mortality Weekly Report, 57,* 1226–1228.

restriction of blood flow through narrowed or blocked coronary arteries; **arteriosclerosis,** in which the walls of arteries harden and lose their elasticity; **atherosclerosis,** in which fatty deposits inside arteries impede blood flow; and **ischemic stroke,** in which interruption or reduction in blood flow causes damage to the brain. In all

arteriosclerosis (ar-TEER-ee-oh-scluh-ROH-sis): A disease in which blood flow is restricted because the walls of arteries harden and lose their elasticity.

atherosclerosis (ATH-er-oh-scluh-ROH-sis): A disease in which blood flow is restricted because of the buildup of fatty deposits inside arteries.

ischemic (iz-SKEE-mic) stroke: A disease in which there is an interruption of or reduction in blood flow to the brain, causing paralysis, sensory loss, cognitive deficits, or a combination of neuropsychological effects.

chronic obstructive pulmonary disease (COPD): A group of diseases characterized by impaired breathing due to an abnormality in the air passages.

chronic bronchitis: A respiratory disease involving inflammation of bronchial tissue following a buildup of excess mucus in air passages.

emphysema (EM-fuh-SEE-mah): An enlargement of air sacs in the lungs and abnormalities in the air sac walls, causing great difficulty in breathing.

these diseases, cigarette smoking increases the risk dramatically.

We know now that smoking is responsible for approximately 30 percent of all CHD deaths. The risk of CHD doubles if you smoke and quadruples if you smoke heavily. On average, smoking also raises the risk of a sudden death (such as from a fatal heart attack) by two to four times, with the degree of risk increasing as a direct function of how many cigarettes are smoked per day. To put it even more bluntly, it has been estimated that unless smoking patterns change dramatically in the future, about 10 percent of all Americans now alive may die prematurely from some form of heart disease as a result of their smoking behavior.[27]

These statistics are strengthened by our understanding of how cigarette smoking actually produces these dangerous cardiovascular conditions. The major villains are nicotine and carbon monoxide. Nicotine, as a stimulant drug, increases the contraction of heart muscle and elevates heart rate.

At the same time, nicotine causes the constriction of blood vessels, leading to a rise in blood pressure, and also increases *platelet adhesiveness* in the blood. As a result of a greater adhesiveness, platelets clump together and increase the risk of developing a blood clot. When a clot forms within coronary arteries, a heart attack can occur; a clot traveling into the blood vessels of the brain can produce a stroke. Finally, nicotine increases the body's serum cholesterol and fatty deposits, leading to the development of atherosclerosis.

While nicotine is doing its dirty work, carbon monoxide makes matters worse. A lack of oxygen puts further strain on the ability of the heart to function under already trying circumstances.[28]

Respiratory Diseases

The general term **chronic obstructive pulmonary disease (COPD)** refers to several conditions in which breathing is impaired because of some abnormality in the air passages either leading to or within the lungs. Although only 20 percent of smokers in the United States develop COPD, 80 to 90 percent of all COPD cases are the result of smoking. Historically, COPD has been viewed as "a man's disease," but since 1980 the death rate in women has tripled, and since 2000, more women than men have died or been hospitalized each year as a result of COPD. With the exception of a rare genetic defect, smoking is the only established cause of clinically significant COPD.

Two examples of COPD are **chronic bronchitis,** in which excess mucus builds up in air passages, leading to an inflammation of bronchial tissue, and **emphysema,** in which air sacs in the lungs are abnormally enlarged and the air sac walls either become inelastic or rupture, leading to extreme difficulty in inhaling oxygen and exhaling carbon dioxide. In the case of advanced emphysema, more than 80 percent of a patient's energy is required merely to breathe. These two diseases account for more than one hundred thousand deaths each year, and many additional thousands are forced to lead increasingly debilitating lives, gasping and struggling each day to breathe.

Pulmonary damage, however, is not limited to adults who have been smoking for many years. Cigarette smoking is also associated with airway obstruction and slower growth of lung function in younger populations. Adolescents who smoke five or more cigarettes a day are 40 percent more likely to develop asthma and 30 percent more likely to have symptoms of wheezing but not asthma than those who do not smoke. Among smokers, girls show a greater loss of pulmonary function than boys, even though boys report that they smoke more cigarettes.[29]

Lung Cancer

It is hard to believe that at the beginning of the twentieth century, lung cancer was a rare disease. Its steady increase in the United States as well as the rest of the world since then has occurred in direct proportion to the growing prevalence of cigarette smoking and other tobacco use. About 80 percent of an estimated 226,000 new cases of lung cancer in the United States in 2012 have been determined by the American Cancer Society to be smoking-related. Male smokers, in particular, are 23 times more likely to develop lung cancer than lifelong nonsmokers. Although there has been a steady decline in deaths due to lung cancer among American males overall since 1990, there remains an approximately 35 percent greater mortality rate among African American males due to smoking than among white males.

Another important change has occurred over the years with respect to the incidence of lung cancer among women. Like COPD, lung cancer was once considered to be limited largely to male smokers. More recently, however, increasing numbers of women have contracted lung cancer as a result of their increased level of cigarette smoking. The age-adjusted mortality rate for women is still about one-half that for men, and the decline in mortality rates seen among men since 1990 is only beginning to be realized among women. Since 1988, lung cancer has exceeded breast cancer as the leading cause of cancer deaths among women (Figure 10.2). In general, females who are currently smoking incur a risk of lung cancer that is about thirteen times higher than that for nonsmokers.

As discussed earlier in the chapter, the exposure to tar in cigarette smoke disrupts the indispensable action of ciliary cells in the bronchial tubes leading to the lungs. Without their protective function, the lungs are open to attack. Several carcinogenic compounds in the smoke can now enter the lungs and stimulate the formation of cancerous growths, **carcinomas**, in lung tissue. One of these compounds, *benzopyrene*, has been found to cause genetic mutations in cells that are identical to the mutations observed in patients who have developed carcinomas in their lungs. This finding is important because it establishes a causal link between a specific ingredient in tobacco smoke and human cases of cancer.[30]

Other Cancers

Certainly lung cancer is the best-known and most common example of smoking-related cancers, but other organs are affected in a similar way. In the United States, approximately 30 percent of cancer deaths *of all types* have been linked to smoking. It has been estimated that smokers increase their risk by two to twenty-seven times for cancer of the larynx, thirteen times for mouth or lip cancer, two to three times for bladder cancer, two times for pancreatic cancer, and five times for cancers of the kidney or uterine cervix.[31]

Despite a widespread belief to the contrary, using smokeless tobacco, in the form of chewing tobacco or snuff, does not prevent the user from incurring an increased risk of cancer. Continuing contact with tobacco in the mouth has been shown to produce precancerous cell changes, as revealed by **leukoplakia** (white spots) and **erythroplakia** (red spots) inside the mouth and nasal cavity. Even though smokeless tobacco obviously avoids the problems associated with tobacco smoke, it does not prevent the user from being exposed to carcinogens, specifically a class of compounds called

---

carcinomas (CAR-sih-NOH-mas): Cancerous tumors or growths.

leukoplakia (LOO-koh-PLAY-kee-ah): Small white spots inside the mouth and nasal cavity, indicating precancerous tissue.

erythroplakia (eh-RITH-ro-PLAY-kee-ah): Small red spots inside the mouth and nasal cavity, indicating precancerous tissue.

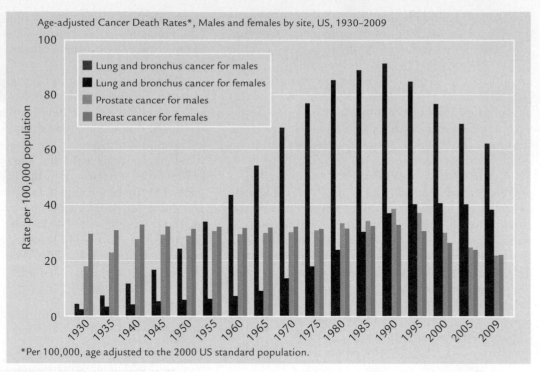

FIGURE 10.2

Age-adjusted death rates from lung and bronchus cancer and other cancers among males and females in the United States, 1930–2009.

Note: Since about 1990, lung and bronchus cancer deaths among women have exceeded breast cancer deaths. In addition, lung and bronchus cancer rates for women have remained relatively stable while rates for men have declined significantly.

Source: American Cancer Society (2013). *Cancer Facts and Figures 2013.* Atlanta: American Cancer Society, Inc., pp. 2–3.

nitrosamines that are present in all tobacco products. As a result of federal legislation enacted in 1986, all forms of smokeless tobacco must contain, on the package, a set of specific warnings that these products may cause mouth cancer as well as gum disease and tooth loss (Health Alert). To reinforce the idea that grave dangers lurk in smokeless tobacco, one of these warnings reads, "This product is not a safe alternative to cigarette smoking."

Special Health Concerns for Women

Tobacco use presents specific health risks for women. Women who smoke have a more than three times greater risk of dying from stroke due to brain hemorrhaging and an almost two times greater risk of dying from a heart attack. Added to these concerns is the toxic interaction of tobacco smoke with birth control pills. If a woman is using birth control pills as well, the risk increases to twenty-two times and twenty times, respectively.

The higher risk of low birth weight and physical defects in the newborn due to the mother's smoking during pregnancy was discussed in Chapter 2. In addition, there is a specific elevation in systolic blood pressure at about 2 months of age among infants whose mothers smoked during pregnancy.[32] Even though there has been a decline in smoking in recent years among pregnant women, more than one in six pregnant women (17 percent) have smoked in the past month, with more of them smoking in their first trimester of pregnancy (22 percent) than in their second and third trimesters (14 percent and 15 percent, respectively).

The Hazards of Environmental Smoke

In the early days of development of methods for detecting the effects of nicotine in the bloodstream, scientists were puzzled to find traces of a nicotine

> **nitrosamines (nih-TRAW-seh-meens):** A group of carcinogenic compounds found in tobacco.

metabolite in nonsmokers. They suspected at first that there was some flaw in their analysis but later had to conclude that their measurements were indeed accurate. Nonsmokers testing positive had shared car rides or workplaces with smokers shortly before their tests. Today, a large body of evidence indicates not only the presence of tobacco smoke compounds in the bodies of nonsmokers but also the adverse consequences that such "involuntary smoking" can provoke. In other words, environmental tobacco smoke is a significant health hazard even to people who are not actively smoking.

Approximately 85 percent of the smoke in an average room where people are smoking cigarettes is generated by sidestream smoke, and about three-fourths of the nicotine originating from these cigarettes ends up in the atmosphere. In some cases, the carcinogens released in environmental tobacco smoke (ETS) are so potent that they are dangerous even in their diluted state. For example, N-nitrosamine (an example of a group of carcinogens mentioned earlier in connection with smokeless tobacco) is so much more concentrated in sidestream smoke than in mainstream smoke that nonsmokers end up inhaling as much of it after one hour in a very smoky room as will a smoker after smoking ten to fifteen cigarettes.[33]

The U.S. surgeon general's report on involuntary exposure to tobacco smoke in 2006 has confirmed previous data on this question and extended its conclusions to the following:

- For nonsmoking adults, exposure to environmental smoke raises the risk of heart disease by 25 to 30 percent in both men and women. The risk of lung cancer is increased by 20 to 30 percent among nonsmokers who live with a smoker.
- Environmental smoke is a cause of sudden infant death syndrome (SIDS), accounting for 430 deaths per year in the United States. The risk is higher for children whose mothers were exposed to tobacco smoke during pregnancy and for children exposed during infancy.
- Among children of parents who smoke in the home, there is an increased risk of lower respiratory illnesses such as bronchitis, middle ear disease, wheezing, and childhood asthma.

It is estimated that environmental smoke exposure accounts for 46,000 premature deaths from heart disease and 3,400 premature deaths from cancer among adults in the United States each year. Although the proportion of nonsmokers has declined substantially as a result of publicity about the hazards of ETS and extensive smoking bans and restrictions, more than 126 million Americans remain subject to exposure at some time in their lives.[34]

Patterns of Smoking Behavior and Use of Smokeless Tobacco

In 1965, about 40 percent of all American teenagers and adults smoked cigarettes, and it is estimated that more than 50 percent did in the 1940s. In 2011, however, according to the National Survey on Drug Use and Health, approximately 22 percent of people aged twelve or older smoked a cigarette within the past month, qualifying as current smokers. Although this percentage is significantly less than it was, it still represents a very large number of people. Extrapolating to the U.S. population, a 22 percent prevalence rate corresponds to about 57 million Americans. American Indians and Alaska natives are more likely to smoke than any other group in the United States, with 37 percent of adults defined as smokers. In contrast, individuals of Asian descent are the least likely to smoke; just 12 percent of them report having smoked a cigarette in the past month.

There has been only a small decline in the percentage of American adult smokers in the last few years. Among college students, thirty-day prevalence rates increased from 1990 to 1999, but since then they have declined by 50 percent. In 2011, about 15 percent of college students had smoked cigarettes within the previous month, considerably below the national average. In 2011, about 12 percent of tenth graders and 19 percent of high school seniors reported cigarette smoking within the previous month. Compared to peak levels reached in 1996, these figures represent a 61 percent decline for tenth graders and 49 percent decline for seniors. It is generally considered that if high school seniors have not begun smoking at this point in their lives, it is unlikely that they will do so in the future.[35]

The Youngest Smokers

In the 2011 University of Michigan survey, approximately 18 percent of eighth graders reported that they had tried cigarettes in their lifetime, and about 6 percent reported smoking at least once in the previous month. These figures are down substantially from the 49 and 21 percent figures, respectively, reported in 1996. Approximately 2 percent of eighth graders smoked on a daily basis in 2011, and less than 1 percent smoked at least half a pack a day, once again down substantially from 10 and 4 percent, respectively, in 1996.

The peak year for starting to smoke has been reported to be in the seventh grade, although a significant number of eighth graders qualifying as regular smokers have said that they had started earlier. About six percent report that they had begun *prior to the sixth grade*. In general, it has been estimated that between 80 and 90 percent of regular smokers began to smoke by the age of eighteen.[36]

Attitudes toward Smoking among Young People

Adolescent attitudes toward cigarette smoking have changed dramatically in the early years of the twenty-first century. In general, young people in middle school and high school have become less accepting of cigarette smoking. About 88 percent of eighth graders, for example, reported in 2011 their disapproval of someone smoking a pack of cigarettes per day, and 63 percent reported that people engaging in such behavior would present "great risk" of harming themselves physically or otherwise.

Interestingly, adolescent attitudes toward the *social* aspects of smoking have become more negative as well. Currently, more than half of tenth and twelfth graders agree with the statement "I strongly dislike

Cigarette smoking among minors is a continuing social and public health problem.

being near people who are smoking." About 80 percent of them prefer to date nonsmokers. About six out of ten view smoking as a behavior that reflects poor judgment on the part of those who smoke, and at least seven out of ten consider smoking to be a "dirty habit." The continuing disinclination toward dating smokers over recent years has been observed equally among males and females.[37] As Lloyd D. of the University of Michigan has observed,

> It now appears that taking up smoking makes a youngster less attractive to the great majority of the opposite sex, just the opposite of what cigarette advertising has been promising all these years. I think this is something that teens need to know, because it may be the most compelling argument for why they should abstain from smoking or, for that matter, quit if they have already started.[38]

Since 1997, all fifty U.S. states have been required to establish eighteen as the minimum age at which tobacco products can be purchased. Vendors have been required to verify the age of purchasers up to the age of twenty-seven as a means of reducing the access of young people to tobacco. In some U.S. states, efforts are under way to raise the minimum age for tobacco purchases to nineteen or twenty-one, and other states have this higher minimum age already in effect. Any upward change from the national standard reduces the incidence of high school seniors buying cigarettes for their younger friends.

With regard to standards set in federal regulations on underage smoking, compliance rates on the part of tobacco retail vendors nationwide reached 91 percent in 2011, substantially higher than the 60 percent rate reported in 1996. Nonetheless, about 52 percent of eighth graders said in 2011 that cigarettes were fairly easy or very easy to get. This percentage is significantly lower than percentages reported in the 1990s, but it still reflects relatively easy access.[39]

Smokeless Tobacco

Smokeless tobacco is ingested, as the name implies, by absorption through the membranes of the mouth rather than by inhalation of smoke into the lungs (Table 10.1). The two most common forms are the traditional loose-leaf chewing tobacco (brand names include Red Man and Beech Nut) and moist, more finely shredded tobacco called **moist snuff** or simply snuff (brand names include Copenhagen and Skoal). Snuff, by the way, is no longer sniffed into the nose, as in the eighteenth century, but rather placed inside the cheek or alongside the gum under the lower lip. Some varieties of snuff are available in a small absorbent-paper sack (like a tea bag) so that the tobacco particles do not get stuck in the teeth. The practice is called "dipping."

According to the 2011 University of Michigan survey, about 4 percent of eighth graders, 7 percent of tenth graders, and 8 percent of high school seniors had used smokeless tobacco within the previous thirty days. Although more than 80 percent of eighth graders disapprove of others using smokeless tobacco, only about 40 percent perceive great risk in this form of tobacco use.[40]

Currently, the form of smokeless tobacco showing the most consistent gains in recent sales is moist snuff;

TABLE 10.1

Forms of smokeless tobacco

TYPE	DESCRIPTION
Chewing tobacco	
Loose-leaf	Made of cigar-leaf tobacco, sold in small packages, heavily flavored or plain
Fine-cut	Similar to loose-leaf but more finely cut so that it resembles snuff
Plug	Leaf tobacco pressed into flat cakes and sweetened with molasses, licorice, maple sugar, or honey
Twist	Made of stemmed leaves twisted into small rolls and then folded

(Chewing tobacco is not really chewed but rather is held in the mouth between the cheek and lower jaw.)

Snuff	

Dry, moist, sweetened, flavored, salted, scented

(A pinch of snuff, called a *quid*, is typically tucked between the gum and the lower lip. Moist varieties are currently the most popular.)

Source: Adapted from Popescu, C. (1992). The health hazards of smokeless tobacco. In Kristine Napier (Ed.), *Issues in tobacco.* New York: American Council on Science and Health, pp. 11–12.

moist snuff: Damp, finely shredded tobacco, placed inside the cheek or alongside the gum under the lower lip.

some brands are sold in cherry or wintergreen flavors. As with cigarette tobacco, variations in the alkalinity of different brands of moist snuff allow for different percentages of the nicotine in the tobacco to be absorbed through the membranes of the mouth. Thus, snuff users typically start with brands that release relatively low levels of nicotine and then "graduate" to more potent brands. The most potent brand on the current market, Copenhagen, is also the best-selling snuff in the United States.[41]

Despite continuing warnings that smokeless tobacco presents great risk to one's health, its popularity persists. As we have noted, although smokeless tobacco presents no immediate danger to the lungs, there are substantial adverse effects on other organs of the body. At the very least, regular use of smokeless tobacco increases the risk of gum disease, damage to tooth enamel, and eventually the loss of teeth. More seriously, the direct contact of the tobacco with membranes of the mouth allows carcinogenic nitrosamines to cause tissue changes that can lead to oral cancer. Delay in the treatment of oral cancer increases the likelihood of the cancer spreading to the jaw, pharynx, and neck. When swallowed, saliva containing nitrosamines can produce stomach and urinary tract cancer. Moreover, all the negative consequences of ingesting nicotine during tobacco smoking are also present in the use of smokeless tobacco.

In recent years, a moist snuff product called *snus*, the name derived from the Swedish word for snuff, has gained in popularity. In 2009, Altria, the leading tobacco company in the United States, began an aggressive marketing campaign for "Marlboro snus", a spit-less, "mess-free" smokeless tobacco product to be slid under the upper lip (with the slogan "When smoking isn't your option, reach for Marlboro snus"). A Camel-snus product was introduced as well. Since 2010, FDA regulations have stipulated warning labels on all such products as they have appeared on other forms of smokeless tobacco.[42]

Cigars

For a brief time in the 1990s, there was a resurgence in the popularity of cigars, spurred on by images of media stars, both male and female, who had taken up cigar smoking. The cigar suddenly was fashionable. By the end of the decade, however, the cigar-smoking craze had "gone up in smoke." This was partly because of changing market conditions for imported cigars, but a major contributing factor was increasing recognition that cigars could not be regarded as a safe alternative to cigarettes.[43] Cigar smoke is more alkaline than cigarette smoke, so the nicotine content in cigars can be absorbed directly through tissues lining the mouth rather than requiring inhalation into the lungs. In addition, due to the tar content, the risk of lung cancer is five times higher for those who smoke cigars than for nonsmokers, eight times higher for those smoking three or more cigars per day, and eleven times higher for those inhaling the smoke of cigars. Regular cigar smokers have a doubled risk, relative to nonsmokers, for cancers of the mouth, throat, and esophagus; they also incur a 45 percent higher risk of COPD and a 27 percent higher risk of coronary heart disease (Portrait). Major cigar manufacturers have now agreed to place warning labels on their products, alerting consumers to the risk of mouth and throat cancer, lung cancer, and heart disease and to the hazards to fertility and unborn children.

While cigars are eligible for FDA regulation under the Tobacco Control Act of 2009, no steps have yet been taken. In 2012, congressional resolutions were passed exempting "premium cigars" from future regulation, on the argument that they are unlikely to appeal or be affordable to minors.[44]

Tobacco Use around the World

Since the seventeenth century, the practice of tobacco smoking has spread throughout the world, but until the 1980s the behavior itself outside the United States had been largely independent of American tobacco corporations. Today, the picture has changed dramatically. Between 1985 and 1994 alone, U.S. cigarette exports to Japan increased 700 percent and to South Korea increased 1,200 percent. In the late 1990s, American-made cigarettes moved into significant markets in Eastern Europe and Russia, where smoking prevalence rates are substantially higher than those in the United States (Figure 10.3). Presently, U.S. tobacco exports total more than $6 billion each year.

Unfortunately, the prevalence rate of smoking in many foreign countries far exceeds that of the United States, coupled with substantially less public concern for the consequences of smoking on health. In the Russian Federation, Kenya, South Korea, and China, for example, more than 60 percent of all adult men smoke cigarettes. In Japan, as in many nations of the world, no-smoking sections in restaurants and

Sigmund Freud—Nicotine Dependence, Cigars, and Cancer

Probably the best-known photograph of Sigmund Freud, founder of psychoanalysis and one-time proponent of cocaine use (see Chapter 4), shows him with a cigar in hand. Given that Freud typically smoked twenty cigars each day, it is not surprising that he did not set it aside merely to have his picture taken. But there is a story behind this photograph, a lesson about the power of smoking over the will to stop and the tragic health consequences when one's will succumbs.

In 1923, at the age of sixty-seven, Freud noted sores on his palate and jaw that failed to heal, a sign of oral cancer. Surgery was indicated and fortunately proved successful in removing the cancerous tissue. This would be only the first of thirty-three surgical

operations on the jaw and oral cavity that Freud was to endure for the remaining sixteen years of his life. As the leukoplakia and finally genuine carcinomas returned to his mouth, he was repeatedly warned by specialists that his practice of smoking cigars was the root of his problems and that he must stop. Despite these warnings, Freud kept on smoking.

Freud tried very hard to stop; indeed, sometimes he would not smoke for a few weeks at a time. In addition to his problems with cancer, he suffered from chest pains called "tobacco angina." In 1936, the angina became acutely painful. His biographer, Ernest Jones, noted that it was obvious to him and to others that the pain was exacerbated by nicotine and relieved as soon as he stopped smoking.

By this time, Freud's jaw had been entirely removed and an artificial jaw substituted in its place. He was now almost constantly in pain, often could not speak, and sometimes could not eat or swallow. Despite the agony, Freud still smoked a steady stream of cigars until he finally died at the age of eighty-three.

Here was a man whom many consider to be one of the intellectual giants of the twentieth century. Yet the giant was a slave to his cigars.

Source: Brecher, R.; Brecher, E.; Herzog, A.; Goodman, W.; Walker, G.; and the Editors of *Consumer Reports* (1963). *The Consumer Union's report on smoking and the public interest.* Mount Vernon, NY: Consumer Union, pp. 91–95.

---

offices are uncommon; approximately half a million outdoor vending machines allow minors to purchase cigarettes easily; and only recently have there been governmental efforts to reduce smoking in general.[45]

Clearly, tobacco use on a global scale presents one of the most significant public health challenges we face in the twenty-first century. According to the World Health Organization (WHO), an estimated 5.4 million people worldwide die each year from tobacco-related diseases, and this figure is projected to increase to more than 810 million by 2030. In the twentieth century, tobacco smoking contributed to the deaths of 100 million people worldwide. During the twenty-first century, the death toll could rise as high as a billion people.

Making matters worse, global approaches to reducing the deadly effects of tobacco use are discouragingly weak or absent. Approximately 40 percent of countries in the world still allow smoking in hospitals and schools; only 5 percent of the world's population lives in a country that imposes a comprehensive national ban on tobacco advertising. Only 5 percent of the world's population lives in a country in which full services to treat tobacco dependence are widely available.[46]

In recognition of the enormous health crisis that exists at present and the potential calamity that looms in the future, a Framework Convention on Tobacco Control has been signed by more than 175 members of the World Health Organization, an agency of the United Nations. Implementation of the tobacco-use reduction initiatives in the agreement is voluntary, however, and progress on a global level has been slow. One major reason is that governments around the world collect more than $200 billion each year in taxes imposed on tobacco sales. In some cases, governments are dependent on these tax revenues to sustain their economies. In other cases, governments receive direct profits from state-owned tobacco corporations.[47]

Quitting Smoking: The Good News and the Bad

There is no question that tobacco use of any kind is harmful to your health, as well as your wallet, and it is indeed hard to quit once you have started. But

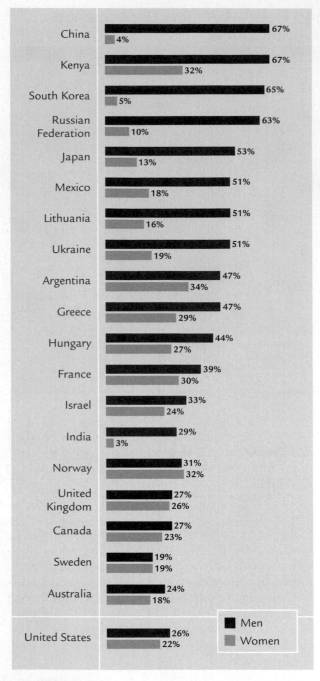

FIGURE 10.3

Smoking rates for men and women over fifteen years old in twenty countries, including the United States.

Note: As a consequence of differences in criteria and age range, percentages for the United States differ slightly from data in the National Survey on Drug Use and Health.

From *The Tobacco Atlas* - www.int/tobacco/en/atlas ISBN 0-92-4156-209-9. Reprinted by permission of WHO.

there's some good news with respect to the consequences of quitting.

The Good News: Undoing the Damage

Given the grim story of all the documented health risks associated with tobacco, it is at least reassuring to know that if a smoker does succeed in quitting, some of the damage can be undone. Here are the benefits:

- Within eight hours—Carbon monoxide levels in the blood drop to normal.
- Within twenty-four hours—Chances of a heart attack decrease.
- Within two weeks to three months—Circulation improves. Lung function increases by up to 30 percent.
- Within one to nine months—Coughing, sinus congestion, fatigue, and shortness of breath decrease. Cilia regain normal function in the lungs and become increasingly able to handle mucus, clean the lungs, and reduce infection.
- Within one year—Excess risk of coronary heart disease is half that of a smoker.
- Within five to ten years—Risk of stroke is reduced to that of a nonsmoker.
- Within ten years—Lung cancer death rate is about half that of a continuing smoker.
- Within fifteen years—Risk of coronary heart disease is equal to that of a nonsmoker.[48]

The Bad News: How Hard It Is to Quit

The advantages of quitting are real and most people are aware of them, but the fact remains that, in the words of the surgeon general's report in 1988, "The pharmacologic and behavioral processes that determine tobacco addiction are similar to those that determine addiction to drugs such as heroin and cocaine."[49] It may be easy to quit smoking for a short while, but it is very difficult to avoid a relapse, as any former or present smoker will tell you see Health Line on page 268.

About one-third of all smokers in the United States try to quit each year, the vast majority of them without any treatment, but only about 3 to 5 percent succeed with their initial attempt. Nonetheless, about half of all smokers do eventually manage to achieve

An antismoking billboard in California, alluding to the Marlboro cowboy of past cigarette ad campaigns.

long-term abstinence from the nicotine in tobacco products, but only after an average of eight attempts at quitting. The fact that a higher level of smoking is consistently related to a lower level of education and family income makes it vital that smoking-cessation programs be available to those who ordinarily would not be able to afford them.[50]

The options available to smokers who want to quit are numerous. In addition to behaviorally oriented social support groups (Smokers Anonymous, SmokeEnders, Smoke-Stoppers), counseling either in person or through telephone "quit-lines," hypnosis, acupuncture, and specific prescription drugs can help reduce the withdrawal symptoms and feelings of nicotine craving. One example is a sustained-release form of the antidepressant drug bupropion. Originally marketed as a treatment for depression under the name Wellbutrin, it was approved by the FDA in 1997 for use as an aid in smoking cessation and renamed Zyban when marketed for this purpose. It is recommended that Zyban be taken daily for a week prior to the last cigarette to allow drug levels to build up in the bloodstream and buffer the loss of nicotine when smoking stops. About 44 percent of individuals taking Zyban have refrained from smoking after seven weeks, and 23 percent remain smoke-free after one year—roughly twice the percentage among those who receive a placebo. Since 1999, the costs of all prescription medications and quit-smoking programs have been tax-deductible as medical expenses.[51]

In 2006, a twice-daily tablet called Chantix became available in the United States as a nicotine-free stop-smoking medication. Clinical trials of Chantix have shown that users have a rate of abstinence from tobacco of 22 percent, compared to 16 percent among those taking Zyban. Forty-eight percent of long-time, one-pack-per-day smokers quit after a twelve-week treatment with Chantix, compared to 33 percent among Zyban patients.[52]

However, despite FDA approval for both Chantix and Zyban, health risks have been identified with their use, which has resulted in the products currently carrying a FDA warning label that there is "a risk of serious mental health events including changes in behavior, depressed mood, hostility, and suicidal thoughts." At the request of the FDA, the Pfizer company has begun additional clinical trials (see Chapter 14) to study the

Health Line

How to Succeed in Quitting Smoking—By Really Trying

Everyone knows how hard it is to quit smoking and how powerfully addictive nicotine can be. But everyone also knows that the long-term adverse consequences of continuing are just too severe to ignore. Here are some guidelines that can help along the way to a smoke-free life:

- Understand why you want to quit smoking in the most concrete manner you can imagine. Success comes from having a very good reason to quit, not just a nebulous notion that "it's not good for me."
- Don't try it cold turkey. Nicotine is just too much a factor in your brain to let it go all at once. Do it gradually, but have a plan. Mark down dates (benchmarks) when you will be smoking less and less until you reach your goal. Understand that the first few days without a cigarette will be the most difficult.
- Try nicotine replacements to control your cravings, but don't smoke when taking these replacements. Otherwise, you will be doubling up on your nicotine and that is the last thing you want to do.
- Don't do it alone. Seek and accept encouragement from your non-smoking family and friends. They need to be the cheerleaders in your life as you go through this difficult time.
- Try to reduce the stress in your life. Meditate or simply listen to soothing music when you feel the urge to smoke.
- Avoid the behavioral triggers that you had for smoking. This may include alcohol and coffee. Remember how Pavlovian conditioning works (Chapter 2) in connecting environmental cues with drug-taking behavior.
- Sweep away (maybe literally) all signs of cigarette smoking in your house. You don't need reminders.
- Increase your level of physical exercise. Besides giving yourself an alternative activity in your life, you will be surprised to see the improved breathing ability and stamina you will have as you rid yourself of inhaled smoke.
- Reward yourself for success. Do something nice for yourself as you reach your quit-smoking goals.
- Finally, if you relapse, understand that failures will occur and that this is an uphill battle. As the saying goes: If you don't succeed, try, try again.

Some helpful online resources for those who want to quit smoking:

The American Cancer Society web site: http://www.cancer.org/healthy/stayawayfromtobacco/guidetoquittingsmoking/indexorg

WebMd Health, LLC, web site: www.webmd.com/smoking-cessation/quit-smoking

The American Lung Association web site: www.lung.org/stop-smoking

link between its product Chantix and psychological side effects. The results are due in 2017. In the meantime, some public health experts have suggested that smokers should be discouraged from using these drugs as their first attempt to stop smoking.[53]

Nicotine Gums, Patches, Sprays, and Inhalers

The long-term goal in quitting smoking is to withdraw from dependence-producing nicotine altogether and to be totally free of any hazard associated with tobacco. In the meantime, however, it is possible to employ an alternative route of ingestion for nicotine that avoids inhaling carbon monoxide and tar into the lungs. Chewing gum containing nicotine (brand name: Nicorette), available since the early 1970s as a prescription drug, is now marketed on a nonprescription basis. Transdermal nicotine patches are marketed on a nonprescription basis as well. Prescription nicotine-substitute options include a nasal spray (brand name: Nicotrol NS) and an oral inhalation system (brand name: Nicotrol Inhaler) in which nicotine is inhaled from a cartridge through a plastic mouthpiece, and lozenges (brand name: Commit).[54]

The Role of Physicians in Smoking Cessation

Owing to the fact that tobacco use is the leading cause of preventable death in the United States, it is clear that physicians must play a critical role in addressing the

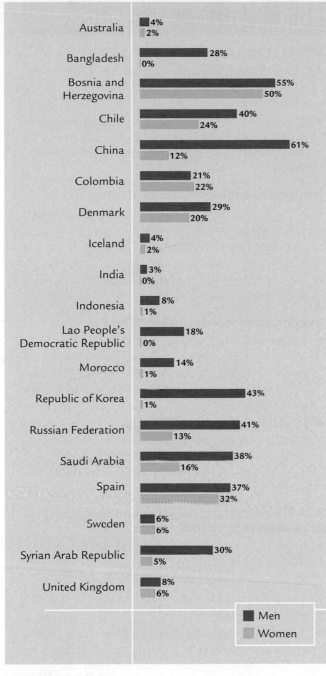

FIGURE 10.4

Percentages of physicians who smoke, worldwide

From *The Tobacco Atlas* - www.int/tobacco/en/atlas
ISBN 92-4156-209-9. Reprinted by permission of WHO.

issue of tobacco use in their patients as part of an intervention to help them quit smoking. Suggestions for a greater role of the physician in this regard have been dubbed the "Five A's":

- *Ask about tobacco use.* Identify and document tobacco-use status for every patient at every visit.
- *Advise to quit.* In a clear, strong, and personalized manner, urge every tobacco user to quit.
- *Assess willingness to make a cessation attempt.* Is the tobacco user willing to make a cessation attempt at this time?
- *Assist in cessation attempt.* For the patient willing to make a cessation attempt, use counseling and pharmacotherapy to help him or her quit.
- *Arrange follow-up.* Schedule follow-up contact, preferably within the first week after the cessation date.[55]

A recent study suggests that when physicians tell smokers their "lung age," as determined by the age of an average healthy nonsmoker with a comparable level of breathing strength, smokers evidently get the message. They are twice as likely to quit, compared to smokers who are not informed of this fact. Unfortunately, however, the campaign encouraging physicians or other health professionals to communicate any sort of quit-smoking information to patients has a long way to go. It has been estimated that as many as 42,000 additional lives in the United States would be saved each year if 90 percent of smokers were advised by a health professional to quit and were offered medication or other assistance to do so. Presently, only 28 percent of smokers receive such services. Meanwhile, a disturbingly high percentage of physicians worldwide continue to be smokers themselves (Figure 10.4).[56]

A Final Word

The best strategy to stop smoking, of course, is never to start in the first place, which brings us back to the teenage years, when virtually all adult smokers pick up the habit. The challenge as we progress through the twenty-first century will be to maintain the communication of effective messages that prevent the initiation of cigarette smoking as well as other forms of tobacco use by young people (see Chapter 16).[57]

Tobacco Use through History

- Tobacco use originated among the original inhabitants of North and South America, and its introduction to Europe and the rest of the world dates from the first voyage of Columbus. Europeans used tobacco initially in the form of pipe smoking and later in the form of snuff.

- In the nineteenth-century United States, the most popular form was tobacco chewing and later cigar smoking. It was not until the late nineteenth century and early twentieth century that cigarette smoking became popular.

Health Concerns and Smoking Behavior

- The 1964 surgeon general's report, the first official statement on the connection between smoking and adverse health consequences, produced a general reversal in the previously climbing per capita consumption of cigarettes.

- Since 1964, the surgeon general's reports have solidified the position that nicotine is a clearly addicting component of tobacco and that tobacco use, whether in smoked or smokeless form, causes significant health risks.

- Since 1964, there has been increased use of filtered, low-tar, and low-nicotine cigarettes.

Tobacco Today: An Industry on the Defensive

- Since the early 1990s, most U.S. states, cities, and communities have enacted laws mandating smoke-free environments in all public and private workplaces. It is now typical for restaurants, hotels, and other commercial spaces to be at least partially smoke-free.

- Additional pressure on the tobacco industry has come from proposals to increase the federal excise tax on tobacco products.

- Increased public pressure since the mid-1990s has resulted in a greatly limited marketing approach for tobacco products, particularly with respect to sales to young people.

- In 1998, the major American tobacco corporations entered into a $246 billion settlement agreement with all fifty U.S. states to resolve claims that the states should be compensated for the costs of treating people with smoking-related illnesses.

- In 2009, the Tobacco Control Act was signed into law, authorizing the FDA to regulate tobacco products sold in the United States.

What's in Tobacco?

- The principal ingredients consumed during the smoking of tobacco are nicotine, tar, and carbon monoxide.

- The smoker inhales smoke in the form of mainstream smoke (through the cigarette itself) and sidestream smoke (released from the cigarette tip into the air).

The Dependence Potential of Nicotine

- Nicotine ingestion produces both tolerance effects and physical withdrawal symptoms. A prominent feature of nicotine withdrawal is the strong craving to return to tobacco use.

- Smokers typically adjust their smoking behavior to obtain a stable dose of nicotine.

Health Consequences of Tobacco Use

- Tobacco smoking produces an increased risk of cardiovascular diseases such as coronary heart disease and stroke, lung cancer and other forms of cancer, and respiratory diseases such as chronic bronchitis and emphysema.

- In addition to the hazards to the smoker through the inhalation of mainstream smoke, there are hazards to the developing fetus when the mother is smoking and hazards to nonsmokers who inhale environmental tobacco smoke.

Patterns of Smoking Behavior and Use of Smokeless Tobacco

- In 2011, the past-month prevalence rate for cigarette smoking in the United States among people aged twelve years or older was approximately 22 percent.

- The peak years for starting to smoke are in the sixth and seventh grades of school.

- A steady increase in the prevalence of smoking among secondary school students during the 1990s has been reversed. As these young people get older, the prevalence rates for cigarette smoking among college students and young adults are likely to decline.

- A global trend of unabated smoking rates in Asia, Eastern Europe, Russia, and elsewhere threatens the future health of huge populations of people worldwide.

Quitting Smoking: The Good News and the Bad

- Research has clearly shown that when people quit smoking, many health risks diminish rapidly.

Unfortunately, nicotine dependence is very strong, and it is difficult to quit smoking. Nonetheless, a wide range of smoking cessation treatments are available, and about 50 percent of smokers eventually succeed in quitting on a permanent basis.

● Present-day approaches to smoking cessation include behavioral treatment programs, hypnosis, acupuncture, and prescription drugs to reduce withdrawal symptoms and craving, as well as a variety of nicotine substitutes.

Key Terms

arteriosclerosis, p. 258
atherosclerosis, p. 258
carbon monoxide, p. 255
carcinomas, p. 259
chronic bronchitis, p. 258
chronic obstructive
   pulmonary disease
   (COPD), p. 258

cigarettes, p. 251
cigars, p. 250
cilia, p. 255
ciliary escalator,
   p. 255
coronary heart disease
   (CHD), p. 257
emphysema, p. 258

environmental tobacco
   smoke (ETS), p. 253
erythroplakia, p. 259
gaseous phase, p. 255
ischemic stroke, p. 258
leukoplakia, p. 259
mainstream smoke, p. 255
moist snuff, p. 263

nicotine, p. 256
nitrosamines, p. 260
particulate phase, p. 255
sidestream smoke, p. 253
snuff, p. 250
snuffing, p. 250
tar, p. 255
titration hypothesis, p. 256

Endnotes

1. Brooks, J. E. (1952). *The mighty leaf: Tobacco through the centuries.* Boston: Little, Brown, pp. 11–14. Fairholt, F. W. (1859). *Tobacco: Its history and associations.* London: Chapman and Hill, p. 13.
2. Brooks, *The mighty leaf*, pp. 74–80. White, J. M. (1991). *Drug dependence.* Englewood Cliffs, NJ: Prentice-Hall, pp. 32–33.
3. Austin, G. A. (1978). *Perspectives on the history of psychoactive substance use.* Rockville, MD: National Institute on Drug Abuse, pp. 1–12.
4. Brooks, *The mighty leaf*, p. 181. Lehman Brothers (1955). *About tobacco.* New York: Lehman Brothers, pp. 18–20.
5. Kluger, R. (1996). *Ashes to ashes: America's hundred-year cigarette war, the public health, and the "unabashed" triumph of Philip Morris.* New York: Knopf, p. 14. Tate, C. (1989). In the 1800s, antismoking was a burning issue. *Smithsonian, 20*(4), 111.
6. Quotation originally in Bain, John, and Werner, C. (1905). *Cigarettes in fact and fancy.* Boston: H. M. Caldwell. Cited in Brooks, *The mighty leaf*, p. 259.
7. Kluger, *Ashes to ashes*, pp. 16–20. Lehman Brothers, *About tobacco*, pp. 24–27. Slade, J. (1992). The tobacco epidemic: Lessons from history. *Journal of Psychoactive Drugs, 24*, 99–109.
8. Lehman Brothers, *About tobacco*, p. 30.
9. Ibid., p. 31.
10. Connolly, G. N.; Alpert, H. R.; Wayne, G. F.; and Koh, H. (2007, January). Trends in smoke nicotine yield and relationship to design characteristics among popular U.S. cigarette brands 1997–2005. A report of the Tobacco Research Program, Harvard School of Public Health, Boston. Federal Trade Commission Report to Congress (1992). Pursuant to the Federal Cigarette Labeling and Advertising Act, p. 31. Centers for Disease Control and Prevention (Updated 2010, September 17). Consumption data: Total and per capita adult yearly consumption of manufactured cigarettes and percentage changes in per capita consumption—United States, 1900–2006. Atlanta GA: Centers for Disease Control and Prevention, Bethesda, MD: National Cancer Institute. Wilson, D. (2010, February 19). Coded to obey law, lights become Marlboro Gold. *New York Times*, pp. B1, B5.
11. The official web site for Philip Morris, USA, www.philipmorrisusa.com.
12. Campaign for Tobacco Free Kids, American Heart Association, American Lung Association, and American Cancer Society Cancer Action Network (2011, November 30). *A broken promise to our children. The 1998 State Tobacco Settlement thirteen years later.* Washington, DC: Campaign for Tobacco Free Kids.
13. Office of the Press Secretary, The White House (2009, June 22). Fact sheet: The Family Smoking Prevention and Tobacco Control Act of 2009. Washington, DC: Office of the President. Wilson, D. (2011, January 6). Firms told to divulge all changes to tobacco. *New York Times*, p. B3.
14. U.S. Department of Agriculture (2006, September 26). Tobacco outlook. Electronic Outlook Report from the Economic Research Service, Center for Tobacco Grower Research (2011, November). U.S. tobacco situation and outlook. Knoxville, TN: Center for Tobacco Grower Research.
15. Centers for Disease Control and Prevention (2008). Smoking and tobacco use: Frequently asked questions. Atlanta, GA: Centers for Disease Control and Prevention. Payne; Wayne A; Hahn D. B.; and Lucas, E. B. (2009). *Understanding your health* (10th ed.) New York: McGraw-Hill, p. 270.

16. Schlaadt, R. G. (1992). *Tobacco and health.* Guilford, CT: Dushkin Publishing, p. 41.

17. Gahagan, D. D. (1987). *Switch down and quit: What the cigarette companies don't want you to know about smoking.* Berkeley, CA: Ten Speed Press, p. 44. Payne and Hahn, *Understanding your health,* pp. 273–275.

18. Jacobs, M. R., and Fehr, K. O'B. (1987). *Drugs and drug abuse: A reference text* (2nd ed.). Toronto: Addiction Research Foundation, pp. 417–425. Julien, R. M. (2005). *A primer of drug action* (10th ed.). New York: Worth, pp. 233–234

19. Meier, B. (1998, February 23). Cigarette maker manipulated nicotine, its records suggest. *New York Times,* pp. A1, A15. Pankow, J. F.; Mader, B. T.; Isabelle, L. M.; Luo, W. T.; et al. (1997). Conversion of nicotine and tobacco smoke to its volatile and available free-base form through the action of gaseous ammonia. *Environmental Science & Technology, 31,* 2428–2433.

20. Julien, *A primer of drug action,* pp. 234–238. Phillips, S., and Fox, P. (1998). An investigation into the effects of nicotine gum on short-term memory. *Psychopharmacology, 140,* 429–433. Schuckit, M. A. (2006). *Drug and alcohol abuse: A clinical guide to diagnosis and treatment* (6th ed.). New York: Springer, p. 289.

21. Brecher, E. M., and the editors of *Consumer Reports* (1972). *Licit and illicit drugs.* Boston, Little, Brown, pp. 220–228. DiFranza, J. R. (2008, May). Hooked from the first cigarette. *Scientific American,* pp. 82–87.

22. Pontieri, F. E.; Tanda, G.; Orzi, F.; and DiChiara, G. (1996). Effects of nicotine on the nucleus accumbens and similarity to those of addictive drugs. *Science, 382,* 255–257. Risso, F.; Parodi, M.; Grilli, M.; Molfino, F.; et al. (2004). Chronic nicotine causes functional upregulation of ionotropic glutamate receptors mediating hippocampal noradrenaline and stratal dopamine release. *Neurochemistry International, 44,* 293–301.

23. Herning, R. I.; Jones, R. T.; and Fischman, P. (1985). The titration hypothesis revisited: Nicotine gum reduces smoking intensity. In J. Grabowski and S. M. Hall (Eds.), *Pharmacological adjuncts in smoking cessation* (NIDA Research Monograph 53). Rockville, MD: National Institute on Drug Abuse, pp. 27–41. Scherer, G. (1999). Smoking behavior and compensation: A review of the literature. *Psychopharmacology, 145,* 1–20.

24. Julien, *A primer of drug action,* pp. 232–247.

25. Koslowski, L. T.; Wilkinson, A.; Skinner, W.; Kent, C.; Franklin, T.; and Pope, M. (1989). Comparing tobacco cigarette dependence with other drug dependencies. *Journal of the American Medical Association, 261,* 898–901.

26. Centers for Disease Control and Prevention (2008, November 14). Cigarette smoking–attributable morbidity, years of potential life lost, and productivity losses — United States, 2000–2004. *Morbidity and Mortality Weekly Report, 57,* 1226–1228.

27. Howard, G.; Wagenknecht, L. E.; Burke, G. L.; Diez-Roux, A.; et al. (1998). Cigarette smoking and progression of atherosclerosis. *Journal of the American Medical Association, 279,* 119–124. U.S. Department of Health and Human Services (2004), *The health consequences of smoking:* A *report of the Surgeon General.* Atlanta, GA: Centers for Disease Control and Prevention, Chapter 3. U.S. Department of Health and Human Services (1983). *The health consequences of smoking: Cardiovascular disease* (A report of the surgeon general). Rockville, MD: U.S. Public Health Service, pp. 63–156.

28. Payne, W. A.; Hahn D. B.; and Lucas, E. B. (2009). *Understanding your health* (10th ed.), pp. 272–273.

29. Gold, D. R.; Wang, X.; Wypij, David; Speizer, F. E.; Ware, J. H.; et al. (1996). Effects of cigarette smoking on lung function in adolescent boys and girls. *New England Journal of Medicine, 335,* 931–937. U.S. Department of Health and Human Services, Public Health Service, Office of Smoking and Health (1984). *The health consequences of smoking: Chronic obstructive lung disease* (A report of the surgeon general). Rockville, MD: U.S. Public Health Service, pp. 329–360. U.S. Department of Health and Human Services (2004), *The health consequences of smoking,* Chapter 4.

30. American Cancer Society (2013). *Cancer facts and figures 2013. Tobacco and cancer.* Atlanta, GA: American Cancer Society. Rotunno, M.; Hu, N.; Su, H.; Wang, C., Goldstein, A. M.; et al. (2011). A gene expression signature for peripheral whole blood for Stage 1 lung adenocarcinoma. *Cancer Prevention Research, 4,* 1599–1608.

31. Schuckit, *Drug and alcohol abuse,* pp. 296–297.

32. Geerts, C. C.; Grobbee, D. E.; van der Ent, C. K; de Jong, B. M.; et al. (2007). Tobacco smoke exposure of pregnant mothers and blood pressure in their newborns. *Hypertension, 50,* 572–578. Li, Y-F.; Langholz, B.; Salam, M. T., and Gilliland, F. D. (2005). Maternal and grandmaternal smoking patterns are associated with early childhood asthma. *Chest, 127,* 1232–1241. U.S. Health and Human Services (2004), *The health consequences of smoking,* Chapter 5.

33. Davis, R. M. (1998). Exposure to environmental tobacco smoke: Identifying and protecting those at risk. *Journal of the American Medical Association, 280,* 1947–1949. Ginzel, K. H. (1992). The ill-effects of second hand smoke. In K. Napier (Ed.), *Issues in tobacco.* New York: American Council on Science and Health, pp. 6–7.

34. Aligne, C. A.; Moss, M. E.; Auinger, P.; and Weitzman, M. (2003). Association of pediatric dental caries with passive smoking. *Journal of the American Medical Association, 289,* 1258–1264. Fielding, J. E., and Phenow, K. J. (1989). *Health effects of involuntary smoking.* Atlanta, GA: American Cancer Society. Kawachi, I.; Colditz, G. A.; Speizer, F. E.; Manson, J. E.; et al. (1997). A prospective study of passive smoking and coronary heart disease. *Circulation, 95,* 2374–2379. Nafstad, P.; Fugelseth, D.; Qvigstad, E.; Zahlsen, K.; et al. (1998). Nicotine concentration in the hair of nonsmoking mothers and size of offspring. *American Journal of Public Health, 88,* 120–124. U.S. Department of Health and Human Services, Public

Health Service, Office of Smoking and Health (2006). *The health consequences of involuntary exposure to tobacco smoke* (A report of the surgeon general). Rockville, MD: U.S. Public Health Service.

35. Johnston, L. M.; O'Malley, P. M.; Bachman, J. G.; and Schulenberg, J. E. (2012). *Monitoring the Future: National survey results on drug use, 1975–2011. Volume II. College students and adults ages 19–5*. Ann Arbor, MI: Institute for Social Research, The University of Michigan, Table 2-3. Substance Abuse and Mental Health Administration (2012). *Results from the 2011 National Survey on Drug Use and Health: Detailed tables*. Rockville, MD: Substance Abuse and Mental Health Administration,. Tables 2-1A, 2-1B, and 2-22B. Wechsler, H.; Rigotti, N. A.; and Gledhill-Hoyt, J. (1998). Increased levels of cigarette use among college students: A cause for national concern. *Journal of the American Medical Association, 280*, 1673–1678.

36. Centers for Disease Control and Prevention (2003). Tobacco use among middle and high school students— New Hampshire, 1995–2001. *Morbidity and Mortality Weekly Report, 52*, 7–9. Johnston, O'Malley, Bachman, and Schulenberg, Decline in teen smoking resumes, Table 1. Johnston, L. D.; O'Malley, P. M.; Bachman, J. G., and Schulenberg, J. E. (2012). *Monitoring the future: National results for adolescent drug use 1975–2011. Volume 1: Secondary school students*. Ann Arbor, MI: Institute for Social Research, The University of Michigan, Tables 2-1 and 6-1.

37. Johnston, L. D.; O'Malley, P. M.; Bachman, J. G.; and Schulenberg, J. E. (2011, December 14), Decline in teen smoking resumes in 2011. University of Michigan News Service, Ann Arbor, MI, Tables 2 and 3.

38. Johnston, L. D.; O'Malley, P. M.; and Bachman, J. C. (2002, December 16). Teen smoking declines sharply in 2002, more than offsetting large increases in the early 1990s. University of Michigan News and Information Service, Ann Arbor, pp. 4–5. Quotation by L.D. Johnston, p. 5.

39. Johnston, O'Malley; Bachman; and Schulenberg, *Monitoring the future, 2004-2011*, Volume 1, Table 9-6. Rigotti, N. A.; DiFranza, J. R.; Chang, Y.; Thelma, T.; et al. (1997). The effect of enforcing tobacco-sales laws on adolescents' access to tobacco and smoking behavior. *New England Journal of Medicine, 337*, 1044–1057. Substance Abuse and Mental Health Services Administration (2012). *FY 2011 annual Synar reports: Youth tobacco sales*. Rockville, MD: Substance Abuse and Mental Health Services Administration.

40. Johnston; O'Malley; Bachman; and Schulenberg, *Monitoring the future, 2004–2001*, Volume 1, Tables 2-3, 8-1, and 8-4.

41. Freedman, A. M. How a tobacco giant doctors snuff brands to boost their "kick." (1994, October 26). *Wall Street Journal*, pp. A1, A14.

42. Information courtesy of the U.S. Food and Drug Administration, Silver Springs, MD. Wilson, D., and Creswell, J. (2010, January 31). Where there's no smoke, Altria hopes there's fire. *New York Times*, pp. B1, B5.

43. Hamilton, K. (1997, July 21). Blowing smoke. *Newsweek*, pp. 54–60.

44. Ackerman, E. (1999, November 29). The cigar boom goes up in smoke. *Newsweek*, p. 55. Associated Press (2012, June 20). Cigar industry braces for new regulations. Baker, F., et al. (2000). Health risks associated with cigar smoking. *Journal of the American Medical Association, 284*, 735–740. Substance Abuse and Mental Health Services Administration (2001, December 21). *The NHSDA report: Cigar use*. Rockville, MD: Substance Abuse and Mental Health Services Administration.

45. Strom, S. (2001, June 13). Japan and tobacco revenue: Leader faces difficult choice. *New York Times*, pp. A1, A14. Tagliabue, J.(2005, September 8). The ash may finally be falling from the Gauloise. *New York Times*, p. A4. Watts, J. (1999). Smoking, sake, and suicide: Japan plans a healthier future. *The Lancet, 354*, p. 843. Winter, G.(2001, August 24). Enticing Third World youth. *New York Times*, pp. C1, C4.

46. Hampton, T. (2008, April 2). Global report highlights tobacco use, offers countermeasures for nations. *Journal of the American Medical Association, 299*, 1531–1552.

47. Marsh, B. (2008, February 24). A growing cloud over the planet. *New York Times*, p. 4. Shafey, O.; Eriksen, M.; Ross, H.; and MacKay, J.(2009). The Tobacco Atlas (3rd ed.). Atlanta, GA: American Cancer Society, pp. 22–23. World Health Organization (2008). *WHO report on the global tobacco epidemic 2008: The MPOWER package*. Geneva, Switzerland: World Health Organization. World Health Organization (2010). *2010 Global Progress Report on implementation of the WHO framework convention on tobacco control*. Geneva, Switzerland: World Health Organization.

48. American Cancer Society, Atlanta, GA. Cited in *The world almanac and book of facts 2000* (1999). Mahwah, NJ: Primedia Reference, p. 733.

49. U.S. Department of Health and Human Services, Public Health Service, Office of Smoking and Health (1988). *The health consequences of smoking: Nicotine addiction* (A report of the surgeon general). Rockville, MD: Public Health Service, p. 9.

50. American Legacy Foundation (2003). Factsheet: Quitting smoking. Washington, DC: American Legacy Foundation. Ehrich, B., and Emmons, K. M. (1994). Addressing the needs of smokers in the 1990s. *The Behavior Therapist, 17*(6), 119–122. Freudenheim, M. (2007, October 26). Seeking savings, employers help smokers quit. *New York Times*, pp. A1, A18. Hughes, J. R.; Keely, J.; and Naud, S. (2004). Shape of the relapse curve and long-term abstinence among untreated smokers. *Addiction, 99*, 29–38. Lichtenstein, E.; Zhu, S-H.; and Tedeschi, G. J. (2010, May–June). Smoking cessation quitlines: An underrecognized intervention success story. *American Psychologist*, 253–261. Munafò, M. R.; Clark, T. G.; Johnstone, E. C.; Murphy, M. F. G.; et al. (2004). The genetic basis for smoking behavior: A systematic review and meta-analysis. *Nicotine and Tobacco Research, 6*, 583–597.

51. Ahluwalia, J. S.; Harris, K. Jo; Catley, D.; Okuyemi, K. S.; and Mayo, M. S. (2002). Sustained-release bupropion for smoking cessation in African Americans: A randomized controlled trial. *Journal of the American Medical Association, 288,* 468–474. Benowitz, N. L. (1997). Treating tobacco addiction—Nicotine or no nicotine? *New England Journal of Medicine, 337,* 1230–1231. Jain, A. (2003). Treating nicotine addiction. *British Medical Journal, 327,* 1394–1395. Zickler, P. (2003). Genetic variation may increase nicotine craving and smoking relapse. *NIDA Notes, 18*(3), 1, 6.

52. Nides, M.; Oncken, C.; Gonzales, D.; Rennard, S.; Watsky, E. J.; et al. (2006). Smoking cessation with varenicline, a selective alpha-4-beta-2 nicotinic receptor partial agonist. *Archives of Internal Medicine, 166,* 1561–1568.

53. Park, A. (2011, November 3). Trying to quit smoking? Don't start with Chantix, say some experts. http:/heartland.time.com/2001/11/03.

54. Franzon, M.; Gustavsson, G.; and Korberly, B. H. (2002). Effectiveness of over-the-counter nicotine replacement therapy. *Journal of the American Medical Association, 288,* 3108–3110. Mathias, R. (2001). Nicotine patch helps smokeless tobacco users quit, but maintaining abstinence may require additional treatment. *NIDA Notes, 16*(1), 8–9. Shiffman, S.; Dresler, C. M.; and Rohay, J. M. (2004). Successful treatment with a nicotine lozenge of smokers with prior failure in pharmacological therapy. *Addiction, 99,* 83–92.

55. Fiore, M. C.; Hatsukami, D. K.; and Baker, T. B. (2002). Effective tobacco dependence treatment. *Journal of the American Medical Association, 288,* 1768–1771. Spangler, J. G.; George, G.; Foley, K. L.; and Crandall, S. J. (2002). Tobacco intervention training: Current efforts and gaps in U.S. medical schools. *Journal of the American Medical Association, 288,* 1102–1109.

56. Parkes, G.; Greenhaigh, T.; Griffin, M.; and Dent, R. (2008). Effect on smoking quit rate of telling patients their lung age: The Step2quit randomized controlled trial. *British Medical Journal, 336,* 598–600. Partnership for Prevention (2008). New study: Boosting five preventive services would save 100,000 lives each year. Washington, DC: Partnership for Prevention, National Commission on Prevention Priorities. World Health Organization (2002). *The tobacco atlas.* Geneva, Switzerland: World Health Organization, pp. 24–25.

57. Goldman, L. K., and Glantz, S. A. (1999). Evaluation of antismoking advertising campaigns. *Journal of the American Medical Association, 279,* 772–777. Raising kids who don't smoke (2003), created by Philip Morris USA Youth Smoking Prevention. Story, L. (2007, January 2). Kicking an addiction, with real people. *New York Times,* p. C7. Two questions to identify future smokers (2008, July 15). *New York Times,* p. F6.

Caffeine

For a while, Steve couldn't understand why he was suffering those headaches. Every Sunday afternoon, sometimes earlier in the day, he would get a pounding headache and feel grumpy and out of sorts. Steve would notice that he felt achy, as though he were coming down with the flu.

Then it occurred to him. On the weekends at home, he was able to sleep late and drank decaffeinated coffee instead of his regular brew at the office. He realized that he was going through caffeine withdrawal. "I had better cut down," he said to himself, "or stick with regular on the weekends."

If you enjoy a cup of caffeinated coffee or caffeinated tea, a piece of chocolate, or a can of "regular" Coke or Pepsi, you may be surprised to know that you are engaging in the most popular form of drug-taking behavior in the world. To varying degrees, all these products contain caffeine, a psychoactive stimulant drug. It should be added, however, that you need not be overly concerned. Among the range of psychoactive stimulants that exist (the major ones were examined in Chapters 4 and 10), caffeine is considerably weaker than most, and research suggests that caffeine consumption is relatively benign. Nonetheless, as will be shown, caffeine can be a dependence-producing drug, and several precautions against its use should be heeded. This is particularly true in light of the recent popularity of highly caffeinated energy drinks, with stimulant potential far exceeding that of traditional caffeinated beverages.

Caffeine belongs to a family of stimulant compounds called **xanthines**. Two other major examples of xanthines, **theobromine** (found in chocolate) and **theophylline** (found in small amounts in tea), also have stimulating effects. In general, theophylline and caffeine have approximately equal stimulatory effects; theobromine is only about one-tenth as strong. This chapter will focus on what we know about caffeine itself, beginning with a look at three natural sources of caffeine: coffee, tea, and chocolate.

Coffee

We do not know exactly when coffee drinking began, but we do know that the plant *Coffea arabica*, from which coffee beans were first harvested, originated in Ethiopia, and its cultivation spread to Yemen and Arabia at some time between the eleventh and the fifteenth centuries. Coffee has been called "the wine of Islam," suggesting that it was viewed as a substitute for alcoholic beverages, which are forbidden by the Koran.

A popular legend concerning the beginnings of coffee drinking has it that a young Yemenite or Ethiopian

caffeine: A xanthine stimulant found in coffee, tea, chocolate, soft drinks, and several medications.

xanthines (ZAN-theens): A family of CNS stimulant drugs that includes caffeine, theophylline, and theobromine.

theobromine (THEE-oh-BROH-meen): A xanthine stimulant found in chocolate.

theophylline (thee-OFF-ill-lin): A xanthine stimulant found in small amounts in tea. It is used as an antiasthma medication.

by the numbers . . .

80   Milligrams of caffeine in an 8.3-ounce can of Red Bull, the leading "energy drink" in the U.S. market. The caffeine content in a 12-ounce serving is approximately 3 times that in a 12-ounce can of Coca-Cola Classic.

260   Milligrams of caffeine in a 12-ounce Starbucks Tall coffee, approximately 7½ times that of a 12-ounce can of Coca-Cola Classic.

9   The number of ounces in an average cup of coffee in the United States. The "standard drink size" for coffee has traditionally been five ounces.

Sources: Energyfiend.com, 2013.

goatherd named Khaldi, while tending his flock, noticed that his goats were unusually hyperactive and unable to sleep after nibbling some red berries in the field. Khaldi tried some himself and, upon feeling as exhilarated as his goats, took the berries to the local Islamic monastery. The chief holy man there prepared a beverage from these berries and found the effect to be so invigorating that he was able to stay awake during a long night of prayers in the mosque. According to this legend, the fame of the "wakeful monastery" and its remarkable potion spread through the whole kingdom and to other countries of the region.[1]

At first, coffee was banned on religious grounds because some Islamic clerics considered it to be as much an intoxicant as an alcoholic beverage, but these ecclesiastic disputes were eventually settled and coffee drinking became a fixture of daily life. In the words of one historian, "The growth of coffee and its use as a national beverage became as inseparably connected with Arabia as tea is with China."[2]

Coffee in Britain and North America

The practice of coffee drinking reached England in the middle of the seventeenth century, just in time to be associated with one of the most turbulent periods of political, social, economic, and religious unrest in its history. It was in establishments specializing in the sale of coffee, known as coffee houses, that intellectuals met and argued their respective points of view. Until the end of the eighteenth century, when tea began to replace coffee as the dominant British drink, coffee was the principal alternative social beverage to alcohol. The British coffee house enjoyed the reputation of being a place where men could socialize with one another and enjoy a nonintoxicating beverage in sober company. (Women rarely frequented coffee houses, although they often managed them.)

The emphasis was on keeping a clear head, which was certainly not likely after an hour or two at the local tavern. In fact, historians have credited coffee houses with helping to moderate the widespread drunkenness that was rampant as a result of the "gin epidemic" in England during the 1700s (see Chapter 8). A popular nickname for coffee houses was "penny universities," since the conversation there was considered to be as stimulating as a university education and a lot cheaper.[3]

Coffee houses in colonial America served a similar purpose. One such political gathering place, the Green Dragon in Boston, was the setting for meetings of John Adams, Samuel Adams, Paul Revere, and their compatriots as they planned their strategy against the British. After the Revolutionary War, coffee emerged as the American national drink, especially after 1830 when alcohol consumption began to decline (see Chapter 8). During the settling of the American frontier, coffee was an indispensable provision for the long trek westward. By 1860, Americans were consuming three-fourths of the world's entire production of coffee.

Today, the United States remains the world's top importer of coffee (Germany being a close second), with most of our imported coffee originating in Brazil, Colombia, and Vietnam. However, in terms of per capita coffee consumption, the United States barely ranks among the top twenty-five nations of the world. Most European countries exceed the U.S. in per capita consumption, with Finland being number one (about 27 pounds/12.2 kilograms in a year). Since roughly 1960, domestic coffee consumption has gradually declined as American drinking habits have shifted to an increased consumption of colas, particularly among young adults.[4]

Major Sources of Coffee

The global coffee market is represented by two species of coffee beans. *Coffea arabica*, the original coffee bean as far as Westerners are concerned, is grown mostly in Brazil and Colombia, having been brought to South America by the French in the early 1700s. The other species, *Coffea robusta*, was originally grown primarily in formerly Dutch plantations on the Indonesian island of Java (hence the phrase "a cup of java" for a cup of coffee). Vietnam is currently the leading grower of robusta coffee, followed by Brazil, India, and several countries in Africa. *Coffea arabica* beans represent about 80 percent of the world's coffee production.

Expert coffee tasters in a German coffee company sample the possibilities before deciding on a particular blend.

Coffee blends are made up of combinations of these two types of beans, with the ratio dictated by local tastes and economic concerns. Robusta beans are considered by coffee experts to be inferior to arabica beans because of their harsher taste, but robusta beans have approximately twice the caffeine content and are cheaper to buy. In recent years, "100 percent Arabica bean" coffee has become the norm for most coffee retailers in the United States.

The Caffeine Content in Coffee

Caffeine is the only xanthine found in coffee (see Drugs . . . in Focus), with the caffeine content in a "standard" 5-ounce cup of coffee ranging from about 57 to 145 milligrams (mg). The precise caffeine dosage depends on the method of brewing, the amount of coffee used, brand of coffee, and brewing time. Roughly speaking, the caffeine content in coffee can be

Coffea arabica (KOFF-ee-uh air-RAB-beh-ka): A type of coffee bean native to the Middle East but now grown principally in South America. It is typically referred to simply as arabica.

Coffea robusta (KOFF-ee-uh row-BUS-tah): A type of coffee bean grown principally in Indonesia, Brazil, and Africa.

Drugs . . . in Focus

Why There Are No (Live) Flies in Your Coffee

Chemical compounds found naturally in plants are generally there because they confer some selective advantage, although it may take a while for scientists to figure out what that advantage may be. In the case of plants containing xanthines, the benefit lies in the area of insect control.

We now know that xanthines interfere with an insect's ability to feed on a plant because they increase the level of octopamine, an excitatory chemical in the nervous system of invertebrates. As a result, contact with xanthine-containing plants causes insects to become overly stimulated and die. Fortunately, octopamine plays little or no role in mammalian nervous systems. One extra benefit in knowing how xanthines affect insects is the possibility in the future of developing xanthine-based pesticides that are effective on cockroaches but a good deal safer for human beings.

Sources: Hirashima, A.; Morimoto, M.; Kuwane, E.; and Eto, M. (2003). Octopaminergic agonists for the cockroach neuronal octopamine receptor. *Journal of Insect Science, 3,* 1–9. Nathanson, J. A. (1984). Caffeine and related methylxanthines: Possible naturally occurring pesticides. *Science, 226,* 184–187.

estimated to be about 100 mg (20 mg per fluid ounce). Comparable amounts of instant coffee have about 60 mg of caffeine (12 mg per fluid ounce).[5]

Bear in mind, however, that the average regular-size cup of coffee holds about 9 ounces, and a 12- to 24-ounce cup is often the preferred serving size, so you have to do the math carefully to determine the actual amount of caffeine you are ingesting in a given day.

Tea

By the standard of historical records, tea is the world's oldest caffeine-containing beverage. The legendary Chinese emperor Shen Nung is credited with its discovery in 2737 B.C., along with other stimulants such as the anti-asthma medication we now know as ephedrine (see Chapter 4) and marijuana (see Chapter 7). Tea is a brew of leaves from the *Camellia sinensis* (tea plant), a large evergreen tree that is typically trimmed back to look more like a bush. The Latin word *sinensis* refers to its origin in China.[6]

Dutch traders brought tea from Asia to Western Europe in the early 1600s, where it met with mixed reviews. The Germans tried tea drinking for a while, but then returned to beer; the French also tried it, but

Camellia sinensis (ka-MEE-yah sin-EHN-sis): The plant from which tea leaves are obtained.

then returned to coffee and wine. The Chinese traded directly with the Russians, who became enamored with tea and made drinking it a national pastime. Giant tea urns, called *samovars*, kept tea available for drinking throughout the day.

Tea in Britain and North America

The principal Dutch success with tea in Europe was in Britain, where it eventually became the national drink. Chinese tea, as noted in Chapter 5, was in such great demand by the British that the Chinese were forced to trade their tea in exchange for opium imported by the British into their own country. By 1842, the problems with this odd arrangement escalated into the Opium War, pitting China against Britain and later France and the United States.

By the end of the nineteenth century, however, China was no longer the principal source for British tea. Tastes had shifted away from the subtle flavor of Chinese green tea leaves and toward a stronger, blacker tea that was being grown in India and Ceylon (now Sri Lanka). It also did not hurt that a greater number of cups could be made from a pound of Indian or Ceylonese tea, making it more economical for the average consumer. Today's teas are blends of black tea leaves, chiefly from India, Sri Lanka, and Indonesia, although there is a growing market for green tea from China and Japan.[7]

We do not know whether the gentlemen at the Green Dragon coffee house in Boston were drinking coffee or tea during the months of growing unrest and resentment against the British prior to the beginning of the Revolutionary War, but much of the talk certainly *concerned* tea. In 1773, the British government had decided to allow British agents to sell cheap tea directly to the American colonies, bypassing American tea merchants in the process. In the eyes of the Americans, the policy was another instance of British tyranny and one more reason why the colonies should be independent.

We do know what happened next. On the night of December 16, 1773, while three British ships loaded with chests of British tea lay at anchor in Boston Harbor, fifty to sixty colonists, some of them dressed as Mohawk Indians, boarded the vessels and proceeded to break open the tea chests and dump the contents into the water. Thus the Boston Tea Party entered the pages of history. Strangely enough, the initial reaction to this event in British newspapers focused not on the political ramifications but rather on the pharmacological effect of the tea on the unfortunate fish in Boston Harbor. One London newspaper reported that the fish "had contracted a disorder not unlike the nervous complaints of the body." Assuming this story is true, we can only conclude that all that tea had given the fish a large dose of xanthines, specifically caffeine and theophylline (see below).[8]

Largely as a result of continuing anti-British sentiment during the early history of the United States, drinking tea was viewed as unpatriotic, and coffee became the preferred beverage. Today, American consumption of tea is only approximately one-eighth that of Ireland and Great Britain, who lead the world, as you might suspect, in per capita tea drinking. More than 80 percent of all tea consumed in the United States is in the form of iced tea, a beverage that was introduced at the Louisiana Purchase Exposition in St. Louis in the summer of 1904.

The Chemical Content in Tea

Tea contains caffeine and theophylline. The caffeine content of a 5-ounce cup of medium-brewed tea is approximately 60 mg. If the tea is a strong brew, the caffeine content approaches that of regular coffee, especially if the tea is produced in Britain rather than the United States. A strong brew of Twining's English Breakfast tea, for example, contains approximately 107 mg of caffeine in a 5-ounce cup. Of course, as with coffee, caffeine amounts in the tea consumed will be higher if the drink size is greater.[9]

The other xanthine found in tea, theophylline, is found in much smaller concentrations than caffeine.

As will be noted later, its bronchodilating effect is clinically useful for the treatment of asthma and other respiratory problems.

A growing medical literature points to the potential health benefits in the consumption of a group of non-xanthine chemicals in tea, called *polyphenols*. Polyphenols are plentiful in green tea and, to a lesser degree, in black or pekoe tea. Although both types of tea are harvested from the *Camellia sinensis* plant, they are processed differently. Black tea leaves are fermented prior to drying, whereas green tea leaves are not. During the fermentation process, black tea loses most of its polyphenol content. Beneficial effects have been studied in the prevention of cardiovascular disease, inflammatory disorders, neurogenerative disorders such as Parkinson's disease and Alzheimer's disease, as well as some forms of cancer. Whether green tea is a "miracle drink" remains, however, to be determined. Green tea may not be beneficial in all circumstances. For example, green tea contains vitamin K (a clotting factor), raising the potential for interfering with blood-thinning medications, and it can reduce the absorption of iron from the diet. There is also evidence that polyphenols can interfere with the action of certain anti-cancer treatment drugs.[10]

Chocolate

Chocolate comes from **cocoa bean pods** growing directly on the trunk and thick main branches of cacao trees. Cacao trees are native to Mexico and Central America, but now they are grown in tropical regions of the Caribbean, South America, Africa, and Asia. The leading exporters of cocoa beans to the United States are the Ivory Coast, Ghana, and Indonesia.[11]

According to popular legend, chocolate was a gift from the Aztec god Quetzalcoatl to give humans a taste of paradise. At the time of Hernando Cortés's expedition to Mexico in 1519, chocolate (*xocoatl* or *chocolatl* as the Aztecs called it) was a prized beverage, to be enjoyed only by the rulers and the upper classes of society. Cortés took some cocoa bean pods back to Spain in 1528 and made a preparation as he had learned it from the Aztecs, but with an important difference: the addition of sugar. Now, in a sweetened form called *molinet*, chocolate became an instant

cocoa bean pods (COH-coh): Parts of the cacao tree that are the raw material for cocoa and chocolate. Not to be confused with coca, the source of cocaine.

success—and a closely guarded secret of the Spanish emperor Charles V and his royal court. Inevitably, however, word leaked out to the other royal courts of Europe that the Spanish were enjoying an exotic new drink that came from the New World.

When the fourteen-year-old Spanish princess arrived in Paris to marry the fourteen-year-old Louis XIII of France in 1615, she carried with her a betrothal gift of Spanish chocolate. It was the beginning of the traditional connection of chocolate with romance. Later, in 1660, a similar betrothal gift at the wedding of another Spanish princess and Louis XIV of France sealed its reputation as the gift of love. It also has not hurt chocolate's image that the eighteenth-century Italian lover Casanova credited his considerable sexual prowess to a habit of drinking chocolate each morning. Of course, the true explanation could have been either the stimulating effects of caffeine, or simply a powerful placebo effect (see Chapter 1).

Chocolate took hold in England not so much as a symbol of romance but simply as another good-tasting beverage that could be sold in the growing number of coffee houses in English cities. From the beginning, chocolate was sold in shops rather than hidden away behind palace walls. It was not cheap, but at least it was available to all who could afford to buy it. By 1700, the specialty chocolate house rivaled the coffee house as a place to gather and discuss current events.

How Chocolate Is Made

The preparation of modern-day chocolate begins with the roasting of cocoa beans to such temperatures that the natural fat within the beans, called **cocoa butter**, melts. The result is a deep-colored chocolaty-smelling paste called **chocolate liquor**. When it later cools and hardens, the paste is called **baking chocolate**. As chocolate, it is as pure as you can get, but since there is no sugar content it has an "extra-bittersweet" flavor, suitable only for cakes, brownies, and other baking purposes.

cocoa butter: The fat content of the cocoa bean.

chocolate liquor (lih-KOOR): A deep-colored paste made when roasted cocoa beans are heated so that the cocoa butter in the beans melts.

baking chocolate: A hardened paste, consisting of chocolate liquor, produced by heating roasted cocoa beans.

To make chocolate that is eaten by itself, several additional processing steps are required, many of which were developed by the Swiss chocolatier Rodolphe Lindt in 1879. A ratio of cocoa liquor and cocoa butter is combined with milk, sugar, and vanilla to make milk chocolate. Just how much cocoa liquor is added depends on the type of chocolate. Dark (semisweet) chocolate is made with much less milk and less sugar than milk chocolate, with the percentage of cocoa liquor typically in the 60% to 75% range. The percentage of cocoa liquor is higher in "extra dark" versions.

Fortunately, unlike other fats, cocoa butter almost never goes rancid. In other words, chocolate keeps. It might turn white after a while, but that simply means that the cocoa butter is starting to separate from the mixture. It is all right to eat, although chocolate connoisseurs would surely disagree. All that is needed to produce commercial chocolate is to refine the texture to achieve that degree of smoothness the world has come to know and love—not to mention a consumable product that, despite its detrimental effect on the waistline, appears to have genuine health benefits (Health Line).[12]

The Chocolate Industry Today

Present-day domestic sales of chocolate in the United States are dominated by the Hershey Company and Mars, Incorporated, which together hold approximately 75 percent of an annual market (see Portrait). Overall, the annual per capita consumption of chocolate in the United States is approximately 11 pounds, which puts the country well below that of other chocolate-loving nations of the world. Not surprisingly, Switzerland ranks first in the world, consuming about twice as much on an annual per capita basis.[13]

The Xanthine Content in Chocolate

The amounts of xanthines are much smaller in chocolate than in coffee or tea. A typical 1-ounce piece of milk chocolate, for example, contains about 6-8 mg of caffeine and about 40 mg of theobromine. With theobromine packing about one-tenth the stimulant power of caffeine, the total effect of this quantity of chocolate is roughly equivalent to that of 10–12 mg of caffeine. Of course, eating more than 1 ounce will change these figures (a typical chocolate bar is approximately 1.5 ounces), but even so, it is unlikely that chocolate will keep you up at night.[14]

Health Line

Chocolate, Flavanols, and Cardiovascular Health

Are we running any risk to our health by indulging in our obvious love for chocolate? It is true that chocolate is rich in saturated fatty acids, many of which are villains when it comes to raising cholesterol and clogging our coronary arteries. Yet the particular saturated fatty acid in the cocoa butter of chocolate turns out to be quite benign. The main component of cocoa butter is a fatty acid known as stearic acid, which is rapidly converted in the liver to oleic acid, a mono-unsaturate that neither raises nor lowers serum cholesterol. One study found that healthy young men on a twenty-six-day diet in which a total of 37 percent of calories came from fat and 81 percent of those fat calories came from cocoa butter had no increase in their serum cholesterol, and their cholesterol levels were no higher than if they had been on a comparable diet in which the fat came from olive oil (see Chapter 1).

Recent evidence suggests that chocolate may even *protect* arteries from disease. Cocoa liquor has a concentration of compounds called *flavanols* that are known to function as antioxidants of the bloodstream. The greater the level of antioxidants, the lower the probability that artery-clogging cells will develop. This is consistent with recent studies indicating that dark chocolate is associated with reducing the risk of cardiovascular disease and stroke. Dark chocolate has twice the flavanols of milk chocolate. This is not to say that chocolate should be considered a substitute for fruits and vegetables, foods that have obvious nutritional virtues. Nor should chocolate necessarily be viewed as a health food. Milk chocolate contains by definition (and by law) a minimal amount of milk-derived butterfat in addition to cocoa butter. Some chocolates also contain palm oil or coconut oil, two saturated fats that *do* raise cholesterol levels. And no one should expect to lose weight on a chocolate diet. Even so, nutritionists are concluding that there is little harm in eating two or three chocolate bars a week, which is welcome news for chocolate lovers everywhere.

Sources: Barnett, C. F., and DeMarco, T. (2011). A chocolate a day keeps the doctor away? *Journal of Physiology, 589,* 5921–5922. Buitrago-Lopez, A.; Sanderson, J.; Johnson, L.; Warnakule, S.; Wood, A.; et al. (2011). Chocolate consumption and cardiometabolic disorders: Systematic review and meta-analysis. *British Medical Journal,* accessed BMJ 2011; 343:d4488 doi. Grassi, D.; Lippi, C.; Necozione, S.; Desideri, G.; and Ferri, C. (2005). Short-term administration of dark chocolate is followed by a significant increase in insulin sensitivity and a decrease in blood pressure in healthy persons. *American Journal of Clinical Nutrition, 81,* 611–614. Waterhouse, A. J.; Shirley, J. R.; and Donovan, J. I. (1996). Antioxidants in chocolate. Lancet, 348, 834.

Soft Drinks

The fourth and final major source of caffeine in our diet is soft drinks. Table 11.1 shows the caffeine content of prominent soft-drink brands. Although most of the caffeinated drinks are colas, it is possible for a noncola to be caffeinated as well. The reason is that more than 95 percent of the caffeine in caffeinated soft drinks is added by the manufacturer during production; less than 5 percent actually comes from the West African kola nut, from which cola gets its name.

In general, the United States leads the world in per capita consumption of soft-drink products, about 45 gallons annually (a bit less than two 8-ounce servings per day). Traditionally, almost all of the major caffeinated soft drinks (Coca-Cola and Pepsi-Cola products being the leaders), have contained caffeine levels in the range of 3–5 mg per fluid ounce. Recently, a new category of highly caffeinated soft-drinks (such as Red Bull and Monster Energy) have entered the market and are currently the fastest-growing segment of the beverage industry (see Table 11.3, page 285). In addition, new products of highly concentrated caffeinated beverages, so-called energy shots, have been introduced (see Drugs . . . in Focus, page 289).[15]

Caffeine from OTC Drugs and Other Products

Caffeine is sold purely as a stimulant in over-the-counter (OTC) drugs such as NoDoz and Vivarin tablets and as one of several ingredients in a number of other products ranging from pain relievers and cold remedies to diuretics and weight-control aids. As Table 11.2 shows, the equivalent caffeine level in these products ranges approximately from that of one-third cup to two cups of regular coffee.

The availability of caffeine in OTC drugs has recently been supplemented by novelty products such as caffeinated lip balm, caffeinated sunflower seeds, caffeinated beer, and even caffeinated soap (promoted as waking you up while the coffee is brewing). Inhalable caffeine (brand name: AeroShot), equivalent to a large-size coffee and sold in lipstick-sized canisters, became available in

PORTRAIT

Milton S. Hershey and the Town Built on Chocolate

When Milton Hershey made a decision in 1893 to go into the chocolate business, he was already an experienced confectioner with a prosperous caramel company in Lancaster, Pennsylvania. At the time, caramels were the dominant candies in America, but he could see that the future was in chocolate. New German-built machinery was now available to mass-produce milk chocolate. As Hershey had observed during a trip to Switzerland a few years earlier, chocolate was already all the rage in Europe. He wanted to be in the business on the ground floor.

Hershey bought the equipment and started to experiment on a special recipe, using fresh milk from the local dairy farms instead of powdered milk. The proportions of milk and sugar, the blend of cocoa beans, and the roasting time are secrets to this day. All we know is that somehow Hershey devised a recipe that was a winner.

The new Hershey bar was an instant hit.

By 1903, the Hershey chocolate business had become so successful that it needed a new factory. Defying conventional wisdom, however, Hershey did not look for a town or city for the factory but rather went into the surrounding countryside. He bought a thousand acres of prime Pennsylvania Dutch farmland, built his factory, then decided to build a town around it.

By 1930, the town of Hershey had grown to include residents beyond the six thousand factory workers. The Hershey business was now worldwide, with its chocolate "kisses" and chocolate syrup in addition to other products. During hard economic times, Hershey went on a construction spree to maintain employment. He built the famous Hershey Hotel, Hershey Gardens, a football stadium and sports arena, and a convention center. Because he was childless, he turned his attention to

building a Milton Hershey school for orphaned boys and girls.

Milton Hershey died in 1945 at the age of eighty-eight, but his corporate heirs continued in his spirit. Today, there is the Milton S. Hershey Medical Center of the Pennsylvania State University, endowed by the Hershey Company. And of course there is Hersheypark, an enlargement of an old amusement park Hershey had built in 1905, all powered by a best-selling chocolate bar and a man with a very sweet dream.

Sources: D'Antonio, M. (2006). *Hershey: Milton S. Hershey's extraordinary life of wealth, empire, and utopian dreams.* New York: Simon and Schuster. Kennedy, P. (2013, January 13). Who made that? (Hershey bar). *New York Times Magazine,* p. 15. Morton, M., and Morton, F. (1986). *Chocolate: An illustrated history.* New York: Crown Publishers, pp. 89–125

TABLE 11.1

Caffeine levels and domestic U.S. market share of leading brands of soft drinks

BRAND NAME (COMPANY)	MARKET SHARE (2011)	CAFFEINE CONTENT (MG/12 OZ.)
Coke (Coca-Cola)	17.0%	34
Diet Coke (Coca-Cola)	9.7%	45
Pepsi-Cola (PepsiCo)	9.2%	38
Mountain Dew (PepsiCo)	6.7%	55
Sprite (Coca-Cola)	5.7%	none
Diet Pepsi (PepsiCo)	4.9%	36
Diet Mountain Dew (PepsiCo)	2.0%	55
Fanta (Coca-Cola)	1.9%	41
Diet Dr Pepper (Dr. Pepper Snapple)	1.8%	none

Note: Diet Coke became the Number Two brand for the first time in history in 2011.

Sources: Energyfiend.com, 2013. Top soft drink brands, 2011. *Market Share Reporter* (2012). Detroit: Gale. Business Insights: Essentials Web. April 2013.

2011, not requiring FDA approval since it is marketed as a dietary supplement (Chapter 1). Nonetheless, the FDA has since issued a warning letter to the manufacturer that the product label must address issues of safety, possible use by children and adolescents, and possible use with alcohol. Concerns that AeroShot might become another club drug are similar to those that had been raised with respect to the briefly popular caffeinated alcohol drink Four Loko (see Drugs . . . in Focus, Chapter 8).[16]

Caffeine as a Drug

When ingested orally, caffeine is absorbed in about thirty to sixty minutes. Caffeine levels peak in the bloodstream in one hour, and reactions in the central nervous system peak in about two hours. Many coffee drinkers notice a boost of energy, or "buzz," almost immediately, but this effect is attributable either to the sugar in the coffee or to a conditioned learning effect, not to the caffeine itself. From three to seven hours after caffeine is consumed, approximately half of it still remains in the bloodstream.

The biotransformation of caffeine and the time it takes to eliminate it vary according to a number

TABLE 11.2

Caffeine content in common over-the-counter medications

MEDICATION	CAFFEINE PER TABLET OR CAPSULE (in milligrams)	CAFFEINE PER RECOMMENDED DOSAGE (in milligrams)
Stimulants		
NoDoz	100	200
Vivarin	200	200
Pain relievers		
Anacin	32	64
Excedrin	65	130
Midol	32	64
Vanquish	33	66
Cold remedies		
Coryban-D	30	30
Dristan	16	32
Triaminicin	30	30
Diuretics		
Aqua-Ban	100	200

Note: Caffeine is also found in prescription remedies for migraines (Cafergot and Migral) and in pain relievers (Darvon Compound and Fiorinol).

Source: Updated from Gilbert, R. J. (1986). *Caffeine: The most popular stimulant.* New York: Chelsea House, p. 51.

Quick Concept Check 11.1

Understanding Caffeine Levels in Foods and Beverages

Check your understanding of the relative amounts of caffeine in various foods and beverages by rank ordering the following caffeine-containing foods or beverages, from 1 (most) to 6 (least). If any examples have caffeine levels close enough to be considered a tie, indicate this in your ranking.

a. 1-ounce bar of milk chocolate

b. 5-ounce cup of drip brewed coffee

c. 5-ounce cup of tea

d. 12-ounce can of Coca-Cola

e. 5-ounce cup of instant coffee

f. 5-ounce cup of decaffeinated coffee

Answers: a. 5   b. 1   c. 2 (tie)   d. 4   e. 2 (tie)   f. 6

of factors. For example, women in late stages of pregnancy and those using oral contraceptives eliminate caffeine from their systems more slowly than either men or women in general. Infants and the elderly also show a slower elimination of caffeine. In contrast, smokers eliminate caffeine about 100 percent more quickly than nonsmokers. As a result, smokers on average experience the effect of the caffeine they consume for a relatively shorter period of time; it is possible that smokers tend to drink more caffeinated coffee than nonsmokers to compensate for their faster elimination of caffeine.[17]

Effects of Caffeine on the Body

The stimulant effects of caffeine, as well as those of the other xanthines, are a result of a "double-negative effect." Essentially, caffeine is a stimulant because it inhibits an inhibitory factor in brain functioning. In this case, caffeine blocks the effects of an inhibitory neurotransmitter called **adenosine**. Normally, adenosine binds to receptors on the surface of cells and consequently produces sleepiness, dilation of blood vessels, and constriction of bronchial passageways. It also protects the body against seizures; slows down the body's reaction to stress; and lowers heart rate, blood pressure, and body temperature.

By inhibiting the effects of adenosine, caffeine and other xanthines cause the opposite responses to occur, although the actual results are complex. In general, peripheral blood vessels are dilated, while cerebral blood vessels in the head are constricted. Because dilated blood vessels in the head can frequently result in headache pain, caffeine can help headache sufferers, and that is why it is found in many over-the-counter pain relievers. Heart rate is slightly elevated when caffeine is consumed, but the effect is dose-dependent and often is not observed at all.

The fact that caffeine has a bronchodilating effect makes it helpful in treating asthmatic conditions in which the bronchial passageways are abnormally constricted. Theophylline, however, has a stronger bronchodilating effect than caffeine and so can be prescribed at lower doses. Caffeine is effective, but patients often report unpleasant side effects of "jitteriness" prior to improvement in their asthmatic condition.[18]

Effects of Caffeine on Behavior

As a stimulant, caffeine excites neuronal activity in the brain. As the dose increases, the effects expand from the

adenosine (a-DEN-oh-seen): An inhibitory neurotransmitter that is blocked, or neutralized, by caffeine and other xanthines. The action on adenosine receptors in the body is the basis for the stimulant properties of these drugs.

cerebral cortex downward to lower systems in the brain and finally to the spinal cord (Chapter 3). The behavioral consequence of this excitation is a feeling of mental alertness and lack of fatigue.

On the basis of these effects, you might expect that caffeine would also improve human performance, but reports in this regard are mixed. Subjects in controlled experimental settings feel stimulated and more alert, but whether their performance improves after caffeine depends on the type of task, their personal characteristics, and even the time of day when the experiment is conducted. In a recent study of possible performance-enhancing effects among competitive cyclists, it was found that caffeine administration increased their performance during timed trials overall, but the effect was greater when the cyclists were (falsely) informed that they had not ingested it.[19]

Nonetheless, it is possible to make some generalizations about caffeine's effect on performance. In general, caffeine increases vigilance and attentiveness in tasks at which subjects become easily bored, and it decreases the response time to simple visual or auditory signals. For more complex tasks in which subjects need to make decisions or in situations that require motor coordination, however, caffeine either has little effect or can be disruptive. Most reports of improvements under caffeine involve conditions in which the subject is already either bored or fatigued. In these circumstances, caffeine helps either to maintain a level of performance that would otherwise have declined or to restore performance from a state degraded by boredom or fatigue. Caffeine, therefore, can serve to support a moderate level of arousal and attention that is optimal for the task at hand.[20]

Caffeine is typically most effective for warding off sleep and improving performance on tedious tasks, at home, at school, and in the workplace.

The best-known effect, however, is the impact on sleep. Caffeine lengthens the time it takes to fall asleep and reduces the quality of sleep once it comes. Generally, studies investigating caffeine effects have involved coffee drinking, and the sleep effects are seen more strongly in nondrinkers of coffee than in habitual heavy coffee drinkers.[21]

As a final note, it is important to understand what interacting effects caffeine may or may not have on alcohol intoxication. First of all, caffeine does *not* have the ability to sober up a person recently intoxicated with alcohol. Despite the widespread notion that a cup of strong black coffee will help someone who is drunk, the evidence is simply not there. If anything, the behavioral consequences of alcohol intoxication can worsen. Second, the ingestion of highly caffeinated energy drinks (see Table 11.3) as mixers with alcohol at bars and clubs will not reduce alcoholic intoxication, as measured by objective tests. The combination reduces people's perception of intoxication, leading them to believe that they are more in control than they actually are. As a result, caffeinated energy drinks can make it more likely that greater amounts of alcohol will be consumed.[22]

Potential Health Benefits

In 2000, an intriguing connection was found between caffeine consumption and a lower risk of developing Parkinson's disease. In a follow-up of about eight thousand Japanese American men in Honolulu, the incidence of Parkinson's disease was about one-fifth in men who consumed at least 28 ounces of coffee per day, compared to those who consumed none at all. A lower risk of Parkinson's disease was observed no matter what the source of the caffeine and independent of intake levels of milk and sugar.

A second study in 2001 involving a larger sample of men confirmed this relationship, but it is presently uncertain whether the same relationship exists in women. In studies in which a lower risk is found in women, there is a U-shaped function for women, with either low or high consumption levels being less protective than moderate ones; for men, the higher the caffeine intake, the better the protection. The gender differences in the health consequences of caffeine consumption appear to be related to hormonal factors in women, specifically the interaction of caffeine and estrogen. A recent study has shown that caffeine reduces the risk of Parkinson's disease among postmenopausal women who do not take replacement estrogen; for those women who do take this therapy, caffeine increases the risk of the disorder. There is also evidence

TABLE 11.3

Current leading "energy drinks" in the U.S. market

BRAND	DOMESTIC MARKET SHARE (2011)	CAFFEINE CONTENT (mg)	SERVING QUANTITY (oz)	CAFFEINE (mg/oz)*
Red Bull	39.7%	80	8.4	9.6
Monster Energy	20.7%	160	16.0	10.0
Rockstar	7.4%	160	16.0	10.0
NOS	3.7%	260	16.0	16.2
Mega Monster Energy	3.1%	240	24.0	10.0

Note: Some brands also contain taurine, guarana, or bitter orange. All of these ingredients have stimulant properties and have the potential to elevate heart rate and blood pressure. Checking the list of ingredients is a good idea, even though manufacturers are not required to specify the milligram quantities.

*Comparable caffeine content in Coca-Cola Classic is 2.9 mg/oz.

Sources: www.energyfiend.com, 2013. Top energy drink brands, 2011. *Market Share Reporter* (2012). Detroit: Gale. Business Insights: Essentials. Web. April 2013.

that caffeine intake may reduce the risk of the cognitive decline, though the effects are stronger for women than for men.[23]

Potential Health Risks

Studies investigating the potential adverse health consequences of caffeine consumption have been conducted for more than a century, and the conclusions have varied considerably. In some cases, earlier concerns have been determined to be unfounded. For example, a 1971 study indicating an association between caffeine consumption and urinary tract cancer and a 1981 study indicating an association with pancreatic cancer were both compromised methodological design flaws. At present, the medical consensus is that caffeine consumption is not causally related to these or other types of cancer.[24]

Cardiovascular Effects

Because it is known that caffeine stimulates cardiac muscle as well as skeletal muscle throughout the body, it is only natural to be concerned with the possibility that caffeine consumption would be a risk factor for a heart attack or cardiac arrhythmia (irregular heart beat). In 1973, a great deal of publicity was generated by a study called the Boston Collaborative Drug Surveillance Program in which a large number of individuals at Boston metropolitan hospitals were surveyed as to their use of many different drugs, including caffeine, and the incidence of various disease states. The researchers reported that the consumption of more than six cups of caffeinated coffee a

day more than doubled the risk of a heart attack. Further studies, however, have failed to find any connection at all between caffeine and heart attacks.[25]

What do we do when the medical literature is so inconclusive and contradictory? First of all, in caffeine studies that show some cardiovascular health risk, the consumption levels are rather high (five to six cups or more a day). Drinking less caffeine has not been identified as a risk factor. Even so, potential health problems associated with caffeine consumption have to be considered in the context of other behaviors. For example, caffeine consumption is highly associated with cigarette smoking. Therefore, increased rates of coronary heart disease in heavy coffee drinkers who smoke may be a result of the cigarette smoking, not the caffeine consumption (Health Line).[26]

At the same time, we should be aware that a four-year-old child drinking a 20-ounce cola drink is consuming a very high dose of caffeine per body weight, and we should not be surprised to observe marked behavioral and physiological effects.

Osteoporosis and Bone Fractures

A 1990 study analyzing caffeine consumption and the incidence of hip fractures among more than three thousand elderly men and women found that those who reported drinking 2.5 to 3 cups of caffeinated coffee or 5 to 6 cups of caffeinated tea per day had a 69 percent greater risk of osteoporosis (bone loss and brittleness) than caffeine abstainers. Those who reported drinking more than 3.5 cups of caffeinated coffee or 7 cups of caffeinated tea had an 82 percent greater risk. Because one of the effects of caffeine is to increase the urinary excretion

The known stimulant effect of caffeine on cardiac muscle has raised suspicions about the potential risk of a heart attack due to coffee intake. As described in this chapter, the medical findings are often confusing, and a number of explanations have been advanced to explain contradictions in the data.

A major study points to the role of an enzyme that controls the metabolism of caffeine in the body. Researchers studied 2,000 patients who had suffered heart attacks and 2,000 healthy subjects. Analysis of their DNA revealed a gene sequence that allowed caffeine to break down up to four times more slowly than normally. Individuals with the relatively "slow" version of this gene had an increased risk of a heart attack with as little as two cups of coffee per day. However, those individuals with the relatively "fast" version had no increased risk, even with four or more cups per day. Indeed, for individuals younger than 50 years of age who had the fast version of the gene, the consumption of one to three cups per day was associated with a *lower* risk. In other words, for this particular group, caffeine had a protective effect with respect to a potential heart attack.

The stimulant effect of caffeine on the nervous system is not related to this particular gene sequence, so whether individuals had the slow or the fast version did not change their behavioral response to coffee. Nonetheless, the increasing attention being paid to genomic variations among individuals is certain to shed light on previously inconclusive medical research concerning the health risks of various orally administered drugs (see Chapter 3).

Source: Cornelis, M. C.; El-Sohemy, A.; Kabagambe, E. K.; and Campos, H. (2006). Coffee, CYP1A2 genotype, and risk of myocardial infarction. *Journal of the American Medical Association, 295,* 1135–1141.

---

of calcium and to inhibit the absorption of calcium from the diet in the elderly, it makes sense that there might be an adverse effect on bone tissue in this age group.[27]

Breast Disease

A 1981 report indicated a relationship between caffeine consumption and the formation of benign (that is, non-cancerous) lumps in the breasts called *fibrocystic lesions.* However, the study was severely criticized as not being based on randomized sampling and as not having methodological controls that would shield the researchers from imposing their bias in observing fibrocystic lesion cases. Subsequent studies that were more carefully executed showed no relationship between the incidence of this frequently painful condition and caffeine consumption.[28]

Effects during Pregnancy and Breastfeeding

At one time, caffeine use was suspected to be linked to infertility in women. A study in 1990 reported that women who consumed three cups of coffee a day reduced their chances of getting pregnant by 25 percent. More recent studies, however, have found no relationship between caffeine intake and infertility.[29]

Nonetheless, there can be potential problems later in pregnancy. Caffeine consumption (more than three or four cups of coffee a day) during the first three months of pregnancy is related to a greater incidence of low birth weight in the newborn, although the incidence of premature birth or birth defects is not increased. There is also a relationship between very high levels of caffeine consumption (more than six cups of coffee per day) during pregnancy and an increased risk of miscarriage. Therefore, the cautionary advice of the FDA is warranted: Women should abstain from caffeine if at all possible during pregnancy.[30]

Afterward, in the case of breastfeeding, it is also a good idea to continue a caffeine-free diet. Enzymes that normally break down caffeine in the liver are not present in the liver of a newborn baby, and as a consequence, the elimination half-life of caffeine is much longer than in the adult—up to eighty-five hours. Although there is no evidence of specific harm from having a stimulant such as caffeine in the nervous system for such intervals of time, it seems to be a situation that might well be avoided.[31]

Panic Attacks

Consumption of caffeine equivalent to about four to five cups of coffee a day has been associated with the onset of panic attacks in those individuals suffering from a panic disorder. This finding is consistent with the known effects of caffeine as a CNS stimulant. Any person with a history of panic attacks should be careful to avoid caffeine, and mental health professionals should be aware of the possibility that caffeine consumption could trigger a panic episode.[32]

Dependence, Acute Toxicity, and Medical Applications

More than 85 percent of the adult U.S. population consume caffeine in one form or another each day. The average daily intake of caffeine among caffeine consumers is about 280 mg, equivalent roughly to three standard cups of coffee. Estimates of daily caffeine intake in Europe and other nations of the world are considerably higher. Clearly, caffeine consumption is a cultural norm in the United States and the rest of the world. The fact that caffeinated beverages in particular are embedded in the diet of this country makes it difficult to think of caffeine as a drug, much less one that could cause dependence.[33]

Tolerance

When individuals who do not usually use caffeine are administered repeated doses equivalent to amounts that would ordinarily be acquired from the diet, the initial increases in heart rate and blood pressure start to decline after approximately seventy-two hours.[34] In other words, with respect to the cardiovascular effects of caffeine, a classic tolerance effect, as defined in Chapter 2, can be observed.

With respect to the behavioral and psychological effects of caffeine, tolerance effects are more difficult to evaluate, despite the fact that most of us have noticed at some time in our lives that caffeine was having a progressively smaller effect on us as we started to be habitual caffeine consumers. The problem appears to be that once we are in a laboratory setting, most of us are already tolerant to the effects of caffeine. Recent studies that have specifically controlled for variations in the subject's recent dietary intake of caffeine have shown tolerance effects for dosage levels as low as 100 mg, the equivalent of one to two cups of coffee.

Withdrawal

A stronger case for caffeine being a drug that produces physical dependence comes from research findings concerning withdrawal. As you may yourself have experienced, a sudden cessation in the intake of coffee or other caffeinated products results in symptoms of headache, impaired concentration, drowsiness, irritability, muscle

aches, and other flu-like symptoms. A headache is a typical withdrawal symptom, usually appearing from twelve to eighteen hours after the last dose of caffeine, peaking over the next two days or so, and persisting in some individuals for up to a week. This pain is associated with an increase in blood flow to the brain, at levels above what a person normally experiences. A reintroduction of caffeine causes the pain and other withdrawal symptoms to disappear. One study on the pattern of withdrawal symptoms from coffee found significant symptoms even when subjects had been consuming as little as 100 mg per day.[35]

Craving

The case for physical dependence is clear; the case for psychological dependence, however, is presently uncertain. We do not know whether the tendency to have that next cup of coffee or other caffeinated product is a matter of desiring to have it or an effort to avoid withdrawal symptoms that would ensue if we did not have it.

Acute Toxicity of Caffeine

Too much caffeine can produce toxic effects on the body, but the amount that might do so is substantial and generally beyond what we typically consume. Approximately 1,000 mg of caffeine (equivalent to about ten cups of caffeinated coffee), consumed over a short period of time, results in extreme nervousness and agitation, muscle hyperactivity and twitching, profound insomnia, heart palpitations and arrhythmias, gastrointestinal upset, nausea, and diarrhea. The condition is referred to as **caffeinism**. In a few individuals, particularly those who do not typically ingest caffeine, these symptoms might arise from a much lower dose level. There is also growing concern that caffeine use might magnify emotional difficulties in mental health patients and reduce the benefits of medications they are taking.

Caffeinism is not officially recognized as a psychological disorder by the American Psychiatric Association, but the DSM-IV-TR and the newer DSM-5 manuals (see Chapter 2) define a condition called *caffeine intoxication*, resulting from a caffeine intake in excess of 250 mg and producing caffeinism-like behavioral symptoms. It is admittedly unusual to observe such behaviors from a caffeine level equivalent to two or three cups of coffee, but as the dose rises above this level, the probability of observing a toxic reaction can be expected to increase.[36]

> **caffeinism:** A dangerous state of behavioral and physiological overstimulation from a very large dose of caffeine.

The adult lethal dose is approximately 5 to 10 grams (5,000 to 10,000 mg), which is equivalent to somewhere between fifty and one hundred cups of caffeinated coffee. The lowest caffeine dose known to have been fatal in an adult is 3.2 grams (3,200 mg), administered mistakenly by a nurse who believed the syringe contained another drug. A caffeine-induced fatality was reported in 2010 following an intentional ingestion of 10,000 mg. Naturally, lethal doses for children are lower, and a number of accidental deaths have resulted from children eating large quantities of caffeine-containing medications.[37]

Prescription Drugs Based on Xanthines

Owing to the superiority of theophylline over caffeine in its ability to relax smooth muscle, theophylline has been used medically to treat a number of clinical conditions. Its application as a bronchodilator for asthmatics has been mentioned earlier. One particular medication, *aminophylline*, combines theophylline with methylediamine, an inert compound that increases the absorption of theophylline and enhances its clinical benefit. Because theophylline also stimulates cardiac muscle, it is sometimes prescribed for patients with congestive heart disease.

Caffeine and Young People: A Special Concern

There is little doubt that caffeine consumption among young people in the United States under the age of eighteen has risen significantly in the last decade or so. One reason has to do with the consumption of caffeinated soft drinks. It has been estimated that teenagers consume about sixty-four gallons of soft drinks each year, largely in caffeinated forms. Mega-sized soft drinks, sometimes with free refills, are standard offerings in fast-food restaurants and convenience stores; soft-drink vending machines that provide 20-ounce bottles, instead of 12-ounce cans, are not uncommon. You might recall a similar issue in Chapter 8, related to calculating the total amount of alcohol in a given number of alcoholic "drinks."

Another major opportunity for caffeine consumption in this age group comes from patterns of coffee drinking at coffee bars, where highly caffeinated espresso drinks served sweet, cold, and in "grande" quantities are enormously popular. Although the level of caffeine intake in multiple soft drinks and coffee may be equivalent to levels experienced by many adults, the physiological and behavioral effects are actually greater, since body weight in a younger population is only one-half to two-thirds that of an adult. In other words, the dosage level of caffeine, expressed as milligrams per kilogram (mg/kg), ends up exceeding levels typically ingested by adults (Table 11.3). In some European countries (the United Kingdom, Sweden, and Finland) per capita caffeine consumption among young people exceeds that in the United States.

The extent of caffeine consumption in this population raises some significant health concerns. Drinking caffeinated beverages instead of milk can result in obesity as well as deficient levels of calcium and phosphorus, minerals that are needed for normal bone growth during adolescence. Although research is presently lacking on the issue of whether significant caffeine consumption in the early years will lead to osteoporosis in adulthood, the research showing an increased risk among the elderly suggests that a similar risk might exist for younger people as well. Finally, the evidence is quite clear that soft-drink consumption and the substantial calorie intake associated with it have significant adverse metabolic effects, resulting in obesity and increased risk of Type 2 diabetes. Indeed, soft-drink consumption is widely viewed as a factor in the increased prevalence of childhood obesity in American youths.[38]

On a behavioral level, there are concerns about insomnia, nervousness, and anxiety among young people who ingest large amounts of caffeine. On the other hand, some evidence suggests that moderate levels of caffeine consumption may reduce the hyperactivity and impulsiveness associated with attention-deficit/hyperactivity disorder (ADHD). In this sense, caffeine acts as a CNS stimulant in much the same way as the stronger stimulant medications, such as methylphenidate (Ritalin) and amphetamine, that are prescribed for this disorder (Chapter 4).[39]

The large doses of caffeine ingested by young people on a daily basis have raised health concerns.

Drugs . . . in Focus

Energy Shots

Highly caffeinated "power drinks" such as Red Bull and Monster Energy, containing an approximate caffeine dosage of 10 mg per fluid ounce (compared to Coca-Cola Classic at 2.9 mg per fluid ounce), have become a major part of the current soft drink industry market. Recently, a new class of highly concentrated caffeinated products, so-called energy shots, have appeared on the scene, packaged in two-ounce plastic bottles. A major brand, 5-Hour Energy, has been reported to contain about 215 mg of caffeine. Sales in energy drinks in general in 2012 exceeded $10 billion, more than iced tea and sports beverages like Gatorade.

Health and nutrition professionals, however, have great concerns about young people indulging in energy-shot products. Although the product manufacturers recommend taking no more than two bottles per day, spaced several hours apart, there are no restrictions on its sale and use by the consumer. There are reports of people taking energy shots combined with alcohol as a new form of club drug. Of particular concern is the combination of energy shots with the nonmedical use of stimulant medications such as Adderall (see Chapter 4).

In 2012, the FDA disclosed that it had received reports of 13 deaths over a four-year period that cited the possible involvement of 5-Hour Energy, as well as more than 30 incidences of serious or life-threatening injuries such as heart attacks and convulsions. The reports had been submitted by the manufacturer; since 2008, when products are classified as dietary supplements (as is the case with 5-hour Energy), producers are required to make such reports when they become aware of product-related death or serious injury. Producers of energy drinks marketed as beverages (as is the case with Red Bull and similar products) are not required to do so, though they can notify the FDA on a voluntary basis. In 2010, German health authorities issued a statement warning against overconsumption of energy shots and have deemed the products unsafe.

Sources: Energyfiend.com, 2013. Garnier, L. M.; Arria, A. M.; Caldeira, K. M.; Vincent, K. B.; et al. (2009). Nonmedical prescription analgesic and concurrent alcohol consumption among college students. *American Journal of Drug and Alcohol Abuse*, 35, 334–338. Meier, B. (2013, January 2). Energy drinks promise edge, but experts say proof is scant. *New York Times*, pp. A1, B4. Meier, B. (2012, November 15). Caffeinated drink cited in reports of 13 deaths. *New York Times*, pp. B1, B10. Neuman, W. (2009, July 11). Little bottle, big punch: "Energy shots" stimulate power drink sales. *New York Times*, pp. B1, B5. Starling, S. (2010, February 4). Germans call for energy shot ban. Nutra ingredients.com.

Summary

Caffeine

- Caffeine belongs to a family of stimulant drugs called xanthines. It is found in coffee, tea, chocolate, many soft drinks, and some medications.
- Other xanthines are theophylline (found in tea) and theobromine (found in chocolate).

Coffee

- Coffee drinking originated in the Middle East and later was introduced to England in the seventeenth century. Coffee houses in Britain and in colonial America sprang up as establishments where political and social discussions could be held.
- On average, a 5-ounce cup of coffee contains roughly 100 mg of caffeine, the actual level being determined by the type of coffee beans used and the method of brewing.

Tea

- Tea drinking originated in China and later was introduced to Europe by Dutch traders in the early seventeenth century. It became most popular in Britain and Russia. Today, tea consumption is greatest in Britain and Ireland.
- On average, a 5-ounce cup of tea contains roughly 60 mg of caffeine, the actual level being determined by the method of brewing and brand.

Chocolate

- Chocolate originated in pre-Columbian Central America and was introduced into Europe by the return of Cortés to Spain in 1528. Its popularity spread across Europe in the seventeenth century. By the 1880s, techniques for producing present-day milk chocolate had been perfected.

- The caffeine level in chocolate is relatively low, roughly 6 mg per ounce.

Soft Drinks

- Caffeinated colas have most of the caffeine content added to the beverage during production. Levels of caffeine in these beverages are approximately 34–45 mg per 12 ounces.
- In recent years, a category of highly caffeinated soft-drinks (such as Red Bull and Monster Energy) has entered the market and represents currently the fastest-growing segment of the beverage industry.

Caffeine from Medications

- Like drugs, caffeine and other xanthines are stimulants of the CNS and of peripheral musculature. Theophylline, in particular, has a strong broncho-dilating effect and is useful for treating asthmatic conditions.

Caffeine as a Drug

- The behavioral effects of caffeine can be characterized principally as a reduction in fatigue and boredom, as well as a delay in the onset of sleep.
- Recent evidence suggests that caffeine might lower the risk of developing Parkinson's disease in men.

A comparable protective role in women is currently uncertain.

- Health risks from moderate consumption of caffeine are not clinically significant, except for the adverse effects on fetal development during pregnancy, the development of bone loss among the elderly, a possible adverse effect on the cardiac condition of patients already suffering from cardiovascular disease, and the aggravation of panic attacks among patients with this disorder.
- Continued consumption of caffeine produces tolerance effects; when caffeine consumption ceases, withdrawal symptoms are observed. High levels of caffeine consumption can produce toxic effects, although deaths are extremely rare.

Kids and Caffeine

- Young people in the United States ingest increasingly large quantities of caffeine through the drinking of caffeinated soft drinks and coffee. The actual dosage level is substantial, since body weight is less than that of an adult.
- Health concerns regarding caffeine consumption in this population include potential deficiencies in calcium and phosphorus for normal bone growth as well as behavioral problems such as insomnia, nervousness, and anxiety. The current popularity of highly caffeinated "energy drinks" has added to these problems.

Key Terms

adenosine, p. 283
baking chocolate, p. 280
caffeine, p. 276
caffeinism, p. 287

Camellia sinensis, p. 278
chocolate liquor, p. 280
cocoa bean pods, p. 279
cocoa butter, p. 280

Coffea arabica, p. 277
Coffea robusta, p. 277
theobromine, p. 276
theophylline, p. 276

xanthines, p. 276

Endnotes

1. Austin, G. A. (1978). *Perspectives on the history of psychoactive substance use.* Rockville, MD: National Institute on Drug Abuse, p. 50. Jacob, H. E. (1935). *Coffee: The epic of a commodity.* New York: Viking Press, pp. 3–10.
2. Robinson, E. F. (1893). *The early history of coffee houses in England.* London: Kegan Paul, p. 26. Cited in E. M. Brecher and the editors of *Consumer Reports* (1972), *Licit and illicit drugs.* Boston: Little, Brown, p. 197.
3. Ukers, W. H. (1935). *All about coffee.* New York: Tea and Coffee Trade Journal Co., p. 61. Wellman, F. L. (1961).

Coffee: Botany, cultivation, and utilization. New York: Interscience Publishers, p. 22–23.
4. International Coffee Organization, London, 2013. Pendergrast, M. (1999). *Uncommon grounds: The history of coffee and how it transformed our world.* New York: Basic Books. Starbird, E. A. (1981, March). The bonanza bean: Coffee. *National Geographic Magazine*, pp. 398–399.
5. Barone, J. J., and Roberts, H. (1984). Human consumption of caffeine. In P. B. Dews (Ed.), *Caffeine: Perspectives from recent research.* Berlin: Springer-Verlag, pp. 60–63.

6. Shalleck, J. (1972). *Tea*. New York: Viking Press.
7. MacFarlane, A., and MacFarlane, I. (2003). The empire of tea: The remarkable history of the plant that took over the world. New York: Overlook. Maitland, D. (1982). *5000 years of tea: A pictorial companion.* Hong Kong: CFW Publications Limited, pp. 80–89.
8. Gilbert, R. (1986). *Caffeine: The most popular stimulant.* New York: Chelsea House, p. 23.
9. Grosser, D. S. (1978). A study of caffeine in tea. *American Journal of Clinical Nutrition, 31,* 1727–1731.
10. Pastore, R. L., and Fratellone, P. (2006). Potential health benefits of green tea (Camellia sinensis): A narrative review. *Explore, 2,* 531-539. Shah, J. J.; Kuhn, D. J.; and Orlowski, R. Z. (2009). Bortezomib and EGCG: No green tea for you? *Blood, 113,* 5695-5696. Weinreb, O.; Mandel, S., Amit, T.; and Youdim, M. B. H. (2009). Neurological mechanisms of green tea polyphenols in Alzheimer's and Parkinson's diseases. *Journal of Nutritional Biochemistry, 2004,* 506–516. Yang, C. S.; Lambert, J. D.; and San, S. (2009). Antioxidative and anti-carcinogenic activities of tea polyphenols. *Archives of Toxicology, 83,* 11-21. Zijp, I. M.; Korver, O.; and Tijberg, L. B. M. (2000). Effect of tea and other dietary factors on iron absorption. *Critical Reviews in Food Science and Nutrition, 40,* 371–398.
11. Courtesy of the Food and Agriculture Organization (FAO) of the United Nations, 2008.
12. Morton, M., and Morton, F. (1986). *Chocolate: An illustrated history.* New York: Crown Publishers, pp. 77–87.
13. Information for 2012 courtesy of the Chocolate Manufacturers' Association and the CAOBISCO Secretariat, Brussels.
14. Apgar, J. L., and Tarka, S. M. (1998). Methylzanthine composition and consumption patterns of cocoa and chocolate products. In G. A. Spiller (Ed.), *Caffeine.* Boca Raton, FL: CRC Press, pp. 163–192. Courtesy of the Hershey Company, Hershey, PA
15. Noonan, D. (2001, May 14). Red Bull's good buzz. *Newsweek,* p. 39. Schwartz, N. D. (2012, August 29). New inquiry into energy drink firms. *New York Times,* pp. B1, B2. Substance Abuse and Mental Health Services Administration (2011, November 22). Emergency Department visits involving energy drinks. *The DAWN Report.* Rockville, MD: Substance Abuse and Mental Health Services Administration. Warner, M. (2006, March 6). Soda sales are showing their age. *New York Times,* pp. C1, C6.
16. FDA issues warning letter to makers of AeroShot "caffeine inhaler." (2012, March 6). Press Release of the U.S. Food and Drug Administration, Silver Springs, MD. Kuchment, A. (2007, July 30). Make that a double: Our desire for caffeinated "energy" products is soaring. *Newsweek,* p. 48. Shute, N. (2007, April 23). Over the limit: Americans young and old crave high-octane fuel and doctors are jittery. *Newsweek,* pp. 60–68. Tumolillo, M. A. (2010, November 17). Company to drop caffeine from alcoholic drinks. *New York Times,* p. A22.
17. Fredholm, B. B.; Bättig, K.; Homén, J.; Nehlig, A.; and Zvartau, E. E. (1999). Actions of caffeine in the brain with special reference to factors that contribute to its widespread use. *Pharmacological Reviews, 51,* 83–133. Gilbert, *Caffeine,* pp. 76–79. Julien, R. M. (2005). *A primer of drug action* (10th ed.). New York: Worth, pp. 225–231. Quinlan, P.; Lane, J.; and Aspinall, L. (1997). Effects of hot tea, coffee and water ingestion on physiological responses and mode: The role of caffeine, water, and beverage type. *Psychopharmacology, 134,* 164–173. Reid, T. R. (2005, January). Caffeine. *National Geographic Magazine,* pp. 2–32.
18. Davis, A. M.; Zhao, Z.; Stock, H. S.; Mehl, K. A.; et al. (2003). Central nervous system effects of caffeine and adenosine on fatigue. *American Journal of Physiology, 53,* R399. Schiwall, S. I. (1986, November). Asthma relief that's brewed by the cup. *Prevention, 38,* 127. Spiller, G. A. (1998). Basic metabolism and physiological effects of the methylxanthines. In G. A. Spiller (Ed.), *Caffeine.* Boca Raton, FL: CRC Press, pp. 225–231.
19. Foad, A. J.; Beedie, C. J.; and Coleman, D. A. (2008). Pharmacological and psychological effects of caffeine ingestion in 40-km cycling performance. *Medicine and Science in Sports and Exercise, 40,* 158–165.
20. Brice, C., and Smith, A. (2001). The effects of caffeine on simulated driving, subjective alertness, and sustained attention. *Human Psychopharmacology: Clinical and Experimental, 16,* 523–531. Lane, J. D., and Phillips-Bute, B. G. (1998). Caffeine deprivation affects vigilance performance and mood. Physiology and Behavior, 65, 171–175. Snel, J.; Lorist, M. M.; and Tieges, Z. (2004). Coffee, caffeine, and cognitive performance. In A. Nehlig (Ed.), *Coffee, tea, chocolate, and the brain.* Boca Raton, FL: CRC Press, pp. 53–71. Watters, P. A.; Martin, F.; and Schreter, Z. (1997). Caffeine and cognitive performance: The nonlinear Yerkes-Dodson Law. *Human Psychopharmacology: Clinical and Experimental, 12,* 249–257.
21. Curatolo, P., and Robertson, D. (1983). The health consequences of caffeine. *Annals of Internal Medicine, 98,* 641–653. Snel, J.; Lorist, M. M.; and Tieges, Z. (2004). Effects of caffeine on sleep and wakefulness: An update. In A. Nehlig (Ed.), *Coffee, tea, chocolate, and the brain.* Boca Raton, FL: CRC Press, pp. 13–33.
22. Attwood, A. S. (2012). Caffeinated alcohol beverages: A public health concern. *Alcohol and alcoholism, 47,* 370–371. Fillmore, M. T.; Roach, E. L.; and Rice, J. T. (2002). Does caffeine counteract alcohol-induced impairment? The ironic effects of expectancy. *Journal of Studies on Alcohol, 63,* 745–754.
23. Ascherio, A.; Chen, H.; Schwarzschild, M. A.; Zhang, S. M.; Colditz, C. A., et al. (2003). Caffeine, postmenopausal estrogen, and risk of Parkinson's disease. *Neurology, 60,* 790–795. Santos, C.; Lunet, N.; Azevedo, A.; de Mendoca, A.; Ritchie, K.; et al. (2010). Caffeine intake is associated with a lower risk of cognitive decline: A cohort study from Portugal. *Journal of Alzheimer's Disease, 20,* S175–S185. Schwarzschild, M. A., and Ascherio, A. (2004). Caffeine and Parkinson's disease. In A. Nehlig (Ed.), *Coffee, tea, chocolate, and the brain.* Boca Raton, FL: CRC Press, pp. 147–163.

24. Curatolo and Robertson, The health consequences of caffeine. Gierach, G. L.; Freedman, N. D.; Andaya, A.; Hollenbeck, A. R., Park, Y.; et al. (2012). Coffee intake and breast cancer risk in the NIH-AARP diet and health study cohort. *International Journal of Cancer, 131,* 452–460. Michels, K. B.; Willett, W. C.; Fuchs, C. S.; and Giovannucci, E. (2005). Coffee, tea, and caffeine consumption and incidence of colon and rectal cancer. *Journal of the National Cancer Institute, 97,* 282–292. Ishitani, K.; Lin, J.; Manson, J. E.; Buring, J. E.; and Zhang, S. M. (2008). Caffeine consumption and the risk of breast cancer in a large prospective cohort of women. *Archives of Internal Medicine, 168,* 2022–2031.

25. Jick, H.; Miettinen, O. S.; Neff, R. K.; Shapiro, S.; Heinonen, O.; et al. (1973). Coffee and myocardial infarction. *New England Journal of Medicine, 289,* 63–67. Myers, M. G. (1992, November). Caffeine under examination—A passing grade. *The Western Journal of Medicine,* pp. 586–587.

26. Bonita, J. S.; Mandarano, M.; Shuta, D.; and Vinson, J. (2007). Coffee and cardiovascular disease: *In vitro,* cellular, animal, and human studies. *Pharmacological Research, 55,* 187–198. Julien, R. M. (1998). *A primer of drug action* (8th ed.). New York: Freeman. Quotation on p. 163.

27. Bruce, B., and Spiller, G. A. (1998). Caffeine, calcium, and bone health. In G. A. Spiller (Ed.), *Caffeine.* Boca Raton, FL: CRC Press, pp. 345–356. Wetmore, C. M.; Ichikawa, L.; LaCroix, A. Z.; Ott, S. M.; and Scholes, D. (2007). Association between caffeine intake and bone mass among young women: Potential effect modification by depot medroxyprogesterone acetate use. *Osteoporosis International, 19,* 517–529.

28. Levinson, W., and Dunn, P. M. (1986). Nonassociation of caffeine and fibrocystic breast disease. *Archives of Internal Medicine, 146,* 1773–1775. Minton, J. P.; Foecking, M. K.; Webster, J. T.; and Matthews, R. H. (1979). Caffeine, cyclic nucleotides, and breast diseases. *Surgery, 86,* 105–109. Russell, L. C. (1989). Caffeine restriction as initial treatment for breast pain. *Nurse Practitioner, 14,* 36–37.

29. Caan, B.; Quesenberry, C. P.; and Coates, A., O. (1998). Differences in fertility associated with caffeinated beverage consumption. *American Journal of Public Health, 88,* 270–274. Riduan J. M.; Beral, V.; Rolfs, R. T.; Aral, S. O.; and Cramer, D. W. (1990). Are caffeinated beverages risk factors for delayed conception? *Lancet, 335,* 136–137.

30. Grady, D. (2008, January 21). Pregnancy problems tied to caffeine. *New York Times,* p. A10. Savitz, D. A.; Chan, R. L.; Herring, A. H.; Howards, P. P.; and Hartmann, K. E. (2008). Caffeine and miscarriage risk. *Epidemiology, 19,* 55–62. Weng, X.; Odouli, R.; and Li, D. K (2008). Maternal caffeine consumption during pregnancy and the risk of miscarriage: A prospective cohort study. *American Journal of Obstetrics and Gynecology, 198,* 279e1–279e8.

31. Bakker, R.; Steegers, E.; Obradov, A.; Raat, H.; Hofman, A.; et al. (2010). Maternal caffeine intake from coffee and tea, fetal grown, and the risks of adverse birth outcomes: The Generation R Study. *American Journal of Clinical Nutrition, 91,* 1691–1698. Peck, J. D.; Leviton, A.; and Cowan, L. D. (2010). A review of the epidemiologic evidence concerning the reproductive health effects of caffeine consumption: A 2000-2009 update. *Food and Chemical Toxicology, 48,* 2549–2576.

32. Charney, D. S.; Heniger, G. R.; and Jatlow, P. L. (1985). Increased anxiogenic effects of caffeine in panic disorders. *Archives of General Psychiatry, 42,* 233–243.

33. Juliano, L. M., and Griffiths, R. R. (2004). A critical review of caffeine withdrawal: Empirical validation of symptoms and signs, incidence, severity, and associated features. *Psychopharmacology, 176,* 1–29.

34. Robertson, D.; Wade, D.; Workman, R.; and Woosley, R. L. (1981). Tolerance to the humoral and hemodynamic effects of caffeine in man. *Journal of Clinical Investigation, 67,* 1111–1117.

35. Nehlig, A. (2004). Dependence upon coffee and caffeine: An update. In A. Nehlig (Ed.), *Coffee, tea, chocolate, and the brain.* Boca Raton, FL: CRC Press, pp. 133–145. Sigmon, S. C.; Herning, R. L.; Better, W.; Cadet, J. L.; and Griffiths, R. R. (2009). Caffeine withdrawal, acute effects, tolerance, and absence of net beneficial effects of chronic administration: Cerebral blood flow velocity, quantitative EEG, and subjective effects. *Psychopharmacology, 204,* 573–585. Stiley, C. L. W.; Griffiths, R. R.; and Cottler, L. B. (2011). Evaluating dependence criteria for caffeine. *Journal of Caffeine Research, 1,* 219–225.

36. American Psychiatric Association (2000). *Diagnostic and statistical manual of mental disorders (DSM-IV)* (4th ed.). *Text Revision.* Washington, DC: American Psychiatric Association, p. 232. American Psychiatric Association (2013). *Diagnostic and statistical manual of mental disorders (DSM-5)* (5th ed.). Washington, DC: American Psychiatric Association.

37. Gilbert, *Caffeine,* pp. 108–109. Rudolph, T., and Knudsen, K. (2001). A case of caffeine poisoning. *Acta Anaesthesiologica Scandinavica, 54,* 521–523.

38. Dhingra, R.; Sullivan, L.; Jacques, P. F.; Wang, T. J.; Fox, C. S.; et al. (2007). Soft drink consumption and risk of developing cardiometabolic risk factors and the metabolic syndrome in middle-aged adults in the community. *Circulation, 116,* 480–488.

39. Cordes, H. (1998, April 27). Generation wired. *The Nation,* pp. 11–16. Heatherley, S. V.; Hancock, K. M. F.; and Rogers, P. J. (2006). Psychostimulant and other effects of caffeine in 9- to 11-year-old children. *Journal of Child Psychology and Psychiatry, 47,* 135–142. James, J. E.; Kristjansson, A. L., and Sigfusdottir, I. D. (2011). Adolescent substance use, sleep, and academic achievement: Evidence of harm due to caffeine. *Journal of Adolescence, 34,* 665–673. Pollak, C. P., and Bright, D. (2003). Caffeine consumption and weekly sleep patterns in U.S. seventh-, eighth-, and ninth-graders. *Pediatrics, 111,* 42–46.

Performance-Enhancing Drugs and Drug Testing in Sports

After you have completed this chapter, you should have an understanding of

- The history of performance-enhancing drugs in sports
- How anabolic steroids work
- The health risks of steroid abuse
- Patterns of steroid abuse
- Performance-enhancing nonsteroid hormones
- Dietary supplements marketed as performance-enhancing aids
- Nonmedical use of stimulant medications in baseball
- Present-day drug testing in amateur and professional sports

Have I used steroids? You bet I did. Did steroids make me a better baseball player? Of course they did. If I had it all to do over again, would I live a steroid-enriched life? Yes, I would. Do I have any regrets or qualms about relying on chemicals to help me hit a baseball so far? To be honest, no, I don't.

—*José Canseco,* Juiced *(2005)*

. . . .I was immature and I was stupid . . . I blame myself. . . . I knew we weren't taking Tic Tacs.

—*Alex Rodriguez (2009),* On admitting steroid use during the 2001–2003 baseball seasons[1]

I think she [Pat Maris] was shocked that I called her. I felt that I needed to do that. They've been such great supporters of me. She was disappointed, and she has every right to be. I couldn't tell her how so sorry I was.

—*Mark McGwire (2010),* On apologizing to Roger Maris's widow prior to admitting steroid use during the 1990s[2]

For the modern-day athlete in a high-pressure world of competitive sports, running a hundredth of a second faster can mean the difference between an Olympic gold medal and a silver; throwing a javelin a few centimeters farther, lifting a kilogram more, or hitting a baseball a few feet farther can make you either the champion or an also-ran. The stakes have never been higher. The winning edge might be a matter of a novel technique in training, a new attitude toward winning, a special diet—or the use of drugs. This chapter focuses on issues surrounding performance-enhancing drugs in the world of sports, with particular attention to the abuse of anabolic steroids. We will also look at the continuing efforts by regulatory organizations at both the local and international levels to develop testing procedures to detect the presence of such drugs in the athlete's body.

The use of performance-enhancing drugs is a concern not only among athletes who are in the public eye but also among a growing number of young people who simply want to look better by developing their muscles. The serious dangers in such drug-taking behavior, whether the motivation lies in competitive drive or in personal vanity, are major problems that need to be explored. As we will see, performance-enhancing drugs have been part of competitive sports for a very long time.

Drug-Taking Behavior in Sports

The first recorded athletic competition, the Olympic Games in ancient Greece, is also the place where we find the first recorded use of psychoactive drugs in sports. As early as 300 B.C., Greek athletes ate hallucinogenic mushrooms, either to improve their performance in the competition or to achieve some kind of mystical connection to the gods. Later, Roman gladiators and charioteers used stimulants to sustain themselves longer in competition, even when injured.

By the end of the nineteenth century, world-class athletes were experimenting with a variety of stimulant and depressant drugs, including cocaine, caffeine, alcohol, nitroglycerine, opioids, strychnine, and amphetamines. In 1886, while competing in a cross-country race, a Welsh cyclist died of an overdose of a combination of morphine and cocaine (now referred to as a speedball), the first drug-related death ever recorded in sports. During the 1904 Olympics, U.S. marathoner Tom Hicks

ergogenic (ER-go-JEN-ik): Performance-enhancing.

androgenic (AN-droh-JEN-ik): Acting to promote masculinizing changes in the body.

collapsed after winning the race and lost consciousness. When he was revived, doctors were told that he had taken a potentially lethal mixture of strychnine (a CNS stimulant when administered in low doses) and brandy.

With the introduction in the 1930s of anabolic steroid drugs specifically patterned after the male sex hormone testosterone, however, a new element entered the arena of competitive sports. Here was a class of performance-enhancing drugs that did more than alter the behavior or experience of the athlete; these particular drugs actually altered the structure of the athlete's body.

Anabolic steroid drugs had been studied since the 1930s as a treatment for anemia (low red blood cell count) and for conditions that caused muscles to waste away. Following the end of World War II, steroid drugs were administered to people who were near death from starvation and weight loss. It quickly became apparent, however, that steroids could be useful when given to otherwise healthy individuals as well. As pharmaceutical companies began to introduce dozens of new body-building drugs based on the testosterone molecule, it was natural that information about anabolic steroids would come to the attention of athletes, as well as their coaches and trainers.[3]

What Are Anabolic Steroids?

To understand how testosterone-based steroids produce ergogenic (performance-enhancing) changes, we first have to recognize that testosterone itself has two primary effects on the human body. The first and most obvious effect is **androgenic** (literally, "man-producing"), in that the hormone promotes the development of male sex characteristics. As testosterone levels rise during puberty, boys acquire an enlarged larynx (resulting in a deeper voice), body hair, and an increase in body size, as well as genital changes that make them sexually mature adults. The second effect is **anabolic** (upward-changing), in that it promotes the development of protein and, as a result, an increase in muscle tissue. Muscles in men are inherently larger than muscles in women because of the anabolic action of testosterone in the male body.

Steroid drugs based on alterations in the testosterone molecule are therefore called **anabolic-androgenic steroids**. Obviously, with respect to performance-enhancement, the goal has been to develop drugs that emphasize the anabolic function while retaining as little of the androgenic function as possible. For that reason, they are most often called simply **anabolic steroids**. Unfortunately, as we will see, it has not been possible to develop a testosterone-derived drug without at least some androgenic effects (Table 12.1).

It is important that anabolic steroids not be confused with **adrenocortical steroids**, drugs that are patterned after glucocorticoid hormones secreted by the adrenal gland. The major drug of this latter type is *hydrocortisone* (brand name, among others: Hydrocortone injection or tablets). The molecular structure of these drugs qualifies them to belong to the steroid family, but there is no relationship to testosterone or any testosterone-like effects. Adrenocortical steroids are useful in the medical treatment of tissue inflammation; in sports; they reduce the inflammation associated with muscle injuries. Their effects on muscle development can be viewed as *catabolic* (downward-changing), in that they produce a weakening of the muscles, an obviously undesirable option for athletes on a long-term basis.[4]

Anabolic Steroids at the Modern Olympic Games

Steroid use was clearly out in the open during the 1968 Olympic Games in Mexico City. An estimated one-third of the entire U.S. track and field team, not merely the strength-event and field-event competitors but sprinters and middle-distance runners as well, were using anabolic steroids. Any controversy over their use, however, did not concern the appropriateness or morality of taking steroids, only which particular steroids worked best.

TABLE 12.1

Anabolic steroids

TYPE OF STEROID	GENERIC NAME	BRAND NAME
Oral	danazol	Danocrine
	drostanolone	Masteron
	methandrostenolone	Dianabol
	methyltestosterone	Android, Testred, Virilon
	oxandrolone	Oxandrin, Anavar
	oxymetholone*	Anadrol
	stanozolol	Winstrol
Intramuscular injection	nandrolone decanoate	Deca-Durabolin IM
	nandrolone phenpropionate	Durabolin IM
	testosterone proprionate*	Testex IM
	testosterone enantrate*	Delatestryl IM
Transdermal patch	testosterone	Androderm transdermal system, Testoderm transdermal system

Note: Anabolic steroids are Schedule III controlled substances. As such, they are considered illicit drugs under federal guidelines when not obtained with a medical prescription and restricted to medical use along with other Schedule III controlled substances. Several "brand names" marketed for performance-enhancing purposes are combinations of various steroids.

*Approved outside the United States.

Sources: Julien, R. M. (2005). *A primer of drug action* (10th ed.). New York: Worth, p. 631. National Institute on Drug Abuse (2000, April). Anabolic steroids. *Community drug alert bulletin.* Bethesda, MD: National Institute on Drug Abuse. *Physicians' desk reference* (67th ed.) (2013). Montvale, NJ: PDR Network.

anabolic (AN-ah-BALL-ik): Acting to promote protein growth and muscle development.

anabolic-androgenic steroids: Drugs that promote masculinizing changes in the body and increase muscle development.

anabolic steroids: Drugs patterned after the testosterone molecule that promote masculine changes in the body and increased muscle development. The full name is "anabolic-androgenic steroids."

adrenocortical steroids: A group of hormones secreted by the adrenal glands. Their anti-inflammatory action makes them useful for treating arthritis and muscle injuries.

Strength-event athletes were taking at least two to five times the therapeutic recommendations (based on the original intent of replacing body protein). The following year, an editor of *Track and Field News* dubbed anabolic steroids "the breakfast of champions." In 1971, one U.S. weight lifter commented, in reference to his Soviet rival,

> Last year the only difference between me and him was I couldn't afford his drug bill. Now I can. When I hit Munich [in 1972] I'll weigh in at about 340, or maybe 350. Then we'll see which is better, his steroids or mine.[5]

In the meantime, the notable masculine features of many female athletes from eastern European countries in the 1960s and 1970s, not to mention the number of Olympic records that were suddenly broken, prompted many observers to ask whether they were either men disguised as women or genetic "mistakes." Questions about the unusually deep voices of East German women swimmers prompted their coach, at one point, to respond, "We came here to swim, not to sing."

From information that subsequently came to light, we now know that the effects were due to large doses of steroids. Until the late 1980s, the East German government was conducting a scientific program specifically to develop new steroid formulations that would benefit their national athletes and, at the same time, would be undetectable by standard drug screening procedures. In 2000, the principal physician in the East German Swimming Federation at the time when these steroids were being administered was convicted on charges that from 1975 to 1985 the program caused bodily harm to more than four dozen young female swimmers.[6]

The 2000 Summer Olympic Games in Sydney, Australia, instituted the strictest drug-testing procedures to date for all competing athletes. For the first time, a specific phrase was inserted into the Olympic Oath, recited by all athletes at the beginning of the games: ". . . committing ourselves to a sport without doping and without drugs."

In 2004, the World Anti-Doping Code was created. It included an agreed-upon list of prohibited performance-enhancing drugs and performance-enhancing methods in international sports competitions, testing procedures for their use, and specific penalties for violations. Under the auspices of the World Anti-Doping Agency (WADA), rules and regulations have been formally accepted by more than 200 National Olympic Committees, as well as by professional leagues (such as the National Basketball Association and the National Hockey League) representing the United States in the

Russian pentathlon champion Nadezhda Tkachenko was one of several world-class female athletes in the 1970s who later tested positive for anabolic steroids.

Olympic Games and other international competitions. The Code has been updated over the years as the development and availability of new drugs of this kind have changed.

Although the 2012 Olympic Games in London were the first in recent history to report no incidences of performance-enhancing drug use among competing athletes, drug-related scandals in sports continue. In 2012, the United States Anti-Doping Agency announced that international cycling champion Lance Armstrong would be banned for life from cycling and stripped of his seven Tour de France titles as well as his bronze medal from the 2000 Olympic Games, after finding that Armstrong had used red-blood-cell booster erythropoietin (EPO), testosterone, corticosteroids and masking agents, as well as engaging in the trafficking of performance-enhancing drugs and participating in a widespread cover-up of doping activities. In 2013, after years of denials, Armstrong admitted using performance-enhancing drugs during his cycling career (Portrait).[7]

Lance Armstrong—From Honor to Dishonor

The athletic and personal record of professional cyclist Lance Armstrong has made him an icon in modern-day sports. He won the Tour de France a record seven consecutive times between 1999 and 2005. In 1997, barely a year after his diagnosis of testicular cancer that had spread to his brain and lungs, Armstrong had conquered it through surgery and chemotherapy. He was the founder of the Lance Armstrong Foundation for cancer support and was instrumental in raising more than 500 million dollars for the cause. By 2009 he had returned to competitive cycling, finishing third in the Tour de France of that year. Armstrong himself referred to his life as a "mythic, perfect story."

It was in 2012 that it came apart. Shortly after his decision to renew his entry in the triathlon competitions (he had been in triathlon competition earlier in his life), the United States Anti-Doping Agency (USADA) charged Armstrong with a longstanding record of having used illicit performance-enhancing drugs. In other words, the USADA was charging him with doping. Two months later, the agency imposed a lifetime ban from athletic competition.

Armstrong never appealed the USADA decision that effectively ended his career. Unlike other athletes for whom suspicions of performance-enhancing drug use have made them live only under a shadow of doubt that their achievements were warranted, there would not be an asterisk in the record books for Lance Armstrong; there would be nothing in the official record books to acknowledge his achievements in the first place. The name of the foundation he created would now simply known as the LIVESTRONG Foundation, severing all ties to Armstrong. Nonetheless, for a time, Armstrong continued to deny the accusations against him, as he had done through most of his career.

In January of 2013, on a televised interview, Oprah Winfrey asked Armstrong whether he had used during his cycling career performance-enhancing drugs and blood-transfusions (specifically prohibited in competitive sports since 2000). He replied with a simple "yes." What followed was a series of measured responses. No details were revealed, no names of teammates or other sports associates were mentioned, nor did he elaborate on the ways he had managed through his career to evade the authorities.

After years of denial, Armstrong's less-than-complete confession of guilt has been viewed as too little and too late. He is a *persona non grata* in the world of sports, and he faces the possibility of major lawsuits from the investors in his professional cycling team. It is unclear where it will end.

Sources: Austin, I. (2013, January 19). Armstrong's critics largely unmoved by interview. *New York Times*, p. D2. Macur, J. (2013, January 20). As Armstrong decides next move, agencies are watching. *New York Times*, p. SP4.

Anabolic Steroids in Professional and Collegiate Sports

The widespread use of anabolic steroids in international athletics in the 1960s quickly filtered down to sports closer to home. Trainers in the National Football League began to administer anabolic steroids to their players. By the 1970s and 1980s, virtually all the NFL teams were familiar with these drugs. Estimates of how many NFL players were on anabolic steroids varied from 50 to 90 percent. We will never know the full extent of the practice, but it was certainly substantial.

Several professional football players remarked at the time that their steroid use had begun while they were playing on collegiate teams, and indeed, football players in several colleges and universities during the 1980s were implicated in steroid use. Football players were not alone in this regard. Use of anabolic steroids had found its way into other collegiate and even high school sports, including track and field, baseball, basketball, gymnastics, lacrosse, swimming, volleyball, wrestling, and tennis. It is fair to say that until the late 1980s, when screening procedures became commonplace, there was no sport, professional or amateur, for which the use of anabolic steroids was not an accepted element in athletic training programs.[8]

Performance-Enhancing Drug Abuse and Baseball

Record-breaking home-run performances in the late 1990s and early 2000s raised suspicions that these achievements in baseball were due not solely to athletic prowess but to some pharmacological assistance as well. Matters were made worse by the fact that major league baseball (MLB) had stood apart from other professional sports in the United States and sports organizations around the world by failing to establish regulatory policies regarding steroid abuse and the use of other performance-enhancing drugs.

In 2004, a prominent track coach, two executives of BALCO, a nutritional supplements laboratory in California, and the personal trainer for outfielder Barry Bonds were indicted on charges of illegally distributing steroids and other performance-enhancing drugs to dozens of professional athletes in baseball and other sports. In a subsequent development, a New York Mets clubhouse assistant pleaded guilty to having supplied performance-enhancing drugs to dozens of current and former major MLB players and their associates between 1995 and 2005, and subsequently laundering the proceeds from these transactions.

Under intense pressure from public opinion and from government officials, the MLB players union agreed in early 2005 to a policy of steroid testing that was more in line with those of the National Football League and the National Basketball Association. In late 2005, MLB penalties for steroid use were stiffened. Testing procedures and penalties for the use of amphetamine and other stimulants, which had been omitted from consideration in the earlier agreement, were added and later extended to minor league players (see Drugs . . . in Focus).

Despite changes in policy with regard to performance-enhancing drugs in MLB baseball, it became evident that these kinds of abuses had not ended. In 2007, a major investigation under the direction of former U.S. senator and federal prosecutor

Drugs . . . in Focus

Suspension Penalties for Performance-Enhancing Drug Use in Sports

The 2005 agreement on regulations against performance-enhancing drug use in major league baseball (MLB) included a ban on "all substances regarded now, or in the future, by the federal government as steroids" as well as human growth hormone and steroid precursor hormones such as androstenedione. Suspension penalties for positive-test infractions under these new regulations are shown in comparison to previous MLB regulations and those of other U.S. and international athletic organizations. In 2013, MLB announced an expansion of their drug-testing program, with players required to undergo in-season (as opposed to spring-training and off-season) blood testing for human growth hormone as well as a new test for synthetic testosterone.

	POSITIVE TEST				
	First	Second	Third	Fourth	Fifth
Major League Baseball					
Pre-2005	counseling	15 days	25 days	50 days	1 year
Late 2005	50 games	100 games	lifetime suspension, with right of reinstatement after two years		
Minor League Baseball	15 days	30 days	60 days	1 year	lifetime
National Football League	4 games	6 games	1 year	1 year	1 year
National Basketball Association	5 games	10 games	25 games	25 games	25 games
National Hockey League			—no testing for steroids—		
World Anti-Doping Association (Olympic sports)	2 years	lifetime			

Sources: Curry, J. (2006, November 16). Baseball lacks stiffer penalties for steroid use. *New York Times,* pp. A1, D2. Schmidt, M. S. (2013, January 13). Baseball to expand drug-testing program. *New York Times,* pp. B13, B17. Schmidt, M. S. (2010, February 24). Baseball plans to start testing for human growth hormone in minors. *New York Times,* p. B11. NFL will ban amphetamines as enhancers (2006, June 28). *Newsday,* p. A53.

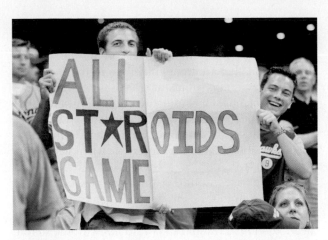

Fans expressed their opinion on steroid use at Major League Baseball's All-Star Game in 2002. Between 5 and 7 percent of MLB players tested positive for anabolic steroids when randomized screening was conducted during spring training in 2003. Players involved in steroid use have been dubbed "the syringe generation."

George J. Mitchell concluded that MLB policies had reduced the use of steroids but that other, nonsteroid performance-enhancing drugs, particularly human growth hormone, had increased in popularity and were widely used. In 2011, Barry Bonds was convicted of one felony count of obstruction of justice in connection with BALCO investigations, although acquitted of charges of perjury. In 2012, pitcher Roger Clemens was found not guilty of lying to Congress in 2008, when he testified that he never administered performance-enhancing drugs during his baseball career. Whether there will be future high-profile trials of this type remains to be seen.[9]

The Hazards of Anabolic Steroids

One of the problems in evaluating the adverse effects of steroid abuse is that the dosage levels can vary over an enormous range. Since nonmedical steroid use is illegal, it is virtually impossible to know the exact dosage levels or even the exact combinations of steroids a particular individual may be taking. It is estimated that a "typical" body builder on anabolic steroids takes in a minimum of five to twenty-nine times the therapeutic doses recommended for the medical use of these drugs, but in some cases, the estimates have gone as high as

a hundred to a thousand times the recommended therapeutic dose.[10]

Effects on Hormonal Systems

At these huge dosages, anabolic steroids are literally flooding into the body, upsetting the delicate balance of hormones and other chemicals that are normally controlled by testosterone. The primary effect in men is for the testes gland to react to the newly increased testosterone levels in the blood by producing *less* testosterone on its own. In other words, the gland is getting the incorrect message that its services are no longer needed. As a result, the testicles shrink, and a lower sperm count leads to sterility, reversible for most men but irreversible in a small number of cases. Paradoxically, the male breasts enlarge (a condition called **gynecomastia**) because steroids break down eventually into estradiol, the female sex hormone. Other related consequences include frequent, sustained, and often painful penile erections (a condition called **priapism**) and an enlargement of the prostate gland. Severe acne, particularly on the shoulders and back, results from an increase in the secretions of the sebaceous glands in the skin. Other testosterone-related effects include two changes in hair growth patterns: increased facial hair growth and accelerated balding on the top of the head.

Some athletes have attempted to counter these undesirable hormonal effects by combining anabolic steroids with human chorionic gonadotropin (HCG), a hormone that ordinarily stimulates the testes to secrete testosterone. In theory, this strategy can work, but the dosages have to be carefully controlled, something that self-medicating athletes are unlikely to do. Repeated HCG treatments actually can have the opposite effect from the one that is intended, making matters worse rather than better. In addition, HCG itself has its own adverse effects, including headaches, mood swings, depression, and retention of fluids.[11]

Among women taking anabolic steroids, the dramatically increased levels of testosterone in bodies that normally have only trace amounts produce major physiological changes, only some of which return to normal when steroids are withdrawn. Table 12.2 lists the major reversible and irreversible effects among women.

gynecomastia (GUY-neh-coh-MAST-ee-ah): An enlargement of the breasts.

priapism (PRY-ah-pih-zem): A condition marked by persistent and frequently painful penile erections.

Whether or not aided by performance-enhancing drugs, massive development of musculature continues to be a prized asset in competitive bodybuilding.

Effects on Other Systems of the Body

Given the fact that the liver is the primary mechanism for clearing drugs from the body (see Chapter 3), it is

TABLE 12.2

Reported side effects of anabolic steroids in ten women

EFFECT	NUMBER REPORTING THE EFFECT	REVERSIBLE AFTER END OF USE
Lower voice	10	no
Increased facial hair	9	no
Enlarged clitoris	8	no
Increased aggressiveness	8	yes
Increased appetite	8	unknown
Decreased body fat	8	unknown
Diminished or stopped menstruation	7	yes
Increased sexual drive	6	yes
Increased acne	6	yes
Decreased breast size	5	unknown
Increased body hair	5	no
Increased loss of scalp hair	2	no

Note: The ten women were all weight-trained athletes.

Sources: Strauss, R. H., and Yesalis, C. E. (1993). Additional effects of anabolic steroids in women. In C. E. Yesalis (Ed.), *Anabolic steroids in sport and exercise.* Champaign, IL: Human Kinetics Publishers, pp. 151–160. Strauss, R. H.; Ligget, M. T.; and Lanese R. R. (1985). Anabolic steroid use and perceived effects in ten weight-trained women athletes. *Journal of the American Medical Association, 253,* 2871–2873.

not surprising that large doses of anabolic steroids take their toll on this organ. The principal result is a greatly increased risk of developing liver tumors. The type of liver tumors that are frequently seen in these circumstances are benign (noncancerous) blood-filled cysts, with the potential for causing liver failure. In addition, a rupture in these cysts can produce abdominal bleeding, requiring life-saving emergency treatment. Fortunately, these liver abnormalities are reversible when steroids are withdrawn from use.

There is evidence from animal studies that increased steroid levels in the body can produce high blood pressure and high cholesterol levels, as well as heart abnormalities. In human studies, chronic steroid abuse has been associated with an increased risk of cardiovascular disease. There are documented cases of heart-related sudden death among athletes who have been steroid users, even though there was no history of illness or any family history that would predispose them to heart trouble. Cardiac abnormalities such as enlargement of the left ventricle are not reversible when steroid use is discontinued.[12]

Psychological Problems

Stories abound of mood swings and increased aggressiveness, often referred to by athletes as 'roid rage, when taking anabolic steroids. Numerous anecdotal reports force us to consider the possibility that real psychological changes are going on.[13]

Beyond the well-publicized anecdotal reports, however, more rigorous laboratory investigations into the relationship between anabolic steroid use and psychological problems are needed to provide a better understanding of the phenomenon. In a major study addressing this issue, a group of male volunteers were randomly administered intramuscular injections of either testosterone cyprinate or a placebo over a period of twenty-five weeks. All of them were screened for current or prior psychological problems. One subgroup was engaged in weight training but had no prior history of steroid use. A second subgroup had no training experience and had not used steroids. A third group reported a history of steroid use but had refrained from any use for a minimum of three months prior to the beginning of the study.

The results showed that, on average, testosterone significantly increased manic behavior and feelings of aggressiveness, but the individual reactions were quite variable. Only eight of the fifty men in the study showed any mood changes at all. Two of them showed marked symptoms. One of these men experienced an aggressive outburst at work and, on one occasion, reacted to being cut off in traffic by following the person in his car for several miles. The other man developed extreme euphoria and reported a decreased need for sleep. Six other study participants showed more moderate changes. One man in this category found himself wanting to beat up his opponent in a college sports competition, even though he had never had such aggressive feelings before in the course of a game. All of the other participants in the study showed minimal or no effects, and in no case was there an incident of actual violent behavior. Neither previous steroid use nor regular weight training was associated with the symptoms observed in the men responding to testosterone.

Because the study used a double-blind design, neither the experimenters nor the men being studied knew whether they were being injected with testosterone or a placebo (see Chapter 3); half of the men started with the active drug condition, and half started with the placebo condition. Therefore, in interpreting the results, we can eliminate any possible influences of expectations and preconceptions about what different behaviors and experiences might result from anabolic steroids. On the basis of this information, mood changes and aggressiveness seem genuinely to result from an elevation in testosterone levels, although the reactions of people taking anabolic steroids are far from uniform. It has been estimated, by extrapolating from the available research literature, that somewhere between 2 and 20 percent of men will develop mood-related psychological problems from anabolic steroid use.

However, it is important to realize that experimental studies *underestimate* the extent of the phenomenon in the real world. In the study reported here, the maximum dosage of testosterone was 600 mg per week. In actual practice, steroid abusers often take drugs that boost testosterone to as much as 1,000 to 1,500 mg per week—levels that far exceed those that can be safely studied in the laboratory. As a consequence, the percentage of individuals developing significant mood changes and behavioral problems is likely to be much higher, and the changes and problems themselves can be expected to be substantially greater.[14]

Special Problems for Adolescents

During puberty, a particularly crucial process among boys is growth of the long bones of the body, which results in an increase in height. Anabolic steroids suppress growth hormones; as a result, muscular development is enhanced but overall body growth is stunted. Among girls, testosterone-related drugs delay the onset

of puberty, making the body shorter, lighter, and more "girl-like," while enhancing the user's overall strength. On a psychological level, feelings of euphoria and aggression that adolescents experience while using anabolic steroids can be replaced by lethargy, loss of confidence, and depression when these drugs are discontinued.[15]

Patterns of Anabolic Steroid Abuse

In 1990, as a response to increasing awareness of the abuse of anabolic steroids both in and outside of competitive sports, Congress passed the Anabolic Steroid Control Act, reclassifying anabolic steroids as Schedule III controlled substances. Jurisdiction was transferred from the Food and Drug Administration (FDA) to the Drug Enforcement Administration (DEA). As a result of this legislation, pharmacies are permitted to fill anabolic-steroid prescriptions only up to a maximum of five times. Penalties for violating the law can result in a five-year prison term and a $250,000 fine for illegal nonmedical sales, and a one-year term and a $1,000 fine for nonmedical possession. Penalties are doubled for repeated offenses or for selling these drugs to minors. States are permitted to draft their own laws regarding the definition of anabolic steroids and to set sentencing guidelines for steroid offenders. Although most states follow the federally mandated Schedule III classification, New York lists steroids in Schedule II, while other states have their own classification systems. In some states, possession of small quantities of steroids is regarded as a misdemeanor; other states regard it as a felony. In most but not all states, first-time offenses do not result in imprisonment, unless there are aggravating circumstances, such as possession of large quantities or evidence of intent to sell or distribute the drugs.[16]

Despite the regulations now in effect, steroid abuse today remains a major problem. Steroid distribution has become an enormous black-market enterprise. With their use commonly referred to as being "on the juice," these drugs are channeled principally through people associated with body-building gyms and through Internet web sites that frequently change a company's name and location in an effort to stay one step ahead of the law. Some Internet-based suppliers include a warning on their web sites, "Due to their profound effects and potencies, it is recommended to seek the guidance of a physician prior to use," to protect themselves from liability, although few if any customers would voluntarily divulge their steroid abuse, much less seek medical guidance.

It is estimated that the illicit anabolic steroid market is valued at between $300 million and $400 million each year, and the drugs are smuggled into the United States from Europe, Canada, and Mexico. In 2011, the University of Michigan survey reported that between 1 and 2 percent of eighth graders, tenth graders, and high school seniors had used anabolic steroids in their lifetime.[17]

The Potential for Steroid Dependence

Some anabolic steroids can be taken orally and others through intramuscular injections, but abusers often administer a combination of both types in a practice called *stacking*. Hard-core abusers may take a combination of three to five different pills and injectables simultaneously, or they may consume any steroid that is available ("shotgunning"), with the total exceeding a dozen. In addition to the complications that result

muscle dysmorphia (dis-MORF-ee-ah): The perception of one's own body as small and weak and of one's musculature as inadequately developed, despite evidence to the contrary. Also known as megorexia, the condition of muscle dysmorphia is a form of body dysmorphic disorder.

from so many different types of steroids being taken at the same time, multiple injections into the buttocks or thighs, with 1.5-inch needles (called "darts" or "points"), are painful and inevitably leave scars. If these needles are shared, as they frequently are, the risk of hepatitis or HIV contamination is significant.

Steroid abusers often follow a pattern called *cycling*, in which steroids are taken for periods lasting from four to eighteen weeks, the "on" periods being separated by "off" periods of abstinence. Unfortunately, when the drugs are withdrawn, the newly developed muscles tend to "shrink up," throwing the abuser into a panic that his or her body is losing the gains that have been achieved. In addition, abstinence from steroids can lead to signs of depression, such as problems sleeping, lack of appetite, and general moodiness. All these effects encourage a return to steroids, frequently in even larger doses, and generate a craving for the euphoria that the person felt while on them.

A variation of the cycling pattern is the practice of *pyramiding*. An individual starts with low doses of steroids, gradually increases the doses over several weeks prior to an athletic competition, and then tapers off entirely before the competition itself in an attempt to escape detection during drug testing. However, pyramiding leads to the same problems during abstinence and withdrawal as cycling, except that the symptoms occur during the competition itself.

A major problem associated with steroid abuse is the potential for an individual to believe that his or her physique will forever be imperfect. In a kind of "reverse anorexia" that has been called **muscle dysmorphia**, some body builders continue to see their bodies as weak and small when they look at themselves in the mirror, despite their greatly enhanced physical development. Peer pressure at the gyms and clubs is a factor in never being satisfied with the size of one's muscles, but it is becoming apparent that societal pressures play a role as well. In the case of males, it is interesting to examine the evolution of the design of G.I. Joe action figures over the years, from the original toy introduced in 1964 to the most recent incarnation introduced in 1998 (Figure 12.1). Just as the Barbie doll has been criticized as setting an impossible ideal for the female body among girls, male-oriented action figures can be criticized on the same basis for boys.[18]

Traditional estimates of substance dependence among steroid users range from 13 to 18 percent, but more recent studies indicate that the prevalence rate may be somewhat higher. In an Internet survey, about one in four weight lifters and body builders using steroids have reported that they were taking larger amounts of steroids over a longer period of time than originally

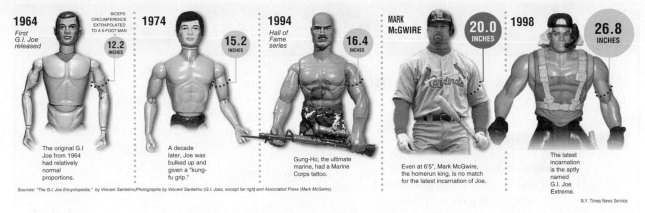

1964
First G.I. Joe released

BICEPS CIRCUMFERENCE EXTRAPOLATED TO A 6-FOOT MAN
12.2 INCHES

The original G.I Joe from 1964 had relatively normal proportions.

1974

15.2 INCHES

A decade later, Joe was bulked up and given a "kung-fu grip."

1994
Hall of Fame series

16.4 INCHES

Gung-Ho, the ultimate marine, had a Marine Corps tattoo.

MARK McGWIRE

20.0 INCHES

Even at 6'5", Mark McGwire, the homerun king, is no match for the latest incarnation of Joe.

1998

26.8 INCHES

The latest incarnation is the aptly named G.I. Joe Extreme.

Sources: "The G.I. Joe Encyclopedia," by Vincent Santelmo.Photographs by Vincent Santelmo (G.I. Joes, except far right and Associated Press (Mark McGwire).

N.Y. Times News Service

FIGURE 12.1

The muscle development of the G.I. Joe action figure has increased dramatically since its introduction in 1964. The estimated bcep circumference for a six-foot man, based on dimensions of the action figure, more than doubled from 1964 to 1998.

Source: GI Joe figures courtesy of Vincent Santelmo from his book *The Complete Encyclopedia of GI Joe,* (3rd ed.) August 2001. Photo of Mark McGwire © Getty Images.

intended, that they needed increased amounts of steroids to achieve the desired effect, or that they experienced physical or emotional problems when steroids were discontinued. One in eight admitted that they had resumed steroid use to relieve a problem that occurred when they stopped (Health Alert). About one-third of them met the criteria for substance dependence, according to DSM-IV guidelines (see Chapter 2).[19]

In light of the potential for steroid dependence and the adverse effects of acute steroid use, prevention programs have been instituted to address the problems of steroid abuse, particularly among male adolescents involved in sports. The most prominent example, developed by Linn Goldberg at Oregon Health and Science University at Portland, is called the Adolescents Training and Learning to Avoid Steroids (ATLAS) program. Young athletes, team coaches, and team captains receive instruction on both sides of the issue—the desirable effects as well as the adverse effects of steroid use. This approach is taken because a failure to acknowledge potential benefits reduces the credibility of the intervention.

Evaluations of the ATLAS program have shown that program participants were better informed than a control group about proper exercise, had a better understanding of the harmful effects of steroids, developed a more negative attitude toward others who used steroids, and were more likely to engage in healthful eating habits. They also showed a 53 percent reduction in new use of anabolic steroids after one year, as well as a 63 percent reduction in the intention to use these drugs in the future. Another prevention and education program originating at the Oregon Health and Science

University called Athletes Targeting Healthy Exercise and Nutrition Alternatives (ATHENA), is specifically oriented toward female athletes, addressing issues such as the connection between disordered eating behaviors and use of body-shaping and performance-enhancing drugs. The program promotes healthful sports nutrition and strength-training alternatives, as well as the training needed to make healthy choices in sports and throughout their lives.[20]

Counterfeit Steroids and the Placebo Effect

As with many illicit drugs, some products marketed to look like anabolic steroids are not the real thing. The problem here is that athletes are notoriously superstitious and easily leave themselves open to placebo effects. On the one hand, in the case of anabolic steroids, the effects on muscle development are usually so dramatic that it is difficult to mistake the response as simply a result of a placebo effect. On the other hand, some performance-enhancing drugs have far more subtle effects, and psychological factors can end up playing a greater role. In relating his own experience with steroids, MLB superstar Alex Rodriguez spoke of the placebo effect:

I'm not sure what the benefit was. . . . I will say this: when you take any substance, especially in baseball, it's half mental and half physical. If you take this glass of water and say you're going to be a better baseball player, if you believe it, you probably will be. I certainly felt more energy, but it's hard to say.[21]

HEALTH ALERT!

The Symptoms of Steroid Abuse

For Both Sexes

1. Rapid increases in strength and/or size beyond what you would expect in a relatively short time. Putting on ten to twenty pounds of solid muscle within a period of a few weeks or so should be a major warning.

2. Involvement in activities in which steroid abuse is known to be condoned or encouraged

3. Sudden increases in appetite and preoccupation with changes in one's physical condition

4. Recent appearance of acne, particularly on the upper back, shoulders, and arms

5. Premature male-pattern baldness, including a rapidly receding hairline or loss of hair from the top rear of the head

6. A puffy appearance in the face, as if the individual is retaining water

7. An increase in moodiness or unusual shifts in mood

8. A reddening of the face, neck, and upper chest, appearing as if one is constantly flushed

9. A yellowing of the skin or the whites of the eyes, stemming from a disturbance in liver function

For Men

1. An enlargement of the breasts, often accompanied by protruding nipples

2. An increase in sexual interest and a tendency to display that interest more aggressively

For Women

1. A lowering of the vocal range

2. Smaller or flatter breasts (see Table 12.1)

Where to go for assistance:
www.nida.nih.gov/Infofacts/Steroids.html
www.steroidabuse.gov

The National Institute on Drug Abuse sponsors a vast array of web sites related to drug use and abuse. The first web site on steroid abuse includes a comprehensive list of potential adverse effects of anabolic steroids; the second web site emphasizes issues of prevention and education.

Source: Wright, J. E., and Cowart, V. S. (1990). *Anabolic steroids: Altered states.* Carmel, IN: Benchmark, pp. 71–91.

Nonsteroid Hormones and Performance-Enhancing Supplements

Certainly anabolic steroids have dominated the performance-enhancing drug scene, but other products have been promoted as having performance-enhancing properties. They include human growth hormone, androstenedione, and creatine.

Human Growth Hormone

One illicit alternative, **human growth hormone (hGH)**, has become increasingly popular, according

human growth hormone (hGH): A naturally occurring hormone promoting growth, particularly in the long bones of the body.

acromegaly (A-kroh-MEG-ah-lee): A condition resulting in structural abnormalities of the head, hands, and feet, as well as damage to internal organs.

to experts in this field, because it is more widely available and cheaper than in previous years, in contrast to the ever more costly illicit steroids. Those who take this pituitary hormone, however, face the increased risk of developing a significant side effect called **acromegaly**, a condition resulting in a coarse and misshapen head, enlarged hands and feet, and damage to various internal organs.

Prior to 1985, hGH was obtained from the pituitary glands of human cadavers, but now genetically engineered hGH (brand names: Protropin and Humatrope) is available, having been approved by the FDA for the treatment of rare cases of stunted growth in children. Although the distribution of these drugs is controlled by their manufacturers as carefully as possible, supplies manage to get diverted for illicit use.

Testimony in 2008 that prominent major league baseball players had used hGH for performance-enhancing purposes revealed the abuse potential of this hormone in professional sports. It is doubtful, however, that its reputation for performance enhancement is justified, according to a major review of more than forty studies of hGH in healthy athletes, conducted between 1966 and 2007. The conclusion is that hGH use increases lean body mass, but the increased bulk does not raise levels of strength or endurance. Indeed, hGH produces higher levels of lactate in muscle tissue, leading to fatigue; hGH users are more likely than others to develop joint pain and carpal tunnel syndrome. In the absence of scientific evidence of any performance-enhancing effects, it has been suggested that reports by athletes that hGH helped to increase their athletic performance are probably due to a placebo effect. Nonetheless, despite hGH's dubious value, hGH screening, capable of differentiating naturally produced hGH from synthetic hGH, became a fixture of drug testing at the 2008 Summer Olympic Games in Beijing. Because hGH has a relatively short half-life, athletes tested positive only if the drug had been injected in the previous twelve to twenty-four hours. No major hGH-related scandals occurred in the 2010 Winter Olympic Games in Vancouver, although, with the number of urine and blood tests exceeding 2,000, it will take up to eight years to determine whether any participating athlete violated anti-doping regulations.[22]

Dietary Supplements as Performance-Enhancing Aids

As recently as ten to twenty years ago, fitness-oriented young people might have taken only basic vitamins and minerals to help them build muscle mass or improve cardiovascular performance. Today, the fitness market is inundated with a growing number of dietary supplement products with presumed performance-enhancing properties; sales of such products exceed $2 billion each year in the United States. They are sold under short, appealing names such as Adenergy and Lean Stack, alongside impressive before-and-after photographs or under long, pseudoscientific names like Vaso XP Xtreme Vasodilator and Xenadrine-NRG that are accompanied by complex molecular diagrams.[23]

A prominent example of a dietary supplement used for performance-enhancing purposes is **androstenedione**. Technically, androstenedione is not an anabolic steroid because it is not based on the specific structure of testosterone itself. Nonetheless, it is testosterone-related because it is a naturally occurring metabolic precursor to testosterone. In other words, the body converts androstenedione to testosterone via the action of specific enzymes in the liver. At the recommended daily dose of 300 mg, androstenedione has been found to increase testosterone levels by an average of 34 percent above normal. Despite the increase in testosterone, however, no change in body composition or strength is observed when its effect is compared to that of placebo controls.

There is no evidence that androstenedione promotes muscle protein synthesis at these dosage levels.[24] Androstenedione rose to prominence in the late 1990s when it became public that St. Louis Cardinals baseball player Mark McGwire had been taking the supplement during his phenomenal 1998 hitting season (seventy home runs, far eclipsing the previous record). A storm of controversy ensued, with some commentators suggesting that McGwire's record be disallowed because of his androstenedione use. Although it had been banned by the National Football League and other professional and amateur sports organizations, androstenedione had not yet been banned in major league baseball at that time, so McGwire's use of it was not illegal. The publicity surrounding McGwire's use of androstenedione and its easy availability were blamed for a 30 percent increase among eighth-grade boys and a 75 percent increase among tenth-grade boys in the use of anabolic steroids from 1998 to 2000.

In 2005, the FDA banned the over-the-counter sale of androstenedione (Andro) and other testosterone precursors. By this time, the Anabolic Steroid Control Act of 2004 had expanded the Schedule III classification (see Chapter 2) to include androstenedione and other testosterone precursors, along with anabolic steroids themselves. In early 2010, it was disclosed that androstenedione had not been the only performance-enhancing drug in McGwire's life. He admitted what had been suspected for some time: that during the 1990s he had used anabolic steroids as well. McGwire has denied that his home-run record-breaking achievements could be attributed to steroid use, but it will never be known whether the performance-enhancing drugs he took did indeed enhance his performance.[25]

Another dietary supplement marketed as a performance-enhancing agent is **creatine** (brand names: Creatine Fuel, Muscle Power, and many other products), a nonprotein amino acid synthesized in the kidney, liver, and pancreas from L-arginine, glycine, and L-methionine. Ingestion of creatine has been found to enhance the retention of water by muscle cells, causing them to expand in size. One hypothesis is that water retention might stimulate protein synthesis and increase muscle mass as a result, but there is no evidence from controlled studies that this is the case. Although creatine appears to enhance performance in repetitive bouts of

androstenedione (AN-dro-steen-DYE-own): A dietary supplement, acting as a metabolic precursor to testosterone and used as an ergogenic agent.

creatine (CREE-ah-teen): A dietary supplement available for ergogenic uses.

high-intensity cycling and sprints, the weight gain experienced by creatine users makes it undesirable for runners or swimmers. Short-term use of creatine has been found to produce muscle cramping, and its long-term adverse effects have not been fully explored.[26]

Nonmedical Use of Stimulant Medication in Baseball

Earlier in the chapter, we cited nineteenth-century examples of world-class athletes experimenting with stimulants in attempts to achieve some level of performance enhancement in their sport. More than a century later, stimulants have continued to be an attractive option. Amphetamines were officially banned from major league baseball in 2005, but before that time, amphetamine use may have been a mainstay for players to stay focused and ward off fatigue in a grueling and lengthy competitive season. According to a professional baseball team psychiatrist, testifying in congressional hearings in 2008, "Amphetamines are the real performance-enhancing drugs that people should always have been worried about."

It is therefore not surprising that since 2005, some players have attempted to circumvent the amphetamine ban by taking stimulant medications intended for the treatment of attention-deficit/hyperactivity disorder (ADHD). In 2007, 103 therapeutic-use exemptions for ADHD were approved for MLB players—a suspiciously high number considering that only 28 players received such approval in 2006. Whether these exemptions reflected a fourfold increase in the incidence of ADHD symptoms over a single year or an effort to benefit from the performance-enhancing effects of stimulant drugs, without violating the amphetamine ban, continues to be a matter of concern to MLB management as well as baseball fans (see Point/Counterpoint II, pages 116–117).[27]

Current Drug-Testing Procedures and Policies

Since the mid-1960s, organizers of major athletic competitions have attempted to develop effective screening

enzyme immunoassay (EIA): One of the two major drug-testing techniques for detecting banned substances or drugs.

procedures to prevent the use of performance-enhancing drugs from giving one competitor an unfair advantage over another. Needless to say, these procedures have neither proved perfect nor served as an effective deterrent for drug use among athletes. We are used to hearing about championship events accompanied by reports of an athlete disqualified from competing or denied the honor of winning because he or she tested positive for a particular banned substance. Ironically, the present status of drug testing as a fact of life in modern sports has brought with it a new form of contest, pitting the skill and ingenuity of the laboratory scientist whose job it is to detect the presence of performance-enhancing drugs against the skill and ingenuity of the athlete in devising ways to use them without detection (Drugs . . . in Focus).[28]

This section looks at drug-testing techniques designed to detect not only performance-enhancing drugs that are relevant to sports but also a wider range of illicit drugs, such as heroin, cocaine, and marijuana. Within some sports organizations, such as the National Collegiate Athletic Association (NCAA), drug tests are conducted not only for the presence of performance-enhancing drugs but also for the presence of drugs that have no particular performance-enhancing benefits. In the case of marijuana, for example, the proper description for its effects with regard to athletic competitions might be *ergolytic* ("performance-reducing"). The policy is defended on the premise that athletes are likely to be exposed to illicit substances, and no collegiate athlete should be permitted to compete while engaging in illegal activity. Related issues surrounding drug testing in the general population, particularly in the workplace, will be examined in Chapter 17.

The Forensics of Drug Testing

Present-day drug-testing procedures begin with a urine sample from the individual in question. The advantages lie in the ease and noninvasiveness of collecting urine, the ease with which urine can be analyzed for specific factors, and the fact that drugs or their metabolites (by-products) are usually very stable in frozen urine. Therefore, it is possible to provide long-term storage of positive samples, in case the results are disputed. The disadvantages are that many perceive urine collection to be a humiliating experience, a dehydrated athlete may find it difficult to urinate immediately after competing, and there may be ways to tamper with the urine sample prior to testing.

The two major urinalysis methods are the **enzyme immunoassay (EIA)** technique and a procedure

Drugs . . . in Focus

Pharmaceutical Companies and Anti-Doping Authorities: A New Alliance

Through the years of scandals involving performance-enhancing drugs, while the World Anti-Doping Agency (WADA) engaged in a continuing and often frustrating game of "cat and mouse" with competitive athletes, major pharmaceutical companies for the most part remained on the sidelines. Now it appears that they are getting increasingly in the game.

A case in point is the medication erythropoietin, marketed in its natural form as Epogen (Amgen Pharmaceuticals) or in synthetic forms as Aranesp (Amgen) and NeoRecorman (Roche Pharmaceuticals). On the one hand, erythropoietin (also known as EPO) is an effective hormonal treatment for millions of anemia patients who suffer from a deficiency in production of red blood cells in bone marrow. On the other hand, the use of EPO for its performance-enhancing (red blood cell boosting) effect in normal individuals, particularly trained athletes, is clearly a form of cheating, a classic example of "doping." Prominent headlines regarding accusations and later confirmation of EPO use by world-champion cyclist Lance Armstrong (see Portrait) have been a public-relations problem of sorts for those manufacturing EPO-related drugs. Would the public now associate a valuable medicinal agent with the dark world of doping? Even worse, would some people accuse these companies of developing drugs that could be misused by athletes essentially as a way of enhancing sales?

In a major gesture of good "corporate citizenship," GlaxoSmithKline Pharmaceuticals sponsored the drug-testing laboratories for the 2012 London Summer Olympic Games, carrying the costs for the facilities and the more than 1,000 staff involved in drug screening. It was the first time in Olympic history that an anti-doping operation had a specific corporate sponsor. But the relationship between pharmaceutical companies and international anti-doping efforts has gone beyond simply the contribution of financial support. Two major manufacturers, Glaxo and Hoffman-LaRoche, are now evaluating every new drug candidate in their development pipeline (see Chapter 14) for potential abuse as a performance-enhancing drug. Customarily, when developing a new drug, a number of reagents are also created in company laboratories that react to the molecular structure of the drug. These reagents remain proprietary compounds, and information about them is kept secret. These particular companies took the unusual step of sharing the reagents with WADA, since it is precisely those reagents that can be "markers" for future drug screening tests.

The actions of Glaxo and Roche are not entirely new. Amgen, for example, was asked by WADA officials to help develop a screening test for Aranesp, released for marketing in 2001, in anticipation of possible doping incidents in the 2002 Salt Lake City Winter Olympic Games. However, not all pharmaceutical companies have been as eager to cooperate with anti-doping authorities in this regard. There remains some reluctance on the part of companies in releasing proprietary information in such a highly competitive business as pharmaceuticals. Nonetheless, there is an increasing awareness that the benefits outweigh the costs.

It must be pointed out that performance-enhancing drugs are also being developed in illicit laboratories around the world, having contacts with athletes in nations that have less strict control over doping than the United States. These laboratories work in the shadows of competitive athletics and have little or no incentive to cooperate with WADA or any other anti-doping agency.

Sources: Salyer, K. (2012, July 18). At London Games, a new record for doping tests. *BloombergBusinessweek*, http://www.businessweek.com/articles/2012-07-18/at-london-games-a-new-record-for-doping-tests#p2. Thomas, K. (2013, February 19). An unexpected drug reaction. Manufacturers increasing join the fight against doping. *New York Times*, pp. B1, B4.

---

combining **gas chromatography and mass spectrometry (GC/MS)**. In both methods, the collected urine is divided into two samples prior to being sent off to the laboratory so that if the analysis of one sample yields a positive outcome, the analysis can be repeated on the other sample. This reanalysis procedure is often required if an individual appeals the original test result.[29]

With the EIA method, a separate test must be run on each particular drug that is being screened. First, at an earlier time, the substance to be tested for (THC or

gas chromatography/mass spectrometry (GC/MS): A drug-testing technique based on the combination of gas chromatography and mass spectrometry.

cocaine, for example) has been injected into an animal, eliciting specific immunological antibodies to that substance. The antibodies are then purified into a testing substrate. The combination of the collected urine and the testing substrate will yield a specific reaction if the urine contains the banned substance. A popular commercial testing kit for screening major controlled substances (opioids, amphetamines, cocaine, benzodiazepines, and marijuana), called **EMIT (enzyme multiplied immunoassay technique)**, has been marketed by Syva Laboratories, a subsidiary of Syntex Corporation in Palo Alto, California, since the early 1970s. This kit is relatively inexpensive and can be used to screen large numbers of urine samples. It is so widely available that its trademark name, EMIT, is often used to mean any form of EIA method.

With the GC/MS method, the urine is first vaporized and combined with an inert gas and then passed over a number of chemically treated columns. Through the process of gas chromatography, technicians are able to identify the presence of a banned substance by the different colorations that are left on the columns. After this has been done, the gas is ionized (converted into an electrically active form) and sent through an electric current and magnetic field that separates out each of the different ions (electrically charged particles) in the gas. Through the process of mass spectrometry, a particular "fingerprint," or "signature," of each chemical substance can be detected and measured. The GC/MS technique is considered more definitive than the EIA technique, but it is considerably more expensive and time-consuming. It is also the only testing procedure that adequately screens for anabolic steroids.[30]

Until the late 1990s, urinalysis was the sole means for drug testing. Since then, however, there has been increasing interest in oral fluid testing. In this procedure, a collection pad is placed between the lower cheek and gum for two to five minutes. The collection pad is then sealed and later analyzed by EIA. The sensitivity and specificity of the results (see the next section) are comparable to those obtained through urinalysis. As with positive urinalysis tests, a confirmation of positive oral fluid results is made by GC/MS.

Currently available FDA-approved drug-testing systems using oral fluid samples can now provide test results in approximately fifteen minutes. The advantages over traditional urinalysis are obvious. Samples are analyzed on-site rather than having to be sent to laboratories.

> **EMIT (enzyme multiplied immunoassay technique):** A commercial testing kit for screening for major controlled substances, based on enzyme immunoassay analysis.

Specimen collection can be performed face-to-face (literally) with the donor, with little risk of sample substitution, dilution, or adulteration. Embarrassment on the part of the donor is eliminated, as are privacy concerns.[31]

Sensitivity and Specificity

As you might imagine, two general questions can be posed with regard to drug-testing methods.

- What is the *sensitivity* of the test? The sensitivity is determined by the likelihood that a specimen containing drugs (or drug metabolites) will test positive. This outcome is referred to as a "true positive." If a drug test has a high degree of sensitivity, then there will be very few "false negatives." If a test is sensitive, the subject will seldom test negative when drug-taking behavior has actually occurred.

- What is the *specificity* of the test? The specificity is determined by the likelihood that a drug-free (or drug metabolite-free) specimen will test negative. This outcome is referred to as a "true negative." If a drug test has a high degree of specificity, then there will be very few "false positives."

In other words, sensitivity indicates the ability of the test to correctly report the presence of drugs. Specificity indicates the ability of the test to correctly report the absence of drugs. In this regard, the GC/MS test is more sensitive and specific than the EIA test.

Frequently, the GC/MS analysis is performed as a confirmation of a positive EIA test. Nonetheless, false positives can occur even with the GC/MS test. Eating a poppy seed roll prior to drug testing or taking quinolone antibiotic medications such as ofloxacin (brand name: Floxin) and ciprofloxacin (brand name: Cipro), for example, has resulted in false-positive indications of opiate use. Therapeutic levels of ibuprofen (brand names: Advil, Motrin, and Nuprin, among others) have resulted in false-positive indications of marijuana smoking. In addition, the passive inhalation of marijuana smoke can leave sufficient levels of THC metabolites to result in false-positive indications of marijuana smoking, although the density of smoke that needs to be present for this to happen makes it unlikely that individuals would be completely unaware that they were being exposed to marijuana.[32]

Masking Drugs and Chemical Manipulations

Two specific tactics have been employed to disguise the prior use of anabolic steroids so that the outcome of a drug test becomes, in effect, a false negative; both are now relatively obsolete. The first strategy was to take the anti-gout drug probenecid (brand name: Benemid). Available since 1987, it does mask the presence of anabolic steroids, but it is now on the list of banned substances for competitive athletes and is easily detected by GC/MS techniques. The second strategy was to increase the level of epitestosterone in the body. The standard procedure for determining the present or prior use of anabolic steroids is to calculate the ratio of testosterone against the level of epitestosterone, a naturally occurring hormone that is usually stable at relatively low levels in the body. International athletic organizations now use the standard of a 4:1 ratio (formerly 6:1) or higher as indicating steroid use. If epitestosterone is artificially elevated, the ratio can be manipulated downward so as to indicate a false-negative result in drug testing. However, suspiciously high levels of epitestosterone can now be detected by GC/MS techniques, so this form of manipulation is no longer successful.[33]

Pinpointing the Time of Drug Use

It is important to remember that a positive result in a drug test indicates merely that the test has detected a minimal level of a drug or its metabolite. It is difficult to determine *when* that drug was introduced into the body or *how long* the drug-taking behavior continued. In the case of urinalysis testing, the time it takes for the body to get rid of the metabolites of a particular drug varies considerably, from a few hours to a few weeks (Table 12.3). In the case of oral-fluid (saliva) drug testing, the window of detection may be different, depending on the drug of interest. Opioids and cocaine are detected within two to three days of ingestion; THC in marijuana is detected within a period ranging from one hour after ingestion to fourteen hours later. Because THC metabolites are excreted into the urine for several days or in some cases for several weeks, oral-fluid testing for marijuana is better suited for determining when marijuana has been last used. In effect, the "window of detection" is narrower. If the interval between use and testing has been longer than fourteen hours or so but shorter than a few days, urinalysis would pick up a positive result, but oral-fluid testing would not.[34]

Owing to the expense of randomized drug-testing programs, not every institution can afford the costs. Large corporations may be able to budget for potentially thousands of tests for preemployment screening purposes, but relatively few colleges and considerably fewer high schools are able to establish the level of funding needed to test their student populations. Even if the costs were lower, it is questionable

TABLE 12.3

Detection periods for various drugs in urinalysis testing

DRUG	DETECTION PERIOD
Alcohol	1-12 hours
Amphetamines in general	1-2 hours
Barbiturates	
Short-acting	2 days
Long-acting	1-3 weeks
Benzodiazepines	
Therapeutic use	3 days
Chronic use (>one year)	4-6 weeks
Cocaine	2-4 days
Marijuana (THC)]	
Single use	2-7 days
Chronic, heavy use	1-2 months
MDMA (Ecstasy)	1-2 days
Methamphetamine	1-2 hours
Opioids	
Codeine	2 days
Heroin or morphine	2 days
Darvon, Darvocet	6 hours to 2 days
Phencyclidine (PCP)	
Casual use	14 days
Chronic, heavy use	up to 30 days

Note: The detection periods vary according to the sensitivity of the test or the subject's physical condition, fluid balance, and state of hydration. Detection periods are relatively longer for hair samples and detection periods are relatively shorter for blood or saliva samples than for urine samples. Detection times for steroids vary from days to months, depending on the steroid and the length of use.

Sources: Drugs of abuse reference guide (2007). Occupational testing services, LabCorp, Research Triangle Park, NC.; Verstraete, A. G. (2004). Detection times of drugs of abuse in blood, urine, and oral fluid. *The Drug Monitor, 26,* 200–205.

whether illicit drug-taking behavior would be reduced in the long run as a result. Interestingly, recent evidence indicates that the prospect of randomized drug testing in schools fails to act as a deterrent among students. University of Michigan researchers in 2003 found virtually identical rates of illicit drug use in schools that had drug-testing programs and schools that did not. This general finding was replicated in a study reported in 2008. The deterrent effect of drug testing on illicit drug use in schools clearly has not been demonstrated.[35]

It is also worth considering the following fact regarding abusers of steroids and related

the ones who have made the determination that appearance and winning are all important. We're telling kids in our society that sports is more than a game. Until we change those signals, for the most part, we might as well tell people to get used to drug use.[36]

Unfortunately, there seems to be little reason to believe that the temptations to indulge in performance-enhancing drugs will go away anytime soon. Numerous surveys taken among young athletes and nonathletes alike indicate that the social signals are crystal clear, and they are more than willing to take up the challenge, despite the risks. Variations of the following question have been asked of them: "If you had a magic drug that was so fantastic that if you took it once you would win every competition you would enter, from the Olympic decathlon to Mr. Universe, for the next five years, but it had one minor drawback—it would kill you five years after you took it—would you still take the drug?" More than half of those polled have answered "yes" to this question.[37]

There is a more general sense of competition that goes beyond dreams of athletic achievement. It is apparent that an idealized body image is part of today's

performance-enhancing drugs: Individuals who are no longer students in a public institution or participants in an organized athletic program do not need to fear a positive drug test because they will never be required to undergo *any* form of drug testing, random or otherwise.

The Social Context of Performance-Enhancing Drugs

Anabolic steroids and other performance-enhancing agents are quite different from many of the abused drugs covered in previous chapters in that they affect the way we look and how we compare to others, rather than the way we feel. Charles E. Yesalis, one of the leading experts in steroid abuse, has put it this way:

> *If you were stranded on a desert island, you might use cocaine if it were available, but nobody would use steroids. On a desert island, nobody cares what you look like and there is nothing to win. We are*

The pressure to be number one exists in all areas of athletic competition. The intensity of competition in our culture, however, extends beyond the world of sports. Temptations to secure a competitive edge in the corporate world have led to a growing and disturbing acceptance of stimulant abuse as a means of keeping pace with increasingly rapid technologies for communication and business transactions.

standard for a sense of sexuality and social acceptance. This standard will not be news at all to women, but it is a fairly recent development in men. Anabolic steroids as a way of accelerating the effects of weight training are increasing in our culture. One high school senior has said, "The majority now are guys that don't do it for sports. They do it for girls. For the look." Another senior has remarked on a different kind of lifter in weight rooms and gyms: the vanity body builder. As he expressed it, "We notice a lot of kids now; they just want this certain type of body—with the abs and the ripped chest—and they want it quick."[38] An exercise physiologist has remarked on the intense social pressures that are involved:

> *The teenage years are the skinniest and most awkward, and the idea of being the skinniest kid in the locker room is absolutely terrifying to a teenage boy.*[39]

As usual, Internet web sites deliver mixed messages, promoting anabolic steroids as well as steroid precursors such as androstenedione with the promise "You'll get huge!" while saying on the labels of their products that people younger than age eighteen should not take them or that they should consult a physician first.

Summary

Drug-Taking Behavior in Sports

- The use of performance-enhancing (ergogenic) drugs in athletic competition has a long history, dating from the original Olympic Games in ancient Greece.

- In the modern era, the principal type of performance-enhancing drugs has been anabolic steroids. These synthetic drugs are all based on variations of the testosterone molecule.

- Since the late 1980s, anabolic steroids have been popular with body builders as well as competitive athletes. This latter group typically takes steroids in enormous quantities and administers them in a largely unsupervised fashion.

- Recently, great concerns have been raised about the use of anabolic steroids, as well as other performance-enhancing drugs, in major league baseball.

The Hazards of Anabolic Steroids

- The hazards of steroid use include liver tumors, mood swings, and increased aggressiveness.

- For men, the effects include lower sperm count, enlargement of the breasts, atrophy of the testicles, baldness, and severe acne. For women, masculinizing changes occur, only some of which are reversible when steroids are withdrawn.

Patterns of Anabolic Steroid Abuse

- Since 1990, anabolic steroids have been classified as Schedule III controlled substances, making their possession and sale without a specific medical prescription illegal. In 2004, steroid precursors were added to the category of Schedule III controlled substances. These drugs are now distributed through illicit black-market channels.

- About 13 to 18 percent of individuals taking large doses of steroids develop both physical and psychological dependence.

Nonsteroid Hormones and Performance-Enhancing Supplements

- Human growth hormone (hGH) is a nonsteroid hormone that has been used for performance-enhancing purposes.

- Two dietary supplements, androstenedione and creatine, have been prominent recently as performance-enhancing aids.

Nonmedical Use of Stimulant Medication in Baseball

- Although amphetamines were officially banned in major league baseball (MLB) in 2005, for a long time players had been taking amphetamines to stay focused and ward off fatigue.

- In 2007, an unusually large number of MLB players reported taking stimulant medications for ADHD treatment, raising suspicions that this was an effort to circumvent prohibitions against nonmedical stimulant use.

Current Drug-Testing Procedures and Policies

- Drug-testing procedures, chiefly for those in organized athletics, have become increasingly sophisticated in their ability to detect the presence of banned substances.

- Two major techniques, based either on urine or on oral-fluid (saliva) samples, are enzyme immunoassay (EIA) and a combination of gas chromatography and mass spectrometry (GC/MS).

- The ultimate goal of drug-testing procedures is to make it impossible to yield either a false-negative or false-positive result. A sensitive test yields few false negatives, and a specific test yields few false positives.

Key Terms

acromegaly, p. 304
adrenocortical steroids, p. 295
anabolic, p. 295
anabolic-androgenic
steroids, p. 295
anabolic steroids, p. 295

androgenic, p. 295
androstenedione, p. 305
creatine, p. 305
EMIT (enzyme multiplied
immunoassay technique),
p. 308

enzyme immunoassay (EIA),
p. 306
ergogenic, p. 294
gas chromatography/mass
spectrometry (GC/MS),
p. 307

gynecomastia, p. 299
human growth hormone
(hGH), p. 304
muscle dysmorphia, p. 302
priapism, p. 299

Endnotes

1. Kepner, T. (2009, February 18). "We weren't taking Tic Tacs." As team looks on, Rodriguez details his use of steroids. *New York Times*, pp. B1, B15. Quotation on p. B1.

2. Kepner, T. (2010, January 12). McGwire admits steroid use in 1990s, his years of magic. *New York Times*, pp. B10, B14. Quotation on p. B10.

3. Dolan, E. F. (1986). *Drugs in sports* (rev. ed.). New York: F. Watts, pp. 17–18. Meer, J. (1987). *Drugs and sports*. New York: Chelsea House, pp. 2, 61–75. Quotation from Scott, J. (1971, October 17). It's not how you play the game, but what pill you take. *New York Times Magazine*, pp. 40–41, 106–113. Taylor, W. N. (1991). *Macho medicine: The history of the anabolic steroid epidemic*. Jefferson, NC: McFarland and Co., pp. 3–16. Wadler, G. I., and Hainline, B. (1989). *Drugs and the athlete*. Philadelphia: F. A. Davis, pp. 3–17.

4. Bhasin, S.; Storer, T. W.; Berman, N.; Callegari, C.; Clevenger, B.; et al. (1996). The effects of supraphysiologic doses of testosterone on muscle size and strength in normal men. *New England Journal of Medicine, 335*, 1–7. Lombardo, J. (1993). The efficacy and mechanisms of action of anabolic steroids. In C. E. Yesalis (Ed.), *Anabolic steroids in sport and exercise*. Champaign, IL: Human Kinetics Publishers, p. 100.

5. Scott, J., It's not how you play the game, p. 41.

6. Catlin, D. H., and Murray, T. H. (1996). Performance-enhancing drugs, fair competition, and Olympic sport. *Journal of the American Medical Association, 276*, 231–237. Maimon, A. (2000, February 6). Doping's sad toll: One athlete's tale from East Germany. *New York Times*, pp. A1, A6. Yesalis, C. E.; Courson, S. P.; and Wright, J. (1993). History of anabolic steroid use in sport and exercise. In Yesalis, *Anabolic steroids*, pp. 1–33.

7. Litsky, F. (2003, March 6). International drug code is adopted. *New York Times*, p. D5. Longman, J. (2003, October 24). Steroid is reportedly found in top runner's urine test. *New York Times*, p. D2. Macur, J. (2008, October 9). Beijing Games blood samples to be retested for new drug. *New York Times*, pp. B17, B20. Macur, J. (2012, October 11). Details of doping scheme paint Armstrong as leader. *New York Times*, pp. A1, B15. Macur, J. (2013, January 5). In reversal, Armstrong is said to weigh admitting drug use. *New York Times*, kjpp. A1, D4. Starr,

M. (2003, November 3). Blowing the whistle on drugs: A raid on a California laboratory threatens to blemish America's athletes—again. *Newsweek*, pp. 60–61. Vecsey, G. (2002, March 1). More curious material in skiing's closet. *New York Times*, pp. D1, D4. World Anti-Doping Association, Montreal.

8. W. W. F.'s McMahon indicted (1993, November 19). *New York Times*, p. B12. Yesalis, Courson, and Wright, History of anabolic steroid use, pp. 40–42.

9. Curry, J. (2005, November 16). Baseball backs stiffer penalties for steroid use. *New York Times*, pp. A1, D2. Kepner, T. (2009, July 31). A stain keeps spreading. *New York Times*, pp. B10, B11. Macur, J. (2011, April 14). Bonds guilty of obstruction, but not of perjury. *New York Times*, p. A1. B15. Macur, J. (2012, June 19). Clemens found not guilty of lying about drug use. *New York Times*, p. A1. Vecsey, G. (2008, January 16). Spring training and the syringe generation. *New York Times*, pp. D1, D3.

10. Council on Scientific Affairs (1990). Medical and non-medical uses of anabolic-androgenic steroids. *Journal of the American Medical Association, 264*, 2923–2927. Hartgens, F., and Kuipers, H. (2004). Effects of androgenic-anabolic steroids in athletes. *Sports Medicine, 34*, 513–554. Perry, P. J.; Lund, B. C.; Deninger, M. J.; Kutscher, E. C.; and Schneider, J. (2005). Anabolic steroid use in weightlifters and bodybuilders: An Internet survey of drug utilization. *Clinical Journal of Sport Medicine, 15*, 326–330.

11. Neri, M.; Bello, S.; Bonsignore, A.; Cantatore, S.; Riezzo, I., et al. (2011). Anabolic androgenic steroids and liver toxicity. *Mini Reviews in Medicinal Chemistry, 11*, 430–437. Van Amsterdam, J.; Opperhuizen, A.; and Hartens, F. (2010). Adverse health effects of anabolic-androgenic steroids. *Regulatory Toxicology and Pharmacology, 57*, 117–123.

12. DiPaolo, M.; Agozzino, M.; Toni, C.; Luciani, A. B; et al. (2005). Sudden anabolic steroid abuse–related death in athletes. *International Journal of Cardiology, 114*, 114–117. Karch, S. B. (2009). *Pathology of drug abuse* (4th ed.). Boca Raton, FL: CRC Press, pp. 617-623. Maravelias, C.; Dona, A.; Stefanidou, M.; and Spiliopoulou, C. (2005). Adverse effects of anabolic steroids in athletes: A constant threat. *Toxicology Letters, 158*,

167–175. Urhausen, A.; Albers, T.; and Kindermann, W. (2004). Are the cardiac effects of anabolic steroid abuse in strength athletes reversible? *Heart, 90,* 496–501.

13. Su, T-P.; Pagliaro, M.; Schmidt, P. J.; Pickar, D.; Wolkowitz, O.; et al. (1993). Neuropsychiatric effects of anabolic steroids in male normal volunteers. *Journal of the American Medical Association, 269,* 2760–2764.

14. Pope, H. G., Jr.; Kouri, E. M.; and Hudson, J. I. (2000). Effects of supraphysiologic doses of testosterone on mood and aggressiveness in normal men: A randomized controlled trial. *Archives of General Psychiatry, 57,* 133–140. Stocker, S. (2000). Study provides additional evidence that high steroid doses elicit psychiatric symptoms in some men. *NIDA Notes, 15*(4), pp. 8–9. Trenton, A. J., and Currier, G. W. (2005). Behavioural manifestations of anabolic steroid use. *CNS Drugs, 19,* 571–595.

15. Adler, J. (2004, December 20). Toxic strength. *Newsweek,* pp. 45–52. Bahrke, M. S. (1993). Psychological effects of endogenous testosterone and anabolic-androgenic steroids. In Yesalis, *Anabolic steroids,* pp. 161–192. Doff, W. (2005, March 10). After a young athlete's suicide, steroids called the culprit. *New York Times,* pp. A1, D8. Estrada, M.; Varshney, A.; and Ehrlich, B. E. (2006). Elevated testosterone induces apoptosis in neuronal cells. *Journal of Biological Chemistry, 281,* 25492–25501. Longman, J. (2003, November 26). An athlete's dangerous experiment: Using steroids enhanced his physique, but he died trying to stop. *New York Times,* pp. D1, D4.

16. National Institute on Drug Abuse (2000, April). Anabolic steroids. *Research report series.* Bethesda, MD: National Institute on Drug Abuse. Collins, R. (2003, January 5). Federal and state steroid laws. Posted on the web site of C., McDonald, and Gann, P. C., Attorneys-at-law, Nassau County and New York, NY, www.steroidlaw.com.

17. DEA leads largest steroid bust in history (2005, December 15). Drug Enforcement Administration, U.S. Department of Justice. Johnston, L. D.; O'Malley, P. M.; Bachman, J. G.; and Schulenberg, J. E. (2012v). Monitoring the Future: National survey results on drug use, 1975–2011. Vol. I: Secondary school students 2011. Ann Arbor, MI: Institute for Social Research, The University of Michigan, Table 2-1.

18. Pope, C. G.; Pope, H. G.; Menard, W.; Fay, C.; Olivardia, R.; et al. (2005). Clinical features of muscle dysmorphia among males with body dysmorphic disorder. *Body Image, 2,* 395-400. Wroblewska, Anna-M. (1997). Androgenic-anabolic steroids and body dysmorphia in young men. *Journal of Psychosomatic Research, 42,* 225–234.

19. Bahrke, M. S.; Yesalis, C. E.; and Brower, K. J. (1998). Anabolic-androgenic steroid abuse and performance-enhancing drugs among adolescents. *Sport Psychiatry, 7,* 821–838. Beel, A.; Maycock, B.; and McLean, N. (1998). Current perspectives on anabolic steroids. *Drug and Alcohol Review, 17,* 87–103. Kashkin, K. B., and Kleber, H. D. (1989). Hooked on hormones? An anabolic steroid addiction hypothesis. *Journal of the American Medical Association, 262,* 3166–3169. Monaghan, L. F. (2000). *Bodybuilding, drugs, and risk.* New York: Routledge. Perry, Lund, Deninger, Kutscher, and Schneider, Anabolic steroid use. Schrof, J. M. (1992, June 1). Pumped up. *U.S. News and World Report,* pp. 55–63.

20. Goldberg, L.; Mackinnon, D. P.; Elliot, D. L.; Moe, E. L.; Clarke, G.; and Cheong, J. (2000). The Adolescents Training and Learning to Avoid Steroids program. *Archives of Pediatrics and Adolescent Medicine, 154,* 332–338. Information courtesy of the Oregon Health and Science University, Portland, 2008. Moe, E. L.; Goldberg, L. D.; MacKinnon, D. P.; and Cheong, J. (1999). Reducing drug use and promoting healthy behaviors among athletes: The ATLAS program. *Medical Science Sports Exercise, 31*(5), S122.

21. Kepner, "We weren't taking Tic Tacs." Quotation from Alex Rodriguez on p. B15.

22. Interlandi, J. (2008, February 25). Myth meets science. *Newsweek,* p. 48. Juhn, M. S. (2003). Popular sports supplements and ergogenic aids. *Sports Medicine, 33,* 921–939. Liu, H.; Bravata, D. M.; Olkin, I.; Friedlander, A.; et al. (2008). Systematic review: The effects of growth hormone on athletic performance. *Annals of Internal Medicine, 148,* 747–748. Macur, J. (2008, June). Who has the horse tranquilizers? *Play,* p. 18. Macur, J. (2008, October 9). Olympic blood samples to be retested. *New York Times,* p. B17. Macur, J. (2010, February 28). No doping scandals at Games, but time will tell. *New York Times,* Sportspage 9.

23. Tuller, D. (2005, January 18). For sale: "muscles" in a bottle. *New York Times,* pp. F5, F10.

24. Androstenedione (2001). *PDR for nutritional supplements* (1st ed.). Montvale, NJ: Thomson HealthCare, pp. 26–28. Juhn, Popular sports supplements. Leder, B. Z.; Longcope, C.; Catlin, D. H.; Ahrens, B.; and Schoenfeld, J. S. (2000). Oral androstenedione administration and serum testosterone concentrations in young men. *Journal of the American Medical Association, 283,* 779–782.

25. Denham, B. E. (2006). The Anabolic Steroid Control Act of 2004: A study in the political economy of drug policy. *Journal of Health and Social Policy, 22,* 51–78. Kepner, T. (2010, January 12). McGwire admits steroid use. *New York Times,* pp. B10, B14. Mravic, M. (2000, February 21). Ban it, bud. *Sports Illustrated,* pp. 24, 26.

26. Buford, T. W.; Kreider, R. B.; Stout, J. R.; et al. (2007). International Society of Sports Nutrition position stand: Creatine supplementation and exercise. *Journal of the International Society of Sports Nutrition, 4,* 6. Creatine,. *PDR for nutritional supplements,* pp. 114–117. Freeman, M. (2003, October 21). Scientist fears athletes are using unsafe drugs: Discovery of an undetected steroid confirms suspicions. *New York Times,* p. D2. Gregory, A. J. M., and Fitch, R. W. (2007). Sports medicine: Performance-enhancing drugs. *Pediatric Clinics of North America, 54,* 797–806.

27. Schmidt, M. S. (2008, January 16). Baseball is challenged on rise in stimulant use. *New York Times*, pp. A1, A16. Quotation on p. A16. Schmidt, M. S. (2009, January 10). Baseball officials give report on amphetamine use among players. *New York Times*, p. D5.
28. Hamilton, M. McNeil (2003, February 23). Beating drug screening builds cottage industry. Evaders change faster than testing technology. *Houston Chronicle*, p. 2.
29. Wadler and Hainline, *Drugs and the athlete*, pp. 201–202.
30. Hatton, C. K. (2007). Beyond sports-doping headlines: The science of laboratory tests for performance-enhancing drugs. *Pediatric Clinics of North America*, 54, 713–733. Meer, *Drugs and sports*, pp. 92–95.
31. Alternate specimen testing policies may be set soon (2005, September). *Occupational Health and Safety*, p. 26. Cone, Edward J.; Presley, L.; Lehrer, M.; Seiter, W.; Smith, M.; et al. (2002). Oral fluid testing for drugs of abuse: Positive prevalence rates by Intercept immunoassay screening and GC-MS-MS confirmation and suggested cutoff concentrations. *Journal of Analytical Toxicology*, 26, 540–546.
32. *Allen and Hanbury's athletic drug reference* (1994). Durham NC: Clean Data, pp. 65–66. Baden, L. R.; Horowitz, G.; Jacoby, H.; and Eliopoulos, G. M. (2001). Quinolones and false-positive urine screening for opiates by immunoassay technology. *Journal of the American Medical Association*, 286, 3115–3119. Struempler, R. E. (1987, May/June). Excretion of codeine and morphine following ingestion of poppy seeds. *Journal of Analytical Toxicology*, 11, 97–99. Wadler and Hainline, *Drugs and the athlete*, pp. 208–209.
33. Catlin, D.; Wright, J.; Pope, H.; and Liggett, M. (1993). Assessing the threat of anabolic steroids: Sportsmedicine update. *The Physician and Sportsmedicine*, 21, 37–44.
34. Rosenberg, R. (2000, October 12). Citgo to use Avitar drug tests, job applicants to undergo new saliva-based exam. *Boston Globe*, p. C3.
35. Brookman, R. R. (2008). Unintended consequences of drug and alcohol testing in student athletes. *AAP (American Academy of Pediatrics) Grand Rounds*, 19,
15–16. Editorial: To test or not to test: Screening for substance use in adolescents. *Journal of Adolescent Health*, 38, 329-331. Yamaguchi, R.; Johnston, L. D.; and O'Malley, P. M. (2003). Relationship between student illicit drug use and school drug-testing policies. *Journal of School Health*, 73, 159–164.
36. Quotation from C. E. Yesalis. In Wright, J. E, and Cowart, V. S. (1990). *Anabolic steroids: Altered States*. Traverse City, MI: Cooper Publishing, p. 196. Schwerin, M. J.; Corcoran, K. J.; Fisher, L.; Patterson, D.; Askew, W.; et al. (1996). Social physique anxiety, body esteem, and social anxiety in bodybuilders and self-reported anabolic steroid users. *Addictive Behaviors*, 21, 1–8.
37. Goldman, B., and Klatz, R. (1992). *Death in the locker room II: Drugs and sports*. Chicago: Elite Sports Medicine Publications, pp. 23–24. McHenry, C. R. (2007, December). Presidential address to the American Association of Endocrine Surgeons: The illicit use of hormones for enhancement of athletic performance: A major threat to the integrity of organized athletic competition. *Surgery*, 785–792. Shermer, M. (2008, April). The doping dilemma. *Scientific American*, pp. 82–89.
38. Egan, T. (2002, November 22). Body-conscious boys adopt athlete's taste for steroids. *New York Times*, pp. A1, A24. Quotations on p. A24. Kolata, G.; Longman, J.; Weiner, T.; and Egan, T. (2002, December 2). With no answers on risks, steroid users still say "yes." *New York Times*, pp. A1, A19. Pope, H. G., Jr., Phillips, K. A., and Olivardia, R. (2002). *The Adonis complex: How to identify, treat, and prevent body obsession in men and boys*. New York: Simon and Schuster. Roosevelt, M. (2010, January 14). When the gym isn't enough. *New York Times*, pp. E1, E8.
39. Kilgannon, C. (2001, May 27). Strong Island: More youngsters seek great physiques, and risky ways to get them. *New York Times*, Section 14 (Long Island), pp. 1, 9. Quotation on p. 9. Kolata, With no answers on risks, steroid users still say "yes," pp. A1, A10. Morgan, R. (2002). The men in the mirror. *Chronicle of Higher Education*, 49, A53–A54.

Depressants and Inhalants

"I remember," Julio says, taking quick, nervous puffs from his cigarette, "when I was a little kid, maybe eight or nine, and I used to take the garbage out for my mother, I'd always see tubes from airplane glue under the stairwell in our apartment house and in the alley out back. At first, glue just meant building models to me. But I'd see people sniffing it, under the stairwell. I was curious, and one day I tried it. It made me feel like I was in a trance. It wasn't really exciting, but I did it again and again until we moved, and in the new neighborhood people weren't into glue and I didn't see the empty tubes to remind me anymore."[1]

— A teenager relating his early experience with inhalant abuse

Just as cocaine, amphetamines, and other stimulants bring us up, depressants bring us down. Just as people desire to be stronger, faster, and more attuned to the world, they also desire to move apart from that world, reduce the stress and anxiety of their lives, and fall asleep more easily. We examined in Chapter 5 the powerful effects of opioids not only to relieve pain but also to provide the means to retreat from the world around them. In Chapter 8, we examined the age-old allure of alcohol to relax our mind and body.

In the first part of this chapter, we will focus on a group of non-opioid, nonalcoholic depressant drugs called **sedative-hypnotics**, so named because they calm us down (from the Latin verb *sedare*, meaning "to calm or be quiet") and produce sleep (from the Greek noun *hypnos*, meaning "sleep"). Several types of sedative-hypnotic drugs exist, ranging from drugs that were introduced more than two hundred years ago to others that have become available only recently.

A separate but related category consists of prescription drugs that provide specific relief from stress and anxiety without sedating us. These drugs have often been referred to as *tranquilizers* because of their ability to make us feel peaceful or tranquil, but we will call them by their currently accepted name, **antianxiety drugs**. Unfortunately, sedative-hypnotics and antianxiety drugs have been subject not only to legitimate medical use but to misuse and abuse as well. Many of them can be obtained through illicit sources as street drugs and are consumed for recreational purposes. The psychological problems and physical dangers associated with the misuse and abuse of these depressants are of particular concern.

This chapter also looks at a category of depressant drugs known as **inhalants**, a group of chemicals that emit breathable vapors and produce intoxicating effects. These chemicals do not need to be acquired in a pharmacy, a convenience store, a liquor store, or even on the street. They can be found under the sink, in kitchen or bathroom cabinets, in the basement, or in the garage.

---

sedative-hypnotics: A category of depressant drugs that provide a sense of calm and sleep.

antianxiety drugs: Medications that make the user feel more peaceful or tranquil; also called tranquilizers.

inhalants: Chemicals that produce breathable vapors. They produce euphoriant and depressant effects when sniffed or inhaled.

barbiturate (bar-BIT-chur-rit): A drug within a family of depressants derived from barbituric acid and used as a sedative-hypnotic and antiepileptic medication.

Ordinary household products frequently have the potential to intoxicate if they are sniffed or inhaled. When you consider that these substances are readily available to anyone in a family, including its youngest members, the consequences of their abuse become especially troubling. Glues, solvents, and other inhalant products will be examined as dangerous recreational drugs in our society today.

Barbiturates

In 1864, the German chemist Adolf von Baeyer combined a waste product in urine called *urea* and an apple extract called *malonic acid* to form a new chemical compound called *barbituric acid*. There are two oft-told stories about how this compound got its name. One story has it that Von Baeyer had gone to a local tavern to celebrate his discovery and encountered a number of artillery officers celebrating the feast day of St. Barbara, the patron saint of explosives handlers. Von Baeyer was inspired by their celebration, and the name "barbituric acid" came to mind. The other story attributes the name to a relationship with a certain barmaid (perhaps at the same tavern) whose name was Barbara.[2]

Whichever story is true (if either is), Von Baeyer's discovery of barbituric acid set the stage for the development of a class of drugs called **barbiturates.** Barbituric acid itself has no behavioral effects, but when additional molecular groups combine with the acid, depressant effects are observed. In 1903, the first true barbiturate, diethylbarbituric acid, was created and marketed under the name Veronal. Over the next thirty years, several major barbiturate drugs were introduced: **phenobarbital** (brand name: Luminal), **amobarbital** (brand name: Amytal), **pentobarbital** (brand name: Nembutal), and **secobarbital** (brand name: Seconal).

Categories of Barbiturates

Barbiturates all share a number of common features. They are relatively tasteless and odorless, and at sufficient dosages, they reliably induce sleep, although the quality of sleep is a matter that will be discussed later. Because they slow down neural activity in the central nervous system (CNS), an important therapeutic application of barbiturates has been in the treatment of seizure disorders (epilepsy).

Barbiturates have elimination half-lives that range from 10 to 40 hours (in the case of amobarbital) to 50 to 120 hours (in the case of mephobarbital). All other factors being equal, injectable forms of barbiturates are shorter-acting than orally administered forms of the same drug because it takes longer for the drug to be absorbed when taken by mouth and longer for it to be eliminated from the body (Table 13.1). Naturally, a higher dose of any drug lasts longer than a lower dose because it takes longer for all of the drug to be eliminated from the body. Thiopental (brand name: Pentothal), a barbiturate used in surgical anesthesia, takes effect extremely rapidly (within seconds) and lasts only a few minutes unless administered in a continuous fashion. For this reason, it is referred to as an *ultra-short-acting barbiturate*.

Because this feature has little appeal to a person seeking a recreational drug, ultra-short-acting barbiturates are not commonly abused.

Acute Effects of Barbiturates

You can visualize the effects of barbiturates on the body and the mind in terms of points along a scale ranging from mild relaxation on one end to coma and death on the other. In this sense, barbiturate effects are the same as the effects of depressants in general. The particular point that is achieved depends on the dose level that is taken.

At very low doses, the primary result of oral administrations of a barbiturate is relaxation and, paradoxically, a sense of euphoria. These effects derive chiefly from a disinhibition of the cerebral cortex, in which normal inhibitory influences from the cortex are reduced. These symptoms are similar to the inebriating or intoxicating effects that result from low to moderate doses of alcohol (Drugs . . . in Focus).

As the dose level increases, lower regions of the brain concerned with general arousal become affected.

phenobarbital (FEEN-oh-BAR-bih-tall): A long-acting barbiturate drug, usually marketed in generic form.

amobarbital (AY-moh-BAR-bih-tall): An intermediate-acting barbiturate drug. Brand name is Amytal.

pentobarbital (PEN-toh-BAR-bih-tall): A short-acting barbiturate drug. Brand name is Nembutal.

secobarbital (SEC-oh-BAR-bih-tall): A short-acting barbiturate drug. Brand name is Seconal.

TABLE 13.1

Major barbiturates

GENERIC NAME	BRAND NAME	ELIMINATION HALF-LIFE IN HOURS	RELATIVE POTENTIAL FOR ABUSE
phenobarbital	Luminal*	24–120	low
mephobarbital	Mebaral	50–120	low
butalbarbital	Pheniline Forte†	34–42	moderate
amobarbital	Amytal	10–40	high
pentobarbital	Nembutal	15–50	high
secobarbital	Seconal	15–40	High

Note: Barbiturates take effect in a range of fifteen minutes to one hour, depending upon the type. Generally, the shorter-lasting barbiturates begin to act sooner.

*Phenobarbital is also available in combination with hyoscyamine, atropine, and scopolamine under the brand name Donnatal.

†Several brands combine butalbarbital with acetaminophen.

Sources: Julien, R. M. (2005). *A primer of drug action* (10th ed.). New York: Worth, p. 146. *Physicians' desk reference* (67th ed.) (2013). Montvale, NJ: PDR Network.

Drugs . . . in Focus

Is There Any Truth in "Truth Serum"?

The idea that a sedative-hypnotic drug such as amobarbital (Amytal, or "sodium amytal") may function as a "truth serum" is not at all new. It has been known for centuries that depressants can produce remarkable candor and freedom from inhibition. The oldest example is simple alcohol, whose effect on loosening the tongue led to the Latin proverb *in vino veritas* ("in wine, there is truth").

Whether we are guaranteed truthfulness under any of these circumstances, however, is another matter entirely. Courts have ruled that expert opinion in criminal cases based *solely* on drug-assisted testimony cannot be admitted as evidence. Controlled laboratory studies have shown that individuals under the influence of Amytal, when pressed by questioners, are as likely to give convincing renditions of fabrications (outright lies) or fantasies as they are to tell the truth. So perhaps Amytal might be better described as a "say anything serum."

Recently, the question of whether Amytal or other depressant drugs should be used to gain information has arisen in connection with the interrogation of captured al Qaeda prisoners following the September 11, 2001, attacks. Legal scholars have argued that the practice constitutes torture under international law. The United States has determined that such individuals are unlawful combatants, a designation that excludes them from protection under the Geneva Convention guidelines prohibiting such practices for prisoners of war. On the record, U.S. officials deny that depressant drugs are being used to gain information from captives under American jurisdiction. It is possible that this practice is in effect in other countries to which captives have been transferred.

There is still no evidence that truthful information can be gained through the use of depressant drugs. Nonetheless, military and intelligence experts point to the potential for gaining some relevant information that might be "buried" in drug-induced ramblings.

Sources: CBS News (2003, April 23). Truth serum: A possible weapon. www.cbsnews.com. Keller, L. (2005). Is truth serum torture? *American University International Law Review, 20,* 523–612. Lillienfeld, S. O., and Landfield, K. (2008). Science and pseudoscience in law enforcement. *Criminal Justice and Behavior, 35,* 1215–1230. Michaelis, J. I. (1966). Quaere, whether "in vino veritas": An analysis of the truth serum cases. *Issues in Criminology, 2* (2), 245–267.

At therapeutic doses (one 100-mg capsule of secobarbital, for example), barbiturates make you feel sedated and drowsy. For this reason, patients are typically warned that barbiturates can impair the performance of driving a car or operating machinery. At higher doses, a hypnotic (sleep-inducing) effect is achieved.

Historically, the primary use of barbiturates has been in the treatment of insomnia, and they were widely recommended for this purpose from 1903, when they were first introduced, until the development of safer alternatives in the 1960s. One of the reasons why barbiturates fell from favor was that the sleep induced by these drugs turned out to be far from normal. Barbiturates tend to suppress rapid eye movement (REM) sleep, which represents about 20 percent of everyone's total sleep time each night. REM sleep is associated with dreaming and general relaxation of the body. If barbiturates are consumed over many evenings and then stopped, the CNS will attempt to catch up for the lost REM sleep by producing longer REM periods on subsequent nights. This **REM-sleep rebound** effect produces vivid and upsetting nightmares, along with a barbiturate hangover the next day, during which the user feels groggy and out of sorts. In other words, barbiturates may induce sleep, but a refreshing sleep it definitely is not.

The most serious acute risks of barbiturate use involve the possibility of a lethal overdose either from taking too high a dose level of the drug alone or from taking the drug in combination with alcohol, such as when a barbiturate is taken after an evening of drinking. In these instances, the sleeper can all too easily slip into coma and death, since an excessive dose produces an inhibition of the respiratory control centers in the brain. The mixture of barbiturates with alcohol produces a synergistic effect (see Chapter 1) in which the combined result is greater than the sum of the effects of each drug alone.[3]

REM-sleep rebound: A phenomenon associated with the withdrawal of barbiturate drugs in which the quantity of rapid eye movement (REM) sleep increases, resulting in disturbed sleep and nightmares.

Half of the lethal dose of secobarbital combined with one-fourth the lethal dose of alcohol can kill in a synergistic double whammy. In another typical case of accidental overdose, a person takes a sleeping pill and awakens drugged and confused a few minutes later, annoyed at being aroused. The person then forgetfully takes another pill, or several, from the nightstand, and goes to sleep forever. This is called "drug automatism," a good reason not to keep medications within reach of the bed.[4]

During the period between 1973 and 1976, barbiturates were implicated in more than half of all drug-related deaths labeled as suicide by medical examiners. In fact, the potential of barbiturates for a lethal overdose is the major reason for their decline as a prescription sedative.[5]

Chronic Effects of Barbiturates

The use of barbiturates as sleep medications often initiates a cycle of behavior that can lead to dependence. Even after brief use of barbiturates, anxiety may be temporarily increased during the day, and there may be an even greater degree of insomnia than before. In addition, because a barbiturate-induced sleep typically leaves a person feeling groggy the next morning, it is tempting to take a stimulant drug during the day to feel completely alert. At bedtime, the person still feels the stimulant effects and is inclined to continue taking a barbiturate to achieve any sleep at all. To make matters worse, the brain builds up a pharmacological tolerance to barbiturates quite quickly, requiring increasingly higher doses for an equivalent effect.

The withdrawal symptoms observed when barbiturates are discontinued indicate a strong physical dependence on the drug. A person may experience a

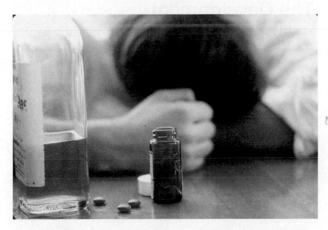

Barbiturates and alcohol have frequently been combined in attempts to commit suicide.

combination of tremors ("the shakes"), nausea and vomiting, intense perspiring, general confusion, convulsions, hallucinations, high fever, and increased heart rate. Not surprisingly, considering the parallels mentioned so far with alcohol, the barbiturate withdrawal syndrome closely resembles that of withdrawal after chronic alcohol abuse.

Professionals in the treatment of drug dependence often view the effects of barbiturate withdrawal as the most distressing, as well as the most dangerous, type of drug withdrawal. From a medical perspective, the withdrawal process is life-threatening unless it is carried out in gradual fashion in a hospital setting. Without medical supervision, abrupt withdrawal from barbiturates carries approximately a 5 percent chance of death.[6]

Current Medical Uses of Barbiturates

Considering the problems of barbiturate use in the treatment of insomnia, it should not be surprising that the clinical use of barbiturates for this problem is essentially "obsolete."[7] Nonetheless, barbiturates continue to play an important role in the treatment of epileptic seizures. Phenobarbital and mephobarbital (two relatively long-acting barbiturates) are prescribed to prevent convulsions. Dose levels need to be adjusted and monitored carefully because the concentration must be high enough to control the development of seizures (despite the tendency for tolerance effects to occur over time) without being so high as to produce drowsiness. Other nonbarbiturate antiseizure medications commonly in use will be described in Chapter 15.

Patterns of Barbiturate Abuse

There are clear indications that taking barbiturate drugs is positively reinforcing. Laboratory animals will eagerly press a lever to deliver intravenous injections of barbiturates, particularly the shorter-acting types, at rates that are equal to those for cocaine.[8] When given the choice between pentobarbital and a nonbarbiturate depressant, and given no knowledge as to the identity of the drugs, human drug abusers reliably select an oral dose of pentobarbital.[9]

Barbiturate abuse reached its peak in the 1950s and 1960s. (Table 13.2). The principal reason for its decline after 1970 was that barbiturates became less widely available as prescription drugs. Stricter controls were placed on obtaining excessive amounts of barbiturates from pharmacies, whereas physicians, concerned with the potential of barbiturates for intentional suicide or unintentional lethal overdose, became reluctant to prescribe them on a routine basis.

TABLE 13.2

Street names for various barbiturates

TYPE OF BARBITURATE	STREET NAME
pentobarbital (Nembutal)	blockbusters, nebbies, nembies, nemmies, yellow bullets, yellow dolls, yellow jackets, yellows
amobarbital (Amytal)	blue angels, bluebirds, blue bullets, blue devils, blue dolls, blue heavens, blues
secobarbital (Seconal)	F-40s, Mexican reds, R.D.s, redbirds, red bullets, red devils, red dolls, reds, seccies, seggies,
secobarbital and amobarbital (Tuinal)	Christmas trees, reds & blues, trees, tuies
barbiturates in general	barbs, downers, down, goofballs, G.B.s, goofers, idiot pills,

Note: Like any other street drug, illicit barbiturate capsules often contain an unknown array of other substances, including strychnine, arsenic, laxatives, and milk sugars. Any yellow capsule is likely to be "marketed" as Nembutal, any blue capsule as Amytal, and any red capsule as Seconal.

Source: Drug Enforcement Administration (2011). *Drugs of abuse: A drug resource guide.* Washington, DC: Drug Enforcement Administration, U.S. Department of Justice, p. 79. Henningfield, J. E., and Ator, N. A. (1986). *Barbiturates: Sleeping potion or intoxicant?* New York: Chelsea House, p. 82.

Despite their decline as major drugs of abuse, however, barbiturates are still being abused. The 2011 University of Michigan survey of high school seniors found that 7 percent of them had used some form of barbiturates during their lifetime, down from 17 percent in 1975, and 4 percent had taken them within the past year, down from 11 percent in 1975.[10]

Nonbarbiturate Sedative-Hypnotics

As the hazards of barbiturate use became increasingly evident, the search was on for sedative-hypnotic drugs that were not derivatives of barbituric acid and had

chloral hydrate: A depressant drug once used for the treatment of insomnia. It is highly reactive with alcohol and can severely irritate the stomach.

methaqualone (MEH-tha-QUAY-lone): A nonbarbiturate depressant drug once used as a sedative. Brand name is Quaalude.

fewer undesirable side effects. Unfortunately, these objectives were not realized.

One such drug, **chloral hydrate**, had been synthesized as early as 1832. As a depressant used for the treatment of insomnia, it has the advantage of not producing the REM-sleep rebound effect or bringing on the typical barbiturate hangover. A major disadvantage, however, is that it can severely irritate the stomach. Like other depressants, it is also highly reactive when combined with alcohol. In the nineteenth century, a few drops of chloral hydrate in a glass of whiskey became the infamous "Mickey Finn," a concoction that left many an unsuspecting sailor unconscious and eventually "shanghaied" onto a boat for China. You might say that chloral hydrate was an early precursor of the modern-day "date-rape" drug (see pages 326–327).

The development of **methaqualone** (brand names: Quaalude, Sopor), first introduced in the United States in 1965, was a further attempt to achieve the perfect sleeping pill. In 1972, methaqualone had become the sixth-best-selling drug for the treatment of insomnia. During the early 1970s, recreational use of methaqualone (popularly known as "ludes" or "sopors") was rapidly spreading across the country, aided by its unfounded reputation of having aphrodisiac properties. In 1984, this drug's legal status changed to that of a Schedule I controlled substance, the most restricted classification, which indicates a high potential for abuse and no medical benefits. Although it is no longer manufactured by any pharmaceutical company, methaqualone is still available as an illicit drug and qualifies as a "date-rape" drug.[11] It is either manufactured in domestic underground laboratories or smuggled into the country from underground laboratories abroad.

The Development of Antianxiety Drugs

If social historians consider the 1950s "the age of anxiety," then it is appropriate that this period also would be marked by the development of drugs specifically intended to combat that anxiety. These drugs were originally called *minor tranquilizers*, to distinguish them from other drugs regarded as *major tranquilizers* and developed at about the same time to relieve symptoms of schizophrenia. This terminology is no longer used today, for we now know that the pharmacological differences between the two drug categories are more than simply a matter of degree. Anxious people (and even people who are not bothered by anxiety) are not affected by drugs designed to treat schizophrenia. The current, and more logical, practice is to refer to drugs in terms of a specific action and purpose. The minor tranquilizers are now called *antianxiety drugs* or *anxiolytic* ("anxiety-reducing") *medications*.

The first antianxiety drug to be developed was **meprobamate** (brand name: Miltown), named in 1955 for a New Jersey community near the pharmaceutical company that first introduced it. Miltown became an immediate hit among prescription drugs, making its name a household word and essentially a synonym for tranquilizers in general. It was the first psychoactive drug in history to be marketed specifically as an antianxiety medication.[12]

Meprobamate had advantages and disadvantages. On the positive side, the toxic dose was relatively high, so the possibility of suicide was more remote than with alcohol, barbiturates, and other depressants. In addition, judging from the reduction in autonomic responses to stressors, there were genuine signs that people on this medication were actually less anxious. On the negative side, motor reflexes were diminished, making driving more hazardous. People often complained of drowsiness, even at dose levels that should have only been calming them down. Meprobamate also produced both physical and psychological dependence, at slightly more than twice the normal recommended daily dose.[13] This was not a very wide margin for possible abuse, and as a result, meprobamate was classified as a Schedule IV controlled substance, requiring limits on the number of prescription refills. By 1960, meprobamate had been eclipsed by a newer and quite different class of antianxiety drugs called benzodiazepines.

Benzodiazepines

The introduction of a group of drugs called **benzodiazepines** was a dramatic departure from all earlier attempts to treat anxiety. On the one hand, for the first time, there now were drugs that had a *selective* effect on anxiety itself, instead of producing a generalized reduction in the body's overall level of functioning. It was their "tranquilizing" effects, rather than their sedative effects, that made benzodiazepines so appealing to mental health professionals. On the other hand, it is important to distinguish between the well-publicized virtues of benzodiazepines when they were introduced in the 1960s and the data that accumulated during the 1970s as millions of people experienced these new drugs. Although they are certainly very useful in the treatment of anxiety and other stress-related problems, long-acting benzodiazepines are no longer recognized as the miracle drugs they were promoted to be when they first entered the market.

Medical Uses of Benzodiazepines

The first marketed benzodiazepine, **chlordiazepoxide** (brand name: Librium), was introduced in 1960, followed by **diazepam** (brand name: Valium) in 1963. Table 13.3 lists the major benzodiazepine drugs currently on the market. They are all chemically related, but their potencies and time courses vary considerably. Valium, for example, is five to ten times stronger than

TABLE 13.3

The leading benzodiazepines on the market

TRADE NAME	GENERIC NAME	ELIMINATION HALF-LIFE (IN HOURS)
Long-acting benzodiazepines		
Valium	Diazepam	20–50
Librium	Chlordiazepoxide	8–24
Limbitrol	chlordiazepoxide and amitriptyline (an antidepressant)	8–24
Dalmane	Flurazepam	70–160
Tranxene	Clorazepate	50–100
Intermediate-acting benzodiazepines		
Ativan	Lorazepam	10–24
Klonopin	Clonazepam	18–50
ProSom	estazolam	13–35
Short-acting benzodiazepines		
Restoril	temazepam	8–35
Versed	midazolam	1.5–4.5
Halcion	triazolam	1.5–5
Xanax	alprazolam	11–18

Note: Klonopin is available in orally disintegrating wafers for panic-attack patients who need the medication in an easily administered form.

Sources: Julien, R.M. (2005). *A primer of drug action* (10th ed.). New York: Worth, p. 169. *Physicians' desk reference* (67th ed.) (2013). Montvale, NJ: PDR Network.

meprobamate (MEH-pro-BAYM-ate): A nonbarbiturate antianxiety drug and sedative. Brand name is Miltown.

benzodiazepines (BEN-zoh-dye-AZ-eh-pins): A family of antianxiety drugs. Examples include diazepam (Valium), chlordiazepoxide (Librium), and triazolam (Halcion).

chlordiazepoxide (CHLOR-dye-az-eh-POX-ide): A major benzodiazepine drug for the treatment of anxiety. Brand name is Librium.

diazepam (dye-AZ-eh-pam): A major benzodiazepine drug for the treatment of anxiety. Brand name is Valium.

Librium and takes effect about an hour sooner. The relatively quicker response from Valium is a principal factor in making it more popular than Librium.

The variations in the benzodiazepines' effects have led to different recommendations for their medical use. Oral administration of the relatively long-acting benzodiazepines, in general, is recommended for relief from anxiety, with the effects beginning thirty minutes to four hours after ingestion. Besides Librium and Valium, other examples of this type include flurazepam (brand name: Dalmane) and clorazepate (brand name: Tranxene). When a very quick effect is desired, an injectable form of diazepam is used—for example, to reduce the symptoms of agitation that follow alcohol withdrawal (delirium tremens, or the DTs), as an anticonvulsant for epileptic patients, or as a pre-anesthetic drug to relax the patient just prior to surgery. Shorter-acting oral benzodiazepines are recommended for sleeping problems because their effects begin more quickly and wear off well before morning. Examples of this type include alprazolam (brand name: Xanax) and temazepam (brand name: Restoril).

Interestingly, benzodiazepines work best when the physician prescribing the medication is perceived as being warm, has a positive attitude toward use of antianxiety drugs, and believes that the patient will improve.[14] The positive impact of such psychological factors on the outcome of treatment underscores the importance of the physician–patient relationship, along with the genuine pharmacological effects of the drugs themselves.

Acute Effects of Benzodiazepines

In general, benzodiazepines are absorbed relatively slowly into the bloodstream, so their relaxant effects develop more gradually and last longer than those of barbiturates. This is because benzodiazepines are absorbed from the small intestine rather than the stomach, as is the case with barbiturates. The relatively greater water solubility and, by implication, the relatively lower fat solubility of benzodiazepines also are factors.

The major advantage that benzodiazepines have over barbiturates and other drugs previously used to control anxiety is their higher level of safety. Respiratory centers in the brain are not affected by benzodiazepines, so it is rare for a person to die of respiratory failure from an accidental or intentional overdose. Even after taking fifty or sixty times the therapeutic dose, the person will still not stop breathing. It is almost always possible to arouse a person from the stupor that such a drug quantity would produce. In contrast, doses of barbiturates or

nonbarbiturate sedatives that are ten to twenty times the therapeutic dose are lethal. Yet we must remember that this higher level of safety assumes that *no alcohol or other depressant drugs are being taken at the same time.*[15]

Despite the relative safety of benzodiazepines, this drug family poses a number of medical risks for special populations. For elderly patients, for example, the rate of elimination of these drugs is slowed down significantly, resulting in the risk of a dangerously high buildup of benzodiazepines after several doses. In the case of a long-acting benzodiazepine such as Valium or Librium, the elimination half-life is as long as ten days. An elderly patient with this rate of elimination would not be essentially drug-free until two months had passed since she or he took the drug.

The continued accumulation of benzodiazepines in the elderly can produce a form of drug-induced dementia in which the patient suffers from confusion and loss of memory. Without understanding the patient's medication history, one could easily mistake these symptoms for the onset of Alzheimer's disease. An additional problem with benzodiazepines is the increased risk of falls and bone fractures. It is for these reasons that long-acting benzodiazepines are no longer recommended for this age group, and those who are currently taking these drugs are being encouraged to switch to shorter-acting forms or alternative non-pharmacological treatments.[16]

Chronic Effects of Benzodiazepines

The benzodiazepines were viewed originally as having few, if any, problems related to a tolerance effect or an acquired dependence. We now know that the *anxiety-relieving* aspects of benzodiazepines show little or no tolerance effects when the drugs are taken at prescribed dosages, but there is a tolerance to the *sedative* effects. In other words, when the drugs are taken for the purpose of relieving anxiety, there is no problem with tolerance, but when they are taken for insomnia, more of the drug may be required in later administrations to induce sleep.[17]

We also now know that physiological symptoms appear when benzodiazepines are withdrawn, an indication of benzodiazepine dependence. In the case of long-acting benzodiazepines, the slow rate of elimination delays the appearance of withdrawal symptoms until between the third day and the sixth day following drug withdrawal. The first signs include an anxiety level that may be worse than the level for which the drug was originally prescribed. Later, there are symptoms of insomnia, restlessness, and agitation. In general, however, withdrawal symptoms are less severe than those observed after barbiturate withdrawal, occur only after long-term use, and are gone in one to four weeks.[18]

How Benzodiazepines Work in the Brain

The key factor in the action of benzodiazepines is the neurotransmitter gamma-aminobutyric acid (GABA), which normally exerts an inhibitory effect on the nervous system (see Chapter 3). When benzodiazepines are in the vicinity of GABA receptors, the actions of GABA are increased. The antianxiety drugs attach themselves to their own receptors on the membrane of neurons and, in doing so, heighten the effect of GABA. The facilitation of GABA produces a greater inhibition and a decreased activity level in the neurons involved.[19]

The receptor described in Figure 13.1 is a large protein molecule that has multiple binding locations, arranged like docking sites for different kinds of boats. The receptor consists of three binding sites: one for sedative-hypnotics (including the barbiturates), one for benzodiazepines (and alcohol), and one for GABA. When GABA attaches to its binding site, there is greater inhibition if the benzodiazepine sites are also occupied at the time by a benzodiazepine drug than if they are not so occupied.[20] The successful binding of a chemical at one site facilitates the binding at the others.

It is not difficult to imagine how cross-tolerance among various depressant drugs would occur. If two depressant drugs were to bind to the same receptor, the receptor would not be able to "tell the difference" between them. As far as the receptor is concerned, the effect would be the same. Evidently, sedative-hypnotics and benzodiazepines share this ability to lock into a common receptor with multiple binding locations.[21]

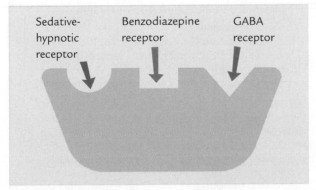

FIGURE 13.1

A simplified view of the benzodiazepine receptor.

Sedative-hypnotic receptor   Benzodiazepine receptor   GABA receptor

Patterns of Benzodiazepine Misuse and Abuse

Benzodiazepines do not present the same potential for abuse that cocaine, alcohol, or the barbiturates do, for two primary reasons. First, benzodiazepines are only weak reinforcers of behavior. When trained to press a lever for an injection of Valium, for example, laboratory animals self-administer the drug, but at far less robust levels than they would self-administer pentobarbital or methaqualone. Studies with normal college student volunteers show that when subjects are given the choice between a placebo and Valium, and the true identity of neither choice is known, they actually prefer the placebo. For these individuals, who presumably are not drug abusers and are relatively anxiety-free, the results show no indication of a positive Valium reaction.[22] Second, the slow onset of a benzodiazepine effect prevents the sudden "rush" feeling that is characteristic of many abused drugs such as cocaine, heroin, and amphetamines.

This is *not* to say, however, that benzodiazepines fail to be abused. It is simply that their abuse exists largely in the context of abusing other drugs as well. Alcoholics, for example, may take benzodiazepines to reduce anxiety and other withdrawal symptoms in the context of their alcoholism. Heroin abusers may take benzodiazepines to augment their euphoria and reduce their anxiety when the opioid levels in their blood begin to fall.[23]

Historically speaking, the principal concern regarding benzodiazepines concerned the enormous quantity of prescriptions that were being written. In 1972, Valium ranked first (and Librium third) among the most frequently prescribed drugs of any type. *At the height of their popularity in 1975, more than 100 million prescriptions for benzodiazepines were processed around the world, 85 million of them in the United States.* It was estimated at the time that in Western Europe and North America, 10 to 20 percent of adults were taking benzodiazepines on a fairly regular basis.[24]

Benzodiazepines have declined substantially in psychiatric practice as newer approaches to anxiety disorders have been pursued. Nonetheless, benzodiazepines remain widely prescribed drugs throughout the world, particularly for people over the age of sixty-five years, to treat problems of insomnia and anxiety. Although they are useful for short-term applications, adverse side effects can arise when benzodiazepines are taken over a long period of time. The potential for cognitive impairment among elderly people and the adverse effects when benzodiazepines are combined with alcohol were discussed earlier in this chapter. These possibilities have been a particular problem in European countries where wine is consumed on a regular basis.[25]

In recent years, considerable publicity has focused on the social and personal concerns surrounding the abuse of a specific benzodiazepine, flunitrazepam (brand name: Rohypnol). This drug is not legally available in the United States but is accessible as a "club drug" through illicit channels (Health Alert).

Nonbenzodiazepine Depressants

Just as benzodiazepines represented a great advance over barbiturates, the development of new nonbenzodiazepine drugs has provided better opportunities to treat sleep disorders and anxiety. Prominent examples of this new generation of medications are zolpidem,

---

HEALTH ALERT!

The Dangers of Rohypnol as a Date-Rape Drug

Flunitrazepam (brand name: Rohypnol) is a long-acting benzodiazepine not unlike diazepam (Valium), except that it is approximately ten times stronger. Because of its extreme potency and the fact that it is highly synergistic with alcohol, Rohypnol is not legally available in the United States. It is, however, approved for medical use in Europe and South America, where it is marketed by Hoffmann–La Roche Pharmaceuticals as a treatment for sleep disorders and as a surgical anesthetic. The U.S. supply of Rohypnol is smuggled into the country from Mexico and South America and sold for recreational use, frequently in its original bubble packaging.

The abuse potential of Rohypnol surfaced in the mid-1990s, when the number of pills seized by the U.S. Customs Service increased by 400 percent from 1994 to 1995 alone. Increased efforts by U.S. Customs and the Drug Enforcement Administration (DEA) have drastically reduced the availability of Rohypnol in the United States, although the drug remains a matter of great concern.

Under such street names as "roofies," "rope," "wolfies," "roches," "R2," and "Mexican Valium," this drug has been promoted as an alcohol enhancer and as a strategy for getting drunk without having a blood-alcohol concentration level that would be defined as legal intoxication. Rohypnol also has been involved in numerous date-rape cases in which victims had been unknowingly slipped the drug, causing them to pass out. The disinhibition of behavior and the subsequent loss of all memory of the experience are similar to an alcohol-induced blackout (see Chapter 8).

At one time, Rohypnol was odorless, colorless, and tasteless, so it could be easily combined with an alcoholic beverage without detection. Recently, in response to instances of abuse, Hoffmann–La Roche has taken steps to reformulate the drug so that it turns blue when dissolved in a clear liquid. This helps to make Rohypnol somewhat

more noticeable to an unsuspecting drinker, but it is difficult to notice changes in beverage color under the dim illumination of a typical bar. Besides, in blue tropical drinks and punches, blue dye produces no color change at all.

Since 1996, U.S. federal law has provided for a twenty-year sentence for the use of Rohypnol in connection with rape or other violent crime. Unfortunately, Rohypnol is an increasingly accessible illicit drug. According to one law-enforcement official in Miami, "It may be easier for teenagers to obtain flunitrazepam (Rohypnol) than alcohol." A recent study has found that a variety of benzodiazepines, all marketed by Hoffmann–La Roche, are being abused and linked to sexual assaults. Because these drugs all bear the same Roche imprint on the tablets, they are collectively known as "roches."

Rohypnol is an example of a group of present-day "club drugs" that have a dangerous potential for abuse as date-rape drugs. Other examples include MDMA, or Ecstasy (see Chapter 6), and GHB (discussed later in this chapter).

Where to go for assistance:

http://www.4woman.gov/faq/rohypnol.htm

This web site is sponsored by the National Woman's Health Information Center, a service of the U.S. Department of Health and Human Services dedicated to women's health issues.

Sources: Community Epidemiology Work Group (1996). *Epidemiologic trends in drug abuse,* Volume 1: *Highlights and executive summary.* Rockville, MD: National Institute on Drug Abuse, pp. 8, 64. Quotation on p. 64. Drug Enforcement Administration, U.S. Department of Justice, Washington, DC, 1997. Office of National Drug Control Policy (2003, February). *ONDCP Drug Policy Clearinghouse fact sheet: Rohypnol.* Washington, DC: Executive Office of the President.

eszopiclone, buspirone, beta blockers, and, strangely enough, antidepressants.

Zolpidem and Eszopiclone

Zolpidem (brand name: Ambien) is not a benzodiazepine drug, but it binds to a specific subtype of GABA receptor. This is probably why it produces only some of the effects usually associated with benzodiazepines and is especially useful in the short-term treatment of insomnia. Its strong but transient sedative effects (with a half-life of about two hours) have led to the marketing of zolpidem, since its introduction in 1993, as a sedative-hypnotic rather than an antianxiety agent. Little or no muscle relaxation is experienced.

Introduced in 2004, **eszopiclone** (brand name: Lunesta, formerly known as Estorra) is also a non-benzodiazepine drug prescribed for the treatment of insomnia. As a result of successful clinical trials lasting six months, the FDA has approved Lunesta for an interval of treatment that is longer than the recommended treatment with Ambien. Because its half-life of six hours is longer than that of Ambien, Lunesta has been helpful for people who have difficulty *staying asleep* during the night as well as difficulty *falling asleep*.[26]

Buspirone

Buspirone (brand name: BuSpar), has a number of remarkable features. It has been found to be equivalent to Valium in its ability to relieve anxiety, but, unlike the benzodiazepines in general, buspirone shows no cross tolerance effects when combined with alcohol or other depressants and no withdrawal symptoms when discontinued after chronic use. When compared with benzodiazepines, side effects are observed less frequently and are less troublesome to the patient; approximately 9 percent report dizziness, and 7 percent report headaches. Animals do not self-administer buspirone in laboratory studies, and human volunteers indicate an absence of euphoria.

Buspirone also fails to cause the impairments in motor skills that are characteristic of benzodiazepines. In other words, the relief of anxiety is attainable without the accompanying feelings and behavioral consequences of sedation. Perhaps anxiety and sedation do not have to be intertwined after all. Unlike benzodiazepines, buspirone does not affect GABA receptors in the brain but rather acts on a special subclass of serotonin receptors. Evidently, the influence of buspirone on serotonin produces the antianxiety effects.

Despite its virtues, however, buspirone has a distinct disadvantage: a very long delay before anxiety relief is felt. It may take weeks for the drug to become completely effective. This feature makes buspirone clearly inappropriate for relieving *acute* anxiety conditions, but patients suffering from long-term generalized anxiety disorder find it helpful as a therapeutic drug. An extra benefit of the delay in the action of buspirone is that it becomes highly undesirable as a drug of abuse. Do not expect to see news headlines in the future warning of an epidemic of buspirone abuse.[27]

Beta Blockers

The traditional medical uses of beta-adrenergic-blocking drugs, commonly known as **beta blockers**, include slowing the heart rate, relaxing pressure on the walls of blood vessels, and decreasing the force of heart contractions. The combination of a beta-blocker drug and a diuretic is a frequent treatment for the control of high blood pressure. These drugs are also prescribed for individuals facing an anxiety-producing event, such as performing on the stage or giving a speech. Examples of beta blockers include atenolol (brand name: Tenormin), metoprolol (brand name: Lopressor), and propranolol (brand name: Inderal).

Antidepressants

Another approach in the treatment of panic disorder, post-traumatic stress disorder, and social anxiety disorder has been the use of antidepressant medications—specifically, selective serotonin reuptake inhibitors (SSRIs) such as sertraline (brand name: Zoloft) and paroxetine (brand names: Paxil, Asima).[28]

zolpidem (ZOL-pih-dem): A nonbenzodiazepine sedative-hypnotic drug, first introduced in 1993, for the treatment of insomnia. Brand name is Ambien.

eszopiclone (es-ZOP-eh-clone): A nonbenzodiazepine sedative-hypnotic, first introduced in 2005, for the treatment of insomnia. Brand name is Lunesta.

buspirone (BYOO-spir-rone): A nonbenzodiazepine antianxiety drug first introduced in 1986. Brand name is BuSpar.

beta blockers: Medicinal drugs that are traditionally used to treat cardiac and blood pressure disorders. They are also prescribed for individuals who suffer from "stage fright" or anxiety regarding a specific event. Examples include atenolol (brand name: Tenormin), metoprolol (brand name: Lopressor), and propanolol (brand name: Inderal).

A Special Alert: The Risks of GHB

Of all the much-publicized club drugs to emerge in recent years, perhaps the most notorious is the CNS depressant **gamma-hydroxybutyrate (GHB)**. First synthesized in the 1960s, GHB is produced naturally in the body in very small amounts, but no one has discovered its function. At one time, GHB was sold in health-food stores and similar establishments. It was considered to have steroid-enhancing and growth-hormone-stimulating effects, leading to interest among body builders (see Chapter 12). Other promotions focused on GHB as a sedative. By 1990, however, numerous reports of GHB-related seizures and comas led the Food and Drug Administration (FDA) to

gamma-hydroxybutyrate (GHB) (GAM-ma heye-DROX-ee-BYOO-tih-rate): A powerful depressant, often abused to induce euphoria and sedation. When slipped into an alcoholic beverage without the knowledge of the drinker, GHB has been employed as a date-rape drug.

remove GHB from the legitimate market. Since then, the drug has gone underground. The manufacture of GHB is currently controlled by small clandestine laboratories, guided in many instances by formulas available on the Internet, and its sale is maintained by networks of illicit drug distributors.

Acute Effects

Present-day GHB abuse focuses on its ability to produce euphoria, an "out-of-body" high, in conjunction with a lowering of inhibitions. Frequently, a combination of GHB and alcohol can lead to unconsciousness in about fifteen minutes and to subsequent amnesia about the experience. The notoriety of GHB as a date-rape drug stems from its being colorless, odorless, and virtually tasteless. As a result, it can be slipped easily into alcoholic beverages without the knowledge of the drinker.[29]

Protective Strategies for Women

The vulnerability of women to being drugged with GHB while consuming alcohol in a club or bar is considerable (Portrait), but a number of protective strategies can be employed to minimize the risk.

- Watch the person who pours you a drink, even if he or she is a friend or a bartender. Even better, do not drink what you cannot open or pour yourself. Avoid punch bowls and shared containers. Never accept a drink offered to you by a stranger.

- Do not leave a drink alone—not while you are dancing, using the restroom, or making a telephone call. If you have left it alone, toss it out.

This commercially available bar coaster is used to test for the presence of GHB in an alcoholic beverage.

Patricia White, a forty-seven-year-old mother of three, was at a party celebrating the birthday of her boss, Lorenzo Feal. According to testimony later given by White, as she was about to leave the party, Feal handed her a bottle of water. She took a gulp. A few hours later, White woke up in Feal's bed, naked and nauseated. She had been drugged and raped. Doctors at the emergency department of the local hospital found traces of GHB in her system, and Feal was eventually convicted of using an anesthetic substance in perpetrating White's rape.

A prosecuting attorney has called GHB "ideal for predators and tough for prosecutors" because it is so easily concealed in a drink. Without toxicological evidence, it is difficult to prove that the rape victim had not given consent to sex. Perhaps GHB should really be called an "acquaintance-rape and date-rape drug."

In 1994, when GHB was relatively new, only 56 GHB-related emergency department "mentions" were reported through the DAWN system (see Chapter 1). By 2002, that number had grown to 3,300 before holding steady at about 1500–2400 between 2004 and 2011. Colleges and universities, as well as commercial bars, have become justifiably alarmed. The Drug Enforcement Administration (DEA) has collaborated with the Rape, Abuse, and Incest National Network (RAINN) in an effort to promote a heightened awareness of GHB and other "predatory" drugs such as Rohypnol.

Patricia White now counsels GHB rape victims and speaks out publicly about her personal story. In the case of GHB, the more you know about this drug, the safer you are.

Sources: Smalley, S. (2003, February 3). "The perfect crime": GHB is colorless, odorless, leaves the body within hours—and is fueling a growing number of rapes. *Newsweek*, p. 52. Substance Abuse and Mental Health Services Administration (2013). *Drug Abuse Warning Network: National estimates of drug-related emergency visits, 2004–2011*. Rockville, MD: Substance Abuse and Mental Health Services Administration, Excel files.

- Appoint a designated "sober" friend to check up on you at parties, bars, clubs, and other social gatherings.

- If a friend seems extremely drunk or sick after a drink and has trouble breathing, call 911 immediately.

- If you have been slipped GHB, the drug will take effect within ten to thirty minutes. Initially, you will feel dizzy or nauseated or will develop a severe headache. You can be incapacitated rapidly. This is the time when having a nondrinking friend nearby is crucial.

- If you wake up in a strange place and believe that you have been sexually assaulted while under the influence of GHB, do not urinate until you have been admitted to a hospital. There is an approximately twelve-hour window of opportunity to detect GHB through urinalysis.

A test strip created by Drink Safe Technology is now available that can detect not only GHB but also Rohypnol and ketamine. A straw can be used to place a few drops of one's drink on the test strip. If the liquid turns blue, there is a positive result. Unfortunately, when the drink contains dairy products, an accurate detection cannot be made. Bar coasters have been developed that incorporate this particular test strip. Never forget, however, that the original and all-time leading date-rape drug is alcohol itself.[30]

Inhalants through History

The mind-altering effects of substances inhaled into the lungs have been known since the beginnings of recorded history. Burnt spices and aromatic gums were used in worship ceremonies in many parts of the ancient world; exotic perfumes were inhaled during Egyptian worship as well as in Babylonian rituals. Inhalation effects also figured prominently in the famous rites of the oracle at Delphi in ancient Greece, where trances induced by the inhaling of vapors led to mysterious utterances that were interpreted as prophecies. We know now, from archeological studies, that limestone faults underneath the temple at Delphi once caused petrochemical fumes to rise to the surface. The oracle was probably inhaling ethylene, a sweet-smelling gas that produces an out-of-body sense of euphoria.[31]

It was not until the latter part of the eighteenth century that reports about the inhalation of specific drugs began to appear. The two most prominent examples were cases involving *nitrous oxide* and *ether*. These anesthetic drugs were first used as surgical analgesics in the 1840s, but they had been synthesized decades earlier. From the very start, word had spread of recreational possibilities.

Nitrous Oxide

In 1798, at the precocious age of nineteen, the British chemist Sir Humphry Davy began formal investigations of a newly synthesized gas called **nitrous oxide**. He immediately observed the pleasant effects of this "laughing gas" and proceeded to give nitrous oxide parties for his literary and artistic friends. By the early 1800s, recreational use of nitrous oxide became widespread both in England and in the United States as a nonalcoholic avenue to drunkenness. In the 1840s, public demonstrations were held in cities and towns, as a traveling show, by entrepreneurs eager to market the drug commercially.

It was at such an exhibition in Hartford, Connecticut, that a young dentist, Horace Wells, got the idea of using nitrous oxide as an anesthetic. One of the intoxicated participants in the demonstration had stumbled and fallen, receiving in the process a severe wound to the leg. Seeing that the man showed no evidence of being in pain, Wells was sufficiently impressed to try out the anesthetic possibilities himself. The next day, he underwent a tooth extraction while under the influence of nitrous oxide. He felt no pain during the procedure, and nitrous oxide has been a part of dental practice ever since, although controversy exists about its routine use as an anesthetic.[32]

During the 1960s, nitrous oxide inhalation reappeared as a recreational drug. Tanks of compressed nitrous oxide were diverted for illicit use, and health professionals, like their counterparts one hundred years earlier, were reportedly hosting nitrous oxide parties. Small cartridges of nitrous oxide called **whippets** (generally used by restaurants to dispense whipped cream) became available through college campus "head shops" and mail-order catalogs. The customary pattern of nitrous oxide abuse was to fill a balloon from

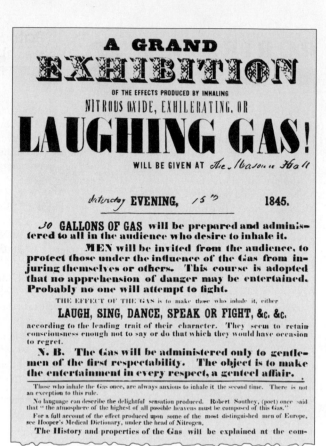

Public demonstrations of nitrous oxide ("laughing gas") inhalation were popular entertainments in the first half of the nineteenth century.

these cylinders and inhale the gas from the balloon. The result was a mild euphoric high that lasted for a few minutes and a sense of well-being that lingered for several hours. Sometimes, there would be a loss of consciousness for a few seconds and an experience of "flying." Once consciousness returned, there was the possibility of sensory distortions, nausea, or vomiting. Ordinary cans of commercial whipped cream, in which nitrous oxide is the propellant gas, currently provide easy access to this inhalant.

Nitrous oxide itself is a nontoxic gas, but its inhalation presents serious risks. As with any euphoriant drug, the recreational use of nitrous oxide can be extremely dangerous when a person is driving under its influence. In addition, if nitrous oxide is inhaled through an anesthetic mask and the mask is worn over the mouth and nose, without being combined with oxygen, the consequences can be lethal. Nitrous oxide dilutes the air that a person breathes. Normally, the oxygen concentration in the air we breathe is 21 percent. If the oxygen concentration falls below 17 percent, symptoms of **hypoxia**

nitrous oxide (NIGH-trus OX-ide): An analgesic gas commonly used in modern dentistry. It is also referred to as laughing gas.

whippets: Small canisters containing pressurized nitrous oxide.

hypoxia (high-POX-ee-ah): A deficiency in oxygen intake.

(literally "oxygen deficiency") such as light-headedness will result; if the concentration falls below 10 percent, there will be a loss of consciousness. The victim will be either asphyxiated and die or else sustain irreversible brain damge.[33]

Ether

Like nitrous oxide, **ether** came into use well before its anesthetic effects were appreciated by the medical profession. It was introduced by Friedrich Hoffmann at the beginning of the 1700s, under the name Anodyne, as a liquid "nerve tonic" for intestinal cramps, toothaches, and other pains. Whether it was swallowed or inhaled (it evaporated very quickly), ether also produced effects that resembled intoxication from alcohol. In fact, during the mid-1800s, when the combination of a heavy tax on alcohol and a temperance campaign in England and Ireland forced people to consider alternatives to alcoholic beverages, both ether drinking and ether inhalation became quite popular. It was used for the same purpose later in the United States during the Prohibition years and in Germany during World War II, when alcohol was rationed. The flammability of ether, however, made its recreational use highly dangerous.[34]

Glue, Solvent, and Aerosol Inhalation

The abuse of nitrous oxide and ether may have a relatively long history, but the more familiar reports of inhalation abuse involving glue and solvent chemicals have appeared only since the late 1950s.

The common products that have been subject to abuse include glues, paint thinners, lighter fluid, and stain removers. In addition, many aerosol products are inhalable: hair sprays, deodorants, vegetable lubricants for cooking, and spray paints. Unfortunately, new products are continually being introduced for genuinely practical uses, with little awareness of (or little regard for) the consequences should someone inhale their ingredients on a recreational basis (Table 13.4). Significant problems are also associated with occupational exposure to solvent vapors. In a study reported in 1999, 125 pregnant women who had been exposed to solvent products at the workplace were studied over a nine-year period. There was a thirteen times greater risk of birth defects among the exposed group, relative to

TABLE 13.4

Household products with abuse potential and their ingredients

HOUSEHOLD PRODUCT	POSSIBLE INGREDIENTS
Glues, plastic cements, and rubber cements	Acetates, acetone, benzene, hexane, methyl chloride, toluene, trichloroethylene
Cleaning solutions	Carbon tetrachloride, petroleum products, trichloroethylene
Nail polish removers	Acetone
Lighter fluids	Butane, isopropane
Paint sprays, paint thinners, and paint removers	Acetone, butylacetate, methanol, toluene, methyl chloride
Other petroleum products	Acetone, benzene, ether, gasoline, hexane, petroleum, tetraethyl lead, toluene
Typewriter correction fluid	Trichloroethylene, trichlorethane
Hair sprays	Butane, propane
Deodorants, air fresheners	Butane, propane
Whipped cream propellants	Nitrous oxide

Sources: Schuckit, M. A. (2006). *Drug and alcohol abuse: A clinical guide to diagnosis and treatment* (6th ed.). New York: Springer, p. 237. Sharp, C. W., and Rosenberg, N. L. (1997). Inhalants. In J. H. Lowinson, P. R., R. B. Millman, and J. G. Langrod (Eds.), *Substance abuse: A comprehensive textbook* (3d ed.). Baltimore: Williams and Wilkins, p. 248.

controls. These women included factory workers, laboratory technicians, artists, printing industry workers, chemists, and painters.[35]

The Abuse Potential of Inhalants

Commercial glues, solvents, and aerosol sprays are prime candidates for drug abuse for a number of reasons. First, because they are inhaled into the lungs, the feeling of intoxication occurs more rapidly than with orally administered alcohol. "It's a quicker drunk," in the words of one solvent abuser.[36] The feeling is often described as a "floating euphoria," similar

ether (EE-ther): An anesthetic drug first introduced to surgical practice by William T. Morton in the 1840s. It is highly flammable.

to the effect of alcohol but with a shorter course of intoxication. The high is over in an hour or so, and the hangover is considered less unpleasant than that following alcohol consumption. Second, the typical packaging of inhalant products makes them easy to carry around and conceal from others. Even if they are discovered, many of the products are so common that it is not difficult to invent an excuse for having them on hand.

Finally, most inhalants are easily available in hardware stores, pharmacies, and supermarkets, where they can be bought cheaply or stolen. Among some inhalant abusers, shoplifting these products from open shelves becomes a routine practice. Inhalants are even more widely available than alcohol in poor households; liquor may be in short supply, but gasoline, paints, and aerosol products are usually to be found around the house or garage.[37] All these factors contribute to the considerable potential for inhalant abuse.

Acute Effects of Glues, Solvents, and Aerosols

The fumes from commercial inhalant products fall into the general category of depressant drugs, in that the central nervous system is inhibited after they are inhaled. Brain waves, measured objectively through an electroencephalograph (EEG), slow down. Subjectively, the individual feels intoxicated within minutes after inhalation. The most immediate effects include giddiness, euphoria, dizziness, and slurred speech, lasting from fifteen to forty-five minutes. This state is followed by one to two hours of drowsiness and sometimes a loss of consciousness. Along with these effects are occasional experiences of double vision, ringing in the ears, and hallucinations.[38]

The Dangers of Inhalant Abuse

Inhalant abuse often involves concentrations of glue and solvent products that are fifty to a hundred times greater than the maximum allowable concentration of exposure in industry. The health of the inhalant abuser, therefore, is obviously at risk (Health Alert).

The dangers of inhalant abuse lie not only in the toxic effects of the inhaled compound on body organs but also in the behavioral effects of the intoxication itself. Inhalant-produced euphoria includes feelings of recklessness and omnipotence. The hallucinations that are sometimes experienced carry their own personal risks. Walls may appear to be closing in, or the sky may seem to be falling. Ordinary objects may be perceived

HEALTH ALERT!

The Signs of Possible Inhalant Abuse

- Headaches and dizziness
- Light sensitivity (from dilation of the pupils)
- Reddened, irritated eyes and rash around the mouth
- Double vision
- Ringing in the ears (tinnitus)
- Sneezing and sniffling
- Coughing and bad breath
- Nausea, vomiting, and loss of appetite
- Diarrhea
- Chest pains
- Abnormal heart rhythm (cardiac arrhythmia)
- Muscle and joint aches
- Slurred speech and unsteady muscle coordination
- Chemical odor or stains on clothing or body
- Rags, empty aerosol cans and other containers
- Plastic and paper bags found in closets and other hidden places

Where to go for assistance:
   www.inhalant.org
The web site is sponsored by the National Inhalant Prevention Coalition, Austin, Texas.

Source: Schuckit, M.A. (2006). *Drug and alcohol abuse: A clinical guide to diagnosis and treatment* (6th ed.). New York: Springer, p. 219.

to be changing their shape, size, or color. Any one of these delusions can lead to impulsive and potentially destructive behavior.[39]

There are also significant hazards related to the ways in which inhalants are administered. Solvents are sometimes inhaled from a handkerchief or from the container in which they were originally acquired ("huffing"), but glues and similar vaporous compounds are often squeezed into a plastic bag and inhaled while the bag is held tightly over the nose and mouth ("bagging"). As in the case of nitrous oxide abuse, a loss of consciousness can result in hypoxia and asphyxiation. Choking can occur if there is vomiting while the inhaler is unconscious. Another danger lies in the inhalation of Freon, a refrigerant gas so cold that the larynx and throat can be frozen upon contact.Identifying the toxic effects of inhalant drugs is complicated by the fact that most products subject to inhalant abuse contain a variety of compounds, and in some cases, the list of ingredients on the product label is incomplete. Therefore, we often do not know whether the medical symptoms resulted from a particular chemical or from its interaction with others. Nonetheless, there are specific chemicals that have known health risks. The most serious concern involves sudden-death cases, brought on by cardiac dysrhythmia, that have been reported following the inhalation of propane and butane, which are commonly used as propellants for many commercial products.[40]

Besides butane and propane, other inhalant ingredients that present specific hazards are *acetone, benzene, hexane, toluene,* and *gasoline*.

- *Acetone:* **Acetone** inhalation causes significant damage to the mucous membranes of the respiratory tract.
- *Benzene:* Prolonged exposure to **benzene** has been associated with carcinogenic (cancer-producing) disorders, specifically leukemia, as well as anemia. Benzene is generally used as a solvent in waxes, resins, lacquers, paints, and paint removers.
- *Hexane:* The inhalation of **hexane**, primarily in glues and other adhesive products, has been associated with peripheral nerve damage leading to muscular weakness and muscle atrophy. There is a latency period of a few weeks before the symptoms appear.
- *Toluene:* **Toluene** inhalation through glue sniffing has been associated with a reduction in short-term memory, anemia, and a loss of hearing, as well as dysfunctions in parts of the brain that result in difficulties in movement and coordination. Toluene also has been implicated as a principal factor in cases of lethal inhalation of spray paints and lacquers, although it is difficult to exclude the contribution of other solvents in these products.
- *Gasoline:* Concentrated vapors from gasoline can be lethal when inhaled. Medical symptoms from gasoline inhalation are also frequently attributed to gasoline additives that are mixed in the fuel. The additive **triorthocresyl phosphate (TCP)**, in particular, has been associated with spastic muscle disorders and liver problems. Lead content in gasoline is generally linked to long-term CNS degeneration, but fortunately, leaded gasoline is no longer commonly available in the United States. On the other hand, present-day gasoline mixtures contain potentially lethal amounts of toluene, acetone, and hexane to help achieve the "anti-knock" property that lead had previously provided.[41]

Patterns of Inhalant Abuse

Among all the psychoactive drugs, inhalants are associated most closely with the young—and often the very young. For those who engage in inhalant abuse, these compounds frequently represent the first experience with a psychoactive drug, preceding even alcohol or tobacco. Overall, inhalant abuse ranks fourth highest in drug experimentation among secondary school students, surpassed only by alcohol, tobacco, and marijuana (in that order). Most of those who engage in inhalant abuse, however, are younger than secondary school age; often they are between eleven and thirteen years old.

The University of Michigan survey of 2011 found that about 13 percent of eighth-grade students had used inhalants at some previous time. About 7 percent reported that they had used inhalants within the past year, and 3 percent within the past month. Inhalants are the only class of drugs for which the incidence of usage in the eighth grade significantly *exceeds* the incidence in the tenth and twelfth grades.

Evidently, awareness of this form of drug-taking activity is quite extensive in the later elementary and middle school student population. According to a recent survey, almost two-thirds of ten- to seventeen-year-olds know the meaning of "huffing" and report

acetone (ASS-eh-tone): A chemical found in nail polish removers and other products.

benzene: A carcinogenic (cancer-producing) compound found in many solvent products, representing a serious health risk when inhaled.

hexane: A dangerous compound present in many glues and adhesive products. Inhalation of these products has been associated with muscle weakness and atrophy.

toluene (TOL-yoo-ene): A compound in glues, cements, and other adhesive products. Inhalation of these products results in behavioral and neurological impairments.

triorthocresyl phosphate (TCP) (tri-OR-thoh-CREH-sil FOS-fate): A gasoline additive. Inhalation of TCP-containing gasoline has been linked to spastic muscle disorders and liver problems.

that they were about twelve years of age when they first became aware of classmates abusing inhalants.[42]

In other cultures and under different circumstances, inhalant abuse affects even younger children and a greater proportion of them. In Mexico City, among street children as young as eight or nine who live without families in abandoned buildings, rates of inhalant abuse are extremely high; 22 percent report engaging in some form of solvent inhalation on a daily basis. Inhalant abuse is reported to be commonplace among street children in Rio de Janeiro and other major cities in Central and South America as well as Asia (Drugs . . . in Focus).[43]

Inhalant abuse on an experimental basis is not restricted by social or geographic boundaries. Chronic inhalant abuse, however, is overrepresented among the poor and those youths suffering emotional challenges in their lives and seeking some form of escape. Studies of young inhalant abusers show high rates of delinquency, poor school performance, and emotional difficulties. They often come from disorganized homes in which the parents are actually or effectively absent or else engage in abuse of alcohol or some other substance themselves.[44]

A group of abandoned Brazilian children inhale glue from bags in Rio de Janeiro. Their dazed expression is a typical sign of inhalant intoxication.

High prevalence rates for inhalant abuse exist among such disparate groups as Latino children in a rural community in the Southwest, American Indian children on a U.S. reservation, and white children

Drugs . . . in Focus

Resistol and *Resistoleros* in Latin America

In the cities of Central and South America, the street children are referred to as *resistoleros*, a name derived from their frequent habit of sniffing a commercial brand of shoemaker's glue called Resistol. Granted, many cases of inhalant abuse among the hundreds of thousands of children in Latin America do not specifically involve Resistol; nevertheless, the frequency of Resistol abuse and the fact that Resistol dominates the market in commercial solvent-based adhesives have focused attention on the company that manufactures it, the H. B. Fuller Company of St. Paul, Minnesota.

Concern for the welfare of these children also has spotlighted a thorny ethical issue: Should a corporation accept the social responsibility when widespread abuse of its product exists, either in the United States or elsewhere in the world? Testor Corporation in 1969 added a noxious ingredient to discourage abuse of its model-kit

glue; in 1994, a German chemical company marketing a Resistol rival halted its distribution in this region. For its part, Fuller did modify the formulation of Resistol in 1992, replacing the sweet-smelling but highly toxic toluene with a slightly less toxic chemical, cyclohexane. However, it continues to sell Resistol, claiming that its legitimate uses benefit the economies of regions where it is marketed. Moreover, the company has funded community programs for homeless children throughout Central America and has limited its Resistol marketing efforts to large industrial customers, rather than marketing to small retailers. Unappeased, foes continue to press Fuller to discontinue the product entirely.

Note: There is no connection between Resistol glue and Resistol Western Hats or any corporation-related sponsorships such as the Resistol Arena in Mesquite, Texas.

Source: Henriques, D.B. (1995, November 26). Black mark for a "good citizen." Critics say H. B. Fuller isn't doing enough to curb glue-sniffing. *New York Times*, Section 3, pp. 1, 11.

in an economically disadvantaged neighborhood in Philadelphia.

Whatever the ethnic identity of the chronic inhalant abuser, a critical factor is peer influence. Most studies indicate that glue, solvent, or aerosol inhalation is generally experienced in small groups, often at the urging of friends or relatives. Young inhalant abusers tend to be more alienated than others at this age, and feelings of alienation can lead youths to others who are also alienated, thus creating a cluster of peers who engage in this form of drug-taking behavior. One survey among American Indian youths, for example, found that when friends strongly encouraged inhalant use or did not try to stop it, 84 percent of the sample reported having tried inhalants and 41 percent reported having used them recently. In contrast, when friends discouraged inhalant use or were perceived as applying strong sanctions against it, only 19 percent reported having tried inhalants and only 3 percent had used them recently.[45]

The Dependence Potential of Chronic Inhalant Abuse

The long-term effects of inhalant abuse are not well documented, because inhalant abuse frequently does not extend over more than a year or two in a person's life and may occur only sporadically. There have been reports of cases showing a tolerance to the intoxicating effects of glues and gasoline. Although it is difficult to determine the dosages that are involved with these tolerance effects, it appears that individuals exposed only to low concentrations for brief periods of time or to high levels on an occasional basis do not show tolerance to the inhalants.

Inhalant dependence occurs frequently. Inhalant abusers have reported feeling restless, irritable, and anxious when prevented from inhaling glues, solvents, or aerosols. Physiological withdrawal symptoms are only rarely observed among inhalant abusers but are frequently observed among animals in laboratory studies, so the question of whether physical dependence exists has yet to be definitively answered.[46]

Responses of Society to Inhalant Abuse

Sniffing gasoline or paint is a grubby, dirty, cheap way to get high. Inhalant users are, therefore, likely to be the social rejects, the emotionally disturbed,

the disadvantaged minorities, the maladjusted, as well as angry and alienated. There is nothing attractive, exciting, or appealing about inhalant use or inhalant users. . . .[47]

Certainly, the concern about inhalant abuse takes a back seat to more widely publicized concerns about cocaine, methamphetamine, and heroin abuse or the recent abuse of club drugs. Despite the relatively low priority given to inhalant abuse, however, steps have been taken to reduce some of its hazards. One major approach has been to restrict the availability and sale of glues to young people—a strategy that, as you might predict, has met with mixed success. Some U.S. cities have restricted sales of plastic cement unless it is purchased with a model kit, but such legislation is largely ineffective when model kits themselves are relatively inexpensive. As with the official restriction of sales of alcohol and tobacco to minors, young people can find a way around these laws.

The Testor Corporation, a leading manufacturer of plastic cement for models, took more direct action in 1969 by incorporating **oil of mustard** into the formula. This additive produces severe nasal irritation similar to the effect of horseradish, while not affecting its use as a glue or the user who does not inhale it directly. Other brands of glues and adhesives, however, may not contain oil of mustard and so could still be available for abuse, and additives in general would not be desirable for certain products that are used for cosmetic purposes.

In an additional step taken to reduce inhalant abuse, concentrations of benzene in many household products sold in the United States have been reduced or eliminated, though it is difficult to determine the exact composition of solutions merely by inspecting the label. Standards for products manufactured and sold in foreign countries are typically far less stringent.

Beyond the difficulty in identifying the toxicity of specific solvent compounds, there is the overriding general problem of the enormous variety and easy availability of solvent-containing products. As one researcher has lamented, "If sales of gold paint or paint thinner are curtailed, people may choose to . . . [sniff] correction fluid, or shoe polish or nail polish remover,

oil of mustard: An additive in Testor brand hobby-kit glues that produces nasal irritation when inhaled, thus reducing the potential for inhalant abuse.

or hundreds of other items that have legitimate uses in everyday life."[48]

Ultimately, some sort of educational strategy must be coordinated that is targeted at children in the elementary grades in school and their parents at home. Different countries have differing educational approaches, ranging from nonalarmist, low-key programs to those urging absolute abstinence, and it is not clear which strategy is most effective in controlling inhalant abuse. A National Inhalants and Poisons Awareness Week is currently held each year in March to promote greater efforts to inform the public about this problem. A 2002 survey conducted by the Partnership for a Drug-Free America has shown that only a small fraction of the parents of teens who have tried inhalants are aware of that fact. On the treatment side, special guidelines are currently being developed for a variety of inhalant-abuse populations—not only the adolescents engaging in transient inhalant abuse but also those individuals who are twenty to twenty-nine years old, have a five-year or longer history of inhalant exposure and have sustained possible brain damage as a result.[49]

Quick Concept Check 13.2

Understanding the History of Inhalants

Check your understanding of the history of inhalant drugs by indicating whether a particular substance was used (a) first recreationally, then as an application in medicine; (b) first as an application in medicine, then recreationally; or (c) recreationally, with no known application in medicine.

1. hexane
2. nitrous oxide
3. toluene
4. ether
5. benzene

Answers: 1. c   2. a   3. c   4. a   5. c

Summary

Barbiturates

- Introduced in 1903 and in use until approximately 1960, the primary sedative-hypnotics (drugs that produce sedation and sleep) belong to the barbiturate family of drugs.

- Barbiturates are typically classified in terms of how long their depressant effects are felt, from long-acting (example: phenobarbital) to intermediate-acting (examples: butalbarbital and amobarbital) to short-acting (examples: pentobarbital and secobarbital).

- A major disadvantage of barbiturates is the potential of a lethal overdose, particularly when the barbiturate is combined with other depressants such as alcohol. In addition, barbiturate withdrawal symptoms are very severe and require careful medical attention.

Nonbarbiturate Sedative-Hypnotics

- Methaqualone (Quaalude) was introduced in the 1960s as an alternative to barbiturates for sedation and sleep. Unfortunately, this drug produced undesirable side effects and became subject to widespread abuse. It is no longer available as a licit drug.

The Development of Antianxiety Drugs

- Beginning in the 1950s, a major effort was made by the pharmaceutical industry to develop a drug that would relieve anxiety (tranquilize) rather than merely depress the CNS (sedate).

- Meprobamate (Miltown) was introduced in 1955 for this purpose, although it is now clear that the effects of this drug result more from its sedative properties than from its ability to relieve anxiety.

Benzodiazepines

- The introduction of benzodiazepines, specifically diazepam (Valium) and chlordiazepoxide (Librium), in the early 1960s was a significant breakthrough in the development of antianxiety drugs. These drugs selectively affect specific receptors in the brain instead of acting as general depressants of the nervous system.

- In general, benzodiazepines are safer drugs than barbiturates, when taken alone. When they are taken in combination with alcohol, however, dangerous synergistic effects are observed.

- Benzodiazepines produce their effects by binding to receptors in the brain that are sensitive to the inhibitory neurotransmitter gamma aminobutyric acid (GABA).

- Social problems related to benzodiazepine drugs during the 1970s centered on the widespread misuse of the drug. Prescriptions were written too frequently and for excessive dosages.

Nonbenzodiazepine Depressants

- Recently developed nonbenzodiazepines have provided better opportunities to treat sleep disorders and anxiety. Two examples are zolpidem and buspirone.

- Zolpidem (brand name: Ambien) and eszopiclone (Lunesta) have been useful as sedative-hypnotics in the treatment of insomnia. They have strong but transient sedative effects and produces little or no muscle relaxation.

- Buspirone (brand name: BuSpar) has been useful as an antianxiety medication that does not cause sedation.

- Beta blockers, traditionally used to treat cardiac and blood pressure disorders, have been prescribed for individuals who are faced with an anxiety-producing event, such as performing on stage or speaking in public.

- Certain antidepressants called selective serotonin reuptake inhibitors (SSRIs) have been successful in treating a variety of anxiety disorders.

The Risks of GHB

- Gamma hydroxybutyrate (GHB) is a CNS depressant, first used by body builders because of the possibility that it had growth-hormone-stimulating effects. Today, GHB is an illicit drug available only through clandestine channels.

- As with Rohypnol, the depressant effects of GHB have made it attractive as a club drug. Its involvement as a potential date-rape drug has raised very serious concerns.

Inhalants through History

- Nitrous oxide was first investigated in 1798 and became a major recreational drug in the early 1800s. It is still used recreationally, but its primary application is for routine anesthesia in dentistry.

- Ether is another anesthetic drug, first introduced in the 1840s. It has also been used as a recreational drug, particularly in times when alcohol availability has been severely reduced.

Glue, Solvent, and Aerosol Inhalation

- Present-day inhalant abuse involves a wide range of commercial products: gasoline, glues and other adhesives, household cleaning compounds, aerosol sprays, and solvents of all kinds.

- These products are usually cheap, readily available, and easily concealed, and their intoxicating effects when inhaled are rapid. All these factors make inhalants prime candidates for abuse.

- The principal dangers of inhalant abuse lie in the behavioral consequences of intoxication and in the possibility of asphyxiation when inhalants are abused via by an airproof bag held over the nose and mouth.

- Specific toxic substances contained in inhalant products include acetone, benzene, hexane, toluene, and gasoline.

Patterns of Inhalant Abuse

- Inhalant abuse respects no social or geographic boundaries, although prevalence rates are particularly high among poor and disadvantaged populations.

- Research studies indicate the presence of psychological dependence, rather than physical dependence, in inhalant abuse behavior.

- Tolerance effects are seen for chronic inhalant abusers when the inhalant concentration is high and exposure is frequent.

Responses of Society to Inhalant Abuse

- Concern about the dangers of inhalant abuse has led to restriction of the sale of model-kit glues to minors and to modification of the formulas for model-kit glue in an attempt to lessen the likelihood of abuse.

- So many products currently on the open market contain volatile chemicals that a universal restriction of abusable inhalants is practically impossible. Therefore, prevention efforts regarding inhalant abuse are critical elements in reducing this form of drug-taking behavior.

Key Terms

acetone, p. 331
amobarbital, p. 317
antianxiety drugs, p. 316

barbiturate, p. 316
benzene, p. 331
benzodiazepines, p. 321

beta blockers, p. 325
buspirone, p. 325
chloral hydrate, p. 320

chlordiazepoxide, p. 321
diazepam, p. 321
ether, p. 329

Endnotes

1. Quotation from Silverstein, A.; Silverstein, V.; and Silverstein, R. (1991). *The addictions handbook.* Hillside, NJ: Enslow, p. 51.
2. Palfai, T., and Jankiewicz, H. (1991). *Drugs and human behavior.* Dubuque, IA: W. C. Brown, p. 203.
3. Julien, R. M. (2005). *A primer of drug action* (10th ed.). New York: Worth, p. 147.
4. Palfai and Jankiewicz, *Drugs and human behavior,* p. 213.
5. Julien (2005), p. 148.
6. Kauffman, J. F.; Shaffer, H.; and Burglass, M. E. (1985). The biological basics: Drugs and their effects. In T.E. Bratter and G.G. Forrest (Eds.), *Alcoholism and substance abuse: Strategies for clinical intervention.* New York: Free Press, pp. 107–136.
7. Sleeping pills and antianxiety drugs (1988). *The Harvard Medical School Mental Health Letter,* 5(6), 1–4.
8. Griffiths, R. R.; Lukas, S. E.; Bradford, L. D.; Brady, J. V.; and Snell, J. D. (1981). Self-injection of barbiturates and benzodiazepines in baboons. *Psychopharmacology,* 75, 101–109.
9. Griffiths, R. R.; Bigelow, G.; and Liebson, I. (1979). Human drug self-administration: Double-blind comparison of pentobarbital, diazepam, chlorpromazine, and placebo. *Journal of Pharmacology and Experimental Therapeutics,* 210, 301–310.
10. Johnston, L. D.; O'Malley, P. M.; Bachman, J. G.; and Schulenberg, J. E. (2012). *Monitoring the Future: National survey results on drug use, 1975–2011.* Vol. I: Secondary school students 2011. Ann Arbor, MI: Institute for Social Research, The University of Michigan, Tables 2-1 and 2-2.
11. Carroll, M., and Gallo, G. (1985). *Quaaludes: The quest for oblivion.* New York: Chelsea House. Julien (2005), p. 150.
12. Julien, *A primer of drug action,* pp. 149–150.
13. Schuckit, M. A. (2006). *Drug and alcohol abuse: A clinical guide to diagnosis and treatment* (6th ed.). New York: Springer, pp. 46–48.
14. Rickels, K. (1981). Benzodiazepines: Clinical use patterns. In S. I. Szara and J. P. Ludford (Eds.), *Benzodiazepines: A review of research results 1980* (NIDA Research Monograph 33). Rockville, MD: National Institute on Drug Abuse, pp. 43–60.
15. Substance Abuse and Mental Health Services Administration. Benzodiazepines in drug abuse-related emergency department visits: 1995–2002 (2004, April). *The DAWN Report.* Rockville, MD: Substance Abuse and Mental Health Services Administration, pp. 1–4. Tanaka, E. (2002). Toxicological interactions between alcohol and benzodiazepines. *Journal of Toxicology— Clinical Toxicology,* 40, 69–75.
16. Cumming, R. G., and LeCouteur, D. G. (2003). Benzodiazepines and risk of hip fractures in older people: A review of the evidence. *CNS Drugs,* 17, 825–837. Salzman, C. (1999). An 87-year-old woman taking a benzodiazepine. *Journal of the American Medical Association,* 281, 1121–1125.
17. Rickels, K.; George C. W.; D. R. W.; and Winokur, A. (1983). Long-term diazepam therapy and clinical outcome. *Journal of the American Medical Association,* 250, 767–771.
18. Longo, L. P., and Johnson, B. (2000). Addiction: Part I. Benzodiazepines—Side effects, abuse risk and alternatives. *American Family Physician,* 61, 2121–2128.
19. Julien, R. M., *A. primer of drug action,* pp. 166–168. Mohler, H., and Okada, T. (1977). Benzodiazepine receptors in rat brain: Demonstration in the central nervous system. *Science,* 198, 849–851. Squires, R. F., and Braestrup, C. (1977). Benzodiazepine receptors in rat brain. *Nature,* 266, 732–734.
20. Ibid.
21. Löw, K.; Crestani, F.; Keist, R.; Benke, D.; Brünig, I.; et al. (2000). Molecular and neuronal substrate for the selective attenuation of anxiety. *Science,* 290, 131–134.
22. Griffiths, R. R., and Ator, N.A. (1981). Benzodiazepine self-administration in animals and humans: A comprehensive literature review. In S. I. Szara and J. P. Ludford (Eds.), *Benzodiazepines: A review of research results, 1980* (NIDA Research Monograph 33). Rockville, MD: National Institute on Drug Abuse, pp. 22–36.
23. Schuckit, *Drug and alcohol abuse,* p. 43.
24. Lickey, M. E., and Gordon, B. *Medicine and mental illness.* New York: Freeman, p. 278.
25. Lagnaouli, R.; Moore, N.; Dartigues, J. F; Fourrier, A.; and Bégaud, B. (2001). Benzodiazepine use and wine consumption in the French elderly. *British Journal of Clinical Pharmacology,* 52, 455–456. Pimlott, N.J. G.; Hux, J.E.; Wilson, L. M.; Kahan, M; Li, C.; et al. (2003). Educating physicians to reduce benzodiazepine use by elderly patients: A randomized controlled trial. *Canadian Medical Association Journal,* 168, 835–839.

26. Gershell, L. (2006). From the analyst's couch: Insomnia market. *Nature Reviews and Drug Discovery, 5*, 15–16.

27. Julien, *A primer of drug action*, p. 182.

28. Kent, J. M.; Coplan, J. D.; and Gorman, J. M. (1998). Clinical utility of the selective serotonin reuptake inhibitors in the spectrum of anxiety. *Biological Psychiatry, 44*, 812–824.

29. Dyer, J. E. (2000). Evolving abuse of GHB in California: Bodybuilding drug to date-rape drug. *Journal of Toxicology—Clinical Toxicology, 38*, 184. Office of National Drug Control Policy (1998, October). *ONDCP Drug Policy Information Clearinghouse fact sheet: Gamma hydroxybutyrate (GHB)*. Washington, DC: Executive Office of the President.

30. Information regarding bar coasters courtesy of Drink Safe Technology, Wellington, Florida. Office of National Drug Control Policy, *ONDCP Drug Policy Information Clearinghouse fact sheet: Gamma hydroxybutyrate (GHB)*.

31. Broad, W. J. (2002, March 19). For Delphic oracle, fumes and visions. *New York Times*, pp. F1, F4. Preble, E., and Laury, G. V. (1967). Plastic cement: The ten cent hallucinogen. *International Journal of the Addictions, 2*, 271–281.

32. Gillman, M. A., and Lichtigfeld, F. J. (1997). Clinical role and mechanisms of action of analgesic nitrous oxide. *International Journal of Neuroscience, 93*, 55–62. Nagle, D. R. (1968). Anesthetic addiction and drunkenness. *International Journal of the Addictions, 3*, 25–39.

33. Kolecki, P., and Shih, R. (2008). Inhalant abuse. In J. Brick (Ed.), *Handbook of the medical consequences of alcohol and drug abuse* (2nd ed.). New York: Routledge, p. 371. Layzer, R. B. (1985). Nitrous oxide abuse. In E. I. Eger (Ed.), *Nitrous oxide/N₂O*. New York: Elsevier, pp. 249–257.

34. Nagle, Anesthetic addiction and drunkenness.

35. Khattak, S.; K Moghtader, C.; McMartin, K.; Barrera, M.; Kennedy, D.; and Koren, G. (1999). Pregnancy outcome following gestational exposure to organic solvents. *Journal of the American Medical Association, 281*, 1106–1109.

36. Cohen, S. (1977). Inhalant abuse: An overview of the problem. In C. W. Sharp and M. L, Brehm (Eds.), *Review of inhalants: Euphoria to dysfunction* (NIDA Research Monograph 15). Rockville, MD: National Institute on Drug Abuse, p. 7.

37. Ibid., pp. 6–8.

38. Schuckit, *Drug and alcohol abuse*, p. 239.

39. Abramovitz, M. (2003, October). The dangers of inhalants. *Current Health 2*, pp. 19–21. Winger, G.; Hofmann, F. G.; and Woods, J. H. (1992). *A handbook on drug and alcohol abuse: The biomedical aspects* (3d ed.). New York: Oxford University Press, pp. 90–91.

40. Kolecki and Shih, Inhalant abuse, pp. 370–376. Schuckit, *Drug and alcohol abuse*, pp. 244–245.

41. Brands, B.; Sproule, B.; and Marshman, J. (1998). *Drugs and drug abuse: A reference text*. Toronto: Addiction Research Foundation, pp. 469–471. Garriott, J. C. (1992). Death among inhalant abusers. In C. W. Sharp, F. Beauvais, and R. Spence (Eds.), *Inhalant abuse: A volatile research agenda* (NIDA Research Monograph 129). Rockville, MD: National Institute on Drug Abuse, pp. 171–193.

42. Edwards, R. W., and Oetting, E. R. (1995). Inhalant use in the United States. In N. Kozel, Z. Sloboda, and M. De La Rosa (Eds.), *Epidemiology of inhalant abuse: An international perspective* (NIDA Research Monograph 148). Rockville, MD: National Institute on Drug Abuse, pp. 8–28. Johnston, O'Malley, Bachman, and Schulenberg, *Monitoring the Future*, Tables 2-1, 2-2, and 2-3. Preboth, M. (2000, February 15). Prevalence of inhalant abuse in children. *American Family Physician*, p. 1206.

43. Howard, M. O.; Walker, R. D.; Walker, P. S.; Cottler, L. B.; and Compton, W. M. (1999). Inhalant use among urban American Indian youth. *Addiction, 94*, 83–95. Kin, F., and Navaratnam, V. (1995). An overview of inhalant abuse in selected countries of Asia and the Pacific region. In N. Kozel, Z. Sloboda, and M. De La Rosa (Eds.), *Epidemiology of inhalant abuse: An international perspective* (NIDA Research Monograph 148). Rockville, MD: National Institute on Drug Abuse, pp. 29–49. Medina-Mora, M. E., and Berenzon, S. (1995). Epidemiology of inhalant abuse in Mexico. In N. Kozel, Z. Sloboda, and M. De La Rosa (Eds.), *Epidemiology of inhalant abuse: An international perspective* (NIDA Research Monograph 148). Rockville, MD: National Institute on Drug Abuse, pp. 136–174. Surratt, H. L., and Inciardi, J. A. (1996). Drug use, HIV risks, and prevention/intervention strategies among street youths in Rio de Janeiro, Brazil. In C. B. McCoy, L. R. Metsch, and J. A. Inciardi (Eds.), *Intervening with drug-involved youth*. Thousand Oaks, MI: Sage Publications, pp. 173–190.

44. Howard, M. O., and Jenson, J. M. (1998). Inhalant use among antisocial youth: Prevalence and correlates. *Addictive Behaviors, 24*, 59–74. Mackesy-Amiti, M. E, and Fendrich, M. (1999). Inhalant abuse and delinquent behavior among adolescents: A comparison of inhalant users and other drug users. *Addiction, 94*, 555–564. Sakai, J. T.; Shannon, K.; Hall, B. A.; Mihulich-Gilbertson, S. K.; and Crowley, T. J. (2004). Inhalant use, abuse, and dependence among adolescent patients: Commonly comorbid problems. Journal of the American Academy of Child and Adolescent Psychiatry, 43, 1080–1088.

45. Oetting, E. R.; Edwards, R. W.; and Beauvais, F. (1988). Social and psychological factors underlying inhalant abuse. In R. A. Crider and B. A. Rouse (eds.), *Epidemiology of inhalant abuse: An update* (NIDA Research Monograph 85). Rockville, MD: National Institute on Drug Abuse, pp. 172–203.

46. Korman, M. (1977). Clinical evaluation of psychological factors. In C. W. Sharp and M. L. Brehm (Eds.), *Review of inhalants: Euphoria to dysfunction* (NIDA Research

Monograph 15). Rockville, MD: National Institute on Drug Abuse, pp. 30–53. Schuckit, *Drug and alcohol abuse*, pp. 239–240.

47. Oetting, E., and Beauvais, Social and psychological factors, p. 197.

48. Kerner, K. (1988). Current topics in inhalant abuse. In R. A. Crider and B. A. Rouse (Eds.), *Epidemiology of inhalant abuse: An update* (NIDA Research Monograph 85). Rockville, MD: National Institute on Drug Abuse, p. 20.

49. Draft of National Inhalant Prevention Coalition guidelines for inhalant abuse treatment (2003). Information courtesy of the National Inhalant Prevention Coalition, Austin, Texas. Office of National Drug Control Policy (2003, February). *Inhalants: Drug Policy Information Clearinghouse fact sheet*. Washington, DC: White House Office of National Drug Control Policy. Williams, J. F.; Storck, M.; and the Committee on Substance Abuse and Committee on Native American Child Health (2007). Inhalant abuse. *Pediatrics, 119*, 1009–1017.

Prescription Drugs, Over-the-Counter Drugs, and Dietary Supplements

After you have completed this chapter, you should have an understanding of

▷ The distinction between prescription and OTC drugs, as opposed to dietary supplements

▷ The history of U.S. drug regulations

▷ Present-day FDA procedures for approving new drugs

▷ Procedures for approving prescription drugs to be available as OTC drugs

▷ Safety issues with respect to prescription drugs

▷ Types of OTC analgesic drugs

▷ Sleep aids and cough-and-cold remedies

▷ The pharmaceutical industry today

▷ Dietary supplements

The little English graveyard contained a dozen or so monuments, their inscriptions nearly worn away by more than two centuries of wind and rain. Each epitaph told a bit about a life remembered. One of them dated back to 1752 and was in rhyme:

> Here lies the body of Mary Ann Lauders,
> died of drinking Cheltenham waters.
> If she had stuck to Epsom salts,
> she wouldn't be lying in these here vaults.

We can only wonder what the Lauders family might have done today. Would they have sued the Cheltenham Spa for promoting a pharmaceutical product to poor Mary Ann that was neither safe nor effective? Would the British equivalent of the FDA have shut the establishment down? And who says that Epsom salts would have been safer or more effective? Where are the clinical trials? Where are the double-blind controls?

The next time you are in a pharmacy or drugstore, take a minute to look around you. Besides the overwhelming variety of soaps, cosmetics, shaving creams, toothpastes, deodorants, and all the other products that have become part of our daily lives, notice the three broad categories of products that are available for purchase as medicines.

The first group of consumer products, a few thousand of them, placed mostly out of view and behind the pharmacy counter, are **prescription drugs**. Their purchase and use require the submission of a written prescription form with an appropriate signature (or other secure mode of communication), which certifies that you are taking one of these drugs for a medical condition and at a dosage level appropriate for that condition. The quantity of a drug that you are allowed to purchase at any one time is specified, and a limit on the number of prescription refills offers some control over that drug's use for an extended period of time (see Health Line, page 348). By law, only licensed physicians, nurse practitioners, or dentists are permitted to issue prescriptions for their patients, and only registered pharmacists are permitted to fill these prescriptions and dispense these drugs to the consumer. Despite these protective procedures, however, cases of prescription drug misuse and abuse occur in alarming numbers. As detailed in Chapters 4 and 5, prescription stimulant medications and prescription pain medications have become the most prominent sources of concern in today's world of drug-taking behavior.

The second group of products, more than 100,000 of them, are **over-the-counter (OTC) drugs**, encompassing about 800 significant active ingredients. In contrast to prescription drugs, OTC drugs are available to you right off the shelves that line the aisles of the store, and their use is limited only by your ability to pay for them. With OTC drugs, you are your own physician. In most cases, you have diagnosed the ailment yourself and determined the course of treatment. Recommended doses are clearly printed on the label, and you may get some guidance from the pharmacist; however, there is no direct medical supervision over the dosage level that you actually

consume at any given time. No one will tell you when to stop using these drugs or whether they were appropriate to take in the first place.

In the United States, the regulation of both prescription and OTC drugs has been assigned to the U.S. Food and Drug Administration (FDA). The FDA is responsible for determining whether an existing prescription drug should continue to be available for public use and whether a newly developed drug can meet established standards of safety and effectiveness and thus qualify to be marketed as a prescription drug. The agency also oversees the safety and effectiveness of OTC drugs. The strength and concentration of active ingredients in OTC drugs must have a greater margin of safety than active ingredients in prescription drugs to justify their wide availability to the general public under such unsupervised conditions. No drug, however, is totally free of potentially toxic effects, despite extensive efforts to ensure the safety of prescription and OTC drugs. As is the case with prescription drugs, the potential for misuse and abuse of OTC drugs exists, particularly with respect to OTC analgesics, sleep aids, and cough-and-cold remedies.

In contrast to prescription drugs and OTC drugs, a third group called **dietary supplements** are relatively new, but they have become in recent years a major

prescription drugs: Medicinal drugs available to the public only when approved by a medical professional and dispensed by a licensed pharmacist.

over-the-counter (OTC) drugs: Medicinal drugs available to the public without the requirement of a prescription. They are often referred to as nonprescription drugs.

dietary supplements: Products (other than tobacco), distributed with the intention of supplementing the diet, that contain a vitamin, mineral, amino acid, herb or other botanical product, enzyme, organ tissue, metabolites, or any combination of these substances.

Pharmacists are specially trained to dispense approximately 2,500 different prescription drugs, although only about 50 of them account for 95 percent of retail pharmacy sales.

category of drugstore products. Dietary supplements are generally available to the public in the form of vitamin or herbal preparations. They are marketed in a similar manner as OTC drugs, but there is an important difference. According to the Dietary Supplement Health and Education Act in 1994, dietary supplements do not have to be proved safe and effective, as prescription and OTC drugs do, although as of 2010, manufacturers must show that the purity, strength, and composition of these products have been tested and that the labels are accurate descriptions of the contents.[1]

The History of Prescription Drug Regulations

We take for granted that the ingredients in drugs commercially available to us through drugstores, pharmacies, and supermarkets are pure and unadulterated. We assume that they will not harm us when we use them as directed and that they will reliably produce the benefits stated on the package or accompanying information packet.

Prior to 1906, no assumption of any kind could have been made. The consumer of any of the fifty thousand or so patent medicines available for purchase had no guarantee of what he or she was getting. Consumers could order, for example, the White Star Secret Liquor Cure from the 1897 Sears, Roebuck catalog (see Chapter 5) and not be told that they would be consuming opium. The manufacturer was under no obligation to inform the buyer of this—or of anything else, for that matter.

As a response to public outcry over the unregulated patent medicines flooding the market, as well as to publicity about the terrible conditions in the meatpacking industry, the Pure Food and Drug Act was enacted in 1906. This legislation set out to ensure that all foods and drugs in the United States would be inspected for purity and consistency. In addition, all active ingredients in drugs had to be clearly and accurately identified on the label. The 1906 act did not, however, guarantee any more protection than that. Until 1938, drugs could still be useless and/or dangerous as long as the label listed the ingredients in a correct manner.

In 1938, President Roosevelt signed into law the Federal Food, Drug, and Cosmetic (FDC) Act, which has served to the present day as the basic food and drug law in the United States. This law mandated that all ingredients in drug and cosmetic products had to be accurately identified, and drug companies were henceforth required to demonstrate by research studies that new drugs were safe (when used as directed) before they could be marketed commercially. A 1951 amendment to the FDC Act established a clear distinction between prescription and OTC drugs. By that point, the FDA had grown in stature and power as the official guardian of the public interest with regard to food, drugs, and cosmetics. As a result of the Kefauver-Harris Amendment in 1962, drug companies were now required to prove that new drugs were *effective* as well as safe.

The FDA continues to prosecute violators of the drug laws, but enforcement is no longer its sole mission. Regulations since 1938 have given the FDA an active role in preventing problems from arising in the first place (Table 14.1). A major part of this preventive approach is the set of procedures required for the approval of new prescription drugs and the setting of standards for OTC drugs. And a major expansion of FDA regulatory control occurred in 2009, when passage of the Tobacco Control Act gave the FDA authority to regulate tobacco products (see Chapter 10).[2]

TABLE 14.1

Major regulatory laws of the FDA since 1938

ACT OR AMENDMENT	YEAR	EFFECT
Color Additive Amendment	1960	Regulated the use of color additives in drugs and food
Hazardous Substances Labeling Act	1960	Required warning labels on all products intended for home use
Kefauver-Harris Amendment	1962	Required that new drugs be effective as well as safe
Child Protection Act	1966	Regulated the safety of toys sold across state lines
Medical Device Amendment	1976	Required that any health care product or device be effective and safe
Instant Formula Act	1980	Regulated the contents of baby-formula preparations
Anti-tampering Act	1983	Required tamper-resistant packaging for all OTC products
Orphan Drug Act	1983	Allowed drug companies to take tax credits for developing new drugs with low potential for profits
Prescription Drug User Fee Act	1992	Increased FDA efficiency in the review of new drug applications
Dietary Supplement Health and Education Act	1994	Set guidelines for the marketing of vitamin and herbal preparations
FDA Modernization Act	1997	Streamlined procedures for approval of new drugs, food labels, and medical devices
Ryan Haight Online Pharmacy Consumer Protection Act	2008	Restricted access to prescription drugs through the Internet
Family Smoking Prevention and Tobacco Control Act	2009	Initiated FDA regulatory authority over tobacco products sold in the United States

Sources: Updated information from the U.S. Food and Drug Administration, Washington, DC.

Procedures for Approving Prescription Drugs

The current process for introducing a new prescription drug on the market consists of a number of stages or phases of approval required by the FDA. It begins in the laboratories of the drug companies themselves or research facilities around the world, with the identification of the composition of a new compound, the purification of its active ingredients, and a preliminary determination of any possible toxic effects. Extensive toxicity tests in two or more species of laboratory animals are carried out, specifically the determination of the LD50 dosage of the compound—the concentration that leads to death in 50 percent of the animals studied (see Chapter 2). Specific tests are also made on pregnant animals to determine whether administration of the compound might produce birth defects. If the intention is to market the compound

> **Phase 1 trials:** The first stage of clinical testing, in which an experimental drug is administered to healthy volunteers to check for possible side effects and determine patterns of absorption and elimination.

as a drug for chronic disorders, toxicity studies are extended over a period of time that simulates the length of time the drug might be used by human patients.

After these preliminary studies are completed and the new drug has been determined to be safe with animals, the drug company notifies the FDA, through an application known as a Notice of Claimed Investigational Exemption for a New Drug (IND), that this compound has promise as a new prescription drug and that permission is requested to conduct testing in humans.

Phases of Clinical Testing for Prescription Drugs

A sequence of four stages or phases of clinical testing is now begun, with each phase dependent on the success of the preceding one.

- In the first stage of clinical studies, called **Phase 1 trials**, about ten to one hundred healthy volunteers (frequently prison inmates or medical students) are administered the drug, and certain pharmacological questions are answered. How quickly is the new drug absorbed and eliminated? Are any side effects observed? What range of dosages is safe for use? Do any specific

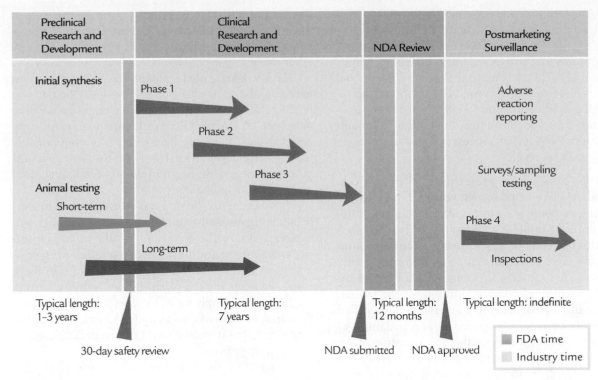

Preclinical Research and Development

Clinical Research and Development

NDA Review

Postmarketing Surveillance

Initial synthesis

Phase 1

Phase 2

Phase 3

Adverse reaction reporting

Animal testing

Short-term

Surveys/sampling testing

Long-term

Phase 4

Inspections

Typical length: 1–3 years

Typical length: 7 years

Typical length: 12 months

Typical length: indefinite

30-day safety review

NDA submitted   NDA approved

■ FDA time
■ Industry time

FIGURE 14.1

Development of new prescription drugs and the FDA approval process. Since 2006, an accelerated procedure has been permitted in which drug companies are allowed to test experimental compounds on fewer than twelve human subjects before animal studies are complete.

Sources: Updated from U.S. Food and Drug Administration (2001, March–April). Making medical progress: A look at FDA approvals in 2000. *FDA Consumer,* pp. 7–8. Zivin, J. A. (2003, April). Understanding clinical trials. *Scientific American,* pp. 69–75.

schedules for administration (one large dose per day versus three small ones) minimize any adverse effects?

■ In the second stage of clinical studies, called **Phase 2 trials**, the new drug is tested on one hundred to five hundred patients who have the medical condition or illness that the drug is intended to treat. Researchers are careful to select only those patients who are free of other health problems so that any improvements will be identified as a genuine effect on the illness in question. All these clinical studies are conducted in a double-blind fashion. Neither the researchers nor the patients are aware of whether the new drug or a look-alike placebo (see Chapter 3) is being administered. As a result, positive effects (if any) are attributed to the therapeutic properties of the drug, free of any expectations or biases that the researchers or patients may have had.

■ If these two trials have been successful, the third clinical stage, called **Phase 3 trials**, is undertaken. At this testing point, the safety, effectiveness, and proper dosage levels are investigated in a population of 1,000 to

3,000 patients. A closer examination of possible side effects (some of which may be observed only rarely) is carried out. Phase III studies are typically lengthy and expensive. If there were a one in a thousand chance of an adverse drug reaction, 3,000 patients would need to be exposed in order for researchers to be reasonably confident of seeing it.

■ After all three stages of clinical trials have been completed, a process that can take three years or more (Figure 14.1), and the drug company considers the results satisfactory, a New Drug Application

Phase 2 trials: The second stage of clinical testing, in which an experimental drug is given to a small population of patients who have the medical condition for which the drug is considered a possible treatment.

Phase 3 trials: The third stage of clinical testing, in which an experimental drug is given to a large population of patients, through which issues of safety, effectiveness, and proper dosage levels are finalized.

(NDA) is submitted for approval by the FDA. This application includes all the data on the animal testing and clinical trials. Less than 30 percent of all compounds that drug companies consider worthy of human clinical trials make it this far. Under usual circumstances, the FDA then has six months to review the application and to either accept or reject the new drug for commercial marketing, although the entire FDA review process at this stage takes up to a year or more.

By the time a new prescription drug is FDA-approved, it is likely that several years will have passed since the compound was first synthesized and considered promising enough to warrant clinical testing.[3] As a further safeguard, a new drug is monitored after release for commercial use for any unforeseen side effects or toxic reactions, in a stage called **Phase 4 trials**. At this point, physicians throughout the United States are instructed, through a federal program called MedWatch, to report to the FDA any instances of adverse effects resulting from the use or misuse of the new drug by their patients. In cases in which significant adverse drug reactions are reported, a special notice referred to as a "black box warning" is inserted in the *Physicians' Desk Reference for Prescription Drugs* (an annual publication that includes detailed information on all FDA-approved prescription medications) and in the consumer information that is provided when the drug is purchased, so that these reactions can be avoided. In extreme cases, FDA approval is rescinded and the drug is withdrawn from the market.[4]

Patents and Generic Forms of Prescription Drugs

Approval by the FDA gives the drug company exclusive rights to manufacture and sell the new drug under its own brand name (beginning with a capital letter and often accompanied by a small, circled letter R just to

---

Phase 4 trials: The fourth stage of clinical testing, in which possible adverse reactions to a drug that is already available to the public are monitored by physicians who have prescribed it.

patent: The exclusive right of a drug company to market a particular drug. The duration of a patent is twenty years.

bioequivalence: A characteristic of two drugs in which all pharmacological and physiological effects are identical.

---

the right of it, signifying that the name is a registered trademark). All other companies are forbidden by law to sell the compound under that brand name or any other name.

These rights, called a **patent**, have a fixed duration of twenty years. The clock starts, however, at the time the original IND is submitted to the FDA, not when the drug enters the commercial market. Consequently, the drug company may, in reality, have patent protection for only ten to twelve years. After that point, the drug "goes off patent," and generic forms of it can be manufactured and sold to the public.

It is typical for the original drug company to market the drug under its brand name even after the patent expires, but now the consumer has the option of having it prescribed and purchased as a brand drug or as a generic (and much less expensive) version. In some cases, when a particular patent expires, a drug company might decide to apply for FDA approval for its prescription drug to be marketed as an OTC drug (as was the case with Claritin in 2002 and Prilosec in 2003), alongside generic versions.[5]

Since 1984, the FDA has required that all generic drugs demonstrate **bioequivalence** with respect to the original, brand-name drug; this means that both versions must be shown to be chemically and pharmacologically identical. However, there may still be significant differences in the *bioavailability* of these generic versions, that is the extent to which or the rate to which a drug enters the bloodstream and reaches the site of action. The issue of bioavailability has becomes particularly important for medications that are used to alter the sensitive neurochemistry of the brain. For example, a brand-name antiepileptic (antiseizure) medication and its generic version may be bioequivalent but have different therapeutic effects in the control of brain seizures due to differences in bioavailability. For this reason, the Epilepsy Foundation in 2009 issued a statement advising caution and close physician monitoring of patients who might be switching their antiseizure medication to generic "bioequivalent" versions in an effort to reduce prescription drug expenses.[6]

Speeding Up the FDA Approval Process

According to current FDA regulations, not all drugs have to travel this long and arduous road to reach the marketplace. Under special circumstances, the process can be accelerated. In 1987, the FDA authorized the use of a "treatment IND" application specially designed

TABLE 14.2

The Billion-Dollar Club: Leading Prescription Drugs, Based on Domestic U.S. Fourth Quarter 2012 Sales

BRAND NAME (MANUFACTURER)	MEDICAL APPLICATIONS	RETAIL SALES (IN BILLIONS OF DOLLARS)
1. Abilify (Otsuka)	Treatment for schizophrenia, depression, or bipolar disorder	1.48
2. Nexium (AstraZeneca)	Treatment for acid reflux and heartburn	1.44
3. Crestor (AstraZeneca)	Treatment for elevated cholesterol	1.28
4. Cymbalta (Eli Lilly)	Treatment for depression and generalized anxiety disorder	1.23
5. Humira (Abbott)	Treatment for arthritis, psoriasis, and ulcerative colitis	1.21
6. Advair Diskus (GlaxoSmithKline)	Treatment for asthma	1.20
7. Enbrel (Amgen)	Treatment for arthritis and psoriasis	1.09

Note 1: Annual sales are, of course, higher than sales in a particular quarter. However, seasonal factors make it difficult to simply multiply by four, and the relative sales ranking among top prescription drugs from quarter to quarter is highly variable.

Note 2: After the Pfizer Inc. patent for Lipitor expired in late 2010, the generic version (atorvastatin) became available. Since then, Pfizer has offered patients the opportunity to purchase Lipitor at generic prices. Formerly best-selling prescription drugs, Plavix, Seroquel, and Singulair went off-patent in 2012.

Source: Thomas, K., and Meier, B. (2013, January 2). Drug makers losing a bid to foil generic painkillers. *New York Times,* pp. B1-B2, www.drugs.com/stats/top100 drugs for Q4 2012 by sales.

for new drugs that show promise for certain seriously ill patients. Without compromising the standards for safety and effectiveness, a streamlined approval procedure has made it possible for a novel drug treatment to reach patients who can benefit from it in a matter of months instead of years. Medical conditions for which drug approval has been "fast-tracked" in this way include AIDS, infection associated with kidney transplants, Alzheimer's disease, Parkinson's disease, and some advanced cancers. One particular drug to treat AIDS and related conditions was approved in 1995 in an agency record-setting ninety-seven days (Table 14.2).[7]

Procedures for Approving OTC Drugs

When the Kefauver-Harris Amendment took effect in 1962, its aim was to ensure that all drugs sold in the United States were both safe and effective. Two governmental study groups were established for this purpose. The Drug Efficacy Study Investigation (DESI) examined all existing prescription medicines, and the Over-the-Counter Review (OTC Review) examined all existing nonprescription medicines. Whether it was in a prescription or nonprescription category, every drug was to be judged as *GRAS* (generally regarded as safe),

GRAE (generally regarded as effective), and *GRAHL* (generally regarded as honestly labeled). If a drug failed to meet any one of these criteria, the drug manufacturer had six months to convince the FDA otherwise, or else the drug would no longer be permitted to be marketed across state lines within the United States.

The OTC Review has produced three important changes in OTC drugs available to the consumer. First, the professional committees examining present-day OTC drugs have recommended, and the FDA has approved, an increase in the recommended dosage for certain OTC drugs. OTC-type antihistamines, for example, are stronger than in previous years as a result. Second, several prescription drugs have been determined to be safe enough to warrant use on an OTC basis, and consequently a growing number of prescription drugs are available for purchase on a non-prescription basis. Table 14.3 lists some of the present-day OTC drugs that were formerly available only on a prescription basis. Third, new regulations require that OTC drugs have consumer-friendly labels so that individuals can easily determine the symptoms that might be relieved by the medications and the safety precautions that must be heeded in their use. Some of these precautions include warnings about possible adverse reactions ("Ask a doctor before use if you have. . . .")

TABLE 14.3

Examples of former prescription drugs now sold on an over-the-counter (OTC) basis

OTC BRAND NAME	GENERIC NAME	CLINICAL USE
Actifed	triprolidine	Antihistamine
Aleve	naproxen	Analgesic and anti-inflammatory
Allegra	fexofenadine	Antihistamine
Benadryl	diphenhydramine	Antihistamine
Claritin, Alavert	loratadine	Antihistamine
Dimetane, Dimetapp	brompheniramine	Antihistamine
Monistat	miconazole	Treatment for vaginal yeast infections
Motrin, Advil, and Nuprin	ibuprofen	Analgesic and anti-inflammatory
Pepcid AC	famotidine	Heartburn relief
Prilosec	omeprazole	Heartburn relief
Rogaine	minoxidil	Hair growth
Tagamet HB	cimetidine	Heartburn relief
Zantac	ranitidine	Heartburn relief
Zyrtec	cetirizine and pseudoephedrine	Antihistamine/ decongestant

Source: Information courtesy of the Nonprescription Drug Manufacturers Association, Washington, DC.

and possible side effects ("When using this product, you may experience. . . .").[8]

Are FDA-Approved Drugs Safe?

The answer to the safety question for FDA-approved drugs, unfortunately, is yes and no. On the one hand, the FDA approval process is designed to prevent the introduction of any new drug, or the continued availability of any present drug, if there is a serious question about its safety when consumed in the recommended dosage for the treatment of certain specified medical disorders. On the other hand, there is no guarantee that some drugs might slip through the approval process without enough scrutiny and cause problems after they have been introduced and made available to the public.

The Issue of Speed versus Caution

It has always been necessary, though far from easy, to balance the need to provide, in an expeditious manner, drugs for people suffering from a variety of physical and mental disorders with the cautious deliberation required to screen out drugs that might be harmful. In recent years, however, the pendulum has swung in the direction of caution rather than speed. According to many public health officials, this new approach is largely due to the FDA decision in 2004 to withdraw the arthritis medication Vioxx from the market after the discovery of a link between the drug and a doubling of the risk of heart attack or stroke. In 2009, the FDA approved only 26 new drugs with active ingredients that had never previously been marketed in the United States, about the same number as in 2008, but more than in 2007, when only 17 were approved. In 2012, 34 new drugs were approved, seven of which were for advanced cancer treatment.[9]

While it is impossible to predict the general trend over an extended period of time, it is likely that a spirit of caution will continue for a while. In an influential

U.S. Supreme Court ruling in 2008, medical-device manufacturers cannot be sued by persons alleging that they had been injured by a defectively designed medical device that the FDA had approved as safe and effective after a full review. In other words, the consumer does not have legal protection for a FDA-approved medical device, should something go wrong. Whether this "preemption" ruling can be applied to FDA-approved drugs remains to be determined, although it is certain that the 2008 decision will be argued as a legal precedent in future cases. Second, in a 2008 study examining FDA drug approvals between 1950 and 2005, it was found that drugs that had been approved just prior to the deadline for doing so were more likely to present safety problems after their introduction than those drugs that had received approval with more time to spare. It is not known whether there has been a change in this pattern since 2008, though it is unlikely that the FDA has been insensitive to the findings of the study.[10]

Patterns of Prescription Drug Misuse

No drug is without side effects. Some of these side effects are quite minor, but others can be severe if the drug is taken by individuals with specific co-existing health problems. A quick look at the full-disclosure statement that is packaged with commercially available drugs will indicate the wide range of possible adverse effects.

The safety issue is further complicated when individuals misuse prescription drugs by either ignoring the manufacturer's precautionary advice or exceeding (deliberately or accidentally) the recommended dosage levels. In these cases, there is the risk of a medical emergency, resulting in a drug-related ED visit.

Historically, prescription and OTC drugs have been the agents for attempted suicide. In 2011, they accounted for about 95 percent of the approximately 228,000 ED visits of this type. In two-thirds of the cases, multiple drugs were reported, and in one-third of the cases, alcohol was involved as well. In some cases, the ingestion of a single medication would not have been problematic. For example, the antianxiety drug diazepam (brand name: Valium) is much more likely to produce a medical emergency or even a life-threatening condition when it is combined with alcohol than when it is ingested alone, even in substantial quantities (see Chapter 13). The tendency to combine drugs with alcohol (categorized as "alcohol-in-combination" in the DAWN statistics) substantially raises the risks of acute toxicity for drugs that are licit as well as for illicit drugs, whether the circumstances are accidental or intentional.[11]

The elderly often have to contend with a multitude of medications, many of which may interact with one another. Four out of five older adults report taking five or more prescription drugs.

Unintentional Drug Misuse through Prescription Errors

The risk of unintentional misuse is a serious concern among the elderly, due to the increasing number of prescription drugs on the market and the growing numbers of elderly patients taking multiple medications on an outpatient basis. An estimated 500,000 preventable adverse reactions, ranging from relatively mild symptoms of nausea to life-threatening kidney failure, are suffered by elderly patients in the United States alone each year. This problem has arisen in part because it is extremely difficult for physicians to monitor the complex array of potential drug interactions among their patients. From the perspective of the pharmacist, handwritten prescriptions from health care professionals can be easily confused, leading to the inappropriate medication being dispensed (see Health Line on page 348).[12]

Health Line
The Potential for Death by Prescription Error

Look carefully at the two prescriptions shown below. The one on the left is for Accupril, a drug used to treat high blood pressure; the one on the right is for Accutane, a drug to treat severe acne. The distinction between the two drugs is by no means trivial. If Accutane is taken instead of Accupril, the patient carries not only an increased risk of stroke from untreated hypertension but also (if the patient is a pregnant female) an increased risk of birth defects in an unborn child.

Even so, the prescriptions look disturbingly similar. This is the essence of the problem facing physicians, pharmacists, and patients in today's world of prescription drugs. Estimates of deaths due to medication errors within the United States range from about four hundred (about one per day) to seven thousand per year.

It is not simply a matter of prescription handwriting. Pharmaceutical companies have increasingly introduced brand names for new drugs that are very difficult to distinguish from each other. In 2008 the United States Pharmacopeia identified 3,370 pairs of drug brand names that either looked or sounded alike—nearly double the number it had identified in 2004.

Here are some examples of how prescription errors might arise from the similarity of prescription brand names. The disorders for which these drugs are prescribed are indicated in parentheses:

Celebrex (arthritis pain), Celexa (depression), Cerebyx (seizures)

Levadopa (Parkinson's disease), Methyldopa (hypertension)

Norflex (muscle spasms), Norfloxacin (bacterial infection)

Procrit (anemia), Proscar (enlarged prostate), ProSom (insomnia), Prozac (depression)

Ranitidine (stomach ulcers), Rimantadine (influenza)

Selegiline (Parkinson's disease), Serentil (schizophrenia), Seroquel (schizophrenia, bipolar disorder), Sertraline (depression)

Xanax (anxiety), Zocor (high cholesterol), Zofran (nausea, vomiting), Zoloft (depression), Zyrtec (allergies)

Where to go for assistance:

www.modernmedicine.com

An extensive listing of pairs of drug brand names that are commonly confused from the United States Pharmacopeia. Search web site under "Commonly confused drug pairs."

Sources: Commonly confused drug pairs. *Drug Topics*, accessed March 10, 2008. Medication mishaps (1997, July–August). *FDA Consumer*, pp. 19–21. Friedman, R. A. (2002, December 17). Curing and killing: The perils of a growing medicine cabinet. *New York Times*, p. F6.

2612 NORTH THIRD STREET
HARRISBURG, PENNSYLVANIA 17110

DEA Reg No._____
Lic. no. MD-032491-L

NAME _____ AGE _____
ADDRESS _____ DATE _____

Rx

☐ LABEL

REFILL _____ TIMES

SUBSTITUTE PERMISSIBLE _____ , M.D.

IN ORDER FOR A BRAND NAME PRODUCT TO BE DISPENSED, THE PRESCRIBER MUST HAND-WRITE "BRAND NECESSARY" OR "BRAND MEDICALLY NECESSARY" IN THE SPACE BELOW.

2612 NORTH THIRD STREET
HARRISBURG, PENNSYLVANIA 17110

DEA Reg No._____
Lic. no. MD-032491-L

NAME _____ AGE _____
ADDRESS _____ DATE _____

Rx

☐ LABEL

REFILL _____ TIMES

SUBSTITUTE PERMISSIBLE _____ , M.D.

IN ORDER FOR A BRAND NAME PRODUCT TO BE DISPENSED, THE PRESCRIBER MUST HAND-WRITE "BRAND NECESSARY" OR "BRAND MEDICALLY NECESSARY" IN THE SPACE BELOW.

Health Line

Doctor Shopping for Prescription Drugs

A new patient comes into Dr. Smith's office in a New York suburb, complains of severe pain and asks for a prescription for a specific drug (typically Percocet) without talking about other symptoms, The explanation may be that "Oh, two weeks ago I fell down the stairs and hurt my back and it's been killing me ever since."

Dr. Smith is bound to be suspicious of this patient's motives, but until recently there has been an inefficient system for checking on the patient's prescription drug history. Doctors across the country have had little assistance in striking a balance between treating people who legitimately need pain medication and those who are in the growing numbers of prescription drug abusers. In 2012, New York became the first U.S. state to establish a mandatory online reporting of prescriptions in real time—when they are written by the doctors themselves and filled by pharmacists. The new law is likely to be a model for future regulatory policy aimed at reducing the incidence of "doctor shopping," a practice that is widely regarded to be a major contributing factor

in the current epidemic of prescription pain medication abuse.

Nearly all U.S. states have prescription database systems and reporting procedures of some kind, but often information is updated only on a periodic basis. The New York system had previously worked on a 45-day reporting basis; now all prescriptions have to be electronically transmitted. Other states had focused only on the pharmacists' records, and not the doctor's orders.

There is also progress toward a sharing of information among states (particularly in locations where a community is close to a state border), but ultimately a nationwide system is necessary if "doctor shopping" has any chance of being contained.

Sources: Centers for Disease Control and Prevention (2012, July 11). Law: Doctor Shopping. Atlanta, GA: Centers for Disease Control and Prevention. Associated Press (2012, June 6). Deal on online prescription reporting. *New York Times,* p. A24.

Even in the more controlled settings of hospitals and clinics, prescription errors have occurred with alarming frequency, affecting patients of all ages. In 2004, an FDA regulation went into effect, mandating the use of bar-coded identifications, similar to those on commercial products, for all prescription and OTC drugs administered in a health care facility. Each patient admitted to a hospital receives a bar-coded identification bracelet linked to his or her individual medical records. When the patient receives his or her medication, the bar codes on the bracelet and the medication container are checked against the patient's medical chart to make sure that the right amount of the right medication is being given at the right time. The FDA has estimated that over a period of twenty years, the barcode-based medication administration system will have prevented a half-million adverse drug events and achieved a 50 percent reduction in the likelihood of medication errors.[13]

Patterns of Prescription Drug Abuse

Nonmedical use of prescription drugs, principally those opioid medications intended to relieve pain (see Chapter 5) and stimulant medications intended to treat attention deficit disorder (see Chapter 4), has grown to be a dominating element in today's drug scene. Prescription drug abuse has become increasingly prevalent among

high school and college students, as well as older adults. Essentially, prescription drug abuse has spread across the age span of Americans.[14] In 2011, the Drug Abuse Warning Network (DAWN) system reported approximately 175,000 drug-related emergency hospital visits due to the use of oxycodone or OxyContin, more than three times than in 2004.[15]

In light of the increase in prescription drug abuse, an intensive effort is underway to reduce the incidence of "doctor-shopping" a practice in which a patient manages to secure multiple prescriptions for abused drugs such as Percocet or OxyContin (Health Line, see above).

Major OTC Analgesic Drugs

Four classes of OTC drugs currently constitute the nonprescription analgesic market: aspirin, acetaminophen, ibuprofen, and naproxen. Of these, aspirin, ibuprofen, and naproxen are often referred to as **nonsteroidal anti-inflammatory drugs (NSAIDs).** This name identifies

nonsteroidal anti-inflammatory drug (NSAID): Any of a group of OTC analgesics (including aspirin, ibuprofen, and naproxen) or prescription analgesics (Celebrex) that are unlike cortisone-based drugs but nonetheless reduce pain and swelling caused by injury or disease.

them as useful in reducing the swelling and pain that often result from injury or illness (anti-inflammatory) but unrelated to the cortisone-based steroids often prescribed for this purpose (nonsteroidal). Acetaminophen, as we will see, is an effective analgesic, but because it does not reduce inflammation, it is not classified as an NSAID.

NSAIDs are not limited to OTC drugs. Prominent prescription NSAIDs, used primarily for the treatment of arthritis pain, are celecoxib (brand name: Celebrex) and diclofenac (brand name: Voltaren). The latter became available in 2008 as an analgesic patch (brand name: Flector). Rofecoxib (brand name: Vioxx) and valdecoxib (brand name: Bextra) were withdrawn from the market in 2004.

Aspirin

When American pioneers traveled west in the nineteenth century, they encountered Native American tribes who were treating pain and fever by chewing willow bark, reminiscent of a remedy that had been popular in Europe from as early as 400 B.C. It turns out that willow bark contains an analgesic compound called **salicylic acid,** named from *Salix,* the botanical name for willow.

The beneficial effect of pure salicylic acid on pain, however, was for a long time limited by the fact that most digestive systems could not handle it easily. In 1898, Felix Hoffman, a chemist at the Bayer Company in Germany, found that adding an acetyl group (making the result **acetylsalicylic acid, or ASA**), reduced this side effect without lessening the compound's therapeutic power. To arrive at a name that was easier to say, company officials noted that salicylic acid also came from spirea plants; thus the name **aspirin** was born.[16]

salicylic acid (SAL-ih-SIL-ik ASS-id): A drug developed in the nineteenth century to treat mild to moderate pain; it is extremely irritating to the stomach.

acetylsalicylic acid (ASA) (a-SEE-til-SAL-ih-SIL-ik ASS-id): A modification of salicylic acid that makes the drug less irritating to the stomach without reducing its analgesic powers.

aspirin: Any analgesic drug containing acetylsalicylic acid (ASA).

anti-inflammatory: Having an effect that reduces inflammation or soreness.

antipyretic: Having an effect that reduces body temperature and fever.

prostaglandins (PROS-tah-GLAN-dins): Hormone-like substances that are blocked by many OTC analgesic drugs.

The three principal medical applications of aspirin are well known. It is an effective *analgesic* drug for mild to moderate pain (hence its use in treating headaches), an **anti-inflammatory** drug in that it relieves inflammation and tenderness in joints of the body (hence its use in treating rheumatoid arthritis), and an **antipyretic** drug in that it lowers elevated body temperature when the body is fighting infection (hence its use in treating fever). A recommended adult dosage of 325 to 650 mg (one to two tablets or capsules), taken every four hours, is considered adequate for these purposes, with a recommended limit of 3,900 mg (twelve tablets or capsules) per day.[17]

Aspirin works as an analgesic not on a CNS level (like morphine or other opioid drugs) but rather on a peripheral level by blocking the synthesis of **prostaglandins,** a group of hormone-like chemicals normally produced by all body cells when injured in some way. When released, prostaglandins also encourage inflammation. Since prostaglandins act on the hypothalamus of the brain to elevate body temperature, blocking the synthesis of prostaglandins has a fever-reducing effect. Therefore, a combination of anti-prostaglandin effects, in both the central and the peripheral nervous systems, explains the three therapeutic actions of aspirin.[18]

However, three significant adverse side-effects of aspirin should be noted:

■ Aspirin-treated patients have a higher risk of developing gastric bleeding because the drug has a direct erosive effect on the stomach wall. This effect has serious implications for individuals taking a "baby" aspirin (81 mg) on a regular basis to lower the risk of heart attack. A recent study found that an aspirin regimen reduced heart-related medical incidents by 10 percent and a non-fatal heart attack by 20 percent, but increased the chances of serious gastrointestinal bleeding by 30 percent. It has been recommended that aspirin treatment be considered more selectively than in the past, on a case-by-case basis. Certainly, anyone with a history of stomach ulcers or related stomach problems should avoid taking aspirin.[19]

■ Aspirin increases the time it takes for blood to clot. Surgical patients should not have their bleeding time increased, so they are frequently advised *not* to take aspirin a week to ten days prior to surgery. Aspirin can be beneficial for individuals who are susceptible to small clots that can potentially block either coronary arteries, leading to a heart attack, or blood vessels in the brain, which could lead to an ischemic (blood flow–interrupting) stroke. On the other hand, aspirin increases the risk of a hemorrhagic (bleeding) stroke, because the normal clotting process is diminished.[20]

- The third caution involves children who have contracted a viral infection such as chicken pox or the flu. Aspirin has been found to be related to the development of **Reye's syndrome**, a rare but very dangerous condition marked by lethargy, nausea and severe vomiting, disorientation, and coma. Approximately 26 percent of Reye's syndrome cases are fatal. Because it is difficult to tell whether even a common cold may be the beginning of the flu, it is advisable to refrain from giving aspirin to anyone under the age of twenty.[21]

Acetaminophen

Since the 1950s, **acetaminophen** (brand names: Tylenol, Datril, Anacin-3, and Panadol, among others) has been available as an OTC drug, but it is only since the 1970s that it has been a popular alternative to aspirin for analgesic and antipyretic purposes. You may notice that no mention of an anti-inflammatory purpose appears. Indeed, acetaminophen does not reduce inflammation and, except for reducing the associated pain, does not help in the treatment of arthritis. However, acetaminophen does not produce gastric distress, nor does it interfere with the clotting process, so there are significant benefits for those individuals who might be adversely affected by aspirin.

The fact that acetaminophen has an effect on pain equivalent to that of aspirin without some of aspirin's side effects has made acetaminophen leading form of OTC pain reliever in the United States. This is not to say that acetaminophen is completely benign. Three areas of concern have arisen with respect to its use.

- A serious problem is its relatively high potential for causing liver damage. About 7,500 mg of acetaminophen (equivalent to fifteen 500-mg tablets of Extra-Strength Tylenol) can produce liver damage, and the combination of acetaminophena with alcohol greatly increases the risk of such a toxic reaction. In 1993, an FDA advisory panel recommended that warnings on acetaminophen labels refer to the particular risk of combining acetaminophen with alcohol. It has been recommended that individuals who have up to two drinks a day restrict their intake of acetaminophen to 2,000 mg per day (equivalent to four extra-strength tablets or about six regular-strength tablets). The normal maximal recommended dose per day is 4,000 mg. Anyone who has taken acetaminophen in this dosage range in combination with alcohol should seek medical attention immediately, prior to the appearance of symptoms related to liver disease. As an emergency medical procedure, an injection of acetylcysteine (brand name: Mucosil) can be used as an antidote for acetaminophen overdose, but this treatment is successful only if begun immediately. It may take as long as forty-eight to ninety-six hours before the symptoms of acetaminophen overdose appear, and by this time liver damage will have reached an advanced stage. Approximately one hundred people in the United States have died, and more than two thousand are hospitalized, each year as a result of liver damage from unintentional overdoses of acetaminophen. As a result of this evidence, the FDA in 2002 mandated a strongly worded warning on nearly two hundred OTC products containing acetaminophen that taking more than the recommended dose could cause liver damage.[22]

- A second concern is the risk of kidney damage as a result of heavy average use or moderate cumulative use of acetaminophen. The risk of kidney failure doubles in people who have taken more than 365 acetaminophen pills over a year's time (averaging one per day) or 1,000–5,000 pills over a lifetime. Aspirin use has not been found to increase the chances of kidney damage, although, as noted earlier, aspirin has its own health risks.[23]

- A third concern with acetaminophen is the risk of enhancing the effect of prescription anticlotting medications such as warfarin (brand name: Coumadin). A reduction of clotting is often indicated for patients who suffer from clogged arteries, but acetaminophen creates a situation in which the reduction of clotting is excessive, leading to hemorrhage. To this extent, acetaminophen shares the same interactive effect as aspirin and other NSAIDs.[24]

In the United Kingdom and other nations outside North America, generic acetaminophen is referred to as paracetamol (brand name: Panadol).

Ibuprofen

Ibuprofen is marketed as an OTC drug under a variety of brand names, most prominently as Advil, Medipren, Midol, Motrin, and Nuprin. It is effective in reducing pain, inflammation, and elevated temperature due to

Reye's syndrome (RYES SIN-drohm): A rare but very dangerous childhood disorder that has been associated with the administration of ASA-type analgesic drugs for the treatment of certain viral infections.

acetaminophen (a-SEE-tuh-MIN-oh-fen): A type of OTC analgesic drug. A major brand name is Tylenol.

ibuprofen (EYE-buh-PRO-fin): A type of OTC analgesic drug. Major brand names include Advil, Motrin, and Nuprin.

fever. In addition, ibuprofen has been found to be particularly effective in the treatment of menstrual cramps. As with aspirin, the mechanism behind ibuprofen's effects is to block the production of prostaglandins.

The recommended adult dosage of ibuprofen is 200 mg (one tablet) every four to six hours. Two tablets may be used, but no one should exceed 1,200 mg (six tablets) in a twenty-four-hour period. Less gastric irritation results from taking ibuprofen than from taking aspirin, although some discomfort can be experienced and the warning label suggests that one should consume milk or food when taking the drug. An additional concern is the potential for kidney damage or kidney failure. As a result, it is not advisable for individuals who have a history of kidney disease to take ibuprofen. In general, ibuprofen shares the anticlotting feature associated with aspirin, although there is evidence indicating that it interferes with aspirin's ability to protect against recurring heart attacks.[25]

Naproxen

The newest OTC analgesic drug, **naproxen**, is actually a well-known prescription drug that has been FDA-approved since 1994 for nonprescription use. When it was marketed as a prescription drug, it was known under the brand names Naprosyn and Anaprox. As an OTC drug, naproxen is available at a slightly lower dosage under the brand name Aleve.

Naproxen has analgesic, anti-inflammatory, and antipyretic effects, with a duration of action of eight to twelve hours, substantially longer than the other types of OTC analgesic drugs. The principal problem with naproxen is gastrointestinal irritation. Chronic naproxen treatment may cause gastric bleeding, ulceration, or perforation. It is important to be alert to signs of these problems while taking naproxen and to discontinue its use if any difficulties arise. It also has anticlotting effects.[26]

OTC Analgesic Drugs and Attempted Suicide

If we were to combine the four types of OTC analgesic drugs, we would see that they were represented in approximately one in four drug-related ED visits involving a

---

naproxen (na-PROX-sin): An analgesic drug, formerly available only by prescription (brand names: Naprosyn and Anaprox). It is now available as an OTC drug under the brand name Aleve.

diphenhydramine (DYE-fen-HIGH-druh-meen): One of two FDA-approved active ingredients in OTC sleep-aid products, such as Nytol and Sleepinal.

---

suicide attempt in 2010. In the overwhelming number of cases, the circumstance includes the ingestion of alcohol. As noted with respect to prescription drug overdoses, combining OTC analgesic drugs with alcohol is far more dangerous than taking them alone.[27]

Other Major Classes of OTC Drugs

In addition to analgesic products, a number of other product categories play a major role in the overall OTC market. Two of them will be considered here: sleep aids and cough-and-cold remedies.

Sleep Aids

The only FDA-approved active ingredients in OTC sleep aids are **diphenhydramine**, an antihistamine to be taken in either a 25-mg or a 50-mg dosage once a day (it is also available in various types of Benadryl), and **doxylamine succinate**, another antihistamine to be taken in a 25-mg dosage once a day. Brand names of such sleep aids containing diphenhydramine include Nytol QuickCaps and Sleepinal Night-time Sleep Aid; Unisom is the brand name for a sleep aid containing doxylamine succinate. Some of these products are also marketed in combination with acetaminophen as a "sleep-aid pain-relief formula" medication (Tylenol PM, for example). Individuals taking this kind of medication should be aware that they are dealing with a CNS depressant, and any combination with other depressants, such as alcohol or antihistamines contained in cough-and-cold remedies, can inadvertently enhance the overall effect.

Cough-and-Cold Remedies

As we all know, a cold can be a miserable experience. It can be frustrating as well because it is a viral infection, and there are few if any medications that can prevent a cold, cure a cold, or even reduce the length of time that we have to endure a cold. The best we can do is attempt to reduce its symptoms. This is where OTC remedies come into the picture.

One's choice of a cough-and-cold "remedy" (or of similar medications that treat allergic symptoms) depends on the symptoms that are present. Basic ingredients can include an *antitussive* agent, or cough suppressant, for the control of a cough; an *expectorant* to reduce the thickness of mucus in the throat and pharynx (making it easier to cough up); a *decongestant* to widen blocked nasal passages and sinuses; an *antihistamine* to relieve the itching, sneezing, teary eyes, and runny nose; and an *analgesic* and *antipyretic* agent to reduce the sinus pain, headache, or fever. Most cough-and-cold medications combine these ingredients in various proportions, so it is important to read the labels carefully to identify the specific product that is best suited for a particular combination of symptoms.

Potential problems can occur as a result of five major factors in current cough-and-cold medications.

- Antihistamines are CNS depressants. Although antihistamines can sometimes act paradoxically in young children (just as stimulants can act paradoxically as depressants), they produce drowsiness and sleep in most adults. This effect might be fine for bedtime, but it is very important to refrain from driving a car or engaging in any task that requires full attention while taking an antihistamine product.
- Several cough-and-cold remedies contain considerable amounts of alcohol. With levels of alcohol sometimes reaching 25 percent, these cough-and-cold remedies function essentially as alcoholic beverages.

An additive interaction of alcohol and antihistamine will occur (Chapter 3), making a person even drowsier than he or she would have been with the antihistamine alone. A person should take great care not to consume alcoholic beverages while being treated with an antihistamine medication.

- Because of the alcohol content, there is a potential for abuse of cough-and-cold remedies by young people who use them to get drunk. Even though this form of alcohol consumption is undoubtedly less than pleasant, some may see these products as an opportunity to bypass present restrictions on alcohol sales to underage customers. Mouthwashes also have this potential for alcohol-related abuse.
- Cough-and-cold remedies, particularly those containing the nasal decongestant pseudoephedrine, present health risks in young children. On the advice of the U.S. Centers for Disease Control and Prevention and the American College of Chest Physicians, manufacturers in 2008 changed their products' labels to say that they should not be used in children under age 4.
- Cough-and-cold remedies often contain dextromethorphan (abbreviated DM or DMX), an opioid used to suppress coughing. As discussed in Chapter 1, consuming large amounts of dextromethorphan for the purpose of getting high ("robo-tripping" or "skittling") is an increasingly serious problem. In 2011, one out of twenty high school seniors and one out of sixteen tenth graders reported having taken cough-and-cold medications for nonmedical purposes in the past year.[28]

Fortunately, most cough-and-cold products include on their labels specific warnings citing potential difficulties that might arise if the individual is diabetic, has high blood pressure, or suffers from heart or thyroid disease. Women who are pregnant or nursing should consult their physicians or other health professionals before taking any cough-and-cold remedy.[29]

The Pharmaceutical Industry Today

For several years, major pharmaceutical companies have faced increasing strains and pressures not only within their own industry but also from governmental

doxylamine succinate (DOX-il-a-meen SUK-sih-nate): One of two FDA-approved active ingredients in OTC sleep-aid products, such as Unisom.

agencies and the public at large. They have been criticized for runaway prescription drug prices, excessive corporate profits, commercial ties to physicians and scientists conducting drug research, and an apparent willingness to spend nearly as much on advertising and promotion as on research and development (see Point/Counterpoint IV on pages 360–361). Despite federal legislation regarding prescription drug reimbursement (Medicare Part D, enacted in 2003) and health care insurance in general (the Patient Protection and Affordable Care Act of 2010), these issues are bound to continue.[30]

In addition, there has been considerable concern about the ease with which prescription drugs can be obtained through Internet web sites, without proper supervision of physicians ordering the prescription or pharmacists filling it. In 2008, the Ryan Haight Online Pharmacy Consumer Protection Act was enacted in an effort to tighten procedures for gaining access to prescription drugs via the Internet (Portrait).

PORTRAIT

Ryan Haight and the Ryan Haight Act of 2008

Ryan Haight, a multisport scholar–athlete from La Mesa, California, died in 2001, at the age of eighteen, from an overdose of Vicodin he had obtained over the Internet. He had no intention of using Vicodin for recreational purposes; the purpose was to help him deal with back pain he had been suffering. He had secretly placed the order after claiming, in an online questionnaire, to be a twenty-five-year-old with back pain (he would not have been able to order the drug if he had admitted to being younger than twenty-one).

"Just the night before," his mother Francine Haight (see photo), a registered nurse, remembers, "We had dinner together after he came home from work at a nearly retail store. He used my Jacuzzi tub because he . . . said his back bothered him from lifting things at work." Ryan had never seen a doctor about his back, yet he got Vicodin delivered to his home in a matter of days. After one of his friends told his parents that Ryan got the Vicodin tablets via the Internet, they gave Ryan's computer to the DEA to investigate. To her amazement, his mother later found hundreds of Internet pharmacy web sites selling controlled substances that included generic versions of OxyContin and Vicodin, as well as antianxiety medications such as Xanax and Valium and stimulants like Ritalin and Adderall— all without the usual requirement of a written medical prescription. She decided to create a web site of her own, dedicated to the memory of young people like her son who have died from prescription drug overdose, and she set about persuading lawmakers of the need to curb the dangerous proliferation of Internet pharmacies.

The Ryan Haight Online Pharmacy Consumer Protection Act (the Ryan Haight Act, for short) was signed into law in 2008 and implemented in 2009. It stipulates that a doctor must conduct a face-to-face examination of a patient before dispensing any medication for a legitimate medical condition. Internet pharmacies are not illegal, but they must post truthful information about their physical location, provide the license numbers of their pharmacists, and get an additional endorsement from the DEA in order to conduct business over the Internet, even if the pharmacy already exists as a brick-and-mortar establishment. The act also makes it a crime to use the Internet to advertise the illegal sale of a controlled substance. Penalties of up to twenty years can be imposed for violations of the Ryan Haight Act. It is also easier now for states' attorneys general to prosecute violations committed by online pharmacies outside their states. This is a particular problem inherent in transactions carried out by the Internet businesses.

Prior to enactment of the Ryan Haight Act, the DEA found that 85 percent of all Internet prescription sales involved controlled substances, compared to 11 percent of prescriptions filled by regular pharmacies. It is evident that online sales were particularly suited to encourage drug misuse. One DEA official has expressed the issue in vivid terms: "Cyber-criminals illegally peddling controlled substances over the Internet have invaded households and threatened America's youth for far too long by supplying pharmaceuticals with a few clicks of a mouse and a credit card number." In effect, the Ryan Haight Act has established the new standard for legitimate online pharmaceutical sales.

Sources: Eckholm, E. (2008, July 9). Abuses are found in online sales of medications. *New York Times.* McKenna, C. (2008, October 2). Ryan Haight Act will require tighter restrictions on Internet pharmacies. *Government Technology*, www.govtech.com/gt/419355. McKenna, C. (2009, April 15). New rules implement Ryan Haight Act. *Government Technology*, www.govtech.com/gt/639985.

Dietary Supplements

There are well over one hundred dietary supplements available to the public. Approximately seventy are herbal preparations, purporting to enhance mood, energize the mind, or relieve feelings of anxiety. Although they are clearly not as problematic as illicit drugs such as heroin and hallucinogens or club drugs, these products need to be closely examined for their potential to create as well as resolve health problems. In a national survey in 2007, approximately 18 percent of American adults reported using "natural products" (dietary supplements other than vitamins and minerals) in the past year. In the vast majority of cases, people are taking supplement preparations without any communication with a physician or other health professional. In addition, herb-based dietary supplements are now commercially available in products such as iced tea, soft drinks, fruit juices, and yogurts. Sales of food and drink products that promise benefits beyond basic nutrition presently exceed $40 billion each year.[31]

Because dietary supplements are not officially classified as drugs, governmental regulations for them are different from those that apply to prescription and over-the-counter medications. The Dietary Supplement Health and Education Act of 1994 does not require dietary supplements to be tested for safety or effectiveness, although as of 2010 they must be determined to be free of contaminants, and the labels must accurately reflect the contents. Federal law requires that supplement labels contain the statement that any claims made by the manufacturer "have not been evaluated by the U.S. Food and Drug Administration." In effect, this disclaimer allows these products to be marketed and sold in the United States without any rigorous process of review and evaluation to assure the consumer that they are safe to take and effective for medicinal purposes.

What medical claims can be made for these preparations? On the one hand, the 1994 law clearly prohibits manufacturers from making any claim that refers to a form of disease. On the other hand, a federal ruling in 2000 stipulated that certain common physical conditions associated with different stages of life (such as aging, adolescence, pregnancy, and menopause) are not diseases, and therefore dietary supplement claims for helping with these conditions are allowed. Uncommon or more serious conditions associated with these life stages would still be considered diseases, and supplement labels are required to indicate that the products are not intended to "diagnose, treat, cure, or prevent" any such conditions.

Unfortunately, the distinction between disease and non-disease can be difficult to make. For example, "nutraceutical" manufacturers can now claim that certain supplements may be able to treat muscle pain but are prohibited from mentioning joint pain, because the latter is a symptom of arthritis. They can claim to treat "mild memory loss associated with aging" but not more severe memory problems associated with Alzheimer's disease. Federal officials admit that, at best, it is a difficult line to draw. At worst, there are serious concerns that consumer protections are being compromised. Science and common sense are far less influential in decisions about using dietary supplements than are feelings of hope, publicity hype, and simple word of mouth. As a prominent nutritionist has expressed it, "A lot of the information about supplements is generated by the manufacturers or by personal testimonials. Someone at the machine next to you in the gym says, 'You've got to try this.'"[32]

Dietary supplements are generally classified as either non-herbal or herbal. We discussed two examples of non-herbal supplements, androstendione and creatine, in the context of performance-enhancing drugs in Chapter 12. Herbal supplements are much more widely available to the public. The instrumental use of these compounds is directed toward the enhancement of health. However, claims by herbal supplement manufacturers are likely to be wildly exaggerated, when compared to the results of scientific studies of their effectiveness. Nine of the most prominent herbal supplements are examined in Drugs . . . in Focus. Note that one of these, ephedra, has been officially banned since 2004 as a consequence of potentially life-threatening side effects.

It is important to remember that the risks associated with the instrumental use of dietary supplements are also present when they are used for recreational purposes by individuals seeking a so-called natural "herbal high." The idea that herbal supplements are somehow safer than non-herbal supplements because they derive from natural, botanical sources is completely false. For example, an herbal product that claims to increase alertness may also produce extreme euphoria, disorientation, and dangerous cardiovascular changes.[33]

Drugs . . . in Focus

What We Know about Nine Herbal Supplements

Supplement	(Effective/Ineffective/Inconclusive) Therapeutic Applications	Risks and Side Effects
Ephedra	Nasal congestion, weight loss, increased energy performance enhancement	Nausea, high blood pressure, irregular heart for rhythms. Banned in 2004 as having an unreasonable risk of injury or illness
Ginkgo	Asthma, bronchitis, tinnitus (ringing in the ears). Ineffective for improving memory or treating dementia	Nausea, stomach upset, diarrhea, risk of increased bleeding, risk of seizures with prolonged use
Ginseng	Elevated blood glucose. Inconclusive evidence for improved health recovery following illness or increased stamina	Headache, stomach upset. Generally well-tolerated. Diabetics should show extra caution, since blood glucose can decline more so than with non-diabetics.
Hawthorn	Relieving mild heart problems	Mild upset stomach, headache, dizziness. Considered safe for most adults for short periods of times
Kava	Anxiety. No proven effectiveness as therapy for other uses	Liver damage, including hepatitis and liver failure, abnormal muscle spasm or involuntary muscle movements
St. John's wort	Ineffective therapy for major depression, although studies are under way for use in mild depression	Interactions with birth-control pills, anticoagulants, anti-immune drugs, and certain cancer drugs
Saw palmetto	Ineffective therapy for benign prostate hyperplasia (BPH, enlarged prostate gland).	Mild stomach discomfort
Turmeric	Indigestion, inflammatory disorders. Effects are uncertain at present.	Safe for most adults. High doses may cause indigestion or worsening of gall bladder disease.
Valerian	Insomnia and other sleep disorders	Safe for short periods of time. Mild headaches, dizziness, upset stomach, and tiredness the morning after its use

Note: Consumers, particularly young people, should recognize that scientific verification of claims is often lacking or incomplete. Tell your health care provider about any complementary and alternative health practices you use. This will help ensure coordinated and safe care.

Sources: Gold, P. E.; Cahill, L.; and Went, G. L. (2003, April). The lowdown on *Ginkgo biloba. Scientific American*, pp. 87–91. Klein, J. D.; Wilson, K. M.; Sesselberg, T. S.; Gray, N. J.; et al. (2005). Adolescents' knowledge of and beliefs about herbs and dietary supplements: A qualitative study. *Journal of Adolescent Health, 37,* 409, e1–e7. National Center for Complementary and Alternative Medicine, National Institutes of Health, Rockville, MD, nccam.nih.gov.

Summary

Categories of Medicinal Products

- Three categories of medicinal products are available for purchase: prescription drugs (which require medical approval), over-the-counter (OTC) drugs, and dietary supplements (both of which are available without any restrictions).
- The U.S. Food and Drug Administration (FDA) is responsible for setting the standards of safety, effectiveness, and honesty in labeling for the first two categories.

How the Regulation of Prescription and OTC Drugs Began

- A series of federal laws, put into effect since 1906, have established the FDA as the authority for safeguarding the public health with regard to prescription and OTC drugs, as well as food products, cosmetics, and medical devices.

Procedures for Approving Prescription and OTC Drugs

- The FDA process for the approval of new prescription drugs begins with animal studies to determine their safety limits and relative toxicity. If these standards are met, clinical trials, first with healthy human volunteers and later with actual patients, are conducted to identify the optimal dosage levels and degree of effectiveness.
- Only a small proportion of new compounds developed by drug companies make it successfully through these clinical trials and are eventually approved by the FDA for marketing as new prescription drugs. The process often takes several years.
- Since 1962, all prescription and OTC drugs have been required by the FDA to be generally recognized as safe (GRAS), as effective (GRAE), and as honestly labeled (GRAHL).

Are FDA-Approved Drugs Safe?

- There is considerable concern that although prescription and OTC drugs are FDA-approved for use when taken in the recommended dosages and under the recommended circumstances, their misuse can result in medical emergencies and fatalities. Issues of misuse and abuse has been particularly prominent recently in light of the enormous increase in pain medication prescriptions.
- Prescription drug misuse, whether intentional or unintentional (through prescription errors), is a growing public health problem as the number of available medications increases. Nationwide, regulations are being tightened to reduce the incidence of "doctor-shopping," a practice in which a patient manages to secure multiple prescriptions for abused drugs such as Percocet or OxyContin.

Major OTC Analgesic Drugs

- Acetylsalicylic acid (aspirin), acetaminophen, ibuprofen, and naproxen are four types of OTC analgesic drugs available to the public.
- Because each of these types has its benefits *and* hazards, recommended dosage levels should be observed, and anyone with specific health problems should be aware that analgesic drugs may be harmful.

Other Major Classes of OTC Drugs

- Two other classes of OTC drugs are notable for their popularity and their potential for misuse. The first is the variety of sleep aids, with the active ingredient of either diphenhydramine or doxylamine succinate. The second is the variety of cough-and-cold remedies that generally contain some combination of antihistamine and decongestant. The recreational use of cough-and-cold remedies containing dextromethorphan (DM, DMX) is a continuing drug-abuse problem.
- Careful use of all of these products is advised.

The Pharmaceutical Industry Today

- In the present-day pharmaceutical industry, companies have diversified their prescription and OTC products in an effort to maintain their share of a highly competitive market.
- Pharmaceutical companies are also under pressure to reduce the prices of their products as a component of controlling overall health care costs, particularly for patients who lack adequate insurance to cover their pharmaceutical expenses.

Dietary Supplements

- A large number of products, referred to as dietary supplements, are available to the public. Unlike OTC preparations, dietary supplements have not been evaluated by the FDA for safety and efficacy.
- Claims of medical benefits for both herbal and nonherbal supplements are often exaggerated and are difficult to verify because well-controlled scientific studies of their effectiveness are either nonexistent or incomplete. Therefore, considerable caution should be exercised when using them.

Key Terms

acetaminophen, p. 351
acetylsalicylic acid (ASA), p. 350
anti-inflammatory, p. 350
antipyretic, p. 350
aspirin, p. 350
bioequivalence, p. 344

dietary supplements, p. 340
diphenhydramine, p. 352
doxylamine succinate, p. 353
ibuprofen, p. 351
naproxen, p. 352

nonsteroidal anti-inflammatory drug (NSAID), p. 349
over-the-counter (OTC) drugs, p. 340
patent, p. 344
Phase 1 trials, p. 342

Phase 2 trials, p. 343
Phase 3 trials, p. 343
Phase 4 trials, p. 344
prescription drugs, p. 340
prostaglandins, p. 350
Reye's syndrome, p. 351
salicylic acid, p. 350

Endnotes

1. F.D.A. approves vitamin rules (2007, June 23). *New York Times*, p. A8. *Physicians' desk reference* (67th ed.) (2013). Montvale, NJ: PDR Network. Center for Drug Evaluation and Research, U.S. Food and Drug Administration, Washington, DC.

2. Burkholz, H. (1994). *The FDA follies*. New York: Basic Books. Carpenter, D. (2010). *Reputation and power: Organizational image and pharmaceutical regulation by the FDA*. Princeton, NJ: Princeton University Press, pp. 744–746. Hilts, P. J. (2003). *Protecting America's health: The FDA, business, and one hundred years of regulation*. New York: Knopf. Rados, C. (2006). FDA law enforcement critical to product safety. *FDA Consumer, 40*, 21–27. Sinclair, U. (1906). *The jungle*. New York: Doubleday, Page, and Company.

3. Zivin, J. A. (2003, April). Understanding clinical trials. *Scientific American*, pp. 69–75.

4. Haas, J. F. (2011). Managing benefits and risks of pharmaceutical drug treatment . In M. L. Finkel (Ed.), *Public health in the 21st century, Volume 1: Global issues in public health*. Santa Barbara, CA: Praeger, pp. 159–176.

5. Yorke, J. (1992, September). FDA ensures equivalence of generic drugs. *FDA Consumer*, pp. 11–15.

6. Position on switching of antiepileptic drugs. Statement approved by Epileptic Foundation Board of Directors, May 2009.

7. Als-Nielsen, B.; Chen, W.; Gluud, C.; and Kjaergard, L. L. (2003). Association of funding and conclusions in randomized drug trials. *Journal of American Medical Association, 290*, 921–928. Henkel, J. (1993, October). User fees to fund faster reviews. *FDA Consumer*, pp. 19–21. Zivin, Understanding clinical trials.

8. Brass, E. P. (2001). Changing the status of drugs from prescription to over-the-counter availability. *New England Journal of Medicine, 345*, 810–816. Nightingale, S. L. (1999). From the Food and Drug Administration: New easy-to-understand labels for OTC drugs. *Journal of the American Medical Association, 281*, 1164.

9. Information courtesy of the U.S. Food and Drug Administration, Washington, DC.

10. Carpenter, D.; Zucker, E. J.; and Avorn, J. (2008). Drug-review deadlines and safety problems. *New England Journal of Medicine, 358*, 1354–1361. Glantz, L. H., and Annas, G. J. (2008). The FDA, preemption, and the Supreme Court. *New England Journal of Medicine, 358*, 1883–1885. Lipsky, M. S., and Sharp, L. K. (2001). From idea to market: The drug approval process. *Journal of the American Board of Family Practice, 14*, 362–367.

11. Substance Abuse and Mental Health Services Administration (2013). *National estimates of drug-related emergency department visits, 2004–2011*. Rockville, MD: Substance Abuse and Mental Health Services Administration, Excel files. Substance Abuse and Mental Health Services Administration. (2012). *Results from the 2011 National Survey on Drug Use and Health: Summary of national findings*. Rockville, MD: Substance Abuse and Mental Health Services Administration, p. 58.

12. Gurwitz, J. H.; Field, Terry S.; Harrold, L. R.; Rothschild, J.; Debellis, K.; et al. (2003). Incidence and preventability of adverse drug events among older patients in the ambulatory setting. *Journal of the American Medical Association, 289*, 1107–1116.

13. Lyall, S. (2001, December 20). More deaths in England, due to error, report says. *New York Times*, p. A6. McNeil, D. G., Jr. (2003, March 14). To cut errors, F.D.A. orders drug bar codes. *New York Times*, pp. A1, A22. NEPS reduces hospital medication errors (2008, April 16). News release, NEPS LLC, Salem, New Hampshire.

14. Compton, W. M., and Volkow, N. D. (2006). Abuse of prescription drugs and the risk of addiction. *Drugs and Alcohol Dependence, 83S*, S4–S7. Editorial: Prescription drug use by adolescents: What we are learning and what we still need to know (2009) *Journal of Adolescent Health, 45*, 539–540. Ford, J. A., and Arrastia, M. C. (2008). *Addictive Behaviors, 33*, 934–941. Simoni-Wastila, L., and Yang, H. K. (2006). Psychoactive drug abuse in older adults. *American Journal of Geriatric Pharmacotherapy, 4*, 380–294.

15. Executive Office of the President (2011). *Epidemic: Responding to America's prescription drug abuse crisis.*

Washington, DC: Office of the President. Substance Abuse and Mental Health Services Administration, *National estimates of drug-related emergency department visits.*

16. Krantz, J. C. (1974). Felix Hoffman and aspirin. *Historical medical classics involving new drugs.* Baltimore: Williams & Wilkins, pp. 37–41. Levinthal, C. F. (1988). *Messengers of paradise: Opiates and the brain.* New York: Anchor Press/Doubleday, p. 112.

17. *Physicians' desk reference for nonprescription drugs, dietary supplements, and herbs* (32nd ed.) (2011). Montvale, NJ: PDR Network.

18. Stix, G. (2007, January). Better ways to target pain. *Scientific American,* pp. 84–86.

19. Mayo Foundation for Medical Education and Research (2012, May 24). Daily aspirin therapy: Understand the benefits and risks. Mayo Clinic, Rochester, MN. Parker-Pope, T. (2012, January 17). Daily aspirin is not for everyone, study suggests. *New York Times,* p. D5.

20. He, J.; Whelton, P. K.; Vu, B.; and Klag, M. J. (1998). Aspirin and risk of hemorrhagic stroke: A meta-analysis of randomized controlled trials. *Journal of the American Medical Association, 280,* 1930–1935.

21. Zamula, E. (1990, November). Reye's syndrome: The decline of a disease. *FDA Consumer,* pp. 21–23.

22. Schiødt, F. V.; Rochling, F. A.; Casey, D. L.; and Lee, W. M. (1997). Acetaminophen toxicity in an urban county hospital. *New England Journal of Medicine, 337,* 1112–1117. Stolberg, S. G. (2002, September 20). Warning sought for popular painkiller: F.D.A. panel says many used toxic doses of acetaminophen. *New York Times,* p. A25.

23. Perneger, T. V.; Whelton, P. K.; and Klag, M. J. (1994). Risk of kidney failure associated with the use of acetaminophen, aspirin, and nonsteroidal anti-inflammatory drugs. *New England Journal of Medicine, 331,* 1675–1679.

24. Hylek, E. M.; Heiman, H.; Skates, S. J.; Sheehan, M. A.; and Singer, D. E. (1998). Acetaminophen and other risk factors for excessive warfarin anticoagulation. *Journal of the American Medical Association, 279,* 657–662.

25. Ibuprofen interferes with aspirin's benefits (2003, April). *Health News,* p. 6. Whelton, A.; Stout, R.; Spilman, P.; and Klassen, D. (1990). Renal effects of ibuprofen, piroxicam, and sulindac in patients with asymptomatic renal failure. *Annals of Internal Medicine, 112,* 568–576.

26. *Physicians' desk reference for nonprescription drugs and dietary supplements* (24th ed.) (2003). Montvale, NJ: PDR Network , p. 2.

27. Substance Abuse and Mental Health Services Administration (2012). *National estimates, Suicide attempt visits.*

28. Ford, J. D. (2009). Misuse of over-the-counter cough or cold medications among adolescents: Prevalence and correlates in a national sample. *Journal of Adolescent Health, 44,* 505–507. Johnston, L. D.; O'Malley, P. M.; Bachman, J. G.; and Schulenberg, J. E. (2012a). Monitoring the Future: National survey results on drug use, 1975–2011. Vol. I: Secondary school students 2011. Ann Arbor, MI: Institute for Social Research, The University of Michigan, Table 2-2.

29. Gunn, V. L.; Taha, S. H.; Leibelt, E. L.; and Serwint, J. R. (2001). Toxicity of over-the-counter cough and cold medications. *Pediatrics, 108,* p. e52. Schneider, M. K.; Shehab, N.; Cohen, A. L.; and Budnitz, D. S. (2008). Adverse events attributable to cough and cold medications in children. *Pediatrics, 121,* 783–787.

30. Christian Science Monitor (2010). New health care bill pros and cons: Will it cut costs? http//www.csmonitor.com/USA/2010/0322/New-health-care-bill-pros-and-cons-Will-it-cut-costs. Accessed July 20, 2012. *Forbes Magazine* (2012, May 23). Why closing Medicare's 'Donut Hole' is a terrible idea. http://www.forbes.com/sites/aroy/2012/05/23/why-closing-medicares-donut-hole-is-a-terrible-idea/ Accessed July 20, 2012.

31. Brody, J. E. (2003, February 4). Herbal and natural don't always mean safe. *New York Times,* p. F7. De Smet, P. (2002). Herbal remedies. *New England Journal of Medicine, 347,* 2046–2056. National Center for Complementary and Alternative Medicine, National Institutes of Health, Rockville, MD. Straus, S. E. (2002). Herbal medicines—What's in the bottle? *New England Journal of Medicine, 347,* 1997–1998.

32. Fontanarosa, P. B.; Rennie, D.; and DeAngelis, C. D. (2003). The need for regulation of dietary supplements—Lessons from ephedra. *Journal of the American Medical Association, 289,* 1568–1570.

33. Klein, J. D.; Wilson, K. M.; Sesselberg, T. S.; Gray, N. J.; et al. (2005). Adolescents' knowledge of and beliefs about herbs and dietary supplements: A qualitative study. *Journal of Adolescent Health, 37,* 409, e1–e7. National Center for Complementary and Alternative Medicine, National Institutes of Health, Rockville, MD. Roosevelt, M. (2010, January 14). When the gym isn't enough. *New York Times,* pp. E1, E8.

Point/Counterpoint IV

Should Prescription Drugs Be Advertised to the General Public?

The following discussion of viewpoints represents the opinions of people on both sides of the controversial issue of prescription drug advertisement. Read them with an open mind. You don't have to come up with the final answer, nor should you necessarily agree with the argument you read last. Many of the ideas in the feature come from sources listed.

POINT

You have seen the DTC (direct-to-consumer) prescription drug advertising images on TV and in practically every magazine you read: good-looking people, apparently in superb health, enjoying the outdoors under an azure sky—all because they had taken Flonase, a prescription drug that could only have been obtained with a doctor's assent. It is as if the consumer now exclaims, "Wow, this Flonase must really be good. Besides, it makes me realize I have hay fever!" This is blatant manipulation. Why does a prescription drug have to be advertised to the public when the public couldn't obtain it legally on its own?

COUNTERPOINT

You obviously don't understand the evolving pharmaceutical marketplace. The more information presented to the patient, the better the health care system will be. Without advertising, you don't have a choice in your health care, and television is the most efficient outlet. Health care

consumers should make choices for themselves.

POINT

Wait a minute. Since the FDA relaxed the rules on direct-to-consumer advertising in 1997, things have gotten out of hand. Every major prescription drug available now has been promoted to the public through the media, and lately this use of the media has been extended to the advertising of medical devices. (One commercial that aired during a Thanksgiving Day football game in 2007 promoted a new coronary stent used in angioplasty surgery.) The American Medical Association gave up trying to ban the practice in 2006. Shouldn't it be the physician who makes the decision about a pharmaceutical treatment for his or her patients? Drug ads are not-so-subtle ways of getting patients to bring up the subject (and the drug they have heard about) when they see a doctor. And these ads are very big business that offer huge advantages to the pharmaceutical companies. It's been estimated that every dollar spent on DTC advertising yields more than four dollars in drug sales. Obviously, the patient inquiries stimulated by this advertising are working on the physicians. A study in 2005 showed that women who went to their physician pretending to have major depression were prescribed an antidepressant 53 percent of the time if they specifically mentioned

that they had seen a Paxil ad on TV, compared to 31 percent of the time if no drug was mentioned—a whopping 74 percent increase in antidepressant sales. And this was from patients who only *pretended* to be depressed!

COUNTERPOINT

Patients are encouraged to speak to their physician for truly appropriate health care. FDA regulations require that consumers receive a balanced and clear description of a drug's potential application, as well as its effectiveness, major side effects, and overall risks.

POINT

Pharmaceutical companies have a cagey way of abiding by these regulations. What about the following tag line for Adderall XR, an extended-release version of the popular psychostimulant treatment for attention deficit disorder? "Talk to your doctor to see if the all-day symptom control of Adderall XR can add new meaning to your child's life." The headline reads "Already Done with My Homework, Dad!"—a clever play on the letters ADHD. It's as if a prescription drug is being marketed as if it were breakfast cereal.

COUNTERPOINT

The viewing audience can tell the difference between medicine and cereal. DTC advertising in a thirty-second or sixty-second television spot or on a full page of a magazine simply empowers consumers to make informed decisions about their drug therapy when they go to a health care professional. People aren't dummies.

POINT

What you call "empowerment" amounts to $4.8 billion spent on DTC advertising in a single year (2006 figures, double the expenditure in 2000), just for promotional purposes. This is money that could have been directed toward the actual costs of research into new drugs that could save lives. Advertising costs are picked up by the consumer in the form of exorbitantly high prescription drug prices. Some people simply can't afford these drugs.

COUNTERPOINT

People don't complain that they now can't afford food because all the grocery stores advertise.

Ironically, advertising lowers costs. Pharmaceutical companies can't add the advertising cost on top of the product if there are other competitively priced alternatives already on the market. The health insurance companies will see to it that they don't. It is the high costs for research and development that are to blame for high prescription drug prices, not the expense of advertising.

Critical Thinking Questions for Further Debate

1. You are a physician, and your patient comes to you with the name of a prescription medication that he or she heard about on TV in a drug commercial. The drug in question is equivalent to the drug the patient is currently taking for a certain disorder. Do you switch the prescription to the new drug, in light of your patient's feeling that it might be more effective? How would the placebo effect figure into your thinking about this question?

2. You are a physician, and your patient comes to you with the name of a prescription medication that he or she heard about on TV in a drug commercial. The patient believes that he or she has the symptoms that this drug is designed to treat. The patient also hints that if you do not supply a written prescription for this drug, he or she will consult another physician. Do you prescribe the drug to the patient, even though you have some reservations about whether the patient really has the symptoms in question?

Point/Counterpoint V can be found on pages 405–406.

Sources: Boden, W. E., and Diamond, G. A. (2008). DTCA for PTCA—Crossing the line in consumer health education. *New England Journal of Medicine, 358,* 2197–2200. Kaiser Family Foundation (2001, November). Impact of direct-to-consumer advertising on prescription drug spending. Menlo Park, CA: Kaiser Family Foundation. Kravitz, R. L.; Epstein, R. M.; Feldman, M. D.; Franz, C. E.; et al. (2005). Influence of patients' requests for direct-to-consumer advertised antidepressants. *Journal of the American Medical Association, 293,* 1995–2002. Rados, C. (2004, July–August). Truth in advertising: Rx drug ads come of age. *FDA Consumer,* pp. 20, 27. Salazar, V. (2008, May 15). Our view on pharmaceutical advertising: Can you believe what you see on TV? Ask your doctor. *USA Today.* http://blogs.usatoday.com/oped/2008/05/edit15 .html. Thomaselli, R. (2006). AMA gives up push to ban DTC drug ads. *Advertising Age, 77,* p. 4.

Drugs for Treating Schizophrenia and Mood Disorders

I got to tell you, Doc, it was getting awful weird. It was like my thoughts were paralyzed. Cousin Sam's great-great-grandmother last week told me herself that I better be on my guard about those paralyzing thoughts in my head. Now lately, I suppose the medicine has killed off that stuff. That old woman's voice don't visit me no more. And I don't mind. I'm a lot calmer now. My brain's working better.

That's how it seems to me. I reckon the medicine just took those bad thoughts away. Don't ask me how it did it, 'cause I don't know. But it did.

—*A schizophrenia patient being treated with Thorazine*

We are fortunate to have drugs with the potential to liberate the mind from symptoms of mental illness, either moderate or severe in degree. The first part of Chapter 13 dealt with the use of psychoactive drugs in the treatment of anxiety disorders. This chapter will look at another set of psychoactive drugs that are used in the treatment of more severe mental disorders, specifically schizophrenia and mood disorders. As we will see, drugs of this type can help to reduce intense personal suffering and enable deeply troubled people to lead relatively normal lives.

Drugs used in treating mental illness are often referred to as **psychiatric drugs**, because they are generally prescribed and supervised by psychiatrists (medical specialists trained to deal with patients with mental illness). An alternative term, **psychotropic medication**, refers to the fact that their pharmacological effects move the patient closer to a normal state of mind (*trop*, meaning "to turn toward"). Over the last sixty years or so, the development of psychiatric drugs has brought about nothing short of a revolution in the quality of mental-health care, as well as major insights into the neurochemical nature of mental illness. Millions of individuals suffering from schizophrenia, depression, mania, and other serious mental disorders have benefited from psychiatric drugs.

The Biomedical Model

Using the term "mental illness" to describe the symptoms of disorders such as schizophrenia, depression, and mania implies that we are viewing abnormal psychological and behavioral symptoms as being no different from symptoms arising from a physical disease such as pneumonia or a stroke. This perspective, which is commonly referred to as the **biomedical model**, holds that abnormal thoughts and behaviors result from abnormal biochemical processes in the brain. According to this model, the effectiveness of psychiatric drugs in changing such symptoms is a function of altering these biochemical processes toward a more normal state.

Not everyone believes wholeheartedly in the biomedical model, and some mental-health professionals have considered alternative points of view. It can be argued that adverse sociological factors, psychodynamic factors, or behavioral and cognitive factors also play a role in producing abnormal thoughts and behaviors. The fact remains, however, that for many patients the administration of psychiatric drugs is an effective means of treating serious mental disorders. Because these drugs are affecting the functioning of neurons in the brain, the inference is inescapable that the improvements observed in such patients are directly related to the biochemical changes that the drugs produce. In other words, from the perspective of developing therapeutic approaches toward these patients, the biomedical model seems to work.

We can also look at the genetic evidence in favor of the biomedical model, particularly in the case of patterns of schizophrenia. For example, the concordance rate for schizophrenia in pairs of identical twins (corresponding to the probability of one twin becoming schizophrenic if the other twin already is) has been estimated to be 46 percent, compared to a concordance rate of 15 percent in pairs of fraternal twins. Given the essentially equivalent environmental influences on identical and fraternal twins, the difference between the two concordance rates indicates a strong genetic component. Recent evidence indicates that specific genes predispose individuals to the development of schizophrenia as well as other major psychiatric disorders.[1]

by the numbers . . .

25	Percentage of adults in the United States who have suffered some form of mental illness in the previous year.
15	Percentage of the U.S. population who will suffer from clinical depression at some time during their lifetime
121 million	Estimated number of people worldwide suffering from depression.

Sources: American Foundation for Suicide Prevention, New York, 2012. Reeves, W. C.; Strine, T. W.; Pratt, L. A.; Thompson, W.; Abluwalia, I.; et al. (2011). Mental illness surveillance among adults in the United States. *Morbidity and Mortality Weekly Report, Supplement, 60,* 1–32. World Health Organization World Mental Health Survey Initiative, Geneva, Switzerland, 2011.

psychiatric drugs: Medications used to treat forms of mental illness.

psychotropic medication: An alternative term for psychiatric drugs.

biomedical model: The theoretical position that mental disorders are caused by abnormal biochemical processes in the brain.

Antipsychotic Drugs and Schizophrenia

Drugs specifically intended to treat schizophrenia are traditionally referred to as **antipsychotic drugs**. Before considering these drugs in detail, however, it is helpful first to take a careful look at the often misunderstood symptoms of schizophrenia itself.

The Symptoms of Schizophrenia

The name **schizophrenia** literally means "split-mind," a term that unfortunately has led to a widespread misconception about how schizophrenic patients typically think and behave. *Schizophrenia patients do not have a split or multiple personality. Such psychiatric conditions exist, but they are referred to as dissociative disorders.* The accurate way of viewing a schizophrenia patient is in terms of an individual being "split off" or "broken off" from a firm sense of reality. The presence of **delusions** (beliefs not rooted in reality), leading to feelings of persecution or paranoia, and the presence of auditory hallucinations, commonly in the form of "voices," often torment the patient on a daily basis.

This is not to say that all schizophrenia patients have delusions or hallucinations. Some may display a significant "split" in the connections that normally exist among the processes of thinking, emotion, and action. The expression of emotion may be dulled or altogether absent; verbal expressions or mannerisms may be entirely inappropriate to a given situation; odd postures may be assumed for long periods of time (a condition called **catatonia**). Given the wide variety in schizophrenic behaviors, it is sometimes difficult for mental-health professionals to tell whether they are dealing with schizophrenia itself or with organic brain damage due to the toxicity of some ingested compound. The consumption of a number of solvent products and common metals (such as mercury) can produce schizophrenia-like symptoms (Health Line). In such cases, these substances are referred to as *neurotoxins*.

Overall, the prevalence rate of schizophrenia is approximately 1 percent of the U.S. adult population, representing more than 2 million people, roughly uniform across cultures throughout the world. Schizophrenia affects men and women with equal frequency, but the disorder often appears earlier in men, usually in their late teens or early twenties, than in women, who generally begin to show symptoms in their twenties or early thirties.[2]

The Early Days of Antipsychotic Drug Treatment

To appreciate the impact that antipsychotic drugs have had on the treatment of schizophrenia, we need to go back to the mid-1950s. Prior to that time, the principal methods of dealing with schizophrenia patients included the heavy administration of barbiturates and neurosurgical interventions such as prefrontal lobotomies. The side effects of these treatments included apathy and a general loss of emotional expression. By 1955, the total population of hospitalized psychiatric patients in the United States (of which schizophrenia patients represented the majority) had risen to about 560,000, roughly 50 percent of all those hospitalized for *any* reason. The demand for facilities to house psychiatric patients was quickly reaching crisis proportions.[3]

With the introduction of antipsychotic drugs around 1955, the tide turned. For the first time, symptoms of a major mental disorder such as schizophrenia were genuinely alleviated. Many schizophrenia patients could now be successfully treated on an outpatient basis.

Over the next thirty years, the resident population in U.S. mental hospitals decreased by 80 percent as a result of two factors. The first was the beneficial effect of antipsychotic medications on approximately half the schizophrenia patient population, allowing them to lead relatively normal lives outside a mental hospital. The second was a policy of deinstitutionalization, in which psychiatric patients of all types were admitted to mental hospitals only

---

antipsychotic drugs: Medications used to treat symptoms of schizophrenia.

schizophrenia: A major mental illness, characterized by being "cut off" from a sense of reality. Symptoms of schizophrenia may include hallucinations and delusional thinking.

delusions: Ideas that have no foundation in reality.

catatonia (CAT-ah-TONE-yah): A symptom displayed by some schizophrenic patients, characterized by a rigid, prolonged body posture.

for limited periods of time. The social consequences of deinstitutionalization will be considered later in this chapter 4.

Antipsychotic Drug Treatment

For most schizophrenia patients, antipsychotic drugs are administered orally in daily doses. In a few cases, intravenous or intramuscular injections are given when a highly agitated patient has to be subdued quickly. When the drugs are administered orally, the benefits appear slowly, over a period of a few weeks. During the initial days of treatment, patients usually feel sedated, but the degree of sedation generally declines as the antipsychotic effects begin to appear. In general, activity levels tend to become normal, with agitated patients becoming more relaxed and withdrawn patients becoming more sociable. When receiving the proper dosage, patients remain reasonably alert. Because they do not produce euphoria, tolerance, or psychological dependence, antipsychotic drugs have a low potential for misuse or abuse.[5]

The currently available, FDA-approved antipsychotic medications can be classified in three major "generational" groups (Table 15.1). We will begin with the first generation of drugs for schizophrenia treatment, which were introduced in the mid-1950s.

First-Generation Antipsychotic Drugs

The earliest medications for schizophrenia included chlorpromazine (brand name: Thorazine), haloperidol (brand name: Haldol), thiothixene (brand name: Navane), thioridazine (brand name: Mellaril), and trifluoperazine (brand name: Stelazine). Although they have been demonstrated to significantly reduce the hallucinatory and delusional behavior that is characteristic of many schizophrenia patients, these agents are not effective in reducing "less active" problems such as social withdrawal, apathy, and disorientation. A number of adverse side effects also arise with their long-term use. In fact, the side effects of first-generation drugs are so predictable (that is, typical) that the medications have frequently been referred to as **typical antipsychotic drugs**.

The adverse side effects of first-generation drugs range from relatively minor inconveniences to severe neurological difficulties. Patients may develop a dry mouth, blurred vision, dizziness, or weight gain. The skin can become oversensitized to the sun so that burning occurs even after a minimum of exposure. More significant reactions, however, include a severe disturbance in movement-control systems in the brain (see Chapter 3). Patients may develop a stiff, shuffling walk, a lack of spontaneity, restlessness, a fixed facial expression, and loss of coordinated movements such as the free swinging of the arms during walking. These problems are called **Parkinson's-like symptoms** because they resemble many of the features of Parkinson's disease.[6] A related side effect associated with first-generation antipsychotic drugs is a condition called **tardive dyskinesia**, a neurological syndrome that may appear after two or more years of continual drug treatment. Tardive dyskinesia, which literally means "a movement disorder arriving late," consists of jerky, tic-like movements of the lips, tongue, jaw, and face. Patients may smack their lips or flick their tongues in and out as frequently as twenty times in thirty seconds; their walking may become progressively unsteady, or they may rock back and forth while seated. It has been estimated that the likelihood of developing tardive dyskinesia as a result of long-term treatment with first-generation antipsychotic drugs is more than 10 percent, depending on the dosage and age of the patient. It is most common to observe this side effect in patients older than 50.[7]

---

typical antipsychotic drugs: A majority of available antipsychotic medications, all of which are associated with the possibility of Parkinson's-like side effects.

Parkinson's-like symptoms: Side effects of typical antipsychotic drugs, involving a fixed facial expression and difficulty walking.

tardive dyskinesia (TAR-div DIS-keh-NEEZ-ee-ah): A serious side effect affecting about 15 percent of schizophrenic patients who have undergone chronic treatment with first-generation (typical) antipsychotic drugs. Characterized by jerky movements of the face and lips, unsteadiness in walking, and rocking when seated.

atypical antipsychotic drugs: Antipsychotic medications that, unlike earlier medications used for treating schizophrenia, do not produce Parkinson's-like side effects. Clozaril, Risperdal, Zyprexa, Geodon, and Abilify are examples.

TABLE 15.1

Currently available, FDA-approved antipsychotic medications

GENERIC NAME	BRAND NAME*	RANGE OF DAILY ORAL DOSAGE (IN MILLIGRAMS)
First-generation drugs (typical antipsychotic drugs)		
chlorpromazine	Thorazine	100–500[†]
perphenazine	generic, Etrafon[‡]	12–24[†]
pimozide	Orap	1–2
prochlorperazine	Compazine	50–150[†]
thioridazine	Mellaril	150–600
thiothixene	Navane	10–30[†]
trifluoperazine	Stelazine	10–30[†]
Second-generation drugs (atypical antipsychotic drugs)		
clozapine	Clozaril	300–900
loxapine	Loxitane	20–60[†]
lurasidone	Latuda	40–80
molindone	Moban	100–225
olanzapine	Zyprexa	10
paliperidine	Invega	Extended release
quetiapine	Seroquel	50–400
risperidone	Risperdal	1–3
asenapine	Saphris	5–10 sublingual
ziprasidone	Geodon	20–160[†]
Third-generation drugs (newer atypical antipsychotic drugs)		
aripiprazole	Abilify	10–30

*Many of these medications, particularly those in the first-generation category, have been off-patent for many years and are prescribed in generic form, even though they are often still referred to by their original brand names.

[†]Also available in injectable forms.

[‡]Etrafon is a combination of perphenazine and amitriptyline (an antidepressant).

Source: U.S. Food and Drug Administration, Washington, DC.

Second-Generation Antipsychotic Drugs

A second generation of antipsychotic drugs, developed in the 1980s, has allowed for more complete treatment of schizophrenic symptoms without the potential for Parkinson's-like side effects. Because this particular problem is minimized or absent altogether, these medications are often referred to as **atypical antipsychotic drugs**.

Second-generation antipsychotic drugs have, in general, outperformed first-generation drugs in treating a wider spectrum of schizophrenic symptoms without inducing undesirable movement difficulties, but they are not without adverse side effects of their own. For example, clozapine (brand name: Clozaril) is effective in treating many schizophrenia patients who have not been helped by chlorpromazine, haloperidol, or other drugs in that category. Parkinson's-like symptoms and tardive dyskinesia are rare. However, a unique feature of Clozaril is the 1 to 2 percent chance of developing a potentially lethal blood disease called **agranulocytosis**, a condition involving the loss of white blood cells and a decline in the immune system as a result. If early signs of agranulocytosis are detected, Clozaril can be withdrawn and the patient will recover. As a safeguard, Clozaril-treated patients must undergo regular blood tests for the entire time they are under treatment. The need for blood testing has made Clozaril treatment far more expensive than traditional treatment with first-generation antipsychotic drugs.

More recently developed second-generation drugs share Clozaril's wide spectrum of effectiveness in treating schizophrenia, as well as its very low incidence of Parkinson's-like symptoms and tardive dyskinesia. They include olanzapine (brand name: Zyprexa), risperidone (brand name: Risperdal), quetiapine (brand name: Seroquel), and ziprasidone (brand name: Geodon). Fortunately, none of these drugs is linked to agranulocytosis, so there is no need for frequent blood tests.

However, some patients taking Zyprexa, Risperdal, and related antipsychotic medications experience considerable weight gain. In addition, there is an increased risk of hyperglycemia (high blood sugar) and the development of diabetes. The FDA now issues a strong warning that Zyprexa, Risperdal, and related drugs should not be administered to treat psychotic symptoms related to dementia among elderly individuals, because these medications nearly double the risk of death due to heart-related problems or respiratory infections such as pneumonia. However, a genetic link has been recently discovered that promotes the weight-gain effect in patients taking these medications. A simple saliva test can identify those patients who can benefit without the undesirable side-effect.[8]

Third-Generation Antipsychotic Drugs

The latest category of atypical antipsychotic drugs, referred to as third-generation medications for schizophrenia, is represented by aripiprazole (brand name: Abilify), available since 2002, has been shown to be an effective treatment for schizophrenia, without the risk of Parkinson's side effects, tardive dyskinesia, agranulocytosis, weight gain, or diabetes. As a consequence, the discontinuance rate (that is, the percentage of patients who no longer wish to take the drug) is only about 9 percent, a very low level when compared to the discontinuance rate for antipsychotic drugs in general. As we will see shortly, Abilify is categorized as a third-generation antipsychotic drug on the basis of its unique mechanism of action in the brain.[9]

Effects of Antipsychotic Drugs on the Brain

When the first antipsychotic drugs were introduced in the 1950s, *how* they worked at the neuronal level in the brain was a total mystery. In those days, drugs were "discovered" quite accidentally. Chlorpromazine, for example, was first administered as a treatment for severe vomiting (which remains one of its applications today) and as a sedative for presurgical patients. Only later was it recognized as having beneficial effects on certain schizophrenic symptoms.

As haphazard as the development of psychiatric drugs was at that time, a common thread frequently connected them, suggesting that the same neural mechanism might be responsible for their actions. In the case of antipsychotic drugs, there was an unmistakable connection between the improvement in schizophrenic symptoms and the often observed signs of Parkinson's-like motor problems. Could this connection provide a clue to the underlying biochemistry of schizophrenia?

By 1963, the biochemical nature of Parkinson's disease was beginning to be understood. Essentially, its symptoms were found to be a result of a deficiency in dopamine-releasing neurons in an area of the midbrain called the substantia nigra (see Chapter 3).[10] One result was the development of new drugs that helped Parkinson's patients by boosting the activity of dopamine systems in the brain.

The second result was an insight into the mechanism behind antipsychotic drugs. The reasoning was that if Parkinson's-like symptoms were appearing when

agranulocytosis (A-GRAN-yoo-loh-sigh-TOH-sis): A potentially lethal blood disorder associated with the antipsychotic drug clozapine (brand name: Clozaril).

patients' schizophrenic symptoms were improving, and if Parkinson's disease was due to a dopamine deficiency, then perhaps the antipsychotic drugs were reducing the activity level of dopamine in the brain. By implication, schizophrenia would be tied to an excessively high level of dopamine activity, and treating it would be a matter of bringing that level down.

Evidence that dopamine is involved in schizophrenia comes from a variety of sources. You would predict that an overdose of L-Dopa, an anti-Parkinson's drug that elevates the activity of dopamine systems in the brain, would produce schizophrenic-like behavior, and it does. Parkinson's patients need to be careful about the dose levels of their medication to avoid displaying signs of disorientation, disturbed thinking, paranoia, or catatonia. Another prediction is that the mechanism behind the action of antipsychotic drugs would be specifically associated with a decline in dopamine activity. It turns out that all the typical antipsychotic drugs block the stimulation of dopamine-sensitive receptor sites. In fact, the drugs that are most effective in blocking dopamine are the very same drugs that are most effective in treating schizophrenia. Likewise, drugs that are relatively weak blockers of dopamine are relatively ineffective in treatment.

Other evidence, however, points to the possibility that recognizing the dopamine connection might be only a first step toward understanding schizophrenia. Researchers know that dopamine-sensitive receptors in the brain can be broken down into subtypes—and in some cases, into subtypes within subtypes. At least six major subtypes of dopamine receptors (called D_1 through D_6) have been identified so far.

Understanding distinctions within neurotransmitter receptors has provided some insight into the effectiveness of various drugs, as well as into side effects that might or might not occur. For example, first-generation (typical) antipsychotic drugs block D_2 receptors to varying degrees. The incidence of Parkinson's-like side effects and tardive dyskinesia is considered to be linked to the reduction in D_2 receptor activity, without the protection that might be provided by changes in other neurotransmitters.

Second-generation (atypical) antipsychotic drugs operate in a somewhat different way. Clozaril, for example, blocks D_4 receptors to a greater extent than it inhibits D_2 receptors, which helps to explain why motor difficulties do not arise, but there is a link to an increased risk of agranulocytosis. Geodon, Risperdal, and Zyprexa block D_2 receptors, but the Parkinson's-like side effects and tardive dyskinesia are avoided, evidently because these drugs also block a special subtype of serotonin receptor.

Third-generation (also atypical) antipsychotic drugs are unique in that D_2 receptors are not necessarily blocked, as with other medications, but rather are modulated. Abilify increases the functioning of D_2 receptors when the neural pathways are hypodopaminergic (that is, when dopamine activity is too low) and decreases it when neural pathways are hyperdopaminergic (that is, when dopamine activity is too high). In other words, Abilify stabilizes the activity at this subtype of dopamine receptors. The additional feature of blocking certain serotonin receptors (the same ones that are involved in second-generation drugs) appears to be helpful in avoiding Parkinson's-like side effects and tardive dyskinesia.[11]

Drugs Used to Treat Depression

Severe and debilitating depression, usually referred to as *major depression*, is the most common form of mood disorder. It has been estimated that one in six American adults will be severely depressed at some time in their lives and that one in twelve has had a major depressive episode in the past year. The disorder strikes both young people and adults, both rich and poor. Not surprisingly, a large number of famous men and women in history—from the Roman emperor Tiberius and Queen Victoria to Peter Tchaikovsky, Fyodor Dostoevski, Abraham Lincoln, and Sigmund Freud—suffered depressive symptoms. The particular case of Abraham Lincoln is reviewed in this chapter's Portrait.

Major depression is an emotional state far beyond ordinary feelings of sadness, grief, or remorse. Many depressed individuals have turned to alcohol for relief. As we know, however, the depressant action of alcohol on the nervous system not only makes matters worse but also sets the stage for alcohol dependence and alcoholism (see Chapter 9).

A more immediate concern, obviously, is the risk of suicide. Not all people who either attempt or actually commit suicide are depressed, but the tendency toward depression increases the risk substantially. On the one hand, only about 15 percent of depressed people are suicidal; on the other, most suicide-prone people are or have been depressed. Ironically, the likelihood of a suicide attempt is increased in the initial phase of an upswing in mood after a deep period of depression. When the depression is at its most intense, the depressed individual has little energy to engage in suicidal feelings and thoughts.[12]

PORTRAIT

The Melancholy President: Abraham Lincoln, Depression, and Those "Little Blue Pills"

It is well known to historians that Abraham Lincoln suffered from long bouts of melancholy, a condition that would today be diagnosed as major depression. He suffered two major depressive episodes early in his life, in 1835 and 1841. What is less known is that Lincoln had been advised by his physician in the late 1850s to take what Lincoln called his "little blue pills" to help him elevate his mood. A few months into his presidency, in 1861, however, Lincoln stopped taking these pills, complaining that they made him "cross." During the late 1850s, Lincoln had experienced episodes of bizarre behavior that included towering rages and mood changes that either appeared out of nowhere or were responses to innocuous and sometimes trivial circumstances. It is reasonable to assume that these behaviors were, as Lincoln himself surmised, due to the "little blue pills."

It is a good thing that Lincoln made this decision. The medication he was taking was a common nineteenth-century remedy for depression called *blue mass*. It consisted of licorice root, rosewater, honey, sugar, and rose petals. But the main ingredient in these blue-colored pills, about the size of peppercorns, was approximately 750 micrograms of mercury, a highly neurotoxic substance. At the common dosage level of two or three pills per day, individuals ingested nearly nine thousand times the amount of mercury that is considered safe by current health standards.

If Lincoln had continued to take blue mass for his depression, he undoubtedly would have continued to experience the behavioral and neurological symptoms common to chronic mercury poisoning (see Health Line on page 365) as he led the nation during the Civil War. Fortunately, the symptoms of mercury poisoning in Lincoln's case were reversible after he stopped taking blue mass. Lincoln would suffer from severe bouts of depression until his death in 1865, but America was spared what might have been a catastrophe of historic proportions.

Like most Americans in the nineteenth century, Lincoln had no reluctance in securing any number of "over-the-counter" psychoactive medicines to help reduce his depressive episodes. While in Springfield, Illinois, he maintained a charge account at a local drugstore, where he bought opium on a regular basis and, on one occasion, cocaine (it cost him fifty cents). After his unsatisfactory experience with blue mass, Lincoln adopted non-pharmacological strategies to elevate his mood, turning to humor for help. His comic storytelling became legendary. As Lincoln would write, "If it were not for these stories—jokes—jests I should die; they give vent—are the vents of my moods and gloom." In the words of a Lincoln biographer, humor gave Lincoln "some protection from his mental storms."

Sources: Hirschhorn, N.; Fieldman, R. G.; and Greaves, I. (2001, Summer). Abraham Lincoln's blue pills: Did the 16th president suffer from mercury poisoning? *Perspectives in Biology and Medicine*, pp. 315–322. Shenk, J. W. (2005). *Lincoln's melancholy: How depression challenged a president and fueled his greatness.* New York: Houghton Mifflin. Both quotations on p. 116.

Drugs used to treat major depression are referred to as **antidepressants**. Like the antipsychotic drugs discussed earlier, these medications can be classified in terms of three generations of drug development.

First-Generation Antidepressant Drugs

Like the earliest antipsychotic medications, the first-generation antidepressants were discovered accidentally, and their original applications often had little to do with psychological disorders. One early antidepressant was first intended for the treatment of tuberculosis. It was soon recognized that the improvement in the patient's spirits was not merely a matter of reduced symptoms of this disease. When depressed but otherwise healthy individuals were given the drug, a significant improvement in mood was observed. Eventually, it was discovered that other chemically similar drugs were also effective antidepressants. The key factor connecting them all was their ability to inhibit the enzyme **monoamine oxidase (MAO)**—hence their classification as **MAO inhibitors**. Two MAO inhibitors are currently marketed for the treatment of

antidepressants: Drugs prescribed and used for the treatment of depression.

monoamine oxidase (MAO) (MON-oh-AY-meen OX-ih-dace): An enzyme that breaks down dopamine, norepinephrine, or serotonin at their respective synapses in the brain.

MAO inhibitors: A class of first-generation antidepressants that reduce the effects of monoamine oxidase (MAO) in the brain.

depression: phenelzine (brand name: Nardil) and tranyl-cypromine (brand name: Parnate).

Despite their benefits in the treatment of depression, MAO inhibitors are safely administered only to patients whose dietary habits can be carefully supervised or who can be relied on to observe certain specific dietary restrictions. The problem is that MAO inhibitors inhibit MAO not only in the brain but elsewhere in the body as well. In the liver, MAO serves a useful function in breaking down a chemical called *tyramine*. Too high a level of tyramine produces a highly toxic reaction by elevating the blood pressure and increasing the chances of a stroke. Therefore, although MAO inhibitors are useful at the level of the brain, they remove the individual's natural safety barrier against the harmful effects of excessive tyramine. Ordinarily, this action would not be a problem, except for the fact that tyramine is contained in many foods and drinks.

Because any food product or drink that involves fermentation or aging in its processing contains high levels of tyramine, combining one with an MAO inhibitor can be highly dangerous. Therefore, patients on MAO-inhibitor antidepressants must avoid any such food or drink. MAO inhibitors continue to be an option in the treatment of depression, but the difficulty in maintaining this kind of restricted diet for long periods of time has until recently been a major problem for many patients. Another set of first-generation antidepressants all have a three-ring portion in their molecular structure. They are referred to as **tricyclic antidepressants** for this reason. The most prominent examples are amitriptyline (brand name: Elavil), nortriptyline (brand name: Pamelor), desipramine (brand name: Norpramin), and imipramine (brand name: Tofranil). Because tricyclic drugs do not operate specifically on MAO, the problems inherent in a potentially high level of tyramine are not an issue, and dietary restrictions are unnecessary. As a result, depressed patients being treated on an outpatient basis can be given these types of antidepressants more safely. Those patients with cardiovascular problems, however, need to be monitored regularly because high doses of tricyclic drugs can produce an irregular or elevated heart rate. Some patients with cardiovascular disease cannot be treated with tricyclic drugs at all.[13]

Second-Generation Antidepressant Drugs

The 1980s saw the introduction of a second generation of antidepressants that bore no chemical similarity to either MAO inhibitors or tricyclic drugs. These antidepressants are referred to as **selective serotonin reuptake inhibitors (SSRIs)**, because they slow the reuptake of serotonin from its receptors at the synapse. The net effect is to prolong the action of serotonin at receptors that are sensitive to it. SSRI antidepressants include citalopram (brand name: Celexa), escitalopram (brand name: Lexapro), fluoxetine (brand name: Prozac), paroxetine (brand name: Paxil), and sertraline (brand name: Zoloft). Prozac was the first SSRI to become available, so it has attracted the most attention.

By all accounts, Prozac (along with other second-generation antidepressants) can be viewed as a genuine breakthrough in the treatment of major depression. It quickly became the number-one antidepressant medication on the strength of its effectiveness in reducing depressive symptoms with fewer side effects than other antidepressants available at the time.[14]

Unfortunately, Prozac had significant adverse side effects, as do all SSRIs to varying degrees. Some patients reported agitation and a feeling of nausea, as well as sexual dysfunction. There was an increased risk of seizures, though this side effect could be controlled either by lowering the dose or by combining the drug with antiseizure medication. Another source of concern was the tendency for Prozac and other SSRIs to be overprescribed, not only as a treatment for major depression but also for milder episodes of depression and related ailments that might better have been treated by traditional psychotherapy or counseling (Health Alert). Fortunately, there is no evidence for tolerance or physical withdrawal symptoms with Prozac or other SSRIs.[15]

Third-Generation Antidepressant Drugs

The newest generation of antidepressants include duloxetine (brand name: Cymbalta), mirtazapine (brand name: Remeron), venlafaxine (brand name: Effexor), and desvenlafaxine (Pristiq). Like SSRIs, these medications act on serotonin in the brain, but not exclusively so. As we will see in the next section, third-generation

---

tricyclic antidepressants: A class of first-generation antidepressant drugs. Brand names include Elavil, Norpramin, and Tofranil.

selective serotonin reuptake inhibitors (SSRIs): A group of antidepressants that slow down the reuptake of serotonin at synapses in the brain. Prozac, Celexa, Lexapro, Paxil, and Zoloft are prominent examples.

SSRI Antidepressants and Elevated Risk of Suicide among Children and Adolescents

In September 2004, a federal advisory committee recommended to the FDA that "black box" warnings be issued to physicians, indicating that SSRI antidepressants may cause some children and adolescents to become suicidal and may indeed not be effective in reducing depressive symptoms. Such warnings on standard drug references and information sheets are printed in boldface type with a black border around them and are positioned at the top of the warning label for these drugs. Although the incidence of suicide is roughly twice as high as when a placebo is administered, the overall risk of taking SSRIs is low. The likelihood of suicide would be 2 or 3 percent higher among patients taking SSRIs than among those taking a placebo. Considering the increased practice of prescribing antidepressant medication to this age group in recent years, the precaution has been deemed necessary. Physicians are still permitted to prescribe these drugs but must be careful in doing so.

Concerns that SSRI antidepressants might cause a small number of patients to develop suicidal thoughts have been raised since the introduction of Prozac in the late 1980s. In 1991, the question seemed to be settled when an FDA panel concluded that there was no convincing evidence linking increased suicide risk to Prozac itself. Nonetheless, later studies reawakened the controversy, particularly with respect to a young population and the wider availability of different forms of SSRI medications. In July 2005, the FDA issued a second warning that physicians prescribing SSRI antidepressants should carefully monitor their depressed patients of all ages at early stages of SSRI treatment or when dosage levels are adjusted upward or downward.

> **Where to go for assistance:**
> www.fda.gov/CDER/Drug/antidepressants/default.htm
> This web site is sponsored by the U.S. Food and Drug Administration (FDA) and is specifically designed to address potential adverse effects of SSRI antidepressants in adolescent patients.

Sources: Carey, B., and Harris, G. (2006, May 12). Antidepressants may raise young adult suicide risk. *New York Times*, p. A26. Grady, D., and Harris, G. (2004, March 24). Overprescribing prompted warning on antidepressants. *New York Times*, p. A13. Harris, G. (2004, September 15). F.D.A. panel urges stronger warning on antidepressants. *New York Times*, pp. A1, A19.

antidepressants affect the activity level of norepinephrine as well. For this reason, these medications are referred to as **serotonin-norepinephrine reuptake inhibitors (SNRIs)**.

Effects of Antidepressant Drugs on the Brain

When MAO inhibitors were discovered to be effective in reducing symptoms of depression, theories concerning the mechanism behind the action of these drugs turned to the properties of MAO itself. As enzymes, MAO molecules were known to inactivate dopamine, norepinephrine, and serotonin (collectively referred to as monoamines) at the synapses where these neurotransmitters operate. We can think of a drug as producing a double-negative effect on these neurotransmitters. By inhibiting MAO, we are inhibiting an inhibitor, and the net result will be a rise in the activity level of dopamine, norepinephrine, or serotonin. If so, then it would be logical to theorize that depression is associated with a lower-than-normal level of any one of these neurotransmitters or some combination of the three.

With the discovery of tricyclic antidepressants, it has been possible to focus on a more specific biochemical theory. Unlike MAO inhibitors, tricyclic drugs do not act on enzymes in the synapse. Instead, they slow down the reuptake of norepinephrine and serotonin at their respective synapses. Since the reuptake process allows neurotransmitter molecules to be reabsorbed from the receptor sites back to the neuron that released them in the first place (see Chapter 3), a slowing down means that these neurotransmitter molecules now remain in the receptor site for a longer period of time. When the neurotransmitter stays in the receptors longer, the receptors are stimulated more intensely. In other words, the effect of tricyclic drugs

> **serotonin-norepinephrine reuptake inhibitors (SNRIs):** A group of antidepressants that slow down the reuptake of serotonin and norepinephrine at synapses in the brain. Remeron, Cymbalta, and Effexor are prominent examples.

is to increase the activity level of norepinephrine and serotonin. Following the line of reasoning presented earlier, depression would be associated with a lower-than-normal level of activity with respect to these neurotransmitters.

Prozac was unique in that it was not so much "discovered" as designed with a specific purpose in mind. The intent was to identify a chemical that slowed the reuptake of serotonin alone—hence its eventual designation as a selective serotonin reuptake inhibitor (SSRI). Since its introduction, Prozac has been joined by other SSRIs that share this pharmacological feature. On a theoretical level, the successful development of Prozac and other SSRIs as effective antidepressants has provided strong evidence for the involvement of serotonin in providing the optimal level of mood in a person's life.

This fact does not necessarily mean, however, that serotonin is the exclusive neurotransmitter system in the regulation of mood. As noted earlier, a sizable proportion of depressive patients benefit from the administration of drugs such as tricyclic drugs, and this implies that a norepinephrine system is involved as well. Third-generation antidepressants, such as Cymbalta, Effexor, Pristiq, and Remeron, are desirable for some patients because they affect both neurotransmitters. Cymbalta, Effexor, and Pristiq, for example, slow the reuptake of both norepinephrine and serotonin. In this respect, Cymbalta, Effexor, and Pristiq resemble tricyclic antidepressants, but their chemical structure and effects on other neurotransmitters are different. As a result, treatment with these antidepressants makes it possible to avoid the adverse side effects associated with tricyclic medications. In the case of Remeron; greater amounts of norepinephrine and serotonin are allowed to be released at their respective synapses. At the same time, only certain subtypes of serotonin receptors are involved.[16]

The Effectiveness of Specific Antidepressant Drugs

Approximately 65 percent of patients taking any antidepressant drug will show significant improvement in their mood, compared to about 35 percent who will feel improvement with a placebo. This finding is sufficient to warrant the use of antidepressants in general, but the question of which antidepressant is best remains. Comparative studies of various antidepressants indicate that

mania: A mood disorder characterized by agitation, bursts of energy, and impulsiveness.

bipolar disorder: A mood disorder in which the patient swings back and forth between feelings of depression and mania.

roughly the same percentage of patients show improvements, no matter which antidepressant is used.

However, despite the fact that the percentage of patients who improve is the same *overall*, there can be substantial individual differences. For example, hypothetically, if 100 patients are given a tricyclic antidepressant (such as Tofranil), 65 are likely to show improvement, and if 100 patients are given an SSRI, 65 will also respond, *but not the same 65*. It may be that depression is expressed in different neurochemical ways in different people. The key to future success in treating depression in the most effective way will be finding a way to determine, ahead of time, which patients are likely to respond to which neurochemical manipulation and, in turn, to which medication. One group of patients might respond best to a higher level of norepinephrine activity; another group might respond to a higher level of serotonin activity; and a third group might respond to a higher level of serotonin activity, but only at specific subtypes of serotonin receptors.[17]

Recently, some question has even arisen about whether antidepressants are effective treatments (relative to placebo controls) for all forms of depression, no matter whether the symptoms are mild or severe. Examining studies that have used a randomized, double-blind, placebo-controlled design, a procedure that is considered the "gold standard" for teasing out genuine effects from placebo effects (see Chapter 3), reveals that antidepressant medications do produce a substantial reduction in symptoms associated with severe depression, but minimal or non-existent positive effects, on average, in patients with mild or moderate symptoms.[18]

Drugs for Other Types of Mental Disorders

In addition to drugs designated specifically for the treatment of schizophrenia and depression, there is a range of psychotropic drugs that are useful in dealing with other mental disorders. Two examples are described here.

Mania and Bipolar Disorder

A mood disorder can encompass forms other than simple depression. Some individuals may display symptoms of **mania** that are as disruptive to themselves and their families as depression. Symptoms of mania include sleeplessness, impulsiveness (a manic patient and a credit card are a dangerous combination), irritability, and feelings of grandeur. Others may display mood swings back and forth between depression and mania (a condition referred to as **bipolar disorder**, formerly known as manic-depression).

Until recently, the primary psychiatric drug for the treatment of either mania or bipolar disorder has been **lithium carbonate**. Unfortunately, lithium carbonate is effective for only 50 percent of patients showing these symptoms, and those who respond well to it must undergo periodic blood testing to avoid potential toxic effects to the thyroid gland and kidneys.

The drug valproate (brand name: Depakote) has now been found to help patients suffering from either mania or bipolar disorder, as an alternative to lithium carbonate. Recently, it has been found also to be useful in conjunction with antipsychotic medication when psychotic symptoms are accompanied by an unstable mood. Valproate was originally introduced for the treatment of epilepsy, for which it continues to be prescribed. The mechanism by which it is effective in the treatment of a variety of psychiatric disorders is unclear.[19]

Since 2005, a number of second-generation antipsychotic medications have been FDA-approved for the treatment of bipolar disorder. These medications include Risperdal, Geodon, Seroquel, and a combination of Zyprexa with Prozac (brand name: Symbyax). However, they presently carry a "black box" warning (see Chapter 14) that they should not be administered to elderly patients with dementia, on the basis of evidence showing an elevated risk of death from cardiovascular disease or infections such as pneumonia. In addition, Abilify has been found to be effective in treatment of

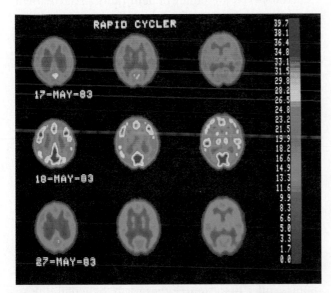

These PET scans show significant differences in the neural activity (yellow and red areas being the highest) of a bipolar disorder patient during times of alternating depression (top and bottom rows) and hypomania, a mild form of mania (middle row). Similar scans have identified differences in neural activity between normal and schizophrenic individuals.

bipolar disorder as well, although it has not been FDA-approved for patients younger than 10 years old.[20]

Autism

Autism is a complex developmental disability that typically appears during the first three years of life and impairs the social connectedness that a person shares with others. In some cases, behavioral problems among autistic individuals include aggressiveness, severe temper tantrums, and self-injury. In 2006, the FDA approved

lithium (LITH-ee-um) carbonate: A psychiatric drug used in the treatment of mania or bipolar disorder.

autism: A form of developmental disability, typically appearing during the first three years of life, that affects the normal development of the brain in areas of social communication and communication skills. Autistic children and adults have difficulties in verbal and nonverbal communication and emotional responses.

Risperdal as a treatment for these behavioral problems in autistic children and adolescents. In 2009, Abilify received FDA approval for use in treating irritability and aggressive behavior in autistic patients aged 6 to 17.[21]

Off-Label Usage of Psychotropic Medications

Increasingly, psychotropic medications have been used for purposes other than those specified by the FDA when they were first approved. This practice, referred to as off-label usage, is common not only for psychotropic medications but for prescription drugs in general. By law, physicians are given considerable latitude to prescribe, for their patients, drugs that they consider appropriate for a specific set of symptoms, even if there is no official sanction for that particular application.[22]

In circumstances of mental-health treatment, some antidepressants may be useful in the treatment of anxiety, and some antianxiety medications may be useful in the treatment of depression. For example, Zoloft has been shown to be effective in the treatment of post-traumatic stress disorder and Cymbalta and Effexor for generalized anxiety. In response to these developments, the FDA has made official changes to widen the possible applications from those originally designated when the drug was introduced. In general, this kind of "cross-over" pharmacotherapy in psychiatry is on the rise and is part of the challenge we face in our attempt to understand specific neurochemical systems that underlie normal as well as abnormal behavior.[23]

Psychiatric Drugs, Social Policy, and Deinstitutionalization

Prior to the 1960s, the dominant approach to treating severely impaired psychiatric patients was institutionalization in large, state-supported mental hospitals. In such places the treatment of choice, medication, could be controlled by psychiatrists and hospital staff. During the 1960s, the approach to treating the mentally ill

> **off-label usage:** The practice of prescribing the use of a particular medication, even if the drug in question has not been FDA-approved for that purpose.
>
> **deinstitutionalization:** The social policy of encouraging mentally ill individuals to be treated in community-based programs rather than in large mental hospitals.

started to change. A 1960 U.S. Supreme Court decision, later to form the basis for the mental-health policy known as the "least restrictive alternative," established that involuntary admission to psychiatric hospitals was permitted only if there were no other feasible means of treatment that would allow patients greater freedom. As a result, responsibility for treatment largely shifted from centralized institutions to decentralized community mental-health clinics. Patient advocates argued that these smaller centers could provide a more humane setting for psychiatric treatment. The process of deinstitutionalization was greatly accelerated by the expansion of federal Medicaid and Medicare programs, enabling thousands of patients to sustain themselves financially in the community.

Today, the concept of deinstitutionalization is the subject of considerable ambivalence. When large numbers of institutionalized patients were released, theories about psychiatric rehabilitation were largely untested, and not enough planning was conducted to anticipate and meet the needs of people with serious mental illnesses in the community at large. Community mental-health centers failed to live up to their promise to provide comprehensive mental-health care, particularly for patients with substance-abuse problems. The large numbers of homeless young adults, displaying obvious signs of disorientation and distress, received considerable media attention.

Where has the policy of deinstitutionalization left psychiatric patients? With court decisions upholding the illegality of involuntary commitment (patients being hospitalized against their will) for more than a limited period of time, unless there is a clear danger to society, many patients have ended up drifting into and out of mental-health facilities, no longer supervised carefully enough to take their medication regularly or attend to their personal needs. Estimates are that between one-third and one-half of all homeless adults have been diagnosed with a severe mental disorder. It has been said that, at its worst, deinstitutionalization moved some psychiatric patients from the "back wards" of mental hospitals to the back alleys of our communities. More than 250,000 patients with severe mental illness are in jails or prisons, where psychiatric treatment is often unavailable, and there are increasing rates of substance-abuse problems. More than 400,000 elderly individuals in nursing homes suffer from some form of severe mental illness, and these facilities are so hard-pressed in dealing with their residents' physical needs that mental-health treatment is often poor or nonexistent (Drugs . . . in Focus).

Nonetheless, despite these very real problems, most mentally ill patients lead better lives now than their

Psychiatric Drugs and the Civil Liberties Debate

Let's imagine that you are a hospitalized psychiatric patient, either voluntarily or involuntarily committed to a mental-health facility on the basis of a diagnosis of schizophrenia. You are handed your daily medication that has been prescribed by a staff psychiatrist. There has been a careful diagnosis of your mental illness and a determination that the medication is appropriate and effective in reducing your symptoms. Can you refuse to take it? Do you even have to give a reason for your refusal? If you are asked to participate in a study in which a new experimental drug is being tested against a placebo, should you be required to do so? If you signed an informed-consent form, are you mentally competent to know what you are agreeing to do? If you state that you are mentally competent but have been diagnosed as a schizophrenic, will your self-assessment be considered valid?

These are a few of the difficult questions currently being faced in mental-health treatment facilities and in the development of new therapeutic drugs. Few of them have been totally resolved. In the late 1960s in Minnesota and New York, physicians were successfully sued for *not* medicating committed, drug-refusing patients. However, in 1975 in Massachusetts, physicians were successfully sued *for* medicating drug-refusing patients. Court decisions since 1979 regarding a patient's right to refuse medication have

generally been in the patient's favor, although the decision about the mental competence of an individual patient is frequently left to a judge's ruling. According to a survey in 2006, 28 percent of Americans support the policy of forcing people with mental illness to take psychiatric medication.

Another controversy has arisen surrounding the rights of patients in the development of new drugs, particularly with regard to the treatment of schizophrenia. Should these patients participate in clinical testing trials for experimental antipsychotic medications? On the one hand, there are no animal models for hallucinations or other symptoms of schizophrenia, disorders that antipsychotic medications are intended as potential treatments. On the other hand, civil rights attorneys have argued that people with significant psychiatric disorders should never be "guinea pigs," even for the benefit of humanity. What do you think?

Sources: Amarasingham, L. R. (1980). Social and cultural perspectives on medication refusal. *American Journal of Psychiatry, 137,* 353–358. Applebaum, P. D. (1988). Antipsychotic medications: Retrospect and prospect. *American Journal of Psychiatry, 145,* 413–419. Gutheil, T. G. (1980). In search of true freedom: Drug refusal, involuntary medication, and "Rotting with your rights on." *American Journal of Psychiatry, 137,* 327–328. Mossakowski, K. N.; Kaplan, L. M.; and Hill, T. D. (2011). Americans' attitudes toward mental illness and involuntary psychiatric medication. *Society and Mental Health, 1,* 200–2016.

counterparts in the days of institutionalized care. About two-thirds of these people who are provided with a comprehensive range of services, including social support, can live outside of mental hospitals. Patients themselves overwhelmingly prefer living in the community than to living in a mental hospital. The challenges that lie ahead involve addressing more effectively the needs of those patients who are "falling through the cracks" in the system. It is unlikely that anyone will be advocating a return to the era of massive institutionalized care.[24]

Summary

Mental Illness and the Biomedical Model

- The development of psychiatric drugs to treat major mental illnesses such as schizophrenia and mood disorders has both revolutionized the field of mental health and provided insights into the biochemical basis for mental illness.

- The biomedical model, the prevailing viewpoint among mental-health professionals, asserts that

abnormal thoughts and behaviors result from faulty biochemical processes in the brain.

Antipsychotic Drugs and Schizophrenia

- Therapeutic medications for schizophrenia patients are classified as first-generation, second-generation, and third-generation antipsychotic drugs. First-generation drugs include chlorpromazine (brand name: Thorazine) and haloperidol (brand name: Haldol). Second-generation drugs include clozapine (brand name: Clozaril) and risperidone (brand name: Risperdal). The newest third-generation drugs include aripiprazole (brand name: Abilify).

- First-generation antipsychotic drugs have been effective in reducing symptoms for many patients, but they also carry the potential for the development of severe movement-related motor problems.
- Second-generation and third-generation antipsychotic medications do not produce this particular side effect.
- Antipsychotic medications are believed to be clinically effective, and to involve the least number of adverse side effects, by virtue of a combination of actions upon subtypes of dopamine and serotonin receptors in the brain.

Drugs Used to Treat Depression

- First-generation antidepressant drugs can be divided into two groups: MAO inhibitors and tricyclic antidepressants.
- The MAO inhibitors were the first group to be developed for the treatment of depression. Although they are effective, patients need to be on a restricted diet to avoid serious adverse side effects.
- Tricyclic antidepressants do not require dietary restrictions, but their effects on the cardiovascular system make them undesirable for certain patients.
- Second-generation antidepressants include the well-known drug fluoxetine (brand name: Prozac) and

similar drugs that slow the reuptake of serotonin. Collectively, they are referred to as selective serotonin reuptake inhibitors (SSRIs).

- Third-generation antidepressants slow the reuptake of both serotonin and norepinephrine in the brain.

Drugs for Other Types of Mental Disorders

- Mania and extreme mood swings between mania and depression (bipolar disorder) are two mood disorders that have been treated successfully with lithium carbonate or valproate (brand name: Depakote), as well as antipsychotic medications such as risperidone (brand name: Risperdal) and ziprasidone (brand name: Geodon), or a combination of antipsychotic and antidepressant medications (brand name: Symbyax).
- Risperidone (brand name: Risperdal) has been approved as a treatment for symptoms of autism in children and adolescents.

Psychiatric Drugs, Social Policy, and Deinstitutionalization

- Since the 1960s, a growing number of psychiatric patients have been treated outside a centralized hospital or institution and placed in treatment-care clinics in the community. Although the policy of deinstitutionalization has sparked great debate and significant social problems remain, there is a growing consensus that mental-care treatment implemented in this manner is superior to institutionalization.

Key Terms

agranulocytosis, p. 367
antidepressants, p. 369
antipsychotic drugs, p. 364
atypical antipsychotic drugs, p. 366
autism, p. 373
biomedical model, p. 363
bipolar disorder, p. 372
catatonia, p. 364

deinstitutionalization, p. 374
delusions, p. 364
lithium carbonate, p. 373
mania, p. 372
MAO inhibitors, p. 369
monoamine oxidase (MAO), p. 369
off-label usage, p. 374

Parkinson's-like symptoms, p. 366
psychiatric drugs, p. 363
psychotropic medication, p. 363
schizophrenia, p. 364
selective serotonin reuptake inhibitors (SSRIs), p. 370

serotonin-norepinephrine reuptake inhibitors (SNRIs), p. 371
tardive dyskinesia, p. 366
tricyclic antidepressants, p. 370
typical antipsychotic drugs, p. 366

Endnotes

1. Walsh, T.; McClellan, J. M.; McCarthy, S. E.; Addington, A.; et al. (2008). Rare structural variants disrupt multiple genes in neurodevelopmental pathways in schizophrenia. *Science, 320,* 539–543. Pogue-Geile, M. F., and Yokley, J. L. (2010). Current research on the genetic contributors to schizophrenia. *Current*

Directions in Psychological Science, 19, 214–219. Tarbox, S. I., and Poguek-Geile, M. F. (2011). A multivariate perspective on schizotypy and familial association with schizophrenia: A review. *Clinical Psychology Review, 31,* 1169–1182. Wilffert, B.; Zaal, R.; and Brouwers, J. R. (2005). Pharmacogenetics as a tool in the therapy of schizophrenia (2005, February). *Pharmacy World and Science*, pp. 20–30.

2. American Psychiatric Association (2013). Highlights of changes from DSM-IV-TR to DSM-5. Washington, DC: American Psychiatric Association. American Psychiatric Association (2000). *Diagnostic and statistical manual of mental disorders*. Text revision (4th ed.). Washington, DC: American Psychiatric Association, pp. 278–290. National Institute of Mental Health (1999, revised 2002). *Schizophrenia*. Bethesda, MD: National Institute of Health.

3. Levinthal, C. F. (1988). *Messengers of paradise: Opiates and the brain*. New York: Anchor Press/Doubleday, pp. 60–61. Snyder, S. H. (1974). *Madness and the brain*. New York: McGraw-Hill, pp. 19–21.

4. Grob, G. N. (1995, July/August). The paradox of deinstitutionalization. *Society*, pp. 51–58. Krieg, R. G. (2001). An interdisciplinary look at the deinstitutionalization of the mentally ill. *Social Science Journal*, 38, 367–380.

5. Julien, R. M (2005). *A primer of drug action* (10th ed.). New York: Worth, pp. 337–359. Picchioni, M. M., and Murray, R. M. (2007). Schizophrenia. *British Medical Journal*, 335, 91–95. Van Os, J., and Kapur, S. (2009). Schizophrenia. *The Lancet*, 374, 635–645.

6. Julien, *A primer of drug action*, pp. 350–356.

7. Ibid, p. 353.

8. Lenz, T.; Robinson, D.; Napolitano, B.; Sevy, S.; Kane, J.; et al. (2010). DRD2 promoter region variation predicts antipsychotic-induced weight gain in first episode schizophrenia. *Pharmacogenetics and Genomics*, 20, 569–572. Lieberman, J. A.; Stroup, T. S.; McEvoy, J. P.; Swartz, M. S.; et al. (2005). Effectiveness of antipsychotic drugs in patients with chronic schizophrenia. *New England Journal of Medicine*, 353, 1209–1223. U.S. Food and Drug Administration (2004, March 1). Medwatch: 2004 safety alert: Zyprexa (olanzapine). Washington, DC: U.S. Food and Drug Administration. U.S. Food and Drug Administration (2005, April 11). FDA Talk Paper: FDA issues public health advisory for antipsychotic drugs used for treatment of behavioral disorders in elderly patients. Washington, DC: U.S. Food and Drug Administration.

9. Belgamwar, R. B., and El-Sayeh, H. G. G. (2012). Aripiprazole vs. placebo for schizophrenia. *Schizophrenia Bulletin*, 38, 382–383. Burris, K. D.; Molski, T. F.; Xu, C.; Ryan, E.; Tottori, K.; et al. (2003). Aripiprazole, a novel antipsychotic, is a high-affinity partial agonist at human dopamine D2 receptors. *Journal of Pharmacology and Experimental Therapeutics*, 302, 381–389. Stroup, T. S.; McEvoy, J. P.; Ring, K. D.; Hamer, R. H.; LaVange, L. M.; et al. (2011). A randomized trial examining the effectiveness of switching from olanzapine, quetiapine, or risperidone to aripiprazole to reduce metabolic risk: Comparison of antipsychotics for metabolic problems (CAMP). *American Journal of Psychiatry*, 168, 947–956.

10. Hornykiewicz, O. (1974). The mechanisms of L-dopamine in Parkinson's disease. *Life Sciences*, 15, 1249–1259.

11. Plotkin, S. G.; Saha, A. R.; Kujawa, M. J.; Carson, W. H.; Ali, M.; et al. (2003). Aripiprazole, an antipsychotic with a novel mechanism of action, and risperidone vs. placebo in patients with schizophrenia and schizoaffective disorder. *Archives of General Psychiatry*, 60, 681–690. Rivas-Vazquez, RA. (2003). Aripiprazole: A novel antipsychotic with dopamine stabilizing properties. *Professional Psychology: Research and Practice*, 34, 108–111.

12. Kessler, R. C.; Berglund, P.; Demler, O.; Jin, R.; Koretz, D.; et al. (2003). The epidemiology of major depressive disorder. *Journal of the American Medical Association*, 289, 3095–3105. Substance Abuse and Mental Health Services Administration (2009, July 2). Treatment for substance use and depression among adults, by race/ethnicity. *The NSDUH Report*. Rockville, MD: Substance Abuse and Mental Health Services Administration.

13. Julien, *A primer of drug action*, pp. 263–272.

14. Kramer, P. D. (1993). *Listening to Prozac*. New York: Viking. G. Cowley (1990, March 26). The promise of Prozac. *Newsweek*, p. 39.

15. Glenmullen, J. (2000). *Prozac backlash: Overcoming the dangers of Prozac, Zoloft, Paxil, and other antidepressants with safe, effective alternatives*. New York: Simon and Schuster. Julien, *A primer of drug action*, pp. 276–284.

16. Martinez, J. M.; Katon, W.; Greist, J. H.; Kroenke, K.; Thase, M. E.; et al. (2012). A pragmatic 12-week, randomized trial of duloxetine versus generic selective serotonin-reuptake inhibitors in the treatment of adult outpatients in a moderate-to-severe depressive episode. *International Clinical Psychopharmacology*, 27, 17–26. Westanmo, A. D.; Gayken, J.; and Haight, R. (2005). Duloxetine: A balanced and selective norepinephrine- and serotonin-reuptake inhibitor. *American Journal of Health-System Pharmacy*, 62, 2481–2490.

17. SSRIs: Prozac and company—Part I (2000, October). *Harvard Mental Health Letter*, p. 7

18. Begley, S. (2010, February 8). The depressing news about antidepressants. *Newsweek*, pp. 34–42. Fournier, J. C.; DeRubeis, R. J.; Hollon, S. D.; Dimidjian, S.; et al. (2010). Antidepressant drug effects and depression severity: A patient-level meta-analysis. *Journal of the American Medical Association*, 303, 47–53. Klitzman, R. (2010, February 8). A doctor disagrees: Antidepressants have helped not only my patients, but myself. *Newsweek*, p. 42.

19. Johnson, F. N. (1984). *The history of lithium therapy*. New York: Macmillan. Shelton, R. C. (1999). Mood-stabilizing drugs in depression. *Journal of Clinical Psychiatry*, 60 (Suppl. 5), 37–40.

20. Findling, R. L, Youngstrom, E. A.; McNamara, N. K.; Stansbrey, R. J.; Wynbrandt, J. L.; et al. (2012). Double-blind, randomized, placebo-controlled long-term maintenance study of aripiprazole in children with bipolar disorder. *Journal of Clinical Psychiatry*, 73, 57–63. Keck, P. E., Jr.; Marcus, R.; Tourkodimitris, S.; Ali, M.; Liebeskind, A.; et al. (2003). A placebo-controlled, double-blind study of the efficacy and safety of aripiprazole in patients with acute bipolar mania. *American Journal of Psychiatry*,

160, 1651–1658. U.S. Food and Drug Administration (2005, April 11). FDA Talk Paper: FDA issues public health advisory for antipsychotic drugs used for treatment of behavioral disorders in elderly patients. Washington, DC: U.S. Food and Drug Administration. Waring, E. W.; Dewan, V. K.; Cohen, D.; and Grewal, R. (1999). Risperidone as an adjunct to valproic acid. *Canadian Journal of Psychiatry, 44*, 189–190.

21. McCracken, J. T.; McGough, J.; Shah, B.; Cronin, P.; Hong, D.; et al. (2002). Risperidone in children with autism and serious behavioral problems. *New England Journal of Medicine, 347*, 314–321. Associated Press (2009, November 21). FDA OK's Abilify for autism-linked irritability.

22. Alexander, G. C.; Gallagher, S. A.; Mascola, A.; Moloney, R. M.; and Stafford, R. S. (2011). Increasing off-label use of antipsychotic medications in the United States, 1995–2008. *Pharmacoepidemiology and Drug Safety, 20*, 177-184. Beck, J. M., and Azari, E. D. (1998). FDA, off-label drug use, and informed consent: Debunking myths and misconceptions. *Food and Drug Law Journal, 53*, 71–104.

23. Barlow, D. H.; Gorman, J. M.; Shear, M. K.; and Woods, S. W. (2000). Cognitive-behavioral therapy, imipramine, or their combination for panic disorder. *Journal of the American Medical Association, 283*, 2529–2536. Brady, K.; Pearlstein, T.; Asnis, G. M.; Baker, D.; Rothbaum, B.; et al. (2000). Efficacy and safety of sertraline treatment of posttraumatic stress disorder. *Journal of the American Medical Association, 283*, 1837–1844. Gelenberg, A. J.; Lydiard, R. B.; Rudolph, R. L.; Aguiar, L.; Haskins, J. T.; et al. (2000). Efficacy of venlafaxine extended-release capsules in nondepressed outpatients with generalized anxiety disorder: A 6-month randomized controlled trial. *Journal of the American Medical Association, 283*, 3082–3088.

24. Doyle, R. (2002, December). Deinstitutionalization: Why a much maligned program still has life. *Scientific American*, p. 38. Lamb, H. R., and Bachrach, L. L. (2001). Some perspectives on deinstitutionalization. *Psychiatric Services, 52*, 1039–1045. Wallace, C.; Mullen, P. E.; and Burgess, P. (2004). Criminal offending in schizophrenia over a 25-year period marked by deinstitutionalization and increasing prevalence of comorbid substance use disorders. *American Journal of Psychiatry,161*, 716–727.

Substance-Abuse Prevention

After you have completed this chapter, you should have an understanding of

▶ The three major levels of intervention in substance-abuse prevention

▶ Strategies for substance-abuse prevention

▶ Measurements of success in a substance-abuse prevention program

▶ Approaches to substance-abuse prevention that have failed

▶ Successful school-based substance-abuse prevention programs

▶ Community-based prevention and the impact of mass media

▶ The importance of family systems in substance-abuse prevention

▶ Multicultural issues in substance-abuse prevention

▶ Substance-abuse prevention in the workplace

▶ Substance-abuse prevention in colleges and universities

Your daughter is pretty and popular. She's the homecoming queen and the editor of the school paper. So you think you're safe. You're not. Your son is on the swimming team, a star athlete. He's talking about going to medical school. So you think you're safe. You're not....

Drugs are everywhere and they're everybody's problem. They're in big cities and in small rural communities. They strike troubled families and families whose children are seeming achievers, good students, athletes, prom queens.

—*Beth Polson,* Not My Kid:
A Parent's Guide to Kids and Drugs

The impact of drug-taking behavior on our lives, whether we are referring to the abuse of illicit drugs or of licit drugs, continues to be one of the most emotion-laden social issues of our day. Perhaps the most disturbing aspect of statistical reports regarding the incidence of drug-taking behavior concerns the youngest age category studied: eighth graders who are thirteen or fourteen years old. The need for effective prevention programs to reduce drug use and abuse among young people, as well as among individuals of all ages, is a deeply personal issue, and we ask ourselves: What can be done?

We need to be reminded once again about the wide range of potentially abusable substances that are involved in drug-taking behavior: Illicit drugs, alcohol, and nicotine, as well as prescription and non-prescription medications. As a result, it is hard to come up with a single phrase for abuse prevention that incorporates all the possible forms of drug-taking behavior. The admittedly awkward phrase "alcohol, tobacco, and other drug (ATOD) prevention" has been used to describe prevention strategies for illicit drugs, alcohol, and tobacco. But, in this chapter, we will use a more concise phrase, "substance-abuse prevention," with a primary focus on prevention strategies related to the abuse of illicit drugs and alcohol. Nonetheless, the principles of substance-abuse prevention that we will review here are applicable to a wide variety of life-style situations, including tobacco use, the nonmedical use of prescription and non-prescription medications, and a number of high-risk social behaviors. Effective substance-abuse prevention programs have been applied in all of these contexts.

Levels of Intervention in Substance-Abuse Prevention

Prevention programs can work on one of three possible levels of intervention: primary, secondary, and tertiary prevention. Each intervention has its own target population and goals, based largely on the extent of prior drug use.

- In **primary prevention**, efforts are directed at those who have not had any experience with drugs or have been only minimally exposed. The objective is to prevent substance abuse from starting in the first place — "nipping the problem in the bud." Targets in primary prevention programs are most frequently elementary school or middle school youths, and intervention usually occurs within a school-based curriculum or specific educational program, although community involvement is encouraged. For example, a primary prevention program would include the development of peer-refusal skills that students can use when offered marijuana, alcohol, or cigarettes (that is, teaching "ways to say no").

- In **secondary prevention**, the target population has already had some experience with alcohol, nicotine, and other drugs. The objective is to limit the extent of substance abuse (reducing it, if possible), to prevent the spread of abuse behavior beyond the drugs the individual has already encountered, and to teach strategies for the responsible use of alcohol if the legal minimum age has been met. Ordinarily, those individuals receiving secondary prevention efforts are older than those involved in primary prevention programs. High school students who are identified as users of alcohol or other drugs, for example, may participate in a program that emphasizes social alternatives to drug-taking behavior (after-school programs, sports, etc.).

primary prevention: A type of intervention in which the goal is to forestall the onset of drug use by an individual who has had little or no previous exposure to drugs.

secondary prevention: A type of intervention in which the goal is to reduce the extent of drug use in individuals who have already been exposed to drugs to some degree.

College students may focus on the skills necessary to restrict their behavior to the moderate use of alcohol, on the significant dangers of combining drinking and driving, and on the signs of chronic alcohol abuse. Secondary prevention efforts are consistent with the philosophy of harm reduction rather than zero tolerance of drug-taking behavior (see Health Line on page 383).

- In **tertiary prevention,** the objective is to ensure that an individual who has entered treatment for some form of substance abuse or substance dependence becomes drug-free after treatment has ended and does not revert to former patterns of drug-taking behavior. Successful prevention of relapse is the ultimate indication that the treatment has taken hold.

In the case of primary prevention, we are assuming that the target population for these interventions may have been exposed to drug-taking behavior in other people but have not had significant drug experiences of their own. We recognize that the potential for young people to engage in drug use themselves is substantial, and only through effective primary prevention programs can we keep that potential from turning into reality. It is increasingly clear that the *age of onset* for drug-taking behavior of any kind is a key factor in determining problems later in life, particularly with respect to licit drugs. For example, a young person who begins drinking before the age of fifteen is twice as likely to develop a pattern of alcohol abuse and four times as likely to develop alcohol dependence as an individual who begins drinking at the age of twenty-one. In general, if the age of onset can be delayed significantly, or even moderately, it may be possible to reduce the incidence of substance abuse or dependence later in life.[1]

In the case of secondary prevention, we are concentrating on the life-style of a somewhat older population, and our goal is to minimize the problems associated with drug-taking behavior, assuming that some level of that behavior already exists. Emphasis is placed on social alternatives to behaviors involving alcohol and other drugs among high school students. At the college level, the moderate use of alcohol, the avoidance of alcohol binging in particular, and education about the personal risks of some of the newer club drugs and the nonmedical use of prescription medications are all elements in a program of secondary prevention.

Chapter 17 will deal with programs that focus on tertiary prevention.

Quick Concept Check 16.1

Understanding Levels of Intervention in Substance-Abuse Prevention Programs

Check your understanding of the three basic levels of intervention in drug-abuse prevention by matching each of the following five scenarios with (a) primary, (b) secondary, or (c) tertiary prevention.

1. Midnight basketball sessions keep teenagers from drinking on weekends out of boredom.

2. Young children receive lessons on how to refuse the offer of drugs from a friend or acquaintance.

3. A child learns about "good drugs" and "bad drugs" in the first grade.

4. A man learns how to live without cocaine following a successful cocaine-abuse treatment program.

5. College students organize a "responsible drinking" program on campus.

Answers: 1. b 2. a 3. a 4. c 5. b

Strategies for Substance-Abuse Prevention

The U.S. federal agency specifically charged with prevention programs is the Center for Substance Abuse Prevention (CSAP), which is a division of the Substance Abuse and Mental Health Services Administration (SAMHSA), which is in turn a division of the U.S. Department of Health and Human Services. According to CSAP guidelines, substance-abuse prevention is accomplished through two principal strategies. The first is the promotion of constructive life-styles and norms that discourage substance abuse. The second is the development of social and physical environments that facilitate drug-free life-styles that can act as a buffer against the development of substance-abuse behaviors.

tertiary (TER-shee-eh-ree) prevention: A type of intervention in which the goal is to prevent relapse in an individual following recovery in a drug-treatment program.

You may recall from Chapter 1 that two groups of factors play a major role in predicting the extent of drug-taking behavior in a given individual: (1) risk factors that increase the likelihood of drug-taking behavior and (2) protective factors that decrease it. You can think of the goals of substance-abuse prevention in those terms. The optimal substance-abuse prevention program effectively reduces the impact of risk factors in an individual's life and, at the same time, enhances the impact of protective factors.

Resilience and Primary Prevention Efforts

Successful primary prevention programs are built around the central idea that an individual is less inclined to engage in substance abuse if the protective factors in his or her life are enhanced and the risk factors are diminished. Only then can a young person be resilient enough to overcome the temptations of alcohol, tobacco, and other drugs. **Resilience**, defined as the inclination to resist the effect of risk factors through the action of protective factors, can be a make-or-break element in one's social development. The promotion of positive social skills and the encouragement of a proactive rather than a passive approach to problem solving enhance the "buffering effect" of protective factors with respect to drug-taking behavior and other forms of deviant behavior. Since a young population is the principal target for primary prevention, programs are customarily implemented in the school. To be most effective, however, these programs must incorporate aspects of a young person's life outside of school. In a later section, we will turn to primary prevention programs that involve the community at large.[2]

Measuring Success in a Substance-Abuse Prevention Program

Evaluating the success or failure of a substance-abuse prevention program is more complicated than people often think. In the public mind, a school-based substance-abuse prevention program might be considered successful, for example, if it enjoys support from parents, administrators, and teachers. There might be a long list of testimonials in which participants attest to their belief that they have benefited from the program. It might also be considered successful if there is evidence of a change in a child's view toward drug use or a change in a child's stated inclination to engage in drug use in the future.

However gratifying these outcomes might be to the community, and however persuasive they might be to the general public, they do not get to the core issue: Is the prevalence of substance abuse reduced as a result of the program? *The goal of any prevention program, particularly a primary prevention program aimed at young people, is to lower the numbers of new drug users or to delay the first use of alcohol and tobacco to an age at which the young people are considered adults.* To be considered "evidence-based," primary prevention programs must be evaluated against a control group that did not receive the intervention; otherwise, it is impossible to determine whether the effect of the program itself was greater than that of doing nothing at all. Positive change per se is not enough. For example, if drug use among eighth graders has declined as a result of a prevention program, but this decline is not greater than the decline among eighth graders in the control group, then the prevention program is essentially ineffective. Secondary prevention programs are judged to be effective by a similar comparison against a control group. When successful prevention programs are reviewed later in this chapter, their effectiveness will have been measured by this rigorous "yardstick" of performance. As we will see in Chapter 17, the effectiveness of substance-abuse treatment programs is evaluated in the same way.[3]

A Matter of Public Health

It is important to recognize that a drug-free life is a major aspect of a healthy life and, in turn, of a healthy society. Figure 16.1 shows dramatically how substance abuse affects the nation's health in general. As you can see, about half of all preventable deaths in the United States are accounted for by the abuse of alcohol products (7 percent), tobacco products (38 percent), or illicit drugs (2 percent). Each year, an estimated 537,000 deaths are attributed to these three circumstances (Health Line).[4]

In addition, the monetary impact is immense, with the estimated costs of substance abuse exceeding $1 trillion each year. Some of these costs are incurred through accidents, crime, academic underachievement from underage drinking ($64 billion), drug-related hospital

---

resilience: The inclination to resist the negative impact of risk factors in a person's life through the positive impact of protective factors. Sometimes referred to as resiliency.

FIGURE 16.1

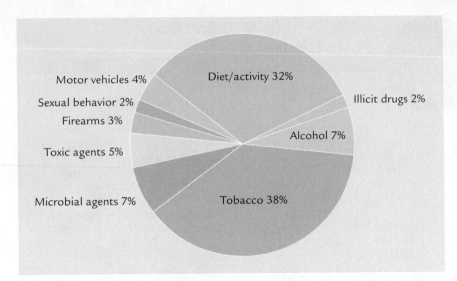

The relative incidence of causes of preventable death annually in the United States.

Source: Mokdad, A. H.; Marks, J. S.; Stroup, D. F.; and Gerberding, J. L. (2004). Actual causes of death in the United States, 2000. *Journal of the American Medical Association, 291,* 1238–1245, Table 2.

emergency visits ($4 billion), incarceration of individuals who commit drug-law offenses ($30 billion), alcohol-related workplace injuries and absenteeism ($28 billion), and DWI-related collisions on highways ($230 billion). Looking at prescription pain medication abuse alone (Chapter 5), the societal costs exceed $56 billion a year, driven primarily by workplace costs (lost earning from premature deaths and reduced compensation or lost employment) and health care costs (excess medical and prescription expenses).[5]

Health Line

The Public Health Model and the Analogy of Infectious Disease Control

The idea that reducing the negative consequences of drug-taking behavior is a desirable goal for the enhancement of the overall health of society is often referred to as the Public Health Model. As Avram Goldstein, a prominent drug-abuse researcher and policy analyst, has pointed out, the problems of reducing drug-taking behavior have many similarities to wresting control over an infectious disease. A virus, for example, infects some people who are more susceptible than others (in other words, there are risk factors), while some people will be relatively immune (in other words, there are protective factors). Public health measures can be established to reduce or eradicate the virus (just as we attempt to reduce the supply of illicit drugs reaching the consumer); and specific vaccinations can be discovered to increase a person's resistance to the virus (just as we search for effective primary prevention programs in drug abuse).

We can carry the analogy further. Medical treatment for an infectious disease is considered uncontroversial and necessary for two reasons. First, we are alleviating the suffering of the infected individual; second, we are reducing the pool of infection to limit its spread to others. Analogously, drug-abuse treatment is desirable to relieve the negative consequences of drug abuse, as well as to reduce the social influence of drug abusers on nondrug abusers in our society.

Goldstein asks a provocative question:

There are individuals who contribute to the AIDS epidemic by having promiscuous sexual contacts without taking elementary precautions. Are those behaviors, which contribute to the spread of infectious disease, really different in principle from that of pack-a-day cigarette smokers who will not try to quit, despite all the evidence of physical harm to themselves and their families?

There is certainly no consensus on how the problem of drug abuse should be conceptualized. Some have objected to the implications of the Public Health Model, arguing that it ignores the moral and ethical choices that are made in establishing a pattern of drug-taking behavior. You may be reminded of a similar controversy, discussed in Chapter 9, regarding the question of whether alcoholism should be considered a disease.

Sources: Goldstein, A. (1994). *Addiction: From biology to drug policy.* New York: Freeman. Quotation on p. 10. Jonas, S. (1997). Public health approaches. In J. H. Lowinson, P. Ruiz, R. B. Millman, and J. G. Langrod (Eds.), *Substance abuse: A comprehensive textbook.* Baltimore, MD: Williams & Wilkins, pp. 775–785.

Dr. A. Thomas McLellan Goes to Washington (Briefly)

Administrators in the Office of National Drug Control Policy have traditionally been recruited from positions of authority, military or otherwise, So when, in early 2009, President Obama announced Dr. A. Thomas McLellan as his choice for deputy director, it sent a clear signal that the decades-long approach to substance abuse and dependence in America was about to change. For McLellan it was not an easy decision to accept the offer. "A Washington insider he ain't, and damn proud of it," it has been reported. A promising sign was the announcement by Gil Kerlikowske, the newly-appointed "Drug Czar," that the decades-long government phrase "war on drugs" would be retired since it implied doing battle against addicts instead of the disease of addiction. This perspective fit nicely with McLellan's view, where the focus was on substance-abuse prevention and treatment, with an emphasis on full community involvement. A principal supporter in this work, Dr. Nora D. Volkow, director of the National Institute on Drug Abuse (see Portrait in Chapter 3) remarked at the time that this would be "an extraordinary moment of opportunity."

Dr. McLellan was no ordinary governmental appointee. A professor of psychiatry at the University of Pennsylvania School of Medicine, author of more than 400 papers on substance dependence, and author of two of the most practical and widely used methods of assessing the severity of substance dependence and potential success of treatment, Dr. McLellan had the academic credentials to examine national drug policy with fresh and unbiased eyes. He also had a unique personal story. Three months prior to his appointment, his son had died of a drug overdose, a mixture of antianxiety medication and Scotch. Another son was in residential treatment for alcohol and cocaine dependence. Married to a recovering cocaine abuser, Dr. McLellan had been surrounded by substance abuse and dependence in life as well as in his work. His family was a personal battlefield that mirrored the nation's own struggle with drug-taking behavior.

It turns out that McLellan's stay in Washington was shorter than even he might have imagined, a little over a year, but it was a productive time for him and the nation. The Patient Protection and Affordable Care Act as well as the Mental Health Parity and Addiction Equity Act were enacted, changing the landscape of health-care and addiction-treatment forever. Now back at his former post at the prestigious Treatment Research Institute in Philadelphia, McLellan continues the work of achieving smarter prevention and treatment programs for substance abusers nationwide. In the end, the goal is to move treatment for substance abuse from a "segregated" part of health care to the mainstream. According to McLellan, "I want to show businesses and local governments that they can actually save money by addressing all 60 million people through prevention and early intervention. If we can do that successfully, the forces of the marketplace will take over."

Sources: Clark, J. C. (2009, December). Kicking the national drug habit. *Monitor on Psychology*, pp. 36–38. Kershaw, S. (2009, December 8). Addiction on 2 fronts: Work and home. *New York Times*, pp. D1, D4. Volkow quotation on p. D4. Treatment Research Institute (2012, March 21). A. Thomas McLellan, PhD returns to TRI as Chief Executive Officer. Press release, Treatment Research Institute, Philadelphia. Why Obama's deputy drug czar ditched DC. Accessed 2012 with quotations from www.thefix.com/content/interview-mclellan.

It should not be surprising that in the 1990s, when the U.S. Public Health Service established a comprehensive, national health promotion and disease prevention agenda for a program called Healthy People 2000 (recently updated to Healthy People 2020), a major component concerned behaviors related to substance abuse (Portrait).[6]

Lessons from the Past: Prevention Approaches That Have Failed

When deciding how to solve a problem, it always helps to look at what has *not* worked in the past. That way, we can avoid wasting time, effort, and money on nonsolutions. In the general opinion of health professionals and researchers, the following primary prevention efforts have been largely unsuccessful when positioned as the major thrust of a particular program. Nonetheless, some of these approaches have been incorporated successfully, with several other components, into an effective primary prevention package.

Reducing the Availability of Drugs

It is reasonable to expect that the incidence of illicit drug abuse could be reduced if the availability of these drugs were reduced or eliminated altogether. This "supply/availability" argument in drug prevention accounts for almost 60 percent of about $26 billion of the federal budget spent each year on drug control.

This portion of the drug-control budget comprises three categories of programs: (1) domestic law enforcement through the Department of Justice, Homeland Security, and the High-Intensity Drug Trafficking Area Tasks Forces, (2) interdiction at points of entry through the Departments of Homeland Security and Defense, and (3) international support for drug trafficking programs in partner nations such as Colombia, Mexico, and Afghanistan.[7]

According to the economic principle of supply and demand, however, a decline in supply or availability of a commodity can result in either an increase in its cost or in an increase in demand. If one accepts the first viewpoint, then reductions in supply or availability should help prevent drug-taking behavior because the drug would be too expensive to obtain. If one accepts the second viewpoint, then such reductions should exacerbate the situation; people would want the drug even more than before. Which theoretical viewpoint is operating with respect to illicit drugs (or with respect to alcohol, tobacco, and other licit drugs) is a point of contention among health professionals both inside and outside the government.

How successful have we been in reducing the supply or availability of illicit drugs? Have we been able, for example, to reduce the production of illicit drugs around the world and their influx into the United States? Unfortunately, drug cultivation (such as the harvesting of opium, coca leaves, and marijuana) and the exportation of processed illicit drugs from their points of origin are so deeply entrenched in many regions of the world, and the resourcefulness of drug producers is so great, that our global efforts have been frustratingly inadequate. As noted in Chapter 2, a production crackdown in one region merely serves to create a marketing vacuum, which another region quickly fills. Moreover, efforts to control international drug trafficking have been embarrassingly unsuccessful, despite well-publicized drug busts, arrests, and seizures. It is estimated that only a small fraction of illicit drugs is interdicted (intercepted) at U.S. borders, and drug trafficking within foreign countries remain substantial.[8]

On the other hand, efforts to reduce alcohol availability among young people have been more successful (see Chapter 8). Alcohol sales to minors continue to be a problem, but there has been a reduction in underage alcohol drinking since the nationwide minimum age standard (21 years of age) for the possession and purchase of alcohol beverages were into effect in the mid-1980s. With respect to impaired driving behavior among underage drinkers, two additional regulatory actions, a nationwide standard of .02 percent BAC or less for legal intoxication while driving for minors (better known as the "zero tolerance" law) and a "use it-or lose it" law in some U.S. states that sets a penalty of suspension or revocation of driving privileges for underage purchase, possession, or consumption of alcohol, have been successful in reducing alcohol-related fatal crashes of young drivers. Proposals to limit alcohol availability through increases in the price of alcohol are also possible options. A recent analysis has indicated that as little as a 25-cent-per-drink tax increase would result in more than a 10 percent reduction in heavy drinking among individuals of all ages.[9]

Punitive Measures

There is a common expectation, when policies related to law enforcement and the criminal justice system are considered, that individuals will be less inclined to use and abuse illicit drugs if they are afraid of being arrested, prosecuted, convicted, and incarcerated. The available statistics show that this threat has little effect as a deterrent. The enticements of many psychoactive drugs are extremely powerful, and the imposition of harsh penalties has frequently been delayed or inconsistent. Mandatory minimum-sentencing laws (see Chapter 17) have resulted in a clogged judicial system and vastly overcrowded prisons, without making any noticeable dent in the trafficking in or consumption of illicit drugs. Although the enforcement of these penalties may be defended in terms of an overall social policy toward illicit drugs, it has evidently failed as a means for either primary or secondary prevention. The current trend toward greater flexibility in sentencing guidelines for drug-law offenses will be reviewed in the next chapter.[10]

Scare Tactics and Negative Education

In the late 1960s, the suddenly widespread use of marijuana, amphetamines, barbiturates, LSD, and other hallucinogens, first among students on college campuses and later among youth at large, spawned a number of hastily designed programs based on the arousal of fear and on exaggerated or blatantly inaccurate information about the risks involved. They were the products of panic rather than careful thought.

As might be imagined, such efforts turned young people *off* precisely at the time when they were turning themselves on to an array of exotic and seemingly innocuous drug-taking experiences. Professionals have called these misguided efforts the "reefer madness approach," an allusion to the government-sponsored movie of the 1930s that attempted to scare people away from experimenting with marijuana (see Chapter 7). These programs accomplished little, except to erode even further the credibility of the adult presenters in the eyes of youths who often knew (or thought they knew) a great deal more about drugs and their effects than their elders.[11]

Objective Information Approaches

At the opposite end of the emotional spectrum are programs designed to present information about drugs and their potential dangers in a straightforward, nonjudgmental way. Unfortunately, evaluations of this "just the facts, ma'am" approach have found that youths exposed to such primary prevention programs are no less likely—and sometimes are *more* likely—to use drugs later in their lives. These programs tend to increase their curiosity about drugs in general, obviously something the program planners want to avoid.[12]

Despite these failures, however, it would be a mistake to dismiss the informational aspect of any substance-abuse prevention program, particularly when the information is presented in a low-fear atmosphere.[13] The overall value of an informational approach appears to depend on whether the target population consists of high-risk or low-risk children. The evidence indicates that when low-risk young people are presented with drug-related information, they really understand the dangers, and the chances of remaining drug-free are increased. High-risk youths, on the other hand, may not be so easily dissuaded, and additional intervention appears to be necessary.[14]

Magic Bullets and Promotional Campaigns

A variety of anti-drug promotional materials, such as T-shirts, caps, rings, buttons, bumper stickers, posters, rap songs, school assembly productions, books, and brochures, are available and are frequently seen as "magic bullets" that can clinch success in substance-abuse prevention programs. Their appeal lies in their high visibility; these items send a clear signal to the public at large, ever eager for signs that the drug-abuse problem might easily go away, that something is being done. Yet, although they may be helpful in deglamorizing drug-taking behavior and providing a forum for young people to express their feelings about drugs, promotional items are inadequate by themselves to reduce substance abuse overall. They do, however, remain viable components of more comprehensive programs that will be examined later in the chapter.[15]

affective education: An approach in substance-abuse prevention programs that emphasizes the building of self-esteem and an improved self-image.

values clarification: An approach in substance-abuse prevention programs that teaches positive social values and attitudes.

Elementary school children display their handprint art projects. Designations of drug-free pledges are prominent features of many school-based drug-abuse prevention programs.

Self-Esteem Enhancement and Affective Education

In the early 1970s, several substance-abuse prevention programs were developed that emphasized the affective or emotional component of drug-taking behavior, rather than specific information about drugs. In the wake of research that showed a relationship between drug abuse and psychological variables such as low self-esteem, poor decision-making skills, and poor interpersonal communication skills, programs were instituted that incorporated role-playing exercises with other assignments designed to help young people get in touch with their own emotions and feel better about themselves.

This effort, called **affective education**, was an attempt to deal with underlying emotional and attitudinal factors rather than specific behaviors related to drug use (in fact, alcohol, tobacco, and other drugs were seldom mentioned at all). Affective education was based on the observation that drug users had difficulty identifying and expressing emotions such as anger and love. In a related set of programs called **values clarification**, moral values were actively taught to children, on the assumption that they frequently had a poorly developed sense of where their life was going and lacked a "moral compass" to guide their behavior.

Difficulties arose, however, when parents, community leaders, and frequently educators themselves argued that the emphasis of affective education on values clarification was inappropriate for public schools. There was concern that a system of morality was being imposed on students without respecting their individual backgrounds and cultures. This kind of instruction, it was felt, was more suited for faith-based education settings.[16]

Above and beyond these social considerations, neither affective education nor values clarification was effective in preventing drug-taking behavior. Some researchers have recently questioned the basic premise that self-esteem is a major factor at all. As a result, affective issues are no longer viewed as central considerations in primary or secondary substance-abuse prevention. Nonetheless, they can be found as components in more comprehensive prevention programs, discussed later, that have been more successful.[17]

Hope and Promise: Components of Effective School-Based Prevention Programs

One of the major lessons to be learned from evaluations of previous substance-abuse prevention efforts is that there is a far greater chance for success when the programs are multifaceted than when they focus on only a single aspect of drug-taking behavior. The following are elements of school-based substance-abuse prevention programs that have been shown to work.

Peer-Refusal Skills

A number of school-based programs developed during the 1980s have included the teaching of personal and social skills, as well as techniques for resisting various forms of social pressure to smoke, drink, or use other drugs (often referred to as **peer-refusal skills**). The emphasis is directed toward an individual's relationships with his or her peers and the surrounding social climate. Rather than simply prodding adolescents to "just say no," these programs teach them *how to do so* when they find themselves in uncomfortable social circumstances. Health Line lists some specific techniques that have been taught to help deflect peer pressure regarding drug-taking behavior.

Primary prevention programs using peer-refusal skill training have been shown to reduce the rate of tobacco smoking, as well as the rates of alcohol drinking and marijuana smoking, by 35 to 45 percent—considerably better than any change observed in control groups. With respect to tobacco smoking, this approach has been even more effective for young people identified as being in a high-risk category (in that their friends or family smoked) than for other students.[18]

Anxiety and Stress Reduction

Adolescence can be an enormously stressful time, and drug-taking behavior is frequently seen as a way to reduce feelings of anxiety, particularly when an individual has inadequate coping skills to deal with that anxiety. It is therefore useful to learn techniques of self-relaxation and stress management and to practice the application of these techniques to everyday situations.

Social Skills and Personal Decision Making

Peer-refusal skills are but one example of a range of assertiveness skills that enable young people to express their feelings, needs, preferences, and opinions directly and honestly, without fear that they will jeopardize their friendships or lose the respect of others. Learning assertiveness skills not only helps advance the goals of primary prevention but also fosters positive interpersonal relationships throughout life. Tasks in social skills training include the ability to initiate social interactions (introducing oneself to a stranger), offer a compliment to others, engage in conversation, and express feelings and opinions. Lessons generally involve a combination of instruction, demonstration, feedback, reinforcement, behavioral rehearsal, and extended practice through behavioral homework assignments.

A related skill is the ability to make decisions in a thoughtful and careful way. Emphasis is placed on identifying problem situations, formulating goals, generating alternative solutions, and considering the probable consequences of each. Lessons also focus on identifying persuasive advertising appeals and exploring counterarguments that can defuse them. Primary prevention programs that employ a social skills training approach have been shown to reduce by 42 to 75 percent the likelihood that a young person will try cigarette smoking and to reduce by 56 to 67 percent the likelihood that a nonsmoker will be a regular smoker in a one-year follow-up.[19]

An Example of an Effective School-Based Prevention Program

Substance-abuse prevention professionals are in general agreement that the most effective programs should be comprehensive in nature, with special emphasis on

peer-refusal skills: Techniques by which an individual can resist peer pressure to use alcohol, tobacco, or other drugs.

Health Line

Peer-Refusal Skills: Ten Ways to Make It Easier to Say No

- Make it simple. There is no need for explanations. Keep your refusal direct and to the point.
- Know the facts. If you know something is bad for you, it is easier to make it part of your refusal.
- Have something else to do. You can suggest some alternative activity.
- Walk away. If the pressure begins to feel threatening to you, just leave.
- Avoid the situation. Stay away from places where you might be pressured. If there is a party where you might be pressured, simply don't go.
- Change the subject. Surprisingly, this works.
- Hang out with friends who aren't substance abusers. Pressure won't be there.

- Be a broken record. You can be firm without sounding angry or irritated. A little repetition may be needed.
- Use the "fogging" technique of passive resistance. If they criticize you for refusing, simply agree and let it pass over you. Don't let their reactions get to you.
- Refuse to continue discussing it. Tell them you made up your mind and you are not going to talk about it anymore.

Source: Center for Substance Abuse Prevention, Substance Abuse and Mental Health Services Administration, Rockville, MD.

---

the teaching of specific social decision-making skills, such as resisting peer pressure to engage in drug-taking behavior.[20] An example of a successful school-based prevention effort is the Life Skills Training (LST) program developed by Gilbert Botvin at the Cornell University Medical College in New York City. Three LST programs have been designed with developmentally appropriate content for young people in elementary school, middle school, and high school, respectively. The elementary school program can be taught either during the third grade or over the course of the fourth, fifth, and sixth grades. The middle school program is taught over the course of the seventh, eighth, and ninth grades. The high school program is taught in one year, either as a stand-alone program or as a maintenance program in conjunction with earlier sessions in middle school. The major elements of the LST programs are

- A *cognitive component* designed to provide information about the short-term consequences of using alcohol, tobacco, and other drugs. Unlike traditional prevention approaches, LST includes only minimal information on the long-term health consequences of drug-taking behavior. Evidently, it is not useful to tell young people about what might happen when they are "old." Instead, information is provided concerning immediate negative effects, the impact on social acceptability, and actual prevalence rates among adults and adolescents. This last element of the lesson is to counter the myth that drug-taking behavior is

the norm in their age group—the misconception that "everyone's doing it."

- A *decision-making component* designed to facilitate critical thinking and independent decision making. Students learn to evaluate the role of the media in shaping behavior, as well as to formulate counterarguments and other cognitive strategies to resist advertising pressures.
- A *stress-reduction component* designed to help students develop ways to lessen anxiety. Students learn relaxation techniques and cognitive techniques to manage stress.
- A *social skills component* designed to teach social assertiveness and specific techniques for resisting peer pressure.
- A *self-directed behavior-change component* designed to facilitate self-improvement and encourage a sense of personal control and self-esteem. Students are assigned to identify a skill or behavior that they would like to change or improve and to develop a long-term goal over an eight-week period and short-term objectives that can be met week by week.

Originally designed as a smoking-prevention program, LST presently focuses on issues related to the entire spectrum of drug-taking behavior. Over a period of as long as six years following exposure to the program, participants have been found to have a 50 to 75 percent lower incidence of alcohol, tobacco, and marijuana use, a 66 percent lower incidence of multiple-drug use, a 25 percent lower incidence of pack-a-day cigarette smoking, and a lower incidence of inhalant, opioid, and hallucinogen use, relative to controls.[21] Reductions in drug use have been seen among inner-city minority students as well as among white middle-class youths, an encouraging sign that these primary prevention strategies can have a positive influence on adolescents from varying social backgrounds. In effect, as Botvin has expressed it, LST and similar programs work "in cities and towns and villages across the United States without having to develop separate intervention approaches for each and every different population."[22]

LST programs also exert a positive influence in a number of high-risk social behaviors beyond simply drug-taking behavior. Reductions in violence and delinquency have been observed among sixth-grade LST participants, relative to controls. There has also been a reduction in risky driving behaviors among adolescent participants. Young adults who have participated in LST programs engage in a reduced level of HIV-risk behaviors, as indicated by multiple sex partners, frequency of intercourse while drunk or high, and recent high-risk substance use (for example, administration by needle injection). In addition, LST programs are useful for adolescents and young adults in workplace settings (such as supermarkets) in promoting communication, problem-solving, conflict resolutions as well as drug resistance and related life skills. These studies illustrate the long-term protective results of effective primary and secondary prevention programs for a range of life decisions.[23]

Drug Abuse Resistance Education (D.A.R.E.)

The Drug Abuse Resistance Education program, commonly known as D.A.R.E., is undoubtedly the best-known school-based primary prevention program in the United States and perhaps the world. It was developed in 1983 as a collaborative effort by the Los Angeles Police Department and the Los Angeles United School District to bring uniformed police officers into kindergarten and elementary grade classrooms to teach basic drug information, peer-refusal skills, self-management techniques, and alternatives to drug use. Since the controversies surrounding this program are also well-known, it is important to provide details of its history and its present status.

Shortly after its inception, the D.A.R.E. program expanded at a rapid pace. By 1999, more than 75 percent

Quick Concept Check 16.2

Understanding Primary Prevention and Education

Judging on the basis of available research, check your understanding of primary prevention and education strategies by deciding whether each of the following approaches would or would not be effective (in and of itself) in reducing drug and alcohol use or delaying its onset.

	Would Be Effective	Would Not Be Effective
1. Scare tactics	☐	☐
2. Life skills training	☐	☐
3. Peer-refusal skills training	☐	☐
4. Values clarification	☐	☐
5. Objective information	☐	☐
6. Anxiety reduction and stress management	☐	☐
7. Assertiveness training	☐	☐
8. Training in problem solving and goal setting	☐	☐

Answers: 1. would not   2. would   3. would
4. would not   5. would not   6. would   7. would
8. would

of school districts in the U.S. had participated in D.A.R.E., along with school systems in 44 countries. An estimated 33 million young people have participated in the program since 1983. It has been referred to as one of the most popular prevention programs in the world.[24] Responses to Project D.A.R.E. from teachers, principals, students, and police officers have been typically enthusiastic, and it is clear that the program struck a responsive chord over the years for a public eager to establish active drug-abuse prevention programs in the schools. Part of this enthusiasm stemmed from a strategic decision on the part of local police departments to develop better community relations, recognizing the need to shift their enforcement role as agents of "supply reduction" to a more proactive social role as agents of "demand reduction." Nonetheless, D.A.R.E. is an expensive program, since the average cost per uniformed police officer can be as high as $50,000 per year and the cost per student as high as $100.

Yet, despite its success in the area of public relations, several large-scale evaluation studies carried out in the 1990s were unanimous in their conclusion that the D.A.R.E. program was ineffective in achieving genuine reductions in drug use, particularly in long-term follow-up analyses. It was found that children who participated in the D.A.R.E. program had a more negative attitude toward drugs one year later than children who did not, as well as a greater capability to resist peer pressure and a lower estimate of how many of their peers smoked cigarettes. However, in terms of comparisons between D.A.R.E. and non-D.A.R.E. control groups, there was little or no differences in drug use or self-esteem.[25]

The D.A.R.E. program was also criticized for advocating that children be questioned about possible drug offenders in their families. A D.A.R.E. lesson called "The Three R's: Recognize, Resist, Report" encouraged them to tell friends, teachers, or police if they found drugs at home. Critics of D.A.R.E. viewed this and related elements of the program as a mechanism for turning young children into informants.[26]

In light of the criticisms leveled against it, federal funding for the D.A.R.E. program was drastically reduced in the late 1990s, and D.A.R.E. was eventually removed from the National Registry of Effective Programs. As a response to these actions, the D.A.R.E. program was modified in 2003 as a more comprehensive prevention approach that met National Health Education Standards. Not surprisingly, several of the components that had been established as effective in fostering resilience were incorporated into "New D.A.R.E." A greater emphasis, for example, was placed on student interaction and opportunities for children to participate on an individual basis rather than hearing lectures by police officers. In 2006, a middle school curriculum was added, called "keepin' it REAL," formed as an acronym for "Refuse, Explain, Avoid, and Leave." Recent research on the effectiveness of the "New D.A.R.E." curriculum or "keepin' it REAL" has yielded only mixed results, at best. However, more studies need to be carried out before definitive conclusions can be made.[27]

Why D.A.R.E. continued in many communities around the country for so many years when there was widely publicized information about its lack of effectiveness is an intriguing question. Some health professionals in this field theorize that the popularity of D.A.R.E. continued, in part, from the perception among parents and D.A.R.E. supporters that it appeared to work, through a process of informally comparing children who went through D.A.R.E. with unfounded assumptions about children who did not:

The adults rightly perceive that most children who go through D.A.R.E. do not engage in problematic drug use. Unfortunately, these individuals may not realize that the vast majority of children, even without any intervention, do not engage in problematic drug use.... That is, adults may believe that drug use among adolescents is much more frequent than it actually is. When the children who go through D.A.R.E. are compared to this "normative" group of drug-using teens, D.A.R.E. appears effective.[28]

The Point/Counterpoint V Debate (pages 405–406) examines the continuing controversy surrounding the D.A.R.E. program.

Community-Based Prevention Programs

Community-based prevention programs offer several obvious advantages over those restricted to schools. The first is the greater opportunity to involve parents and other family members, religious institutions, and the media as collaborative agents for change. The most important factor here is the comprehensive nature of such programs. They draw on multiple social institutions that have been demonstrated to represent protective factors in an individual's life, such as the family, religious groups, and community organizations. In addition, corporations and businesses can be contributing partners, in both a financial and a nonfinancial sense. Undoubtedly, we are in a better position to tackle the complexities of drug-taking behavior through the use of multiple strategies rather than a single approach.

Components of an Effective Community-Based Program

Typically, many of the prevention components that have been incorporated into the schools are also components of community-based programs, such as the dissemination of information, stress management, and life skills training. Other approaches can be handled better in a community setting. For example, although schools can promote the possibility of alternative student activities that provide positive and constructive means for addressing feelings of boredom, frustration, and powerlessness (activities such as Midnight Basketball and Boys and Girls Clubs), the community is in a better position than the schools to actually provide these activities.

There is also a greater opportunity in the community to elicit the involvement of significant individuals to act as positive role models, referred to as **impactors**, and to enlist the help of the mass media to promote anti-drug messages in the press and on television. In addition, community-based programs can be more influential in promoting changes in public policy that foster opportunities for education, employment, and self-development.[29]

Alternative-Behavior Programming

It is easier to say no to drugs when you can say yes to something else. In community-based prevention programs, a major effort is made to provide the activities and outlets that steer people away from high-risk situations. Because adolescents spend a majority of their time outside school, and it is outside school that the preponderance of drug-taking behavior occurs, community programs have the best chance of providing the necessary interventions. In fact, high-risk adolescents are the least likely even to be attending school on the days that prevention efforts are delivered.[30]

One way of thinking about alternative-behavior programming is that a person is trading a negative dependence (on alcohol, tobacco, or other drugs) that causes harm on a physical or psychological level for a positive dependence that causes no harm and taps into one's potential for personal growth and achievement.[31]

The Influence of Media

In the words of a major 2005 study analyzing the lifestyles of eight- to eighteen-year-olds, young people today live "media-saturated lives, spending an average of nearly 6½ hours a day with media." Since about one-fourth of the time they are engaged in media multitasking (reading, listening to music, text messaging with friends, for example), they are actually crowding about 8 hours of media into each day—the equivalent of a full-time job. These individuals (who have been dubbed "Generation M" to reflect the dominance of media in their lives) are the first generation to have grown up with easy access to computers and particularly the Internet.[32]

Because of the unprecedented media access available at home (frequently in the privacy of their bedrooms), it is important to evaluate the impact of media messages on drug-taking behavior in their lives and the potential for media exposure to promote primary prevention. It has been estimated that young people are exposed to more than eighty explicit references to substance use per day, in the course of listening to

popular music. A statistical relationship has been identified between the amount of exposure among young people ten to fourteen years old to alcohol drinking in popular movies and early-onset teen drinking, even after controlling for variables such as socioeconomic status, personality characteristics, school performance, and gender. In other words, exposure to alcohol use in movies can be viewed as an independent risk factor for drinking behavior in this population.[33]

Traditionally, anti-drug messages have been largely confined to public-service announcements, brief commercials, and limited program series. Even so, the potential impact can be substantial. A prominent example is a series of memorable and persuasive anti-drug advertisements on TV, on the radio, in print, and in other media sources, sponsored by the Partnership for a Drug-Free America (PDFA), a nonprofit coalition of professionals in the communications industry whose mission is to reduce demand for drugs in America. In the early 1990s, a number of PDFA spots targeted inner-city youths living in high-risk drug-use environments, and a 1994 study indicated that these messages had a significant effect in promoting increasingly anti-drug attitudes, particularly among African American children attending schools in areas where many families had incomes below the poverty line.[34]

Unfortunately, Internet media have undermined these efforts. A rapidly growing number of Internet web sites are devoted to information about marijuana cultivation, drug paraphernalia, and illicit drug use in general. These pro-drug outlets have proliferated since the advent of online services. Making matters worse, the percentage of adolescents reporting that they remember seeing or hearing substance-abuse prevention messages has declined.[35]

An Example of an Effective Community-Based Prevention Program

An intensive and coordinated program of preventive services and community-based law enforcement has been designed by the National Center on Addiction and Substance Abuse at Columbia University in New York, called CASASTART (the first part of the acronym refers to the center that designed it, and the latter part stands for "Striving Together to Achieve Rewarding

impactors: Individuals in the community who function as positive role models for children and adolescents in substance-abuse prevention programs.

Tomorrows"). The target population for the program is defined as children between eight and thirteen years of age who have at least four risk factors for substance-abuse problems. These risk factors may involve school (such as poor academic performance, in-school behavior problems, or truancy), family (such as poverty, violence at home, or a family member involved with gangs, drug use or sales, or a criminal conviction within five years), or the individual child (such as a history of known or suspected drug use or sales, past arrest, gang membership, or being a victim of child maltreatment).

In the CASASTART program, a case manager serving fifteen children and their families coordinates a variety of services, including social support, family and educational services, after-school and summer activities, mentoring, incentives, and juvenile justice intervention. The objective is to build resilience in the child, strengthen families, and make neighborhoods safer for these children and their families. Relative to controls, CASASTART children have been found to be 60 percent less likely to sell drugs, 20 percent less likely to have used drugs in the past thirty days, 20 percent less likely to commit a violent act, and more likely to be promoted to the next grade in school.[36]

Family Systems in Primary and Secondary Prevention

It can be argued that family influences form the cornerstone of any successful substance-abuse prevention program; we will see the significant impact of the family on substance-abuse treatment in Chapter 17. In effect, the family is the first line of defense against substance abuse (Figure 16.2). Reaching the parents or guardians of youths at greatest risk, however, is a difficult task. Too often, substance-abuse prevention programs are attended by those parents or guardians who do not really need the information; those who need the information the most—parents who are in denial, too embarrassed, or out of control themselves—are notably absent. Other parents or guardians may need and genuinely want to participate, but they may have difficulty attending because of lack of child care at home, lack of transportation, scheduling conflicts with their employment, or language differences. Several of the factors that discourage their attendance are the same factors that increase the risk of substance abuse among their children. In addition, the significant level of substance among primary caretakers themselves, specifically young mothers,

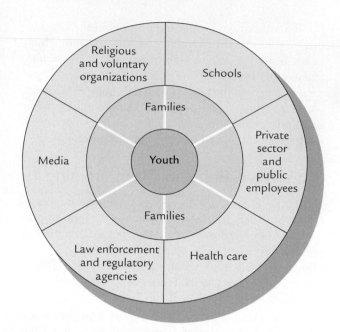

FIGURE 16.2

Various factors that have an impact on families, and youth in turn, in substance-abuse prevention.

Source: Adapted from Attorney General John Van De Kamp's Commission of Drug and Alcohol Abuse, 1986. Sacramento, CA. Reprinted by permission of the California Attorney General's Office.

adds a major complication for the development of prevention programs aimed at reducing future substance abuse in their children (Drugs...in Focus).[37]

Special Role Models in Substance-Abuse Prevention

Although obstacles exist, comprehensive substance-abuse prevention programs strive to incorporate parents or guardians, as well as other family members, such as grandparents, into the overall effort. The reason lies in the variety of special roles they play in influencing children:

- As role models, parents or guardians may drink alcoholic beverages, smoke, or drink excessive amounts of caffeinated coffee, not thinking of these habits as drug-taking behaviors. They can learn to avoid sending their children signals about abstinence that are inconsistent at best, hypocritical at worst.

- As educators or resources for information, they can help by conveying verbal messages about health risks that are accurate and sincere.

Substance Use and Abuse among Young Mothers

Adolescents are in a high-risk demographic category for substance abuse in the first place (Chapter 2) but when female adolescents are mothers themselves at this stage of life, the risk factor for future substance abuse among their children increases dramatically. Here are some facts about substance use and abuse among an annual average of 528,000 young mothers in the U.S., aged 15 to 17, who were living with one or more of their children from 2005 to 2009:

- About 28 percent reported smoking cigarettes in the past month, compared to 16 percent among counterparts who were not mothers.

- About 25 percent reported drinking alcohol in the past month, the same as among counterparts.

- About 18 percent reported smoking marijuana in the past month, compared to 10 percent among counterparts.

An understanding of this special group of people is essential in designing specific prevention programs, with lasting consequences to a future generation. What programs might be designed for young mothers?

Source: Substance Abuse and Mental Health Services Administration (2011, March 10). Substance use among young mothers. *The NSDUH Report.* Rockville, MD: Substance Abuse and Mental Health Services Administration.

- As family policymakers and rule setters, they can convey a clear understanding of the consequences of drug-taking behaviors. If a parent or guardian cannot or will not back up family rules with logical and consistent consequences, the risk increases that rules will be broken.

- As stimulators of enjoyable family activities, parents or guardians can provide alternative behavior programming necessary to steer youths away from high-risk situations.

- As consultants against peer pressure, parents or guardians can help reinforce the peer-refusal skills of their children. Children and adolescents frequently report that a strongly negative reaction at home was the single most important reason for their refusing alcohol, tobacco, and other drugs from their peers.

Parental Communication in Substance-Abuse Prevention

In recognition of the importance of parental communication in efforts to reduce drug-taking behavior, the program "Parents: The Antidrug" has been a dominant feature in public-service announcements in recent years.[38] The need for better lines of communication between parents and teenagers is illustrated in a PDFA survey. When asked whether they had talked

The power of a Grandpa.

Children have a very special relationship with Grandma and Grandpa. That's why grandparents can be such powerful allies in helping keep a kid off drugs.

Grandparents are cool. Relaxed. They're not on the firing line every day. Some days a kid hates his folks. He never hates his grandparents. Grandparents ask direct, point-blank, embarrassing questions you're too nervous to ask:

"Who's the girl?"

"How come you're doing poorly in history?"

"Why are your eyes always red?"

"Did you go to the doctor? What did he say?"

The same kid who cons his parents is ashamed to lie to Grandpa. Without betraying their trust, a loving, understanding grandparent can discuss the danger of drugs openly with the child he adores. And should.

• The average age of first-time drug use among teens is 13. Some kids start at 9.

• 1 out of 4 American kids between 9 and 12 is offered illegal drugs. 22% of these kids receive the offer from a friend. And 10% named a family member as their source.

• Illegal drugs are linked to increased violence in many communities, to AIDS, to birth defects, drug-related crime, and homelessness.

As a grandparent, you hold a special place in the hearts and minds of your grandchildren. Share your knowledge, your love, your faith in them. Use your power as an influencer to steer your grandchildren away from drugs.

If you don't have the words, we do. We'll send you information on how to talk to your grandkids about drugs. Just ask for your free copy of *Keeping Youth Drug-Free.* Call 1-800-788-2800 or visit our websites, www.projectknow.com or www.drugfreeamerica.org.

Grandma, Grandpa. Talk to your grandkids. You don't realize the power you have to save them.

Office of National Drug Control Policy
Partnership for a Drug-Free America

Communication between grandparents and grandchildren can be an important tool in substance-abuse prevention.

An outdoor public-service announcement urges parents to begin a dialogue early about the short-term and long-term dangers of underage drinking. Parents generally underestimate the extent of alcohol use in their children and find it hard to decide how or when to begin this important conversation.

to their teenagers about drugs at least once, 98 percent of parents reported that they had done so, but only 65 percent of teenagers recalled such a conversation. Barely 27 percent of teenagers reported learning a lot at home about the risks of drug use, even though virtually all of their parents said they had discussed the topic.

> **sociocultural filters:** A set of considerations specific to a particular culture or community that can influence the reception and acceptance of public information.

Justifiably, anti-drug media campaigns have focused on parent–child communication skills, specifically on the difficulty many parents have in talking to their children about sensitive subjects such as drugs and the role of drug-taking behavior in their children's social lives.[39]

The Triple Threat: Stress, Boredom, and Spending Money

Substance-abuse prevention in young people can sometimes be simpler and more straightforward than we realize. A recent survey of teenagers aged twelve to seventeen measured the effects of three circumstances on the likelihood that a teenager would engage in some form of substance abuse: (1) the degree of stress they feel they are under, (2) the frequency with which they are bored, and (3) the amount of money they have to spend in a typical week. High-stress teens (one-fourth of teens interviewed) were twice as likely as low-stress teens (a little more than one-fourth of teens interviewed) to smoke, drink, get drunk, and use illicit drugs. Teens reporting that they were frequently bored were 50 percent more likely than not-often-bored teens to engage in these behaviors. Teens with $25 or more a week in spending money were nearly twice as likely as teens with less spending money to smoke, drink, and use illicit drugs, and they were more than twice as likely to get drunk. Combining two or three of these risk factors (high stress, frequent boredom, and too much spending money) made the risk of smoking, drinking, and illicit drug use three times higher than when none of these characteristics was present.[40]

Multicultural Issues in Primary and Secondary Prevention

In the case of substance-abuse prevention messages, it is important to remember that information intended to reach individuals of a specific culture passes through a series of **sociocultural filters**. Understanding this filtering process is essential to maximizing the reception and acceptance of substance-abuse prevention information.

Prevention Approaches in Latino Communities

A good example of the need to recognize sociocultural filters is the set of special concerns associated with communicating drug-related information to Latinos, a diverse group representing more than 13 percent of the U.S. population and expected to represent more than 25 percent

INHALANTS...
(Sprays / Aerosols / Glues)

EVIL SPIRITS THAT BREAK THE BONDS BETWEEN OURSELVES AND OUR ELDERS, DISRUPT THE CIRCLE OF OUR FAMILY SYSTEM, DESTROY THE HARMONY BETWEEN US AND ALL CREATION.

FOR OUR OWN SURVIVAL, THE SURVIVAL OF OUR FAMILY, OUR TRIBE AND THE INDIAN NATION, WE MUST RESIST THESE SPIRITS OF DEATH.

This substance-abuse prevention message focuses on inhalant abuse among Native American children, adolescents, and young adults through the sociocultural filter of their community.

by 2050. The following insights concerning elements of the Latino community can enhance the chances of success in a Latino-targeted prevention program.

- Because of the importance that Latinos attach to the family and religious institutions, prevention and treatment efforts should be targeted to include the entire family and, if possible, its religious leaders. Prevention efforts will be most effective when counselors reinforce family units and value them as a whole.

- Prevention programs are needed to help Latino fathers recognize how important their role or example is to their sons' and daughters' self-image regarding alcohol and other drugs. Because being a good father is part of *machismo*, it is important that the men become full partners in parenting. Mothers should be encouraged to learn strategies for including their husbands in family interactions at home.

- Because a Latina woman with alcohol or other drug problems is strongly associated with a violation of womanly ideals of purity, discipline, and self-sacrifice, educational efforts should concentrate on reducing the shame associated with her reaching out for help.

One particular web site (www.nlcatp.org) that addresses the needs of the Latino community is sponsored by the National Latino Council on Alcohol and Tobacco Prevention (NLCATP).[41]

Prevention Approaches in African American Communities

Another set of special concerns exist with regard to communicating drug-related information in African American communities. Some basic generalizations have proved helpful in optimizing the design of prevention programs.

- African American youths tend to use drugs other than alcohol after they form social attitudes and adopt behaviors associated with delinquency. The most common examples of delinquency include drug dealing, shoplifting, and petty theft. With regard to the designing of media campaigns, it is deglamorization of the drug dealer that appears to be most helpful in primary prevention efforts among African American youths.

- Drug use and social problems are likely to be interrelated in primarily African American neighborhoods. The effects of alcohol and other drug use are intensified when other factors exist, such as high unemployment, poverty, poor health care, and poor nutrition.

- Several research studies have shown that most African American youths, even those in low-income neighborhoods, do manage to escape from the pressures to use alcohol and other drugs. The protective factors of staying in school, solid family bonds, strong religious beliefs, high self-esteem, adequate coping strategies, social skills, and steady employment all build on one another to endow high-risk children and adolescents with resilience. As noted before, prevention programs developed with protective factors in mind have the greatest chance for success.[42]

Substance-Abuse Prevention in the Workplace

The workplace has been recognized as an important focus for substance-abuse prevention. According to statistics from the 2011 National Survey on Drug Use and Health (see Chapter 1), more than 71 percent of current illicit drug users were employed either full-time or part-time, as were 87 percent of adult binge drinkers and persons reporting heavy alcohol use. Workers have reported being put in danger, having been injured, having to work harder or re-do work, or having to cover for a coworker as a result of a fellow employee's drinking. Small businesses are particularly affected by worker substance abuse.[43]

The 1988 Drug-Free Workplace Act requires that all companies and businesses receiving any U.S. federal contracts or grants provide a drug-free workplace. Specifically, organizations must initiate a comprehensive and continuing program of drug education and awareness. Employees must also be notified that the distribution, possession, or unauthorized use of controlled substances is prohibited in that workplace and that action will be taken against any employee who violates these rules. Supervisors are advised to be especially alert to changes in a worker that might signal early or progressive stages in the abuse of alcohol and/or other drugs. These signals include chronic absenteeism, a sudden change in physical appearance or behavior, spasmodic work pace, unexpectedly lower quantity or quality of work, partial or unexplained absences, a pattern of excuse-making or lying, the avoidance of supervisors or coworkers, and on-the-job accidents or lost time from such accidents.

In effect, achieving a drug-free workplace is made possible by a combination of secondary prevention and tertiary prevention. Secondary prevention programs will be covered in this chapter, and tertiary prevention (treatment-oriented) programs will be reviewed in Chapter 17.

The Economic Costs of Substance Abuse in the Workplace

High-profile instances of on-the-job accidents involving the effects of either illicit drugs or alcohol are often given as examples of the scope of substance abuse in the workplace and the need for workplace drug testing. In 1991, for example, a New York subway operator crashed his train near a station in lower Manhattan, resulting in five deaths and 215 injuries. The operator admitted that he had been drinking prior to the crash, and his BAC level was measured at 0.21 percent, more than twice the legal limit of 0.10 percent in New York at that time. In 1987, a Conrail train brakeman and an engineer were found to be responsible for a collision that resulted in sixteen deaths and 170 injuries. Drug testing revealed traces of marijuana in their systems.

There are two reasons why such examples do not accurately reflect the impact of alcohol and other drug abuse in the workplace. First, the likelihood of an adverse effect is not adequately reflected in news reports, any more than the impact of drug toxicity on our society can be assessed by reading the news stories of public figures and celebrities who have died of a drug overdose (Chapter 2). Second, in many cases, it is very difficult to

determine the extent to which we can connect drug use with the tragic consequences of an accident, because some drugs leave metabolites in the system long after they have stopped producing behavioral effects. In the case of the Conrail incident, the continued presence of marijuana metabolites for weeks after marijuana use (see Chapter 12) can make the positive test results irrelevant.

We must turn instead to estimates gathered from other sources of information. Unfortunately, these estimates are "soft," having large margins of error. Even so, they leave little doubt that the abuse of alcohol and other drugs has a major impact on workplace productivity. On the basis of its own studies, CSAP estimates that, relative to nonabusers, abusers of alcohol and other drugs are

- 5 times more likely to file a workers' compensation claim
- 3.6 times more likely to be involved in an accident on the job
- 5 times more likely to be personally injured on the job
- 3 times more likely to be late for work
- 2.2 times more likely to request early dismissal from work or time off
- 16 times more likely to take sick leave

Overall, the estimated costs from productivity lost as a result of such behavior amount to $60 billion–$100 billion each year.[44]

Drug Testing in the Workplace

By executive order of President Reagan in 1986, preemployment drug screening was mandated for all federal employees, along with periodic, random drug testing afterward. (It is not known whether President Reagan or subsequent presidents since 1986 have been included in this requirement.) Federal statutes have not required drug testing for employees other than those working for the federal government. By 1996, 81 percent of employers reported having a drug-testing program in place. By 2004, however, an American Management Association survey reported that the percentage had gone down considerably. Approximately 62 percent of all companies tested for illicit drugs; 55 percent conducted testing as part of the job application process, and 44 percent conducted testing among current employees on a periodic basis. Surveys have not been conducted more recently, but the chances are that there has been a further decline.[45]

Although it is easy to understand the rationale for drug testing in the workplace in the overall scheme of drug prevention, the procedure has raised a number of important issues regarding individual rights. Does taking a urine sample violate a person's freedom from "unreasonable search and seizure" as guaranteed by the Fourth Amendment to the U.S. Constitution? It turns out that if the government requires it, the decision rests on the question of whether there is reasonable or unreasonable cause for the drug testing to occur. In cases in which a threat to public safety is involved, the cause has been ruled reasonable. However, if a private business requires it, the legal rights of employees are somewhat murky. An employee typically accepts his or her job offer with the assumption and agreement that periodic monitoring of drug use will take place, but whether this understanding is a form of implied coercion is an open question.

If you lose your job as a result of testing positive in a drug test, has there been a violation of your right to "due process" as guaranteed by the Fifth Amendment? The courts have ruled that this right would be violated only if the method of drug screening were unreliable, if the analysis and reporting were carried out in an unreliable manner, or if it could not be shown that the presence of any one of the screened substances had a relationship to job impairment. In general, screening methods are not perfectly reliable, the handling of drug tests is not perfectly controlled, and the relationship between drug use and a decline in job performance is not perfectly clear, but drug tests have nonetheless been judged to have met reasonable standards, and the practice is allowed. The bottom line is that drug testing, despite its obvious infringements on individual privacy, has become a fact of life in corporate America.[46]

Nonetheless, despite the increasing acceptance of drug testing as a tool for drug-abuse prevention in the workplace, there will always be questions about the impact on workers themselves. For example, the possibility of false positives (when an individual tests positive but has not been using a particular drug) and false negatives (when an individual who, on the basis of prior drug use, should test positive for a particular drug, does not do so) can have unfortunate consequences. Consider this possible preemployment screening scenario:

> *Suppose that the EMIT test were 100 percent effective in spotting drug users (it is not) and that it has a false-positive rate of 3 percent (which is not unreasonable). In a group of 100 prospective employees, one person has recently taken an illegal drug. Since the test is 100 percent effective, that person will be caught, but three other people (the 3 percent false-positive rate) will also. Therefore, 75 percent of those who fail the test are innocent parties.*[47]

Another problem is that companies are not required to follow up a positive EMIT test result with another, more sensitive method, such as one using the GC/MS procedure (Chapter 12). Some companies allow for retesting in general, but most do not.

The Impact of Drug-Free Workplace Policies

Given the adverse effects of drug abuse on productivity, we should expect to see substantial economic and personal benefits when drug-free workplace policies are in effect. In one well-documented case, a program developed by the Southern Pacific Railroad Company in the 1980s, extensive drug testing was required for all employees who had been involved in a company accident or rule violation. As a result, the annual number of accidents decreased from 911 to 168 in three years, and the financial losses from such accidents decreased from $6.4 million to $1.2 million. During the first few months of the new testing program, it was found that 22 to 24 percent of employees who had experienced some human-factor-related accident tested positive for alcohol or other drugs, a figure that fell to 3 percent three years later.[48]

It makes sense that substance-abuse prevention programs would have the greatest impact in companies within the transportation industry, owing to the close relationship between drug-induced impairments in performance and the incidence of industrial accidents. Beyond this application, however, it is widely recognized that a similar impact, if not one as dramatic in magnitude, can be demonstrated in any business setting. The reasons are related to the basic goals of prevention, as discussed earlier: deterrence and rehabilitation. The practice of testing for illicit drug use in the workplace functions as an effective deterrent among workers, because the likelihood is strong that illicit drug use will be detected. As we will see in Chapter 17, substance-abuse treatment programs in the workplace can function as an effective rehabilitative tool, because those workers who might otherwise not receive help with drug-abuse problems will be referred to appropriate agencies for treatment services.[49]

Yes, You: Substance-Abuse Prevention and the College Student

Effective substance-abuse programs among college students present an unusual challenge, in that we are hardly speaking of a homogeneous population. U.S. college students represent all racial, ethnic, and socioeconomic groups and are likely to come from all parts of the world. They include undergraduate and graduate students, full-time and part-time students, residential students and commuters, students of traditional college age and students who are considerably older. Each of these groups has a different perspective on drug-taking behavior, different opportunities for drug-taking behavior, and different life experiences.

In particular, there are marked differences in the objectives of a prevention program for those under twenty-one years of age and for those who are older. In the former group, the goal may be "no use of" (or abstinence from) alcohol, tobacco, and other drugs, whereas in the latter group the goal may be the low-risk (that is, responsible) consumption of alcohol and no use of tobacco and other drugs. The term "low-risk consumption" refers to a level of use restricted by considerations of physical health, family background, pregnancy risk, the law, safety, and other personal concerns.

With respect to alcohol, secondary prevention guidelines might stipulate that pregnant women, recovering alcoholics, those with a family history of alcoholism, people driving cars or heavy machinery, people on medications, and those under the age of twenty-one should not drink alcohol at all. But even though the distinction between under-twenty-one and over-twenty-one preventive goals is applicable in many community-oriented programs, it is an especially difficult challenge for prevention efforts on a college campus, where the target population contains both subgroups so closely intermingled.[50]

Changing the Culture of Alcohol and Other Drug Use in College

A major challenge with regard to prevention programs at colleges and universities comes from the widely regarded expectation that heavy alcohol drinking, as well as some illicit drug use, during the college years represents something of a rite of passage. College alumni (and potential benefactors) frequently oppose the implementation of drug and alcohol crackdowns, arguing that "we did it when we were in school."[51] Moreover, national surveys in 2011 indicate that by the end of high school, about 70 percent of all students have consumed alcoholic beverages, 51 percent have been drunk at least once, and 46 percent have smoked marijuana. Therefore, we cannot say that use of these drugs present a new experience for many college students.[52] Given this prior exposure, it is not surprising that further experimentation and more extensive patterns of

drug-taking behavior will occur. There is a compelling argument for secondary and tertiary prevention programs to be in place at this point.

The emphasis on most campuses is on the prevention and control of alcohol problems (Health Line). However, it is less common for college administrators to focus on the problems associated with drugs other than alcohol. Frequently, the only policy in place involves punitive action if a student athlete tests positive for an illicit drug. And although no-smoking campuses are the norm, few if any programs are in place to help reduce the level of tobacco use among college students.

Substance-Abuse Prevention on College Campuses

On the positive side, college campuses have the potential to be ideal environments for comprehensive substance-abuse prevention programs, because they combine features of both school and community settings. Here are some suggested strategies for prevention on the college campus:

- Develop a multifaceted prevention program of assessment, education, policy, and enforcement. Involve students, faculty, and administrators in determining the degree of availability and demand for alcohol and other drugs on campus and in the surrounding community and to initiate public information and education efforts.

- Incorporate alcohol and other drug education into the curriculum. Faculty members can use drug-related situations as teachable moments, include drug topics in their course syllabi, and develop courses or course projects on issues relating to alcohol and other drugs.

- Ensure that hypocrisy is not the rule of the day. Substance-abuse prevention is not a goal for college students only but is a larger issue that affects all members of the academic community, including faculty and administration.

- Encourage environments that reduce the pressures to engage in drug-taking behavior. Foster more places where social and recreational activities can take place spontaneously and at hours when the most enticing alternative may be the consumption of alcohol and other drugs. A recent promising sign is the growing popularity of drug-free dormitories on many college campuses, where student residents specifically choose to refrain from using alcohol, tobacco, and other drugs.[53]

The seriousness of the drug-taking behavior on college campuses could not be demonstrated more clearly

Health Line

Alcohol 101 on College Campuses

A familiar experience among many students entering college for the first time is referred to by public health officials as the "college effect"—defined as an increase in drinking and negative behaviors associated with it (Chapter 8). One increasingly popular approach intended to minimize this phenomenon is a three-hour web-based online course called AlcoholEdu, developed by Outside the Classroom, Inc. More than 500 colleges and universities nationwide are currently participating in this program.

AlcoholEdu is oriented toward responsible drinking behavior rather than abstinence. Topics include an understanding of blood alcohol concentrations, activities that increase the likelihood of blacking out, discredited remedies for hangovers, and an appreciation of the alcohol beverage industry's role in fostering the image of alcohol consumption as a means for advancing social and interpersonal relationships. Participants are given an exam that tests their knowledge of the information provided in the course.

Colleges and universities have varying policies about students taking AlcoholEdu. Some require students to complete and pass the course with a minimum score on the exam prior to the first day of classes or before registering for the next semester. Others convey an expectation that the AlcoholEdu should be completed and warn that severe consequences will be imposed for those students who fail to finish the course and commit an alcohol violation in the future. There are early indications that student participation in AlcoholEdu results in significantly fewer negative consequences of drinking, such as missing class, attending class with a hangover, blacking out, and abusive behavior. However, intensive studies of effectiveness, both short-term and long-term, need to be carried out.

In the meantime, additional programs addressing a wider range of alcohol problems on campuses have been developed. AlcoholEdu for Sanctions is an intervention program suited for students who have violated academic policies on alcohol; its goal is to reduce recidivism rates. Alcohol Innerview is a brief motivational intervention tool for students who have experienced alcohol problems or are in alcohol-abuse counseling. AlcoholEdu for Parents is designed to support parents with college-age children in fostering conversations that can help shape healthy decisions about alcohol use at college.

Recent developments in online prevention programs by Outside the Classroom, Inc., include MentalHealthEdu (raising campus community awareness of college student mental-health issues) and SexualAssaultEdu (focusing on relationships and decision making to reduce the incidence of sexual assaults on campus).

Sources: Fact sheet on alcohol issues, University of Colorado at Boulder (2004, August 11). Boulder, CO: Office of News Services, University of Colorado. Kesmodel, D. (2005, November 1). Schools use web to teach about booze. *Wall Street Journal Online.* Outside the Classroom (2008). www.outsidetheclassroom.com.

---

than in the context of alcohol drinking among members of college fraternities. A statement in a 1994 decision of the Arizona Supreme Court expressed this concern in no uncertain terms:

> We are hardpressed to find a setting where the risk of an alcohol-related injury is more likely than from under-age drinking at a university fraternity party the first week of the new college year.[54]

Since 2000, when one in five fraternity chapters in the United States began to phase in a policy forbidding alcohol of any kind anywhere in the fraternity house, even in rooms of members who were of legal drinking age, there has been a steady upward trend in the number of alcohol-free fraternity (and sorority) houses around the country.[55]

Substance-Abuse Prevention Information

Fortunately, information and guidance about prevention issues and strategies are available from many sources, tailored for any age group. As we have noted, the specific prevention of prescription drug misuse among adolescents is currently a major issue of public health concern (see Chapters 1, 4, and 5). The National Council on Patient Information and Education issues extensive resource materials on the prevention of prescription drug misuse; these materials are available through its web site, www.talkaboutrx.org. The most comprehensive source for substance-abuse prevention information is the Substance Abuse and

Mental Health Services Administration (SAMHSA). Prevention information and educational materials regarding virtually every aspect of substance use, misuse, or abuse are available through the SAMHSA web site, www.samhsa.gov.

For residents of Canada, the Canadian Centre on Substance Abuse (CCSA) is a useful source of help; it can be accessed through the web site, www.ccsa.ca. For residents of the United Kingdom, the following web site is available: www.talktofrank.com.

Summary

Levels of Intervention in Substance-Abuse Prevention

- Substance-abuse prevention efforts fall into three basic levels of intervention: primary, secondary, and tertiary.

- Primary prevention focuses on populations that have had only minimal or no exposure to drugs. Secondary prevention focuses on populations whose drug experience has not yet been associated with serious long-term problems. Tertiary prevention focuses on populations who have entered treatment; the goal is to prevent relapse.

Strategies for Substance-Abuse Prevention

- The U.S. federal agency specifically charged with prevention programs is the Center for Substance Abuse Prevention (CSAP), a division of the Substance Abuse and Mental Health Services Administration (SAMHSA), which is in turn a division of the U.S. Department of Health and Human Services.

- The overall strategy for substance-abuse prevention is to minimize the risk factors in a person's life with respect to drug-taking behavior and to maximize the protective factors. The inclination to resist the effects of risk factors for drug-taking behavior through the action of protective factors is referred to as resilience.

- In order to be "evidence-based," primary and secondary prevention programs must be evaluated against a control group that did not receive the intervention. Positive change per se is not enough for a judgment of success.

- The estimated costs of substance abuse in the United States exceed $1 trillion each year. The federal program Healthy People 2020 has set specific objectives regarding a wide range of health behaviors, including those that pertain to substance abuse.

Lessons from the Past: Prevention Approaches That Have Failed

- Several strategies have been largely unsuccessful in meeting the goals of substance-abuse prevention.

They include the reliance on supply/availability reduction, punitive judicial policies, scare tactics, objective information, and affective education.

Hope and Promise: Components of Effective School-Based Prevention Programs

- Effective school-based programs have incorporated a combination of peer-refusal skills training, relaxation and stress management, and training in social skills and personal decision making.

- The Life Skills Training (LST) program is an example of a comprehensive program that incorporates several of these school-based components for effective substance-abuse prevention. The Drug Abuse Resistance Education (D.A.R.E.) program, in its original form, has been shown to have little effect in primary prevention, although later versions have incorporated many of the components that have been demonstrated to be effective.

Community-Based Prevention Programs

- Community-based programs make use of a broader range of resources, including community leaders and public figures as positive role models, opportunities for alternative-behavior programming, and the mass media.

- Recent efforts by the media have had a major impact on the image of drug-taking behavior in both high-risk populations and others in the community.

- CASASTART is an example of a community-based program that incorporates intensive community-wide components of substance-abuse prevention.

Family Systems in Primary and Secondary Prevention

- Community-based prevention programs are increasingly mindful of the importance of the family, particularly parents, as the first line of defense in prevention efforts.

- A major emphasis in primary and secondary prevention programs has been on the special roles of parents, grandparents, guardians, and other family members. Improved lines of communication within the family are crucial elements.

Multicultural Issues in Primary and Secondary Prevention

- Cultural considerations are important when communicating about substance abuse with specific population subgroups, such as Latinos and African Americans.

Substance-Abuse Prevention in the Workplace

- The 1988 Drug-free Workplace Act mandated that any company or business receiving U.S. federal contracts or grants provide a drug-free workplace. This is carried out through a comprehensive and continuing program of drug education and awareness. It is estimated that substance abuse costs as much as $60 billion–$100 billion each year.
- One element of most drug-free workplace programs is an employee assistance program (EAP), serving to help workers with abuse problems. Where unions exist, member assistance programs (MAPs) supplement and complement the work of EAPs.

Yes, You: Substance-Abuse Prevention and the College Student

- On college campuses, substance-abuse prevention programs are incorporating features of both school-based and community-based approaches. There is a compelling need to change the culture of alcohol and other drug use in college.
- Substance-abuse prevention programs should involve faculty and administrators, as well as students, in an overall comprehensive strategy. College fraternities have taken important strides toward banning alcohol in fraternity houses, even when members are of legal drinking age.

Key Terms

affective education, p. 386
impactors, p. 391
peer-refusal skills, p. 387

primary prevention, p. 380
resilience, p. 382

secondary prevention, p. 380
sociocultural filters, p. 394

tertiary prevention, p. 381
values clarification, p. 386

Endnotes

1. Grant, B. F., and Dawson, D. A. (1997). Age at onset of alcohol use and its association with DSM-IV alcohol abuse and dependence: Results from the National Longitudinal Alcohol Epidemiological Survey. *Journal of Substance Abuse, 9,* 103–110. Grant, B. F., and Dawson, D. A. (1998). Age at onset of drug use and its association with DSM-IV drug abuse and dependence: Results from the National Longitudinal Alcohol Epidemiological Survey. *Journal of Substance Abuse, 10,* 163–173. Stagman, S.; Schwartz, S. W.; and Powers, D. (2011, May). Fact sheet: Adolescent substance use in the U.S.: Facts for policy makers. National Center for Children in Poverty, New York.
2. Brook, J. S., and Brook, D. W. (1996). Risk and protective factors for drug use. In C. B. McCoy, L. R. Metsch, and J. A. Inciardi (Eds.), *Intervening with drug-involved youth.* Thousand Oaks, CA: Sage Publications, pp. 23–44. Fagan, A. A., and Eisenberg, N. (2012). Latest developments in the prevention of crime and anti-social behavior: An American perspective. *Journal of Children's Services, 7,* 64–72. Wong, M. M.; Nigg, J. T.; Zucker, R. A.; Puttler, L. I.; et al. (2006). Behavioral control and resiliency in the onset of alcohol and illicit drug use: A prospective study from preschool to adolescence. *Child Development, 77,* 1016–1033.
3. Backer, T. E. (2000). The failure of success: Challenges of disseminating effective substance abuse prevention programs. *Journal of Community Psychology, 28,* 363–373. Biglan, A.; Mrazek, P. J.; Carnine, D.; and Flay, B. R. (2003). The integration of research and practice in the prevention of youth problem behaviors. *American Psychologist, 58,* 433–441. Ennert, S. T.; Haws, S.; Ringwalt, C. L.; Vincus, A. A.; Hanley, S., et al (2011). Evidence-based practice in school substance use prevention: Fidelity of implementation under real-world conditions. *Health Education, 26,* 361–371. Office of National Drug Control Policy (2010, February). *National drug control budget: FY 2011 funding highlights.* Washington, DC: White House Office of National Drug Control Policy.
4. Mokdad, A. H.; Marks, J. S.; Stroup, D. F.; and Gerberding, J. L. (2004). Actual causes of death in the United States, 2000. *Journal of the American Medical Association, 291,* 1238–1245. Mokdad, A. H.; Marks, J. S.; Stroup, D. F.; and Gerberding, J. L. (2005). Correction: Actual causes of death in the United States, 2000. *Journal of the American Medical Association, 293,* 298.
5. Birnbaum, H. G.; White, A. G.; Schiller, M.; Waldman, T.; Cleveland, J. M.; et al. (2011). Societal costs of prescription opioid abuse, dependence, and misuse in the United States. *Pain Medicine, 12,* 657–667. Califano,

J. A. Jr. (2007). *High society: How substance abuse ravages America and what to do about it.* New York: Public Affairs. Center for Substance Abuse Prevention (2009). *Substance abuse prevention dollars and cents: A cost-benefit analysis.* Rockville, MD: Substance Abuse and Mental Health Services Administration.

6. Koh, H. K. (2011). A 2020 vision for healthy people. *New England Journal of Medicine, 362,* 1653–1655. Riegelman, R. K., and Garr, D. R. (2011). Healthy People 2020 and education for health: What are the objectives? *American Journal of Preventive Medicine, 40,* 203–206.

7. Office of National Drug Control Policy (2013). *National drug control budget—FY 2013 funding highlights.* Washington, DC: Office of National Drug Control Policy.

8. Goode, E. (2008). *Drugs in American society* (7th ed.). New York: McGraw-Hill, pp. 400–403. National Drug Intelligence Center (2011, August). *National drug threat assessment 2011.* Washington, DC: U.S. Department of Justice, pp. 25–32.

9. Carazos-Rehg, P. A.; Krauss, M. J.; Spitznagel, E. I.; Chalouipka, F. J.; Schottman, M.; et al. (2012). Associations between selective state laws and teenagers' drinking and driving behaviors. *Alcoholism: Clinical and Experimental Research (doi/10.1111/j.1530-0277.2012.01764.x/full).* Daley, J. I.; Stahre, M. A.; Chaloupka, F. J.; and Naimi, T. S. (2012). The impact of a 25-cent-per-drink alcohol tax increase. *American Journal of Preventive Medicine, 42,* 382–389. Fell, J. C.; Fisher, D. A.; Voas, R. B. K; Blackman, K.; and Tippetts, A. S. (2009). The impact of underage drinking laws on alcohol-related fatal crashes of young drivers. *Alcoholism: Clinical and Experimental Research, 33,* 1208–1219. Wechsler, H., and Nelson, T. F. (2010). Will increasing alcohol availability by lowering the minimum legal drinking age decrease drinking and related consequences among youths? *American Journal of Public Health, 100,* 986–989.

10. Goode, *Drugs in American society,* pp. 385–417. Greenhouse, L. (2007, December 11). Justices restore judges' control over sentencing. *New York Times,* pp. A1, A28. Levinthal, C. F. (2012). *Drugs, society, and criminal justice* (3rd ed.). Upper Saddle River, NJ: Pearson Education, Prentice-Hall.

11. Funkhouser, J. E., and Denniston, R. W. (1992). Historical perspective. In M. A. Jansen (Ed.), *A promising future: Alcohol and other drug problem prevention services improvement* (OSAP Prevention Monograph 10). Rockville, MD: Office of Substance Abuse Prevention, pp. 5–15.

12. Flay, B. R., and Sobel, J. L. (1983). The role of mass media in preventing adolescent substance abuse. In T. J. Glynn, C. G. Leukenfeld, and J. P. Ludford (Eds.), *Preventive adolescent drug abuse.* Rockville, MD: National Institute on Drug Abuse, pp. 5–35.

13. Williams, R.; Ward, D.; and Gray, L. (1985). The persistence of experimentally induced cognitive change: A neglected dimension in the assessment of drug prevention programs. *Journal of Drug Education, 15,* 33–42.

14. Meeks, L.; Heit, P.; and Page, R. (1994). *Drugs, alcohol, and tobacco.* Blacklick, OH: Meeks Heit Publishing, p. 201.

15. Ibid., p. 202.

16. McBride, D. C.; Mutch, P. B.; and Chitwood, D. D. (1996). Religious belief and the initiation and prevention of drug use among youth. In C. B. McCoy, L. R. Metsch, and J. A. Inciardi (Eds.), *Intervening with drug-involved youth.* Thousand Oaks, CA: Sage Publications, pp. 110–130.

17. Schroeder, D. S.; Laflin, M. T.; and Weis, D. L. (1993). Is there a relationship between self-esteem and drug use? Methodological and statistical limitations of the research. *Journal of Drug Issues, 22,* 645–665. Yuen, F. K. O., and Pardeck, J. T. (1998). Effective strategies for preventing substance abuse among children and adolescents. *Early Child Development and Care, 145,* 119–131.

18. Allan B. J.; Flay, B. R.; Towson, S. M. J.; Ryan, K. B.; et al. (1984). Smoking prevention and the concept of risk. *Journal of Applied Social Psychology, 14,* 257–273. Pandina, R. J.; Johnson, V. L.; and White, H. R. (2010). Peer influences on substance use during adolescence and emerging adulthood. In L. M. Scheier (Ed.), *Handbook of drug use etiology: Theory, methods, and empirical findings.* Washington, DC: American Psychological Association, pp. 383–402.

19. Botvin, G. J., and Griffin, K. W. (2010). Advances in the science and practice of prevention: Targeting individual-level etiological factors and the challenge of going to scale. In Scheier, *Handbook of drug use etiology,* pp. 631–650.

20. Culpers, P. (2002). Effective ingredients of school-based drug prevention programs: A systematic review. *Addictive Behaviors, 27,* 1009–1023. Faggiano, F.; Vigna-Taglianti, F.; Versino, E.; Zambon, A.; and Lemma, P. (2005). School-based prevention for illicit drugs' use. *Cochrane Database of Systematic Reviews,* Issue 2. Article No.: CD003020. DOI: 10.1002/14651858.CD0030.pub2.

21. Botvin, G. J.; Baker, E.; Dusenbury, L.; Botvin, E. M.; and Diaz, T. (1995). Long-term follow-up results of a randomized drug abuse prevention trial in a white middle-class population. *Journal of the American Medical Association, 273,* 1106–1112. Botvin, G. J.; Epstein, J. A.; Baker, E.; Diaz, T.; and Ifill-Williams, M. (1997). School-based drug abuse prevention with inner-city minority youth. *Journal of Child and Adolescent Substance Abuse, 6,* 5–19. Botvin, G. J.; Griffin, K. W.; and Murphy M. M. (2011). Adolescent substance abuse prevention and cessation. *In* M. L. Finkel (Ed.), *Public health in the 21st century. Volume 1: Global issues in public health.* Santa Barbara: Praeger, pp. 287–305.

22. Mathias, R. (1997, March/April). From the 'burbs to the 'hood … This program reduces student's risk of drug use. *NIDA Notes,* pp. 1, 5–6. Quotation on p. 6.

23. Botvin, G. J.; Griffin, K. W.; and Nichols, T. D. (2006). Preventing youth violence and delinquency through a universal school-based prevention approach. *Prevention Science, 7,* 403–408. Griffin, K. W.; Botvin, G. J.; and

Nichols, T. D. (2006). Effects of a school-based drug abuse prevention program for adolescents on HIV risk behaviors in young adulthood. *Prevention Science, 7,* 103–112. Griffin, K. W.; Botvin, G. J.; and Nichols, T. D. (2004). Long-term follow-up effects of a school-based drug abuse prevention program on adolescent risky driving. *Prevention Science, 5,* 207–212. Williams, C.; Samuolis, J.; Griffin, K. W.; and Botvin, G. J. (2011). LifeSkills Training Wellness Program: An application for young adults in supermarkets. In J. W. Bray, D. M. Galvin, and L. A. Cluff (Eds.), *Young adults in the workplace: A multisite initiate of substance use prevention programs.* Research Triangle, NC: RTI International, pp. 117–132.

24. Griffith, J. S. (1999). Daring to be different? A drug prevention and life skills education programme for primary schools. *Early Child Development and Care, 158,* 95–105.

25. Clayton, R. R.; Cattarello, A. M.; and Johnstone, B. M. (1996). The effectiveness of Drug Abuse Resistance Education (Project D.A.R.E.): 5-year follow-up results. *Preventive Medicine, 25,* 307–318. Lynam, D. R.; Milich, R.; Zimmerman, R.; Novak, S. P.; Logan, T. K.; et al. (1999). Project D.A.R.E.: No effects at 10-year follow-up. *Journal of Consulting and Clinical Psychology, 67,* 590–593. Pan, W., and Bai, H. (2009). A multivariate approach to a meta-analytic review of the effectiveness of the D.A.R.E. program. *International Journal of Environmental Research and Public Health, 6,* 267–277.

26. Miller, J. (2004). *Bad trip: How the war against drugs is destroying America.* New York: Nelson Thomas.

27. Lynam et al., Project D.A.R.E., p. 593. Ringwalt, C.; Hecht, M. L.; and Hopfer, S. (2010). Drug prevention in elementary schools: An introduction to the Special Issue. *Journal of Drug Education, 40,* 1–9. Singh, R. D.; Jimerson, S. R.; Renshaw, T.; Saeki, E.; Hart, S. R.; et al. (2011). A summary and synthesis of contemporary empirical evidence regarding the effects of the Drug Abuse Resistance Education Program (D.A.R.E.). *Contemporary School Psychology, 15,* 93–102.

28. Zernicke, K. (2001, February 15). Antidrug program says it will adopt a new strategy. *New York Times,* pp. A1, A29.

29. Gardner, M.; B. R. Gabriela; and Brooks-Gunn, J. (2010). Neighborhood influences on substance use etiology: Is where you live important? In Scheier, *Handbook of drug use etiology,* pp. 423–442. Snyder, L. B., and N. P. Gayle (2010). Youth substance use and the media. In Scheier, *Handbook of drug use etiology,* pp. 475–492. Wandersman, A., and Florin, P. (2003). Community interventions and effective prevention. *American Psychologist, 58,* 441–448.

30. Firesheets, E. K.; Francis, M.; Barnum, A.; and Rolf, L. (2012). Community-based prevention support: Using the interactive systems framework to facilitate grassroots evidence-based substance-abuse prevention. *American Journal of Community Psychology, published online March 23, 2012,* 10.1007/s10464-012-9506-x. Hill, L. G.; Goates, S. G.; and Rosenman, R. (2010). Detecting selection effects in community implementation of family-based substance abuse prevention programs. *American Journal of Public Health, 100,* 623–630.

31. Tobler, N. S. (1986). Meta-analysis of 143 adolescent drug prevention programs: Quantitative outcome results of program participants compared to a control group. *Journal of Drug Issues, 16,* 537–567.

32. Ridout, V.; Roberts, D. F.; and Foehr, U. G. (2005, March). *Generation M: Media in the lives of 8–18-year-olds: Executive summary.* Menlo Park, CA: Kaiser Family Foundation. Quotation on p. 6.

33. Masten, A. S.; Faden, V. B.; Zucker, R. A.; and Spear, L. P. (2008). Underage drinking: A developmental framework. *Pediatrics, 121,* S235–S251. Primack, B.; Dalton, M. A.; Carroll, M. V.; Agarwal, A. A.; and Fine, M. J. (2008). Content analysis of tobacco, alcohol, and other drugs in popular music. *Archives of Pediatric and Adolescent Medicine, 162,* 169–175. Sargent, J. D.; Wills, T. A.; Stoolmiller, M.; Gibson, J.; and Gibbons, F. X. (2006). Alcohol use in motion pictures and its relation with early-onset teen drinking. *Journal of Studies in Alcohol, 67,* 54–65.

34. Partnership for a Drug-Free America (1994, July 12). Press release: New study shows children in NYC becoming more anti-drug, bucking national trends. Partnership for a Drug-Free America, New York.

35. Office of National Drug Control Policy (2006, July 21). Media campaign fact sheets: Teens and technology fact sheet. National Youth Anti-drug Media Campaign, Office of National Drug Control Policy, Washington, DC. Partnership for a Drug-Free America, New York. Substance Abuse and Mental Health Services Administration (2009, April 3). SAMHSA News Release: National survey finds a decrease in the percentage of adolescents seeing substance use prevention messages in the media. Rockville, MD: Substance Abuse and Mental Health Services Administration.

36. Information courtesy of the Substance Abuse and Mental Health Services Administration, Rockville, MD. Murray, L. F., and Belenko, S. (2005). CASASTART: A community-based, school-centered intervention for high-risk youth. *Substance Use and Misuse, 40,* 913–923.

37. Kliewer, W. (2010). Family processes in drug use etiology. In Scheier, *Handbook of drug use etiology:* pp. 365–382. National Center on Addiction and Substance Abuse at Columbia University (1999). No safe haven: Children of substance-abusing parents. New York: National Center on Addiction and Substance Abuse.

38. The Ad Council. (2008, March/April). Underage drinking prevention: Alcohol initiation rates highest during summer. *PSA Bulletin,* p. 1. Lac, A., and Crano, W. D. (2009). Monitoring matters: Meta-analytic review reveals the reliable linkage of parental monitoring with adolescent marijuana use. *Perspectives on Psychological Science, 4,* 578–586. Wooldridge, L. Q. (2007, March/April). Ads, billboards highlight younger children. *SAMHSA News,* p. 11.

39. The National Center on Addiction and Substance Abuse at Columbia University (2005, September). The importance of family dinners II. New York: National Center on Addiction and Substance Abuse at Columbia University. The National Center on Addiction and Substance Abuse at Columbia University (2006, August). National Survey of American Attitudes on Substance Abuse XI: Teens and parents. New York: National Center on Addiction and Substance Abuse at Columbia University. Partnership for a Drug-Free America (1998). Partnership attitude tracking survey: Parents say they're talking, but only 27% of teens—1 in 4—are learning a lot at home about the risk of drugs. Partnership for a Drug-Free America (1999). Partnership attitude tracking survey: More parents talking with kids about drugs more often, and appear to be having an impact. Information courtesy of Partnership for a Drug-Free America, New York.

40. The National Center on Addiction and Substance Abuse at Columbia University (2003, August). National Survey American Attitudes on Substance Abuse VIII: Teens and parents. New York: National Center on Addiction and Substance Abuse at Columbia University.

41. Gallardo, M. E., and Curry, S. J. (2009). Shifting perspectives: Culturally responsive interventions with Latino substance abusers. *Journal of Ethnicity in Substance Abuse*, 8, 314–329. Hernandez, L. P., and Lucero, Ed (1996). *La Familia* community drug and alcohol prevention program: Family-centered model for working with inner-city Hispanic families. *Journal of Primary Prevention*, 16, 255–272. Substance Abuse and Mental Health Services Administration (2009, July 16). Substance use treatment need and receipt among Hispanics. *The NSDUH Report*. Rockville, MD: Substance Abuse and Mental Health Services Administration.

42. Clark, T. T.; Belgrave, F. Z.; and Abell, M. (2012). The mediating and moderating effects of parent and peer influences upon drug use among African American adolescents. *Journal of Black Psychology*, 38, 52-80. Hahn, E. J., and Rado, M. (1996). African-American Head Start parent involvement in drug prevention. *American Journal of Health Behavior*, 20, 41–51.

43. Lehman, W. E. K.; Farabee, D. J.; and Bennett, J. B. (1998). Perceptions and correlates of co-worker substance use. *Employee Assistance Quarterly*, 13, 1–22. Substance Abuse and Mental Health Services Administration (2012). *Results from the 2011 National Survey on Drug Use and Health: Detailed tables*. Rockville, MD: Substance Abuse and Mental Health Services Administration, Tables 1.21B and 2.44B.

44. Center for Substance Abuse Prevention (1994). *Making the link: Alcohol, tobacco, and other drugs in the workplace*. Rockville, MD: Center for Substance Abuse Prevention. Substance Abuse and Mental Health Services Administration.

45. American Management Association (2004). *AMA 2004 workplace testing survey: Medical testing*. New York: American Management Association, p. 3. Substance Abuse and Mental Health Services Administration (2008, March 15). *Making your workplace drug-free: A kit for employers*.

Rockville, MD: Substance Abuse and Mental Health Services Administration.

46. Comerford, A. W. (1999). Work dysfunction and addiction. *Journal of Substance Abuse Treatment*, 16, 247–253. Normand, J.; Lempert, R.; and O'Brien, C. (Eds.) (1994). *Under the influence? Drugs and the American work force*. Washington, DC: National Academy Press.

47. Avis, H. (1996). *Drugs and life* (3rd ed.). Dubuque, IA: Brown and Benchmark, p. 256.

48. National Transportation Safety Board (1988). *Alcohol/drug use and its impact on railroad safety: Safety study*. Washington, DC: U.S. Department of Transportation.

49. Blum, T. C., and Roman, P. M. (1995). *Cost-effectiveness and preventive implications of employee assistance programs*. Rockville, MD: Substance Abuse and Mental Health Services Administration. Carpenter, C. S. (2007). Workplace drug testing and worker drug use. *Health Research and Educational Trust*, 42, 795–810.

50. Castro, R. J., and Foy, B. D. (2002). Harm reduction: A promising approach for college health. *Journal of American College Health*, 51, 89–91. Lewis, D. C. (2001). Urging college alcohol and drug policies that target adverse behavior, not use. *Journal of American College Health*, 50, 39–41. Weitzman, E. R.; Nelson, T. F.; Lee, H.; and Wechsler, H. (2004). Reducing drinking and related harms in college: Evaluation of the "A Matter of Degree" program. *American Journal of Preventive Medicine*, 27, 187–196.

51. Cronce. K. M., and Larimer, M. E. (2011). Individual-focused approaches to the prevention of college student drinking. *Alcohol Research and Health*, 34, 210–221. Freedman, S. G. (2007, September 12). Calling the folks about campus drinking. *New York Times*, p. B6. National Institute on Alcohol Abuse and Alcoholism (2002, October). Changing the culture of campus drinking. *Alcohol Alert*, No. 58. Rockville, MD: National Institute on Alcohol Abuse and Alcoholism.

52. Johnston, L. D.; O'Malley, P. M.; Bachman, J. G.; and Schulenberg, J. E. (2012). Monitoring the Future: National survey results on drug use, 1975–2011. Vol. I: Secondary school students 2011. Ann Arbor, MI: Institute for Social Research, The University of Michigan, Table 2-1.

53. Office of Educational Research and Improvement (1990). *A guide for college presidents and governing bodies: Strategies for eliminating alcohol and other drug abuse on campuses*. Washington, DC: U.S. Department of Education.

54. Denizet-Lewis, B. (2005, January 9). Band of brothers. *New York Times Magazine*, pp. 32–39, 52, 73. Quotation on p. 35. Office of Educational Research and Improvement, *A guide for college presidents*.

55. Busteed, B. (2010, March 19). Is high-risk drinking at college on the way out? *Chronicle of Higher Education*, p. A76. Crump, S. (2008, March 6). Fraternity life without keg parties safer, saner, say Phi Delta Theta guys, www.cleveland.com/lifestyles/2008. Schackner, B. (2000, August 18). Fraternity houses turn off the taps and sober up, www.post-gazette.com.

Point/Counterpoint V

Should We Continue to D.A.R.E. or Should We Give It Up?

The following discussion of viewpoints presents the opinions of people on both sides of the controversial issues surrounding the Project D.A.R.E. prevention program. You don't have to come up with the final answer, nor should you necessarily agree with the argument you read last. Many of the ideas in this feature come from sources listed.

POINT

No program in recent years has had the success of Project D.A.R.E. in reaching millions of schoolchildren with a prevention message. D.A.R.E. is now the primary educational program in our war on drugs in America. Every year, in school district after school district, police officers from the community serve to administer D.A.R.E. sessions, and all of them have received eighty hours of training for the job, at no cost to the educational districts that receive this service.

COUNTERPOINT

No one questions the success of D.A.R.E. in terms of its popularity, but how effective is it in reducing drug-taking behavior among the children it serves? More than fifteen evaluation studies of the long-term effects of D.A.R.E. have been conducted by reputable researchers or research centers since the early 1990s, and the results are remarkably consistent. When D.A.R.E. programs are compared with control groups, the studies show little or no differences in the level of drug use or onset of use among adolescents.

POINT

That position continues on and on. It's quite possible the researchers don't know how to measure things. There is more at stake here than good statistics. If those researchers could just see the kids' faces during the D.A.R.E. sessions, they'd know how much good it's doing. Besides, a D.A.R.E. police officer in the classroom is a symbol that the community at large is involved in substance-abuse prevention, that law enforcement is on the side of the kids, that it is a matter not just of reducing the supply of drugs but also of reducing the demand for them at the grass-roots level. It's amazing to see the improvement in the relationships between kids and the police.

COUNTERPOINT

But don't you think there would be some indication of effectiveness among all these studies? It's true that students, teachers, administrators, parents, police, and political leaders feel good about D.A.R.E. because it means something is being done about substance abuse, but we are talking about a program budget of approximately $750 million a year with $600 million coming from federal, state, and local sources. A publicly funded program like D.A.R.E., therefore, ought to be accountable for what it achieves. How can D.A.R.E. maintain this standard of accountability?

POINT

First of all, there were positive effects in the studies you referred to. There was a significant increase in the level of self-esteem among children in the D.A.R.E. program. Second, those evaluation studies were working with the D.A.R.E. program before it was substantially revised. D.A.R.E. sessions are now much more interactive than they were in the past. In other words, the whole curriculum has been redesigned.

COUNTERPOINT

To coin a phrase, show me the data. The evaluation studies in 1999 show no advantages gained from the D.A.R.E. program after a six-year and a ten-year follow-up. The results simply aren't there. In the meantime, given the situation as it stands now, why should D.A.R.E. remain the dominant primary prevention program in the United States?

POINT

Granted that evaluations of the D.A.R.E. program have been less than positive, but we now have an enhanced new D.A.R.E. program that addresses the criticisms that have been directed at it. The revised program is more interactive than instructional, more active-learning oriented than passive. The early evaluation results are positive.

COUNTERPOINT

Yes, D.A.R.E. has changed to a new and improved D.A.R.E., but in doing so the program has simply co-opted the components of other school-based programs that we know are effective. Besides, because the enhanced D.A.R.E. program is so new, the long-term positive effects you refer to remain to be determined. In the meantime, given the situation as it stands now, why should D.A.R.E. retain its exalted position as the dominant drug-related prevention program in the United States? Why should there continue, as late as 2010, to be a National D.A.R.E. Day, proclaimed by the President himself? Why not substitute for it a prevention program with a track record of research-based success? What is so sacred about D.A.R.E.?

Critical Thinking Questions for Further Debate

1. The original D.A.R.E. seemed like such a good idea. Why do you think it failed to reduce drug use?

2. Suppose you are a sixteen-year-old teenager using illicit drugs as well as smoking cigarettes. What program back in the fifth or sixth grade, do you think, would have prevented this from happening? Suppose you are a sixteen-year-old teenager *not* engaging in this behavior. Did D.A.R.E. make a difference in your life?

Sources: Birkeland, S.; Murphy-Graham, E.; and Weiss, C. (2005). Good reasons for ignoring good evaluation: The case of the drug abuse resistance education (D.A.R.E.) program. *Evaluation and Program Planning, 28,* 247-256. Lynam, D. R.; Milich, R.; Zimmerman, R.; Novak, S. P.; Logan, T. K.; et al. (1999). Project D.A.R.E.: No effects at 10-year follow-up. *Journal of Consulting and Clinical Psychology, 67,* 590–593. Toy, V.S. (2004, February 1). D.A.R.E. program: Sacred cow or fatted calf? *New York Times,* Section 14, pp. 1, 5. Wysong, E., and Wright, D. W. (1995). A decade of D.A.R.E.: Efficacy, politics, and drug education. *Sociological Focus, 28,* 283–311. Zernike, K. (2001, February 15). Antidrug program says it will adopt a new strategy. *New York Times,* pp. A1, A29.

Substance-Abuse Treatment: Strategies for Change

I would lie about everything, and I lied to everybody. It was so easy to play off my family's denial. What is all that drug stuff in my room? Oh, I'm just holding it for a friend. It made me so angry that the lies worked so well with them. It became a way of life. But after a while I got sick and tired of all the lying. And I kept thinking about where my life was heading. Half of my friends are dead; the other half are in jail. That's why I'm here to get help.

—Excerpted from the explanation of a seventeen-year-old about why he came to Daytop Village

After you have completed this chapter, you should have an understanding of

▶ The challenges in designing effective substance-abuse treatment programs

▶ The biopsychosocial model for substance-abuse treatment

▶ Prison-alternative and prison-based treatment programs

▶ Drug courts in the criminal justice system

▶ Efforts to create a drug-free workplace in the United States

▶ The stages of change in substance-abuse treatment and recovery

▶ The importance of family dynamics in treatment and recovery

▶ Available options for substance-abuse treatment

In this final chapter, as we turn to the question of substance-abuse treatment and recovery, the focus will be on programs that help individuals who have problems specifically associated with the abuse of illicit drugs and alcohol. On an annual basis, approximately 4 million Americans receive some form of treatment for problems arising from the abuse of alcohol or illicit drugs; about half of these individuals are receiving this treatment in a facility licensed or certified to provide treatment programs. However, approximately 22 million Americans are in need of treatment services in the first place. Therefore, some form of treatment is received by only one out of five Americans who need it. The disparity between the number who need treatment and the number who receive it is one of the challenges we face in health care today.

In most respects, the overall drug profile of substance-abuse treatment admissions has remained

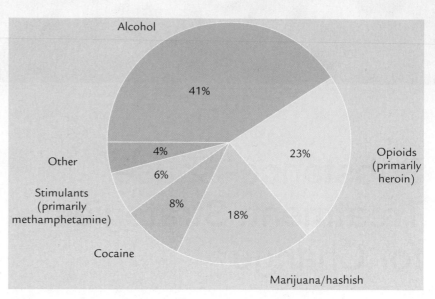

FIGURE 17.1

Five groups of abused substances account for **96 percent** of all reasons for treatment in facilities licensed or certified to provide treatment programs.

Source: Substance Abuse and Mental Health Services Administration (2012). 2000–2010 *Treatment Episode Data Set (TEDS): National admissions to substance abuse treatment services.* Rockville, MD: Office of Applied Studies, Substance Abuse, and Mental Health Services Administration, p. 1.

essentially unchanged from 2000 to 2010. Five groups of abused substances account for 96 percent of all reasons for individuals seeking and receiving treatment (Figure 17.1), and alcohol is, by far, the most prominent substance of abuse for individuals seeking and receiving treatment, comprising 41 percent of all admissions. The other drug groups are, in descending order, opioids (23 percent), marijuana (18 percent), cocaine (8 percent), and methamphetamine/amphetamines (6 percent). While heroin accounted for 91 percent of opioid treatment admissions in 2000, the percentage fell to 62 percent in 2010, due to the increase in problems related to opioid pain medications (see Chapter 5).[1]

Previous chapters of this book covered treatment options for clinical diagnoses of substance abuse or dependence (according to DSM-IV-TR) or substance use disorder (according to DSM-5) that were related to cocaine and amphetamines (Chapter 4), heroin (Chapter 5), marijuana (Chapter 7), and alcohol (Chapter 9). Smoking cessation options for nicotine dependence were covered in Chapter 10. In this chapter, we will deal with issues surrounding treatment in general. As we will see, there are important considerations that are relevant for any treatment program, regardless of the substance (or substances) of abuse.

by the numbers . . .

21.6 million	Estimated number of individuals aged twelve or older in the United States who needed treatment for a problem with alcohol or illicit drugs in 2011
2.3 million	Estimated number of individuals who received such treatment in 2011
$4 to $7	Estimated reduction in the cost of drug-related crime, criminal justice costs, and theft alone for every $1 invested in substance-abuse treatment programs. When savings related to health care are included, total savings exceed costs by a ratio of 12 to 1.

Source: National Institute on Drug Abuse (2009, April). *Principles of drug addiction treatment: A research-based guide* (2nd ed.). Rockville, MD: National Institute on Drug Abuse, p. 13. Substance Abuse and Mental Health Services Administration (2012). *Results from the 2011 National Survey on Drug Use and Health: Summary of national findings.* Rockville, MD: Substance Abuse and Mental Health Services Administration, pp. 83–88.

Designing Effective Substance-Abuse Treatment Programs

In designing effective substance-abuse treatment programs, it is important to recognize a key fact of life with regard to drug-taking behavior: Not one but several types of drugs, either licit or illicit, are often represented in an individual's "abuse or dependence profile." Nearly 40 percent of clients report the abuse of alcohol along with at least one other drug. A heroin abuser, for example, will also frequently smoke marijuana or dabble in any of a variety of available street drugs. As discussed in the context of emergency department visits in Chapter 2, these individuals are referred to as **polydrug abusers**. It is clear that the most effective treatment program is one that acknowledges the problems of an individual with a history of *multiple substance abuse*.

It is also important to recognize that about 30 percent of clients in substance-abuse treatment are also contending with a co-occurring mental health condition such as depression, generalized anxiety, or other types of psychiatric disorder. These individuals are often referred to as *dual-diagnosis patients* or *dual-diagnosis clients*. In many cases, substance-abuse behavior has been a form of "self-medication" undertaken to reduce feelings of depression or anxiety. In these circumstances, a psychiatrist, psychologist, or clinical social worker plays a crucial role in finding the most appropriate mix of pharmacological (medication) and behavioral treatment.[2]

The Biopsychosocial Model for Substance-Abuse Treatment

In a number of cases, a treatment program tailored for individuals who have problems with one particular class of drugs will be inappropriate for individuals who have problems with a different class of drugs. A methadone maintenance program or buprenorphine treatment, for example, is not appropriate for cocaine dependence or alcoholism, because the intent of the treatment is to substitute, for an illicit, unpredictable opioid (heroin), an opioid that can be medically supervised (methadone or buprenorphine). The use of disulfiram (Antabuse) is restricted to the treatment of chronic alcohol abuse, because it is a specific inhibitor of enzymes involved in the breakdown of alcohol, and its effects are not felt if alcohol is not in the system.

However, several approaches to substance-abuse treatment cut across different forms of drug-taking behavior.

We have seen how a *twelve-step program* can be useful not only for those individuals contending with chronic alcohol abuse or alcoholism in the traditional Alcoholics Anonymous format, but also for individuals seeking help with chronic heroin abuse (Narcotics Anonymous) or cocaine abuse (Cocaine Anonymous). You may recall that one particular location in the brain, the nucleus accumbens, is known to be stimulated by a variety of dependence-producing drugs (opioids, cocaine, alcohol, and nicotine). The current use of naltrexone (brand names: ReVia, Vivitrol) and nalmefene (brand name: Revex), both opioid antagonists, in the treatment of alcoholism and heroin abuse is a good example of the "crossover value" of current substance-abuse treatment strategies. Given the evidence for a common neural and neurochemical basis for drug dependence in general, it makes sense that a common approach should work in its treatment.[3]

Inevitably, success in a treatment program rests upon the recognition that there are multiple pathways to substance abuse. For each individual, some specific combination of biological, psychological, and social factors has played a role in getting that person to the point where treatment is necessary. This integrated approach to treatment has often been called the **biopsychosocial model** (Figure 17.2). Unfortunately, through much of the history of the United States, there has been a tendency to view the problems of substance abuse, particularly illicit substance abuse, from a limited, punitive perspective. The next section reviews intervention and treatment efforts in the context of law enforcement and punishment.

Intervention through Incarceration and Other Punitive Measures

A natural response to the presence of an individual whose behavior poses a significant threat to society is to remove that individual from society and provide some form of containment or **incarceration** in a prison, jail, or other secure environment. Besides protecting society

---

polydrug abusers: Individuals whose drug-taking behavior involves the abuse of multiple licit or illicit drugs. Also referred to as *multiple substance abusers*.

biopsychosocial model: A perspective on drug-abuse treatment that recognizes the biological, psychological, and social factors underlying drug-taking behavior and encourages an integrated approach, based on these factors, in designing an individual's treatment program.

incarceration: Imprisonment for a fixed length of time.

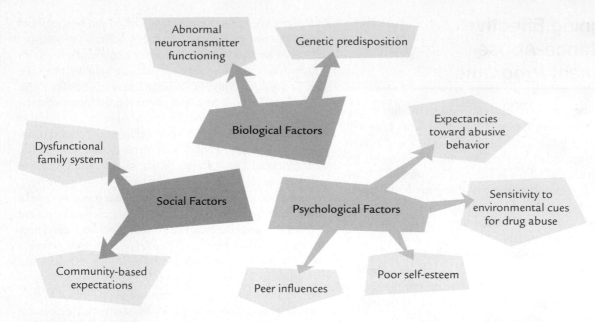

FIGURE 17.2

The biopsychosocial model asserts that there are multiple pathways to drug abuse.

Source: Modified from Margolis, R. D., and Zweben, J. E. (1998). *Treating patients with alcohol and other drug problems: An integrated approach.* Washington, DC: American Psychological Association, pp. 76–87.

at large, incarceration is intended to be preventive in the long run by (1) reducing the likelihood that the individual will behave in a similar way in the future, after the sentence is completed, and (2) conveying the message to others who might contemplate engaging in similar behavior that a comparable punishment would apply to them as well. The first goal is referred to as **rehabilitation**; the second goal is referred to as **deterrence**.

Substance-Abuse Treatment and Law Enforcement

Drug-control laws in general have been formulated over the years according to the philosophy that punitive measures such as incarceration or financial penalties (fines)

lead to rehabilitation on a personal level and to deterrence on a societal level. The five categories or schedules of controlled substances, adopted by the Comprehensive Drug Abuse Prevention and Control Act of 1970, were designed not only to set limitations on public access to different types of drugs but also to establish different levels of criminal penalties for unauthorized behavior related to these drugs, based on their potential for abuse.

Specifically, the law defined **drug trafficking** as the unauthorized manufacture, distribution by sale or gift, or possession (with intent to distribute) of any controlled substance (Tables 17.1 and 17.2).

rehabilitation: A process of change through which there is a reduced likelihood that a pattern of problematic behavior will recur.

deterrence: The reduced likelihood that a person might engage in a pattern of problematic behavior in the future.

drug trafficking: The unauthorized manufacture of any controlled substance, its distribution by sale or gift, or possession of such a substance with intent to distribute it.

Police officers arrest drug offenders in a drug bust in Tampa, Florida.

TABLE 17.1

Federal Trafficking Penalties—Controlled Substances Other Than Marijuana

DRUG/SCHEDULE	QUANTITY	PENALTIES	QUANTITY	PENALTIES
Powder cocaine (Schedule II)	500–4999 g mixture*	**First Offense** Not less than 5 yr, and not more than 40 yr. If death or serious injury, not less than 20 yr or more than life. Fine of not more than $2 million if an individual, $5 million if not an individual. **Second Offense** Not less than 10 yr, and not more than life. If death or serious injury, life imprisonment. Fine of not more than $4 million if an individual, $10 million if not an individual.	5 kg or more mixture	**First Offense** Not less than 10 yr, and not more than life. If death or serious injury, not less than 20 yr or more than life. Fine of not more than $4 million if an individual, $10 million if not an individual. **Second Offense** Not less than 20 yr, and not more than life. If death or serious injury, life imprisonment. Fine of not more than $8 million if an individual, $20 million if not an individual. **2 or More Prior Offenses** Life imprisonment
Cocaine base including crack cocaine (Schedule II)	28–279 g mixture*		50 g or more mixture	
Fentanyl (Schedule II)	40–399 g mixture		400 g or more mixture	
Fentanyl analogue (Schedule 1)	10–99 g mixture		100 g or more mixture	
Heroin (Schedule 1)	100–999 g mixture		1 kg or more mixture	
LSD (Schedule 1)	1–9 g mixture		10 g or more mixture	
Methamphetamine (Schedule II)	5–49 g pure or 50–499 g mixture		50 g or more pure or 500 g or more mixture	
PCP (Schedule II)	10–99 g pure or 100–999 g mixture		100 g or more pure or 1 kg or more mixture	

DRUG/SCHEDULE	QUANTITY	PENALTIES
Other Schedule I and II drugs (and any drug product containing gamma hydroxybutyric acid)	Any amount	**First Offense** Not more that 20 yr. If death or serious injury, not less than 20 yr, or more than life. Fine of $1 million if an individual, $5 million if not an individual. **Second Offense** Not more than 30 yr. If death or serious injury, not less than life. Fine of $2 million if an individual, $10 million if not an individual.
Flunitrazepam (Schedule IV)	1 g or more	
Other Schedule III drugs	Any amount	**First Offense** Not more than 5 yr. Fine of not more than $250,000 if an individual, $1 million if not an individual. **Second Offense** Not more than 10 yr. Fine of not more than $500.000 if an individual, $2 million if not an individual.
Flunitrazepam (Schedule IV)	30 to 999 mg	
All other Schedule IV drugs	Any amount	**First Offense** Not more than 3 yr. Fine of not more than $250,000 if an individual, $1 million it not an individual. **Second Offense** Not more than 6 yr. Fine of not more than $500,000 if an individual, $2 million if not an individual.
Flunitrazepam (Schedule IV)	Less than 30 mg	
All Schedule V drugs	Any amount	**First Offense** Not more than 1 yr. Fine of not more than $100,000 if an individual, $250,000 if not an individual. **Second Offense** Not more than 2 yr. Fine not more than $200,000 if an individual, $500,000 if not an individual.

*Under the Fair Sentencing Act of 2010, equivalent penalties for possessing quantities of powder cocaine or crack cocaine have been changed from a 100-to-1 ratio to an 18-to-1 ratio.

Note: Trafficking penalties distinguish between Schedule I drugs excluding marijuana and marijuana itself (Table 17.2).

Sources: Associated Press (2010, August 4). Obama signs new cocaine bill. Drug Enforcement Administration, U.S. Department of Justice, Washington, DC.

TABLE 17.2

Federal Trafficking Penalties—Marijuana

DRUG	QUANTITY	1ST OFFENSE	2ND OFFENSE
Marijuana	1,000 kg or more mixture; or 1,000 or more plants	• Not less than 10 yr, not more than life • If death or serious injury, not less than 20 yr, not more than life • Fine of not more than $4 million if an individual, $10 million if other than an individual	• Not less than 20 yr, not more than life • If death or serious injury, mandatory life • Fine of not more than $8 million if an individual, $20 million if other than an individual
Marijuana	100 kg to 999 kg mixture; or 100 to 999 plants	• Not less than 5 yr, not more than 40 yr • If death or serous injury, not less than 20 yr, not more than life • Fine of not more than $2 million if an individual, $5 million if other than an individual	• Not less than 10 yr, not more than life • If death or serious injury, mandatory life • Fine of not more than $4 million if an individual, $10 million if other than an individual
Marijuana	more than 10 kg hashish; 50 to 99 kg mixture more than 1 kg of hashish oil; 50 to 99 plants	• Not more than 20 yr • If death or serious injury, not less than 20 yr, not more than life • Fine of $1 million if an individual, $5 million if other than an individual	• Not more than 30 yr • If death or serious injury, mandatory life • Fine of $2 million if an individual, $10 million if other than individual
Marijuana	1 to 49 plants; less than 50 kg mixture	• Not more than 5 yr • Fine of not more than $250,000, $1 million if other than individual	• Not more than 10 yr • Fine of $500,000 if an individual, $2 million if other than individual
Hashish	10 kg or less		
Hashish oil	1 kg or less		

Sources: Associated Press (2010, August 4). Obama signs new cocaine bill. Drug Enforcement Administration, U.S. Department of Justice, Washington, DC.

The severity of the penalties that were established by federal laws enacted in 1970, and revised in 1986 and 1988, has varied according to the schedule of the controlled substance involved. Schedule I violations are the most severely punished and Schedule V violations the least (Chapter 2). As a result of the Anti-Drug-Abuse Acts of 1986 and 1988, a number of special circumstances also are considered in arriving at the penalty imposed:

■ Penalties are doubled for first-offense trafficking of Schedule I or II controlled substances if death or bodily injury results from the use of such substances.

■ Penalties for the sale of drugs by a person over twenty-one years old to someone under the age of eighteen are increased to up to double those imposed for sale to an adult.

simple possession: Having on one's person any illegal or nonprescribed controlled substance for one's own use.

■ Penalties for the sale of drugs within 1,000 feet of an elementary or secondary school are increased to up to double those imposed when the sale is made elsewhere.

■ Fines for companies or business associations are generally 2½ times greater than those for individuals. In either case, penalties include the forfeiture of cars, boats, or planes that have been used in the illegal conveyance of controlled substances.

■ If a family is living in public housing, the entire family can be evicted if a family member is convicted of criminal activity, including drug trafficking, on or near the public-housing premises.

Federal penalties for **simple possession**, defined as having on one's person any illegal or nonprescribed controlled substance in *any* of the five schedules for one's own use, are much simpler. First-offense violators face a maximum of one year of imprisonment and a fine of between $1,000 and $5,000. Second-offense violators

Drugs . . . in Focus

Penalties for Crack versus Penalties for Cocaine: Correcting an Injustice

Under the 1986 Anti-Drug Abuse Act, the penalties for possession of crack (the smokable form of cocaine) were much more severe than those for possession of cocaine itself (the powder form). A mandatory minimum prison sentence of five years was imposed upon conviction of possessing more than 500 grams of powder forms of cocaine, whereas the possession of as little as 5 grams of crack could result in the same penalty. This became known as the 100-to-1 penalty ratio. In 1988, the federal penalty for possession of more than 5 grams of cocaine powder was set at a minimum of one-year imprisonment; the penalty for possessing an equivalent amount of crack was set at a minimum of five years.

This disparity, according to critics of this policy, had resulted in far more African Americans in prison for five years or more than white drug offenders. Why? Statistics showed that whites were more likely to snort or inject cocaine, whereas African Americans were more likely to smoke cocaine in its cheaper crack form. The differential effects of drug-law enforcement for the two forms of cocaine were reflected in a drug offense inmate population that was clearly divided along racial lines. On the one hand, 90 percent of crack cocaine convictions involved African Americans; on the other, nearly two-thirds of powder cocaine abusers in the United States were white. Moreover, it was more common for offenses relating to the possession of powder cocaine to be prosecuted under state regulations, under which mandatory minimum sentences frequently did not apply.

In 2007, the United States Sentencing Commission, the agency that establishes guidelines for federal prison

sentences, unanimously voted to lighten punishments retroactively for some crimes related to crack cocaine possession. As a result, the stark disparity that had existed for more than twenty years in penalties for powder cocaine and crack cocaine was narrowed, and more than 19,000 prisoners became eligible for early release. As many as 17,000 others incarcerated for a crack-related offense, however, could not benefit from the change. These prisoners had been given the absolute minimum term in the first place or were arrested with huge amounts of crack cocaine.

In 2010, the Fair Sentencing Act was signed into law, narrowing the gap between penalties involving crack cocaine and powder cocaine. Under the new regulations, the amount of crack cocaine subject to the five-year minimum sentence was increased from 5 grams to 28. The former 100-to-1 rule (500 versus 5) now would be the 18-to-1 rule (500 versus 28). In addition, the Sentencing Commission has been directed to review and amend its guidelines to increase penalties for persons convicted of using violence while trafficking in illicit drugs. The Congressional Budget Office estimates that the new law will reduce the current prison population by 1,550 person-years (years of incarceration) over the 2011–2015 period, with a savings of $42 million dollars in prison expenditures.

Sources: Congressional Budget Office (2010, March 19). Cost estimate. S.1789 Fair Sentencing Act of 2010. www.cbo.gov/ftpdocs/114xx/doc11413/s1789.pdf. Hatsukami, D. K., and Fischman, M.W. (1996). Crack cocaine and cocaine hydrochloride. Are the differences myth or reality? *Journal of the American Medical Association, 276,* 1580–1588. Stout, D. (2007, December 12). Retroactively, panel reduces drug sentences. *New York Times,* pp. A1, A31. Weinreb, A. (2010, August 4). Obama signs fair sentencing act into law. http://news.suite101.com.

face a minimum of fifteen days up to a maximum of two years and a fine of up to $10,000 (Drugs. . . in Focus).[4]

Federal penalties set the standard for the punishment of drug offenses in the United States, but most drug-related offenses are prosecuted at the state rather than the federal level, and state regulations for simple possession and drug trafficking can vary widely. In cases of simple possession of small amounts of marijuana, most U.S. states are generally more lenient than the federal government or even consider such cases as not illegal at all (see Chapter 7), whereas in cases of heroin possession, some states might be more stringent. Certain aspects of

drug-taking behavior, such as the day-to-day regulation of alcohol sales and distribution, are regulated primarily by state and local municipalities, unless interstate commerce is involved. The federal government, as well as the states and local municipalities, have also taken on regulatory authority with regard to **drug paraphernalia**—products whose predominant use is to administer, prepare,

drug paraphernalia: Products that are considered to be used to administer, prepare, package, or store illicit drugs.

package, or store illicit drugs. Nearly all U.S. states have statutes making it unlawful to sell these items to minors, unless they are accompanied by a parent or legal guardian. In addition, the importation, exportation, and advertising of drug paraphernalia are prohibited.[5]

Unfortunately, the enforcement of drug laws since the passage of the Comprehensive Drug Abuse Prevention and Control Act has created a bloated prison system around the nation. Drug-law offenders serving time in federal prisons currently constitute approximately 51 percent of the total prisoner population, an increase from 16 percent in 1970. In 2011, approximately 1.6 million arrests were made in this category, accounting for about one in eight of the total number. It is estimated that a drug arrest was made every 20 seconds. About 82 percent were for drug possession.

Although drug-related offenses are the reason for the incarceration of approximately one out of two of all inmates presently in federal prisons, it is more likely that a drug offender is serving his or her time in a state prison, because state inmates in general outnumber federal inmates by more than six to one. [6]

What happens to people who are arrested and convicted of drug-law violations? Does the criminal justice system provide a deterrent against drug abuse by others in society? Considering the enormous number of drug offenders in the current prison population and the continuing level of substance abuse in the United States, the criminal justice system appears to be ineffective as a deterrent measure. To what extent, then, does the criminal justice system offer opportunities for rehabilitation?

Prison-Alternative Treatment Programs

A large number of drug offenders who could potentially be incarcerated are instead offered treatment as an alternative to imprisonment or other punitive measures. Approximately 50 percent of all individuals who enter a publicly funded drug treatment program have done so because of direct or indirect legal pressure. Since the late 1980s, it has been common for arrestees demonstrating drug dependence to be "steered" toward drug treatment as a condition for having prosecution postponed, a prison sentence reduced or avoided, or some form of probationary status approved.

> **drug court:** Specialized court system that handles adult, nonviolent offenders who have violated drug laws and incorporates a supervised treatment program instead of standard criminal sentencing.

Most U.S. states presently make provisions, in some manner, for a treatment option in drug-offense sentencing, but some states have gone further. In 2000, California enacted a law that *requires* judges to offer nonviolent drug offenders probation with substance-abuse treatment instead of incarceration for their first two offenses. The judge may choose from diverse state-licensed treatment programs and may require community service, literacy training, family counseling, and vocational training as conditions for probation. The benefits of this approach have been indicated by follow-up studies in Arizona, a state that instituted a similar policy in 1996. Results showed that 75 percent of its participants remained drug-free in the program's first year, saving the state approximately $2.5 million.[7]

Drug Courts

A growing presence in the criminal justice system has been the establishment of specialized judicial proceedings called **drug courts** in which adult, nonviolent drug offenders are provided intensively supervised treatment as a "sentence" instead of being incarcerated. More than 2,600 drug courts presently operate in the United States.[8]

The initial step in drug-court programs begins with defense attorneys, probation officers, or prosecutors referring a potential candidate to the drug court itself. Candidates must be judged to be serious drug abusers, cannot be on parole, and cannot have a prior conviction for a serious or violent felony. Upon accepting a drug-court procedure, the candidate waives his or her right to a jury trial and enters a treatment program for a year, during which he or she is subject to random drug tests. Participants are supervised by a probation officer to ensure that they adhere to program rules. In many cases, a therapeutic community approach, such as Daytop Village, Samaritan Village, or a similar organization (Portrait) is chosen as the placement for treatment.

Numerous studies have shown that drug-court programs are successful in providing effective rehabilitation. First of all, they decrease the rate of criminal recidivism (repeated arrests). In a study sampling approximately 17,000 drug-court graduates nationwide within one year of their graduation from the program, only 16 percent had been rearrested and charged with a felony offense—approximately one-third the level of recidivism observed in drug offenders not participating in a drug court. Second, drug-court programs are cost-effective. Approximately $250 million in incarceration costs has been saved each year in New York State alone by diverting 18,000 nonviolent drug offenders into treatment. Third, drug courts increase the length

In 1957, Monsignor William O'Brien was a simple parish priest in Tuckahoe, New York, a quiet suburban town north of New York City. He was quite unprepared for the gritty facts of life on urban streets when he was assigned to serve at St. Patrick's Cathedral in the center of Manhattan. For the first time, he came face to face with the desperate and the despondent victims of drug abuse. Both crushed and touched, he wanted to help them as a priest and counselor, but he soon discovered how difficult such cases can be. In his own words,

I was the biggest disaster in New York. Because it's just the thing you can't do with alcoholics and drug addicts. They'd go in the parish house bathroom and shoot up behind your back.

After two years of failure, Monsignor O'Brien realized that he had to deal with the "human" before he could deal with the "divine." In 1963, he helped establish a small center in New York, based on a then-unique concept of drug-treatment intervention: an intensive, therapeutic community where drug-dependent people could relearn how to live their lives and move toward a drug-free way of thinking. The center was called Daytop (short for Drug Addicts

Yielding to Persuasion) Village, and it was the beginning of what is today the oldest and largest drug-free, therapeutic community program for substance dependence in the United States. By the 1980s, Daytop Village had expanded beyond its twenty-seven centers in this country to more than sixty-six locations around the world.

More than 100,000 individuals have participated in Daytop, and the overwhelming majority of them have reclaimed their lives as a result of its programs. As a reflection of the growing levels of drug use among young people in the 1990s, it is not surprising that teenagers, who once accounted for scarcely 25 percent of the Daytop client population, now at times represent up to half the total. Referrals to Daytop increase steadily, and there is an extensive waiting list for new entrants.

Daytop and a number of similar therapeutic community organizations continue to evolve in substance-dependence treatment strategies, adopting evidence-based practices such as motivational interviewing, cognitive-behavioral therapy, and gender-specific programming for women. In recent years, Daytop and others have broadened the range of services provided to clients, creating outpatient facilities to accommodate

the needs of those whose problems and circumstances indicate a shorter residency or outpatient treatment. There is also increasing collaboration with drug courts, when legally mandated (court-ordered) treatment is feasible and recommended.

Despite these successes, however, the organization has recently suffered major financial difficulties. In April 2012, Daytop Village New York filed for Chapter 11 bankruptcy protection after five years of losses and increasing pressure from creditors. The expectation is that this move will enable Daytop to continue its operations as it pays off bank loans and other liabilities through the sale of specific assets.

Sources: Associated Press (2012, April 7). Drug rehabilitation agency files for bankruptcy protection. *New York Times,* p. 14. DeLeon, G. (2000). *The therapeutic community: Theory, model, and method.* New York: Springer. Marriot, M. (1989, November 13). A pioneer in residential drug treatment reaches out. *New York Times,* p. B2. Nieves, E. (1996, August 25). Wresting a life from the grip of addiction. *New York Times,* p. 41. O'Brien, W. B., and Henican, E.(1993). *You can't do it alone.* New York: Simon and Schuster. Daytop Village, Inc., New York, NY, 1997. Updated information courtesy of Daytop Village, Inc., 2013. www.daytop.org.

of time an individual remains in treatment. The coercive power of the criminal justice system with respect to getting into treatment and staying in treatment is dramatic. Ordinarily, between 40 and 80 percent of drug abusers drop out of treatment within ninety days, and between 80 and 90 percent drop out within twelve months. In sharp contrast, more than two-thirds of drug-court participants complete a treatment program lasting a year or more. The benefits of drug-court programs have been demonstrated in nonurban as well as urban communities.[9]

According to experts in the field of drug-abuse treatment, the mandated treatment approach in drug-court

programs is more likely to result in a successful outcome than in circumstances where the decision to go into treatment is made on a voluntary basis. Recently, the drug-court concept has been expanded to the establishment of drug courts specifically for juvenile drug offenders.[10]

Clearly, the drug-court movement represents a shift away from a criminal justice policy oriented toward punishing illicit drug users to a policy that focuses on treatment and recovery. Since the early 1990s, a number of problem-solving court programs, modeled after drug courts, have been created to foster treatment for other psychosocial difficulties. Mental-health courts, for example, provide a means for mentally ill defendants who have committed nonviolent criminal offenses to receive psychiatric evaluation and treatment. Driving-under-intoxication (DUI) courts and courts addressing problems of domestic violence have been developed as well.

Prison-Based Treatment Programs

For those drug offenders who *are* sentenced to prison, a previous history of drug abuse or dependence continues to present difficulties that do not go away just because the inmate is now behind bars. It is estimated that one out of every two prisoners (including prisoners sentenced for other than drug offenses) meet the criteria for substance abuse or substance dependence. Yet less than 20 percent of these prisoners receive any formal treatment at all. For those who do receive treatment, there is little or no continuity of substance-abuse treatment after the prisoner is released. Without a program of post-incarceration treatment in place, a range of stressors increase the risk of relapse. These stressors include the stigma of being labeled an ex-offender, the need for housing and legal employment, being reunited with an often indifferent or hostile family, and returning to a high-risk environment for drug-taking behavior. Public health officials have described the dismal state of prison-based treatment programs as representing a fundamental "disconnect" between two cultures: the criminal justice system organized to punish the offender in the interest of public safety, and the substance-abuse treatment system organized to help the individual achieve some level of recovery in the interest of public health.[11]

Substance-Abuse Treatment in the Workplace

The same executive order issued by President Reagan in 1986 that mandated drug testing among federal employees (see Chapter 16) also directed all U.S. federal agencies to establish **employee assistance programs (EAPs)** in order to identify and counsel workers who

employee assistance programs (EAPs): Corporate-based services designed to identify and counsel employees with personal problems that are connected to substance abuse or dependence and to provide referrals to community agencies where these individuals can get further help.

member assistance programs (MAPs): Corporate-based services similar to employee assistance programs (EAPs) that are sponsored and supervised by labor unions.

have personal problems associated with substance abuse or dependence and to provide referrals to community agencies where these individuals can get further help. Nongovernmental organizations have since been encouraged (but not required) by the Drug-Free Workplace Act of 1988 to establish EAP services as well. Thus, though they are not technically required to do so, steadily increasing numbers of American businesses have set up EAPs and are becoming committed to treatment as well as prevention. Traditionally, the emphasis in EAPs, as well as in union-supported **member assistance programs (MAPs)**, has been on problems resulting from alcohol abuse; this is understandable, given that alcohol abuse represents such a large proportion of substance abuse in general (Chapter 9). In recent years, EAPs and MAPs have expanded their services to focus on psychological problems that do not necessarily concern substance abuse. An optimal strategy for both treatment and prevention has been a collaborative effort between management and unions that combines EAP and MAP

It's amazing how Dave's car broke down for the fifth straight Monday.

Dave doesn't really have a car problem. He has a drug problem. And if he works for you, it's your problem. Drug users have almost double the normal absentee rate, which you certainly can't afford.

So call **1-800-843-4971** for a free guide on how to set up a drug-free workplace.

It's surprisingly easy. And a lot cheaper than Dave's car problem.

1-800-843-4971
Partnership for a Drug-Free America

Drug and alcohol problems are major sources of worker absenteeism and decreased productivity.

approaches into one comprehensive substance-abuse program. Even a modest amount of treatment that results from an EAP or MAP intervention can prove beneficial to both the employee and the employer. In one study, heavy drinkers who received brief interventions over a two-month period had significantly fewer accidents, hospital visits, and other events related to problem drinking during the following year. The cost of each brief intervention was $166 per employee, and the medical savings to the employee amounted to $523.[12]

The Personal Journey to Treatment and Recovery

A person's early days in recovery might be compared to a climber's first step up a great mountain. There's a lot of work ahead. As time passes, healing occurs not only for the person in recovery but also for relatives, coworkers, business associates, and the community at large.

At its core, the philosophy of recovery embraces and encourages an individual's capacity for change and personal transformation. But that change does not happen overnight. Challenges can and often do crop up every step of the way.[13]

Individuals who seek help in a treatment program have typically been "jolted" by some external force in their lives. They may have no other option except imprisonment for drug offenses; they may be at risk of losing their job because their supervisor has identified an unproductive pattern of behavior; a spouse may have threatened to leave if something is not done; a friend may have died from a drug overdose or a drug-related accident. Any of these crises or others similar to them can force the question and the decision to seek treatment.

The prospect of entering a treatment program is probably the most frightening experience the abuser has ever had in his or her life. Treatment counselors frequently hear the questions "Couldn't I just cut down?" and "Couldn't I just give up drugs temporarily?" and "How will I be able to take the pain of withdrawal?" and "How will I be able to stand the humiliation?" Far from stalling tactics, these questions represent real fears and significant obstacles to taking the crucial first steps to recovery.[14]

Rehabilitation and the Stages of Change

Rehabilitation from substance abuse and dependence has three major goals. First, the long decline in physical and psychological functioning that has accumulated over the years must be reversed. Drugs take a heavy toll on the user's medical condition and his or her personal relationships. Second, the use of all psychoactive substances must stop, not simply the one or two that are causing the immediate problem, and not merely for a limited period of time. Thus, the motivation to stop using alcohol and other drugs and to remain abstinent on a permanent basis must be strong and stay strong. Third, a life-style free of alcohol and other drugs must be rebuilt, from scratch if necessary. This frequently means giving up the old friends and the old places where drugs were part of an abuser's life, and finding new friends and places that reinforce a drug-free existence. A determination to stay clean and sober requires avoiding high-risk situations, defined as those that increase the possibility of relapse.

Unfortunately, it is hard to ascertain the success rates of substance-abuse and dependence treatment options. Relatively few treatment programs allow outside evaluators to determine whether or not treatment has conferred a genuine benefit. The need for evidence-based treatment strategies is no less urgent than the need for evidence-based prevention strategies, and the judgment of effectiveness must be made in the same way (see Chapter 16). A major public official in the field of substance-abuse treatment has expressed the lack of proper evaluation of treatment outcomes: "You're discharged [after 60 visits or 60 days] and everyone's crying and hugging and feeling proud—and you're supposed to be cured."[15]

However uncertain the outcome of substance-abuse treatment, there is little disagreement about the process an individual must follow to reach some level of recovery: There are five distinct "stages of change" through which the recovering individual must pass.[16] These stages are (1) precontemplation, (2) contemplation, (3) preparation, (4) action, and (5) maintenance. The following is a description of each stage in detail.

- *Precontemplation.* Individuals who are in the **precontemplation stage** may *wish* to change but lack the serious intention to undergo change in the foreseeable future or may be unaware of how significant their problems have become. They may be entering treatment at this time only because they perceive that a crisis is at hand. They may even

precontemplation stage: A stage of change in which the individual may wish to change but either lacks the serious intention to undergo change in the foreseeable future or is unaware of how significant his or her problem has become.

demonstrate a change in behavior while the pressure is on, but once the pressure is off, they revert to their former ways. It is often difficult for a counselor to deal with a drug abuser during the precontemplation stage, because the abuser still feels committed to positive aspects of drug use. A principal goal at this point is to induce inconsistencies in the abuser's perception of drugs in general.

■ *Contemplation.* In the **contemplation stage,** individuals are aware that a problem exists and are thinking about overcoming it but have not yet made a commitment to take action. At this point, drug abusers may struggle with the prospect of the tremendous amount of effort and energy needed to overcome the problem. Counselors can help them by highlighting the negative aspects of drug use, making reasonable assurances about the recovery process, and building the self-confidence necessary to change.

■ *Preparation.* Individuals in the **preparation stage** are those who are seriously considering taking action in the next thirty days and have unsuccessfully taken action over the past twelve months. Alcohol abusers or tobacco smokers may at this point set a "quit date," and a heroin abuser may make a firm date to enter a therapeutic community within the next month. Because drug abusers are fully capable of stating a clear commitment to change at the preparation stage, counselors can begin to discuss the specific steps in the recovery process, strategies for avoiding problems or postponements, and ways to involve friends and family members.

■ *Action.* The **action stage** is the point at which individuals actually modify their behavior, their experiences, and their environment in an effort to overcome their problem. Drug use has now stopped. This is the most fragile stage; abusers are at a high

risk of giving in to drug cravings and experiencing mixed feelings about the psychological costs of staying clean. If they successfully resist these urges to return to drug use, the counselor should strongly reinforce their restraint. If they slip back into drug use temporarily and then return to abstinence, the counselor should praise their efforts to turn their life around. An important message to be conveyed at this stage is that a fundamental change in life-style and a strong support system of friends and family will reduce the chances of relapse.

■ *Maintenance.* Individuals in the **maintenance stage** have been drug-free for a minimum of six months. They have developed new skills and strategies to avoid backsliding and are consolidating a lifestyle free of drugs. Here, the counselor must simultaneously acknowledge the success that has been achieved and emphasize that the struggle will never be totally over. The maintenance stage is ultimately open-ended, in that it continues for the rest of the ex-user's life. Therefore, it may be necessary to have booster sessions from time to time so that the maintenance stage is itself maintained.

Rather than thinking of these stages as a linear progression, it is more accurate to think of them as points along a spiral (Figure 17.3); a person will probably recycle through the stages many times before he or she is totally rehabilitated. Unfortunately, relapse is the rule rather than the exception in the process of recovery.

Stages of Change and Other Problems in Life

If the stages of change listed above seem vaguely familiar to you, even without a drug-related problem, it is no accident. Problems may take many different forms, but the difficulties that we face when we confront these problems have a great deal in common. We may wish to lose weight, get more exercise, stop smoking, end an unhappy relationship, seek out a physician to help with a medical condition, or any of a number of actions that might lead toward a healthier and more productive life. We only have to witness the popularity of New Year's Eve resolutions to appreciate the fact that our desire to take steps to change is part of being human. And yet, we often feel frustrated when our good intentions do not prevail and those New Year's Eve resolutions are left unfulfilled. You may find it helpful to look at your own personal journey toward resolving a problem in your life in terms of the five stages of change.[17]

contemplation stage: A stage of change in which the individual is aware that a problem exists and is thinking about overcoming it but has not yet made a commitment to take action.

preparation stage: A stage of change in which the individual seriously considers taking action to overcome a problem in the next thirty days and has unsuccessfully taken action over the past twelve months.

action stage: A stage of change in which the individual actually modifies his or her behavior and environment to overcome a problem.

maintenance stage: A stage of change in which the individual has become drug-free for a minimum of six months and has developed new skills and strategies that reduce the probability of relapse.

FIGURE 17.3

A spiral model of the stages of
change in the recovery from
drug abuse and dependence.

Source: Prochaska, J. O.;
DiClemente, C. C.; and Norcross,
J. C. (1992). In search of how
people change: Applications to
addictive behaviors. *American
Psychologist, 47,* 1102–1114.

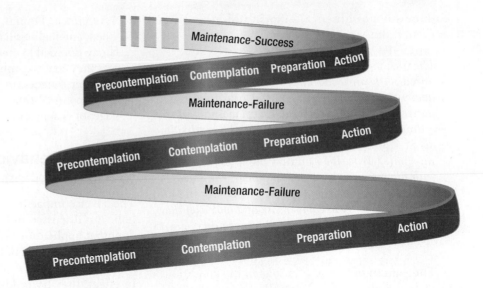

Quick Concept Check 17.1

Understanding the Stages of Change in Substance-Abuse Treatment

Check your understanding of the stages of change by
matching each quotation on the left with the appropriate
stage in treatment on the right. Quotations are assumed
to be statements made by a substance abuser at a particular point in the process of treatment and recovery.

1. "Yeah, I know I drink too much,
   but I'm not ready to do something about it yet."

2. "I may need a boost right now to
   help me hold on to the changes
   I've made. It's been nearly two
   years since I used drugs."

3. "I don't have any big problems. I
   have a right to do whatever I want."

4. "Although I like snorting coke, it
   might be time to quit."

5. "It's New Year's Eve and I've set two
   weeks from now as the day I'm quitting. I want everyone to know that."

6. "It's been six weeks since I smoked
   a joint, and I can tell already how
   different things seem to be."

a. precontempla-
   tion stage

b. contemplation
   stage

c. preparation
   stage

d. action stage

e. maintenance
   stage

Answers: 1. b   2. e   3. a   4. b   5. c   6. d

The Impact of Family Systems on Treatment and Recovery

An estimated 8.3 million children under 18 years
of age live with one or more parents who have been
diagnosed as having a substance-abuse or substance-
dependence condition. This is equivalent to one out
of ten children in the United States.[18] These numbers
not only indicate the impact that substance abuse
or dependence has on family life but also reflect the
potential impact that children can have on the treatment and recovery process of one or both of their parents. Unfortunately, family members can be highly
resistant to becoming involved in the treatment process, often abdicating any responsibility for the problems that abuse has produced. Their embarrassment,
shame, and personal feelings of inadequacy in the
face of the abuser's drug-dominated life-style are overwhelming. Resistance to change may also come from
a family's assumption that they are responsible for the
situation instead of the substance abuser. As we will
see, obstacles to treatment can derive from a pattern of
enabling behavior.

Family Dynamics in Drug Abuse

Learning how the family has coped with having
a substance abuser as a family member is crucial
not only to understanding the origins of the abuse
but also to maximizing the chances of successful

treatment. A prominent therapist and author has expressed it this way:

> The alcoholic/addict family system could be compared with an unbalanced toy top, one so top-heavy that when it tries to spin in a functional pattern, it instead swerves to one side and skids in a diagonal direction until it stops. The individuals in this system are all compensating in different yet similar ways. It's as if they are walking around with a heavy weight on one shoulder; they have to either lean to one side to walk properly or use all their energy to try to compensate and look as if they are walking upright. Both positions require a great deal of energy.[19]

The pattern of family reactions to the conditions of substance abuse are essentially the same stages that people go through when mourning the loss of a loved one.

- *Denial.* Feelings of denial help family members avoid feelings of humiliation and shame, not to mention their own sense of responsibility. They might rationalize that their family is no different from most others. If they talk with people outside the family system, it is typically done to reinforce their denial. They want assurance that their denial of problems is not a delusion.
- *Anger.* Expressed verbally or physically, anger is a strategy for avoiding feelings of shame by blaming others in the family for the problem. Causing a fight at home is sometimes a way for the abuser to get out of the house and escape to a place where the abuse of alcohol or other drugs is more easily tolerated. Needless to say, the pattern of family interaction can be confused and unpredictable.
- *Bargaining.* When a major crisis ensues, family members can no longer deny the problem or react in anger. Implicit agreements are made that if a pattern of drug abuse will stop, the family will respond in a positive way. Conversely, a bargain might be struck that if the family tolerates the continuation of drug abuse, then the abuser will continue to support the family financially.
- *Feeling.* Earlier reactions, now exhausted, are replaced by a pervasive anxiety and obsessiveness toward the entire situation. Family members may cry at the slightest provocation or find themselves immobilized in carrying out their daily lives.

- *Acceptance.* Denial, anger, and bargaining have failed, and feelings have become too disruptive. The family is forced to seek help; family members realize that they have a problem, and they are ready to do whatever is necessary to overcome or resolve it. It is at this point that the contemplation and preparation stages of change begin.[20]

Enabling Behaviors as Obstacles to Rehabilitation

The adverse impact of enabling on the life of an alcoholic was discussed in Chapter 9, but it should be evident that applications hold for all forms of substance abuse. In general, enablers take on themselves the responsibility that has been rejected by someone else. In effect, they try to cushion the consequences that inevitably occur as a result of that other person's irresponsibility. A pattern of enabling behavior can take several forms:[21]

- *Avoiding and shielding.* Enablers make up excuses to avoid social situations where drug abuse is going on and keep up appearances when among friends or neighbors. They may stay away from home as much as they can to avoid dealing with the family situation.
- *Attempting to control.* Enablers might buy gifts in an attempt to divert the abuser from dealing with his or her problems. They might threaten to injure themselves in an attempt to get the family member to stop.
- *Taking over responsibilities.* Enablers might assume the responsibility of waking the substance abuser in time for work in the morning. They might take second jobs to cover the bills that have piled up because money has been squandered on alcohol and other drugs.
- *Rationalizing and accepting.* Enablers might communicate the belief that the episodes of substance abuse were isolated and sporadic, that family members were not *really* endangered, or that there was a positive side to the drug-taking behavior, such as the relief of depression or anxiety.
- *Cooperation and collaborating.* At an extreme level, enablers might facilitate the process of substance abuse by helping to clean and purify drugs, drinking along with an alcoholic, or lending money to purchase street drugs or alcohol so that stealing money is not necessary.

Survival Roles and Coping Mechanisms

The problems of growing up in a dysfunctional family system were examined in Chapter 9 in the context of children of alcoholic parents. Not surprisingly, the interpersonal problems within the family unit are similar for any situation in which substance abuse or dependence is involved. Sharon Wegscheider-Cruse has been an influential theorist in pointing out specific ways of coping with this difficult circumstance. In her view, there are five dysfunctional roles that a family member may assume. Understanding these roles helps the family during the process of counseling and facilitates the eventual reconstruction of family relationships during and following treatment.[22]

- *Chief Enabler.* The chief enabler takes on the principal responsibility for the family member involved in substance abuse. These responsibilities include shielding and denying the extent of dysfunctionality in the family, controlling the abuser's life, and rationalizing the negative effects on others in the family.

- *Family Hero.* As a compensation for the failures of the family, the family hero strives to be the model child, escaping the dysfunctional system through personal achievement. This individual is outwardly successful but feels like an overachiever and a fraud, undeserving of success and happiness.

- *Family Scapegoat.* A family member playing this role tries to divert attention from real problems within the family through antisocial behavior. The family scapegoat role often engages in delinquency in school and elsewhere.

- *The Lost Child.* One plays the role of the lost child by attempting to reduce the pain and suffering within the family, often by isolating oneself from family dynamics and denying one's own feelings and needs. Often, the lost child "fades into the woodwork," becoming disconnected emotionally and physically from the family.

- *Family Mascot.* Through humor and self-disparaging behavior, the family mascot strives to divert attention from the dysfunctionality of the family. However, the price paid for calm and emotional relief is a lack of maturity and a diminished sense of personal self-esteem.

Resistance at the Beginning, Support along the Way

Given the variety of dysfunctional relationships within the family of a substance-abuse individual, it is not surprising that it is often difficult to get a person in need of treatment to seek help in a meaningful way. They may feel protective of their families, not wishing to add more pain and anguish to what the family has already suffered. For their part, families may reinforce these protective feelings by being appreciative that the substance abuser is thinking of them. Abusers may feel that involving the family in treatment might reveal their own communication of inaccurate or distorted information to the counselor. There is also the fear that if counselors criticize family members for sharing the responsibility for substance abuse, family members might later retaliate by making domestic life even worse than it already is.

Whatever the difficulties in family dynamics at the onset of treatment, there is no doubt that family support is crucial as treatment progresses. Counselors frequently emphasize that family members and friends should not feel the burden of responsibility for the problem itself, nor are they responsible for the abuser's decision to enter (or reject) treatment. Instead, their responsibility is to support the abuser along the way to recovery by changing as well. In the case of alcoholism, the establishment of sobriety does not always ensure a smooth, placid relationship within the family. As a therapist has expressed it, the entire family needs to "reestablish communication, work through old resentments, develop trust, and strive to produce a comfortable and rewarding relationship."[23] A drug-free family is more than simply a family without drugs in their lives; it is a family that is completely different from what it has been before.

Finding the Right Substance-Abuse Treatment Program

Adding to the difficulties in deciding to seek treatment, there are important decisions to be made about the type of program that is best suited for a given individual (Figure 17.4). Health professionals have made three general recommendations:

- Outpatient treatment should be given preference over inpatient treatment; among other advantages, an outpatient approach is less costly and concentrates on the adjustment to a drug-free life in the context of functioning in the "real world." Consider inpatient treatment (1) when outpatient treatment has failed, (2) when

FIGURE 17.4

Components of a comprehensive treatment program for drug abuse.

Source: Modified from National Institute on Drug Abuse (2009, April). *Principles of drug addiction treatment: A research-based guide* (2nd ed.). Rockville, MD: National Institute on Drug Abuse, p. 8.

medical or psychiatric problems require hospitalization, (3) when outpatient treatment facilities are a great distance from home, or (4) when problems are so severe as to warrant removal from the current environment for a length of time. If inpatient treatment is chosen, the program should be kept as short as possible, usually two to four weeks, because longer inpatient care has not been demonstrated to be any more effective.

■ Contact should be continued with the treatment facility for at least six to twelve months. This ongoing connection minimizes the probability of the individual's dropping out of the program or undergoing relapse during maintenance.

■ Substance abusers with few sources of social support should consider a half-way or recovery house for three to six months.[24]

Judging the Quality of the Treatment Facility

Claims that sound "too good to be true" are never made by a high-quality drug-abuse treatment facility, and advertisements give only a superficial impression of

what the program might really entail. It is a good idea is to interview key people at the facility in person. Here are some good questions to ask:

■ Does the program accept your insurance? If not, will the facility staff work with you on a payment plan or find other means of support for you?

■ Is the program run by state-accredited, licensed, and/ or trained professionals? Is the facility accredited by the Joint Commission for the Accreditation of Healthcare Organizations (JCAHO)?

■ Does the program encompass the full range of needs of the individual (e.g., medical, including infectious diseases; psychological, including coexisting mental illness; social; vocational; legal)?

■ Does the treatment program address sexual orientation and physical disabilities, as well as provide age-, gender-, and culturally appropriate treatment service?

■ Is long-term aftercare support and/or guidance encouraged, provided, and maintained?

■ Is there ongoing assessment of an individual's treatment plan to ensure that it meets changing needs?

- Does the program offer counseling (individual or group) and other behavioral therapies to enhance the individual's ability to function in the family/ community?
- Is there ongoing monitoring of possible relapse to help guide patients back to abstinence?
- Are services or referrals offered to family members to ensure that they understand the nature of substance dependence and the recovery process, to help them support recovering individuals?[25]

Principles to Maximize the Chances of Successful Treatment

In order to maximize one's chances of stopping a pattern of substance abuse, avoiding relapse, and successfully recovering one's life, one needs to keep a number of key principles in mind:

- Substance abuse and substance dependence are complex but treatable diseases that affect brain function and behavior. Drug-taking behavior has altered the brain's structure and functioning. This is why an individual continues to be at risk of relapse even after long periods of abstinence.
- No single treatment is appropriate for everyone. Finding the right combination of treatment approaches is difficult and requires trained professionals to guide the process of treatment.
- Treatment needs to be readily available. Easy availability makes it possible to intervene at an early stage of substance abuse or dependence, thus increasing the likelihood of successful treatment.
- Effective treatment attends to multiple needs of the individual, not just his or her substance abuse. Associated medical, psychological, social, vocational, and legal problems need to be addressed as well.
- Remaining in treatment for an adequate period of time is critical. Too often treatment is ended too soon, when there are early signs of improvement. Most individuals with substance dependence need at least three months in treatment to achieve a significant reduction or stop their pattern of drug-taking behavior.
- Counseling on an individual or group basis and other behavioral therapies are the most commonly used forms of substance-abuse treatment. Peer support programs during and after treatment help maintain a drug-free lifestyle.
- Medications are an important element of treatment for many patients, especially when combined with counseling and other behavioral therapies.

Cognitive-behavioral therapy has been particularly useful in conjunction with medications.

- An individual's treatment and services plan must be assessed continually and modified as necessary to ensure that it meets his or her changing needs. The intensity of treatment can be adjusted upward or downward on a periodic basis. Medications may be added or withdrawn over time.
- Many substance-abuse or substance-dependence conditions are accompanied by an ongoing mental disorder. Effective treatment needs to address both of these co-occurring problems.
- Medically assisted detoxification is only the first stage of treatment and by itself does little to change long-term patterns of substance abuse.[26]

Needing versus Receiving Substance-Abuse Treatment

According to U.S. government estimates in 2011, more than 7 million people aged twelve or older (about 3 percent of that population) needed treatment for an illicit drug problem, but only one in five received drug-abuse treatment at a specialty substance-abuse facility in the past twelve months. With respect to those identified as having a need for alcohol-abuse treatment, the picture was even worse. In 2011, approximately 17 million people aged twelve or older (about 7 percent of that population) needed treatment for an alcohol-use problem, but only one in ten received it. Figure 17.5 shows, in visual terms, the wide gap between treatment needed and treatment received. The disparity between need and receipt of treatment is even greater among young people and individuals in African-American and Latino communities.

Only a small percentage of people who needed treatment in 2011 for a problem with use of either an illicit drug or alcohol, but did not receive it, personally felt a need to seek help. Of the approximately 5.8 million individuals who needed treatment for an illicit drug problem but did not receive it, only about 500,000 (8 percent) personally felt a need to seek help. Of the approximately 16 million individuals who needed treatment for an alcohol-use problem but did not receive it, only about 500,000 (3 percent) personally felt a need to seek help. About three-fourths of the people in this latter group made no effort at all to receive treatment.[27]

What can be done to reduce this disparity between treatment needed and treatment received?

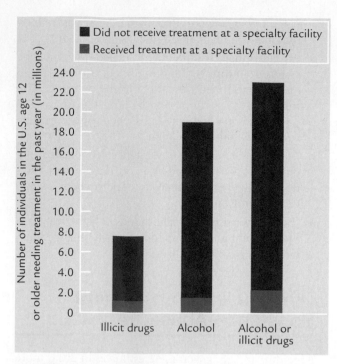

FIGURE 17.5

The gap between treatment needed and treatment received among individuals in the United States over the age of twelve.

Source: Substance Abuse and Mental Health Services Administration (2012). *Results from the 2011 National Survey on Drug Use and Health: Summary of national findings.* Rockville, MD: Substance Abuse and Mental Health Services Administration, pp. 83–88.

First, more work must be done to increase the number of substance abusers who recognize that they need to seek treatment and understand that treatment will not have a negative impact on their lives. This is particularly important in populations of young people and members of minority communities. (See Chapter 16.) An encouraging new program called Screening, Brief Intervention, and Referral to Treatment (SBIRT) is helpful in getting individuals into treatment at an early stage and with less resistance. The program creates a system within community and/or medical settings—including physicians' offices, hospitals, educational institutions, and mental-health centers—that screens for and identifies individuals with or at risk for problems related to substance use. The screening determines the severity of substance use and identifies the appropriate intervention. There is a brief intervention within the community setting, followed by referral to more extensive services if needed. The intent is to make interventions in a relatively nonthreatening manner and to increase the numbers of individuals receiving treatment.[28]

Second, more work must be done to provide accessible and affordable substance-abuse treatment for those individuals who want it and are willing to seek it out. Fortunately, affordable substance-abuse treatment in the United States took a major step forward through the enactment of the Mental Health Parity and Addiction Equity Act of 2008. In the past, Americans seeking help for psychological problems (including problems related to substance abuse) were reimbursed differently from Americans seeking help with medical conditions. After January 2010, individuals seeking treatment for substance use or a mental health disorder no longer faced unfair and arbitrary restrictions on their benefits coverage, relative to coverage for other forms of health care treatment.

It is estimated that more than 113 million Americans are the beneficiaries of this new legislation. It has been particularly helpful in promoting substance-abuse treatment for those in need. In 2011, about more than one in three individuals needing treatment reported that they did not receive treatment it, even though they made the effort, because they had no health insurance coverage and, as a result, they could not afford the cost.[29]

A Final Note: For Those Who Need Help . . .

We must all recognize that throughout our lives, the abuse of licit and illicit substances will surround us, whether they become a significant factor in our personal health, in the lives of family members, and/or in the public health of our communities. From everything that has been reviewed in this introduction to drug-taking behavior in today's society, it is clear that, as decision makers, we need all the help we can get.

As we noted in Chapter 16, a great deal of information and guidance with respect to substance abuse is available. For local referral to treatment programs, you can check out the Yellow Pages of your telephone book under "Alcoholism Information" or "Drug Abuse and Addiction Information." There are also numerous web sites on the Internet that are specifically designed to provide assistance with any alcohol, tobacco, and other drug problem. Once again, the most comprehensive source of substance-abuse treatment information is the Substance Abuse and Mental Health Services Administration (SAMHSA). Treatment options with regard to virtually every aspect of drug use, misuse, or abuse can be accessed through the wide-ranging resources of the SAMHSA web site, www.samhsa.gov. For Canadian residents, the Canadian Centre on Substance Abuse (CCSA) is a useful resource; it can be accessed through its web site, www.ccsa.com. For residents of the United Kingdom, the following web site is available: www.talktofrank.com.

Good luck to you all.

Summary

Designing Effective Substance-Abuse Treatment Programs

- It is important to recognize that not one but several types of drugs, either licit or illicit, are often involved in an individual's "abuse or dependence" profile. Effective treatment programs should address polydrug abusers as well as monodrug abusers.

- Many clients in substance-abuse treatment have co-occurring mental-health problems. These individuals are often referred to as dual-diagnosis clients.

The Biopsychosocial Model for Substance-Abuse Treatment

- Because many individuals experience problems stemming from polydrug abuse, treatment programs must consider common difficulties associated with alcohol and a range of other drugs.

- Chances of success in drug-abuse treatment can be increased by looking at the combination of biological, psychological, and social factors leading to drug abuse. This is referred to as the biopsychosocial model.

Intervention through Incarceration and Other Punitive Measures

- Federal laws since 1970 have established a hierarchy of criminal penalties for drug trafficking, depending on the schedule of the controlled substance, the amounts of drugs that are involved, and special circumstances under which violations have been committed.

- In some cases, abusers of illicit drugs who are arrested for violating drug-control laws are given the option of entering a treatment program rather than undergoing prosecution and imprisonment. For those who are sentenced to a prison term, a limited number of opportunities for drug treatment exist within the prison system.

- A growing number of drug courts, handling the cases of adult, nonviolent drug offenders, operate to adjudicate individual cases through supervised treatment rather than incarceration.

Substance-Abuse Treatment in the Workplace

- Since the mid-1980s, a growing number of companies and other businesses have adopted measures to encourage a drug-free workplace. This involves, in part, the establishment of educational programs that increase workers' awareness of alcohol abuse, the abuse of illicit drugs, and the impact of these behaviors on productivity and the quality of the workers' lives.

- One element of most drug-free workplace programs is an employee assistance program (EAP), serving to help workers with substance abuse problems. Where unions exist, member assistance programs (MAPs) supplement the work of EAPs.

The Personal Journey to Treatment and Recovery

- The road to recovery can be understood in terms of five distinct "stages of change." These stages are precontemplation, contemplation, preparation, action, and maintenance. It is possible to recycle through these stages many times, in a kind of spiraling pattern, before long-term recovery is attained.

- The five stages of change are applicable to the resolution of most life problems, not just those associated with substance abuse.

The Impact of Family Systems on Treatment and Recovery

- It is critical to examine the family dynamics surrounding a drug abuser not only to understand the situational problems that have developed but also to anticipate and deal with the obstacles that might derail treatment. Family units typically pass through the stages of denial, anger, bargaining, feeling, and finally acceptance as treatment is at first rejected and then sought.

- One major way in which family systems can jeopardize successful treatment is through enabling behavior, in which family members assume many of the responsibilities that are rejected by the drug abuser. Forms of enabling behavior include avoiding and shielding, attempting to control, taking over responsibilities, rationalizing and accepting, and cooperation and collaborating.

- Family support is crucial for a treatment program to be successful and for relapse to be avoided, although the responsibility always remains with the substance abuser.

Finding the Right Substance-Abuse Treatment Program

- It is important to consider the goals and objectives of a treatment program to find the one best suited to the person seeking help. Decisions must be made about the inpatient/outpatient format for treatment, the length of treatment, and the possibility of after-care half-way or recovery houses.

- It is also important to inspect the treatment facility in person. The ability of the treatment program to address the full range of individual needs, the availability of diverse forms of treatment, and the licensure and/or accreditation status of the facility are among the major criteria to be weighed.

- Substance-abuse treatment professionals have established ten general principles for maximizing the chances of stopping a pattern of substance abuse, avoiding relapse, and successfully recovering one's life.

Needing versus Receiving Substance-Abuse Treatment

- According to U.S. government estimates, nearly 8 million people, aged twelve or older, need treatment for an illicit drug problem; approximately 19 million people need treatment for an alcohol problem. Only a small fraction, however, have received treatment at a specialized facility—or, indeed, at any facility—in the past twelve months.

- Of those individuals who have needed treatment for problems with illicit drug or alcohol use but have not received it, a very small proportion of them personally felt the need to seek it out. A major reason for not seeking treatment is the lack of financial means to pay for treatment services and inadequate health insurance coverage. As a result of the enactment of the Mental Health Parity and Addiction Equity Act of 2008, individuals in substance-abuse treatment are eligible to receive reimbursement on an equivalent basis as they would in treatment for medical conditions.

A Final Note: For Those Who Need Help . . .

- Two sources for substance-abuse treatment information in the United States are the National Clearinghouse for Alcohol and Drug Information (NCADI) and Substance Abuse and Mental Health Services Administration (SAMHSA). Similar information sources exist in Canada, the United Kingdom, and most other nations.

Key Terms

action stage, p. 418
biopsychosocial model, p. 409
contemplation stage, p. 418
deterrence, p. 410

drug court, p. 414
drug paraphernalia, p. 413
drug trafficking, p. 410
employee assistance programs (EAPs), p. 416

incarceration, p. 409
maintenance stage, p. 418
member assistance programs (MAPs), p. 416
polydrug abusers, p. 409

precontemplation stage, p. 417
preparation stage, p. 418
rehabilitation, p. 410
simple possession, p. 412

Endnotes

1. Holmes, D. (2012). Prescription drug addiction: The treatment challenge. *The Lancet, 379,* 17–18. Substance Abuse and Mental Health Services Administration (2012). *Data Spotlight: Nearly 40 percent of substance abuse treatment admissions report alcohol-drug combinations.* Rockville, MD: Substance Abuse and Mental Health Services Administration. Substance Abuse and Mental Health Service Administration (2012). *Treatment Episode Data Set (TEDS) 2000–2010. National admissions to substance abuse treatment services.* Rockville, MD: Substance Abuse and Mental Health Services Administration, p. 6.
2. Kedia, S.; Sell, M. A.; and Relyea, G. (2007). Mono- versus polydrug abuse patterns among publicly funded clients.

Substance Abuse Treatment, Prevention, and Policy, 2, 33. Substance Abuse and Mental Health Services Administration (2012). *Treatment Episode Data Set,* Table 2.11.
3. Nestler, E. J., and Malenka, R. C. (2004, March). The addicted brain. *Scientific American,* pp. 78–85.
4. Courtesy of the Drug Enforcement Administration. Statutes of the Controlled Substances Act of 1970, as amended and revised in 1986 and 1988. Washington, DC: Drug Enforcement Administration, U.S. Department of Justice.
5. Burns, S.; Welsh, J.; Ng, M.; Li, M.; and Ditzler, A. (2002). State syringe and drug possession laws potentially influencing safe syringe disposal by injection drug users. *Journal of the American Pharmaceutical Association, 42*

(Supplement 1), S94–S98. Healey, K. (1988). *State and local experience with drug paraphernalia laws.* Washington, DC: U.S. Government Printing Office, pp. 69–73. Title 21 United States Code (USC) Controlled Substances, Section 863: Drug Paraphernalia, courtesy of the U.S. Department of Justice, Washington, DC.

6. Bureau of Justice Statistics (2011, December). Correlation population in the United States, 2010. Washington, DC: U.S. Department of Justice. Federal Bureau of Investigation (2012). *Arrests: Crime in the United States 2011.* Washington, DC: U.S. Department of Justice, Table 29.

7. California drug courts: A methodology for determining costs and avoided costs (2004, May). *Journal of Psychoactive Drugs,* SARC Supplement 2, 147–156.

8. National Institute of Justice (2012, May 15). Drug Courts. Washington, DC: Office of Justice Programs, U.S. Department of Justice. Office of National Drug Control Policy (2005, February). The President's National Drug Control Strategy. Washington, DC: Office of National Drug Control Policy. Substance Abuse and Mental Health Services Administration (2006, March/April). Incarceration vs. treatment: Drug courts help substance abusing offenders. *SAMHSA News,* pp. 1–3, 4.

9. Gottfredson, D. C.; Najaka, S. S.; and Kearley, B. (2003). Effectiveness of drug treatment courts: Evidence from a randomized trial. *Criminology and Public Policy,* 2, 401–426. H. C. West; Freeman-Wilson, K.; and Boone, D. L. (2004, May). *Painting the current picture: A national report card on drug courts and other problem solving court programs in the United States.* Alexandria, VA: National Drug Court Institute. Office of Justice Programs (2006, June). *Drug courts: The second decade. NIJ Special Report.* Washington, DC: U.S. Department of Justice.

10. Franco, C. (2010, October 12). *CRS Report to Congress: Drug courts: Background, effectiveness, and policy issues for Congress.* Washington, DC: Congressional Research Service, Funding for juvenile drug courts: Collaborative effort helps potential grantees (2009, March/April). *SAMHSA News,* pp. 1, 7.

11. Chandler, R. K.; Fletcher, B. W.; and Volkow, N. D. (2009). Treating drug abuse and addiction in the criminal justice system: Improving public health and safety. *Journal of the American Medical Association,* 301, 183–190. Larney, S.; Toson, B., Burns, L.; and Dolan, K. (2012). Effect of prison-based opioid substitution treatment and post-release retention in treatment on risk of re-incarceration. *Addiction,* 107, 372–380.

12. Center for Substance Abuse Treatment (2008). Issue Brief #12 for Employers: *What you need to know about substance abuse treatment.* SMA-4-08-4350. Rockville, MD: Substance Abuse and Mental Health Services Administration. Einspruch, E.; O'Neill, C.; Jarvis, K; Vander Ley, K.; and Raya-Carlton, P. (2011). Substance abuse prevention in the electrical industry: The NECA-IBEW team awareness and team vigilance programs. In

J. W. Bray, D. M. Galvin, and L. A. Cluff (Eds.), *Young adults in the workplace: A multisite initiative of substance use prevention programs.* Research Triangle, NC: RTI Press, pp. 73–134. Substance Abuse and Mental Health Services Administration (2009, January/February). Drug-free workplaces: Cost-effective ways to help employees. *SAMHSA News.* Rockville, MD: Substance Abuse and Mental Health Services Administration.

13. Recovery: A philosophy of hope and resilience (2008, September/October). *SAMHSA News,* pp. 1–2. Quotation on p. 1.

14. Connors, G. J.; Donovan, D. J.; and DiClemente, C. C. (2001). *Substance abuse treatment and the stages of change: Selecting and planning interventions.* New York: Guilford Press. DiClemente, C. C.; Bellino, L. E.; and Neavins, T. M. (1999). Motivation for change and alcoholism treatment. *Alcohol Research and Health,* 23, 86–92. Schuckit, M. A. (1995). *Educating yourself about alcohol and drugs: A people's primer.* New York: Plenum Press, pp. 131–153.

15. Carey, B. (2008, December 23). Drug rehabilitation or revolving door? *New York Times,* pp. D1, D4. Quotation of A. T. McLellan on p. D4. Schuckit, *Educating yourself,* pp. 186–216.

16. DiClemente, C. C.; Garay, M.; and Gemmell, L. (2008). Motivational enhancement. In M. Galanter and H. D. Kleber (Eds.), *Textbook of substance abuse treatment* (4th ed.). Washington, DC: American Psychiatric Publishing, pp. 361–372. Dijkstra, A.; Roijackers, J.; and DeVries, H. (1998). Smokers in four stages of readiness to change. *Addictive Behaviors,* 23, 339–350. Prochaska, J. O.; DiClemente, C. C.; and Norcross, J. C. (1992). In search of how people change. *American Psychologist,* 47, 1102–1114.

17. Norman, G. J.; Velicer, W. F.; Fava, J. L.; and Prochaska, J. O. (1998). Dynamic typology clustering within the stages of change for smoking cessation. *Addictive Behaviors,* 23, 139–153. Prochaska, J. O. (1994). *Changing for good.* New York: W. Morrow. Velicer, W. F.; Norman, G. J.; Fava, J. L.; and Prochaska, J. O. (1999). Testing 40 predictions from the transtheoretical model. *Addictive Behaviors,* 24, 455–469.

18. Fields, R. (2007). *Drugs in perspective: A personalized look at substance use and abuse* (6th ed.). New York: McGraw-Hill, p. 155.

19. Children living with substance-dependent or substance-abusing parents: 2002 to 2007 (2009, April 19). *The NSDUH Report,* Figure 1.

20. Fields, *Drugs in Perspective,* pp. 165–171.

21. Ibid., pp. 160–165. Margolis, R. D., and Zweben, J. E. (1998). *Treating patients with alcohol and other drug problems: An integrated approach.* Washington, DC: American Psychological Association. Nelson, C. (1988). The style of enabling behavior. In D. E. Smith and D. Wesson (Eds.), *Treating cocaine dependence.* Center City, MN: Hazelden Foundation.

22. Wegscheider-Cruse, S. (1981). *Another chance: Hope and health for the alcoholic family.* Palo Alto, CA: Science and Behavior Books. Wegscheider-Cruse, S.; Higby, K.; Klontz, T.; and Rainey, A. (1994). *Family reconstruction: The Living Theater Model.* Palo Alto, CA: Science and Behavior Books.

23. Schuckit, *Educating yourself,* pp. 229–230.

24. Schuckit, M. A. (2006). *Drug and alcohol abuse: A clinical guide to diagnosis and treatment* (6th ed.). New York: Springer, pp. 334–383. Sorensen, J. L.; Rawson, R. A.; Guydish, J.; and Zweben, J. E. (2003). *Drug abuse treatment through collaboration: Practice and research partnerships that work.* Washington, DC: American Psychological Association. Substance Abuse and Mental Health Services Administration, *50 strategies for substance abuse treatment.*

25. Center for Substance Abuse Treatment (2006). *Detoxification and substance abuse treatment.* Treatment Improvement Program (TIP) Series 45. Rockville, MD: Substance Abuse and Mental Health Services Administration. Guidelines for finding effective alcohol and drug treatment, courtesy of the Center for Substance Abuse Treatment, Substance Abuse and Mental Health Services Administration.

26. Clay, R. A. (2009, March). New hope for substance abuse treatment. *Monitor on Psychology,* 25–27. National Institute on Drug Abuse (2009). *Principles of drug addiction treatment: A research-based guide* (2nd ed.). Rockville, MD: National Institute on Drug Abuse. Tooley, E. M. and Moyers, T. B. (2012). Motivational interviewing in practice. In S. T. Walters and F. Rotgers (Eds.), *Treating substance abuse.* New York: Guilford Press, pp. 28–47.

27. Markel, H. (2003, October 21). Treatment for addiction meets barriers in the doctor's office. *New York Times,* pp. F5, F8. Substance Abuse and Mental Health Services Administration (2012). *Results from the 2011 National Survey on Drug Use and Health: Summary of national findings.* Rockville, MD: Substance Abuse and Mental Health Services Administration, pp. 83–88 . Substance Abuse and Mental Health Services Administration (2009, July 16). Substance use treatment need and receipt among Hispanics. *The NSDUH Report,* Figures 1 and 2.

28. McLlellan, A. T. (2008). Evolution in addiction treatment concepts and methods. In M. Galanter and H. D. Kleber (Eds.), *Textbook of substance abuse treatment* (4th ed.). Washington, DC: American Psychiatric Publishing, pp. 93–108. Substance Abuse and Mental Health Services Administration (2009, November/December). Screening, brief intervention, and referral to treatment. *SAMHSA News,* 1–2.

29. Parity: What does the new law mean? (2008, November/December). *SAMHSA News,* pp. 1–4. Substance Abuse and Mental Health Services Administration, *Results from 2011 National Survey on Drug Use and Health,* p. 87.

CREDITS

Photos

Chapter 1   Page 3, amenic181 Fotolia; 9, blickwinkel / Alamy; 11, Bettmann/CORBIS; 12, Elliott Landy / The Image Works; 20, John Powell/ Bubbles Photolibrary / Alamy.

Chapter 2   Page 34, Juan Manuel Silva/AGE Fotostock/Getty Images; 37, Arthur Turner / Alamy; 45, RON CORTES KRT/Newscom; 51, AP Photos; 53, AP Photo/Hans Deryk.

Chapter 3   Page 62, Richard Lord / The Image Works; 63, Roy Morsch/AGE Fotostock; 64, Mark R. Prausnitz; 72, Monkey Business Images/Shutterstock.com; 82, Brookhaven National Laboratory; 83, Marcin Balcerzak/Shutterstock.com; 84, Brookhaven National Laboratory.

Chapter 4   Page 91, CORBIS; 92, Bettmann/CORBIS; 95, Piotr Powietrzynski/Getty Images; 98, Wesley Bocxe /Science Source; 101 (center left), AP Photo/Culver City Police Department; 101 (center right), GUS RUELAS/Landov Media; 106, The Partnership at Drugfree.org.

Chapter 5   Page 120, GORAN TOMASEVIC/Landov Media; 121, Aymon de Lestrange/Bridgeman Art Library; 123, Bettmann/CORBIS; 125, Bettmann/Corbis; 138, AP Photos.

Chapter 6   Page 148, Stock Photo/Black Star; 149, Bettmann/CORBIS; 150, David Hoffman / Alamy; 154, Science Picture Library/Science Source; 156, Francois Gohier / Science Source; 158, Scott Houston/Sygma/Corbis.

Chapter 7   Page 169, Stock Photo/Black Star; 170, F1online digitale Bildagentur GmbH / Alamy; 171, Hulton Archive/Getty Images; 185, AP Photos/BEN MARGOT.

Chapter 8   Page 194, The Art Archive at Art Resource, NY; 195, Bettmann/Corbis; 197, Al Golub 032002/ZUMA Press/Newscom; 200, Wallenrock/Shutterstock; 208, Zuma Press/ZUMA/CORBIS; 209, AP Photo/John Durika.

Chapter 9   Page 222, National Clearinghouse for Alcohol & Drug Information; 227 (top), Martin Rotker/Science Source; 227 (bottom) Biophoto Assoc/Science Source; 229, Rick's Photography/Shutterstock; 237 (center left) The Everett Collection; 237 (center right), Dr. Bob's Home; 239, Hank Morgan/Science Source.

Chapter 10   Page 251, Advertising Archives; 254, AP Photo/John Duricka; 262, Science Source; 265, National Library of Medicine; 267, Paul Liebhardt/Alamy.

Chapter 11   Page 277, SAM ABELL/National Geographic Stock; 282, Hershey Community Archives; 284, Science Source; 288, Bob Daemmrich / The Image Works.

Chapter 12   Page 296, AP Photo/STAFF; 297, PCN Photography / Alamy; 299, Reuters/CORBIS; 300, Hassan Ammar/AFP/Getty Images/ Newscom; 303 (top right), DOUG COLLIER/AFP/Getty Images; 303 (top right) Pearson Education; 303 (top left and center) Vincent Santelmo, New York City. The Complete Encyclopedia of GI Joe; 310, Blair Seitz/Science Source.

Chapter 13   Page 319, Will McIntyre/Science Source; 326, AP Photos/ERIC RISBERG; 328, Bettmann/CORBIS; 332, Reuters/CORBIS.

Chapter 14   Page 341, Bill Aron / PhotoEdit; 347, Blend Images/SuperStock; 354, Nelvin Cepeda/ZUMA Press/Newscom.

Chapter 15   Page 369, Alexander Gardner/Library of Congress; 373, Dr Lewis Baxter and Dr. Michael Phelps, UCLA School of Medicine.

Chapter 16   Page 384, Chance Yeh /PatrickMcMullan.com/Sipa Press; 386, Jeff Greenberg / PhotoEdit; 393, Partnership for a Drug-Free America; 394, Ad Council and the U.S. Department of Health & Human Services Substance Abuse & Mental Health Services Administration's Underage Drinking Prevention campaign. Designed by the Kaplan Thaler Group; 395, Blas E. Lopez.

Chapter 17   Page 410, Stefanie Boyar/Newscom; 415, AP Photos/Ed Bailey; 416, Partnership for a Drug-Free America.

Figures and Tables

Chapter 1   **Figure 1.2**, Expanded from Goode, E. (2008). Drugs in American Society (7th ed.). New York: McGraw-Hill, p. 14; **Figure 1.3**, Johnston, L.D.; O'malley, P.M.; Bachman, J.G.; And Schulenberg, J.E. (2012). Monitoring The Future: National Survey Results On Drug Use, 1975–2011, Vol. I Secondary School Students 2011, Table 2-2; **Table 1.1**, Johnston, L.D.; O'Malley, P.M.; Bachman, J.G.; and Schulenberg, J.E. (2012). Monitoring the Future: National survey results on drug use, 1975–2011. Vol. II: College students and adults ages 19–50. Bethesda, MD: National Institute on Drug Abuse, Tables 2-1, 2-2, 2-3, 8-1, 8-2, and 8-3; **Figure 1.4**, Johnston, L.D.; O'malley, P.M.; Bachman, J.G.; And Schulenberg, J.E. (2012). Monitoring the Future: National survey results on drug use, 1975–2011, Vol. I Secondary school students 2011.

Bethesda, MD: National Institute on Drug Abuse; **Table 1.2**, Substance Abuse and Mental Health Services Administration (2012). *Results from the 2011 National Survey on Drug use and Health: Detailed tables*. Rockville, MD: Substance Abuse and Mental Health Services Administration, Tables 1.7A and 1.8A; **Table 1.3**, Wright, D., and Pemberton, M. (2004). Risk and protective factors for adolescent drug use: Findings from the 1999 National Household Survey on Drug Use. Rockville, MD: Substance Abuse and Mental Health Services Administration, Chapter 3 and Appendix A.

Chapter 2   Figure 2.2 Substance Abuse and Mental Health Services Administration (2013). *Drug Abuse Warning Network, 2011: National estimates of drug-related emergency department visits, 2004–2011*. Rockville, MD: Substance Abuse and Mental Health Services Administration; **Figure 2.3** Centers for Disease Control and Prevention (2008, November 14). Cigarette smoking attributable morbidity, years of potential life lost, and productivity losses—United States, 2000–2004. *Morbidity and Mortality Weekly Report*, 57, 1226–1228. Harwood, H. (2011, October 23). Recent findings on the economic impacts of substance abuse. Presented at the American Psychological Association 2011 Science Leadership Conference, Psychological Science and Substance Abuse, Washington DC, Slide 12. Mokdad, A.H.; Marks, J.S.; Stroup, D. F.; and Gerberding, J.L. (2004). Actual causes of death in the United States, 2000. *Journal of the American Medical Association*, 291, 1238–1245; **Table 2.1** Adapted from the American Psychiatric Association: Diagnostic and statistical manual of mental disorders, Text Revision (4th ed.). Washington, DC: American Psychiatric Association. Reprinted with permission from the Diagnostic and statistical manual of mental disorders (4th ed.). Copyright 2000 American Psychiatric Association, pp. 191, 197, and 199. Reed, G.M. (2010). Toward ICD-11: Improving the clinical utili9ty of WHO's International Classification of Mental Disorders. Professional Psychology: Research and Practice, 41, 457-464; **Figure 2.5** Goldstein, P. (1985, Fall). The drug-violence nexus: A tripartite framework. *Journal of Drug Issues*, 493–506; **Table 2.2** Drug Enforcement Administration, U.S. Department of Justice, Washington, DC; **Figure 2.6** Drug Enforcement Administration (2011). FY 2012 Performance budget congressional submission. Washington, DC: Drug Enforcement Administration, U.S. Department of Justice, p. 12.

Chapter 3   Figure 3.3 Baron, Robert A.; Kalsher, Michael J., *Psychology: From Science To Practice*, 2nd Ed., c.2008. Reprinted and Electronically reproduced by permission of Pearson Education Inc., Upper Saddle River, New Jersey; **Figure 3.4** Modified from Kalat, James W. (2007). Biological psychology (9th ed.). Belmont, CA: Wadsworth/ Thomson Learning. Reproduced by permission. www.cengage.com/permissions.

Chapter 4   Figure 4.2 Information courtesy of the Drug Enforcement Administration, U.S. Department of Justice, Washington, DC; **Figure 4.3** Adapted from Shine, B. (2000, March). Some cocaine abusers fare better with cognitive-behavioral therapy, others with 12-step programs. NIDA Notes, 15 (1), 9.

Chapter 5   Figure 5.1 Physicians' desk reference (66th ed.) (2012). Montvale, NJ: Thomson HealthCare. Raj, P. Prithvi (1996). Pain medicine: A comprehensive review. St. Louis: Mosby, pp. 126–153; **Table 5.1** GRILLY, DAVID M.; SALAMONE, JOHN, DRUGS, BRAIN, AND BEHAVIOR, 6th Ed., c.2012. Reprinted and Electronically reproduced by permission of Pearson Education Inc., Upper Saddle River, New Jersey; **Table 5.2** Physicians' desk reference (66th ed.) (2012). Montvale, NJ: Thomson HealthCare.

Chapter 6   Table 6.1 Based on Schultes, R. E., and Hofmann, A. (1979). Plants of the gods: Origins of hallucinogenic use. New York: McGraw-Hill; **Table 6.2** Updated from Milburn, H. T. (1991). Diagnosis and management of phencyclidine intoxication. American Family Physician, 43, 1293.

Chapter 7   Table 7.1 Julien, R.M. (2001). A primer of drug action (9th ed.). New York: Worth, p. 317; **Figure 7.1** Substance Abuse and Mental Health Services Administration (2007). Use of marijuana and blunts among adolescents: 2005. The NSDUH Report, p. 3; **Figure 7.2** Substance Abuse and Mental Health Services Administration (2012). Results from the 2011 National Survey on Drug Use and Health: National findings. Rockville, MD: Substance Abuse and Mental Health Services Administration, p. 13.

Chapter 8   Table 8.1 Based on Becker, C.E.; Roe, R.L.; and Scott, R.A. (1979). Alcohol as a drug: A curriculum on pharmacology, neurology, and toxicology. Huntington, NY: Robert Krieger Publishing, pp. 10–12; **Table 8.2** Updated from A primer of drug action, 8th ed., by R.M. Julien, M.D. © 2001 Worth Publishers. Used with permission; **Table 8.3** Brick, J.; Wallen, M.C.; and Lorman, W.J. (2008). Interaction of alcohol with medications and other drugs. In J. Brick (Ed.), Handbook of the medical consequences of drug and alcohol abuse (2nd ed.). New York, Routledge, pp. 527–563. National Institute on Alcohol Abuse and Alcoholism (1995, January). Alcohol alert: Alcohol–medication interactions. No. 27, PH355. Bethesda, MD: National Institute on Alcohol Abuse and Alcoholism; **Table 8.4** National Highway Traffic Safety Administration, (2000 March), On DWI Laws in Other Countries. U.S. Department of Transportation.

Chapter 9   Figure 9.2 Centers for Disease Control and Prevention (2012). Vital signs: Binge drinking prevalence, frequency, and intensity among adults—United States, 2010. Morbidity and Mortality Weekly Report, 61, 14–19; **Table 9.1** Adapted from Cloninger, C.R. (1987). Neurogenetic adaptive mechanisms in alcoholism. Science, 236, 410–416; **Figure 9.3** Stacy, D.; Clarke, T-K.; and Schumann, G. (2009). The genetics of alcoholism. *Current Psychiatry Reports*, 11, p. 366; **Table 9.2** The Twelve Steps are reprinted with permission of Alcoholics Anonymous World Services, Inc. ("AAWS") Permission to reprint the Twelve Steps does not mean that AAWS has reviewed or approved the contents of this publication, or that AAWS necessarily agrees with the views expressed herein. A.A. is a program of recovery from alcoholism only—use of the Twelve Steps in connection with programs and activities which are patterned after A.A., but which address other problems, or in any other non-A.A. context, does not imply otherwise.

Chapter 10   Figure 10.1 Centers for Disease Control and Prevention (2008, November 14). Cigarette smoking–attributable morbidity, years of potential life lost, and productivity losses—United States, 2000–2004. Morbidity and Mortality Weekly Report, 57, 1226–1228; **Figure 10.2** Based on American Cancer Society. Cancer Facts and Figures 2012. Atlanta: American Cancer Society, Inc.; **Table 10.1** Data from Popescu, Cathy (1992). The health hazards of smokeless tobacco. In Kristine Napier (Ed.), Issues in tobacco. New York: American Council on Science and Health, pp. 11–12; **Figure 10.3** From The Tobacco Atlas—www.int/tobacco/en/atlas ISBN 0-92-4156-209-9. Reprinted by permission of WHO; **Figure 10.4** From The Tobacco Atlas - www.int/tobacco/en/atlas ISBN 92-4156-209-9. Reprinted by permission of WHO.

Chapter 11 **Table 11.1** Energyfiend.com, 2012. Special issue: Top-10 CSD results in 2010 (2011, March 17). Beverage-Digest, 59, No. 5; **Table 11.2** Updated from Gilbert, R.J. (1986). Caffeine: The most popular stimulant. New York: Chelsea House Publishers, p. 51; **Table 11.3** www.energyfiend.com, 2012.

Chapter 12 **Table 12.1** Julien, R.M. (2005). A primer of drug action (10th ed.). New York: Worth, p. 631. National Institute on Drug Abuse (2000, April). Anabolic steroids. Community drug alert bulletin. Bethesda, MD: National Institute on Drug Abuse. Physicians' desk reference (66th ed.) (2012). Montvale, NJ: Thomson HealthCare; **Table 12.2** Strauss, R.H., and Yesalis, C.E. (1993). Additional effects of anabolic steroids in women. In C.E. Yesalis (Ed.), Anabolic steroids in sport and exercise. Champaign, IL: Human Kinetics Publishers, pp. 151–160. Strauss, R.H.; Ligget, M. T.; and Lanese R. R. (1985). Anabolic steroid use and perceived effects in ten weight-trained women athletes. Journal of the American Medical Association, 253, 2871–2873; **Table 12.3** Allen and Hanbury's athletic drug reference (1994). Durham, NC: Clean Data, p. 19. Inaba, D.S., and Cohen, W.E. (1989). Uppers, downers, all arounders. Ashland, OR: Cinemed, p. 206.

Chapter 13 **Table 13.1** Julien, R.M. (2005). A primer of drug action (10th ed.). New York: Worth, p. 146. Physicians' desk reference (66th ed.) (2012). Montvale, NJ: Medical Economics Company; **Table 13.2** Updated from Henningfield, J.E., and Ator, N.A. (1986). Barbiturates: Sleeping potion or intoxicant? New York: Chelsea House, p. 82; **Table 13.3** Julien, R.M. (2005). A primer of drug action (10th ed.). New York: Worth, p. 146. Physicians' desk reference (66th ed.) (2012). Montvale, NJ: Medical Economics Company; **Table 13.4** Schuckit, M. A. (2006). *Drug and alcohol abuse: A clinical guide to diagnosis and treatment* (6th ed.). New York: Springer, p. 237. Sharp, C. W.; and Rosenberg, N. L. (1997). Inhalants. In J. H. Lowinson, P. R., R. B. Millman, and J. G. Langrod (Eds.), *Substance abuse: A comprehensive textbook* (3d ed.). Baltimore: Williams and Wilkins, p. 248.

Chapter 14 **Table 14.1** Updated information from the U.S. Food and Drug Administration, Washington, DC; **Figure 14.1** Updated from U.S. Food and Drug Administration (2001, March–April). Making medical progress: A look at FDA approvals in 2000. FDA Consumer, pp. 7–8. Zivin, J.A. (2003, April). Understanding clinical trials. Scientific American, pp. 69–75; **Table 14.2** www.drugs.com/stats/top 100 sales; **Table 14.3** Information courtesy of the Nonprescription Drug Manufacturers Association, Washington, DC.

Chapter 15 **Table 15.1** U.S. Food and Drug Administration, Washington, DC.

Chapter 16 **Figure 16.1** Mokdad, A.H., et al., (2004). Actual causes of death in the United States, 2000. Journal of the American Medical Association; **Figure 16.2** Adapted from Attorney General John Van De Kamp's Commission of Drug and Alcohol Abuse, 1986. Sacramento, CA. Reprinted by permission of the California Attorney General's Office.

Chapter 17 **Figure 17.1** Substance Abuse and Mental Health Services Administration (2012). 2000–2010 Treatment Episode Data Set (TEDS): National admissions to substance abuse treatment services. Rockville, MD: Office of Applied Studies, Substance Abuse, and Mental Health Services Administration, pp. 1–3; **Figure 17.2** Modified from Margolis, R.D., and Zweben, J.E. (1998). Treating patients with alcohol and other drug problems: An integrated approach. Washington, DC: American Psychological Association, pp. 76–87; **Table 17.1** Associated Press (2010, August 4). Obama signs new cocaine bill. Drug Enforcement Administration, U.S. Department of Justice; **Table 17.2** Associated Press (2010, August 4). Obama signs new cocaine bill. Drug Enforcement Administration, U.S. Department of Justice; **Figure 17.3** Modified from Margolis, R.D., and Zweben, J.E. (1998). Treating patients with alcohol and other drug problems: An integrated approach. Washington, DC: American Psychological Association, pp. 76–87; **Figure 17.4** Modified from National Institute on Drug Abuse (2009, April). Principles of drug addiction treatment: A research-based guide (2nd ed.). Rockville, MD: National Institute on Drug Abuse, p. 8; **Figure 17.5** Substance Abuse and Mental Health Services Administration (2012). Results from the 2011 National Survey on Drug Use and Health: Summary of national findings. Rockville, MD: Substance Abuse and Mental Health Services Administration, pp. 83–88.

INDEX